T0178443

Lecture Notes in Computer Science 13018

Founding Editors

Gerhard Goos
  Karlsruhe Institute of Technology, Karlsruhe, Germany
Juris Hartmanis
  Cornell University, Ithaca, NY, USA

Editorial Board Members

Elisa Bertino
  Purdue University, West Lafayette, IN, USA
Wen Gao
  Peking University, Beijing, China
Bernhard Steffen
  TU Dortmund University, Dortmund, Germany
Gerhard Woeginger
  RWTH Aachen, Aachen, Germany
Moti Yung
  Columbia University, New York, NY, USA

More information about this subseries at http://www.springer.com/series/7412

George Bebis · Vassilis Athitsos ·
Tong Yan · Manfred Lau ·
Frederick Li · Conglei Shi ·
Xiaoru Yuan · Christos Mousas ·
Gerd Bruder (Eds.)

Advances in Visual Computing

16th International Symposium, ISVC 2021
Virtual Event, October 4–6, 2021
Proceedings, Part II

 Springer

Editors
George Bebis
University of Nevada
Reno, NV, USA

Tong Yan
University of South Carolina
Columbia, SC, USA

Frederick Li
School of Engineering and Computing
University of Durham
Durham, Durham, UK

Xiaoru Yuan
Peking University
Beijing, China

Gerd Bruder
IST, School of Modeling, Simulation,
and Training
Orlando, FL, USA

Vassilis Athitsos
University of Texas at Arlington
Arlington, TX, USA

Manfred Lau
City University of Hong Kong
Kowloon, Hong Kong

Conglei Shi
Airbnb
New York, NY, USA

Christos Mousas
Purdue University
West Lafayette, IN, USA

ISSN 0302-9743   ISSN 1611-3349   (electronic)
Lecture Notes in Computer Science
ISBN 978-3-030-90435-7   ISBN 978-3-030-90436-4   (eBook)
https://doi.org/10.1007/978-3-030-90436-4

LNCS Sublibrary: SL6 – Image Processing, Computer Vision, Pattern Recognition, and Graphics

© Springer Nature Switzerland AG 2021
Chapter "Cervical Cancer Detection and Classification in Cytology Images Using a Hybrid Approach" is licensed under the terms of the Creative Commons Attribution 4.0 International License (http://creativecommons.org/licenses/by/4.0/). For further details see license information in the chapter.
This work is subject to copyright. All rights are reserved by the Publisher, whether the whole or part of the material is concerned, specifically the rights of translation, reprinting, reuse of illustrations, recitation, broadcasting, reproduction on microfilms or in any other physical way, and transmission or information storage and retrieval, electronic adaptation, computer software, or by similar or dissimilar methodology now known or hereafter developed.
The use of general descriptive names, registered names, trademarks, service marks, etc. in this publication does not imply, even in the absence of a specific statement, that such names are exempt from the relevant protective laws and regulations and therefore free for general use.
The publisher, the authors and the editors are safe to assume that the advice and information in this book are believed to be true and accurate at the date of publication. Neither the publisher nor the authors or the editors give a warranty, expressed or implied, with respect to the material contained herein or for any errors or omissions that may have been made. The publisher remains neutral with regard to jurisdictional claims in published maps and institutional affiliations.

This Springer imprint is published by the registered company Springer Nature Switzerland AG
The registered company address is: Gewerbestrasse 11, 6330 Cham, Switzerland

Preface

It is with great pleasure that we welcome you to the proceedings of the 16th International Symposium on Visual Computing (ISVC 2021), which was held virtually (October 4–6, 2021). ISVC provides a common umbrella for the four main areas of visual computing including vision, graphics, visualization, and virtual reality. The goal is to provide a forum for researchers, scientists, engineers, and practitioners throughout the world to present their latest research findings, ideas, developments, and applications in the broader area of visual computing.

This year, the program consisted of six keynote presentations, 11 oral sessions, two poster sessions, and three special tracks. We received close to 135 submissions for the main symposium from which we accepted 48 papers for oral presentation and 32 papers for poster presentation. A total of nine papers were accepted for oral presentation in the special tracks from 15 submissions.

All papers were reviewed with an emphasis on the potential to contribute to the state of the art in the field. Selection criteria included accuracy and originality of ideas, clarity and significance of results, and presentation quality. The review process was quite rigorous, involving three independent blind reviews followed by several days of discussion. During the discussion period we tried to correct anomalies and errors that might have existed in the initial reviews. Despite our efforts, we recognize that some papers worthy of inclusion may have not been included in the program. We offer our sincere apologies to authors whose contributions might have been overlooked.

We wish to thank everybody who submitted their work to ISVC 2021 for review. It was because of their contributions that we succeeded in having a technical program of high scientific quality. In particular, we would like to thank the keynote speakers, the program chairs, the steering committee, the international Program Committee, the special track organizers, the tutorial organizers, the reviewers, the sponsors, and especially, the authors who contributed their work to the symposium. We would like to express our appreciation to Springer for sponsoring the "best" paper award again this year and to Vzense for being a bronze sponsor.

Despite all the difficulties due to the pandemic, we sincerely hope that ISVC 2021 offered participants opportunities for professional growth.

September 2021

George Bebis
Vassilis Athitsos
Yan Tong
Manfred Lau
Frederick Li
Conglei Shi
Xiaoru Yuan
Christos Mousas
Gerd Bruder

Organization

Steering Committee Chair

George Bebis   University of Nevada, Reno, USA

Computer Vision Chairs

Vassilis Athitsos   University of Texas at Arlington, USA
Yan Tong   University of South Carolina, USA

Computer Graphics Chairs

Manfred Lau   City University of Hong Kong, Hong Kong
Frederick Li   Durham University, UK

Visualization Chairs

Conglei Shi   Airbnb, USA
Xiaoru Yuan   Peking University, China

Virtual Reality Chairs

Gerd Bruder   University of Central Florida, USA
Christos Mousas   Purdue University, USA

Program Committee

Emmanuel Agu	WPI, USA
Touqeer Ahmad	University of Colorado Colorado Springs, USA
Alfonso Alba	Universidad Autónoma de San Luis Potosí, Mexico
Usman Alim	University of Calgary, Canada
Amol Ambardekar	Microsoft, USA
Zahra Anvari	University of Texas at Arlington, USA
Mark Apperley	University of Waikato, New Zealand
Antonis Argyros	Foundation for Research and Technology - Hellas, Greece
Vijayan K. Asari	University of Dayton, USA
Aishwarya Asesh	Adobe, USA
Vassilis Athitsos	University of Texas at Arlington, USA
Melinos Averkiou	University of Cyprus, Cyprus
George Baciu	Hong Kong Polytechnic University, Hong Kong
Abdul Bais	University of Regina, Canada

Abhishek Bajpayee	Massachusetts Institute of Technology, USA
Peter Balazs	University of Szeged, Hungary
Selim Balcisoy	Sabanci University, Turkey
Reneta Barneva	SUNY Fredonia, USA
Ronen Barzel	Independent, UK
Fereshteh S. Bashiri	University of Wisconsin-Madison, USA
Aryabrata Basu	Emory University, USA
Anil Ufuk Batmaz	Kadir Has University, Turkey
George Bebis	University of Nevada, Reno, USA
Jan Bender	RWTH Aachen University, Germany
Ayush Bhargava	Facebook, USA
Sanjiv Bhatia	University of Missouri at St. Louis, USA
Mark Billinghurst	University of South Australia, Australia
Ankur Bist	Govind Ballabh Pant University of Agriculture and Technology, India
Ayan Biswas	Los Alamos National Laboratory, USA
Dibio Borges	Universidade de Braslia, Brazil
David Borland	University of North Carolina at Chapel Hill, USA
Nizar Bouguila	Concordia University, Canada
Jose Braz Pereira	EST Setúbal/IPS, Portugal
Wolfgang Broll	Ilmenau University of Technology, Germany
Gerd Bruder	University of Central Florida, USA
Tolga Capin	TED University, Turkey
Sek Chai	SRI International, USA
Jian Chang	Bournemouth University, UK
Sotirios Chatzis	Cyprus University of Technology, Cyprus
Rama Chellappa	University of Maryland, USA
Cunjian Chen	Michigan State University, USA
Yang Chen	HRL Laboratories, LLC, USA
Zhonggui Chen	Xiamen University, China
Yi-Jen Chiang	New York University, USA
Isaac Cho	Utah State University, USA
Amit Chourasia	University of California, San Diego, USA
Kichung Chung	SK Infosec, South Korea
Tommy Dang	Texas Tech University, USA
Aritra Dasgupta	New York University, USA
Jeremie Dequidt	University of Lille, France
Daljit Singh Dhillon	Clemson University, USA
Sotirios Diamantas	Tarleton State University, USA
Alexandra Diehl	University of Konstanz, Germany
John Dingliana	Trinity College Dublin, Ireland
Cosimo Distante	CNR, Italy
Ralf Doerner	RheinMain University of Applied Sciences, Germany
Anastasios Doulamis	Technical University of Crete, Greece
Shengzhi Du	Tshwane University of Technology, South Africa
Ye Duan	University of Missouri at Columbia, USA

Soumya Dutta	Los Alamos National Laboratory, USA
Achim Ebert	University of Kaiserslautern, Germany
Mohamed El Ansari	University of Ibn Zohr, Morocco
El-Sayed M. El-Alfy	King Fahd University of Petroleum and Minerals, Saudi Arabia
Barrett Ens	Monash University, Australia
Alireza Entezari	University of Florida, USA
Ali Erol	Sigun Information Technologies, Turkey
Thomas Ertl	University of Stuttgart, Germany
Mohammad Eslami	Technical University of Munich, Germany
Amanda Fernandez	University of Texas at San Antonio, USA
Matteo Ferrara	University of Bologna, Italy
Nivan Ferreira	Universidade Federal de Pernambuco, Brazil
Francesco Ferrise	Politecnico di Milano, Italy
Julian Fierrez	Universidad Autonoma de Madrid, Spain
Robert Fisher	University of Edinburgh, UK
Gian Luca Foresti	University of Udine, Italy
Steffen Frey	University of Groningen, The Netherlands
Ioannis Fudos	University of Ioannina, Greece
Issei Fujishiro	Keio University, Japan
Radovan Fusek	VŠB-Technical University of Ostrava, Czech Republic
Fabio Ganovelli	ISTI-CNR, Italy
Xifeng Gao	Florida State University, USA
M. Gavrilova	University of Calgary, Canada
Krzysztof Gdawiec	University of Silesia, Poland
Robert Geist	Clemson University, USA
Daniela Giorgi	ISTI-CNR, Italy
Wooi-Boon Goh	Nanyang Technological University, Singapore
Roberto Grosso	Friedrich-Alexander-Universität Erlangen-Nürnberg, Germany
Hanqi Guo	Argonne National Laboratory, USA
David Gustafson	Kansas State University, USA
Felix Hamza-Lup	Georgia Southern University, USA
Emily Hand	University of Nevada, Reno, USA
Xuejun Hao	Columbia University, USA
Brandon Haworth	University of Victoria, Canada
Subhashis Hazarika	Los Alamos National Laboratory, USA
Eric Hodgson	Miami University, USA
Chris Holmberg Bahnsen	Aalborg University, Denmark
Jing Hua	Wayne State University, USA
Muhammad Hussain	King Saud University, Saudi Arabia
José A. Iglesias Guitián	University of A Coruña, Spain
Atsushi Imiya	IMIT Chiba University, Japan
Kei Iwasaki	Wakayama University, Japan
Yun Jang	Sejong University, South Korea
Michael Jenkin	York University, Canada

Stefan Jeschke	NVIDIA, Austria
Ming Jiang	LLNL, USA
Sungchul Jung	Kennesaw State University, USA
Ho Chuen Kam	Chinese University of Hong Kong, Hong Kong
George Kamberov	University of Alaska Anchorage, USA
Gerda Kamberova	Hofstra University, USA
Martin Kampel	Vienna University of Technology, Austria
Takashi Kanai	University of Tokyo, Japan
Rajiv Khadka	Idaho National Laboratory, USA
Waqar Khan	Wellington Institute of Technology, New Zealand
Edward Kim	Drexel University, USA
Hyungseok Kim	Konkuk University, South Korea
Min H. Kim	Korea Advanced Institute of Science and Technology, South Korea
James Klosowski	AT&T Labs Research, USA
Stefanos Kollias	National Technical University of Athens, Greece
Takashi Komuro	Saitama University, Japan
Jens Krueger	University of Duisburg-Essen, Germany
Arjan Kuijper	TU Darmstadt, Germany
Yoshinori Kuno	Saitama University, Japan
Hung La	University of Nevada, Reno, USA
Yu-Kun Lai	Cardiff University, UK
Robert S Laramee	University of Nottingham, UK
Manfred Lau	City University of Hong Kong, Hong Kong
D. J. Lee	Brigham Young University, USA
Robert R. Lewis	Washington State University, USA
Frederick Li	University of Durham, UK
Xin Li	Louisiana State University, USA
Kuo-Chin Lien	XMotors.ai, USA
Stephen Lin	Microsoft, China
Peter Lindstrom	LLNL, USA
Shiguang Liu	Tianjin University, China
Zhanping Liu	Old Dominion University, USA
Manuel Loaiza	Universidad Católica San Pablo, Peru
Leandro Loss	QuantaVerse, USA/ITU, USA/ESSCA, China
Joern Loviscach	University of Applied Sciences, Germany
Aidong Lu	University of North Carolina at Charlotte, USA
Xun Luo	Tianjin University of Technology, China
Brendan Macdonald	NIOSH, USA
Sokratis Makrogiannis	Delaware State University, USA
Luigi Malomo	ISTI-CNR, Italy
Dimitrios Kosmopoulos	University of Patras, Greece
Hamid Mansoor	Worcester Polytechnic Institute, USA
Rafael M. Martins	Linnaeus University, Växjö, Sweden
Yoshitaka Masutani	Hiroshima City University, Japan
Sherin Mathews	University of Delaware, USA

Kresimir Matkovic	VRVis Research Center, Austria
Tim McGraw	Purdue University, USA
Tim McInerney	Ryerson University, Canada
Qurban Memon	UAE University, UAE
Daniel Mestre	Aix-Marseille University, France
Jean Meunier	University of Montreal, Canada
Xikui Miao	Brigham Young University, USA
Gabriel Mistelbauer	Otto-von-Guericke University Magdeburg, Germany
Kenneth Moreland	Oak Ridge National Laboratory, USA
Shigeo Morishima	Waseda University, Japan
Brendan Morris	University of Nevada, Las Vegas, USA
Chouaib Moujahdi	Mohammed V University in Rabat, Morocco
Christos Mousas	Purdue University, USA
Soraia Musse	Pontificia Universidade Catolica do Rio Grande do Sul, Brazil
Kawa Nazemi	Darmstadt University of Applied Sciences, Germany
Quang Vinh Nguyen	Western Sydney University, Australia
Mircea Nicolescu	University of Nevada, Reno, USA
Christophoros Nikou	University of Ioannina, Greece
Mark Nixon	University of Southampton, UK
Junyong Noh	Korea Advanced Institute of Science and Technology, South Korea
Klimis Ntalianis	University of West Attica, Greece
Scott Nykl	Air Force Institute of Technology, USA
Yoshihiro Okada	Kyushu University, Japan
Gustavo Olague	CICESE, Mexico
Masaki Oshita	Kyushu Institute of Technology, Japan
Volker Paelke	Hochschule Bremen, Germany
Kalman Palagyi	University of Szeged, Hungary
George Papagiannakis	University of Crete, Greece
George Papakostas	EMT Institute of Technology, Greece
Michael Papka	Argonne National Laboratory/Northern Illinois University, USA
Giuseppe Patanè	CNR-IMATI, Italy
Maurizio Patrignani	Roma Tre University, Italy
Shahram Payandeh	Simon Fraser University, Canada
Helio Pedrini	University of Campinas, Brazil
Jaakko Peltonen	Aalto University and University of Tampere, Finland
Euripides Petrakis	Technical University of Crete, Greece
Giuseppe Placidi	University of L'Aquila, Italy
Vijayakumar Ponnusamy	SRM Institute of Science and Technology, India
Kevin Ponto	University of Wisconsin-Madison, USA
Jiju Poovvancheri	University of Victoria, Canada
Nicolas Pronost	Université Claude Bernard Lyon 1, France
Hong Qin	Stony Brook University, Canada
Christopher Rasmussen	University of Delaware, Canada

Emma Regentova	University of Nevada, Las Vegas, USA
Guido Reina	University of Stuttgart, Germany
Erik Reinhard	InterDigitalm, France
Banafsheh Rekabdar	Southern Illinois University Carbondale, USA
Paolo Remagnino	Kingston University, UK
Hongliang Ren	National University of Singapore, Singapore
Theresa-Marie Rhyne	Independent Consultant, USA
Eraldo Ribeiro	Florida Institute of Technology, USA
Peter Rodgers	University of Kent, UK
Isaac Rudomin	BSC, Spain
Filip Sadlo	Heidelberg University, Germany
Punam Saha	University of Iowa, USA
Naohisa Sakamoto	Kobe University, Japan
Kristian Sandberg	Computational Solutions, Inc., USA
Alberto Santamaria Pang	Microsoft Health AI, USA
Nickolas S. Sapidis	University of Western Macedonia, Greece
Muhammad Sarfraz	Kuwait University. Kuwait
Fabien Scalzo	University of California, Los Angeles, USA
Jacob Scharcanski	Universidade Federal do Rio Grande do Sul, Brazil
Thomas Schultz	University of Bonn, Germany
Jurgen Schulze	University of California, San Diego, USA
Puneet Sharma	UiT-The Arctic University of Norway, Norway
Mohamed Shehata	Memorial University, Canada
Conglei Shi	Airbnb, USA
Gurjot Singh	Fairleigh Dickinson University, USA
Alexei Skurikhin	Los Alamos National Laboratory, USA
Pavel Slavik	Czech Technical University in Prague, Czech Republic
Jack Snoeyink	University of North Carolina at Chapel Hill, USA
Fabio Solari	University of Genoa, Italy
Paolo Spagnolo	CNR, Italy
Jaya Sreevalsan-Nair	IIIT Bangalore, India
Chung-Yen Su	National Taiwan Normal University, Taiwan
Changming Sun	CSIRO
Zehang Sun	Apple Inc., USA
Carlo H. Séquin	University of California, Berkeley, USA
Jules-Raymond Tapamo	Univesity of KwaZulu-Natal, South Africa
Alireza Tavakkoli	University of Nevada, Reno, USA
João Manuel R. S. Tavares	FEUP/INEGI, Portugal
Daniel Thalmann	Ecole Polytechnique Fédérale de Lausanne, Switzerland
Holger Theisel	Otto von Guericke University Magdeburg, Germany
Yuan Tian	Innopeak Tech Inc., USA
Yan Tong	University of South Carolina, USA
Thomas Torsney-Weir	VRVis, Austria
Mehmet Engin Tozal	University of Louisiana at Lafayette, USA
Stefano Tubaro	Politecnico di Milano, Italy

Georg Umlauf	Konstanz University of Applied Sciences, Germany
Daniela Ushizima	Lawrence Berkeley National Laboratory, USA
Serestina Viriri	University of KwaZulu-Natal, South Africa
Athanasios Voulodimos	University of West Attica, Greece
Chaoli Wang	University of Notre Dame, USA
Cuilan Wang	Georgia Gwinnett College, USA
Benjamin Weyers	Trier University, Germany
Thomas Wischgoll	Wright State University, USA
Kin Hong Wong	Chinese University of Hong Kong, Hong Kong
Wei Xu	Brookhaven National Laboratory, USA
Yasuyuki Yanagida	Meijo University, Japan
Fumeng Yang	Brown University, USA
Xiaosong Yang	Bournemouth University, UK
Hsu-Chun Yen	National Taiwan University, Taiwan
Lijun Yin	State University of New York at Binghamton, USA
Zeyun Yu	University of Wisconsin-Milwaukee, USA
Chunrong Yuan	Technische Hochschule Köln, Germany
Xiaoru Yuan	Peking University, China
Xenophon Zabulis	FORTH, Greece
Jiri Zara	Czech Technical University in Prague, Czech Republic
Wei Zeng	Florida International University, USA
Jian Zhao	University of Waterloo, Canada
Ying Zhu	Georgia State University, USA

Steering Committee

George Bebis	University of Nevada, Reno (chair)
Sabine Coquillart	Inria
James Klosowski	AT&T Labs Research
Yoshinori Kuno	Saitama University
Steve Lin	Microsoft
Peter Lindstrom	Lawrence Livermore National Laboratory
Kenneth Moreland	Sandia National Laboratories
Ara Nefian	NASA Ames Research Center
Ahmad P. Tafti	Mayo Clinic

Publicity

Ali Erol	Eksperta Software

Tutorials and Special Tracks

Emily Hand	University of Nevada, Reno
Alireza Tavakkoli	University of Nevada, Reno

Awards

Zehang Sun   Apple
Gholamreza Amayeh   Tesla

Web Master

Isayas Berhe Adhanom   University of Nevada, Reno

International Program Committee

Agu Emmanuel   WPI
Ahmad Touqeer   University of Colorado Colorado Springs
Alba Alfonso   Universidad Autónoma de San Luis Potosí
Alim Usman   University of Calgary
Ambardekar Amol   Microsoft
Anvari Zahra   University of Texas at Arlington
Apperley Mark   University of Waikato
Argyros Antonis   Foundation for Research and Technology - Hellas
Asari Vijayan K   University of Dayton
Asesh Aishwarya   Adobe
Averkiou Melinos   University of Cyprus
Baciu George   Hong Kong Polytechnic University
Bais Abdul   University of Regina
Bajpayee Abhishek   Massachusetts Institute of Technology
Balazs Peter   University of Szeged
Balcisoy Selim   Sabanci University
Barneva Reneta   SUNY Fredonia
Barzel Ronen   Independent
Bashiri Fereshteh S.   UW-Madison
Basu Aryabrata   Emory University
Batmaz Anil Ufuk   Kadir Has University
Bender Jan   RWTH Aachen University
Bhargava Ayush   Key Lime Interactive
Bhatia Sanjiv   University of Missouri at St. Louis
Billinghurst Mark   University of South Australia
Bist Ankur   Govind Ballabh Pant University of Agri. and Tech.
Biswas Ayan   Los Alamos National Laboratory
Borges Dibio   Universidade de Braslia
Borland David   University of North Carolina at Chapel Hill
Bouguila Nizar   Concordia University
Braz Pereira Jose   EST Setúbal/IPS
Broll Wolfgang   Ilmenau University of Technology
Capin Tolga   TED University
Chai Sek   SRI International
Chang Jian   Bournemouth University

Chatzis Sotirios	Cyprus University of Technology
Chellappa Rama	University of Maryland
Chen Yang	HRL Laboratories, LLC
Chen Cunjian	Michigan State University
Chen Zhonggui	Xiamen University
Chiang Yi-Jen	New York University
Cho Isaac	Utah State University
Chourasia Amit	San Diego Supercomputer Center, UCSD
Chung Kichung	SK Infosec
Dang Tommy	Texas Tech University
Dasgupta Aritra	NYU
Dequidt Jeremie	University of Lille
Dhillon Daljit Singh	Clemson University
Diamantas Sotirios	Tarleton State University, Texas A&M System
Diehl Alexandra	University of Konstanz
Dingliana John	Trinity College Dublin
Distante Cosimo	CNR
Doerner Ralf	RheinMain University of Applied Sciences
Doulamis Anastasios	Technical University of Crete
Du Shengzhi	Tshwane University of Technology
Duan Ye	University of Missouri at Columbia
Dutta Soumya	Los Alamos National Laboratory
Ebert Achim	University of Kaiserslautern
El Ansari Mohamed	University of Ibn Zohr
El-Alfy El-Sayed M.	King Fahd University of Petroleum and Minerals
Ens Barrett	Monash University
Entezari Alireza	University of Florida
Erol Ali	Sigun Information Technologies
Ertl Thomas	University of Stuttgart
Eslami Mohammad	Technical University of Munich
Fernandez Amanda	University of Texas at San Antonio
Ferrara Matteo	University of Bologna
Ferreira Nivan	Universidade Federal de Pernambuco
Ferrise Francesco	Politecnico di Milano
Fierrez Julian	Universidad Autonoma de Madrid
Fisher Robert	The University of Edinburgh
Foresti Gian Luca	University of Udine
Frey Steffen	University of Groningen
Fudos Ioannis	University of Ioannina
Fujishiro Issei	Keio University
Fusek Radovan	VŠB-Technical University of Ostrava
Ganovelli Fabio	ISTI-CNR
Gao Xifeng	Florida State University
Gavrilova M.	University of Calgary
Gdawiec Krzysztof	University of Silesia
Geist Robert	Clemson University

Giorgi Daniela	ISTI - CNR
Goh Wooi-Boon	Nanyang Technological University
Grosso Roberto	Friedrich-Alexander-Universität Erlangen-Nürnberg
Guo Hanqi	Argonne National Laboratory
Gustafson David	Kansas State University
Hamza-Lup Felix	Georgia Southern University
Hand Emily	University of Nevada, Reno
Hao Xuejun	Columbia University
Haworth Brandon	University of Victoria
Hazarika Subhashis	Los Alamos National Laboratory
Hodgson Eric	Miami University
Holmberg Bahnsen	ChrisAalborg University
Hua Jing	Wayne State University
Hussain Muhammad	King Saud University
Iglesias Guitián	José A.University of A Coruña
Imiya Atsushi	IMIT Chiba University
Iwasaki Kei	Wakayama University
Jang Yun	Sejong University
Jenkin Michael	York University
Jeschke Stefan	NVIDIA
Jiang Ming	LLNL
Jung Sungchul	HIT Lab NZ
Kam Ho Chuen	The Chinese University of Hong Kong
Kamberov George	University of Alaska Anchorage
Kamberova Gerda	Hofstra University
Kampel Martin	Vienna University of Technology
Kanai Takashi	The University of Tokyo
Khadka Rajiv	Idaho National Laboratory
Khan Waqar	Wellington Institute of Technology
Kim Edward	Drexel University
Kim Hyungseok	Konkuk University
Kim Min H.	Korea Advanced Inst of Science and Technology
Klosowski James	AT&T Labs Research
Kollias Stefanos	National Technical University of Athens
Komuro Takashi	Saitama University
Krueger Jens	University of Duisburg-Essen
Kuijper Arjan	TU Darmstadt
Kuno Yoshinori	Saitama University
La Hung	University of Nevada
Lai Yu-Kun	Cardiff University
Laramee Robert S.	University of Nottingham
Lee D. J.	Brigham Young University
Lewis Robert R.	Washington State University
Li Xin	Louisiana State University
Li Frederick	University of Durham
Lien Kuo-Chin	XMotors.ai

Lin Stephen	Microsoft
Lindstrom Peter	LLNL
Liu Zhanping	Old Dominion University
Liu Shiguang	Tianjin University
Loaiza Manuel	Universidad Católica San Pablo
Loss Leandro	QuantaVerse, ITU, ESSCA
Loviscach Joern	University of Applied Sciences
Lu Aidong	UNC Charlotte
Luo Xun	Tianjin University of Technology
Macdonald Brendan	NIOSH
Makrogiannis Sokratis	Delaware State University
Malomo Luigi	ISTI - CNR
Management Cultural	University of Patras
Mansoor Hamid	Worcester Polytechnic Institute
Martins Rafael M.	Linnaeus University, Växjö
Masutani Yoshitaka	Hiroshima City University
Mathews Sherin	University of Delaware
Matkovic Kresimir	VRVis Research Center
Mcgraw Tim	Purdue University
McInerney Tim	Ryerson University
Memon Qurban	UAE University
Mestre Daniel	Aix-Marseille University
Meunier Jean	University of Montreal
Miao Xikui	Brigham Young University
Mistelbauer Gabriel	Otto-von-Guericke University Magdeburg
Moreland Kenneth	Sandia National Laboratories
Morishima Shigeo	Waseda University
Morris Brendan	University of Nevada, Las Vegas
Moujahdi Chouaib	Mohammed V University in Rabat
Musse Soraia	Pontificia Univ Catolica do Roi Grande do Sul
Nazemi Kawa	Darmstadt University of Applied Sciences
Nguyen Quang Vinh	Western Sydney University
Nicolescu Mircea	University of Nevada, Reno
Nikou Christophoros	University of Ioannina, Ioannina
Nixon Mark	University of Southampton
Noh Junyong	Korea Advanced Inst of Science and Technology
Ntalianis Klimis	University of West Attica
Nykl Scott	Air Force Institute of Technology
Okada Yoshihiro	Kyushu University
Olague Gustavo	CICESE
Oshita Masaki	Kyushu Institute of Technology
Paelke Volker	Hochschule Bremen
Palagyi Kalman	University of Szeged
Papagiannakis George	University of Crete
Papakostas George	EMT Institute of Technology

Papka Michael	Argonne National Laboratory and Northern Illinois University
Patanè Giuseppe	CNR-IMATI
Patrignani Maurizio	Roma Tre University
Payandeh Shahram	Simon Fraser University
Pedrini Helio	University of Campinas
Peltonen Jaakko	Aalto University and University of Tampere
Petrakis Euripides	Technical University of Crete
Placidi Giuseppe	University of L'Aquila
Ponnusamy Vijayakumar	SRM university
Ponto Kevin	University of Wisconsin-Madison
Poovvancheri Jiju	University of Victoria
Pronost Nicolas	Université Claude Bernard Lyon 1
Qin Hong	Stony Brook University
Rasmussen Christopher	University of Delaware
Regentova Emma	UNLV
Reina Guido	University of Stuttgart
Reinhard Erik	InterDigital
Rekabdar Banafsheh	Southern Illinois University Carbondale
Remagnino Paolo	Kingston University
Ren Hongliang	National University of Singapore
Rhyne Theresa-Marie	Consultant
Ribeiro Eraldo	Florida Institute of Technology
Rodgers Peter	University of Kent
Rudomin Isaac	BSC
Sadlo Filip	Heidelberg University
Saha Punam	University of Iowa
Sakamoto Naohisa	Kobe University
Sandberg Kristian	Computational Solutions, Inc.
Santamaria Pang Alberto	General Electric Research
Sapidis Nickolas S.	University of Western Macedonia
Sarfraz Muhammad	Kuwait University
Scalzo Fabien	University of California, Los Angeles
Scharcanski Jacob	UFRGS
Schultz Thomas	University of Bonn
Schulze Jurgen	University of California San Diego
Séquin Carlo H.	University of California, Berkeley
Sharma Puneet	UiT-The Arctic University of Norway
Shehata Mohamed	Memorial University
Singh Gurjot	Fairleigh Dickinson University
Singh Gurjot	Fairleigh Dickinson University
Skurikhin Alexei	Los Alamos National Laboratory
Slavik Pavel	Czech Technical University
Snoeyink Jack	The University of North Carolina at Chapel Hill
Solari Fabio	University of Genoa - DIBRIS
Spagnolo Paolo	National Research Council

Sreevalsan-Nair Jaya	IIIT Bangalore
Su Chung-Yen	National Taiwan Normal University
Sun Zehang	Apple inc.
Sun Changming	CSIRO
Tapamo Jules-Raymond	Univesity of KwaZulu-Natal
Tavakkoli Alireza	University of Nevada, Reno
Tavares João Manuel R. S.	FEUP & INEGI
Thalmann Daniel	Ecole Polytechnique Fédérale de Lausanne
Theisel Holger	Otto-von-Guericke University
Tian Yuan	Innopeak Tech Inc
Torsney-Weir Thomas	VRVis
Tozal Mehmet Engin	University of Louisiana at Lafayette
Tubaro Stefano	Politecnico di Milano
Umlauf Georg	Universityof Applied Science Constance
Ushizima Daniela	Lawrence Berkeley National Laboratory
Viriri Serestina	University of KwaZulu-Natal
Voulodimos Athanasios	University of West Attica
Wang Cuilan	Georgia Gwinnett College
Wang Chaoli	University of Notre Dame
Weyers Benjamin	Trier University
Wischgoll Thomas	Wright State University
Wong Kin Hong	The Chinese University of Hong Kong
Xu Wei	Brookhaven National Lab
Yanagida Yasuyuki	Meijo University
Yang Xiaosong	Bournemouth University
Yang Fumeng	Brown University
Yen Hsu-Chun	National Taiwan University
Yin Lijun	State University of New York at Binghamton
Yu Zeyun	University of Wisconsin-Milwaukee
Yuan Chunrong	Technische Hochschule Köln
Zabulis Xenophon	FORTH
Zara Jiri	Czech Technical University in Prague
Zeng Wei	Florida International University
Zhao Jian	University of Waterloo
Zhu Ying	Georgia State University

Keynote Talks

Embodied Perception in-the-Wild

Deva Ramanan

Carnegie-Mellon University, USA

Abstract. Computer vision is undergoing a period of rapid progress, rekindling the relationship between perception, action, and cognition. Such connections may be best practically explored in the context of autonomous robotics. In this talk, I will discuss perceptual understanding tasks motivated by embodied "in-the-wild" autonomous robots, focusing on the illustrative case of autonomous vehicles. I will argue that many challenges that surface are not well-explored in contemporary computer vision. These include streaming perception with bounded resources, generalization via spatiotemporal grouping, rethinking the interface between perception and action, and robust processing that can recognize anomalous out-of-sample events. I will conclude with a description of open challenges for embodied perception in-the-wild.

Design Tools for Material Appearance

Holly Rushmeier

Yale University, USA

Abstract. The design of material appearance for both virtual and physical design remains a challenging problem. There aren't straightforward intuitive techniques as there are in geometric design where shapes can be sketched or assembled from geometric primitives. In this talk I will present a series of contributions to developing intuitive appearance design tools. This includes studies of material appearance perception which form the basis of the development of perceptual axes for reflectance distribution design. I will also present novel interfaces for design including hybrid slider/image navigation and augmented reality interfaces. I will discuss the unique problems involved in designing appearance for objects to be physically manufactured rather than simply displayed in virtual environments. Finally, I will show how exemplars of spatially varying materials can be inverted to produce procedural models.

Guidance-Enriched Visual Analytics: Challenges and Opportunities

Silvia Miksch

TU Wien, Austria

Abstract. On the one hand, we investigate appropriate, expressive, and effective Visual Analytics concepts and solutions for particular users, their data, and their tasks in mind. On the other hand, we explore the usage and potential of guidance. Guidance aims to support the user while working with Visual Analytics solutions. Guidance assists users with the selection of appropriate visual means and interaction techniques, the utilization of analytical methods, as well as the configuration instantiation of these algorithms with suitable parameter settings and the combinations thereof. After a visualization or Visual Analytics method and parameters are selected, guidance is also needed to explore the data, identify interesting data nuggets and findings, collect and group insights to explore high level hypotheses, and gain new insights and knowledge. In this talk, I will contextualize the different aspects of guidance-enriched Visual Analytics. I will present a framework for guidance designers which comprising requirements, a set of specific phases with quality criteria designers should go through when designing guidance-enriched Visual Analytics. Various examples will illustrate what has been achieved so far and show possible future directions and challenges.

Learning and Accruing Knowledge over Time Using Modular Architectures

Marc'Aurelio Ranzato

Facebook AI Research, USA

Abstract. A typical trait of any intelligent system is the ability to learn new skills quickly without too many interactions with a teacher. Over time we also would expect an intelligent system to become better at solving new tasks, coming up with a better solution in even less time if the new task relates to something already learned in the past. While nowadays machine learning methods excel at learning a single task from large amounts of labeled data, and more recently, even from little labeled data provided suitable pretraining on a vast amount of unlabeled data, knowledge is seldom accrued over time. Whenever more data and compute are available, bigger models are often retrained from scratch. In this talk, I argue that by considering the sequence of learning tasks, and more generally, the sequential nature of the data acquisition process, we may grant our artificial learners an unprecedented opportunity to transfer knowledge and even accrue knowledge over time, potentially leading to more efficient and effective learning of future tasks. From the modeling side, I will introduce a few variants of hierarchical mixtures of experts, which are deep modular networks. These architectures are appealing for a twofold reason. First, since they are modular it is natural to add modules over time to accommodate the acquisition of new knowledge. The modularity also leads to computational efficiency since run time can be made constant with respect to the number of modules. Second, by recombining modules in novel ways compositional generalization emerges, yielding learners that learn faster as time goes by. I will demonstrate these ideas on several learning settings applied to vision, namely compositional 0-shot learning, continual learning and anytime learning. Although these are admittedly baby steps towards our grand goal, I believe there is an untapped potential for more effective and efficient learning once we frame learning as a life-long learning experience.

Combining Brain-Computer Interfaces and Virtual Reality: Novel 3D Interactions and Promising Applications

Anatole Lécuyer

Inria, France

Abstract. In this talk I will present a research path on Brain-Computer Interfaces (BCI) aiming to establish a solid connection with Virtual Reality (VR) and Augmented Reality (AR). I will first evoke the great success of OpenViBE, an open-source software platform dedicated to BCI research used today all over the world, notably with VR systems. Then, I will illustrate how BCI and VR/AR technologies can be combined to design novel 3D interactions and effective applications, e.g. for health, sport, entertainment, or training.

Direct Estimation of Appearance Models for Image Segmentation

Pedro Felzenszwalb

Brown University, USA

Abstract. Image segmentation algorithms often depend on appearance models that characterize the distribution of pixel values in different image regions. We describe a novel approach for estimating appearance models directly from an image, without explicit consideration of the pixels that make up each region. Our approach is based on algebraic expressions that relate local image statistics to the appearance models of spatially coherent regions. The approach leads to two different algorithms for estimating appearance models. We present experimental results that demonstrate the proposed methods work well in practice and lead to effective image segmentation algorithms.

Contents – Part II

Poster

Contents – Part I

Applications

Deep Learning II

Computer Graphics II

3D Vision

Virtual Reality

Motion and Tracking

Object Detection and Recognition

ST: Medical Image Analysis

Video-Based Hand Tracking for Screening Cervical Myelopathy

Ryota Matsui[1] , Takafumi Koyama[2] , Koji Fujita[2] , Hideo Saito[1] ,
and Yuta Sugiura[1](✉)

[1] Keio University, Tokyo, Japan
{r.matsui-1210,hs,sugiura}@keio.jp
[2] Tokyo Medical and Dental University, Tokyo, Japan
{koya.orth,fujiorth}@tmd.ac.jp

Abstract. Cervical myelopathy (CM) is a pathology of the spinal cord
that causes upper limb disorders. CM is often screened by conducting the
10-s grip and release (G&R) test, which mainly focuses on hand dysfunction caused by CM. This test has patients repeat gripping and releasing
their hands as quickly as possible. Spine surgeons observe the quickness
of this repetition to screen for CM. We propose an automatic screening
method of CM that involves patients' hands recorded as videos when they
are performing the G&R test. The videos are used to estimate feature
values, i.e., the positions of each part of the hand, which are obtained
through image processing. A support vector machine classifier classifies
CM patients and controls with these feature values after pre-processing.
We validated our method with 10-fold cross-validation and the videos
of 20 CM patients and 15 controls. The results indicate that sensitivity, specificity, and area under the receiver operating characteristic curve
were 90.0%, 93.3%, and 0.947, respectively.

Keywords: Medical image processing · Hand tracking · Gesture
classification · Cervical myelopathy

1 Introduction

The spine covers the spinal cord, which is a part of the central nervous system, to
protect it. However, the function of the spinal cord decreases if some cause, such
as the degeneration of the intervertebral disks, compresses it. This pathology
is called myelopathy, and this disorder at the cervical level is called cervical
myelopathy (CM). CM causes various symptoms such as upper limb disorders
and gait disturbance.

Spine surgeons often use a computed tomography or magnetic resonance
imaging (MRI) scan to check for spinal cord compression [3,6,10]. They also
use screening methods to determine if certain symptoms of CM have occurred.
The 10-s grip and release (G&R) test, which mainly focuses on hand dysfunction, is one of the most common CM screening methods [17]. In this test, a

© Springer Nature Switzerland AG 2021
G. Bebis et al. (Eds.): ISVC 2021, LNCS 13018, pp. 3–14, 2021.
https://doi.org/10.1007/978-3-030-90436-4_1

patient repeats gripping and releasing their hand as quickly as possible for 10 s. The spine surgeon estimates that the patient may have CM if the repeat count is approximately less than 20. This test is quite simple, no other devices are required. However, spine surgeons often use qualitative evaluation indexes such as the characteristic hand movement of CM patients, which may be difficult to be consistent between spine surgeons. Therefore, screening performance may increase by introducing more quantitative and consistent evaluation indexes.

We propose a CM screening method that involves using videos of the G&R test and machine learning (ML). The procedure of the method is as follows. We place a smartphone on a table with the screen side facing up. Each patient performs the G&R test while holding the tested hand above the smartphone. The hand movement is recorded as a video with the front camera of the smartphone to focus on its characteristics. After the recording, each movement is described as three-dimensional position data through image processing. The data are then converted to frequency components by fast Fourier transform (FFT). These components are classified into CM patients and controls with a support vector machine (SVM) classifier.

The main contributions of this paper are (1) proposing an automatic CM screening method that performs better than other screening methods; and (2) introducing a ML-based classification model that does not require spine surgeons to rely on several qualitative indexes.

2   Related Work

2.1   Development of Medical Treatments for Cervical Myelopathy

In addition to the 10-s G&R test [17], there are various methods for screening CM, e.g., the 30-m walking test [19] and the 10-s step test [22]. Cook et al. evaluated several neurological screening methods such as Hoffmann's, inverted supinator, and Babinski signs. These methods focus on characteristic reflexes of CM patients when their body is stimulated in specific ways [5]. Among these methods, the G&R test is one of the most representative methods because of its simplicity. Therefore, our proposed video-based screening method is based on the G&R test.

Many researchers have aimed to make use of artificial intelligence and ML for spine surgery recently [4,7]. Focusing on CM, Merali et al. suggested an autonomous method of classifying MRI images using ML to detect cervical spinal cord compression [16]. Hoffman et al. used an SVM model to predict CM patients' conditions after surgical operations [11]. These methods can contribute patients get more appropriate medical treatment [14]. We aim to contribute that by screening CM more accurately.

2.2   Expansion of 10-Second Grip and Release Test

Several research projects have contributed to expanding the G&R test [17]. Machino et al. investigated the difference in the appropriate threshold of the repetition count of G&R among different ages of patients and concluded that the threshold decreases with age [15]. Hosono et al. proposed to extend the length of the G&R test to 15 s, and record patients' finger movements with a camera. The resulting video is divided into three segments for three spine surgeons to count the repetition separately [12].

The G&R test is conducted on the premise that a spine surgeon counts the G&R repetitions. Other researchers have considered how to screen CM without this task. Alagha et al. suggested using a Leap Motion Controller (LMC), a non-contact hand-tracking device, to count the repetitions [1]. Watanabe et al. proposed using a random forest classifier to screen for CM with an LMC [21]. Su et al. developed a glove-like sensing device for the G&R test. This device is used to measure the magnitude and period of movement for screening CM [20].

With our proposed method, we use a camera as a hand-tracking device. The tracking data are then used to screen CM with an SVM classifier.

2.3 Automatic Screening Methods for Various Diseases

Such automatic screening methods have been considered for various diseases. For example, Iakovakis et al. focused on hand disorders, an early symptom of Parkinson's disease (PD). It is screened for by hand movements through manipulating the touchscreen of a smartphone [13]. Sharma et al. used patients' voice data to screen for specific language impairment, which delays a child's development of language skills [18].

Video-based screening methods have also been proposed. Gomez et al. focused on hypomimia, a symptom of PD that causes changes in the ability to move one's face. They suggested detecting it from face gestures with video [8]. Bandini et al. used a depth camera to detect amyotrophic lateral sclerosis (ALS), which causes motor disability. The camera is used to track facial movements that can be affected by ALS [2].

3 Method Design

The flow of our proposed CM screening method is shown in Fig. 1. We used Python to implement this method.

3.1 Recording Grip and Release Test

We use the front camera of a smartphone to record the G&R test. The smartphone is placed on a table with the screen facing upward. The patient holds their hand above the smartphone (Fig. 2) and repeats gripping and releasing their hand as quickly as possible. We record a video at a frame rate of 30 frames per second (fps) with the camera while ensuring that the position of the hand does not move out of the field of view. The recording continues until the following two conditions are met: the repetition count reaches 20 and the recording time exceeds 10 s. After the recording, the video is forwarded to a PC for processing.

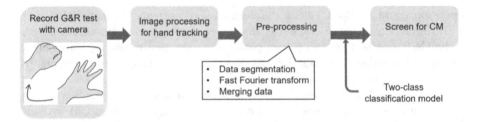

<figure>Fig. 1. Flow of our screening method</figure>

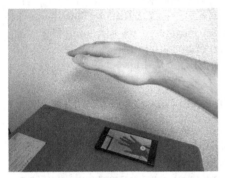

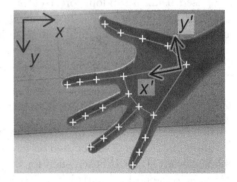

Fig. 2. Recording G&R test. Smartphone is used as camera. Each patient holds their hand above it to record test.

Fig. 3. Image processing with MediaPipe [9]. It estimates 21 positions, shown as cross markers.

3.2 Image Processing

This process extracts feature values of hand movement for screening classification. We use MediaPipe, an image-processing framework provided by Google [9]. MediaPipe estimates 21 positions of the hand and fingers from each video frame (Fig. 3). Since these positions are described as three-dimensional coordinates, each feature value is composed of $3 \times 21 = 63$ dimensions. These values are unified as time-series data.

These data are adjusted through two steps. The first step is the adjustment of the coordinate system. That of MediaPipe is described as three directions: horizontal (x), vertical (y), and depth (z). Each corresponds to the video frame. Thus, x and y are changed if the relative direction of the smartphone and hand is not unified. To align these directions, this step changes these directions to x' and y'; x' is parallel to the line between the wrist and base of the index finger, and y' is orthogonal to x' (Fig. 3). The origins of x' and y' are located at the wrist.

The second adjustment step is the introduction of the velocity components v. These are calculated as

$$v_t = p_t - p_{t-1}, \tag{1}$$

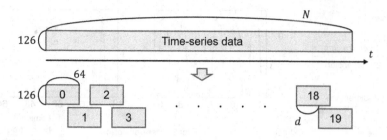

Fig. 4. Segmentation of time-series data

where p and $t \in \{0, 1, \cdots, N-1\}$ are the data and period of the frame, respectively. We directly use v as feature values without any adjustments such as filtering and smoothing. Since v has 63 dimensions as well as p, the number of dimensions of the feature values increase to $2 \times 63 = 126$. We eliminate feature values of the first period p_0 from the data because we cannot calculate v_0.

3.3　Pre-processing of the Data

These data are pre-processed before the screening classification. Three steps compose this pre-processing: data segmentation, FFT, and merging data of multiple trials.

The first step of pre-processing is segmenting the data. The purpose is to align the number of frames of each segment because the length of the time-series data varies depending on the recording time of the video. Data segmentation is visualized in Fig. 4. The time-series data, which have N frames, are divided into 20 segments, numbering 0 to 19. The length of each segment is 64. Each segment corresponds to the hand movement for about 2 s, as the frame rate of the video is 30 fps. The distance of the start frame between the neighboring segments d is determined as

$$d = \frac{N - 64}{19}, \tag{2}$$

which essentially means that d is adjusted to associate the end of the last segment with that of the time-series data.

In the next step, each of the 20 segments and 126 dimensions, which has 64 elements, is transformed into 64 frequency components with one-dimensional FFT (Fig. 5). We can consider the G&R test as a periodic movement. However, the periodic characteristics of each segment are not unified. We thought that this transformation can improve robustness against the characteristics. In this study, we used the amplitude components of the lower 32 frequency components for each dimension to eliminate mirrored and redundant frequencies. Thus, each segment has $32 \times 126 = 4,032$ elements.

We may want to screen CM with more than one trial of the G&R test, such as one trial for each hand. In this case, segments for each trial are merged as the last pre-processing step. By merging them per segment number between 0 and 19, we obtain 20 pre-processed segments.

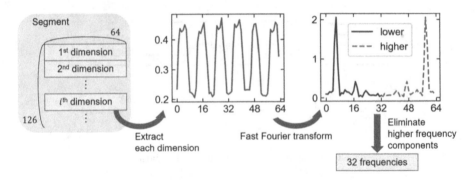

Fig. 5. Flow of fast Fourier transform

3.4 Two-Class Classification

These segments are classified into two classes with an SVM classifier that estimates certain characteristics of CM symptoms. Since the data have been divided into 20 segments, we obtain 20 decision functions that correspond to the estimated probabilities. The final estimation result is determined by the average of these functions.

We do not declare that this design is optimized for screening. This means that some modifications, such as an additional pre-processing step and using another ML method may improve the screening method. We think non-linear transformations of the feature values and convolutional neural network suitable for images as the concrete examples.

4 Experiments

4.1 Overview

We recorded the G&R test once for each hand and participant at our hospital. We collected a total of 70 videos from 35 right-handed participants. They were divided into CM patient group and control group on the basis of the spine surgeons' diagnoses. Detailed information of the participants is shown in Table 1.

After the data processing introduced in Sect. 3, we validated the classification performance with 10-fold cross-validation. The data were divided into training and test data. The training data were used to generate a two-class SVM classifier. The test data were classified using the classifier to select three evaluation indexes, which are sensitivity, specificity, and area under the receiver operating characteristic curve (AUC). We found multiple combinations of sensitivity and specificity depending on the classification threshold. We selected one that maximized $(\text{sensitivity})^2 + (\text{specificity})^2$.

Table 1. Participant information

	CM patient group		Control group	
	Male	Female	Male	Female
Number of participants	10	10	8	7
Mean age	66.8	71.6	57.9	64.9
Standard deviation of age	7.9	11.1	14.4	12.2

Table 2. AUC for each finger

Focused finger	AUC
Thumb	0.907
Index finger	0.900
Middle finger	0.877
Ring finger	0.853
Little finger	0.870

Table 3. AUC for each feature value

Focused type	AUC
FT	0.880
DIPJ	0.867
PIPJ	0.910
MPJ	0.930

4.2 Validation for Each Finger and Feature Value

Before the main validation, we validated the classification performance of our method using only components of one finger. The objective was to select components that mainly contribute to classification. We obtained three-dimensional positions of the fingertip and three joints for each finger, as shown in Fig. 3. Therefore, we used $2 \times 3 \times 4 = 24$ components for this validation. Videos of both the left and right hands were used for this validation.

We also validated this performance for four types of feature values: fingertip (FT), distal interphalangeal joint (DIPJ), proximal interphalangeal joint (PIPJ), and metacarpophalangeal joint (MPJ). This order corresponds to the distance from FT. Focusing on each position of five fingers, we used $2 \times 3 \times 5 = 30$ components. It should be noted that the number of thumb joints is one less than that of the other fingers. MediaPipe obtains the carpometacarpal joint as the fourth position of the thumb. We treated the composition of thumb joints in the same manner as the others for simplicity.

The AUCs for each finger and feature value are shown in Tables 2 and 3, respectively. Sensitivity and specificity were 90.00% and 86.67% for every finger and feature value, respectively. We can see that fingers of the thumb side and feature values of the wrist side tended to show higher AUCs, although the difference was almost within 0.05.

From these results, we manually selected the components to be used in the main validation. We selected PIPJ and MPJ of the thumb and index finger, which showed AUCs of more than 0.900. This combination is composed of $2 \times 3 \times 2 \times 2 = 24$ components.

Table 4. Sensitivity, specificity, and AUCs for selected components

Focused hands	Sensitivity (%)	Specificity (%)	AUC
Both hands	90.0	86.7	0.947
Right hand	90.0	93.3	0.947
Left hand	85.0	80.0	0.890

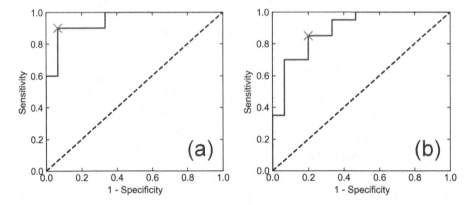

Fig. 6. ROC curves as validation results: (a) and (b) correspond to right and left hands, respectively. Cross markers show combination of sensitivity and specificity we selected.

4.3 Validation for the Selected Components

We used the 24 components selected in Sect. 4.2 for the main validation. We validated the classification performance of our method under three conditions: using videos of the right hand, left hand, and both. Through this validation, we aimed to reveal if our method is effective enough to be used in actual medical settings.

The classification performance of our method is shown in Table 4. The receiver operating characteristic (ROC) curves when focusing on only one hand are shown in Fig. 6. These results indicate that we do not need to focus on both hands to use our method since the performance for the right hand exceeded that for both hands. However, it may be crucial to select which hand to focus on since the classification performance for the left hand is mildly worse. We chose the result for the right hand as the best classification performance of the validation.

5 Discussion

5.1 Consideration of Validation Results

Table 2 shows that fingers of the thumb side tend to result in a higher AUC than ones of the little-finger side. The cause of this is thought to be the direction of

Table 5. Sensitivity, specificity, and AUCs of our method and other methods

Screening method	Sensitivity (%)	Specificity (%)	AUC
The 10-s G&R test [15]	70.3–82.1	42.9–74.0	0.647–0.890
Inverted supinator sign [5]	61	78	N/A
Babinski sign [5]	33	92	N/A
Su et al.'s method [20]	86.73	86	0.929
Our method	90.0	93.3	0.947

finger movement. As shown in Fig. 3, the fluctuation of x' and y' differ between fingers. If the characteristics of CM symptoms mainly appear in either direction, the difference should affect the classification performance. On the other hand, it is medically said that fingers of the little-finger side show more obvious characteristics of CM symptoms than ones of the thumb side [17]. We believe that these two tendencies are conflicting. Although it is difficult to specify a reason for this conflict, we will investigate these tendencies as future work.

Table 4 and Fig. 6 show that the classification performance for the right hand is higher than that of the left hand. We believe that the dominant hand of each patient may affect this difference. As mentioned in Sect. 4.1, all participants were right-handed. We can generally move the dominant hand more easily than the non-dominant hand. This difference may affect the clarity of the difference between CM patients and controls.

5.2 Comparison with Other Screening Methods

As mentioned in Sect. 4.3, sensitivity, specificity, and AUC of our method were 90.0%, 93.3%, and 0.947, respectively. Table 5 shows the comparison between our method and other screening methods: the 10-s G&R test validated by Machino et al. [15], that of Su et al. involving a glove-like device to measure the G&R test [20], inverted supinator sign, and Babinski sign. The latter two methods are the reflex-based methods validated by Cook et al. [5]. The performance of our method was generally higher than that of other methods, indicating that the performance of our method should be adequate to be used in actual medical settings.

5.3 Limitations and Future Work

Although our method performed relatively well, there are limitations. First, our method only focuses on hand movement, although we can also say this for other CM screening methods. CM causes various symptoms in addition to hand dysfunction. Considering various information such as symptoms and image inspections, spine surgeons diagnose CM. Thus, it is not appropriate to diagnose CM with only our method.

Another limitation is that our method does not currently take other pathologies and diseases that cause hand dysfunction into account. This means that our method does not identify the cause of a symptom. To solve this problem, we aim to apply our method to other pathologies and diseases such as carpal tunnel syndrome. A screening method of multiple pathologies and diseases should enables not only detection of symptoms but also differential diagnosis.

Our ultimate goal is to apply our method to the actual medical settings, specifically local doctors' offices and nursing homes, as the initial screening method. It may contribute to the early detection of CM by linking the screening results to further medical services such as consulting spine surgeons and image inspections. We will consider further improvement plans with the opinions of medical professionals for such application. These should be helpful to fill the gap between our method and the needs of a particular medical setting.

6   Conclusion

We proposed an automatic CM screening method that is based on the G&R test. With this method, we record videos of hand movements with a smartphone camera to obtain feature values. These values are classified into two classes corresponding to CM patients and controls after pre-processing.

We validated our method with cross-validation and 70 videos of 20 CM patients and 15 controls. Sensitivity, specificity, and AUC were 90.0%, 93.3%, and 0.947, respectively, which are higher than those of other CM screening methods.

We will apply our method to other causes of hand dysfunction, such as carpal tunnel syndrome. We also aim for our method to be used in actual medical settings.

Acknowledgements. This work was supported by JST PRESTO Grant Number JPMJPR17J4 and JST AIP-PRISM Grant Number JPMJCR18Y2.

References

1. Alagha, M.A., Alagha, M.A., Dunstan, E., Sperwer, O., Timmins, K.A., et al.: Development of a new assessment tool for cervical myelopathy using hand-tracking sensor: part 1: validity and reliability. Eur. Spine J. **26**(4), 1291–1297 (2017). https://doi.org/10.1007/s00586-017-4948-3
2. Bandini, A., Green, J.R., Taati, B., Orlandi, S., Zinman, L., et al.: Automatic detection of amyotrophic lateral sclerosis (ALS) from video-based analysis of facial movements: speech and non-speech tasks. In: 2018 13th IEEE International Conference on Automatic Face and Gesture Recognition (FG 2018), pp. 150–157. IEEE, Xi'an (2018). https://doi.org/10.1109/FG.2018.00031
3. Chanda, P.B., Paul, A., Paul, A., Sarkar, S.: Spondylosis detection and classification of cervical images using ATMFCMC based medical image segmentation methods. In: Proceedings of the International Conference on Advances in Electronics, Electrical and Computational Intelligence (ICAEEC) 2019 (2020). https://doi.org/10.2139/ssrn.3575474

4. Chang, M., Canseco, J.A., Nicholson, K.J., Patel, N., Vaccaro, A.R.: The role of machine learning in spine surgery: the future is now. Front. Surge. **7**(54) (2020). https://doi.org/10.3389/fsurg.2020.00054

5. Cook, C., Roman, M., Stewart, K.M., Leithe, L.G., Isaacs, R.: Reliability and diagnostic accuracy of clinical special tests for myelopathy in patients seen for cervical dysfunction. J. Orthopaedic Sports Phys. Therapy **39**(3), 172–178 (2009). https://doi.org/10.2519/jospt.2009.2938

6. d'Avanzo, S., Ciavarro, M., Pavone, L., Pasqua, G., Ricciardi, F., et al.: The functional relevance of diffusion tensor imaging in patients with degenerative cervical myelopathy. J. Clin. Med. **9**(6) (2020). https://doi.org/10.3390/jcm9061828

7. Galbusera, F., Casaroli, G., Bassani, T.: Artificial intelligence and machine learning in spine research. JOR Spine **2**(1) (2019). https://doi.org/10.1002/jsp2.1044

8. Gomez, L.F., Morales, A., Orozco-Arroyave, J.R., Daza, R., Fierrez, J.: Improving parkinson detection using dynamic features from evoked expressions in video. In: Proceedings of the IEEE/CVF Conference on Computer Vision and Pattern Recognition (CVPR) Workshops, pp. 1562–1570. IEEE, Nashville (2021). https://doi.org/10.1109/CVPRW53098.2021.00172

9. Google: Mediapipe. https://google.github.io/mediapipe/, Accessed 12 July 2021

10. Harrop, J.S., Naroji, S., Maltenfort, M., Anderson, D.G., Albert, T., et al.: Cervical myelopathy: a clinical and radiographic evaluation and correlation to cervical spondylotic myelopathy. Spine **35**(6), 620–624 (2010). https://doi.org/10.1097/BRS.0b013e3181b723af

11. Hoffman, H., Lee, S.I., Garst, J.H., Lu, D.S., Li, C.H., et al.: Use of multivariate linear regression and support vector regression to predict functional outcome after surgery for cervical spondylotic myelopathy. J. Clin. Neurosci **22**(9), 1444–1449 (2015). https://doi.org/10.1016/j.jocn.2015.04.002

12. Hosono, N., Sakaura, H., Mukai, Y., Kaito, T., Makino, T., et al.: A simple performance test for quantifying the severity of cervical myelopathy. J. Bone Joint Surg. Brit. **90**(9), 1210–1213 (2008). https://doi.org/10.1302/0301-620X.90B9.20459

13. Iakovakis, D., Hadjidimitriou, S., Charisis, V., Bostanjopoulou, S., Katsarou, Z., et al.: Early Parkinson's disease detection via touchscreen typing analysis using convolutional neural networks. In: 2019 41st Annual International Conference of the IEEE Engineering in Medicine and Biology Society (EMBC), pp. 3535–3538. IEEE, Berlin (2019). https://doi.org/10.1109/EMBC.2019.8857211

14. Khan, O., Badhiwala, J.H., Grasso, G., Fehlings, M.G.: Use of machine learning and artificial intelligence to drive personalized medicine approaches for spine care. World Neurosurg **140**, 512–518 (2020). https://doi.org/10.1016/j.wneu.2020.04.022

15. Machino, M., Ando, K., Kobayashi, K., Morozumi, M., Tanaka, S., et al.: Cut off value in each gender and decade of 10-s grip and release and 10-s step test: A comparative study between 454 patients with cervical spondylotic myelopathy and 818 healthy subjects. Clin. Neurol. Neurosurg. (2019). https://doi.org/10.1016/j.clineuro.2019.105414

16. Merali, Z., Wang, J.Z., Badhiwala, J.H., Witiw, C.D., Wilson, J.R., et al.: A deep learning model for detection of cervical spinal cord compression in MRI scans. Sci. Rep. **11** (2021). https://doi.org/10.1038/s41598-021-89848-3

17. Ono, K., Ebara, S., Fuji, T., Yonenobu, K., Fujiwara, K., et al.: Myelopathy hand: new clinical signs of cervical cord damage. J. Bone Joint Surg. Brit. **69**(2), 215–219 (1987). https://doi.org/10.1302/0301-620X.69B2.3818752

18. Sharma, G., Prasad, D., Umapathy, K., Krishnan, S.: Screening and analysis of specific language impairment in young children by analyzing the textures of speech signal. In: 2020 42nd Annual International Conference of the IEEE Engineering in Medicine and Biology Society (EMBC), pp. 964–967. IEEE, Montreal (2020). https://doi.org/10.1109/EMBC44109.2020.9176056
19. Singh, A., Crockard, H.A.: Quantitative assessment of cervical spondylotic myelopathy by a simple walking test. The Lancet **354**(9176), 370–373 (1999). https://doi.org/10.1016/S0140-6736(98)10199-X
20. Su, X.J., Hou, C.L., Shen, B.D., Zhang, W.Z., Wu, D.S., et al.: Clinical application of a new assessment tool for myelopathy hand using virtual reality. Spine **45**(24), E1645–E1652 (2020). https://doi.org/10.1097/BRS.0000000000003696
21. Watanabe, M., Sugiura, Y., Saito, H., Koyama, T., Fujita, K.: Detection of cervical myelopathy with Leap Motion Sensor by random forests. In: 2020 IEEE 2nd Global Conference on Life Sciences and Technologies (LifeTech), pp. 214–216. IEEE, Kyoto (2020). https://doi.org/10.1109/LifeTech48969.2020.1570620097
22. Yukawa, Y., Kato, F., Ito, K., Horie, Y., Nakashima, H., et al.: "Ten second step test" as a new quantifiable parameter of cervical myelopathy. Spine **34**(1), 82–86 (2009). https://doi.org/10.1097/BRS.0b013e31818e2b19

NeoUNet: Towards Accurate Colon Polyp Segmentation and Neoplasm Detection

Phan Ngoc Lan[1], Nguyen Sy An[1], Dao Viet Hang[2,3], Dao Van Long[2,3], Tran Quang Trung[4], Nguyen Thi Thuy[5], and Dinh Viet Sang[1(✉)]

[1] Hanoi University of Science and Technology, Hanoi, Vietnam
sangdv@soict.hust.edu.vn
[2] Hanoi Medical University, Hanoi, Vietnam
[3] Institute of Gastroenterology and Hepatology, Hanoi, Vietnam
[4] University of Medicine and Pharmacy, Hue University, Hue, Vietnam
[5] Faculty of Information Technology, Vietnam National University of Agriculture, Hanoi, Vietnam

Abstract. Automatic polyp segmentation has proven to be immensely helpful for endoscopy procedures, reducing the missing rate of adenoma detection for endoscopists while increasing efficiency. However, classifying a polyp as being neoplasm or not and segmenting it at the pixel level is still a challenging task for doctors to perform in a limited time. In this work, we propose a fine-grained formulation for the polyp segmentation problem. Our formulation aims to not only segment polyp regions, but also identify those at high risk of malignancy with high accuracy. We then present a UNet-based neural network architecture called NeoUNet, along with a hybrid loss function to solve this problem. Experiments show highly competitive results for NeoUNet on our benchmark dataset compared to existing polyp segmentation models.

Keywords: Polyp segmentation · Colonoscopy · Deep learning

1 Introduction

Colonoscopy is considered as the most effective procedure for colorectal polyp detection and removal. Among many histopathological types of precancerous polyps, adenomas with high-grade dysplasia carry the highest risks of developing into colorectal cancer (CRC) [7]. With over 640,000 deaths each year [3], CRC is among the most common types of cancer. As such, the importance of performing colonoscopies to detect and remove high-risk polyps is undeniable.

However, a review by Leufkens et al. [17] showed that $20 - 47\%$ of polyps might have been missed during colonoscopies. Several factors are contributing to this situation, including overloading healthcare systems with an overwhelming number of cases per day and reducing withdrawal time, low-quality endoscopy equipment, or personnel's lack of experience. Technologies such as image-enhanced endoscopies and novel accessories were invented and applied to

© Springer Nature Switzerland AG 2021
G. Bebis et al. (Eds.): ISVC 2021, LNCS 13018, pp. 15–28, 2021.
https://doi.org/10.1007/978-3-030-90436-4_2

solve this problem. However, cost-effectiveness is still a barrier, especially for limited-resource settings, while performance is not yet ideal. Thus, computer-aided systems have a lot of potentials to improve colonoscopy quality. Recent years have seen very active research in this domain, mostly focused on automatic polyp segmentation and/or detection. Several such works [6, 9] have achieved very high accuracy on benchmark datasets.

While automatic segmentation can immensely improve endoscopic performance, it leaves out the difficult task of determining whether a polyp is neoplastic. Neoplastic polyps are precursor lesions to CRC. They require different approaches such as conventional polypectomies, endoscopic mucosal resection, endoscopic submucosal dissection, biopsy, marking, staging for further management such as surgery or neoadjuvant chemo-radiotherapy. Non-neoplastic polyps, on the other hand, can be removed or left with/without following up during colonoscopies. Classifying neoplastic polyps could be very challenging, especially when the withdrawal time is under overwhelming pressure. In addition, the task typically requires well-trained endoscopists with many years of experience, who may still be unable to recognize and characterize some lesions due to tiredness. The critical nature of this task calls for a more fine-grained approach to segment polyps as well as to classify the lesions according to the risk of neoplasm with relative confidence.

Polyp segmentation has seen a number of approaches over the years. Traditional machine learning methods based on hand-crafted features [12, 24] rely on color, shape, texture, etc., to learn a classifier to separate polyps from the surrounding mucosa. These approaches are generally limited, as polyps have very high intra-class diversity and low inter-class variation. The state-of-the-art methods for polyp segmentation in recent years have been deep neural networks. These networks can learn highly abstract and complex image representations to accurately find polyp areas. U-Net [22] and related models are among the most successful and widely used, all of which feature an encoder-decoder architecture allowing the combination of low-level concrete features and high-level abstract features. Variants such as UNet++ [31] and ResUNet++ [15] improved on the original U-Net by adopting a nested architecture, while others (e.g. DoubleUNet [13]) went with a stacking approach. More general techniques in deep learning such as attention and deep supervision have also been incorporated in UNet, and have yielded promising results.

Fine-grained object classification seeks to discriminate different subordinate-level of object categories *subclasses* instead of simple coarse-grained classes [29]. For example, an image classified as "Dog" may have more fine-grained classes such as "Golden Retriever" or "Pomeranian". For the polyp detection problem, fine-grained segmentation provides a more semantic meaning of polyp regions, which can help to identify types of lesions at the pixel level. While these problems may seem to be similar to multi-class classification, their high inter-class similarity can easily confuse the learning models, leading to low performance.

In this paper, we first restate the polyp segmentation problem by expanding it with a fine-grained classification aspect. We then propose a UNet-based network architecture to solve it. Specifically, our contributions are:

- A formal statement for the problem of polyp segmentation and neoplasm detection;
- A new deep neural network architecture NeoUNet, designed for the stated problem;
- A new benchmark dataset, called NeoPolyp, for polyp segmentation and neoplasm detection;
- Experimental results for NeoUNet on the NeoPolyp dataset, including comparisons with existing models for polyp segmentation.

The rest of the paper is organized as follows. We provide a brief review of related works in Sect. 2. Section 3 describes the polyp segmentation and neoplasm detection problem in detail. The proposed NeoUNet is presented in Sect. 4. Section 5 showcases our experimental studies. Finally, we conclude the paper and highlight future works in Sect. 6.

2 Related Work

Convolutional neural networks (CNNs) have claimed state-of-the-art performance in almost every computer vision task in the last few years. Some of the earliest breakout models were AlexNet [16] and VGG [25]. These early architectures were still quite limited and suffered from degradation when increasing network depth. ResNet [8] introduced skip connections that helped smooth out the loss landscape and combat gradient vanishing in very deep networks. GoogLeNet [26] proposed a meticulously-designed multi-branch network with good performance. ResNeXt [30] also took up a multi-branch approach and applied it to ResNet. EfficientNet [27] is a family of networks designed using neural architecture search techniques that provides a range of tradeoffs between accuracy and latency. HarDNet [4] focused on reducing inference latency by reducing memory traffic.

Semantic segmentation and segmentation for medical images, in particular, have seen a lot of interest in recent years. Long et al. [19] adopted several well-known architectures for segmentation using transfer learning techniques. DeepLabV3 [5] proposed the use of atrous convolutions for dense feature extraction with positive results. PraNet [6] enhanced an FCN-like model with parallel partial decoder and reverse attention. HarDNet-MSEG [9] adopts the HarDNet backbone as the encoder in an encoder-decoder structure. The network achieved state-of-the-art performance on the Kvasir-SEG dataset [14] while also improving inference latency.

U-Net [22] was one of the first successful CNNs applied in medical imaging. The architecture features an encoder-decoder design, combining low-level features on the encoder branch with high-level features on the decoder branch. Numerous works have proposed improvements to the original UNet. UNet++ [31] and ResUNet++ [15] used a nested architecture, with multiple levels of cross-connections. DoubleUNet [13] stacked two UNets sequentially, using VGG-16 as the encoder backbone, with squeeze and excitation units and ASPP modules. While outperforming previous methods on several datasets, DoubleUNet is limited in terms of information flow between the two UNets. Tang et al. [28] tackled this limitation with Coupled U-Net (CUNet), which adds skip connections between UNet blocks. Attention-UNet [20] introduced attention gates which filters for useful salient features. Abraham et al. [1] proposed a novel loss function in conjunction with the Attention-UNet architecture, combined with multi-scale input and deep supervision.

Due to the heterogeneous quality of different endoscopic systems, the lack of public datasets for polyp characterization is a challenge. Among the most similar research to ours is that of Ribeiro et al. [21], who presented several approaches, including CNNs and hand-crafted features, for polyp classification. The authors extracted a dataset of 100 polyp images from endoscopy videos, each containing exactly one polyp. Several CNN models were tested on this dataset, including VGG, AlexNet, GoogLeNet, etc.... A primary drawback for this approach is that classification has to be done after detection or segmentation. In other words, the problem is approached in two stages. While combining the polyp detection modules with classification is possible, this method can be inefficient and cumbersome, especially for systems with real-time requirements or running on embedded devices. In this paper, we present an end-to-end model for both the segmentation and classification of polyps to overcome these limitations.

3   Polyp Segmentation and Neoplasm Detection

The problem presented in this work is an expansion of polyp segmentation, focusing more on the fine-grained classification to detect neoplasm polyps. In polyp segmentation, given an input image, we need to output a binary mask where each pixel's value is either 1 (the pixel is part of a polyp) or 0 (the pixel is part of the background).

The polyp segmentation and neoplasm detection problem (PSND) expects each pixel in the segmentation mask to have one of three values (see Fig. 1 for examples): 0 if the pixel is part of the image background; 1 if the pixel is part of a non-neoplastic polyp; 2 if the pixel is part of a neoplastic polyp.

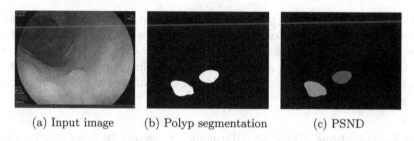

(a) Input image   (b) Polyp segmentation   (c) PSND

Fig. 1. Expected outputs for polyp segmentation and PSND. Black regions denote background pixels. White regions denote polyp regions. Green and red regions denote non-neoplastic and neoplastic polyp regions, respectively. (Color figure online)

PSND presents several unique challenges. First, the surface pattern of a polyp could be homogenous or heterogeneous, with different areas of texture which requires experienced endoscopists to evaluate carefully. Second, a neoplastic area in one lesion may only take up a portion of the polyp's surface, causing further difficulties for machine learning models. This property is the primary distinction between our problem and generic multi-class segmentation. While datasets such as PASCAL-VOC have many more classes, they are primarily well-defined and highly distinguishable (e.g., car, bird, person, etc....). Moreover, from the medical perspective, a misclassification could lead to biased decisions. False positives could result in over indications of endoscopic interventions or surgery, while false negatives could result in delaying suitable treatment.

Due to the challenging nature of neoplasm detection, actual training data for this problem may contain another class: polyps with undefined neoplasticity. These are highly difficult cases where trained physicians are unsure of the classification. Despite their existence, we do not want automatic systems to learn and output "undefined" pixels. Instead, it is much more beneficial to still produce a classification between neoplastic and non-neoplastic, as this provides more insight to physicians while also reducing inter-class similarity. At the same time, "undefined" polyps are still helpful for learning how to segment without classification.

The challenges mentioned above serve as motivation for the proposed NeoUNet model, which we shall describe in detail in the next section.

4   NeoUNet

4.1   Architecture

NeoUNet is a U-Net architecture similar to the one introduced in [1], with several key differences. The encoder backbone uses the HarDNet68 architecture [4], comprising of Harmonic Dense blocks (HDB). Outputs from each encoder level are passed to corresponding decoder blocks through attention gate modules. All decoder blocks also have output layers producing multi-class segmentation masks at their corresponding scale level. These output layers allow us to train the network using deep supervision, which boosts the network's stability and convergence rate. To take advantage of public ImageNet-trained HarDNet models, we keep the backbone structure and thus do not use joint multi-scale inputs. However, the benefits of pretraining can outweigh this limitation. The architecture's overview is shown in Fig. 2.

Encoder Backbone. HarDNet (Harmonic DenseNet) [4] is a CNN architecture inspired by DenseNet [10]. DenseNet's core principle is encouraging feature reuse through skip connections: each layer in a Dense Block receives the concatenated feature map of every preceding layer, essentially having a *global state* through which high-value features can be shared. While achieving high accuracy, DenseNet also has a large memory footprint, leading to low throughput and increased latency due to memory traffic.

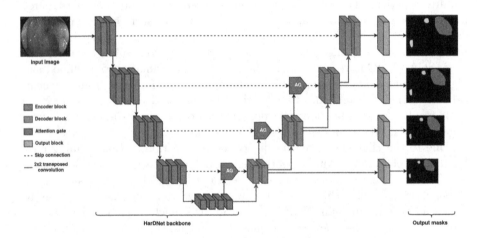

Fig. 2. Overview of NeoUNet's architecture

HarDNet sparsifies DenseNet by reducing the number of skip connections to create a better tradeoff between accuracy and memory. Specifically, a layer k in a HarD Block (HDB) receives a feature map from layer $k-2^n$ if 2^n divides k ($n \geq 0$, $k - 2^n \geq 0$). In addition, layers whose indices are divisible to large powers of 2 are more "influential", as their feature maps are more frequently reused. Such layers are given more convolutional kernels (more output channels). Concretely, the number of output channels for layer l with a growth rate k is $k \times m^n$, where $n = max\{\nu \mid l : 2^\nu\}$. m can be considered as the compression factor, where $m = 2$ means all layers have the same number of input feature maps. HarDNet68 further changes DenseNet architecture by removing the global dense connections, using Max Pooling for downsampling, and having dedicated growth rates for each HDB. In addition, HarDNet68 has 5 "strides" that reduce the feature map size by 2, 4, 8, 16, and 32 times compared to the original image. When incorporated in NeoUNet as the encoder backbone, each stride serves as an encoder block.

Attention Gate. The information carried in skip connections between encoder and decoder blocks can generally be noisy, as finer feature maps contain more local features that may be irrelevant. Thus, we use additive attention gates [20] on all such connections, except for the top-most blocks. An attention gate filters the input tensor using a set of attention coefficients α_i, calculated from the input x^l and the gating signal g (see Eq. (1) and Eq. (2) [20] for details).

$$q_{att}^l = \psi^T(\sigma_1(W_x^T x_i^l + W_g^T g_i + b_g)) + b_\psi \tag{1}$$
$$\alpha_i^l = \sigma_2(q_{att}^l(x_i^l, g_i; \Theta_{att})) \tag{2}$$

where σ_1 denotes the ReLU function, σ_2 denotes the sigmoid function. $\Theta_{att} = (W_x, W_g, b_g, \psi, b_\psi)$ is the set of learnable parameters. The attention gate's output is the filtered tensor $\hat{x}^l = x^l.\alpha$. Figure 3 illustrates the attention gate's structure.

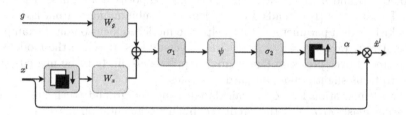

Fig. 3. Diagram of the additive attention gate module [20]

Decoder and Output Block. Each decoder block consists of 2 sequential sets of {Convolution, Batch Norm, Leaky ReLU} layers. The output of the previous decoder block is concatenated with the attention gate output (carrying filtered information from the encoder) to form the current decoder's input.

Each output block is a simple 1×1 convolution layer with two output channels, followed by the sigmoid activation. Each channel corresponds to the output mask for one class. Segmentation maps without classification can be inferred using the element-wise OR operator.

During training, we upsample output masks from all levels to the original image size and compute the loss values for each mask. These values are then summed to form the final loss for backpropagation. This form of deep supervision forces different levels of abstract features to make sense semantically, allowing faster convergence and improving stability.

4.2   Loss Function

The loss function for training NeoUNet is a weighted sum of a segmentation loss and a multi-class loss as follows:

$$\mathcal{L}(M_{ct}, M_{st}, M_{cp}, M_{sp}) = w_c \mathcal{L}_c(M_{ct}, M_{cp}) + w_s \mathcal{L}_s(M_{st}, M_{sp}), \qquad (3)$$

where the parameters w_c and w_s controls the level of effect each loss has on the training process. We find that NeoUNet performs best when $w_c = 0.75$ and $w_s = 0.25$.

The multi-class loss $\mathcal{L}_c$ reflects the difference between the ground truth multi-class mask M_{ct} and the predicted multi-class mask M_{cp}. $\mathcal{L}_c$ is averaged from Binary Cross Entropy loss and Focal Tversky loss [1] (see Eq. (4)). This is the primary loss function that drives the model toward making accurate class-specific segmentation.

$$\mathcal{L}_c(M_{ct}, M_{cp}) = \frac{BCE(M_{ct}, M_{cp}) + FocalTversky(M_{ct}, M_{cp})}{2} \qquad (4)$$

Tversky loss [23] can be seen as a generalization of Dice loss, with two hyper-parameters α and β that control the effect of false positives and false negatives. Focal Tversky loss [1] extends Tversky loss by combining ideas from Focal loss [18], which adds a parameter γ that helps the model to focus on hard examples. For NeoUNet, we set $\alpha = 1 - \beta = 0.3$ for Tversky loss, meaning the model prioritizes recall over precision (since smaller polyps are likely to be missed), and $\gamma = \frac{4}{3}$ to focus slightly more on hard examples.

The segmentation loss $\mathcal{L}_s$ is calculated using the ground truth binary segmentation mask M_{st}, and the predicted binary segmentation mask M_{sp}. M_{sp} can be inferred from the multi-class mask M_{cp} as follows:

$$M_{sp}(i,j) = \begin{cases} 0, \text{ if } M_{cp}(i,j) = 0 \\ 1, \text{ otherwise} \end{cases} \qquad (5)$$

$\mathcal{L}_s$ is averaged from Binary Cross Entropy loss and Tversky loss (see Eq. (6)). This is a secondary loss function that ensures the model maintains high segmentation accuracy. In addition, the segmentation loss allows NeoUNet to take advantage of training data marked as "undefined".

$$\mathcal{L}_s(M_{st}, M_{sp}) = \frac{BCE(M_{st}, M_{sp}) + Tversky(M_{st}, M_{sp})}{2} \qquad (6)$$

During training, pixels that are part of "undefined" polyps only contribute to the segmentation loss and are ignored by the multi-class loss. This mechanism allows the model to freely label "undefined" polyps based on existing features while still benefitting from partially labeled data.

5 Experiments and Discussion

5.1 Benchmark Dataset

There is a number of endoscopic image datasets available for different research purposes in endoscopic image analysis, such as Kvasir-SEG [14], CVC-ColonDB [2], or CVC-ClinicDB, ETIS-Larib in the MICCAI 2015 [3]. However, there is no publicly available dataset for the problem of polyp segmentation and neoplasm detection at the pixel level. Therefore, we have created a benchmark dataset for this research in order to compare the performance of our method with the state-of-the-art methods.

Our dataset contains 7,466 annotated endoscopic images to train and benchmark the proposed NeoUNet. These images are captured directly during endoscopic recording, including all four lighting modes: WLI (White Light Imaging), FICE (Flexible spectral Imaging Color Enhancement), BLI (Blue Light Imaging), and LCI (Linked Color Imaging). The patient's identifying information is removed from each image to ensure anonymity.

Annotations (including segmentation and classification) are added to each image independently by two experienced endoscopists. Matching annotation labels are accepted into the dataset, while those without full consensus from annotators or declared "undefined" by at least one annotator are marked with the label "undefined". Neoplastic polyps take up a majority of the polyps present in NeoPolyp. The number of neoplastic, non-neoplastic and "undefined" polyp pixels account for 80%, 13%, and 7%, respectively. The dataset is randomly split into a training set of 5,966 images and a test set of 1,500 images.

5.2 Experiment Setup

We perform two experiments to validate the effectiveness of our proposed NeoUNet: a comparison with baseline models: we compare NeoUNet with U-Net [22], PraNet [6], and HarDNet-MSEG [9] on the PSND task; and a comparison on NeoPolyp and NeoPolyp-Clean: we compare the performance of NeoUNet when trained on NeoPolyp and NeoPolyp-Clean, in order to show the benefits of learning on "undefined"-labeled data.

In both experiments, common used metrics are employed for performance measurement:

- Polyp segmentation performance (without classification), measured using Dice score and IoU score. We denote these metrics as $Dice_{seg}$ and IoU_{seg};
- Segmentation performance on each class (non-neoplastic and neoplastic), measured using Dice score and IoU score. We denote these metrics as $Dice_{non}$, IoU_{non}, $Dice_{neo}$ and IoU_{neo}, respectively.
- Inference speed for each model, measured as frames per second (FPS). This metric is only of significance in the first experiment.

Dice and IoU are calculated pixel-wise on the entire test set (micro-averaged, not averaged over each image). Evaluation is done on images resized to 352×352.

To measure inference speed for a model, we average the latency of inferring 100 test images with a batch size of 1.

Additionally, the following settings and techniques are applied to the training process in both experiments:

- To avoid bias due to class imbalance in the dataset, we oversample images containing non-neoplastic polyps during training such that $P_{non} \approx P_{neo}$, where P_{non} and P_{neo} are the number of pixels containing non-neoplastic and neoplastic polyps, respectively;
- NeoUNet is trained using Stochastic Gradient Descent with Nesterov momentum and a learning rate of 0.001. The learning rate lr increases linearly up to the target value in the first t_w epochs, then annealed following the cosine function [11].
- Each training batch is put through the network in 3 different scales: 448×448, 352×352, and 256×256;
- Data augmentation is employed to improve models' generality. We use five types of augmentation: rotate, horizontal/vertical flip, motion blur, and color jittering. Augmentation is performed on the fly with a probability of 0.7.

NeoUNet and the original U-Net are implemented in Python 3.6 using the PyTorch framework. We use the official PraNet[1] and HarDNet-MSEG[2] implementations to perform comparison. All training is done on a machine with a 3.7 GHz AMD Ryzen 3970X CPU, 128 GB RAM, and an NVIDIA GeForce GTX 3090 GPU. We use a Google Colab instance with 2 CPU cores and an NVIDIA Tesla V100 GPU to measure inference speed.

Comparison with the Baseline Models. This experiment uses the NeoPolyp-Clean dataset, as the baseline models do not handle "undefined" labels in the input data. Each model is first pretrained for 200 epochs on the polyp segmentation training data from [15] (including images from the Kvasir-SEG [14] and CVC-ClinicDB datasets [3]). We then train each model until convergence on the NeoPolyp-Clean dataset (by swapping the final output layers with 2-channel convolutional blocks).

Comparison on NeoPolyp and NeoPolyp-Clean. For this experiment, NeoUNet is first trained on the polyp segmentation task using data from [15]. We then compare the performance when training this model to convergence on the NeoPolyp and NeoPolyp-Clean datasets.

5.3   Results and Discussion

Comparison with Baseline Models. Table 1 shows the performance metrics for NeoUNet and HarDNet-MSEG on the NeoPolyp-Clean dataset. We can see

---

[1] https://github.com/DengPingFan/PraNet.
[2] https://github.com/james128333/HarDNet-MSEG.

that all four models struggle with the non-neoplastic class. The highest Dice score for this class is only 0.713 from NeoUNet, significantly lower than on the neoplastic class (0.887) and the segmentation task (0.902). This is likely due to the heavy class imbalance in the training dataset. Although oversampling and Focal loss partially mitigates the issue, there is still a noticeable drop in the performance.

NeoUNet significantly outperforms all baseline models in all Dice and IoU metrics. Against the best baseline, PraNet, our model achieves better scores by $\sim 2\%$ in each metric. The segmentation task sees the most improvement from NeoUNet, with a 1.6% increase in Dice score and 2.6% increase in IoU. These results show that the combination of HDB and attention gates used in NeoUNet is very effective for the PSND problem. Additionally, the use of the secondary segmentation loss in NeoUNet has helped in maintaining segmentation accuracy. Meanwhile, U-Net performs significantly worse than the other three methods.

In terms of speed, HarDNet-MSEG is the fastest model by a large margin, achieving 77.1 FPS. This is consistent with the results in [9], as speed is a major focus for this model. PraNet is the slowest of the four models, at only 55.6 FPS. NeoUNet and U-Net have similar speeds at 68.3 and 69.6 FPS, respectively. Overall, despite being slower than HarDNet-MSEG and U-Net, NeoUNet provides a good tradeoff between accuracy and speed while still being faster and more accurate than PraNet.

Table 1. Performance metrics on the NeoPolyp-Clean test set for U-Net, PraNet, HarDNet-MSEG, and NeoUNet

Method	$Dice_{seg}$	IoU_{seg}	$Dice_{non}$	IoU_{non}	$Dice_{neo}$	IoU_{neo}	FPS	Parameters
U-Net [22]	0.785	0.646	0.525	0.356	0.773	0.631	69.6	31,043,651
HarDNet-MSEG [9]	0.883	0.791	0.659	0.492	0.869	0.769	**77.1**	17,424,031
PraNet [6]	0.895	0.811	0.705	0.544	0.873	0.775	55.6	30,501,341
NeoUNet (Ours)	**0.911**	**0.837**	**0.720**	**0.563**	**0.889**	**0.800**	68.3	38,288,397

Comparison on NeoPolyp and NeoPolyp-Clean. Table 2 shows performance metrics for NeoUNet when trained on NeoPolyp and NeoPolyp-Clean. We notice a slight drop in accuracy for the same model when testing on NeoPolyp compared to NeoPolyp-Clean, since images containing "undefined" polyps are typically more challenging. Interestingly, the use of "undefined"-label data shows

Table 2. Performance metrics for NeoUNet when training on NeoPolyp and NeoPolyp-Clean, measured on the NeoPolyp test set

Training dataset	$Dice_{seg}$	IoU_{seg}	$Dice_{non}$	IoU_{non}	$Dice_{neo}$	IoU_{neo}
NeoPolyp-Clean	0.906	0.828	0.725	0.569	0.888	0.799
NeoPolyp	0.908	0.831	0.729	0.573	0.891	0.804

improvement for all metrics, not just segmentation. While the difference is slight $(0.2 - 0.5\%)$, it shows that making use of data for one task can yield benefits in other tasks.

6 Conclusion

This paper has presented the polyp segmentation and neoplasm detection problem, a challenging combination of fine-grained classification and semantic segmentation. To solve this problem, we propose NeoUNet, a UNet-based architecture incorporating attention gates, an efficient HarDNet backbone, and a hybrid loss function to take advantage of "undefined" labels. Our experiments show very competitive results when compared to existing models for polyp segmentation. This work can be a basis for further improvements on this challenging problem. Our future works include designing new network architectures for improving classification accuracy, especially for non-neoplastic polyps, and computational efficiency.

Acknowledgments. This work was funded by Vingroup Innovation Foundation (VINIF) under project code VINIF.2020.DA17. Phan Ngoc Lan was funded by Vingroup Joint Stock Company and supported by the Domestic Master/Ph.D. Scholarship Programme of Vingroup Innovation Foundation (VINIF), Vingroup Big Data Institute (VINBIGDATA), code VINIF.2020.ThS.BK.02.

References

1. Abraham, N., Khan, N.M.: A novel focal tversky loss function with improved attention u-net for lesion segmentation. In: 2019 IEEE 16th International Symposium on Biomedical Imaging (ISBI 2019), pp. 683–687. IEEE (2019)
2. Bernal, J., Sánchez, J., Vilarino, F.: Towards automatic polyp detection with a polyp appearance model. Pattern Recogn **45**(9), 3166–3182 (2012)
3. Bernal, J., et al.: Comparative validation of polyp detection methods in video colonoscopy: results from the miccai 2015 endoscopic vision challenge. IEEE Trans. Med. Imaging **36**(6), 1231–1249 (2017)
4. Chao, P., Kao, C.Y., Ruan, Y.S., Huang, C.H., Lin, Y.L.: Hardnet: a low memory traffic network. In: ICCV, pp. 3552–3561 (2019)
5. Chen, L., Papandreou, G., Schroff, F., Adam, H.: Rethinking atrous convolution for semantic image segmentation. CoRR abs/1706.05587 (2017)
6. Fan, D.P., et al.: PraNet: parallel reverse attention network for polyp segmentation. In: Martel, A.L. (ed.) MICCAI 2020. LNCS, vol. 12266, pp. 263–273. Springer, Cham (2020). https://doi.org/10.1007/978-3-030-59725-2_26
7. Gschwantler, M., et al.: High-grade dysplasia and invasive carcinoma in colorectal adenomas: a multivariate analysis of the impact of adenoma and patient characteristics. Eur. J. Gastroenterol. Hepatol **14**(2), 183–188 (2002)
8. He, K., Zhang, X., Ren, S., Sun, J.: Deep residual learning for image recognition. In: CVPR, pp. 770–778 (2016)
9. Huang, C.H., Wu, H.Y., Lin, Y.L.: Hardnet-mseg: a simple encoder-decoder polyp segmentation neural network that achieves over 0.9 mean dice and 86 fps (2021). arXiv preprint arXiv:2101.07172

10. Huang, G., Liu, Z., Van Der Maaten, L., Weinberger, K.Q.: Densely connected convolutional networks. In: CVPR, pp. 4700–4708 (2017)
11. Ilya, L., Hutter, F.: Sgdr: stochastic gradient descent with restarts. Learning **10**(3) (2016)
12. Iwahori, Y., et al.: Automatic polyp detection in endoscope images using a hessian filter. In: MVA, pp. 21–24 (2013)
13. Jha, D., Riegler, M.A., Johansen, D., Halvorsen, P., Johansen, H.D.: Doubleu-net: a deep convolutional neural network for medical image segmentation. In: 2020 IEEE 33rd International Symposium on Computer-Based Medical Systems (CBMS), pp. 558–564. IEEE (2020)
14. Jha, D., et al.: Kvasir-SEG: a segmented polyp dataset. In: Ro, Y.M. (ed.) MMM 2020. LNCS, vol. 11962, pp. 451–462. Springer, Cham (2020). https://doi.org/10. 1007/978-3-030-37734-2_37
15. Jha, D., et al.: Resunet++: an advanced architecture for medical image segmentation. In: 2019 IEEE International Symposium on Multimedia (ISM), pp. 225–2255. IEEE (2019)
16. Krizhevsky, A., Sutskever, I., Hinton, G.E.: Imagenet classification with deep convolutional neural networks. In: Advances in Neural Information Processing Systems, pp. 1097–1105 (2012)
17. Leufkens, A., Van Oijen, M., Vleggaar, F., Siersema, P.: Factors influencing the miss rate of polyps in a back-to-back colonoscopy study. Endoscopy **44**(05), 470–475 (2012)
18. Lin, T.Y., Goyal, P., Girshick, R., He, K., Dollár, P.: Focal loss for dense object detection. In: ICCV, pp. 2980–2988 (2017)
19. Long, J., Shelhamer, E., Darrell, T.: Fully convolutional networks for semantic segmentation. In: CVPR, pp. 3431–3440 (2015)
20. Oktay, O., et al.: Attention u-net: Learning where to look for the pancreas. CoRR (2018)
21. Ribeiro, E., Uhl, A., Wimmer, G., Häfner, M.: Exploring deep learning and transfer learning for colonic polyp classification. Comput. Math. Methods Med. **2016** (2016)
22. Ronneberger, O., Fischer, P., Brox, T.: U-Net: convolutional networks for biomedical image segmentation. In: Navab, N., Hornegger, J., Wells, W.M., Frangi, A.F. (eds.) MICCAI 2015. LNCS, vol. 9351, pp. 234–241. Springer, Cham (2015). https://doi.org/10.1007/978-3-319-24574-4_28
23. Salehi, S.S.M., Erdogmus, D., Gholipour, A.: Tversky loss function for image segmentation using 3D fully convolutional deep networks. In: Wang, Q., Shi, Y., Suk, H.-I., Suzuki, K. (eds.) MLMI 2017. LNCS, vol. 10541, pp. 379–387. Springer, Cham (2017). https://doi.org/10.1007/978-3-319-67389-9_44
24. Silva, J., Histace, A., Romain, O., Dray, X., Granado, B.: Toward embedded detection of polyps in WCE images for early diagnosis of colorectal cancer. Int. J. Comput. Assist. Radiol. Surg. **9**(2), 283–293 (2014)
25. Simonyan, K., Zisserman, A.: Very deep convolutional networks for large-scale image recognition. In: Bengio, Y., LeCun, Y. (eds.) ICLR (2015)
26. Szegedy, C., et al.: Going deeper with convolutions. In: CVPR, pp. 1–9 (2015)
27. Tan, M., Le, Q.: Efficientnet: rethinking model scaling for convolutional neural networks. In: ICML, pp. 6105–6114 (2019)
28. Tang, Z., Peng, X., Geng, S., Zhu, Y., Metaxas, D.N.: Cu-net: Coupled u-nets. In: BMVC (2019)

29. Xiao, T., Xu, Y., Yang, K., Zhang, J., Peng, Y., Zhang, Z.: The application of two-level attention models in deep convolutional neural network for fine-grained image classification. In: CVPR, pp. 842–850 (2015)
30. Xie, S., Girshick, R., Dollár, P., Tu, Z., He, K.: Aggregated residual transformations for deep neural networks. In: CVPR, pp. 1492–1500 (2017)
31. Zhou, Z., Siddiquee, M.M.R., Tajbakhsh, N., Liang, J.: Unet++: redesigning skip connections to exploit multiscale features in image segmentation. IEEE Trans. Med. Imaging **39**(6), 1856–1867 (2019)

Patch-Based Convolutional Neural Networks for TCGA-BRCA Breast Cancer Classification

Rosiel Jazmine T. Villareal$^{(\boxtimes)}$ and Patricia Angela R. Abu$^{(\boxtimes)}$

Ateneo de Manila University, Quezon City, Philippines
rosiel.villareal@obf.ateneo.edu, pabu@ateneo.edu

Abstract. The current study automatically identified regions of interest and classified breast tumors in whole slide images from The Cancer Genome Atlas Breast Invasive Carcinoma (TCGA-BRCA) using patch-based convolutional neural networks (CNNs). Pre-processing techniques were applied on whole slide images. Then, whole slide images were tiled into patches, and patches containing regions of interest (ROIs) like nuclei-rich areas were identified. Afterwards, features from patches containing ROIs were extracted using CNNs and used to train patch-level classifiers. Finally, patch-level predictions were aggregated into slide-level predictions. Classification metrics like accuracy, precision, recall, and f1-score were used to evaluate results.

Keywords: Computer vision · Convolutional neural networks · Breast cancer classification

1 Introduction

Diagnosis by using histopathological images, or slide images of tissue sections, is needed to provide personalized therapy for breast cancer patients. However, due to the visual richness and complex variety of structures in these images, analyzing them manually becomes a difficult and time-consuming task for pathologists. On the other hand, automating the process by applying deep learning techniques is hindered by lack of annotations and computational complexity. Due to the high resolution of whole slide images (WSIs), generating enough segmentations of tumor cells and other structures and training models on them is costly and tedious. Moreover, processing a large volume of images can result to a slow digital workflow, one of the common reasons why some cases were deferred to manual analysis of tissues in a study on the use of WSIs for primary diagnosis [8]. If the problem of slow processing of WSIs is not addressed, then pathologists would hesitate on adopting digital imaging and image analysis algorithms into clinical applications. The proposed study hopes to address the said concerns through a

Supported by the Engineering Research and Development for Technology (ERDT) graduate scholarship in the Philippines.

© Springer Nature Switzerland AG 2021
G. Bebis et al. (Eds.): ISVC 2021, LNCS 13018, pp. 29–40, 2021.
https://doi.org/10.1007/978-3-030-90436-4_3

patch-based approach where information-rich patches are identified from WSIs, even without segmentations, and are then used for breast cancer classification. More importantly, the study seeks to give pathologists a tool for more efficient and accurate breast cancer diagnosis.

Deep learning has shown potential to deliver significant results in image classification and recognition problems, including medical diagnosis. In the Grand Challenge on BreAst Cancer Histology (BACH) in 2018, convolutional neural networks (CNN) were the most successful method in classifying normal, benign, in situ cancer, and invasive cancer from WSIs [2]. A similar data collection of WSIs is The Cancer Genome Atlas Breast Invasive Carcinoma (TCGA-BRCA). There have been some studies on the dataset to connect breast cancer phenotypes to genotypes. For instance, Saltz et al. (2018) used a deep learning approach to identify tumor-infiltrating lymphocytes (TILs) in H&E (hematoxylin & eosin) stained images of 13 cancer types from TCGA and to correlate TIL maps with molecular data, survival, tumor subtypes, and immune profiles [14]. However, the potential of WSIs from TCGA-BRCA has not been fully exploited due to concerns such as limited annotations and lack of dataset description. For example, while other datasets have pixel-level annotations that segment the tumor areas, TCGA-BRCA only provides slide-level ground truth, i.e., classification of a whole slide image into a tumor type. Thus, analysis on the dataset remains an open area of research.

The goal of the study is to provide an automated method of identifying relevant regions and classifying tumor types in diagnostic whole slide images. The research objectives are to identify in whole slide images the patches that contain regions of interest and to aggregate patch-level features for whole slide-level classification. Experiments were performed to determine the optimal parameters in patch filtering techniques such as nuclei count thresholds and the best combination of classifier and patch aggregation technique based on classification metrics like accuracy and f1-score.

2   Related Literature

Applying CNNs directly to WSIs that are 40,000 by 40,000 pixels in size or higher is computationally expensive, but on the other hand, too much downsampling WSIs may result to loss of discriminative features crucial to classification. Thus, many previous studies on deep learning frameworks for WSIs used patch-based approaches, i.e., WSIs were divided into patches or tiles before CNN modeling. For instance, Cruz-Roa et al. (2017) detected the pixel-level presence and extent of invasive ductal carcinoma (IDC) on H&E slides using patch-based CNN classifiers with 3, 4, and 6 layers on 200 cases from TCGA and achieved a Dice coefficient of 75.86% and a positive predictive value of 71.62% [7]. Furthermore, the study showed that CNN classifiers performed better than hand-crafted features like color, shape, and texture in terms of area under the ROC curve. However, the study required manual segmentations of breast tumors in whole slide images by expert pathologists.

In another study that used a patch-based approach, Araujo et al. (2017) extracted breast cancer patches from H&E slides of the Bioimaging 2015 breast histology classification challenge. Then, they trained CNNs for patch-wise classification by giving patches the same labels as the slides from which they were extracted and achieved accuracies of 66.7% for 4 classes (normal, benign, in situ, invasive) and 65% for 2 classes (cancer, non-cancer). Afterwards, they aggregated patch predictions and achieved image-wise accuracies of 77.8% for 4 classes and 80.6% for 2 classes using majority voting. [1] The study showed the potential of using patch-wise CNN classifiers and decision fusion techniques like voting in the absence of patch-wise ground truth. One limitation of the study, however, is the lack of any filtering approach prior to patch-wise CNN training. All of the patches that contained tissue regions were included in the training even if some patches might not contain information relevant to classification.

The need to train CNNs efficiently by focusing on regions of interest only prompted some breast cancer detection studies to explore nuclei-guided sampling strategies, where only patches with high nuclei densities are extracted [9,10,15].

The current study incorporates the ff. from related studies: preprocessing techniques, such as normalization [3,4,6,11,13]; nuclei-guided patch filtering [9, 10,15]; and patch aggregation techniques, such as voting [1].

The main contribution of the current study is, to the best of the researchers' knowledge, this is the first to use patch-based CNNs for breast cancer classification of whole slide images from the TCGA-BRCA dataset. A whole slide image of a breast tissue section may contain anything from 50% to 90% tumor cells with the rest being normal cells or stromal cells. The extent of breast tumor is not labeled in a whole slide image. Rather, only the final tumor type classification into ductal cancer, lobular cancer, or a mix of ductal and lobular cancer is provided for the whole slide image. Thus, the dataset is more challenging to analyze compared to other datasets from previous studies. Nonetheless, the study addresses the said concern through different CNN architectures.

3   Methodology

3.1   Dataset

The Cancer Genome Atlas Breast Invasive Carcinoma (TCGA-BRCA) dataset, which includes diagnostic, H&E-stained whole slide images of invasive breast cancer (examples shown in Fig. 1), is publicly accessible through the National Cancer Institute's Genomic Data Commons Data Portal [12]. An R package called TCGAbiolinks by Colaprico et al. (2015) [5] was used to query the TCGA database and obtain slide information such as tumor type, e.g., invasive ductal carcinoma (IDC), invasive lobular carcinoma (ILC), and others.

3.2   Preprocessing

Whole slide images (WSIs) of 40,000 by 40,000 pixels were resized into 10,000 by 10,000 pixel images to save memory. Afterwards, contrast stretching was

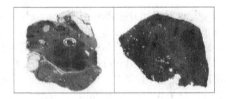

Fig. 1. Sample WSIs from the dataset: (left) IDC (right) ILC

applied to enhance the images while avoiding the problem of unnatural looking images sometimes resulting from histogram equalization. In contrast stretching, the image is rescaled to include intensities falling within a range of values using a linear function. An example of a raw whole slide image and the resulting image and histogram after contrast stretching over the 2nd and 98th percentiles of image pixel values are shown in Fig. 2. Then, WSIs containing multiple copies of the same tissue section were cropped to include only one object. Afterwards, WSIs were normalized by subtracting the mean and dividing by the standard deviation. Finally, WSIs were assigned into 60% training, 20% validation, and 20% test sets.

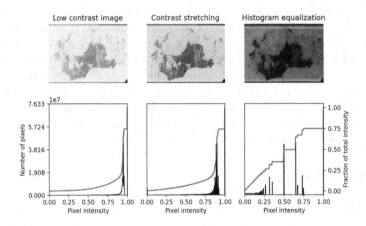

Fig. 2. Pixel intensity distributions (left) of original image, (middle) after contrast stretching, (right) after histogram equalization

3.3 Patch Extraction

Non-overlapping patches were extracted from whole slide images via a simple grid approach, where a window of a specific patch width was slid across the whole slide image. Although a grid approach is inefficient, using all the extracted patches from slides as inputs to classification models would serve as baseline on which to compare models that only use discriminative patches.

Specifically, the images were tiled into 64 by 64 pixel patches with the number of patches per class and per set given in Table 1. A patch width of 64 pixels was chosen so that the model would be able to capture cell-level features.

Table 1. Number of patches in training and test sets

Set	IDC	ILC
Training	145,554	60,726
Test	55,021	24,986

3.4   Patch Filtering

Discriminative patches, or patches containing regions of interest (ROIs), were identified since non-ROIs were filtered out later on through a nuclei-guided approach as illustrated in Fig. 3. The method by Zheng et al. (2017) [15] guided the nuclei detection step for all extracted patches. First, the hematoxylin (H) and eosin (E) stain components were separated via color deconvolution. Second, a Gaussian filter was applied to the H stain component to filter out noise. Third, peak local maxima were identified on the result of the Gaussian filter. These peak local maxima, which are detected nuclei, were counted for each patch. The 50th and 99th percentiles of the nuclei count distribution across all patches were experimentally determined as the optimal lower and upper thresholds. Patches with nuclei counts lower than or equal to the lower threshold and patches with nuclei counts above the upper threshold were excluded from the patch classification step (Fig. 4). Excluded patches were mostly empty patches, i.e., patches that do not contain any tissue or patches that contain mostly cytoplasm.

After a nuclei-guided filtering approach was implemented to include only patches with regions of interest relevant to tumor classification, the number of patches that were included in the classification for each class and set were reduced to an average of 28% of the original number of patches (Table 2).

Table 2. Number of patches in training and test sets after nuclei-guided filtering (% remaining)

Set	IDC	ILC
Training	40,846 (28.1%)	17,810 (29.3%)
Test	15,212 (27.6%)	7,172 (28.7%)

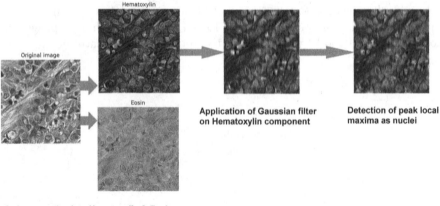

Fig. 3. Nuclei detection process: (1) Stain separation & isolation of Hematoxylin (H) component, (2) Gaussian filter application on H component for noise reduction, (3) Peak local max detection (red dots represent nuclei detected) (Color figure online)

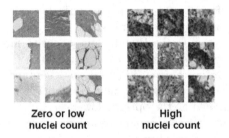

Fig. 4. Nuclei-guided filtering: (left) patches that were filtered out, (right) patches that met the threshold and were included in the classification

3.5 Patch Classification

Different CNN architectures (ResNet50, VGG16, AlexNet, SqueezeNet) that were pretrained on the ImageNet database were finetuned on the extracted patches. The number of layers and parameters of the CNN architectures, as well as the learning rates used, are listed in Table 3. The learning rate for each architecture was chosen by plotting the validation losses across a range of learning rates in a graph and then selecting that which minimized the validation loss. Patches were given the same labels as the whole slide images from which they were extracted. Patches were thus be classified into invasive ductal carcinoma (IDC) or invasive lobular carcinoma (ILC). Furthermore, the output of the classifiers included not just the predicted classes for the patches, but the probabilities for each class as well.

Table 3. Parameters for different CNN architectures

CNN model	Number of layers	Number of parameters	Learning rate
ResNet50	50	26M	2e–6
VGG16	16	138M	1e–6
AlexNet	8	60M	2e–6
SqueezeNet	18	1M	6e–7

3.6   Patch Aggregation

The study by Araujo et al. (2017) [1] served as a guide for decision-level fusion of patches. After patch-level classification, the patch predictions were aggregated using voting methods, namely, majority, maximum probability, and sum of probabilities voting. In majority voting, the predicted label of the slide is the mode of the distribution of individually predicted patch labels. In maximum probability voting, the predicted label of the slide is the label of the patch with the highest probability. In sum of probabilities voting, the classifier provides a probability that a patch belongs to a specific target class. Then, the probabilities are summed for each class across all patches in one slide. The class with the highest sum of probabilities becomes the predicted label of the slide.

3.7   Dataset Augmentation

Both the whole slide images dataset for whole slide image classification and the patches dataset for patch classification were augmented using different transforms like random horizontal flips, rotations of at most 10 degrees, and changes in brightness and contrast of 0.2 (as illustrated in Fig. 5).

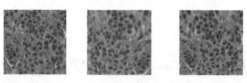

Original   **Patches made by augmentations (e.g.**
patch   **random flips, rotations) on original patch**

Fig. 5. Patch augmentation

4   Results and Discussion

4.1   Whole Slide Image Classification

A pretrained resnet34 model was run directly on whole-slide images for classification into invasive ductal (IDC) or invasive lobular (ILC) carcinoma. Results after 5 epochs of model finetuning did not improve the error rate with the classification accuracy steady at 62.5%. The classification accuracy results show that while training CNNs on whole slides might learn overall tissue organization, CNNs might not be able to learn nuclear features like shape, size, and color and nuclei organization. Thus, it might be worth exploring using patches instead of whole slides to train CNNs and learn features at a smaller scale.

4.2   Patch-Level and Slide-Level Classification After Grid Approach

Patches of size 64 by 64 pixels were classified into IDC or ILC using a pretrained resnet34 model. Results after 5 epochs of model finetuning showed an average classification accuracy of 64.6%. Patch predictions were aggregated using voting methods, and the confusion matrix metrics for the test set are displayed in Table 4. Maximum probability yielded the worst results across all metrics. On the other hand, majority voting and sum of probabilities had the best results among the three voting methods with an f1-score of 80% and an overall accuracy of 70%, which is 7.5% higher than that of using a whole slide image approach. Results show that a patch-based approach can be applied for slide-level classification.

Table 4. Test results for slide-level classification using grid approach

Classification metric	Voting method		
	Majority	Max probability	Sum of probabilities
Precision	75.00%	57.14%	75.00%
Recall	85.71%	57.14%	85.71%
Accuracy	70.00%	40.00%	70.00%
f1-score	80.00%	57.14%	80.00%

4.3   Patch-Level and Slide-Level Classification After Nuclei-Guided Filtering

Results after 5 epochs of model finetuning using different CNN architectures are displayed in Table 5. The average accuracy for patch classification using CNN architectures shows a 31% improvement over the baseline result where no patch filtering was implemented. The significant improvement in accuracy shows that nuclei count is an effective parameter for identifying regions of interest. Specifically, patches with high nuclei counts were shown to be more important to tumor classification than those with low nuclei counts.

The patch classification predictions were aggregated for slide-level classification using three voting methods for all CNN architectures, and the metrics for the test set (precision, recall, accuracy, f1-score) are shown in Tables 6, 7, 8 and 9. Using SqueezeNet as the CNN architecture and maximum probability as the

Table 5. Results of patch-level classification

CNN model	Accuracy
ResNet50	98.62%
VGG16	97.64%
AlexNet	92.33%
SqueezeNet	92.39%

voting method for aggregation of patch-level predictions into slide-level classi-fication yielded the best results across all metrics. Moreover, if the best results of the nuclei-guided filtering approach are compared to those of the grid app-roach (as listed in Table 10), the nuclei-guided filtering approach shows a 10% improvement in precision and accuracy, 5.71% improvement in f1-score, and the same result for recall. Thus, the setup based on the nuclei-guided filtering app-roach not only sped up the training time of CNNs using only about 28% of the patches extracted using the grid approach, but also performed better in terms of classification metrics. The evidence suggests that the patches that remained after nuclei-guided filtering were indeed regions of interest for breast tumor type classification and that voting methods for aggregation of patch-level features for slide-level classification were more effective than whole slide-level classification run directly on the whole slide images.

Table 6. Precision for slide-level classification using nuclei-guided filtering approach

CNN model	Voting method precision		
	Majority	Max probability	Sum of probabilities
ResNet50	**75.00%**	75.00%	**75.00%**
VGG16	71.43%	80.00%	71.43%
AlexNet	71.43%	60.00%	71.43%
SqueezeNet	66.67%	**85.71%**	66.67%

Table 7. Recall for slide-level classification using nuclei-guided filtering approach

CNN model	Voting method recall		
	Majority	Max probability	Sum of probabilities
ResNet50	**85.71%**	42.86%	**85.71%**
VGG16	71.43%	57.14%	71.43%
AlexNet	71.43%	42.86%	71.43%
SqueezeNet	57.14%	**85.71%**	57.14%

Table 8. Accuracy for slide-level classification using nuclei-guided filtering approach

CNN model	Voting method accuracy		
	Majority	Max probability	Sum of probabilities
ResNet50	**70%**	50%	**70%**
VGG16	60%	60%	60%
AlexNet	60%	40%	60%
SqueezeNet	50%	**80%**	50%

Table 9. F1-score for slide-level classification using nuclei-guided filtering approach

CNN model	Voting method F1-score		
	Majority	Max probability	Sum of probabilities
ResNet50	**80.00%**	54.55%	**80.00%**
VGG16	71.43%	66.67%	71.43%
AlexNet	71.43%	50.00%	71.43%
SqueezeNet	61.54%	**85.71%**	61.54%

Table 10. Comparison between grid approach & nuclei-filtering approach

Approach	Classification metric			
	Precision	Recall	Accuracy	f1-score
Grid	75.00%	85.71%	70.00%	80.00%
Nuclei-guided filtering	85.71%	85.71%	80.00%	85.71%

4.4 Voting Methods

Having the same results for majority voting and sum of probabilities voting suggests that the classifiers have high certainty in the predictions they made. In majority voting, the predicted label of the slide is the most common label among the patches in the slide. On the other hand, in sum of probabilities voting, the predicted label of the slide is the class with the largest sum of probabilities across all the patches in the slide. Since both majority and sum of probabilities voting had the same results, the classifiers predicted patch labels with high confidence, i.e., the classifiers gave high probabilities for the predicted classes.

4.5 Comparison to Related Studies

Cruz-Roa et al. worked on the same dataset and achieved a Dice coefficient of 75.8% in predicting the presence and extent of invasive ductal carcinoma (IDC) with manual delineation of breast tumors by expert pathologists as ground truth annotations. [7] Meanwhile, the current study was able to obtain f1-scores of

80% and 85.71% for grid and nuclei-guided filtering approaches, respectively, for slide-level classification of IDC despite lacking breast tumor segmentations.

Araujo et al. (2017) worked on the same problem of not having breast tumor segmentations, albeit with a different dataset. Araujo et al. also used a patch-based approach of training CNNs on patches and then aggregating patch-level predictions into slide-level predictions, but they had a different classification objective. They classified slide images into (1) normal, benign, in situ, and invasive, and (2) cancer and non-cancer. Using majority voting, they achieved slide-level accuracies of 77.8% for 4 classes and 80.6% for 2 classes [1]. Meanwhile, the current study was able to obtain accuracies of 70% and 80% for grid and nuclei-guided filtering approaches, respectively. Although the current study cannot be compared quantitatively with the study by Araujo et al. due to having a different dataset and classification objective, it can be said that both were able to obtain acceptable classification accuracies despite the limitation of working only on slide-level ground truth. Furthermore, the current study builds on the study by Araujo et al. which used a grid approach—using all patches containing tissue regions in patch-level training—by applying nuclei-guided filtering to exclude patches that had no or few nuclei, focus on relevant regions of interest, and speed up training.

5   Conclusions

Convolutional neural networks (CNNs) have been finetuned for the classification of patches extracted from H&E stained whole slide images of invasive breast cancer. Patches are classified as either invasive ductal carcinoma (IDC) or invasive lobular carcinoma (ILC). CNNs were trained on a grid extraction-based patch dataset and a smaller patch dataset after nuclei-guided filtering. Then, patch-level predictions were aggregated into slide-level predictions using voting methods. The initial results have shown that a patch-based approach and a nuclei-guided filtering technique are helpful in the classification of invasive breast cancer even in the absence of tumor segmentations. The best combination of classifier and voting method achieved an f1-score of 85.71% and an accuracy of 80% in classifying breast tumor type. In the future we plan to explore methods such as transfer learning using CNNs for fixed feature extraction, other preprocessing techniques, and refining of patch filtering. Moreover, we plan to investigate patch-based CNNs for other breast cancer classification objectives, e.g., predicting molecular subtypes, stages, and grades.

Acknowledgments. This work is supported by the Engineering Research and Development for Technology consortium in the Philippines.

References

1. Araújo, T., et al.: Classification of breast cancer histology images using convolutional neural networks. PloS one **12**(6), e0177544 (2017)

2. Aresta, G., et al.: Bach: grand challenge on breast cancer histology images. Med. Image Anal. **56**, 122–139 (2019)
3. Chen, C., Huang, Y., Fang, P., Liang, C., Chang, R.: A computer-aided diagnosis system for differentiation and delineation of malignant regions on whole-slide prostate histopathology image using spatial statistics and multi-dimensional densenet. Med. Phys. **47**(3), 1021–1033 (2020)
4. Ciompi, F. et al.: The importance of stain normalization in colorectal tissue classification with convolutional networks. In: Egan, G., Salvado, O. (eds.) 14th International Symposium on Biomedical Imaging (ISBI), pp. 160–163. IEEE (2017). https://doi.org/10.1109/ISBI.2017.7950492
5. Colaprico, A., et al.: Tcgabiolinks: an r/bioconductor package for integrative analysis of TCGA data. Nucleic Acids Res. **44**(8), e71 (2016)
6. Coltuc, D., Bolon, P., Chassery, J.-M.: Exact histogram specification. IEEE Trans. Image Process. **15**(5), 1143–1152 (2006)
7. Cruz-Roa, A., Basavanhally, A., Gilmore, H., Feldman, M.: Accurate and reproducible invasive breast cancer detection in whole-slide images: a deep learning approach for quantifying tumor extent. Sci. Rep. **7**(1), 1–14 (2017)
8. Evans, A., Salama, M., Henricks, W., Pantanowitz, L.: Implementation of whole slide imaging for clinical purposes: issues to consider from the perspective of early adopters. Arch. Pathol. Lab. Med. **141**(7), 944–959 (2017)
9. George, K., Sankaran, P., Joseph, P.: Computer assisted recognition of breast cancer in biopsy images via fusion of nucleus-guided deep convolutional features. Comput. Methods Prog. Biomed. **194**, 105531 (2020)
10. Campilho, A., Karray, F., ter Haar Romeny, B. (eds.): ICIAR 2018. LNCS, vol. 10882. Springer, Cham (2018). https://doi.org/10.1007/978-3-319-93000-8
11. Gurcan, M., Boucheron, L., Can, A., Madabhushi, A., Rajpoot, N., Yener, B.: Histopathological image analysis: a review. IEEE Rev. Biomed. Eng. **2**, 147–171 (2009)
12. National Cancer Institute Genomics Data Commons Data Portal. https://portal.gdc.cancer.gov/, Accessed 24 Apr 2021
13. Reinhard, E., Ashikhmin, M., Gooch, B., Shirley, P.: Color transfer between images. IEEE Comput. Graph. Appl. **21**(5), 34–41 (2001)
14. Saltz, J., et al.: Spatial organization and molecular correlation of tumor-infiltrating lymphocytes using deep learning on pathology images. Cell Rep. **23**(1), 181–193 (2018)
15. Zheng, Y., et al.: Feature extraction from histopathological images based on nucleus-guided convolutional neural network for breast lesion classification. Pattern Recogn. **71**, 14–25 (2017)

CT Perfusion Imaging of the Brain with Machine Learning

Kellen Cheng[1], Kunakorn Atchaneeyasakul[2], Zeid Barakat[3],
David S. Liebeskind[1], and Fabien Scalzo[1,4(✉)]

[1] Department of Neurology, University of California,
Los Angeles (UCLA), CA 90095, USA
`fab@cs.ucla.edu`
[2] School of Medicine, University of Pittsburgh, Pittsburgh, PA 15213, USA
[3] Perfuse, inc., Los Angeles, USA
[4] Seaver College, Pepperdine University, Malibu, CA 90265, USA

Abstract. Computed tomography (CT) perfusion imaging is a routinely used technique in the field of neurovascular imaging. The progression of a bolus of contrast agent through the neurovasculature is imaged in a series of CT scans. Relevant perfusion parameters, such as cerebral blood volume (CBV), flow (CBF) and delay (Tmax), can be computed by deconvolution of the contrast-time curves with the bolus shape measured at one of the feeding arteries. These parameters are crucial in the medical management of acute stroke patients, where they are used to identify the extent of likely salvageable tissue and irreversibly damaged infarct core. Deconvolution is normally achieved using singular value decomposition (SVD). However, studies have shown that such a technique is noise sensitive and easily influenced by artifacts in the source image, and may introduce further distortions in the output parameters. In this study, we present a machine learning approach to the estimation of perfusion parameters from CT imaging. Standard types of regression-based machine learning models were trained on the raw/native CT perfusion imaging data to reproduce the output of an FDA-approved commercial implementation of the SVD deconvolution algorithm. As part of our experiments, Kernel ridge regression and random forest models performed best (SSIM: 82%, 84%), trading off quick run time for better prediction accuracy while requiring a relatively low number of training examples.

1 Introduction

Clinical management of neurovascular diseases, and acute stroke in particular, requires perfusion imaging to quantify blood flow through the brain parenchyma. In computed tomography (CT) perfusion imaging [1,2], or CT perfusion, images are obtained after a bolus of contrast agent, that attenuates the signal intensity on the X-ray receptor, is injected to flow through vessels and tissue while a series of consecutive scans is taken. The spatiotemporal signal attenuation resulting

© Springer Nature Switzerland AG 2021
G. Bebis et al. (Eds.): ISVC 2021, LNCS 13018, pp. 41–52, 2021.
https://doi.org/10.1007/978-3-030-90436-4_4

from the contrast agent can be inferred across the brain over the duration of the acquisition.

Due to the dimensionality of the resulting CT perfusion data (i.e. 4D), these concentration-time curves are not directly interpreted by clinicians. Instead, features are inferred from it and displayed as a set of 2D image slices. Such feature maps include cerebral blood flow (CBF), cerebral blood volume (CBV), mean transit time (MTT), time-to-peak (TTP), and time-to-maximum (Tmax). The computation of these features typically amounts at deconvolving the data with the arterial input function (AIF) to obtain the residue function: a curve characterizing blood flow through a given volume element. These parametric estimations are widely used in assessing neurovascular conditions [3]. In acute stroke, treatment selection is performed by comparing the volume of the ischemic core with that of the hypoperfused tissue which is at risk, but which may still be salvaged. Parameters extracted from perfusion imaging are vital for identifying the tissue at risk. Various studies have shown correlations between the perfusion parameters and clinical outcome in terms of Rankin score and Barthel Index [4].

The problem of inferring the residue function, and thus the feature maps, is ill-posed, and deconvolution techniques such as singular value decomposition (SVD) are unstable in the presence of noise, causing biases [5] that could alter clinical decisions. Certain techniques have been developed to reduce this problem. A smoother residue function can be achieved through a Gaussian process for deconvolution (GPD) [6], Tikhonov Regularization [7], and a physiological model of microvasculature [8]. Attempts to provide better estimates of perfusion parameters have also used Expectation Maximization (EM) [9], and Bayesian estimation [10]. Other groups have focused on reducing the noise of CTP source images prior to the deconvolution using Deep Learning techniques [11] and restoring higher temporal resolution [12]. These novel algorithms have provided encouraging results to mitigate the risk of bias introduced by the deconvolution.

As part of the clinical workflow in acute stroke, perfusion maps are reviewed by visual inspection and by automated processing based on image segmentation. While these interpretations are complementary, both are susceptible to noise and bias in the reported maps. As an alternative to improving the quality of perfusion maps by post-processing, attempts have been made to move beyond thresholds and instead apply machine-learning to compute standard perfusion maps [13,14]. Yu et al. presented a model predicting hemorrhagic transformation severity directly from MRI source perfusion imaging [15]. Similarly, recent models have used source MR [16] and angiographic [17] images to produce perfusion maps and have demonstrated greater robustness when compared to deconvolution-based approaches.

In this paper, we follow a similar strategy and propose to evaluate the use of regression-based machine learning models to compute perfusion maps from CT perfusion data without the use of deconvolution. The models are trained on a large number of concentration-time curves extracted locally. We demonstrate in our experiments the similarity of the maps obtained via machine learning to the ones obtained via deconvolution.

2   Methods

2.1   Overview

The study is based on imaging data taken from patients treated for acute ischemic stroke at the UCLA Ronald Reagan Hospital in Los Angeles. The deidentified medical imaging data composed the training set that was used to train various types of machine learning models, including but not limited to kernel ridge and random forest regression. The model utilizes regression analysis to predict the perfusion parameter scans of a patient based on their time series CT slices. This process was repeated for each patient and their 6 slice locations, outputting perfusion maps that were compared to the ground truth values. Model accuracy and correction were evaluated by the structural similarity index metric (SSIM) between the actual and predicted rCBV and rCBF perfusion maps (Fig. 1).

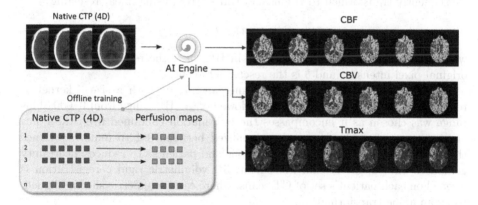

Fig. 1. Machine learning model pipeline for perfusion parameter prediction.

2.2   Dataset

The dataset is a retrospective collection of patients' CT scans gathered from perfusion imaging of the neurovascular artery as part of treatment for acute stroke. The usage of the data was approved by the internal review board (IRB) of our institution. This study uses a total of 38 patients, with the training set composed of 30 patients and the test set composed of 8 patients. Each patient has a total of 360 time series CT scans, split between 6 slice locations for 60 time points each. Additionally, each patient has a total of 24 perfusion maps, split between 6 slice locations and 4 perfusion parameters. For this study, the focus is on the results achieved by the models when predicting the perfusion parameters rCBV and rCBF (Fig. 2).

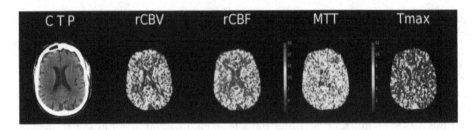

Fig. 2. Illustration of source CTP image (1st acquisition) with corresponding computed perfusion maps, including rCBV, rCBF, MTT, and Tmax using deconvolution.

2.3   Pre-processing

CT Processing. All 360 time series CT scans for each patient are extracted as 2D floating point arrays from their DICOM files. The pixel intensity values are subsequently transformed to Hounsfield Units (HU), using linear rescaling

$$v = mx + b$$

where v is the resultant pixel intensity in HU, m is the rescale slope, x is the original pixel intensity, and b is the rescale intercept.

The timeseries CT scans are then median filtered with a size 3 kernel to reduce intracranial noise, and then windowed on an HU range from 0–600. This range was chosen as it encompasses the information contained from the bolus of a contrast agent. Each scan is normalized between 0–1 to remove variance that exists between different slice locations and patients. To reduce uncertainty generated via patient cranial movement, 3D volumetric rigid coregistration is applied on each patient's set of CT scans, where each volumetric slice is aligned, using an affine transformation.

Grayscale Conversion. All 24 perfusion maps for each patient are converted to grayscale, as the time series CT scans are represented using grayscale intensities. Due to the nature of the JET color map, a standardized conversion formula from RGB to grayscale would fail to accurately retain the neurovascular information, as the maximum and minimum intensities would converge to the same grayscale intensity index. This problem is bypassed by implementing a manual lookup table (LUT), where each RGB pixel value is measured against the LUT. A grayscale index is selected from the LUT based off the entry with the minimum L2 distance to the RGB pixel value.

Sampling Process. The training set is constructed by randomly sampling 25,000 pixels from the timeseries CT scans, spread evenly across all 30 training patients. Each point is sampled randomly, and without replacement, from a region in the scan containing only non-zero intensities, so as to limit the chance of selecting immaterial pixels. The set of selected points is additionally filtered by removing pixels that correspond to the background in the ground truth scan. For a single patient's slice location, the sampled pixel is not a single intensity value but an array containing the spatial location's intensity values for all time points. The data set is adequately represented by a 2D array of dimensions 25,000 by 60, as each pixel is an array of 60 time-varying intensities. The indices of valid points are saved, and then resampled from the perfusion maps to generate the ground truth, represented by a 1D array of 25,000 intensities.

The testing set is constructed by randomly sampling 10,000 pixels from the time series CT scans, spread evenly across all 8 testing patients. Each point is subject to the same requirements as to the training set, to maintain model and result consistency. The indices of valid points are saved in this model, to generate easy access when constructing the ground truth for the testing set. The ground truths are represented by a 1D array of 10,000 intensities spread across all 8 testing patients. For this study, the model used the training set to output prediction scans of the perfusion parameters rCBV and rCBF.

2.4 Training and Deployment

Overview. This study utilizes four different types of regression based machine learning models to predict rCBV and rCBF, specifically kernel ridge regression, random forest regression, regularized linear regression (ridge regression), and linear regression. These models aim to identify general trends and varying observations from the training set in order to build an accurate prediction of the perfusion parameters.

Kernel Ridge Regression Model. The model uses classic kernel ridge regression to predict the perfusion parameter intensities based on their temporal array values, using the equation below to determine the model parameters

$$\theta = (X^T X + \lambda I)^{-1} X^T y \tag{1}$$

where X is the input vector, y is the corresponding pixel output, and λ is the regularization. Note that unlike linear regression, kernel ridge regression aims to provide a more robust testing outlook by introducing both a regularization parameter to combat overfitting and by implementing a kernel transformation on the input, such that the model can predict nonlinear trends by transforming the data into the kernel space. The regularization parameter and kernel standard deviation used to train the model was 0.1 and 8.0, respectively.

Random Forest Regression Model. The model uses an aggregation of singular decision trees, with each tree having its own weight on the influence of the model prediction. For this study, the model utilized 90 decision trees, each with a maximum tree depth of 55. By introducing more trees as opposed to its singular component, the decision tree regression model, the random forest is able to combat severe overfitting on the training set and allows for weighted pixel prediction for the output pixel.

Ridge Regression Model. Linear ridge regression aims to improve upon the basic linear regression model by introducing a regularization parameter, in an effort to weight the model parameters in the cost function analysis. The model cost function is determined by the equation below

$$J = \|y^{(i)} - f(x^{(i)})\|_2^2 + \lambda\|\theta\|_2^2$$

where J is the cost, $y^{(i)}$ is the ground truth value, $f(x^{(i)})$ is the predicted value, λ is the regularization parameter, and θ are the model weights. The regularization parameter of 0.1 was used to train this model.

Linear Regression Model. The baseline linear regression model aims to predict pixel intensity values from the input intensities based on the following equation

$$y^{(i)} = \theta x^{(i)} + b$$

where $y^{(i)}$ represents the predicted output pixel, θ the model parameters, $x^{(i)}$ the input pixel intensity, and b the bias value.

3   Experiments

In order to assess the accuracy of the model, the predicted intensities for each pixel was compared to its corresponding intensity in the ground truth perfusion scan, using the SSIM as a measurement of each model's accuracy. The SSIM is typically used to determine the similarity in image structure and quality between a reference and processed image. The metric considers image degradation as a loss in visual information. We report the SSIM scores of various machine learning models and visualize their predicted rCBV and rCBF perfusion parameter maps compared to the ground truth maps.

Validity of Machine Learning Model. Each machine learning model underwent hyperparameter testing to optimize results. The regression model was trained on a range of data points, from 5,000 to 25,000, with each point containing an array of 60 intensity values for each patient, and outputs the predicted perfusion map. The accuracy of these predictions was compared by their SSIM scores for the rCBV and rCBF perfusion parameters, which we display below. The most accurate model used kernel ridge regression paired with a Gaussian kernel. The kernel ridge regression model performs adequately in regards to both the training and testing set, with a training SSIM of 82.71% and testing SSIM of 82.53% at 25,000 training points.

Tables 1 and 2 illustrate the overall performance of the regression-based machine learning models for predicting rCBV and rCBF, respectively, both in the training set and the testing set. Tables 3 and 4 illustrate the results for the prediction of rCBV and rCBF for 8 representative patients. The effect of smoothing on the overall accuracy can be visualized from column 3 to 5 where an increasingly large Gaussian filter was applied.

Figures 3 and 4 provide a visualization of the accuracy (in terms of SSIM) with respect to the number of training data points. Figure 4 shows that while Kernel ridge and random forest regression can take advantage of a large number of training samples (best results are obtained with 22,500 samples), regularized and standard linear regression reach their best accuracy around 15,000 samples.

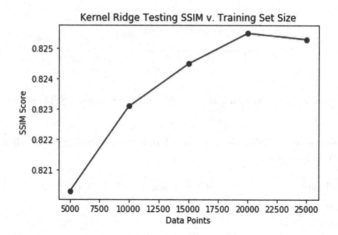

Fig. 3. Effect of training set size on kernel ridge SSIM scores, for regularization parameter 0.1 and gamma value 8.0.

Table 1. Average rCBV SSIM scores from batch model testing for all slice locations on the 8 testing patients.

Model type	rCBV Training SSIM	rCBV Testing SSIM
Linear regression	74.64%	77.01%
Ridge regression	74.34%	76.89%
Kernel ridge regression	82.71%	82.53%
Random forests regression	81.14%	82.59%

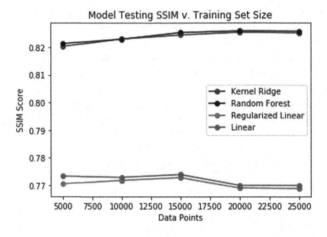

Fig. 4. Effect of training set size on all model testing SSIM scores.

Table 2. Average rCBF SSIM scores from batch model testing for all slice locations on the 8 testing patients.

Model type	rCBF Training SSIM	rCBF Testing SSIM
Linear regression	74.55%	77.46%
Ridge regression	74.51%	77.67%
Kernel ridge regression	82.83%	83.25%
Random forests regression	82.12%	84.19%

Table 3. Visualization of Gaussian filtering on kernel ridge regression rCBV perfusion predictions on slice location 3 for the 8 testing patients, trained on 25000 data points.

	Ground Truth	No Filter	Sigma= 0.9	Sigma= 1.0	Sigma= 1.1
Patient 1					
Patient 2					
Patient 3					
Patient 4					
Patient 5					
Patient 6					
Patient 7					
Patient 8					
Average SSIM	N/A	83.45%	84.79%	84.77%	84.70%

Table 4. Visualization of Gaussian filtering on kernel ridge regression rCBF perfusion predictions on slice location 3 for the 8 testing patients, trained on 25000 data points.

	Ground Truth	No Filter	Sigma= 0.9	Sigma= 1.0	Sigma= 1.1
Patient 1					
Patient 2					
Patient 3					
Patient 4					
Patient 5					
Patient 6					
Patient 7					
Patient 8					
Average SSIM	N/A	84.22%	86.00%	86.09%	83.25%

4   Discussion

There are numerous advantages to applying machine learning to CT imaging techniques. Machine learning models create consistent and reproducible results for analysis, far superior to conventional methods. Proper supervision of the training process entails successful treatment and diagnosis methods, which can become more widespread and reliable for medical use. Specifically, the prediction of perfusion parameters by machine learning models allows near instantaneous and convenient treatment solutions, without relying on expensive or inconvenient industry programs.

To accurately supervise the training process, the size and quality of the data set is the chief concern. CT image data was pruned to remove faulty and unreliable patients, such as those with excessive cranial movement or containing mismatched CT slice locations. This removal allowed the training process to occur only on patients with consistent scans and minimize variance between patients. The process to create the model was not trivial, and for 38 patients took less than 20 min. However, since the model only needs to be generated once, the time for construction can be disregarded. Processing of the model scales linearly with more training data, although this represents a trade-off between fitting the data and model runtime. Additionally, excessive data can give rise to the machine learning problem of overfitting, which occurs if the model fits the training data too well, at the cost of failing to capture and generalize trends.

For this study, the model is able to predict the spatio-temporal intensities of perfusion parameters associated with the intracranial artery. The framework of this study demonstrates that our model can learn these trends automatically, and predict the results with reasonable accuracy. The combination of this model with automatic imaging and training techniques allows for the possibility of a pipeline to process and predict perfusion parameters for any single patient.

Finally, deep learning methods such as neural networks and long short-term memory models could be considered to improve the results of the study. These models will, however, require a much larger data set and significantly more runtime to process.

5   Conclusion

We introduced a framework to utilize machine learning-based models for the computation of neurovascular perfusion parameters from patient CT scans. Overall, the use of machine learning models in automating the processing of patient data has been proven to be a viable alternative to current commercial methods based on deconvolution. This study concluded that machine learning models might improve accuracy in prediction and represent the potential for hospital cost cutting, which can significantly aid neurologists and neurosurgeons on a variety of neurological conditions, including acute stroke. Such results could monumentally facilitate the prediction of outcome based on raw CT perfusion.

References

1. Campbell, B.C., et al.: Imaging selection in ischemic stroke: feasibility of automated ct-perfusion analysis. Int. J. Stroke **10**, 51–54 (2015)

2. Vagal, A., et al.: Automated CT perfusion imaging for acute ischemic stroke: pearls and pitfalls for real-world use. Neurology **93**, 888–898 (2019)
3. Tong, E., Sugrue, L., Wintermark, M.: Understanding the neurophysiology and quantification of brain perfusion. Top Magn. Reson. Imaging **26**, 57–65 (2017)
4. Farr, T.D., et al.: Use of magnetic resonance imaging to predict outcome after stroke: a review of experimental and clinical evidence. J. Cerebral Blood Flow Metab. **30**(4), 703–717 (2010)
5. Kudo, K., et al.: Differences in CT perfusion maps generated by different commercial software: quantitative analysis by using identical source data of acute stroke patients. Radiology **254**, 200–209 (2010)
6. Andersen, I.K., et al.: Perfusion quantification using Gaussian process deconvolution. Magn. Reson. Med. **48**, 351–361 (2002)
7. Calamante, F., Gadian, D.G., Connelly, A.: Quantification of bolus-tracking MRI: improved characterization of the tissue residue function using Tikhonov regularization. Magn. Reson. Med. **50**, 1237–1247 (2003)
8. Mouridsen, K., Friston, K., Hjort, N., Gyldensted, L., Ostergaard, L., Kiebel, S.: Bayesian estimation of cerebral perfusion using a physiological model of microvasculature. Neuroimage **33**, 570–579 (2006)
9. Vonken, E.P., Beekman, F.J., Bakker, C.J., Viergever, M.A.: Maximum likelihood estimation of cerebral blood flow in dynamic susceptibility contrast MRI. Magn. Reson. Med. **41**, 343–350 (1999)
10. Boutelier, T., Kudo, K., Pautot, F., Sasaki, M.: Bayesian hemodynamic parameter estimation by bolus tracking perfusion weighted imaging. IEEE Trans. Med. Imaging **31**, 1381–1395 (2012)
11. Wu, D., Ren, H., Li, Q.: Self-supervised dynamic ct perfusion image denoising with deep neural networks (2020)
12. Zhu, H., et al.: Temporally downsampled cerebral CT perfusion image restoration using deep residual learning. Int. J. Comput. Assist. Radiol. Surg **15**(2), 193–201 (2019). https://doi.org/10.1007/s11548-019-02082-1
13. Stier, N., Vincent, N., Liebeskind, D., Scalzo, F.: Deep learning of tissue fate features in acute ischemic stroke. In: IEEE International Conference on Bioinformatics Biomedicine, Proceedings 2015, pp. 1316–1321 (2015)
14. Scalzo, F., Hao, Q., Alger, J.R., Hu, X., Liebeskind, D.S.: Regional prediction of tissue fate in acute ischemic stroke. Ann. Biomed. Eng. **40**, 2177–2187 (2012)
15. Yu, Y., Guo, D., Lou, M., Liebeskind, D., Scalzo, F.: Prediction of hemorrhagic transformation severity in acute stroke from source perfusion MRI. IEEE Trans. Biomed. Eng. **65**, 2058–2065 (2018)
16. McKinley, R., Hung, F., Wiest, R., Liebeskind, D.S., Scalzo, F.: A machine learning approach to perfusion imaging with dynamic susceptibility contrast MR. Front. Neurol. **9**, 717 (2018)
17. Feghhi, E., Zhou, Y., Tran, J., Liebeskind, D., Scalzo, F.: Angio-ai: cerebral perfusion angiography with machine learning. In: ISVC (2019)

Analysis of Macular Thickness Deviation Maps for Diagnosis of Glaucoma

Bingnan Zhou[1], Farnaz Mohammadi[2], Jung S. Lim[1], Negin Forouzesh[1], Hassan Ghasemzadeh[3], and Navid Amini[1,2(✉)]

[1] California State University Los Angeles, Los Angeles, CA 90032, USA
namini@calstatela.edu
[2] University of California Los Angeles, Los Angeles, CA 90095, USA
[3] Arizona State University, Tempe, AZ 85281, USA

Abstract. There is a growing number of studies showing that analysis of macular parameters provides additional information about ganglion cell loss in glaucoma and compliments traditional markers of glaucoma. In this paper, we develop an image processing pipeline for the macular thickness deviation maps generated by Heidelberg Spectralis optical coherence tomography (OCT) to evaluate the information within the macular measurements for diagnosing glaucoma. Logistic regression is applied to analyze features extracted from the deviation maps and the strength of their relationship with the diagnosis of glaucoma. Our experimental results show that the proportion of regions with thickness significantly below the normative range in the nerve fiber layer thickness deviation maps can be used to detect glaucoma with an accuracy of up to 70.16%. Moreover, the ganglion cell layer deviation maps also possess significant diagnostic ability for detection of glaucoma, which can be combined with the traditional assessments of the optic nerve head and peripapillary retinal nerve fiber layer to improve the reliability of glaucoma diagnosis.

Keywords: Glaucoma · Macula · Feature selection · Logistic regression · Machine learning

1 Introduction

Glaucoma is a group of disorders that progressively damage the optic nerve and is currently considered the second leading cause of blindness in the world. According to prevalence studies, as of 2020, 79.6 million people worldwide suffer from glaucoma [1], and it is believed that the number will increase to more than 111 million by 2040 [2]. Due to the increasing prevalence of glaucoma, there are numerous research studies seeking to effectively detect glaucoma to overcome the economic, psychological, and societal challenges associated with glaucoma. It is widely believed that glaucoma mainly affects three areas of the human retina, namely optic nerve head (ONH), peripapillary retinal nerve fiber layer, and the macula.

The diagnosis of glaucoma has traditionally been based on the discovery of ONH damage in the form of cupping and the thinning of the peripapillary retinal nerve fiber

© Springer Nature Switzerland AG 2021
G. Bebis et al. (Eds.): ISVC 2021, LNCS 13018, pp. 53–64, 2021.
https://doi.org/10.1007/978-3-030-90436-4_5

layer (RNFL) as shown by the red and green circles in Fig. 1; however, the sole utility of these traditional markers falls short of providing accurate glaucoma diagnosis [1, 2]. It has been reported that the macula (delineated by the blue circle in Fig. 1) offers several potential physiological and anatomical advantages for glaucoma detection and management [3, 4].

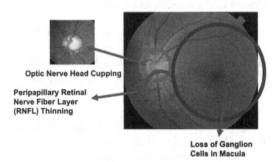

Fig. 1. The optic nerve head (red circle), the peripapillary retinal nerve fiber layer (green circle), and macula (blue circle) are retinal areas that are mostly affected by glaucoma. (Color figure online)

Specifically, the thickness of the inner layers of the macula has been shown to not only correlate with traditional markers in glaucoma, but also to provide additional information that can complement the diagnostic ability of the traditional markers [4–6] The thickness of the three innermost retinal layers in the macular region may represent a surrogate indicator of the degeneration and death of retinal ganglion cells, given the prominent distribution of these cells within the macular region [7, 8]. These three layers include the retinal nerve fiber, ganglion cell, and inner plexiform layers, which contain, respectively, the axons, cell bodies, and dendrites of the ganglion cells.

Optical coherence tomography (OCT) is a non-invasive, micrometer-scale, and cross-sectional imaging technology for biological tissue. It has been widely used for retinal imaging in ophthalmology as it provides high-resolution information of the cross-section and surface of retina. With OCT, tiny tissues such as the retinal layers can be quantified and visualized. In this study, we focus on the diagnosis power of the macula; we investigate the extent of information that resides in the macula and study the relationship between such information and glaucoma diagnosis. With the progression of glaucoma and degeneration of ganglion cells, the first three layers of retina in macula will thin out. We develop an image processing pipeline to extract quantitative features related to the thickness of inner retinal layers from the macular deviation maps generated by Heidelberg Spectralis OCT. The pipeline is mainly used to process the macular deviation maps of each subject and extract the diagnostic data to form the dataset required for the study. We then use logistic regression as our classifier to analyze subjects' macular data and discover the relationship between each macular parameter (feature) and glaucoma diagnosis.

Feature-based machine learning techniques have been extensively used for glaucoma detection. Summary statistics extracted by clinicians such as RNFL thickness, mean deviation measurements from visual field tests, and computer-vision based detection of optic cup-to-disc ratio from fundus images of the eye have been used to aid in automating glaucoma detection [9] with accuracy rates on the order of 87% [9]. Machine learning techniques such as support vector machines (the effort by Dey and Bandyopadhyay [10]), decision trees (the study by Huang and Chen [11]), random forest classifiers (the work of Sugimoto and colleagues [12]), k-nearest neighbors (investigation by Balasubramanian and associates [13]), k-means clustering (by Ayub et al. [14]), linear discriminant analysis (study by Bambo and co-investigators [15]), and Bayesian (the investigation by Bowd et al. [16]) classifiers can be used to detect presence of disease once these summary statistics or features are extracted. However, the initial features are typically human-selected disease markers, resulting in datasets that are small in size, increasing the likelihood of overfitting (obtaining high accuracy on specific datasets without general applicability of an approach), as well as potentially losing important aspects of the data [17, 18]. The above-mentioned studies lack a normative database for the features that they fed as inputs to learning algorithms for glaucoma detection. We argue that comparison of these features (e.g., macular thickness measurements) with a reference, normative database of normal subjects enhances their diagnostic power and improves the visualization of structural defects associated with glaucoma.

The present study is designed to determine the diagnostic performance of commercially available macular thickness deviation maps obtained by Spectralis OCT for glaucoma detection. The deviation maps consist of inner retinal layer thickness parameters. The normality cutoffs and ranges of these thickness parameters are determined by comparisons to Heidelberg Engineering's age-matched normative database.

To the best of our knowledge, this is the first effort to evaluate the diagnostic performance of macular deviation maps in glaucoma. Based on promising results from experiments on 955 deviation maps of 93 glaucomatous eyes and 98 normal eyes, we expect the macular deviation maps and their corresponding normality ranges will improve the ability to detect glaucoma, which will potentially lead to more effective management of this disease. The rest of this paper is organized as follows. Section 2 presents the image processing pipeline for deriving macular features from the deviation maps and methods for evaluation of those features for the detection of glaucoma. Section 3 covers the experimental results and corresponding discussions. Finally, the conclusions of this study are presented in Sect. 4.

2 Methods

2.1 Macular OCT Imaging

OCT devices acquire structural information of the posterior segment of the eye. Many one-dimensional scans (A-scans or depth reflectivity profiles) are performed at several depths to create a two-dimensional cross-sectional image called a B-scan. Macular B-scans, if acquired closely and rapidly, can be translated into a volumetric image of the posterior segment centered on the macula. These B-scans include structures such as vitreous, retina, choroid, and sclera (See Fig. 2). Among these structures, retina is where the eye's visual receptors and various ocular tissues are located. As such, OCT devices usually set their image acquisition properties in such a way that retina can be imaged reliability and with the highest signal-to-noise ratio among these four structures.

Spectralis OCT has developed a specific software tool that provides automated delineation and thickness measurements of 10 retinal layers. The anterior (top) three layers form the inner retina, while the posterior (bottom) seven layers compose the outer retina. It is well established that glaucoma results in a thinning of the inner retina, i.e., decreased retinal nerve fiber layer (RNFL), ganglion cell layer (GCL), and inner plexiform layer (IPL) thickness; however, no changes in outer retinal layer thicknesses have been reported [19, 20]. Therefore, in this study, we only target the thickness levels of RNFL GCL, IPL, or their combinations, such as ganglion cell-inner plexiform layer (GCIPL) and the full retinal thickness (FRT) in the macular region as indicated in Fig. 2.

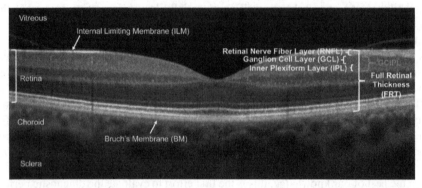

Fig. 2. A macular OCT B-Scan visualizes structures in the posterior segment of the eye, which include vitreous, retina, choroid, and sclera in an anterior to posterior order. Full retinal thickness (FRT) as well as the thickness of the first three layers of retina, i.e., retinal nerve fiber layer (RNFL), ganglion cell layer (GCL), and inner plexiform layer (IPL), or their combinations (e.g., GCIPL) can be used as predictors of glaucoma.

The original OCT scans were acquired from 98 normal and 93 glaucomatous eyes using the Posterior Pole Algorithm of the Spectralis OCT, which acquires 61 horizontal B-scans at approximately 120 μm apart, extending across a 30° × 25° area of the macula. Each B-scan consists of 768 A-scans, with the acquisition process being repeated 9–11 times to decrease speckle noise [21].

A scanning laser ophthalmoscopy (SLO) technology is integrated into most OCT devices to achieve *en face* fundus images, which constitute a useful complement to the cross-sectional B-scans. Figure 3 shows an *en face* fundus image and a cross-sectional OCT B-scan corresponding to the location of the green line on the *en face* image. B-scan images are approximately perpendicular to the retinal surface, while *en face* fundus images are nearly parallel to the retinal surface providing a direct, front view of the retina. Integration of an SLO technology into the OCT device can help localize and visually interpret the key OCT measurements such as thickness values.

Macular thickness measurements for different layers are performed for each individual B-scan. The thickness measurements can be color-coded and overlaid on top of the *en face* fundus image as illustrated in Fig. 4(A). With the help of reference normative

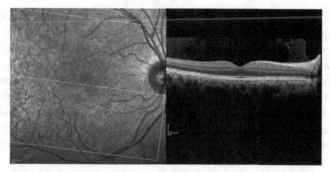

Fig. 3. An *en face* fundus image (left) and a cross-sectional, macular OCT B-scan (right). The green line one the *en face* fundus image shows the exact location of the B-scan. (Color figure online)

databases, Spectralis OCT is able to generate a deviation map to highlight the probability that the thickness measurements of each macular retinal layer are within or outside of normal limits [22]. As shown in Fig. 4(B), the deviation maps reveal regions and associated patterns in specific retinal layers that have statistically significant thinner or thicker values. Comparison of thickness measurements with the reference database enhances their diagnostic value. The deviation maps highlight the probability of measurements that are not within normal limits.

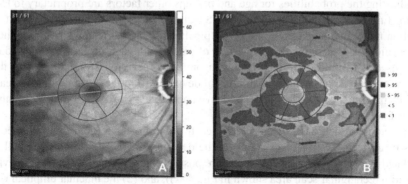

Fig. 4. (A) An example of Heidelberg Spectralis *en face* fundus image overlaid with thickness map. The thickness map is color-coded according to the ganglion cell layer's thickness in μm in this example. (B) Corresponding deviation map overlaid on same *en face* fundus image. The deviation map is a color-coded indication of normative data comparison. Percentile limits of the normal distribution are computed by the device. The meaning of the nth percentile is that n percent of normal subjects from the normative database have a thickness value (ganglion cell thickness in this example) less than or equal to this value. (Color figure online)

For each normal, healthy eye in the normative database, thickness at each macular location and for each inner retinal layer is measured. From these measurements, the age-adjusted percentiles of the eyes in the database are determined. These age-adjusted percentiles form the basis for highlighting a result as being within or outside the normal limits. The meaning of the nth percentile is that n percent of normal subjects from the database sample have a thickness of less than or equal to this value.

A macular deviation map highlights deviation from normal values; in Spectralis macular deviation maps, five ranges of thickness deviations are coded with five different colors from thickness deviation less than 1% to greater than 99% of thickness values of the normal eyes that belong to the normative database of Spectralis OCT. Regions where the thickness deviation lies between 5-percentile and 95-percentile of normal thickness values are considered normal regions and shown in green. Regions with values between 1-percentile and 5-percentile of thickness values of normal eyes are yellow regions, and red regions represent regions with thickness values less than 1-percentile of the normal thickness values. This means that less than 1% of normal eyes from the normative database have a thickness value less than or equal to that of the red regions. Spectralis OCT, also visualizes supernormal (above normal) regions. Supernormal regions contain thickness values greater than the 95-percentile (e.g., >95% or 99% cutoffs). If a macular location has a thickness value between 95-percentile and 99-percentile, it will be shown in blue. Lastly, locations that have very high thickness values to the extent that only 1% of normal eyes in the normative database have thickness above that value will be shown in pink.

2.2 Macular Deviation Map Processing

The normative reference database and the exact methods for the derivation of percentiles and adjusting the probabilities for age and perhaps other factors are proprietary to Heidelberg Engineering, the manufacturer of Spectralis OCT. Nevertheless, we can take deviation maps as inputs to our diagnostic pipeline and define features based on them for detection of glaucoma. The proportion of pixels with each of the five color-codes can be used as features or predictors of glaucoma or its severity. It should be noted that these colors correspond with probabilities of deviation from the normal range for each acquired pixel in the deviation map based on a comparison with an age-matched control group of normal, healthy eyes.

The common approach of calculating each proportion is to count the number of pixels of each of the five color-codes on the deviation map. The proportions will be calculated for two focus areas: (1) the entire posterior pole imaged by the OCT device (the entire rectangular scan area shown in Fig. 4(A)), and (2) the macular elliptical ring (annulus) developed on the macular scan with OCT software (See Fig. 4(C)). The latter focus area is centered around the fovea (central part of macula) and has the highest density of retinal ganglion cells [23]. OCT devices choose to exclude the foveal area where the retinal layers are very thin and difficult to detect accurately. That is why the focus area is effectively between two concentric ellipses forming an elliptical ring. The OCT device divides the elliptical ring into six sectors, as shown in Fig. 4.

As shown in Fig. 5, in order to effectively quantify the deviation maps, the OCT image processing pipeline converts an input deviation map, such as the one shown in Fig. 5(A), into the formats shown in Fig. 5(B) and Fig. 5(C), where all the areas other than the focus areas are masked. We then calculate the proportion of each thickness deviation for each format and form a dataset from those calculations. Therefore, the kernels of the proposed pipeline include masking redundant pixels and ellipse detection.

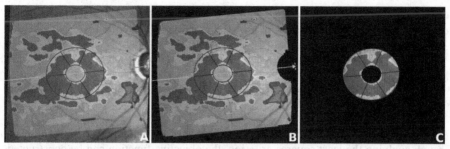

Fig. 5. Illustration of original and processed macular deviation maps. (A) Original deviation map. (B) Deviation map with focus on the entire rectangular scan area. (C) Deviation map of the elliptical ring (annulus) of the ganglion cell layer. In this example, the deviation maps are based on the thickness of the ganglion cell layer.

Masking Redundant Pixels. Since the only elements that we need to quantify are the five color-codes corresponding to the five thickness deviation levels, the first stage of the proposed pipeline is to generate masked deviation maps from the original deviation map. Redundant pixels can be masked by setting color thresholds in five ranges, denoted as C_1, C_2, C_3, C_4, and C_5, where each range includes all possible colors of each thickness deviation level. If a pixel is not within these ranges, the pipeline will classify such a pixel as a redundant pixel whose value will be converted to black. Figure 6 outlines the flowchart for the masking process.

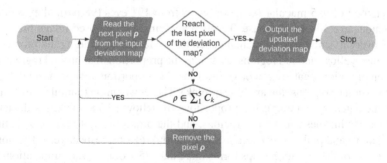

Fig. 6. Flowchart for masking the redundant pixels on macular deviation maps.

Ellipse Detection and Fitting. As mentioned earlier, the elliptical ring in each macular deviation map is the area with the highest density of retinal ganglion cells. However, the location of the two ellipses that form the elliptical ring depends on various characteristics of an eye, such as the curvature of the retina, and it varies from subject to subject. On each deviation map, two ellipses that bound the elliptical ring are extracted using a least-square ellipse fitting algorithm [24–26]. Briefly, an ellipse can be considered a conic section, formed by the intersection of a plane with a right circular cone. The general equation that can be used to represent any conic section can be written as:

$$Ax^2 + Bxy + Cy^2 + Dx + Ey + F = 0, \tag{1}$$

where (x, y) represent coordinates of points lying on the ellipse, and A, B, C, D, E, and F are the coefficients of the ellipse.

If there is a set S of coordinates (at least 5) located on the boundary of the ellipse, through applying the least squares criterion, the objective function can be constructed as follows:

$$\sum_{k=1}^{m} (Ax_k^2 + Bx_k^2y_k^2 + Cy_k^2 + Dx_k + Ey_k + 1)^2 = 0, \tag{2}$$

where (x_k, y_k) is the coordinate from the set S, and m is the number of points to which we fit an ellipse.

There are a number of techniques to detect the boundary of the ellipse to obtain the set S, such as the Hough transform [27]. The proposed pipeline integrates a simple coordinate range test along with the Hough transform to determine five points the boundary of the ellipse. After plugging in all coordinates from the set S, the corresponding system of linear equations can be solved with the partial derivative of each parameter, thereby fitting the ellipse.

2.3 Dataset Overview

There is a total of 955 macular deviation maps from 191 eyes (98 normal eyes and 93 glaucomatous eyes) in the database. Through applying the proposed image processing pipeline, every macular deviation map generates six features including the proportions of pink, blue, yellow, and red regions, as well as the proportion of abnormal regions (i.e., proportion of regions that are red or yellow) and the proportion of supernormal regions (i.e., proportion of regions that are blue or pink). These two union (cumulative) features can be calculated by summing the proportions of yellow ($<5\%$ thickness deviation) and red ($<1\%$ thickness deviation) regions, and the proportions of blue ($>95\%$ thickness deviation) and pink ($>99\%$ thickness deviation) regions, respectively. The normal (green) region of the deviation maps forms more than 75% of the data composition. Furthermore, the normal region is complementary to the other four color-codes. Therefore, we did not include the proportion of green region in the dataset.

For each eye, five macular deviation maps are available in the database. These include the FRT deviation map, the GCIPL thickness deviation map, the GCL thickness deviation map, the IPL thickness deviation map, and the RNFL thickness deviation map. For each deviation map, the six features discussed above are derived for both entire rectangular scan area and the elliptical ring of the macula. Accordingly, in total, 60 features will be extracted and maintained for each eye. The outcome of our analysis is a binary outcome indicating the presence or absence of glaucoma [28].

2.4 Machine Learning for Feature Evaluation

To sort the 50 features based on their relevance and contribution to the binary outcome, we create a logistic regression model comprising all eyes, but considering one feature at a time [29, 30]. As can be seen in Fig. 7, each classification model is based on one feature. Leave-one-out cross-validation is used to train and evaluate the model. For the correlation and ranking of each feature, besides the classification accuracy based on the corresponding classification model, factors such as true positive (TP), true negative (TN), false positive (FP) and false negative (FN) are also considered to gain a comprehensive assessment.

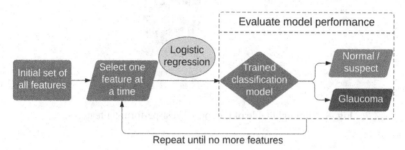

Fig. 7. Flowchart of automatic glaucoma classification with logistic regression.

3 Results and Discussions

Univariate logistic regression models, comprising 98 normal eyes and 93 glaucomatous eyes, are used to evaluate the strength of the relationship between individual features (as independent variables) and the binary outcome of the study, i.e., presence or absence of glaucoma (as the dependent variable). The ranking of the ten most relevant features to binary classification is given in the highlight table of Fig. 8. The values in the table are the average accuracy of the logistic regression classification model of the feature in the first column. If the value appears in the column "Elliptical Ring," it means that the corresponding feature comes from the macular elliptical ring. If the accuracy value appears in the column titled "Entire Rectangle," the feature is derived from the entire rectangular scan area in deviation maps.

The features listed in the first row of the highlight table and the subsequent charts follow the naming convention: the name starts with the name of the retinal layer to which the feature belongs, and the "Rectangle" or "Ring" identification indicates that the feature comes from the entire rectangular scan area in deviation maps or the central elliptical ring of the retinal layer, respectively; lastly, the third word of a feature's name represents the thickness deviation level or levels of a specific retinal layer. For example, "red" means that the thickness is less than that of the bottom 1% of the eyes in the normative database (i.e., <1% cutoff). Similarly, "abnormal" means the cumulative regions of red/yellow, meaning that the thickness is less than that of the bottom 5% or less than that for the bottom 1% of eyes in the normative database (i.e., <5% or <1% cutoffs).

The highlight table indicates that the best performing feature is the proportion of abnormal regions on the RNFL deviation map of the entire rectangular scan area. Such a feature alone can achieve accuracy of 69% in detection of glaucoma. Furthermore, we can observe that none of top six prominent features belongs to the elliptical ring defined by the OCT device. Another observation is that the RNFL-related features from the central elliptical ring do not appear among the best-performing features.

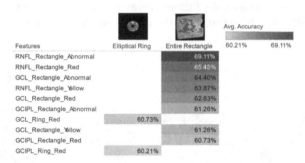

Features	Elliptical Ring	Entire Rectangle
RNFL_Rectangle_Abnormal		69.11%
RNFL_Rectangle_Red		65.45%
GCL_Rectangle_Abnormal		64.40%
RNFL_Rectangle_Yellow		63.87%
GCL_Rectangle_Red		62.83%
GCIPL_Rectangle_Abnormal		61.26%
GCL_Ring_Red	60.73%	
GCL_Rectangle_Yellow		61.26%
GCIPL_Rectangle_Red		60.73%
GCIPL_Ring_Red	60.21%	

Fig. 8. Highlight table of the top 10 best-performing features.

As shown before, the proportion of abnormal regions within the entire rectangular scan area in RNFL thickness deviation maps is the most prominent feature for detection of glaucoma. The univariate logistic regression classifier based on the proportion of red regions as its single predictive feature delivers the accuracy of 64.45% in detecting glaucoma (Fig. 9(A)). If we cumulatively consider red/yellow regions as one feature (i.e., <5% or <1% cutoffs), the univariate logistic regression classifier achieves the accuracy of 69.11% (Fig. 9(B)). We achieve a slightly better accuracy of 70.16% with a bivariate logistic regression with two independent features being the proportion of red regions and the proportion of yellow regions (Fig. 9(C)).

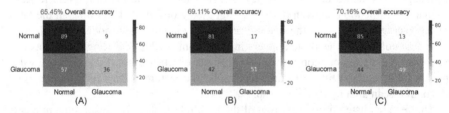

Fig. 9. Comparison of three logistic regression models for glaucoma detection. (A) Confusion matrix based on the proportion of red regions within the entire rectangular scan area in RNFL thickness deviation maps. (B) Confusion matrix based on the cumulative red/yellow regions (i.e., abnormal regions) (C) Confusion matrix based on independent proportions of red and yellow regions, utilized as two predictive features. (Color figure online)

Our experimental results indicate that there is significant information in regard to glaucoma detection in the macula and specifically within the macular thickness deviation maps generated by OCT devices. Furthermore, the features defined based on the macular elliptical ring, despite containing the highest density of retinal ganglion cells, fall behind the features defined in the elliptical ring (e.g., RNFL) in terms of glaucoma diagnosis power. It should be noted that our results do not imply that one should make diagnostic decisions solely based on the macula. In fact, there are several pieces to the glaucoma puzzle. However, our findings can help develop better diagnostic tools for detection of glaucoma.

4 Conclusions

Optical coherence tomography (OCT) allows for non-invasive imaging of glaucomatous structural damage involving the optic nerve head, peripapillary retinal nerve fiber layer, and the macular region. In this paper, we develop an image processing pipeline for the macular thickness deviation maps generated by Heidelberg Spectralis optical coherence tomography (OCT) to evaluate the information within the macular measurements for the diagnosis of glaucoma. Logistic regression is then applied to analyze features extracted from the deviation maps and the strength of their relationship with diagnosis of glaucoma. Our experimental results show that the proportion of regions with thickness significantly below the normative range in the nerve fiber layer thickness deviation maps can be used to detect glaucoma with an accuracy of up to 70.16%. Moreover, the ganglion cell layer deviation maps possess significant diagnostic ability for detection of glaucoma, which can be combined with the traditional assessments of the optic nerve head and peripapillary retinal nerve fiber layer to improve the reliability of glaucoma diagnosis.

References

1. Michelessi, M., et al.: Optic nerve head and fibre layer imaging for diagnosing glaucoma. Cochrane Database Syst. Rev. **11**, 2015 (2015)
2. Tan, O., et al.: Detection of macular ganglion cell loss in glaucoma by fourier-domain optical coherence tomography. Ophthalmology **116**, 2305–2314 (2009)
3. Miraftabi, A., et al.: Macular SD-OCT outcome measures: Comparison of local structure-function relationships and dynamic range. Investig. Ophthalmol. Vis. Sci. **57**, 4815 (2016)
4. Chen, Z., Wang, Y., Wollstein, G., de Los Angeles Ramos-Cadena, M., Schuman, J., Ishikawa, H.: Macular GCIPL thickness map prediction via time-aware convolutional LSTM. In: Proceedings - International Symposium on Biomedical Imaging (2020)
5. Raja, H., Hassan, T., Akram, M.U., Werghi, N.: Clinically verified hybrid deep learning system for retinal ganglion cells aware grading of glaucomatous progression. IEEE Trans. Biomed. Eng. **68**, 2140–2151 (2021)
6. Amini, N., Miremadi, S.G., Fazeli, M.: A hierarchical routing protocol for energy load balancing in wireless sensor networks. In: Canadian Conference on Electrical and Computer Engineering (2007)
7. Ishikawa, H., Stein, D.M., Wollstein, G., Beaton, S., Fujimoto, J.G., Schuman, J.S.: Macular segmentation with optical coherence tomography. Investig. Ophthalmol. Vis. Sci. **46**, 2012 (2005)
8. Amini, N., Vahdatpour, A., Dabiri, F., Noshadi, H., Sarrafzadeh, M.: Joint consideration of energy-efficiency and coverage-preservation in microsensor networks. Wirel. Commun. Mob. Comput. **26**, 1086 (2011)

9. Muhammad, H., et al.: Hybrid deep learning on single wide-field optical coherence tomography scans accurately classifies glaucoma suspects. J. Glaucoma **26**, 1086–1094 (2017)

10. Dey, A., Bandyopadhyay, S.: Automated glaucoma detection using support vector machine classification method. Br. J. Med. Med. Res. **11**, 1–12 (2016)

11. Huang, M.L., Chen, H.Y.: Glaucoma classification model based on GDx VCC measured parameters by decision tree. J. Med. Syst. **34**, 1141–1147 (2010)

12. Sugimoto, K., Murata, H., Hirasawa, H., Aihara, M., Mayama, C., Asaoka, R.: Cross-sectional study: does combining optical coherence tomography measurements using the 'Random Forest' decision tree classifier improve the prediction of the presence of perimetric deterioration in glaucoma suspects? BMJ Open **3**(10), e003114 (2013)

13. Balasubramanian, K., Ananthamoorthy, N.P., Gayathridevi, K.: Automatic Diagnosis and Classification of Glaucoma Using Hybrid Features and k -Nearest Neighbor. J. Med. Imaging Heal. Informatics **8**, 1598–1606 (2018)

14. Ayub, J., et al.: Glaucoma detection through optic disc and cup segmentation using K-mean clustering. In: 2016 International Conference on Computing, Electronic and Electrical Engineering, ICE Cube 2016 - Proceedings (2016)

15. Bambo, M.P., et al.: Diagnostic capability of a linear discriminant function applied to a novel Spectralis OCT glaucoma-detection protocol. BMC Ophthalmol. **20**, 1–8 (2020)

16. Bowd, C., et al.: Bayesian machine learning classifiers for combining structural and functional measurements to classify healthy and glaucomatous eyes. Investig. Ophthalmol. Vis. Sci. **49**, 935 (2008)

17. Maetschke, S., Antony, B., Ishikawa, H., Wollstein, G., Schuman, J., Garnavi, R.: A feature agnostic approach for glaucoma detection in OCT volumes. PLOS ONE **14**(7), e0219126 (2019)

18. Kaiser, W.X., et al.: Method of assessing human fall risk using mobile systemst. 8,823,526 (2014)

19. Hood, D.C., Raza, A.S., de Moraes, C.G.V., Liebmann, J.M., Ritch, R.: Glaucomatous damage of the macula. Progr. Retinal Eye Res. **32**, 1–21 (2013)

20. Takayama, K., et al.: A novel method to detect local ganglion cell loss in early glaucoma using spectral-domain optical coherence tomography. Investig. Ophthalmol. Vis. Sci. **53**, 6904 (2012)

21. Mahmoudinezhad, G., et al.: Detection of longitudinal GCIPL change: comparison of two spectral domain optical coherence tomography devices. Am. J. Ophthalmol. **231**, 1–10 (2021)

22. Heidelberg Engineering. Enhanced Features, Enhanced Diagnostics (2020)

23. Curcio, C.A., Allen, K.A.: Topography of ganglion cells in human retina. J. Comp. Neurol. **300**, 1–5 (1990)

24. Rosin, P.L.: A note on the least squares fitting of ellipses. Pattern Recogn. Lett. **14**(10), 799–808 (1993)

25. Fitzgibbon, A., Pilu, M., Fisher, R.B.: Direct least square fitting of ellipses. IEEE Trans. Pattern Anal. Mach. Intell. **21**(5), 476–480 (1999)

26. Yousefi, H., Mohammadi, F., Mirian, N., Amini, N.: tuberculosis bacilli identification: a novel feature extraction approach via statistical shape and color models. In: Proceedings - 19th IEEE International Conference on Machine Learning and Applications, ICMLA 2020 (2020)

27. Ballard, D.H.: Generalizing the Hough transform to detect arbitrary shapes. Pattern Recogn. **13**(2), 111–122 (1981)

28. Ahmad, S.S.: Glaucoma suspects: a practical approach. Taiwan J. Ophthalmol. **8**(2), 74 (2018)

29. Peng, C.Y.J., Lee, K.L., Ingersoll, G.M.: An introduction to logistic regression analysis and reporting. J. Educ. Res. **96**(1), 3–14 (2002)

30. Peng, C.-Y.J., So, T.-S.H.: Logistic regression analysis and reporting: a primer. Underst. Stat. **1**(1), 31–70 (2002)

Pattern Recognition

Variational Conditional Dependence Hidden Markov Models for Skeleton-Based Action Recognition

Konstantinos P. Panousis[1(✉)], Soritios Chatzis[1], and Sergios Theodoridis[2,3]

[1] Cyprus University of Technology, Limassol, Cyprus
k.panousis@cut.ac.cy
[2] National and Kapodistrian University of Athens, Athens, Greece
[3] Aalborg University, Aalborg, Denmark

Abstract. Hidden Markov Models (HMMs) comprise a powerful generative approach for modeling sequential data and time-series in general. However, the commonly employed assumption of the dependence of the current time frame to a single or multiple immediately preceding frames is unrealistic; more complicated dynamics potentially exist in real world scenarios. This paper revisits conventional sequential modeling approaches, aiming to address the problem of capturing time-varying temporal dependency patterns. To this end, we propose a different formulation of HMMs, whereby the dependence on past frames is dynamically inferred from the data. Specifically, we introduce a hierarchical extension by postulating an additional latent variable layer; therein, the (time-varying) temporal dependence patterns are treated as latent variables over which inference is performed. We leverage solid arguments from the Variational Bayes framework and derive a tractable inference algorithm based on the forward-backward algorithm. As we experimentally show, our approach can model highly complex sequential data and can effectively handle data with missing values.

Keywords: Hidden Markov Models · Approximate inference · Temporal dependence

1 Introduction

Modeling sequential data, typically encountered in many real-world applications such as bioinformatics and computer vision, remains a fundamental task in the field of machine learning. Hidden Markov Models have been a popular approach for modeling such data, but more recently, have largely been replaced by their "deep" variants. Despite their success, these approaches exhibit significant drawbacks such as over-parameterization even in simple tasks as image classification

This work has received funding from the European Union's Horizon 2020 research and innovation program under grant agreement No 872139, project aiD.

© Springer Nature Switzerland AG 2021
G. Bebis et al. (Eds.): ISVC 2021, LNCS 13018, pp. 67–80, 2021.
https://doi.org/10.1007/978-3-030-90436-4_6

[20]. Nevertheless, both models aim to learn hidden representations for sequential data.

Commonly, first-order HMMs are usually considered; this allows for simplicity and low computational complexity. Then, model temporal dynamics are restrained to a simple step back, undermining model effectiveness. This compromise is especially detrimental in many applications where longer temporal dynamics may be present. Researchers have considered alternatives to alleviate this restriction, for example by introducing extended temporal dependencies in the form of second or higher order Markovian dynamics and had successful applications in many domains [2, 13, 17]. However, the increased order introduces three significant drawbacks: (i) additional complexity to the model that may render it unusable in real-world scenarios; (ii) unnecessary burden to the researchers, namely the need to determine the best postulated order for each specific application and dataset; and (iii) unnecessary complex models with strong overfitting tendencies, which may negate the benefits and flexibility of HMMs.

Lastly, a further drawback of conventional HMM approaches is the static and homogeneity assumptions [3, 8, 10], where the possible dynamic temporal dependencies of the data are ignored. The same effect applies to hidden semi-Markov models (HSMMs) [26]; even though the relaxed temporal assumptions allow for more flexible modeling of the dynamics, potential non-homogeneous temporal dynamics in the data are still ignored. Drawing inspiration from there results, researchers have developed HMMs with variable order Markov chains, e.g., [5]. The resulting models have been shown to be effective in a diverse range of applications, nevertheless exhibiting significant drawbacks such as the inability to model continuous observations [12].

Recently, [29] introduced a variant of a simple HSMM model, dubbed Hierarchical Dynamic Model (HDM). Specifically, the proposed model constitutes a hierarchical extension by leveraging on the Bayesian framework to increase the capacity of HSMMs to account for temporal and spatial variations in the Human Action Recognition task. The produced generative model is shown to be more robust to the natural variations of the data; it exhibits increased generalization capabilities, while at the same time requiring less data to train.

This paper draws from these results and attempts to offer a principled way of modeling sequential data with complex dynamics. To this end, we develop a novel variant of HMMs that is able to capture complex temporal dependencies. The considered approach constitutes a hierarchical model: by postulating an *additional latent first-order Markov Chain*, called the *dependence-generator* layer, the model can alter the effective temporal dynamics of the conventional *observation-emitting* Markov Chain. In this way, the proposed approach can effectively infer which past state more strongly affects the current time frame. The proposed inferential construction is enhanced by a fully Bayesian treatment under the Variational Inference framework. We posit that the proposed hierarchical variant, combined with the flexibility and effectiveness of *Variational Bayes*, can greatly increase the capacity of the resulting architecture to model sequential data that exhibit a complex combination of spatial and temporal variations.

We formulate efficient training and inference algorithms for our approach by: (i) deriving a variant of the classical forward-backward algorithm used in HMMs, (ii) relying on Variational Inference and conjugate priors for closed-form solutions. We dub our approach *Variational Bayesian Conditional Dependence Hidden Markov Model* (VB-CD-HMM) and evaluate its performance in the Human Action Recognition domain. Human Action Recognition poses one of the most challenging tasks in the computer vision community. Researchers have devoted significant effort to address this particular area [25] and remarkable progress has been made with the popularization of action recognition through 3D data [1]. In this context, various approaches have been employed in order to model the activity recognition task, such as HMM-based approaches [29], LSTM-based [28] and Gaussian Processes [6,7]. However, the significant spatial and temporal variations arising in the execution of an action, along with variations due to the capturing process, e.g., camera occlusion, leave room for needed improvements in existing approaches. We provided strong empirical evidence for our approach though a series of experiments dealing with Human Action Recognition benchmarks. Our evidence shows competitive predictive accuracy, persistent even in the presence of missing values.

2 Proposed Model

In this work, we consider an extension of a conventional first-order HMM, whereby a hierarchical structure is employed consisting of *two layers*: (i) a *dependence-generator* layer; this comprises a simple first-order Markov Chain that determines the *steps-back* taken into account in the second layer; and (ii) a chain of *observation-emitting* hidden states, where the temporal dependencies are determined from the output of the *dependence-generator* layer. The *temporal dependencies* are *inferred* in a data-driven fashion. An outline of the proposed Conditional Dependence HMM (CD-HMM) model is provided in Fig. 1a.

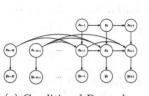

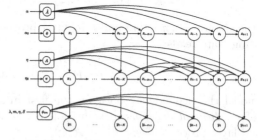

(a) Conditional Dependence Hidden Markov Model.

(b) The resulting hierarchical VB-CD-HMM.

Fig. 1. Graphical representation of the proposed CD-HMM model (Fig. 1a) and its variational counterpart (Fig. 1b).

2.1   Model Definition

Let $Y = \{\boldsymbol{y}_t\}_{t=1}^T \in \mathbb{R}^D$ be an observed data sequence with T time frames and D features. Following the definition of conventional HMMs, let us assume an N-state *emitting state sequence* denoted as $X = \{x_t\}_{t=1}^T, x_t \in [1, \ldots, N]$ where x_t indicates the state from which the tth observation is emitted. Each emission density is modeled by an M-component finite mixture model; the *mixture component indicators* are denoted as $L = \{l_t\}_{t=1}^T, l_t \in [1, \ldots, M]$ with l_t indicating which component generated the tth observation.

The hierarchical construction postulates an additional layer, the *dependence-generator* layer, such that the *latent data* associated with each sequence are augmented with the supplementary sequence of *temporal dependence indicators*, $Z = \{z_t\}_{t=1}^T, z_t \in [1, \ldots, K]$. These denote the current temporal dependencies between the *observation-emitting* states at time t and times $t-1, \ldots, t-K$ as shown in Fig. 1a. Thus, different pairwise state dependencies (x_t, x_{t-z_t}) are valid at each time point t, dictated by the inferred latent variables z_t.

The model parameters comprise $\theta = \{\phi, \psi\}$, where ϕ contains the parameters of the emission distributions of the model and ψ the effective parameters of the latent processes.

For the emission distributions, finite mixture models of multivariate Gaussian distributions are considered, $p(\boldsymbol{y}_t|x_t = i) = \sum_{m=1}^M c_{im} \mathcal{N}(\boldsymbol{y}_t|\boldsymbol{\mu}_{im}, R_{im}), \forall i$ where $\mathcal{N}(\cdot|\boldsymbol{\mu}, R)$ is a multivariate Normal distribution with mean $\boldsymbol{\mu} \in \mathbb{R}^D$ and precision matrix $R \in \mathbb{R}^{D \times D}$ with distinct parameters for each state and mixture; $\boldsymbol{c}_i \in \mathbb{R}^M$ are the mixture component coefficients for state $x_t = i$. Hence, the effective parameters for the model distributions are $\phi = \{\boldsymbol{\mu}_{im}, R_{im}, c_{im}\}_{i,m=1}^{N,M}$.

We proceed with the definition of the parameters and their relationships pertaining to the postulated latent processes. Specifically, the first, *dependence-generator*, layer is a first-order Markov Chain and is described by the following initial and transition probabilities:

$$\hat{\pi}_k \triangleq p(z_1 = k), \quad \forall k \tag{1}$$

$$\hat{A}_{kk'} \triangleq p(z_t = k'|z_{t-1} = k), \quad \forall t > 1, k, k' \tag{2}$$

For the second, *observation-emitting*, layer process, the initial probability of the emitting state reads:

$$\pi_i \triangleq p(x_1 = i), \quad \forall i \tag{3}$$

To model the dependency between the first and second layers, we define the set of *conditional dependence* transition probability matrices $\{A^k\}_{k=1}^K$ on the second-layer process, where $A^k \triangleq [A_{ij}^k]_{i,j=1}^N$,

$$A_{ij}^k \triangleq p(x_t = j|x_{t-k} = i, z_t = k) \tag{4}$$

Thus, based on the inferred dependence of the *dependence-generator* layer, we consider different temporal dependencies in the second layer at each time point; these are regulated through the z_t variables, which are imposed a first-order

Markov chain themselves. Intuitively, the conditional dependence mechanism determines the strength of the dependence of the current state to individual *past states*. The strongest inferred dependence is retained from the model, and is encoded in the z_t values; thus, the model dynamically alters the transition dynamics for the *observation-emitting* state at each time point.

Having fully defined the parameters for the latent processes, the corresponding set comprises $\psi = \{\hat{\boldsymbol{\pi}}, \hat{A}, \boldsymbol{\pi}, \{A^k\}_{k=1}^K\}$. The definition of the model is now concluded.

The joint distribution reads:

$$p(Y, X, Z) = \hat{\pi}_{z_1} \pi_{x_1} \prod_{t=1}^{T-1} \hat{A}_{z_t, z_{t+1}} \prod_{t>1} A_{x_{t-z_t}, x_t}^{z_t} \prod_{t=1}^{T} p(\boldsymbol{y}_t | x_t)$$

2.2 Model Training

We train the CD-HMM model presented in the previous section considering a *variational Bayesian treatment*. The *Variational Bayes* (VB) approach was chosen over MCMC inference methods, e.g., Gibbs Sampling, considering the negligible performance differences and the significantly lower computational complexity. Sampling-based approaches encompass large computational complexity; this restricts the applicability of the model to either more complex applications and datasets or different settings (e.g., streaming).

The VB treatment of the model comprises the introduction of appropriate prior distributions over all model parameters and maximization of the resulting Evidence Lower Bound (ELBO) expression. To obtain closed-form solutions for the updates of the parameters, we employ conjugate priors; a choice accompanied by the benefits of lower computational complexity and interpretability [23].

Priors and Evidence Lower Bound. Dirichlet distributions are imposed as the priors of the initial state probabilities for both layer processes $p(\boldsymbol{\pi}) = \mathcal{D}(\boldsymbol{\pi}|\boldsymbol{\eta}_0)$ and $p(\hat{\boldsymbol{\pi}}) = \mathcal{D}(\hat{\boldsymbol{\pi}}|\boldsymbol{\alpha}_0)$. Analogous Dirichlet priors are imposed on the rows of the state transition probabilities and the mixture coefficients of the emission distributions, i.e.,

$$p(\boldsymbol{c}_{i,:}) = \mathcal{D}(\boldsymbol{c}_{i,:}|\boldsymbol{w}_i), \ \boldsymbol{w}_i \in \mathbb{R}^M, \ i = 1, \ldots, N \tag{5}$$

$$p(\hat{\boldsymbol{A}}_{k,:}) = \mathcal{D}(\hat{\boldsymbol{A}}_{k,:}|\boldsymbol{\alpha}_k), \boldsymbol{\alpha}_k \in \mathbb{R}^K, k = 1, \ldots, K \tag{6}$$

$$p(\boldsymbol{A}_{i,:}^k) = \mathcal{D}(\boldsymbol{A}_{i,:}^k|\boldsymbol{\eta}_i^k), \boldsymbol{\eta}_i^k \in \mathbb{R}^N, i = 1, \ldots, N, \forall k \tag{7}$$

For the prior over the means and precision matrices of the mixture components, we assign a Normal-Wishart distribution with hyperparameters $\lambda_{ij}, \boldsymbol{m}_{ij}, \eta_{ij}, S_{ij}$,

$$p(\boldsymbol{\mu}_{ij}, R_{ij}) = \mathcal{NW}(\boldsymbol{\mu}_{ij}, R_{ij}|\lambda_{ij}, \boldsymbol{m}_{ij}, \eta_{ij}, S_{ij}), \ \forall i, j \tag{8}$$

This concludes the formulation of the prior specification for the VB treatment of the CD-HMM model, henceforth referred to as VB-CD-HMM. A graphical illustration of the fully proposed model can be found in Fig. 1b.

Let $\theta = \{\phi, \psi\}$ be the sets of latent process and emission distribution parameters where a conjugate exponential prior has been imposed. Under the VB treatment, we introduce an arbitrary distribution $q(\theta)$ and derive the Evidence Lower Bound (ELBO) for the model. Maximizing the ELBO is equivalent to the minimization of the KL divergence between the true and the postulated posterior. We introduce the *mean-field* (posterior-independence) assumption on the joint variational posterior, such that $q(\theta)$ factorizes over all latent variables and model parameters. Then, the ELBO can be written as

$$
\text{ELBO} = \mathbb{E}_{q(\theta),X,Y,Z}\left[\log\left(\hat{\pi}_{z_1}\pi_{x_1}\prod_{t=1}^{T-1}\hat{A}_{z_t,z_{t+1}}\prod_{t>1}^{T}A^{z_t}_{x_t,x_{t-z_t}}\prod_{t=1}^{T}p(\boldsymbol{y}_t|x_t)\right)\right]
$$
$$
+ \mathbb{E}_{q(\theta)}\left[\log p(C, \pi, A, \hat{\pi}, \hat{A}, \boldsymbol{\mu}, \boldsymbol{R})\right] - \mathbb{E}_{q(\theta)}\left[\log q(\theta)\right]
$$
(9)

Variational Posteriors. For each variable, the optimal member of the exponential family[1] can be found by maximizing (9). This maximization is performed in an EM-like fashion; in the E-step the parameters of the posterior distributions of the latent processes are updated, while in the M-step the rest of the variational distributions; the resulting iterative procedure is guaranteed to monotonically increase the ELBO.

M-step. Starting from Eq. (9), we collect all relevant terms pertaining to the transition matrix of the first layer process $\hat{A}$; we then maximize the resulting expression, yielding the following variational posterior:

$$
q(\hat{A}) = \prod_{i=1}^{K}\text{Dir}(\hat{A}_{i1}, \ldots, \hat{A}_{iK}|\omega^{\hat{A}}_{i1}, \ldots, \omega^{\hat{A}}_{iK})
$$
(10)

where $\omega^{\hat{A}}_{ij} = \alpha_{ij} + \sum_t \gamma^{\hat{A}}_{ijt}$, $\gamma^{\hat{A}}_{ijt} \triangleq q(z_t = i, z_{t-1} = j)$.

We follow the same procedure for the initial state probabilities, $\hat{\pi}$, the corresponding posteriors for the second layer process parameters π and $A = \{A^k\}_{k=1}^{K}$, and the mixture component weights C. Due to conjugate priors, the emission distributions yield Normal-Wishart distributions with variational parameters $\{\tilde{\lambda}_{ij}, \tilde{m}_{ij}, \tilde{\eta}_{ij}, \tilde{S}_{ij}\}_{i,j=1}^{N,M}$; these are similarly obtained via standard computations, i.e., maximizing the corresponding ELBO expression.

E-step. Turning to the E-step of the iterative procedure, the joint variational posterior optimizer for the latent processes Z and X, and the mixture component indicators L is analogous to the expression of the conditional probability defined in the context of conventional HMMs, e.g., see [9]. Thus, the variational posterior entails the calculation of the corresponding responsibilities that comprise said posterior $q(z_1 = i)$, $q(x_1 = 1)$, $q(z_t = i, z_{t-1} = j)$ and $q(x_t = j, x_{t-k} = i)$; these can easily be computed by means of of the well-known forward-backward algorithm. Thus, in the following, we derive a variant of the forward-backward algorithm for our model.

---

[1] By imposing conjugate priors, we obtain posteriors of the same functional form as their corresponding priors.

Forward-Backward Algorithm. For calculating the forward-backward algorithm, we first define the forward messages as:

$$\alpha_t(\{x_\tau\}_{\tau=t-K+1}^t, z_t) \triangleq p(\{\boldsymbol{y}_\tau\}_{\tau=1}^t, \{x_\tau\}_{\tau=t-K+1}^t, z_t) \tag{11}$$

The defined messages can be computed recursively, using the following initialization:

$$\alpha_1(x_1, z_1) = \begin{cases} \pi_i^* p^*(\boldsymbol{y}_1|x_1 = i), & z_1 = 1 \\ 0, & z_1 > 1 \end{cases} \tag{12}$$

and the induction step reads:

$$\alpha_t(\{x_\tau\}_{\tau=t-K+1}^t, z_t) = p^*(\boldsymbol{y}_t|x_t) \sum_{x_{t-K}} \sum_{z_{t-1}} \hat{A}_{z_{t-1}, z_t}^* A_{x_{t-k}, x_t}^{*z_t} \alpha_{t-1}(\{x_\tau\}_{\tau=t-K}^{t-1}, z_{t-1}) \tag{13}$$

The backward messages are analogously defined as:

$$\beta_t(\{x_\tau\}_{\tau=t-K+1}^t, z_t) \triangleq p(\{\boldsymbol{y}_\tau\}_{\tau=t+1}^T | \{x_\tau\}_{\tau=t-K+1}^t, z_t) \tag{14}$$

The corresponding initialization reads:

$$\beta_T(\{x_\tau\}_{\tau=T-K+1}^T, z_T = k) = 1, \quad \forall k \tag{15}$$

while the recursion becomes:

$$\beta_t(\{x_\tau\}_{\tau=t-K+1}^T, z_t) = \sum_{x_{t+1}} \sum_{z_{t+1}} \hat{A}_{z_t, z_{t+1}}^* p^*(\boldsymbol{y}_{t+1}|x_{t+1}) \times \\ A_{x_{t-k+1}, x_{t+1}}^{*z_{t+1}} \beta_{t+1}(\{x_\tau\}_{\tau=t-K+2}^T, z_{t+1}) \tag{16}$$

Responsibilities. By utilizing the forward-backward messages, the necessary responsibilities for updating the parameters of the model can now be computed.

For the first layer process, the marginal initial state responsibilities yield:

$$\gamma_t^z(k) \triangleq p(z_t = k|\{\boldsymbol{y}_\tau\}_{\tau=1}^T) \propto \sum_X \alpha_t(\{x_\tau\}_{\tau=t-K+1}^t, z_t)\beta_t(\{x_\tau\}_{\tau=t-K+1}^t, z_t)$$

Analogously, for the *observation-emitting* states, we have:

$$\gamma_t^x(i) \triangleq p(x_t = i|\{\boldsymbol{y}_\tau\}_{\tau=1}^T) \propto \sum_{X', z_t} \alpha_t(\{x_\tau\}_{\tau=t-K+1}^t, z_t)\beta_t(\{x_\tau\}_{\tau=t-K+1}^t, z_t)$$

where $X' = \{x_\tau\}_{\tau=t-K+1}^t \setminus \{x_t\} = \{x_\tau\}_{\tau=t-K+1}^{t-1}$.

The state transitions responsibilities for the *temporal dependence* indicators:

$$\gamma_t^z(k, k') \triangleq p(z_t = k', z_{t-1} = k|\{\boldsymbol{y}_\tau\}_{\tau=1}^T) \\ \propto \sum_{X'} \alpha_{t-1}(\{x_\tau\}_{\tau=t-K}^{t-1}, z_{t-1})\hat{A}_{z_{t-1}, z_t}^* A_{x_{t-k}, x_t}^{*z_t} p^*(\boldsymbol{y}_t|x_t)\beta_t(\{x_\tau\}_{\tau=t-K}^t, z_t)$$

Finally, the dependent state transition responsibilities:

$$\gamma_t^x(i, j, k) \triangleq p(x_t = j, x_{t-k} = i|\{\boldsymbol{y}_\tau\}_{\tau=1}^T) \propto \sum_{X'', z_t} \alpha_t(\{x_\tau\}_{\tau=t-K+1}^t, z_t)\beta_t(\{x_\tau\}_{\tau=t-K+1}^t, z_t)$$

where $X'' = \{x_\tau\}_{\tau=t-K+1}^t \setminus \{x_t, x_{t-k}\}$.

2.3   Inference

Let us consider a VB-CD-HMM model, fully trained with data Y. We seek to calculate the predictive density of the test sequence Y^{test}:

$$p(Y^{\text{test}}|Y) = \int d\hat{\theta}\, p(\hat{\theta}|Y)P(Y^{\text{test}}|\hat{\theta}) \tag{17}$$

Using the introduced variational posterior in place of the unknown true posterior $p(\hat{\theta}|Y)$ and similar to [9], we can compute the necessary quantities by utilizing the forward algorithm variant defined in Sect. 2.2. Specifically, the density of a given test set $Y^{\text{test}} = \{\boldsymbol{y}_t^{\text{test}}\}_{t=1}^T$ yields:

$$p(Y^{\text{test}}|\hat{\theta}) = \sum_{z_T}\sum_X \alpha_T(x_{T-K+1}, \ldots, x_T, z_T) \tag{18}$$

3   Experimental Evaluation

3.1   Experimental Details

We use four popular benchmark datasets for the human action recognition task, namely *MSR Action 3D (MSRA)* [15], *UTD-MHAD (UTD)* [11], *Gaming 3D (G3D)* [4] and *UPenn Action (Penn)* [27]. Only skeletal data are used for training the models. The preprocessing and augmentation of the data are the same as in [29]. We extract the motion of the joints for every pair of joints between two consecutive frames. PCA is then employed for dimensionality reduction.

In addition, we further consider evaluation with a more complex dataset, namely NTU [21]. This comprises ≈ 57000 samples of 60 different actions. We adopt the two data splits suggested in the original publication: (i) Cross-View and (ii) Cross-Subject.

3.2   Parameter Initialization and Hyperparameter Selection

The resulting ELBO expression is non-convex with respect to the variational posterior, and potentially many local maxima exist; the obtained solution is thus dependent on parameter initialization. To avoid the rather time-consuming procedure of multiple runs from different initial values, we employ a common initialization scheme: K-Means is used to initialize the posterior parameters of the second layer process and the means and variances of the distributions. The parameters of the first postulated layer are initialized to random values, while for the hyperparameters we use *ad-hoc* uninformative values, similar to [9]. Specifically, the hyperparameters of the Dirichlet priors are set to very small values (10^{-3}). For the parameters of the emission distributions, we set $\lambda_{ij} = \tilde{\lambda}_{ij} = 0.25$ and $\eta_{ij} = \tilde{\eta}_{ij} = D + 2$, where D is the dimensionality of the data.

3.3 States, Mixtures and Temporal Dependencies

We trained different models with varying number of states and mixtures to investigate their effect on model effectiveness. We observed that the recognition accuracy is not considerably sensitive to the chosen configuration; thus, we run multiple configurations and retain the one with the higher ELBO. For all experiments, we set $K = 2$, as we observed that the inferred temporal dependence posteriors rarely assigned high probability (if any) to $p(z_t > 2|z_{t-1})$; this behavior is reasonable considering the physical meaning of the used data features. Nevertheless, we did not observe any drop in accuracy when setting $K > 2$. For $K = 1$, the model reduces to a simple HMM, and exhibits a significant drop in recognition accuracy. This outcome strongly corroborates the benefits of our dynamic temporal dependency inference approach.

3.4 Experimental Results

We follow the train and test splits as suggested by the authors of the respective datasets. We train one model per class and assign the test data to the class with the maximum predictive posterior (Eq. (18)). We compare our approach to related approaches, along with a comparison with HDM [29]. Out of the HDM model variants therein, we focus on the BV variant for comparability, whereby variational inference is utilized for computing the predictive likelihood.

Table 1. Recognition accuracy (%) for individual dataset experiments.

Model	MSRA	UTD	G3D	Penn	Avg.
HMM	67.8	82.8	68.1	82.3	75.3
HMM^2	80.2	83.1	82.6	84.4	82.6
HSMM	66.3	82.3	77.5	78.9	76.35
LSTM	74.7	77.0	82.2	90.3	81.1
HDM-PI	70.3	84.4	79.4	89.8	81.0
HDM-PL	80.6	90.2	87.7	91.6	87.5
HDM-BV	82.1	91.4	87.7	90.8	88.0
VB-CD-HMM	**82.5**	**92.7**	**90.6**	**92.0**	**89.45**

Individual Datasets. We first consider the MRSA dataset, where the recognition rates of our approach can be found in the first column of Table 1. Compared to baseline models such as HMMs, HSMMs and LSTMs, our model performs much better in classification accuracy with an average improvement of 12.9%. Even though the recently proposed HDM [29] consistently improves over the considered alternatives, it falls short compared to the proposed VB-CD-HMM model. This behavior is consistent across all the considered datasets, resulting in an average classification accuracy of 89.45%, outperforming HDM by 1.45%.

Additionally, we observe that our proposed approach consistently and significantly outperforms a second-order HMM (HMM^2) evaluated under the same experimental and modeling setup. Even though HMM^2 improves over simple first-order HMMs, by considering more complex dynamics, it still falls short to the flexibility of modeling dependencies over long horizons, that VB-CD-HMM offers. Note also that the prowness of HMM^2 comes at the cost of a considerable increase in the resulting computational complexity; this is in contrast to our model, which still relies on (a variant of) the forward-backward algorithm.

We additionally compare the recognition accuracy of our approach to other state-of-the-art methods. The corresponding performances are illustrated in Table 2. As we observe, our approach yields clearly improved accuracy compared to the competition for UTD, Penn and NTU datasets. For the G3D dataset, our method slightly outperforms LRBM [19], but R3DG [24] performs better; this is due to the sophisticated feature engineering and combination of several approaches in contrast to our simple joints locations and motion features.

Table 2. Recognition accuracy for all the considered datasets compared to state-of-the-art.

Dataset					
Method ‖ Acc					
MSRA	UTD	G3D	Penn	NTU (x-view)	NTU (x-subject)
ST-LSTM [16] ‖ **94.8**	Fusion [11] ‖ 79.1	LRBM [19] ‖ 90.5	Actemes [27] ‖ 86.5	ST-TSL [22] ‖ 92.4	ST-TSL [22] ‖ 84.8
B-GC-LSTM [28] ‖ 94.5	SOS-CNN [14] ‖ 87.0	R3DG [24] ‖ **91.1**	AOG [18] ‖ 84.8	B-GC-LSTM [28] ‖ 89.0	B-GC-LSTM [28] ‖ 81.8
VB-CDHMM ‖ 92.5	VB-CDHMM ‖ **92.7**	VB-CDHMM ‖ 90.6	VB-CDHMM ‖ **92.0**	VB-CDHMM ‖ **93.0**	VB-CDHMM ‖ **85.0**

The main focus of this Section is to compare and prove the efficacy of our approach within the family of more general HMM-based methods in the tackled application domain. Thus, we did not explore complicated model-based and specific-task tailored feature engineering; this allows for both transparency of comparison to recent related published work, and interpretability of our results. Nevertheless, as we shall see in the next section, our method clearly outperforms R3DG, when we randomly omit observations; this behavior vouches for the improved robustness of our approach. Likewise, ST-LSTM [16] incorporates complicated feature extraction mechanisms, thus explaining the performance gap compared to our approach. For the NTU dataset [21], to the best of our knowledge, there are no results for recent HMM-based methods. As we observe, compared to the state-of-the-art methods ST-LSTM [16] and B-GC-LSTM [28], VB-CD-HMM yields considerable improvements in both splits, despite its simplicity and lower computational complexity.

3.5 Missing Values

Generative models come with the additional benefit of robustness to missing values. This advantage is of great importance in the human action recognition field, especially when using skeletal data, where the dataset may be corrupted with missing observations, e.g., due to occlusion. As an HMM variant, the proposed model is such a generative model; we thus assess the efficacy of our approach when missing values are present. To this end, we train the considered architecture in the UTD, MSRA and G3D datasets, with randomly missing values from both the train and test data. Analogous experiments have been performed in [29], and we adopt the same procedure, including the proportion of missing values with respect to the original data.

Table 3. Recognition accuracy (%) with missing values.

Dataset		UTD			MSRA			G3D		
Missing portion		10%	30%	50%	10%	30%	50%	10%	30%	50%
Model	R3DG [24]	81.5	74.0	72.0	78.0	72.0	70.0	87.0	86.0	83.0
	DLSTM [30]	70.5	66.0	63.0	68.0	63.0	61.0	81.0	76.0	73.0
	HDM [29]	91.0	90.5	90.0	80.5	78.0	76.0	90.0	89.0	88.0
	VB-CD-HMM	**92.55**	**91.6**	**90.2**	**81.7**	**80.1**	**79.1**	**90.2**	**89.3**	**88.5**

Thus, in Table 3, we report the recognition rates when we randomly omit 10%, 30% and 50% of the observations. As we observe, our method clearly outperforms the R3DG [24] and DLSTM [30] methods by a clear margin. The same behavior is observed compared to the more relative HDM approach [29]. Note that even though the reported HDM accuracies are obtained through Gibbs sampling (BG variant), our approach exhibits the smallest decrease in recognition accuracy relative to the increase of missing values.

Further Insights. Finally, we examine the patterns of the first layer process, that is the *dependence generator* layer of the VB-CD-HMM model. We gain further insights to the behavior of the model and assert that the temporal dependencies do not collapse to simple first order dynamics (which would effectively reduce the model to a conventional HMM). To this end, we focus on a trained model on the *UTD* dataset and choose a subset of ten actions to investigate their posterior parameters concerning the generation of dependencies. As is clearly shown in Fig. 2, the distribution of temporal dependencies is essentially different for each action, providing strong empirical evidence that the introduced mechanism can capture complex varying temporal dynamics in the data.

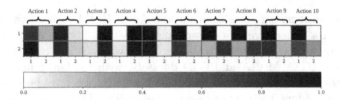

Fig. 2. The inferred temporal dependence probabilities $A_{kk'}$ for the first 10 actions in the UTD dataset. Black denotes very high probability, while white very low. Actions with similar patterns, e.g., 1 (swipe left), 2 (swipe right), 5 (throw), i.e., comprising sequential movements to "one" direction, are dominantly dependent on the previous frame; in contrast, more complicated movements, e.g., 3 (wave), 4 (clap), mainly depend on two steps back, possibly dominated by the reversal in direction. Even more complicated actions, as 7 (basketball shoot) and 8 (draw x) exhibit more complex temporal dependencies, that are captured via the resulting inferred patterns.

4 Conclusions

Our experimental results have provided strong empirical evidence for the efficacy of our approach, yielding competitive recognition accuracy in the Human Action Recognition task. Compared to the commonly considered LSTM-based implementations, our proposed architecture:

- offers the flexibility to model complex sequential data accompanied by the interpretability of its discrete bottlenecks; this is in stark contrast to LSTM-based methods that assume continuous states that essentially entail no probabilistic interpretation.
- enjoys closed-form updates that allow for significantly lower computational and training complexity, devoid of complications, e.g., vanishing gradients, and
- can effectively handle data with missing values, exhibiting the *smallest decrease* in recognition performance relative to other approaches.

We emphasize that the proposed mechanism for inferring the dependencies between the states in our proposed model allows for analyzing the inferred temporal dynamics. Thus, we can gain significant insights and examine how the dynamics adapt to the complexity and variations of different train/test sequences. Therefore, this capacity can be of great benefit to the current effort of the community towards interpretable machine learning models.

References

1. Aggarwal, J., Xia, L.: Human activity recognition from 3d data: a review. Pattern Recogn. Lett. **48**, 70–80 (2014)
2. Aycard, O., Mari, J., Washington, R.: Learning to automatically detect features for mobile robots using second-order hidden markov models. In: IJARS (2005)

3. Begleiter, R., El-Yaniv, R., Yona, G.: On prediction using variable order markov models. J. Artif. Int. Res. **22**, 385–421 (2004)
4. Bloom, V., Makris, D., Argyriou, V.: G3d: a gaming action dataset and real time action recognition evaluation framework. In: CVPRW (June 2012)
5. Bühlmann, P., Wyner, A.J.: Variable length markov chains. Ann. Stat. **27**(2), 480–513 (1999)
6. Chatzis, S.P., Demiris, Y.: Nonparametric mixtures of gaussian processes with power-law behavior. IEEE Trans. Neural Netw. Learn. Syst. **23**(12), 1862–1871 (2012)
7. Chatzis, S.P., Kosmopoulos, D.: A latent manifold markovian dynamics gaussian process. IEEE Trans. Neural Netw. Learn. Syst. **26**, 70–83 (2015)
8. Chatzis, S., Kosmopoulos, D., Papadourakis, G.: A nonstationary hidden markov model with approximately infinitely-long time-dependencies. IJAIT **25**(05), 1640001 (2016)
9. Chatzis, S.P.: A variational bayesian methodology for hidden markov models utilizing student's-t mixtures. Pattern Recogn. **44**(2), 295–306 (2011)
10. Chatzis, S.P.: Margin-maximizing classification of sequential data with infinitely-long temporal dependencies. Expert Syst. Appl. **40**(11), 4519–4527 (2013)
11. Chen, C., Jafari, R., Kehtarnavaz, N.: Utd-mhad: a multimodal dataset for human action recognition utilizing a depth camera and a wearable inertial sensor. In: Proceedings of ICIP (September 2015)
12. Dimitrakakis, C.: Bayesian variable order markov models. In: Proceedings of ICAIS 13 (2010)
13. Engelbrecht, H., du Preez, J.: Efficient backward decoding of high-order hidden markov models. Pattern Recogn. **43**(1), 99–112 (2010)
14. Hou, Y., Li, Z., Wang, P., Li, W.: Skeleton optical spectra-based action recognition using convolutional neural networks. IEEE TCSVT **28**(3), 807–811 (2018)
15. Li, W., Zhang, Z., Liu, Z.: Action recognition based on a bag of 3d points. In: IEEE CVPRW 2010 (07 2010)
16. Liu, J., Shahroudy, A., Xu, D., Kot, A., Wang, G.: Skeleton-based action recognition using spatio-temporal lstm network with trust gates. IEEE Trans. Pattern Anal. Mach. Intell. **40**, 3007–3021 (2018)
17. Nel, E., du Preez, J.A., Herbst, B.M.: Estimating the pen trajectories of static signatures using hidden markov models. IEEE Trans. Pattern Anal. Mach. Intell. **27**(11), 1733–1746 (2005)
18. Nie, B.X., Xiong, C., Zhu, S.: Joint action recognition and pose estimation from video. In: Procs. CVPR, pp. 1293–1301 (June 2015)
19. Nie, S., Wang, Z., Ji, Q.: A generative restricted boltzmann machine based method for high-dimensional motion data modeling. Comput. Vis. Image Underst. **136**, 14–22 (2015)
20. Panousis, K., Chatzis, S., Theodoridis, S.: Nonparametric Bayesian deep networks with local competition. In: Proceedings of ICML, PMLR (June 2019)
21. Shahroudy, A., Liu, J., Ng, T., Wang, G.: Ntu rgb+d: a large scale dataset for 3d human activity analysis. In: Proceedings of CVPR, pp. 1010–1019 (2016)
22. Si, C., Jing, Y., Wang, W., Wang, L., Tan, T.: Skeleton-based action recognition with spatial reasoning and temporal stack learning. In: Proceedings of 15th EC, Munich, Germany, September 2018, Part I, pp. 106–121 (09 2018)
23. Theodoridis, S.: machine learning: a bayesian and optimization perspective. 2nd edn. Academic Press Inc, USA (2020)
24. Vemulapalli, R., Arrate, F., Chellappa, R.: Human action recognition by representing 3d skeletons as points in a lie group. In: Proceedings of CVPR (June 2014)

25. Weinland, D., Ronfard, R., Boyer, E.: A survey of vision-based methods for action representation, segmentation and recognition. Comput. Vis. Image Underst. **115**(2), 224–241 (2011)
26. Yu, S.Z.: Hidden semi-markov models. Artif. Intell. **174**, 215–243 (2010)
27. Zhang, W., Zhu, M., Derpanis, K.G.: From actemes to action: a strongly-supervised representation for detailed action understanding. In: ICCV (December 2013)
28. Zhao, R., Wang, K., Su, H., Ji, Q.: Bayesian graph convolution lstm for skeleton based action recognition. In: Proceedings of ICCV, pp. 6881–6891 (2019)
29. Zhao, R., Xu, W., Su, H., Ji, Q.: Bayesian hierarchical dynamic model for human action recognition. In: Proceedings of CVPR (June 2019)
30. Zhu, W., et al.: Co-occurrence feature learning for skeleton based action recognition using regularized deep lstm networks. In: Proceedings of AAAI (2016)

The Unreasonable Effectiveness
of the Final Batch Normalization Layer

Veysel Kocaman[1]([⊠]) [iD], Ofer M. Shir[2], and Thomas Bäck[1]

[1] LIACS, Leiden University, Leiden, The Netherlands
{v.kocaman,t.h.w.baeck}@liacs.leidenuniv.nl
[2] Computer Science Department, Tel-Hai College and Migal Institute,
Upper Galilee, Israel
ofersh@telhai.ac.il

Abstract. Early-stage disease indications are rarely recorded in real-world domains, such as Agriculture and Healthcare, and yet, their accurate identification is critical in that point of time. In this type of highly imbalanced classification problems, which encompass complex features, deep learning (DL) is much needed because of its strong detection capabilities. At the same time, DL is observed in practice to favor majority over minority classes and consequently suffer from inaccurate detection of the targeted early-stage indications. In this work, we extend the study done by [11], showing that the final BN layer, when placed before the softmax output layer, has a considerable impact in highly imbalanced image classification problems as well as undermines the role of the softmax outputs as an uncertainty measure. This current study addresses additional hypotheses and reports on the following findings: (i) the performance gain after adding the final BN layer in highly imbalanced settings could still be achieved after removing this additional BN layer in inference; (ii) there is a certain threshold for the *imbalance ratio* upon which the progress gained by the final BN layer reaches its peak; (iii) the batch size also plays a role and affects the outcome of the final BN application; (iv) the impact of the BN application is also reproducible on other datasets and when utilizing much simpler neural architectures; (v) the reported BN effect occurs only per a single majority class and multiple minority classes – i.e., no improvements are evident when there are two majority classes; and finally, (vi) utilizing this BN layer with sigmoid activation has almost no impact when dealing with a strongly imbalanced image classification tasks.

1 Introduction

Detecting anomalies that are hardly distinguishable from the majority of observations is a challenging task that often requires strong learning capabilities since anomalies appear scarcely, and in instances of diverse nature, a labeled dataset representative of all forms is typically unattainable. Despite tremendous advances in computer vision and object recognition algorithms in the past few

© Springer Nature Switzerland AG 2021
G. Bebis et al. (Eds.): ISVC 2021, LNCS 13018, pp. 81–93, 2021.
https://doi.org/10.1007/978-3-030-90436-4_7

years, their effectiveness remains strongly dependent upon the datasets' size and distribution, which are usually limited under real-world settings. This work is mostly concerned with hard classification problems at early-stages of abnormalities in certain domains (i.e. crop, human diseases, chip manufacturing), which suffer from lack of data instances, and whose effective treatment would make a dramatic impact in these domains. For instance, fungus's visual cues on crops in agriculture or early-stage malignant tumors in the medical domain are hardly detectable in the relevant time-window, while the highly infectious nature leads rapidly to devastation in a large scale. Other examples include detecting the faults in chip manufacturing industry, automated insulation defect detection with thermography data, assessments of installed solar capacity based on earth observation data, and nature reserve monitoring with remote sensing and deep learning. However, class imbalance poses an obstacle when addressing each of these applications.

In recent years, reliable models capable of learning from small samples have been obtained through various approaches, such as autoencoders [2], class-balanced loss (CBL) to find the effective number of samples required [5], fine tuning with transfer learning [9], data augmentation [18], cosine loss utilizing (replacing categorical cross entropy) [1], or prior knowledge [13].

[11] presented an effective modification in the neural network architecture, with a surprising simplicity and without a computational overhead, which enables a substantial improvement using a smaller number of anomaly samples in the training set. The authors empirically showed that the final BN layer before the softmax output layer has a considerable impact in highly imbalanced image classification problems. They reported that under artificially-generated skewness of 99% vs. 1% in the PlantVillage (PV) image dataset [15], the initial F1 test score increased from the 0.29–0.56 range to the 0.95–0.98 range (almost triple) for the minority class when BN modification applied. They also argued that, a model might perform better even if it is not confident enough while making a prediction, hence the softmax output may not serve as a good uncertainty measure for DNNs.

This shows that DNNs have the tendency of becoming 'over-confident' in their predictions during training, and this can reduce their ability to generalize and thus perform as well on unseen data. In addition, large datasets can often comprise incorrectly labeled data, meaning inherently the DNN should be a bit skeptical of the 'correct answer' to avoid being overconfident on bad answers. This was the main motivation of Müller et al. [16] for proposing the *label smoothing*, a loss function modification that has been shown to be effective for training DNNs. Label smoothing encourages the activations of the penultimate layer to be close to the template of the correct class and equally distant to the templates of the incorrect classes [16]. Despite its relevancy, [11] also reports that label smoothing did not do well in their study as previously mentioned by Kornblith et al. [4] who demonstrated that label smoothing impairs the accuracy of transfer learning, which similarly depends on the presence of non-class-relevant information in the final layers of the network.

In this study, we extend previous efforts done by [11] to devise an effective approach to enable learning of minority classes, given the surprising evidence of applying the final Batch Normalization (BN) layer.

Given these recent findings, we formulate and test additional hypotheses and report our observations in what follows. The concrete contributions of this paper are the following:

- The performance gain after adding the final BN layer in highly imbalanced settings could still be achieved after removing this additional BN layer during inference; in turn enabling us to get a performance boost with no additional cost in production.
- There is a certain threshold for the ratio of the imbalance for this specific PV dataset, upon which the progress is the most obvious after adding the final BN layer.
- The batch size also plays a role and significantly affects the outcome.
- We replicated the similar imbalanced scenarios in MNIST dataset, reproduced the same BN impact, and furthermore demonstrated that the final BN layer has a considerable impact not just in modern CNN architectures but also in simple CNNs and even in one-layered feed-forward fully connected (FC) networks.
- We illustrate that the performance gain occurs only when there is a single majority class and multiple minority classes; and no improvement observed regardless of the final BN layer when there are two majority classes.
- We argue that using the final BN layer with sigmoid activation has almost no impact when dealing with a strongly imbalanced image classification tasks.

The remainder of the paper is organized as follows: Sect. 2 gives some background concerning the role of the BN layer in neural networks. Section 3 summarizes the previous findings and existing hypotheses in the previous work done by [11] and then lists the derived hypotheses that will be addressed throughout this study. Section 4 elaborates the implementation details and settings for our new experiments and presents results. Section 5 discusses the findings and proposes possible *mechanistic* explanations. Section 6 concludes this paper by pointing out key points and future directions.

2   Background

In order to better understand the novel contributions of this study, in this section, we give some background information about the Batch Normalization (BN) [10] concept. Since the various applications of BN in similar studies and related work have already been investigated thoroughly in our previous work [11], we will only focus on the fundamentals of BN in this chapter.

Training deep neural networks with dozens of layers is challenging as the networks can be sensitive to the initial random weights and configuration of the learning algorithm. One possible reason for this difficulty is that the distribution of the inputs to layers deep in the network may change after each mini-batch when the weights are updated. This slows down the training by requiring lower learning rates and careful parameter initialization, makes it notoriously hard to train models with saturating nonlinearities [10], and can cause the learning algorithm to forever chase a moving target. This change in the distribution of inputs to layers in the network is referred to by the technical name *"internal covariate shift"* (ICS).

BN is a widely adopted technique that is designed to combat ICS and to enable faster and more stable training of deep neural networks (DNNs). It is an operation added to the model before activation which normalizes the inputs and then applies learnable scale (γ) and shift (β) parameters to preserve model performance. Given m activation values $x_1 \ldots, x_m$ from a mini-batch $\mathcal{B}$ for any particular layer input $x^{(j)}$ and any dimension $j \in \{1, \ldots, d\}$, the transformation uses the mini-batch mean $\mu_\mathcal{B} = 1/m \sum_{i=1}^{m} x_i$ and variance $\sigma_\mathcal{B}^2 = 1/m \sum_{i=1}^{m} (x_i - \mu_\mathcal{B})^2$ for normalizing the x_i according to $\hat{x}_i = (x_i - \mu_\mathcal{B})/\sqrt{\sigma_\mathcal{B}^2 + \epsilon}$ and then applies the scale and shift to obtain the transformed values $y_i = \gamma \hat{x}_i + \beta$. The constant $\epsilon > 0$ assures numerical stability of the transformation.

BN has the effect of stabilizing the learning process and dramatically reducing the number of training epochs required to train deep networks; and using BN makes the network more stable during training. This may require the use of much larger learning rates, which in turn may further speed up the learning process.

Though BN has been around for a few years and has become common in deep architectures, it remains one of the DL concepts that is not fully understood, having many studies discussing why and how it works. Most notably, Santurkar et al. [17] recently demonstrated that such distributional stability of layer inputs has little to do with the success of BN and the relationship between ICS and BN is tenuous. Instead, they uncovered a more fundamental impact of BN on the training process: it makes the optimization landscape significantly smoother. This smoothness induces a more predictive and stable behavior of the gradients, allowing for faster training. Bjorck et al. [3] also makes similar statements that the success of BN can be explained without ICS. They argue that being able to use larger learning rate increases the implicit regularization of the gradient, which improves generalization.

Even though BN adds an overhead to each iteration (estimated as additional 30% computation [14]), the following advantages of BN outweigh the overhead shortcoming:

- It improves gradient flow and allows training deeper models (e.g., ResNet).
- It enables using higher learning rates because it eliminates outliers' activation, hence the learning process may be accelerated using those high rates.
- It reduces the dependency on initialization and then reduces overfitting due to its minor regularization effect. Similarly to dropout, it adds some noise to each hidden layer's activation.
- Since the scale of input features would not differ significantly, the gradient descent may reduce the oscillations when approaching the optimum and thus converge faster.

– BN reduces the impacts of earlier layers on the following layers in DNNs. Therefore, it takes more time to train the model to converge. However, the use of BN can reduce the impact of earlier layers by keeping the mean and variance fixed, which in some way makes the layers independent from each other. Consequently, the convergence becomes faster.

3   Previous Findings and Existing Hypotheses

In the work done by [11], the authors focused their efforts on the role of BN layer in DNNs, where in the first part of the experiments ResNet34 [19] and VGG19 CNN architectures [8] are utilized. They first addressed the complete PV original dataset and trained a ResNet34 model for 38 classes. Using scheduled learning rates [20], they obtained 99.782% accuracy after 10 epochs – slightly improving the PV project's record of 99.34% when employing GoogleNet [15]. In what follows, we summarize the previous observations borrowed from [11] and then formulate the derived hypotheses that became the core of the current study.

Table 1. Averaged **F1 test set** performance values over 10 runs, alongside BN's total improvement, using 10 epochs with VGG19, with/without BN and with Weighted Loss (WL) without BN.

Plant	Class	Without final BN	With WL (no BN)	With final BN (no WL)	BN total improvement
Apple	Unhealthy	**0.2942**	**0.7947**	0.9562	**0.1615**
	Healthy	0.7075	0.8596	0.9577	0.0981
Pepper	Unhealthy	**0.7237**	**0.8939**	0.9575	**0.0636**
	Healthy	0.8229	0.9121	0.9558	0.0437
Tomato	Unhealthy	**0.5688**	**0.8671**	0.9786	**0.1115**
	Healthy	0.7708	0.9121	0.9780	0.0659

3.1   Adding a Final Batch Norm Layer Before the Output Layer

By using the imbalanced datasets for certain plant types (1,000/10 in the training set, 150/7 in the validation set and 150/150 in the test set), [11] performed several experiments with the VGG19 and ResNet34 architectures. The selected plant types were Apple, Pepper and Tomato - being the only datasets of sufficient size to enable the 99%-1% skewness generation. All the tests are run with batch size 64.

In order to fine-tune the network for the PV dataset, the final classification layer of CNN architectures is replaced by Adaptive Average Pooling (AAP), BN, Dropout, Dense, ReLU, BN and Dropout followed by the Dense and BN layer again. The last layer of an image classification network is often a FC layer with a hidden size being equal to the number of labels to output the predicted confidence scores that are normalized by the softmax operator to obtain predicted probabilities. In their implementation, they added another 2-input BN layer after the last dense layer (before softmax output) in addition to existing BN layers in the tail and 4 BN layers in the head of the DL architecture (e.g., ResNet34 possesses a BN layer after each convolutional layer, having altogether 38 BN layers given the additional 4 in the head).

At first they run experiments with VGG19 architectures for selected plant types by adding the final BN layer. When they train this model for 10 epochs and repeat this for 10 times, they observed that the F1 test score is increased from 0.2942 to 0.9562 for unhealthy Apple, from 0.7237 to 0.9575 for unhealthy Pepper and from 0.5688 to 0.9786 for unhealthy Tomato leaves. They also achieved significant improvements in healthy samples (being the majority in the training set). See Table 1 for details.

3.2 Experimentation on PlantVillage Dataset Subject to Different Configurations

Using the following six configuration variations with two options each, the authors created 64 different configurations which they tested with ResNet34 (training for 10 epochs only): Adding (✓) a final BN layer just before the output layer (BN), using (✓) weighted cross-entropy loss [6] according to class imbalance (WL), using (✓) data augmentation (DA), using (✓) mixup (MX) [21], unfreezing (✓) or freezing (learnable vs pre-trained weights) the previous BN layers in ResNet34 (UF), and using (✓) weight decay (WD) [12]. Checkmarks (✓) and two-letter abbreviations are used in Table 2 to denote configurations. When an option is disabled across all configurations, its associated column is dropped.

Table 2. Best performance metrics over the Apple dataset under various configurations using ResNet34.

Class	Config Id	Test set precision	Test set recall	Test set F1-score	Epoch	BN	DA	UF	WD
Unhealthy (class = 1)	**31**	0.9856	0.9133	**0.9481**	6	✓			
	23	0.9718	0.9200	0.9452	6	✓	✓		
	20	0.9926	0.8933	0.9404	7	✓	✓	✓	✓

As shown in Table 2, just adding the final BN layer was enough to get the highest F1 test score in both classes. Surprisingly, although there is already a BN layer after each convolutional layer in the backbone CNN architecture, adding one more BN layer just before the output layer boosts the test scores. Notably, the 3rd best score (average score for configuration 31 in Table 2) is achieved just by adding a single BN layer before the output layer, even without unfreezing the previous BN layers.

One of the important observations is that the model without the final BN layer is pretty confident even if it predicts falsely. But the proposed model with the final BN layer predicts correctly even though it is less confident. They basically ended up with less confident but more accurate models in less than 10 epochs.

3.3   Derived Hypotheses

Under all these observations and findings mentioned above, we derived the following hypotheses for our new study:

- The added complexity to the network by adding the final BN layer could be eliminated by removing the final BN layer in inference without compromising the performance gain achieved.
- There might be a certain level of skewness upon which the progress reaches its peak without further sizing the minority class.
- Since the trainable parameters in a BN layer also depend on the batch size (i.e., number of samples) in each iteration (mini-batch), its sizing could also play a role on the level of progress with the final BN layer.
- The observations and performance gain with respect to the PV dataset, upon utilizing ResNet and VGG architectures, may not be reproduced with any other dataset or with much simpler neural architectures.
- Since the number of units in the output layer depends on the number of classes in the dataset, the performance gain may not be achieved in multi-classification settings and the number of majority and minority classes can affect the role of the final BN layer.
- Since sigmoid activation is also one of the most widely used activation functions in the output layer for the binary classification problems, the performance gain could be achieved with sigmoid outputs as well.

Next, we report on addressing these hypotheses, one by one, and describe our empirical findings in detail.

4   Implementation Details and Experimental Results

4.1   Removing the Additional BN Layer During Inference (H-1)

Since adding the final BN layer adds a small overhead (four new parameters) to the network at each iteration, we experimented if the final BN layer could be dropped once the training is finished so that we can avoid the cost. Dropping this final BN layer means that training the network from end to end, and then chopping off the final BN layer from the network before saving the weights. We tested this hypothesis for Apple, Pepper and Tomato images from PV dataset under three conditions with 1% imbalance ratio: *Without final BN, with final BN and then removing the final BN during testing.* We observed that removing the final BN layer in inference would still give us a considerable boost on minority class without losing any performance gain on the majority class. The results in Table 3 show that the performance gain is very close to the configuration in which we used the final BN layer both in training and inference time. As a consequence, we confirm hypothesis (H-1) by showing that the final BN layer can indeed be removed in inference without compromising the performance gain.

Table 3. Training with the final BN layer, and then dropping this layer while evaluating on the test set proved to be still useful in terms of improving the classification score on minority classes, albeit not as much as with the final BN layer kept (imbalance ratio 0.01, epoch 10, batch size 64).

	Apple		Pepper		Tomoto	
	Healthy	Unhealthy	Healthy	Unhealthy	Healthy	Unhealthy
With no final BN	0.71	0.22	0.74	0.45	0.74	0.46
With final BN	0.92	0.91	0.94	0.94	0.98	0.98
Train with final BN	0.74	**0.83**	0.75	**0.82**	0.78	**0.85**
Remove while testing						

4.2 Impact Level Regarding the Imbalance Ratio (H-2) and the Batch Size (H-3)

[11] empirically shows that the final BN layer, when placed before the softmax output layer, has a considerable impact in highly imbalanced image classification problems but they fail to explain the impact of using the final BN layer as a function of level of imbalance in the training set. In order to find if there is a certain ratio in which the impact is maximized, we tested this hypothesis (H-1) over various levels of imbalance ratios and conditions explained below. In sum, we ended up with 430 model runs, each with 10 epochs (basically tested with 5, 10, 15, .. 100 unhealthy vs 1000 healthy samples). During the experiments, we observed that the impact of final BN on highly imbalanced settings is the most obvious when the ratio of minority class to the majority is less than 10%; above that almost no impact. As expected, the impact of the final BN layer is more obvious on minority class than it is on majority class, albeit the level of impact with respect to the imbalance ratio is almost same, and levels off around 10%. It is mainly because of the fact that the backbone architecture (ResNet34) is already good enough to converge faster on such data set (Plant Village) and the model does well on both classes after 10% imbalance (having more than 100 unhealthy with respect to 1000 healthy samples can already be handled regardless of final BN trick). During these experiments, we also tested if unfreezing the previous layers in the backbone CNN architecture (ResNet34) would also matter. We observed that unfreezing the pretrained layers helps without even final BN layer, but unfreezing adds more computation as the gradient loss will be calculated for each one of them. After adding the final BN layer and freezing the previous pretrained layers, we observed similar metrics and learning pattern as we did

with unfreezing but not with final BN layer. This is another advantage of using the final BN that allow us to freeze the previous pretrained layers. The results are displayed as charts in Fig. 1a.

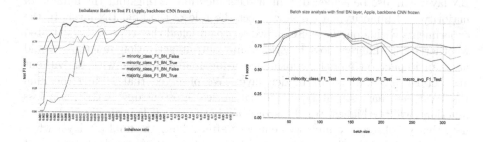

(a) The impact of final BN layer on the F1 test score of each class for Apple plant. The impact is the most obvious when the ratio of minority class to the majority is less than 0.1.

(b) The impact of batch size on the F1 test score when the final BN layer added. The highest score is gained when the batch size is 64 and then the accuracy starts declining.

Fig. 1. Imbalance ratio and batch size analysis with respect to the final BN layer added

We also experimented if the batch size would also be an important parameter for the minority class test accuracy when the final BN is added and found out that the highest score is gained when the batch size is around 64, whereas the accuracy drops afterwards with larger batches. The results are exhibited in Fig. 1b. Consequently, given the reported observations, we confirm hypotheses (H-2) and (H-3).

4.3   Experimentation on the MNIST Dataset: The Impact of Final BN Layer in Basic CNNs and FC Networks [(H-4),(H-5),(H-6)]

In order to reproduce equivalent results on a well known benchmark dataset when utilizing different DL architectures, we set up two simple DL architectures: a CNN network with five Conv2D layers and a one-layer (128-node) FC feed forward NN. Then we sampled several pairs of digits (2 vs 8, 3 vs 8, 3 vs 5 and 5 vs 8) from MNIST dataset that are mostly confused in a digit recognition task due to similar patterns in the pixels. During the experiments, the ratio of minority class to majority is kept as 0.1 and experiments with the simple CNN architecture indicates that, after adding the final BN layer, we gain $\sim 20\%$ boost in minority class and $\sim 10\%$ in majority class. Lower standard deviations across the runs with final BN layer also indicates the regularization effect of using the final BN layer. As a result, we rejected the fourth hypothesis (H-4) that we derived in Sect. 3.3 by showing that the performance gain through the final BN layer can be reproduced with another dataset or with much simpler neural architectures. Another important finding is that the final BN layer boosts the minority class' F1 scores only when there is a single majority class. When two majority classes are set, no improvements are evident regardless of the usage of the final BN layer (see 4th and 5th settings in Table 4). Therefore, we partially confirm hypothesis (H-5) by showing that the performance gain through the final BN layer can also be achieved in multi-classification settings but the number of majority and minority classes may affect the role of the final BN layer. In the experiments with a one-layer FC network, we enriched the scope and also tested whether using different loss functions and output activation functions would have an impact on model performance using final BN layer with or without another BN layer after the hidden layer. We observed that adding the final BN layer, softmax output layer and categorical crossentropy (CCE) as a loss function have the highest test F1 scores for both classes. It is also important to note that we observe no improvement even after adding the final BN layer when we use sigmoid activation in the output layer (Table 4). Accordingly, we reject hypothesis (H-6).

Table 4. Using the same ResNet-34 architecture and skewness (1% vs 99%) and setting up five different configurations across various confusing classes from MNIST dataset, it is clear that adding the final BN layer boosts the minority class F1 scores by 10% to 30% only when there is a single majority class. When we have two majority classes, there is no improvement observed regardless of the final BN layer is used or not. ($\checkmark$) indicates minority classes.

	Setting-1		Setting-2		Setting-3		Setting-4			Setting-5		
	3 ($\checkmark$)	8	2 ($\checkmark$)	8	3 ($\checkmark$)	5	3 ($\checkmark$)	5	8	3 ($\checkmark$)	5 ($\checkmark$)	8
Without final BN	0.19	0.69	0.25	0.70	0.24	0.70	0.06	0.77	0.78	0.28	0.32	0.56
With final BN	0.55	0.76	0.50	0.74	0.54	0.76	0.00	0.77	0.78	0.58	0.59	0.69

5   Discussion

In a previous work done in [11], the authors suggested that by applying BN to dense layers, the gap between activations is reduced (normalized) and then softmax is applied on normalized outputs, which are centered around the mean. Therefore, ending up with centered probabilities (around 0.5), but favoring the minority class by a small margin. They also argued that DNNs have the tendency of becoming 'over-confident' in their predictions during training, and this can reduce their ability to generalize further and thus perform as well on unseen data. Then they also concluded that a DNN with the final BN layer is more calibrated [7]. We assert that 'being less confident' in terms of softmax outputs might be fundamentally wrong and a network shouldn't be discarded or embraced due to its capacity of producing confident or less confident results in the softmax layer as it may not even be interpreted as a 'confidence' (Table 5).

In this study, we empirically demonstrated that the final BN layer could still be eliminated in inference without compromising the attained performance gain.

Table 5. Using one-layer (128 node) NN and the 0.01 skewness ratio, with nine different settings for 3 (minority) and 8 (majority) classes from MNIST dataset (100-epoch). Adding the final BN layer, softmax output layer and CCE as a loss function has the highest test F1 scores for both classes. (CCE - categorical cross entropy, BCE - binary cross entropy, first BN - a BN layer after the hidden layer).

Output activation	Loss function	First BN layer	Final BN layer	Class-3 (minority)	Class-8 (majority)
Sigmoid	BCE			0.17	0.67
Softmax	BCE			0.00	0.67
Softmax	BCE	✓		0.60	0.78
Softmax	CCE			0.67	0.80
Sigmoid	BCE		✓	0.05	0.67
Softmax	BCE		✓	0.85	0.88
Softmax	BCE	✓	✓	0.83	0.87
Softmax	CCE		✓	**0.88**	**0.90**
Softmax	CCE	✓	✓	0.78	0.85

This finding supports the assertion that adding the BN layer makes the optimization landscape significantly smoother, which in turn renders the gradients' behavior more predictive and stable – as suggested by [17]. We argue that the learned parameters, which were affected by the addition of the final BN layer under imbalanced settings, are likely sufficiently robust to further generalization on the unseen samples, even without normalization prior to the softmax layer.

The observation of locating a sweet spot (10%) for the imbalance ratio, at which we can utilize the final BN layer, might be explained by the fact that the backbone ResNet architecture is already strong enough to easily generalize on the PV dataset and the model does not need any other regularization once the number of samples from the minority class exceeds a certain threshold. As the threshold found in our experiments is highly related to the DL architecture and the utilized dataset, it is clear that it may not apply to other datasets, but can be found in a similar way.

As discussed before, the BN layer calculates mean and variance to normalize the previous outputs across the batch, whereas the accuracy of this statistical estimation increases as the batch size grows. However, its role seems to change under the imbalanced settings – we found out that a batch size of 64 reaches the highest score, whereas by utilizing larger batches the score consistently drops. As a possible explanation for this observation, we think that the larger the batches, the higher the number of majority samples in a batch and the lesser the chances that the minority samples are fairly represented, resulting in a deteriorated performance.

During our experiments, we expected to see similar behavior with sigmoid activation replacing softmax in the output layer, but, evidently, the final BN layer works best with softmax activations. Although softmax output may not serve as a good uncertainty measure for DNNs compared to sigmoid layer, it can still do well on detecting the under-represented samples when used with the final BN layer.

6   Conclusions

In this study, we extended the previous efforts done by [11] to devise an effective approach to enable learning of minority classes, given the surprising evidence of applying the final BN layer. Given these recent findings, we formulated and tested additional hypotheses.

We at first noticed that the performance gain after adding the final BN layer in highly imbalanced settings could still be achieved after removing this additional BN layer during inference; in turn enabling us to get a performance boost with no additional cost in production. Then we explored the dynamics of using the final BN layer as a function of the imbalance ratio within the training set, and found out that the impact of final BN on highly imbalanced settings is the most apparent when the ratio of minority class to the majority is less than 10%; there is hardly any impact above that threshold.

We also ran similar experiments with simpler architectures, namely a basic CNN and a single-layered FC network, when applied to the MNIST dataset under various imbalance settings. The simple CNN experiments exhibited a gain of $\sim$ 20% boost per the minority class and $\sim$ 10% per the majority class after adding the final BN layer. In the FC network experiments, we observed improvements by 10% to 30% only when a single majority class was defined; no improvements were evident for two majority classes, regardless of the usage of the final BN layer. While experimenting with different activation and cost functions, we found out that using the final BN layer with sigmoid activation had almost no impact on the task at hand.

We found the impact of final BN layer in simpler neural networks quite surprising. It is an important finding, which we plan to further investigate in the future, as it requires thorough analysis. We also plan to formulate our findings in a generalized way for any neural model, preferably with a combination of softmax activation or a proper loss function that could be used in imbalanced image classification problems.

References

1. Barz, B., Denzler, J.: Deep learning on small datasets without pre-training using cosine loss. In: The IEEE Winter Conference on Applications of Computer Vision, pp. 1371–1380 (2020)
2. Beggel, L., Pfeiffer, M., Bischl, B.: Robust anomaly detection in images using adversarial autoencoders. arXiv preprint arXiv:1901.06355 (2019)
3. Bjorck, N., Gomes, C.P., Selman, B., Weinberger, K.Q.: Understanding batch normalization. In: Advances in Neural Information Processing Systems, pp. 7694–7705 (2018)

4. Chelombiev, I., Houghton, C., O'Donnell, C.: Adaptive estimators show information compression in deep neural networks. arXiv preprint arXiv:1902.09037 (2019)
5. Cui, Y., Jia, M., Lin, T.Y., Song, Y., Belongie, S.: Class-balanced loss based on effective number of samples. In: Proceedings of the IEEE Conference on Computer Vision and Pattern Recognition, pp. 9268–9277 (2019)
6. Goodfellow, I., Bengio, Y., Courville, A.: Deep Learning. MIT Press, Cambridge (2016)
7. Guo, C., Pleiss, G., Sun, Y., Weinberger, K.Q.: On calibration of modern neural networks. In: Proceedings of the 34th International Conference on Machine Learning, vol. 70, pp. 1321–1330 (2017). JMLR. org
8. He, K., Zhang, X., Ren, S., Sun, J.: Deep residual learning for image recognition. In: Proceedings of the IEEE Conference on Computer Vision and Pattern Recognition, pp. 770–778 (2016)
9. Hussain, M., Bird, J.J., Faria, D.R.: A study on CNN transfer learning for image classification. In: Lotfi, A., Bouchachia, H., Gegov, A., Langensiepen, C., McGinnity, M. (eds.) UKCI 2018. AISC, vol. 840, pp. 191–202. Springer, Cham (2019). https://doi.org/10.1007/978-3-319-97982-3_16
10. Ioffe, S., Szegedy, C.: Batch normalization: Accelerating deep network training by reducing internal covariate shift. arXiv preprint arXiv:1502.03167 (2015)
11. Kocaman, V., Shir, O.M., Bäck, T.: Improving model accuracy for imbalanced image classification tasks by adding a final batch normalization layer: An empirical study. arXiv preprint arXiv:2011.06319, Accepted to International Conference on Pattern Recognition, ICPR 2020. (2020)
12. Krogh, A., Hertz, J.A.: A simple weight decay can improve generalization. In: Advances in Neural Information Processing Systems, pp. 950–957 (1992)
13. Lake, B.M., Salakhutdinov, R., Tenenbaum, J.B.: Human-level concept learning through probabilistic program induction. Science 350(6266), 1332–1338 (2015)
14. Mishkin, D., Matas, J.: All you need is a good init. arXiv preprint arXiv:1511.06422 (2015)
15. Mohanty, S.P., Hughes, D.P., Salathé, M.: Using deep learning for image-based plant disease detection. Front. Plant Sci. 7, 1419 (2016)
16. Müller, R., Kornblith, S., Hinton, G.E.: When does label smoothing help? In: Advances in Neural Information Processing Systems, pp. 4696–4705 (2019)
17. Santurkar, S., Tsipras, D., Ilyas, A., Madry, A.: How does batch normalization help optimization? In: Advances in Neural Information Processing Systems, pp. 2483–2493 (2018)
18. Shorten, C., Khoshgoftaar, T.M.: A survey on image data augmentation for deep learning. J. Big Data 6(1), 60 (2019)
19. Simonyan, K., Zisserman, A.: Very deep convolutional networks for large-scale image recognition. arXiv preprint arXiv:1409.1556 (2014)
20. Smith, L.N.: Cyclical learning rates for training neural networks. In: 2017 IEEE Winter Conference on Applications of Computer Vision (WACV), pp. 464–472. IEEE (2017)
21. Zhang, H., Cisse, M., Dauphin, Y.N., Lopez-Paz, D.: mixup: Beyond empirical risk minimization. arXiv preprint arXiv:1710.09412 (2017)

Video Analysis and Event Recognition

Cross Your Body: A Cognitive Assessment System for Children

Saif Sayed[✉] and Vassilis Athitsos

Vision-Learning-Mining Lab, University of Texas at Arlington,
Arlington 76013, TX, USA
saififtekar.sayed@mavs.uta.edu, athitsos@uta.edu

Abstract. While many action recognition techniques have great success on public benchmarks, such performance is not necessarily replicated in real-world scenarios, where the data comes from specific application requirements. The specific real-world application that we are focusing on in this paper is cognitive assessment in children using cognitively demanding physical tasks. We created a system called Cross-Your-Body and recorded data, which is unique in several aspects, including the fact that the tasks have been designed by psychologists, the subjects are children, and the videos capture real-world usage, as they record children performing tasks during real-world assessment by psychologists. Other distinguishing features of our system is that it's scores can directly be translated to measure executive functioning which is one of the key factor to distinguish onset of ADHD in adolescent kids. Due to imprecise execution of actions performed by children, and the presence of fine-grained motion patterns, we systematically investigate and evaluate relevant methods on the recorded data. It is our goal that this system will be useful in advancing research in cognitive assessment of kids.

Keywords: Action recognition · Cognitive assesment · Action segmentation

1 Introduction

Mental illness can cause several undesirable effects on a person's emotional, mental or behavioral states [19]. It is estimated that around 450 million people are currently affected by mental health issues, including schizophrenia, depression, attention-deficit hyperactivity disorder(ADHD) and autism spectrum disorder (ASD) [19]. More specifically, ADHD, which is a psychiatric neurodevelopmental disorder found in children and young adolescents, can have its traces evident as early as age 6 [6]. Such traces may include deficits in executive functions [2] inhibiting them to perform mental processes like planning, organizing, problem-solving as well as managing their impulses, including working memory, cognitive flexibility and inhibitory control [4]. These developmental shortcomings causes detrimental effects not only in their school performances but also at a higher

© Springer Nature Switzerland AG 2021
G. Bebis et al. (Eds.): ISVC 2021, LNCS 13018, pp. 97–109, 2021.
https://doi.org/10.1007/978-3-030-90436-4_8

level, trigger many negative effects in family, employment and community settings which can result into several socio-economic problems, causing low self-esteem and self-acceptance [8]

While current methods use fMRI or sMRI scans [20], facial expressions [14] or clinical notes [7], these methods provide good prognosis of the subject's cognitive condition at the brain activity/blood flow level, but are expensive and not portable. Embodied cognition tackles this problem with an understanding that our sensorimotor experiences with our social and physical environment helps in developing and shaping our higher cognitive processes [24]. Inspired by this approach, research [18] adopted the Head Toe Knee Shoulder(HTKS) task to assess these psychometric measures of self-regulation through physical performance for 208 subjects using obtrusive wearable sensors.

Similarly a recent work [3] created a system called ATEC whose scores showed significant correlation with concurrent measurements of executive functions and significant discriminant validity between At-risk children and Normal Range children on multiple pre-existing tests like the CBCL Competency, CBCL ADHD Combined score, BRIEF-2 Global Executive Composite, BRIEF-2 Cognitive Regulation Index and SNAP-IV ADHD Combined Score. They measure psychometric scores such as Response Inhibition, Self-Regulation, Rhythm and Coordination which constitutes the Executive Function(EF) Score and Working Memory Index Score. These scores provide valuable information for differentiating adolescent kids susceptible to ADHD as compared to normal [16]. They used human annotators to evaluate the activities performed by kids, while current systems like [11,21] use computer vision technique to detect these activities, but they do not produce scores that can be translated to produce these psychometric scores. The main contribution of the paper is to create a system that can produce an automated score of rhythm and accuracy, which is the fundamental component of creating the psychometric measures by utilizing the recording and scoring protocol followed ATEC system for the cross your body task and compare it with the human scores. The data has been recorded in real-time in an indoor environment, and shows children performing fine-grained activities. In this system, the children follow instructions to touch, using each hand, a specific body part (ear, shoulder, knee, or hip) on the other side of the body.

2   Related Work

Neuroimages like fMRI or sMRI have been traditionally used as clinical data for applications such as identification of ADHD [20,26] which use CNN to identify local spatial patterns of modulations of blood flow in a section of brain. While there are compelling research methods that can separate kids with ADHD from control subjects, these techniques require costly acquisition of brain scans and face the issue of portability. Instead of learning such information at a micro-level, one can study the effects of the disorder at macro-level, as human movements and how they can be affected by hyperactivity and/or inattention [1]. This inspired several wearable sensor based approaches [12,15] and a significant difference was evident between non-ADHD controls and ADHD patients, but such methods require obtrusive sensors.

With the advent of sophisticated activity recognition systems, such human movements can be tracked and was first tried on adults using HTKS task [11]. The prior work most related to ours is the method presented in [21], which was also applied to videos of children performing the Cross-Your-Body task.

Our work has significant differences, and advantages, compared to [21] and can be used for fully-automated scoring of the children's performance. The method of [21] cannot be used on its own for fully automated scoring, due to two limitations which our method overcomes: the first limitation was that it required human annotations to convert a child's performance into several segmented videos, each segment corresponding to a specific instance of the hand moving to touch a body part. Second, the output of the system in [21] simply classified each video segment, without providing frame-level labels indicating when exactly the subject touches the instructed body part. Frame-level labels are necessary for scoring the rhythm and timing of each child's performance, which is an important aspect of the human experts' evaluation protocol.

3   Data Acquisition and Protocol Definition

The goal of the system is to facilitate the development of an automated scoring environment, whose output correlates as much as possible with scores produced by human experts for the same videos. Simulated datasets have been previously created for similar tasks using adults [11], but they lack the unique motion dynamics that the children participants display in our recording.

Data Recording. The subjects were recorded at multiple indoor locations and strict quality control was maintained (such as keeping the distance from the subjects to the camera within a specified range), to ensure consistent acquisition quality and every kid was given the same instruction. The data was recorded using Kinect V2. A screen is used to display a music video where the host instructs the kids to perform the task following the song of "Cross-your-body". There are 5 tasks overall and each task has varying sub-segment. In a single sub-segment, the subject is told to perform 3 touches based on the announced body part using the hand from the opposite side and alternate sides, for example "Cross your body touch your hips, hips, hips. For first 2 tasks the subject is required to touch the same body part as instructed, but for the other 3 tasks the challenge becomes cognitively demanding as they are told to follow opposite rules, for example in task 3 subject requires to touch ears when instructed to touch knees and vice versa. Similarly task4 switches shoulders and hips and task5 includes rules of both task 3 and 4. The scoring system is followed according to the research done by Bell [3].

Scoring Scheme. The objective of our data processing module is to apply activity segmentation algorithms to evaluate the performance of the participants. The scoring protocol created by the psychologist experts specifies 2 scores: accuracy and rhythm. The accuracy score depends on the amount of times that the subject touches the desired body part correctly, and the rhythm score depends on the amount of times that the subject touches the desired body part within one second after receiving the instruction. These two scores signify different psychometric measures necessary for measuring self-regulation, response inhibition, working memory, co-ordination and attention [3]. Thus, our system is designed to produce both those scores.

For the accuracy score part, the goal is to detect if the relevant activity is happening or not in a video. A potential approach is to manually segment and annotate these videos, to ensure only one activity happening per video, and then to recognize the activity in each trimmed video. It has limited real-world use, as it requires significant manual effort to produce the trimmed video. Furthermore, as this approach produces a video-level class label, as opposed to frame-by-frame labeling, it could not be used for computing rhythm score, which requires identifying the time when the hand touches the respective body part.

To address these limitations, in this paper we follow a problem formulation where the system output should predict both the body part that is touched, and the time during which it is touched by the hand. The input to the system is a video segment, which typically has more than one action. For the training examples, the ground truth includes frame-level labels. The input video segment is provided automatically by the video capturing system, with no need for manual annotations, based on the time that each instruction is provided to the child. These instructions are pre-recorded, and the time that they are issued is known to the system.

Based on the above considerations, we formulate our problem as an frame-level supervised action segmentation problem, similar to formulations applied on the MPIICooking2 dataset [10] to understand fine-grained activities. We note that our problem could also possibly be tackled as an activity localization problem, but in our work so far we have not pursued that approach.

Annotation Scheme: The annotation scheme we adopted in our system is illustrated in Fig. 3. Here we annotate explicitly those frames where the hand approaches the body part, then touches, and finally leaves the body part. As seen in the figure, a gesture is considered valid only if the hand has crossed the midline of the body and fulfilled the 3 sequential steps. The steps and the corresponding frames are highlighted in the figure. We first identify the time segment when the hand is about to touch the body part. We chose an approximate distance of a few inches around the designated body part. In the subsequent time segment the subject touches the body part, and in the third time segment the hand leaves the body part and gets to a distance of few inches from it. A video segment of video is assigned the appropriate label if it fulfills all these steps, else it is designated as background(BG). A strict protocol was followed as there are cases where a subject keeps the hand crossed and near the body part while using the other hand to touch the other side of the body part.

Dataset Statistics. Overall the dataset consists of 894 total videos recorded for 19 subjects, and has on an average 2.7 activities per video. The average length of a video sample is around 3.3 s, while the maximum and minimum length of the videos are around 3.6 and 3.1 s respectively. There are around 2500 activities in these videos having durations ranging from 0.03 s to 1.36 s. The dataset consists of 8 classes without background. The class-wise distribution of the dataset is as shown in the Table 1. There are 8 classes indicating the combination of hand and body part. The 4 lettered class label is comprised of the first and second letter indicating the side: left(l) or right(l), the second letter stands for hand(h) and the fourth letter stand for the body part: ear(e), shoulder(s), hip(h), knee(k) (Fig. 1).

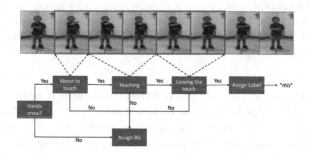

Fig. 1. Annotation scheme for the cross your body system. Highlighted red frames were given annotation as right hand left shoulder(rhls)

Table 1. Class-wise duration distribution of the dataset.

Class label	Index	Min(sec)	Max(sec)	Mean(sec)	Sample Count
lhre	0	0.03	0.93	0.21	319
rhle	1	0.03	0.90	0.23	224
lhrs	2	0.03	1.17	0.20	388
rhls	3	0.03	0.87	0.20	285
lhrh	4	0.03	1.37	0.25	338
rhlh	5	0.03	1.00	0.24	257
lhrk	6	0.03	0.83	0.19	337
rhlk	7	0.03	0.87	0.21	284

Data Properties. The recorded data has several attractive properties that distinguish it from the existing datasets. *High Quality:* All the videos were recorded in Full HD resolution and were recorded in indoor conditions that ensured good illumination quality.

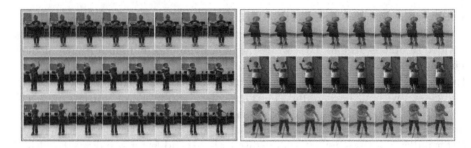

Fig. 2. Examples of action instances in Cross Your Body Data. The left part shows instances belonging to categories within the set of touching-shoulder, from top to bottom "right hand left shoulder", "left hand right shoulder", "right hand left shoulder", illustrating the level of variations that the touching-shoulder action can have. On the right the first 2 samples from top to bottom illustrate examples of touching-shoulder and touching-ear instances in which one hand occludes another, while the third sample illustrates occlusion by head while touching the shoulder.

Richness and Diversity: The only practice that the subjects received was showing them once a video illustrating how to touch each body part. There were no instructions given to the children during the recording phase to improve their gestures or motion patterns. This resulted in a very realistic dataset that has many unique and novel motion patterns, as can be seen in Fig. 2. The dataset has high intra-class variation of and also has occlusions during performance of these activities. Also the diversity in the speed at which a subject touches a body part varies drastically, resulting into cases where the touch of a body part spans just a few frames.

Fine-Grained Action Differences: Since there are classes like touch ear v/s touch shoulder, this dataset is unique from the point of view of inter-class variations, as there are samples belonging to different classes where the body pose looks very similar. Furthermore, since the resolution of the hands is relatively small, hand detection and tracking is a challenge, thus posing a unique use-case for activity detection and recognition algorithms.

4   System Definition

The goal of the system is to recognize and score the fine-grained actions in this dataset. Given the scoring requirements, the system is essentially an action segmentation system. Note that this dataset can also be used to evaluate activity localization algorithms, but we have so far not pursued that approach. Action segmentation involves frame-level predictions of an untrimmed video that may contain one or more activities.

We systematically evaluated 3 action segmentation methods based on Temporal Convolution Networks(TCN), namely MSTCN++ [17], ASRF [13] and DTGRM [23] on the data and also included one pose based activity recognition system ST-GCN [25] to understand the significance of pose. Training protocols follow the original paper unless stated otherwise.

For action segmentation, the setup involves a training set of N videos, where each video is composed of frame-wise feature representations $x_{1:T} = (x_1, ..., x_T)$, where T is the length of the video. Using these features the system outputs the predicted action class likelihoods $y_{1:T} = (y_1, ..., y_T)$, where $y_t \in R^C$ and C is the number of classes. During test time, given only a video, the goal is to predict $y_{1:T}$.

All of the experiments were performed using a user-independent 6-fold cross validation system where it was ensured that, for each split, there is no training video of any person appearing in the test set. The remaining section explains the feature extraction and the analysis on the performance of these methods.

4.1 Feature Extraction

The actions in the video are highly dependent not only on the motion patterns but also on the appearance information. Due to the fine-grained nature of the activities like touching ear v/s touching shoulder, missing on the latter information will lead to incorrect prediction. We used the 2 modalities of data, mainly optical flow and RGB frames to produce intermediate frame-representation using I3D network [5] pretrained on Kinetics dataset. We have chosen a temporal window of 16 frames to compute the I3D features. The I3D features extracted from each modality is concatenated together to produce a feature representation $\mathbf{x}_i \in \mathbb{R}^{2048 \times T_i}$, where T_i is the length of the video i

4.2 Action Segmentation

We chose Temporal Convolution Networks(TCN)-based modelling systems, because TCNs have a large receptive field and work on multiple temporal scales, and thus they are capable of capturing long-range dependencies between the video frames. The reason we chose this multi-scale option is because the instruction given usually follows a theme. For example, if the instruction is "Cross your body touch your Ears, Ears, Ears", the subject is expected to touch ears three times (each time with the opposite hand than the previous time). Consequently, frame-level predictions become easier if the network understands that the actions happening in the video are related to ears, and that hands alternate.

MSTCN++ is an improvement over MSTCN where the system generates frame level pedictions using a dual dilated layer that combines small and large receptive field in contrast to MSTCN [9]. While MSTCN++ has the ability to look at multiple temporal fields, it still lacks the ability for efficient temporal reasoning. This drawback was resolved in DTGRM where they used Graph Convolution Networks(GCN) and model temporal relations in videos. While models like MSTCN++ and MSTCN use smoothing loss to avoid over-segmentation errors, this method introduced an auxilliary self-supervised task to encourage the model to find correct and in-correct temporal relations in videos. DTGRM and MSTCN++ both work predict frames directly and there is no concept of detecting action boundaries. Since in our dataset and task it is necessary to understand when an action starts and ends, and also since the motion is so fine-grained, it is important to accurately detect action boundaries. To resolve this problem, we also employed another method, ASRF, which alleviates over-segmentation errors by detecting action boundaries. For analysis of the importance of the method based on the modality of the data, we trained each method on 3 different modalities: I3D features extracted on RGB frames, I3D features extracted on flow frames, and a third modality consisting of concatenating the I3D features of the first two modalities.

Evaluation metrics: For evaluation, the metrics we employ are framewise accuracy(Acc), framewise accuracy without background(Acc-bg), segmental edit distance (Edit), and segmental F1 score measured at overlapping thresholds of 10%, 25% and 50% denoted by F1-10, F1-25 and F1-50 respectively. The overlapping threshold is based on the metric of Intersection over Union (IoU) ratio. We added the framewise accuracy without background as a metric since a major portion of the frames in the dataset is background.

We did 2 forms of analysis: event-based analysis, where models were trained using all 9 classes including background. The second analysis was done based on a subset of the labels. More specifically we relabeled "left hand right ear" and "right hand left ear" to just ear and similarly for shoulder. This resulted in only 3 classes: ear, shoulder and background.

Table 2 illustrates the performance of all the 3 segmentation models for all the classes. It can be observed that ASRF shows the best performance as compared to MSTCN++ and DTGRM, as it is able to predict action boundaries. Note that the metric of *Acc-BG* is more important than *Acc* as the dataset has a lot of background frames. More importantly, the flow modality produced better results as compared to RGB or even concatenated I3D features, and this is further discussed in the analysis subsection. Other fine-grained activity datasets like [22] have shown similar observations where they illustrate RGB values contribute less due to subtle differences between classes as compared to coarse-grained classes.

We have also investigated how data modality plays a role on capturing temporal dynamics in actions that are very fine. For this, we chose a subset of classes like touching ears and shoulders because they are spatially separated by a very low margin as compared to touching hip and knee. Table 3 illustrates the performance of all the 3 segmentation models for this subset of classes. It is evident that flow plays an important role in understand these motion patterns.

Table 2. Performance of Action Segmentation models for All Classes.

Method	Modality	Acc	Acc-BG	Edit	F1-10	F1-25	F1-50
MSTCN++	RGB	79.59	28.43	67.94	69.53	67.13	55.07
	Flow	82.73	36.10	71.15	74.13	71.81	60.13
	Both	82.11	36.24	71.68	74.71	72.15	59.90
DTGRM	RGB	81.10	26.75	64.83	68.59	66.09	54.75
	Flow	83.55	35.76	71.91	75.35	72.52	61.05
	Both	**83.67**	35.68	70.50	75.07	72.50	60.74
ASRF	RGB	63.34	36.42	55.73	59.90	54.64	42.79
	Flow	80.45	**48.66**	**73.94**	**78.04**	**75.56**	**63.66**
	Both	80.98	44.03	73.45	77.10	74.81	63.27

Table 3. Performance of Action Segmentation models.(Set Level: Ear and Shoulder)

Method	Modality	Acc	Acc-BG	Edit	F1-10	F1-25	F1-50
MSTCN++	RGB	82.41	33.95	71.92	73.51	70.38	59.34
	Flow	86.00	51.36	**80.44**	82.45	80.03	69.76
	Both	85.87	48.08	78.87	81.76	79.90	69.00
DTGRM	RGB	84.00	34.22	72.39	75.65	73.00	61.79
	Flow	**86.69**	50.80	79.09	82.62	80.85	70.23
	Both	86.09	43.45	74.76	80.08	77.43	66.66
ASRF	RGB	83.28	44.22	75.23	77.34	75.74	65.88
	Flow	85.02	**56.55**	79.95	**82.90**	**80.86**	**70.50**
	Both	84.63	49.12	77.79	80.64	78.93	68.69

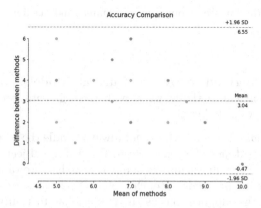

Fig. 3. Accuracy Score comparison of Human and machine scores

4.3   Analysis

Comparison with Human Scores. Using the segmentation results and the times when the instruction was made by accessing the video, the relevant accuracy and rhythm scores for each subject was produced by the system for all the 5 tasks and all subjects. The Bland-Altman plots (Fig. 3 and 4) shows the comparison of the system scores and human scores for the activities performed by the kids. The Y-axis indicates the difference of the scores generated by machines and humans and the X-axis indicates the mean of the scores using both methods. Every point in the scatter plot indicates the measurement for a user which may overlap. For each plot, The blue line indicates the mean of difference of human and machine scores (estimated bias) which is 3.04 for accuracy metric and 3.25 for rhythm. The red lines refers to interval (mean ± 1.96 × standard deviation) which signifies the limits of agreement between human and machine scores. For accuracy the limit of agreement is [6.55,0.47] and [6.66,0.16] for rhythm. Ideally the mean of differences should be closer to 0. This shows that there is a potential of improvement in reliably detecting the touches.

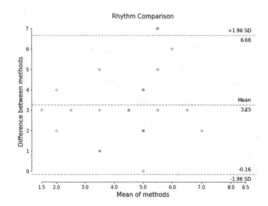

Fig. 4. Rhythm score comparison of human and machine scores

What Cannot Be Handled by the Current Models. To illustrate the limitations of the current methods, we provide the segmentation results of some cases where the network failed.

1) Self Correction: The network cannot always handle the scenario where the user self-corrects the touch. For example in Fig. 5, the subject first intends to touch his shoulder. Then, in the middle of moving the hand towards the shoulder, he corrects himself and proceeds to touch the hip. Such cases are essential in this dataset and the target application, as the subject has to utilize their working memory to decide which body part to touch based on the instruction and type of the rule they are told to follow. The task was intentionally designed by the

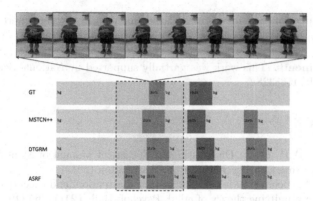

Fig. 5. Segmentation results for different methods. ASRF incorrectly predicts lhrs (highlighted section) when the subject hovered his hand around shoulder and then decided to touch right hip

psychologist experts so that subjects can get easily confused and need to self-correct. The segmentation results show that the best system ASRF incorrectly predicted *lhrs* as it failed to understand that the touch did not happen.

2) Confusion between ear and shoulder: While the pose system clearly illustrated that the system cannot handle spatially fine-grained poses like touch ear v/s touch shoulder for some cases, this issue was echoed in action segmentation results as well, which used much more sophisticated I3D features.

3) Intense motion: Sometimes out of confusion and haste to complete the task, the subject performs touching of body parts at a high speed, and that makes it challenging to predict.

4) Occlusions: As the subjects perform action very quickly, this results into scenarios where the activities overlap and hand from the previous action occludes the other hand which is being used to perform the next action, causing the network difficulty to track.

4.4   Conclusion

In this paper, we introduce a system for Cross-Your-Body task focusing on cognitive assessment using kids as subjects. The system differs from existing works as there is a direct comparison between the scores provided by human experts and machines. The recorded data provides diverse activities which have high intra-class variability and low inter-class variability. It also includes many unique and realistic actions that involve uncoordinated motion patterns that vary in pace and has occlusions. We have empirically investigated significance of pose and I3D features and different data modalities by viewing it as an action segmentation problem. Many interesting findings show that the current state of the art systems find it difficult to recognize these activities. Our system demonstrates creation of 2 fundamental metrics required to measure several executive functions and shows promising potential for future research. This system can be used as a non-intrusive solution for cognitive assessment in kids where there is no need of an expert to manually score the cognitively demanding tasks.

Acknowledgements. This work was partially supported by National Science Foundation grants IIS 1565328.

References

1. Association, A.P., et al.: Diagnostic and Statistical Manual of Mental Disorders (DSM-5®). American Psychiatric Pub, Washington (2013)
2. Barkley, R.A.: Behavioral inhibition, sustained attention, and executive functions: constructing a unifying theory of adhd. Psychol. Bull. **121**(1), 65 (1997)
3. Bell, M.D., Weinstein, A.J., Pittman, B., Gorman, R.M., Abujelala, M.: The activate test of embodied cognition (ATEC): reliability, concurrent validity and discriminant validity in a community sample of children using cognitively demanding physical tasks related to executive functioning. Child Neuropsychol. **27**, 1–11 (2021)
4. Best, J.R., Miller, P.H.: A developmental perspective on executive function. Child Dev. **81**(6), 1641–1660 (2010)
5. Carreira, J., Zisserman, A.: Quo vadis, action recognition? a new model and the kinetics dataset. In: proceedings of the IEEE Conference on Computer Vision and Pattern Recognition, pp. 6299–6308 (2017)
6. Cormier, E.: Attention deficit/hyperactivity disorder: a review and update. J. Pediatr. Nurs. **23**(5), 345–357 (2008)
7. Dai, H.J., Jonnagaddala, J.: Assessing the severity of positive valence symptoms in initial psychiatric evaluation records: should we use convolutional neural networks? PLoS ONE **13**(10), e0204493 (2018)
8. Dendy, C.: Executive function... "what is this anyway?" (2008)
9. Farha, Y.A., Gall, J.: Ms-tcn: Multi-stage temporal convolutional network for action segmentation. In: Proceedings of the IEEE/CVF Conference on Computer Vision and Pattern Recognition, pp. 3575–3584 (2019)
10. Fayyaz, M., Gall, J.: Sct: Set constrained temporal transformer for set supervised action segmentation. In: Proceedings of the IEEE/CVF Conference on Computer Vision and Pattern Recognition, pp. 501–510 (2020)
11. Gattupalli, S., Ebert, D., Papakostas, M., Makedon, F., Athitsos, V.: Cognilearn: A deep learning-based interface for cognitive behavior assessment. In: Proceedings of the 22nd International Conference on Intelligent User Interfaces, pp. 577–587. ACM (2017)
12. Hotham, E., Haberfield, M., Hillier, S., White, J.M., Todd, G.: Upper limb function in children with attention-deficit/hyperactivity disorder (ADHD). J. Neural Transm. **125**(4), 713–726 (2018)
13. Ishikawa, Y., Kasai, S., Aoki, Y., Kataoka, H.: Alleviating over-segmentation errors by detecting action boundaries. In: Proceedings of the IEEE/CVF Winter Conference on Applications of Computer Vision, pp. 2322–2331 (2021)
14. Jaiswal, S., Valstar, M.F., Gillott, A., Daley, D.: Automatic detection of ADHD and ASD from expressive behaviour in RGBD data. In: 2017 12th IEEE International Conference on Automatic Face & Gesture Recognition (FG 2017), pp. 762–769. IEEE (2017)

15. Kam, H.J., Lee, K., Cho, S.M., Shin, Y.M., Park, R.W.: High-resolution actigraphic analysis of ADHD: a wide range of movement variability observation in three school courses-a pilot study. Healthc. Inf. Res. **17**(1), 29–37 (2011)
16. Krieger, V., Amador-Campos, J.A.: Assessment of executive function in ADHD adolescents: contribution of performance tests and rating scales. Child Neuropsychol. **24**(8), 1063–1087 (2018)
17. Li, S.J., AbuFarha, Y., Liu, Y., Cheng, M.M., Gall, J.: Ms-tcn++: Multi-stage temporal convolutional network for action segmentation. IEEE Transactions on Pattern Analysis and Machine Intelligence (2020)
18. McClelland, M.M., et al.: Predictors of early growth in academic achievement: the head-toes-knees-shoulders task. Front. Psychol. **5**, 599 (2014)
19. Organization, W.H.: The world health report 2001: Mental health: new understanding, new hope (2001)
20. Riaz, A., et al.: Deep fMRI: an end-to-end deep network for classification of fMRI data. In: 2018 IEEE 15th International Symposium on Biomedical Imaging (ISBI 2018), pp. 1419–1422. IEEE (2018)
21. Sayed, S.I., Tsiakas, K., Bell, M., Athitsos, V., Makedon, F.: Cognitive assessment in children through motion capture and computer vision: the cross-your-body task. In: Proceedings of the 6th International Workshop on Sensor-based Activity Recognition and Interaction, pp. 1–6 (2019)
22. Shao, D., Zhao, Y., Dai, B., Lin, D.: Finegym: a hierarchical video dataset for fine-grained action understanding. In: Proceedings of the IEEE/CVF Conference on Computer Vision and Pattern Recognition, pp. 2616–2625 (2020)
23. Wang, D., Hu, D., Li, X., Dou, D.: Temporal relational modeling with self-supervision for action segmentation. arXiv preprint arXiv:2012.07508 (2020)
24. Wellsby, M., Pexman, P.M.: Developing embodied cognition: insights from children's concepts and language processing. Front. Psychol. **5**, 506 (2014)
25. Yan, S., Xiong, Y., Lin, D.: Spatial temporal graph convolutional networks for skeleton-based action recognition. In: Proceedings of the AAAI Conference on Artificial Intelligence, vol. 32 (2018)
26. Zou, L., Zheng, J., McKeown, M.J.: Deep learning based automatic diagnoses of attention deficit hyperactive disorder. In: 2017 IEEE Global Conference on Signal and Information Processing (GlobalSIP), pp. 962–966. IEEE (2017)

Privacy-Aware Anomaly Detection Using Semantic Segmentation

Michael Bidstrup[1]([✉]), Jacob V. Dueholm[2], Kamal Nasrollahi[2,3], and Thomas B. Moeslund[2]

[1] Department of Electronic Systems, Aalborg University, Aalborg, Denmark
[2] Visual Analysis and Perception Lab, Aalborg University, Aalborg, Denmark
[3] Research, Milestone Systems, Brøndby, Denmark

Abstract. This paper sets out to investigate if semantic segmentation can be used to achieve anonymity in video surveillance while maintaining the ability to perform anomaly detection. The paper is centered around finding the best model for segmenting the anomaly detection dataset UCHK Avenue without semantic ground truth available. To do this, a series of segmentation models pre-trained on ADE20K and Cityscapes are evaluated against a custom semantic annotation of selected frames from Avenue and the segmentation results are compared both quantitatively and qualitatively. The segmented dataset is then tested on a series of different anomaly detection baselines and the results are compared both in terms of global and anomaly specific accuracy. When comparing the anomaly detection accuracy for RGB and segmented data it was found that anonymity in anomaly detection can be achieved at a small cost in global accuracy but with better accuracy for some specific anomalies.

Keywords: Semantic segmentation · Anomaly detection · Privacy protection · UCHK avenue

1 Introduction

With over 76 countries having adopted artificial intelligence (AI) into surveillance as of 2019, the global video surveillance market is expected to grow within the next many years [6]. With this growth arise both new technologies for improving the efficiency of surveillance and privacy concerns about the use of it.

An important technology with a lot of potential in AI video surveillance is anomaly detection. Anomaly detection, also referred to as abnormal event detection or outlier detection, is the identification of rare events in data. When applied in computer vision this pertains to the detection of abnormal behaviour in among other things people, crowds and traffic. The task of an anomaly detection system is learning regularity in a scene and producing a reaction when irregular events occur, as illustrated in Fig. 1. With manual inspection of surveillance being economically unfeasible and storing footage require increasing amount of

© Springer Nature Switzerland AG 2021
G. Bebis et al. (Eds.): ISVC 2021, LNCS 13018, pp. 110–123, 2021.
https://doi.org/10.1007/978-3-030-90436-4_9

storage, having the ability to automatically determine if footage is relevant or irrelevant through anomaly detection, could greatly reduce the labor required and potentially allow for live investigation of the surveillance. This could result in emergency personal receiving notice of a traffic accident before it is called in by bystanders, care takers to know if an elderly has fallen down or police to be aware of an escalating situation requiring their intercession.

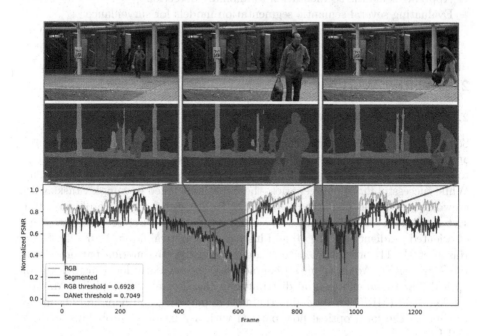

Fig. 1. Anomaly score for UCHK avenue test video in future frame prediction system by Liu et al. [15] subject to RGB (green) and segmented data (blue). Red areas indicate ground truth anomalies and horizontal lines cut-off thresholds for classification. Images bordered by green and red show correct and incorrect classifications, respectively (Color figure online)

In order to meet privacy concerns, a method of anonymizing surveillance while maintaining the ability to detect situations of interest should be investigated. This could be achieved by utilizing semantic segmentation to provide anonymity to scenes while maintaining the global context of the scene. A direct benefit of semantic segmentation is providing the same context humans instinctively derive to computers by transforming singular pixel values to semantic groups. This context includes what objects are in the scene, what their relative positions are and how they move frame-by-frame. As anomaly detection systems have to derive global patterns from singular pixels in RGB space, training a network with global context classifications could prove to be useful. When training on data where people only walk in certain directions, on a subset of surfaces, or objects are found to move at certain velocities between frames, the reduction in information from pixels to semantic classes could potentially remove unwanted noise and help enhance the anomalous behaviour to be more identifiable in the segmented data. The hypothesis of this paper is to test the feasibility of semantic segmentation in anomaly detection to preserve privacy in surveillance.

The contributions of this paper is the following:

- Applying semantic segmentation to anomaly detection
- Evaluating several semantic segmentation models for surveillance.
- Evaluating semantic segmentation in anomaly detection with existing RGB baselines and pricing the privacy preserving aspect in terms of loss in accuracy

2   Related Work

2.1   Custom Feature Methods

Some anomaly detection systems work with custom features. These features are either hand-crafted or learned on a training set. Early work used trajectory features from image coordinates to encode patterns of regularity [22,23,25]. While successful in simple scenarios, these methods failed in complex tasks with crowded scenes and disparity in lighting. To account for these problems later systems [1,11,14,18,29] changed to spatial-temporal features such as histogram of oriented gradients (HOG) [4] and histogram of optical flows (HOF) [5]. Here, Hasan et al. [11] present an auto-encoder reconstructing motion patterns from HOG and HOF. Adam et al. [1] characterize the regularly local histograms of optical flow by an exponential distribution. Zhang et al. [29] exploit a Markov random field (MRF) for modeling the normal patterns, and Kim and Grauman [14] model the local optical flow pattern with a mixture of probabilistic PCA (MPPCA).

2.2   Deep Learning Methods

Deep learning has proven useful in solving a variety of computer vision tasks [24] because of the ability to derive complex patterns in high dimensional space. Among these tasks are anomaly detection [11,15,21,27] and feature extraction for anomaly detection [26]. Xu et al. [26] demonstrate this by designing a multi-layer auto-encoder for feature learning. Besides introducing a feature based auto-encoder, Hasan et al. also propose a fully convolutional auto-ender (Conv-AE) for learning temporal regularity in frames. This method is developed upon by Liu et al. [15] by introducing optical flow as constraint and applying the task to a general adversarial network (GAN) framework.

2.3   Object-Centric Methods

The latest trend in anomaly detection is applying object detector algorithms to scenes and focus on the objects when distinguishing between normal and abnormal frames [10,13]. This focuses the anomaly detection on the parts of the frame responsible for anomalous behaviour and remove redundant data in the form of unchanged background. These object-centric methods use auto-encoders to encode the motion and appearance of the objects. Ionescu et al. has presented two papers on this method. The first [13] applies a single shot detector (SSD) for object detection and auto-encoders for appearance and motion. The encoded features are used to train a support vector machine (SVM) which allows for anomaly detection to be treated as a k-means clustering problem. The second approach [10] differ from the first approach by using a set of classifiers instead of a SVM. Furthermore, the second approach present a method for background agnostic anomaly detection by performing semantic segmentation on the region of interest defined by the object detector, segmenting the object from the background. By doing this, the classifiers rely strictly on the objects in the scene and not on the background.

2.4 Privacy Preserving Anomaly Detection

Research in privacy-aware anomaly detection is a new field of study, which only recently has seen an increase in interest as anomaly detection has shown improvement in accuracy and complexity. Most notably, Angelini et al. publish two papers on the subject [2,28]. The first paper [2] present a method of preserving anonymity in human behaviour anomaly detection from body movements, postures and interactions with surrounding objects using ActionXPose, Single Shot MultiBox Detector and a Support Vector Machine. The second [28] show that instance segmentation using Mask-RCNN and context based information in frames can achieve a reasonably accuracy in human action recognition.

The background agnostic approach by Ionescu et al. [10] is from our knowledge the only existing work using semantic segmentation in an anomaly detection framework. It differs from the proposed work in that semantic segmentation is used as a tool for background removal. The approach by Angelini et al. does segment out humans in the scene, but use instance segmentation which suffer from two problems 1) A failure in the object detection or segmentation result in unmasked subjects and 2) The method only account for anonymity of the subjects and does not account for anonymity in location or objects such as vehicles and road signs. The work presented in this paper will focus on changing entire RGB frames to semantically segmented frames for privacy-aware anomaly detection, and therefore will not risk privacy infringement, as opposed to [28].

3 The Proposed System

The methodology of the proposed solution consists of segmenting an anomaly detection dataset and training an anomaly detection system to test if normal and abnormal events are able to be distinguished from the global context contained in the semantic segmentation. As illustrated in Fig. 2, the experiments consists of two blocks: A segmentation framework and an anomaly detection framework.

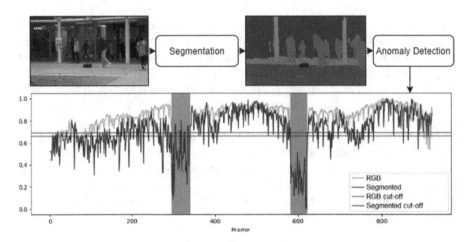

Fig. 2. Overview of methodology. An anomaly detection dataset is segmented using a pre-trained segmentation model and tested on different anomaly detection systems for comparison with RGB baselines.

To test semantic data in an anomaly detection framework, it is either required to perform semantic segmentation on an anomaly detection dataset, for which there exists no ground truth in respect to semantic groups, or reversely, obtain a semantic segmentation dataset with anomaly annotations. As this paper strives to prove that privacy-aware data can work in an anomaly detection setting, using a dataset used for benchmarking existing anomaly detection systems is necessary for result comparison. As annotating a dataset with semantic annotations is a labor intensive task, a segmentation model pre-trained on another dataset will be used. In order to achieve the best segmentation results possible with this method, a dataset which shares resemblance to existing semantic datasets has to be found. Here, UCHK Avenue is selected as it shares features such as view angle, color scheme and objects in the scene with the semantic segmentation datasets ADE20K and Cityscapes, allowing for models pre-trained on these datasets to be tested.

UCHK Avenue is developed by the University of China, Hong Kong [17]. It contains RGB videos roughly 2 min long of people commuting in a public avenue. The set includes 47 abnormal events such as people running, objects being thrown and loitering. The training set consists of 16 videos with 15,328 frames and the test set of 21 videos of 15,324 frames, totalling 30,652 frames for the entire set. The dataset includes two types of anomaly annotations 1) frame annotations with a binary flag indicating frames with abnormal events and 2) region annotations with region of interest of the area with the anomaly. From the 15,324 frames in the test set, 11,504 are normal and 3820 are abnormal frames.

3.1   Segmentation Model Comparison

To find the best pre-trained segmentation model to segment UCHK Avenue with, a comparison of results from a series of models is conducted. To ensure the comparison covers important anomalous scenarios, six frames from the test set are used based on objects and motions in the scene. The first frame is an empty frame, used to create a baseline for the segmentation of the background. The second frame is full of people with a commuter walking in the wrong direction. The third frame is of a person running, to test the models ability to segment blurred objects in motion. The final three frames contain anomalous events with objects such as a bag and papers being thrown and a person walking with a bike. The six frames are illustrated in Fig. 3.

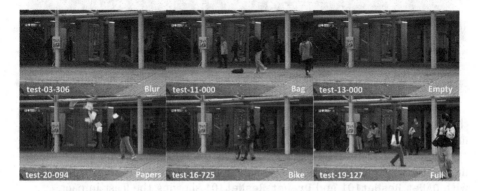

Fig. 3. Six frames from avenue testing set selected for segmentation test

The pre-trained segmentation models tested in the comparison vary on three parameters: network, backbone and pre-trained dataset. They are a mix of five different networks; FCN [16], DeepLab [3], EncNet [30], DANet [8] and Dranet [7] combined with either ResNet-50 or ResNet-101. The full list of models and the results from the test is presented in Table 2. To compare the models, both a quantitative and qualitative analysis of the segmentation results are performed. The quantitative analysis consist of identifying each models ability to segment objects of interest in the scene. The qualitative comparison of the performance is done following the standard evaluation metrics for semantic segmentation models, pixel accuracy (PixAcc) and mean intersection over union (mIoU) [9].

3.2   Quantitative Comparison of Models

In the quantitative comparison of the segmentation models, each frame is compared in respect to the classes detected in the scene and by the amount of noise present on surfaces. As illustrated in Fig. 4, every model is able to segment the people to a satisfying degree. The models DeepLab_ResNeSt50, EncNet_ResNet101s and EncNet_ResNet50s are not able to detect the bag, and

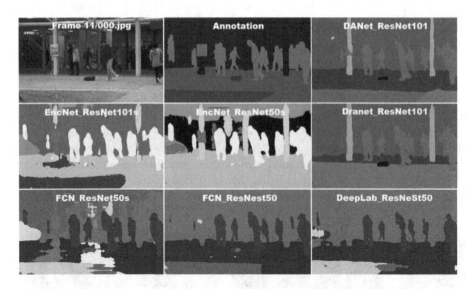

Fig. 4. Segmentation of man throwing bag from selected models.

the models EncNet_ResNet101s, EncNet_ResNet50s and FCN_ResNet50s contain more noise than the remaining models on the ground and background surface.

Figure 5 illustrates how a man walking across the scene on different surfaces impact the segmentations. Here, every model produce noise in the segmentation with DANet_ResNet101 and Dranet_ResNet101 showing the least impact.

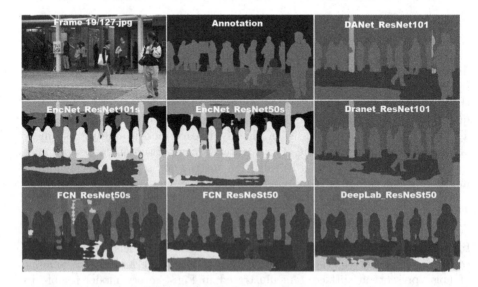

Fig. 5. Segmentation of full frame with man walking towards camera from selected models.

Comparing every frame in the subset showed some general features of every model. In general, models trained on ADE20K contain more noise than those trained on Cityscapes. Furthermore, models trained with ResNeSt as backbone is not able to detect the structure of the building in the background. Table 1 shows each models ability to segment the classes of interest throughout the comparison.

Table 1. Each models ability to detect and segment objects in avenue to a satisfactory level.

	People	Ground	Grass	Building	Background	Bag	Papers	Bike
DeepLab_ResNeSt50	✓	✓	✓		✓			✓
FCN_ResNet50s	✓	✓	✓	✓				
FCN_ResNeSt50	✓	✓	✓		✓			✓
EncNet_ResNet50s	✓	✓		✓				✓
EncNet_ResNet101s	✓	✓	✓	✓				
DANet_ResNet101	✓	✓	✓	✓	✓	✓		✓
Dranet_Resnet101	✓	✓		✓	✓	✓		✓

3.3 Segmentation Results

To compute the PixAcc and mIoU of the segmentation models, the six frames are manually annotated using the LabelMe [20] annotation interface as illustrated in Fig. 6.

Fig. 6. Three of six selected frames and annotated ground truth

It should be noted that a consistent classification of the objects in Avenue is more important than a correct classification, as the specific class predictions can be neglected for the context they provide to the scene. This means the annotations are matched with the predictions for each model and surfaces with multiple predictions are determined by the most present class. Consequently, models with noise in the form of multiple classifications on surfaces achieve a lower accuracy. As the anomalies are performed by the actions of the people and the objects in the scene, each model is also compared based only on the segmentation of these classes. The pixAcc and mIoU for the models can be seen in Table 2. As Dranet produce the best results for the full frame evaluation, this model will be used to segment Avenue for the comparison of the anomaly detection systems.

Table 2. PixAcc and mIoU of segmentation models for full frame, anomalous objects (denoted AO) and people only evaluated on selected frames manually annotated.

Model	Backbone	Dataset	PixAcc			mIoU		
			Full	AO	People	Full	AO	People
FCN	ResNet50s	ADE20K	58.82%	96.57%	96.99%	52.38%	**84.31%**	86.28%
FCN	ResNeSt50	ADE20K	77.59%	96.41%	86.82%	46.81%	77.29%	84.89%
DeepLab	ResNeSt50	ADE20K	72.30%	96.64%	97.14%	47.67%	70.62%	86.02%
EncNet	ResNet50s	ADE20K	51.88%	96.55%	96.96%	53.54%	81.79%	86.75%
EncNet	ResNet101s	ADE20K	62.21%	96.70%	97.11%	46.18%	79.33%	**87.25%**
DANet	ResNet101	Cityscapes	80.58%	**96.83%**	**97.21%**	58.48%	73.11%	87.13%
Dranet	ResNet101	Cityscapes	**81.43%**	96.64%	97.01%	**59.11%**	74.84%	86.52%

3.4   Processing

The segmentation framework is setup on an Ubuntu 16.04 platform running Python 3.6 in an Anaconda environment. It use PyTorch 1.4 with CUDA 10.1 and cudnn 8. The framework for the anomaly detection systems were setup on Windows 10 with Tensorflow 1.4.1, CUDA 8.1 and cudnn 6.1. Both systems are running on a computer with an i7 10700k Intel processor and a Nvidia GeForce 1080ti 11GB graphics card. The processing time for segmenting the 15,234 test frames in Avenue is 14 min 32 s resulting in 17.6 frames segmented per second. Running inference on the Future Frame Prediction system [15] takes 9 min and 45 s resulting in 26 predictions per second. Assuming no external data processing, running the system in a live surveillance setting results in a framerate of 10.6 fps.

4   Results and Discussion

The segmented data is tested on three anomaly detection systems; Future Frame Prediction by Liu et al. [15], MNAD_recon and MNAD_preds by Park et al. [19]. The results are compared with RGB data in terms of global accuracy following the evaluation metrics for frame specific anomaly detection.

4.1 Anomaly Detection Evaluation Metrics

Receiver operating characteristics (ROC) curve is a two-dimensional measure of classification performance in a binary classifier. It maps the true positive rate (TPR), also denoted as the *sensitivity* of the system on the y-axis against the false positive rate (FPR), denoted *(1-specificity)* on the x-axis. TPR and FPR are computed following:

$$TPR = TP/(TP + TN) \ and \ FPR = (FP/FP + FN) \tag{1}$$

An ROC curve following the diagonal reference line $y = x$, produce true positive results at the same rate as false positive results. It follows that the goal of a system is to produce as many true positives as possible, resulting in an ROC curve in the upper left triangle [12]. Here, a classification threshold is decided based on the importance of capturing every true positive at the cost of more false positives. To obtain a global measure of a system's classification performance, the area under the curve (AUC) is used. AUC represents the percentage of true positives in relation to the number of samples in ROC. An AUC of 1.0 represents perfect discrimination in the test with every positive being true positive and every negative being true negative. An AUC of 0.5 represents no discriminating ability with classifications being no better than chance [12].

4.2 Global Accuracy

The accuracy of each system from RGB and segmented data in terms of AUC can be seen in Table 3. The results show that anonymity can be achieved in anomaly detection with a cost in global accuracy. The best performing system for the segmented data overall is the Future Frame Prediction system.

Table 3. The AUC of the different systems for RGB data and segmented data (denoted *SS*).

	AUC	
	RGB	SS
FutureFrame [15]	85%	**74.4%**
MNAD_recon [19]	80.6%	69.3%
MNAD_preds [19]	**86.3%**	67.5%

4.3   Anomaly Specific Accuracy

For a better understanding of the difference between RGB and segmented data in the scope of anomaly detection, an analysis of the performance from the future frame prediction system is conducted. Here, each anomalous frame has been annotated with the anomalous event it contains to test the anomaly specific TPR. In Avenue five anomalies have been identified; A person running, people walking outside the designated walking area, people walking closely to or loitering in front of the camera, kids dancing or playing, and the camera shaking. Only one anomaly happens at a time which allow for each annotated frame to be assigned and summed. A comparison of the TPR for each set of data is presented in Table 4.

Table 4. Performance of RGB and segmented data in comparison to the ground truth annotation (denoted *GT)* in the future frame prediction system for each anomaly. RGB data perform with higher accuracy in object-centric anomalies whereas segmented data perform better in anomalies with a lot of movement from people in the scene.

		Running	Direction	Papers	Bag	Close	Kids playing	Camera shake	Total
GT	Video	1–4	9–11,13–16, 20	13,14,20	5,6,9–12	1,6,19	7–9,17,18,21	2	1–21
	Abnormal events	9	10	3	12	4	8	1	47
	Abnormal frames	377	456	187	1154	743	854	49	3820
RGB	Detected events	9/9	10/10	3/3	12/12	4/4	8/8	1/1	47/47
	True positives	258	281	184	1045	632	600	25	3025
	False negatives	119	175	3	109	111	254	24	795
	TPR	68.44%	61.62%	98.40%	90.55%	85.06%	70.26%	51.02%	79.18%
SS	Detected events	9/9	10/10	3/3	12/12	4/4	8/8	1	47/47
	True positives	293	252	137	823	416	622	28	2571
	False negatives	84	204	50	331	327	232	21	1249
	TPR	77.71%	55.26%	73.26%	71.32%	55.99%	72.83%	57.14%	67.30%

From Table 4 it can be seen that the method based on the segmented data outperforms RGB data for certain anomalies. Specifically, the man running across the scene and the kids playing. This is because the anomaly detection system is more sensitive to changes in the scene for the segmented data. There are two trade-offs from this feature: 1) The segmented data has a higher false positive rate and 2) Objects which are not segmented successfully in every frame, fail to produce an anomalous prediction. The latter is evident when looking at the TPR for the papers and the bag, which the segmentation model had trouble segmenting in the majority of the frames. Figure 7 shows three examples of differences in prediction between RGB and semantic segmentation. The first two frames are correctly classified for the segmented data as a result of the increased sensitivity and the third example illustrates how this results in a false positive.

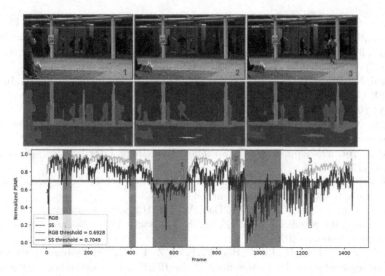

Fig. 7. Three examples of frames where the anomaly detection system react differently to the RGB and segmented data. The first two examples produce true positives for the segmented data and false negative for the RGB data. The last example produce false positive for the segmented data and true positive for RGB.

5 Conclusion

From the segmentation model test it can be concluded that the segmentation models are able to segment Avenue with a high accuracy for the people in the scene. In order to achieve a robust segmentation of all the objects in the scene work have to be put into acquiring semantic annotations for dataset.

From the results it can be concluded that the segmented data is able to retain information to a degree where anomaly detection is possible with a small cost in global accuracy compared to RGB data. It can also be concluded from the anomaly specific results that anomalies from people moving in the scene result in higher accuracy when segmented, eluding to the fact that a higher global accuracy can be achieved from a higher segmentation accuracy.

References

1. Adam, A., Rivlin, E., Shimshoni, I., Reinitz, D.: Robust real-time unusual event detection using multiple fixed-location monitors. IEEE Trans. Pattern Anal. Mach. Intell. **30**(3), 555–560 (2008)
2. Angelini, F., Yan, J., Naqvi, S.M.: Privacy-preserving online human behaviour anomaly detection based on body movements and objects positions. In: ICASSP 2019–2019 IEEE International Conference on Acoustics, Speech and Signal Processing (ICASSP), pp. 8444–8448. IEEE (2019)

3. Chen, L.C., Papandreou, G., Kokkinos, I., Murphy, K., Yuille, A.L.: Deeplab: Semantic image segmentation with deep convolutional nets, atrous convolution, and fully connected crfs. IEEE Trans. Pattern Anal. Mach. Intell. **40**(4), 834–848 (2017)
4. Dalal, N., Triggs, B.: Histograms of oriented gradients for human detection. In: 2005 IEEE Computer Society Conference on Computer Vision and Pattern Recognition (CVPR 2005), vol. 1, pp. 886–893. IEEE (2005)
5. Dalal, N., Triggs, B., Schmid, C.: Human detection using oriented histograms of flow and appearance. In: Leonardis, A., Bischof, H., Pinz, A. (eds.) ECCV 2006. LNCS, vol. 3952, pp. 428–441. Springer, Heidelberg (2006). https://doi.org/10.1007/11744047_33
6. Feldstein, S.: The global expansion of AI surveillance, vol. 17. Carnegie Endowment for International Peace Washington, DC (2019)
7. Fu, J., Liu, J., Jiang, J., Li, Y., Bao, Y., Lu, H.: Scene segmentation with dual relation-aware attention network. IEEE Transactions on Neural Networks and Learning Systems (2020)
8. Fu, J., Liu, J., Tian, H., Li, Y., Bao, Y., Fang, Z., Lu, H.: Dual attention network for scene segmentation. In: Proceedings of the IEEE/CVF Conference on Computer Vision and Pattern Recognition, pp. 3146–3154 (2019)
9. Garcia-Garcia, A., Orts-Escolano, S., Oprea, S., Villena-Martinez, V., Garcia-Rodriguez, J.: A review on deep learning techniques applied to semantic segmentation. arXiv preprint arXiv:1704.06857 (2017)
10. Georgescu, M.I., Ionescu, R.T., Khan, F.S., Popescu, M., Shah, M.: A background-agnostic framework with adversarial training for abnormal event detection in video. arXiv preprint arXiv:2008.12328 (2020)
11. Hasan, M., Choi, J., Neumann, J., Roy-Chowdhury, A.K., Davis, L.S.: Learning temporal regularity in video sequences. In: Proceedings of the IEEE Conference on Computer Vision and Pattern Recognition, pp. 733–742 (2016)
12. Hoo, Z.H., Candlish, J., Teare, D.: What is an roc curve? (2017)
13. Ionescu, R.T., Khan, F.S., Georgescu, M.I., Shao, L.: Object-centric auto-encoders and dummy anomalies for abnormal event detection in video. In: Proceedings of the IEEE/CVF Conference on Computer Vision and Pattern Recognition, pp. 7842–7851 (2019)
14. Kim, J., Grauman, K.: Observe locally, infer globally: a space-time MRF for detecting abnormal activities with incremental updates. In: 2009 IEEE Conference on Computer Vision and Pattern Recognition, pp. 2921–2928. IEEE (2009)
15. Liu, W., Luo, W., Lian, D., Gao, S.: Future frame prediction for anomaly detection-a new baseline. In: Proceedings of the IEEE Conference on Computer Vision and Pattern Recognition, pp. 6536–6545 (2018)
16. Long, J., Shelhamer, E., Darrell, T.: Fully convolutional networks for semantic segmentation. In: Proceedings of the IEEE Conference on Computer Vision and Pattern Recognition, pp. 3431–3440 (2015)
17. Lu, C., Shi, J., Jia, J.: Abnormal event detection at 150 fps in matlab. In: Proceedings of the IEEE international conference on computer vision, pp. 2720–2727 (2013)
18. Mahadevan, V., Li, W., Bhalodia, V., Vasconcelos, N.: Anomaly detection in crowded scenes. In: 2010 IEEE Computer Society Conference on Computer Vision and Pattern Recognition, pp. 1975–1981. IEEE (2010)
19. Park, H., Noh, J., Ham, B.: Learning memory-guided normality for anomaly detection. In: Proceedings of the IEEE/CVF Conference on Computer Vision and Pattern Recognition (CVPR) (June 2020)

20. Russell, B.C., Torralba, A., Murphy, K.P., Freeman, W.T.: Labelme: a database and web-based tool for image annotation. Int. J. Comput. Vis. **77**(1–3), 157–173 (2008)
21. Sabokrou, M., Fayyaz, M., Fathy, M., Klette, R.: Deep-cascade: cascading 3d deep neural networks for fast anomaly detection and localization in crowded scenes. IEEE Trans. Image Process. **26**(4), 1992–2004 (2017)
22. Simonyan, K., Zisserman, A.: Two-stream convolutional networks for action recognition in videos. arXiv preprint arXiv:1406.2199 (2014)
23. Tung, F., Zelek, J.S., Clausi, D.A.: Goal-based trajectory analysis for unusual behaviour detection in intelligent surveillance. Image Vis. Comput. **29**(4), 230–240 (2011)
24. Voulodimos, A., Doulamis, N., Doulamis, A., Protopapadakis, E.: Deep learning for computer vision: a brief review. Comput. Intell. Neurosci. **2018**, (2018)
25. Wu, S., Moore, B.E., Shah, M.: Chaotic invariants of lagrangian particle trajectories for anomaly detection in crowded scenes. In: 2010 IEEE Computer Society Conference on Computer Vision and Pattern Recognition, pp. 2054–2060. IEEE (2010)
26. Xu, D., Ricci, E., Yan, Y., Song, J., Sebe, N.: Learning deep representations of appearance and motion for anomalous event detection. arXiv preprint arXiv:1510.01553 (2015)
27. Xu, D., Yan, Y., Ricci, E., Sebe, N.: Detecting anomalous events in videos by learning deep representations of appearance and motion. Comput. Vis. Image Underst. **156**, 117–127 (2017)
28. Yan, J., Angelini, F., Naqvi, S.M.: Image segmentation based privacy-preserving human action recognition for anomaly detection. In: ICASSP 2020–2020 IEEE International Conference on Acoustics, Speech and Signal Processing (ICASSP), pp. 8931–8935. IEEE (2020)
29. Zhang, D., Gatica-Perez, D., Bengio, S., McCowan, I.: Semi-supervised adapted hmms for unusual event detection. In: 2005 IEEE Computer Society Conference on Computer Vision and Pattern Recognition (CVPR 2005), vol. 1, pp. 611–618. IEEE (2005)
30. Zhang, H., et al.: Context encoding for semantic segmentation. In: Proceedings of the IEEE Conference on Computer Vision and Pattern Recognition, pp. 7151–7160 (2018)

Learning Self-supervised Audio-Visual Representations for Sound Recommendations

Sudha Krishnamurthy$^{(\boxtimes)}$

Sony Interactive Entertainment, San Mateo, CA, USA

Abstract. We propose a novel self-supervised approach for learning audio and visual representations from unlabeled videos, based on their correspondence. The approach uses an attention mechanism to learn the relative importance of convolutional features extracted at different resolutions from the audio and visual streams and uses the attention features to encode the audio and visual input based on their correspondence. We evaluated the representations learned by the model to classify audio-visual correlation as well as to recommend sound effects for visual scenes. Our results show that the representations generated by the attention model improves the correlation accuracy compared to the baseline, by 18% and the recommendation accuracy by 10% for VGG-Sound, which is a public video dataset. Additionally, audio-visual representations learned by training the attention model with cross-modal contrastive learning further improves the recommendation performance, based on our evaluation using VGG-Sound and a more challenging dataset consisting of gameplay video recordings.

Keywords: Self-supervision · Representation learning · Cross-modal correlation

1 Introduction

Learning audio and visual representations based on their correspondence, by training on videos without explicit annotations for the objects and sounds that appear in the videos, is a challenging problem. The learned representations are useful for some of the audio-visual (A-V) content creation tasks. Our motivation is to use these representations to recommend sound effects based on the visual scene, in order to assist sound designers in creating entertaining video content, such as short trailers or video games. Currently, sound effect generation (a technique called Foley) for video game or movie content generation is a time-consuming and iterative process, as shown in Fig. 1. Given a silent video sequence, in the first step the sound designer identifies the relevant sound categories by understanding the visual scene. For example, for the video frame shown in Fig. 1, a designer may identify water-related sounds and human voices as sounds that correspond to the visible objects. Additionally, ambient sounds, such as wind related sounds, may also be relevant, even though this background context may not be visible. Next, specific sound samples for the selected sound categories are retrieved from a sound database. This sound selection and retrieval process is iterative, since there may be numerous variations of sound samples within a category. The selected sound

© Springer Nature Switzerland AG 2021
G. Bebis et al. (Eds.): ISVC 2021, LNCS 13018, pp. 124–138, 2021.
https://doi.org/10.1007/978-3-030-90436-4_10

Fig. 1. Sound matching and mixing for videos (images best viewed in color)

samples are then used to create the desired sound effects for the video. Our goal is to train a neural network model to learn audio and visual representations based on their correspondence and use those representations to assist in the sound selection step, by recommending the top matching sound samples (instances) as well as their respective categories from a given audio list or database, for a visual scene. The recommended sound effects may either correspond to objects directly visible in the scene or may be ambient sounds corresponding to the background context.

Videos in-the-wild provide rich information for learning audio-visual correspondence because of the diversity of objects and sound sources that appear in them. However, it is challenging to get object and sound labels for video datasets with scenes containing an unconstrained number of objects and mixed with noisy audio containing multiple sound sources. Moreover, our goal is to recommend not just the best matching high-level sound categories, but also specific sound instances within those categories, and getting instance-level sound labels for videos, in order to train supervised models is hard. Hence, we propose self-supervised approaches that use the inherent temporal alignment of sounds with video frames in video datasets as implicit labels for learning audio-visual representations. Our self-supervised model uses a two-stream deep convolutional network consisting of a novel attention-based encoder and a projection module, that is trained on audio-visual pairs that are either correlated or uncorrelated. The model is trained to project correlated audio and visual representations closer in the latent space compared to uncorrelated representations. The attention encoder generates audio and visual representations based on the relative importance of local and global convolutional features extracted at different resolutions from the audio and visual streams [11]. The attention mechanism helps in disentangling the latent features extracted from videos having multiple objects and sound sources, without using object detection or audio source separation. Additionally, we trained the attention model to learn audio-visual representations using cross-modal contrastive learning without relying on data augmentation, unlike previous unimodal contrastive learning methods [4, 14] that rely on data augmentations.

We evaluated the learned representations by using them to (1) classify audio-visual correlation, and (2) recommend sound samples corresponding to visual scenes. Our experimental results show that the audio and visual representations generated by the attention model improves the classification accuracy by 18% and the recommendation accuracy by 10% for VGG-Sound [3], which is a public dataset consisting of videos in-the-wild. Additionally, training the attention model with cross-modal contrastive learning results in better representations and improves the recommendation performance further, even without data augmentation, based on our evaluation on VGG-Sound and a more challenging and novel video dataset that we created by recording gameplay sessions of people playing different video games.

2   Related Work

Self-supervised approaches that have been previously proposed to learn audio-visual correspondence and representations, typically assume that the videos either have a single dominant audio signal and visual theme, or a small but fixed number of visual objects and audio sources. For example, the approach in [16] uses a recurrent network to learn A-V correlation from unlabeled videos having a single dominant sound that is generated by a physical impact. The model in [18] learns A-V correspondence from unlabeled videos whose dominant sound is a musical recording, by disentangling and correlating audio mixtures from a pair of videos. In [1,2], a convolutional two-stream network is trained to classify the A-V correspondence based on cross-modal self-supervision using videos that also have a single dominant audio source. Unlike the above approaches, the multi-instance multi-label (MIML) framework in [7] learns from videos with multiple but a small and fixed number of objects and audio sources. It uses a pretrained image classifier to detect a fixed number of objects, then uses this visual guidance to separate the corresponding noisy audio into a fixed number of audio sources, and learns the correlation between the detected objects and separated audio sources. An attention mechanism is used in [17], to localize sound sources in visual scenes and learn A-V representations. In [15], self-supervised A-V representations are learned by predicting the temporal alignment between audio and visual frames.

Our approach also learns audio-visual representations and correlation from unlabeled videos, but does not make any assumptions about the number of visual objects or audio sources in the video. The training videos can be in-the-wild and the learned A-V correspondence may include sounds that are not just related to the visible objects, but also to the ambient context, such as sound of wind blowing. Instead of performing audio source separation or object detection, we use an attention-enhanced model to focus on relevant local and global features extracted at different resolutions from the audio-visual streams, to encode the audio and visual representations based on their correspondence. We also propose the use of cross-modal contrastive approach for learning self-supervised audio and visual representations based on their correlation.

3   Datasets

We used the following video datasets to train and evaluate our self-supervised audio-visual models:

1) **VGG-Sound dataset** [3]: This dataset provides a list of short audio clips corresponding to "in-the-wild" videos posted online by users. We were able to download 5,829 videos from the training split and 428 videos from the test split. Each video clip has a label that indicates the dominant sound or visual theme in the video. However, in some cases these labels are noisy and for some of the videos the sound does not correspond to any visible object in the clip, making it challenging to infer the correlation. After preprocessing, there were 305 unique sound labels in the training set. These sound labels were used only for evaluating the models and not for training.

2) **Gameplay dataset:** As mentioned earlier, one of our motivations for learning audio-visual correlations is to automatically recommend sound effects corresponding to visual

scenes, which can be used to produce entertainment videos, such as video games. Hence, we created a gameplay dataset by recording videos of the gameplay sessions of some video gamers. These videos span different video game genres and most of the visual scenes include complex backgrounds and multiple objects. Unlike the VGG-Sound dataset, which largely comprises videos with a single dominating sound, each gameplay video consists of a noisy monaural audio mixture composed of an unknown number of sound sources, making it hard to separate the noisy mixture into its clean audio sources. Furthermore, there are no annotations for any of the visual objects or sounds that appear in the videos, which makes this dataset considerably more challenging for training and testing compared to the VGG-Sound dataset.

We extracted video frames from each of the videos in the above datasets at 1 fps using *ffmpeg*. We also extracted the audio from each of the videos and segmented it into 1-s audio samples. For each 1-s audio sample, a 64×100-dim log-mel-spectrogram audio feature was generated for training by computing the logarithm on the mel-spectrogram feature extracted for the sample at a sampling rate of 48 KHz, using the *librosa* library [12]. We trained the self-supervised correlation models separately on the two datasets with audio-visual input pairs that are either correlated or uncorrelated. Each input pair consists of a video frame and the log-mel-spectrogram feature extracted from a 1-s audio sample and if both are temporally aligned in a given video, then they are correlated (positive sample). To create uncorrelated pairs (negative samples) for training, we used slightly different methods for the two datasets. For the Gameplay dataset, which has longer videos with varying audio, an uncorrelated pair consists of a video frame paired with a 1-s audio feature extracted either from a different video or from a different timeframe of the same video. To create a negative pair for VGG-Sound, which has shorter video clips, we paired a video frame with a 1-s audio feature extracted from a video with a different sound label.

4   Self-supervised Audio-Visual Representation Learning

Given an input batch of video frames paired with audio, we trained deep convolutional network models to learn audio and visual embeddings (representations) and used the embeddings for downstream tasks, such as recommending sounds relevant to a visual scene. The model has 3 components: *encoder, projector, and a loss function.* The backbone of the network is a two-stream audio-visual encoder, $E = (E_v, E_a)$, which generates the visual embedding $E_v(v_i)$, and audio embedding $E_a(a_i)$ for an input pair (v_i, a_i) consisting of an image (video frame) v_i and audio input a_i. The projector, P, transforms the generated embeddings into suitable inputs for computing the loss function. The encoder and projector are trained together end-to-end by a loss function, L. The goal of training is to learn embeddings such that correlated audio and visual inputs are nearby in the latent space, while uncorrelated audio and visual embeddings are farther apart. After the network is trained, we only use the audio-visual encoder for downstream tasks. In this section, we describe the different architectural choices for the encoder and projector, as well as the loss functions that we experimented with and in Sect. 5, we compare their performance on downstream tasks.

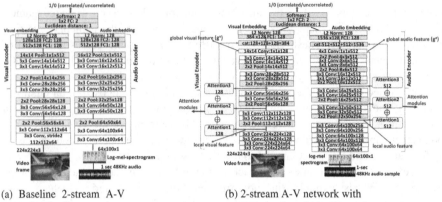

(a) Baseline 2-stream A-V network

(b) 2-stream A-V network with attention-based encoder

Fig. 2. Audio-visual correlation networks. Each layer shows the type of the layer and the dimensions of the output.

4.1 Baseline Model

Our baseline model is shown in Fig. 2a and it is a slight variation of the audio-visual correlation model presented in [2]. The encoder network E in the baseline model uses a two-stream network consisting of a series of convolutional blocks followed by a few fully-connected layers for encoding the visual and audio inputs. Each convolutional block consists of two convolutional (*conv*) and one max-pooling layers. Batch normalization followed by ReLU nonlinearity is applied to the output of each *conv* layer.

The input to the visual stream is a 224×224-dim RGB video frame. The input to the audio stream is a 64×100-dim log-mel-spectrogram feature extracted from a 1-s audio sample, as described in Sect. 3. This audio feature is processed as a grayscale image by the convolutional audio encoder. At the end of the visual and audio encoding pipeline, an $L2$-normalized 128-dim embedding is generated for the visual and audio input, respectively. These audio and visual embeddings are then input to the projection subnetwork P, which uses a fully-connected layer (FC in Fig. 2a) to compute the correlation score as a function of the Euclidean distance between the embeddings and the bias parameter learned by this layer represents the distance threshold that separates the correlated and uncorrelated pairs [2]. The correlation score is used by the binary classification (*softmax*) layer to predict if the audio-visual input pair is correlated or not. The baseline model is trained with batches containing an equal number of correlated and uncorrelated audio-visual pairs extracted from the datasets described in Sect. 3. The network is trained to minimize the binary cross-entropy loss and in the process learns to generate audio-visual representations that are closer in the latent space when they are correlated and farther when they are uncorrelated.

4.2 Attention-Based Model

The baseline model learns a coarse-grained correlation between the image and audio input. However, as mentioned in Sect. 3, the visual scene in a video frame may depict multiple objects and events. Similarly, the noisy audio input may be a mixture of different sound sources, some of them more dominant than the others. Hence, an encoder that weighs the influence of features from different input regions based on their relative importance can learn better encoded representations. To enable this, we enhance the audio and visual convolutional encoders with trainable soft attention layers [11] and combine the encoder with the same projection module used in the baseline model. This attention-based audio-visual correlation network is shown in Fig. 2b.

In the baseline model in Fig. 2a, only the audio and visual embeddings generated at the end of the encoding pipeline were used for learning the A-V correlation. However, in the attention model, we extracted both global and local features representing different audio and visual concepts to generate the audio-visual embeddings and learn the correlation based on that. The local features were extracted at different spatial resolutions from three different intermediate layers of the audio and visual encoder pipelines, as shown in Fig. 2b. Let $L^a = (l_1^a, l_2^a, \ldots, l_n^a)$ and $L^v = (l_1^v, l_2^v, \ldots, l_n^v)$ denote the set of local features extracted from n intermediate layers (in our model $n = 3$) of the audio and visual streams, respectively. Each local feature was extracted after a convolutional block but before the max-pooling layer of that block (local features extracted after the pooling layer lowered the spatial resolution did not result in good performance). Also, let the output of the final convolutional layer of the audio and visual encoding pipelines be denoted as g^a and g^v, which we consider as the global audio and visual feature, respectively (see Fig. 2b). We now explain how the attention-based visual encoder uses the local and global features to generate the visual embeddings (a similar procedure was used to generate the audio embeddings).

1) $w_i^v = conv(l_i^v + g^v), i = 1, \ldots, n$: First, the attention weight w_i^v of each local feature l_i^v is computed with respect to the global feature g^v by adding the two features and passing the sum through a 1×1 convolution operation. Intuitively, these attention weights represent the compatibility between the local and global features. The dot product is an alternative way to compute this compatibility score. If the dimensions of l_i^v and g^v are different, then l_i^v is projected to match the dimension of g^v before the two features are added.

2) $g_i^v = A_i^v * l_i^v, i = 1, \ldots, n$: The attention weights (from Step 1) are normalized through a softmax operation to yield the normalized weights, A_i^v. Then each local feature l_i^v, is weighted through element-wise multiplication with its normalized attention weight A_i^v, to yield the corresponding attention feature g_i^v.

3) $g_{att}^v = g_1^v \oplus g_2^v \oplus \ldots \oplus g_n^v$: The resulting n attention features are then concatenated to yield the global attention feature g_{att}^v for the visual stream.

4) $e^v = norm(project(g_{att}^v))$: Finally, g_{att}^v is projected to a lower dimension (we used 128-dim) and normalized using $L2$-norm to yield the visual embedding e^v. The audio encoder uses the same sequence of operations to generate the 128-dim audio embedding, e^a, for an audio sample.

The 128-dim visual and audio representations, e^v and e^a, generated in Step 4 by the attention-based visual and audio encoders are then input to the projection module, which computes the correlation based on the distance between these representations, as described in Sect. 4.1. This attention model was trained for audio-visual correlation using binary cross entropy loss and the same input as the baseline model. In addition, it was trained with a combination of binary cross entropy (L_{bce}) and margin-based contrastive loss (L_m), $L = L_{bce} + L_m$. Given the visual and audio representations, e^v and e^a, and the ground-truth correlation label, $y \in \{0, 1\}$, indicating if the input audio-visual pair is correlated ($y = 1$) or not ($y = 0$), L_m is defined as follows [9]:

$$L_m(e^v, e^a, y) = (y)dist(e^v, e^a) + (1 - y)max(0, m - dist(e^v, e^a)) \tag{1}$$

where m is a hyperparameter denoting the margin separating the correlated and uncorrelated A-V pairs and $dist$ measures the Euclidean distance between the audio and visual embeddings. The label y is obtained in a self-supervised manner based on the temporal alignment between the video frame and audio sample, as described in Sect. 3. We describe the training hyperparameters and the performance using different loss functions in Sect. 5.

4.3   Unlabeled Contrastive Learning

The two models described above are trained to classify binary audio-visual correlation using balanced batches containing an equal number of correlated and uncorrelated input pairs. In the process, the models learn self-supervised audio-visual representations that are closer in the latent space if they are correlated and farther if they are uncorrelated, which are then used for different downstream tasks. In this section, we present another approach that uses contrastive learning to train a model directly for self-supervised representation learning, without the need for a classification objective. When recommending audio samples from a large database, the fraction of uncorrelated (negative) audio samples is much higher than the fraction of positive samples that correspond to a given visual input. To reflect a similar distribution during training and learn better representations, this third approach compares each visual input with a larger population of negative audio samples, without increasing the batch size.

Recently, contrastive learning methods have been used for self-supervised visual representation learning [4,6,8,10]. These methods minimize the distance between representations of positive pairs comprising augmented views of the same image, while maximizing the distance between representations of negative pairs comprising augmented views of different images. Some of these methods rely on large batch sizes [4,5], large memory banks [6,10,13], or careful negative mining strategies. While these approaches rely on data augmentation to learn self-supervised unimodal representations, we propose a cross-modal contrastive learning approach for learning both audio and visual representations, without relying on data augmentation.

Our contrastive network architecture uses the same attention-based 2-stream audio-visual encoder shown in Fig. 2b as its backbone, but uses a different projection module, training strategy, and loss function. We experimented with two different projection architectures: a single-layer linear MLP and a 2-layer MLP with a ReLU non-linearity between the 2 layers. The projector for contrastive learning does not compute the distance between the audio-visual embeddings output by the encoder, to classify the audio-visual correlation, as was done in the previous two models. Instead, the projected embeddings are used to compute the contrastive loss [4]. Previous contrastive methods introduced two loss functions for unimodal representation learning: (a) normalized temperature-scaled cross-entropy (NT-Xent) loss function [4] and (b) InfoNCE loss function [14], which is based on noise contrastive estimation. We adapted these loss functions to train our model end-to-end for cross-modal representation learning, as follows.

The input batch used to train the baseline and attention models in the previous subsections includes an equal number of positive and negative audio-visual pairs. In contrast, the training batch for contrastive learning models consists of N audio-visual pairs, denoted by $X = \{(v_1, a_1), (v_2, a_2), \ldots, (v_N, a_N)\}$, where each visual input v_i is correlated with audio input a_i, but is not correlated with audio input $a_k, k \neq i$. In other words, each v_i is paired with one positive audio sample, while the remaining uncorrelated $N - 1$ audio samples in the batch serve as negative audio samples for v_i, which obviates the need to explicitly sample negative pairs for training. This allows the model to learn from a larger population of negative pairs without increasing the batch size. The NT-Xent loss function for a positive audio-visual pair (v_i, a_i) is defined in Eq. 2. The training objective is to minimize the average loss computed across all the positive audio-visual pairs.

$$L_{nx}(v_i, a_i) = -log\frac{exp(sim(z_{v_i}, z_{a_i})/\tau)}{\sum_{k=1}^{N} \mathbb{1}_{[k \neq i]}exp(sim(z_{v_i}, z_{a_k})/\tau)} \tag{2}$$

where the embeddings that are output by the A-V encoders (E_v and E_a) for a visual input v_i, and an audio input a_k, are projected by the projection module P to generate $z_{v_i} = P(E_v(v_i))$ and $z_{a_k} = P(E_a(a_k))$, respectively; sim is a similarity function (we used cosine similarity) that computes the similarity between the projected visual and audio representations; τ is the temperature hyperparameter used for scaling the similarity values; $\mathbb{1}_{[k \neq i]} \in \{0, 1\}$ is an indicator function that evaluates to 1 iff $k \neq i$.

We also adapted the InfoNCE loss function to train the contrastive learning model for audio-visual representation learning. The InfoNCE loss function for self-supervised unimodal representation learning was formulated in [14]. Given a batch X of N audio-visual pairs as described above, where each image v_i in the batch is paired with one positive audio sample a_i while the remaining $N - 1$ audio samples serve as negative samples for that image, the InfoNCE loss function computes the categorical cross-entropy of correctly classifying the index of the positive audio sample for each image in the batch. To compute this loss, we first computed the similarity between each image v_i and audio sample a_k in a batch as $f(v_i, a_k) = sim(z_{v_i}, z_{a_k})/\tau$, by using cosine similarity and scaling it by the temperature τ. As in Eq. 2, z_{v_i} and z_{a_k} are the projected representations for v_i and a_k, respectively. These scaled similarity values then serve as the logit values for computing the categorical cross-entropy loss. While the denominator term in Eq. 2 includes only the similarity values for uncorrelated pairs, the InfoNCE loss computation includes the similarity values for correlated and uncorrelated pairs in the denominator.

Table 1. Performance evaluation on VGG-Sound. The encoder, projector, and loss function for each model are described in Sect. 4.

Encoder	Loss	Acc (%)
baseline	BCE	69.5
attention	BCE+margin contrastive	87.4
fine-tuned attention	BCE+margin contrastive	87.8

(a) A-V correlation accuracy for VGG-Sound dataset

ID	Encoder	Projector	Loss function	Category-level acc (%)	Sample-level acc (%)
1	baseline	linear	BCE	14.1	8.6
2	attention	linear	BCE	15.6	13.3
3	attention	linear	BCE+margin-contrastive	24.2	18.8
	Contrastive	Learning	Models		
4	attention	nonlinear	InfoNCE	28.1	23.4
5	attention	linear	InfoNCE	**38.3**	**31.3**
6	attention	nonlinear	NT-Xent	32.0	27.3
7	attention	linear	NT-Xent	33.6	28.9

(b) Top-10 recommendation accuracy for VGG-Sound dataset

5   Performance Evaluation

In this section, we compare the performance of the models presented in Sect. 4 on two tasks: 1) classifying the audio-visual correlation and 2) recommending sound samples relevant to a visual scene. All of the models were trained using the Stochastic Gradient Descent (SGD) optimizer with Nesterov momentum, with a momentum value of 0.9 and weight decay of 10^{-4}. The SGD optimizer achieved better generalization than the Adam optimizer. The models were trained and evaluated using the VGG-Sound and Gameplay datasets described in Sect. 3. The initial learning rate was selected by running a grid search on values in the range $[1 \times 10^{-4}, 1.0]$ and then adaptively decayed during training. When training with VGG-Sound, the best initial learning rate was 0.01, whereas for the larger Gameplay dataset, it was 0.001. We trained all of the models on dual Nvidia 2080Ti GPUs. The baseline model was trained with a batch size of 128, whereas the attention-based models which have a larger number of parameters were trained with a batch size of 32. The training was regularized using early stopping with the training terminated if there was no improvement in the validation performance for 20 consecutive epochs. To train models with margin-based contrastive loss (Eq. 1), we chose margin $m = 0.1$ based on grid search. Similarly, to train the models with InfoNCE and NT-Xent losses (Sect. 4.3), we chose $\tau = 0.5$ for the temperature hyper-parameter, based on grid search.

To train the baseline and attention models for A-V correlation (Sect. 4.1 and 4.2), we used a balanced training dataset containing an equal number of correlated and uncorrelated A-V pairs, by randomly selecting approximately the same number of video frames from each of the videos and pairing them with a 1-s audio sample. This resulted in a balanced training set of 58,290 A-V pairs and validation set of 1280 pairs for VGG-Sound. For the Gameplay dataset, the balanced training set contains 214,168 A-V pairs and validation set contains 35,562 pairs. The contrastive learning models for directly learning audio and visual representations were trained on 5,829 correlated A-V pairs created by pairing one randomly extracted video frame from each VGG-Sound training video with its corresponding 1-s audio sample. As mentioned in Sect. 4.3, uncorrelated (negative) A-V pairs are generated implicitly from within a batch when training contrastive models. No data augmentation was used for any of the models.

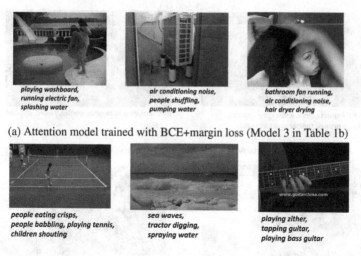

playing washboard,
running electric fan,
splashing water

air conditioning noise,
people shuffling,
pumping water

bathroom fan running,
air conditioning noise,
hair dryer drying

(a) Attention model trained with BCE+margin loss (Model 3 in Table 1b)

people eating crisps,
people babbling, playing tennis,
children shouting

sea waves,
tractor digging,
spraying water

playing zither,
tapping guitar,
playing bass guitar

(b) Attention model trained with InfoNCE loss (Model 5 in Table 1b)

Fig. 3. Top sounds recommended by attention models for VGG-Sound videos

5.1 Audio-Visual Correlation Performance

We evaluated the A-V correlation performance of the models on 3000 audio-visual pairs, each pair consisting of a video frame and 1-s audio sample extracted from the VGG-Sound test videos. The test set consists of an equal number of correlated and uncorrelated pairs. Table 1a shows the correlation accuracy, which measures the percentage of test pairs for which the audio-visual correlation was correctly classified by the 3 approaches in Sect. 4. The first two models were trained to classify the audio-visual correlation. The attention model (Sect. 4.2) trained with a combination of binary cross-entropy (BCE) and margin-based contrastive loss (Eq. 1 with margin = 0.1) improves the correlation accuracy by around 18%, compared to the baseline model without attention. For the third model, the attention-based encoder was first trained with contrastive learning using InfoNCE loss to directly learn A-V representations (Sect. 4.3). This pre-trained encoder was then combined with a binary classifier layer and the whole model was fine-tuned to classify the A-V correlation using BCE+margin-based contrastive loss. All 3 approaches classify the correlation based on the distance between the generated A-V embeddings. From Table 1a, we infer that the attention-based encoder is more effective in predicting the audio-visual correlation because it learns better audio and visual representations that are closer when correlated and farther when they are uncorrelated.

5.2 Sound Recommendation Performance

We also evaluated the A-V representations learned by the trained audio-visual models based on the sound samples they recommended for the VGG-Sound and Gameplay test videos. The models recommended the top-k sound samples from an audio list or

metal impacts, gore-knives and swords,
human grunts, footsteps, animal-cats

gore-knives and swords, gorilla, sword, punches

(a) Recommendations with a good match (images best viewed in color).

knives and swords, machine guns,
impacts and crashes, fights, ape

groan and grunt, impacts and crashes,
explosions, creature footsteps

(b) Recommendations with some mismatch (images best viewed in color).

Fig. 4. Topmost sounds recommended for Gameplay videos by Model 5 in Table 1b. (The frames in (a) are from the video game The Last Guardian^{TM}. ©2016 Sony Interactive Entertainment Inc. The Last Guardian is a trademark of Sony Interactive Entertainment America LLC. The frames in (b) are from Knack^{TM}2. ©2017 Sony Interactive Entertainment Inc. Knack is a trademark of Sony Interactive Entertainment LLC.)

database. Each sample i in the audio search list is labeled as (s_i, c_i), where s_i is the sample label that uniquely identifies the audio sample, while c_i is its category label, which may be shared by multiple audio samples. These labels are used to evaluate the top-k sample-level (or instance-level) and category-level recommendation accuracy, as follows. Let $R(v_j) = [S^R(v_j) = (s_1^R, \ldots, s_k^R); C^R(v_j) = (c_1^R, \ldots, c_k^R)]$ denote the top-k sounds recommended by a model for a video frame v_j, where $S^R(v_j)$ and $C^R(v_j)$ are the list of sample labels and category labels, respectively, for the top-k sounds recommended for v_j. Let $G(v_j) = [S^G(v_j) = (s_1^G, \ldots, s_n^G); C^G(v_j) = (c_1^G, \ldots, c_n^G)]$ denote the ground-truth audio samples for video frame v_j, where $S^G(v_j)$ and $C^G(v_j)$ are the list of sample labels and category labels for the ground-truth audio samples for v_j. If $S^R(v_j) \cap S^G(v_j) \neq \phi$, there is a sample-level match and if $C^R(v_j) \cap C^G(v_j) \neq \phi$, there is a category-level match. Sample-level match is stricter than category-level match. The top-k *sample-level accuracy* and top-k *category-level accuracy* of a model measure the percentage of test video frames for which there is a sample-level match and category-level match, respectively, between the top-k sounds recommended by the model and the ground-truth.

Recommendations for VGG-Sound Dataset: To evaluate the recommendation performance of a model on VGG-Sound, we randomly extracted one video frame v_i and its corresponding 1-s audio sample a_i, from each of the test videos. a_i serves as the ground-truth for v_i and is identified by (s_i, c_i), where the sample label s_i is the unique name of the video and c_i is the category annotation of the video from which a_i is extracted. The audio samples $(a_1, \ldots, a_n)$ that are extracted from the test videos form the search list for sound recommendations. We resized each extracted test video frame to 224×224-dim and normalized it. We then generated the 128-dim visual embeddings for the test video frames and 128-dim audio embedding for each of the samples in the audio search list, using the evaluation model trained on the VGG-Sound training set. To recommend sounds for a video frame, we computed the Euclidean distance between its visual embedding and all of the audio embeddings in the search list and selected the top-k nearest audio samples. We then compared these top-k sound recommendations with the ground-truth to compute the top-k sample-level and category-level accuracy.

Table 1b shows the top-10 category-level and sample-level recommendation accuracy for the VGG-Sound video frames. The first two models are trained with BCE classification loss and learn audio-visual representations while learning to classify the correlation. The attention-based encoder model (Sect. 4.2) has a better performance than the baseline model without attention (Sect. 4.1). When trained with a combination of BCE and margin-based contrastive loss (Eq. 1 with $m = 0.1$), the sample-level and category-level recommendation accuracy of the attention model (Model 3 in Table 1b) improves by around 10% compared to the baseline model. The margin loss term introduces an additional constraint to ensure that the correlated and uncorrelated pairs of audio-visual representations are separated by a margin of at least 0.1. Figure 3a shows the categories of the top sound samples recommended by Model 3 for some of the VGG-Sound test videos. In Models 4–7, contrastive learning is used to train the attention-based encoder with different projection heads and different loss functions (Sect. 4.3). The non-linear projector has 2 fully-connected layers with bias and a ReLU non-linearity in between, whereas the linear projector has only a single fully-connected layer with bias. For InfoNCE as well as NT-Xent loss, the model with linear projection outperforms the corresponding model with non-linear projection. Also, the model with linear projection trained with InfoNCE loss (Model 5) has the best recommendation accuracy and outperforms the linear model trained with NT-Xent loss (Model 7). Figure 3b shows the labels of some of the top sound samples recommended by the best performing model (Model 5) for some of the VGG-Sound video frames.

We now summarize the recommendation results using VGG-Sound: 1) From Fig. 3a and 3b, we see that the attention-based models are able to recommend sound samples that correspond well with the visual scenes, which shows that these models learn effective self-supervised representations and correspondence from audio-visual features extracted at different resolutions, even without explicit annotations, object detection, and sound separation. 2) Models trained with contrastive learning generate better representations and outperform the models that learn the representations using a classification objective for the correlation (Models 1–3). In particular, the best model (Model 5) improved the sample-level and category-level recommendation accuracy by 12% and 14%, respectively, compared to Model 3. We need to explore if cross-modal contrastive learning with data augmentation can further improve the performance.

Recommendations for Gameplay Dataset: We also evaluated the sound recommendation performance on 676 video frames extracted from 30 videos in the Gameplay test dataset. The sounds were recommended from a large internal audio database consisting of more than 200K sound samples grouped into 4000 different categories. We used the same procedure and model architectures for evaluation, as described above for the VGG-Sound dataset. Models 1–3 in Table 1b were first trained on the Gameplay training dataset and then used to generate the visual embeddings for the test video frames and the audio embeddings for the more than 200K samples in the audio database (the audio samples in this database were not used during training). On the other hand, the contrastive learning models that were directly trained to learn A-V representations (Models 4–7 in Table 1b) learn more generic representations. Hence, to evaluate their generalizability, we used the contrastive learning models that were trained only on the VGG-Sound training set to generate the embeddings for the Gameplay test video frames and audio samples in the search database. Each model then used the embeddings it generated to recommend the top-k samples from the audio database for the 676 test scenes.

The Gameplay test videos do not have any sample-level or category-level ground-truth for the sounds. Instead, a few sound designers manually recommended some sound samples from the audio database for our test videos. While our models generate the top-k recommendations by comparing the visual embedding with the audio embeddings of all of the audio samples in the database, the manual recommendations are not based on an exhaustive search of the database. So it is hard to get an exact match between the manual and model recommendations. Nevertheless, the manual recommendations serve as approximate ground-truth to evaluate the relative performance of our models. The sample-level recommendation accuracy of the attention-based model was 10x higher than that of the baseline model. Both of these models were trained with the Gameplay dataset to classify the A-V correlation. The attention model trained with InfoNCE loss (Model 5 in Table 1b) to directly learn the representations, further improved the sample-level and category-level accuracy of the Gameplay recommendations by 7% and 24%, respectively, even though this model was trained on VGG-Sound and there was a significant domain gap between the VGG-Sound and Gameplay dataset. Figure 4 shows the categories of the top sound samples recommended by Model 5 for some of the Gameplay test videos. Figure 4a shows video frames for which the model generated recommendations were a good match for the visual scene, while Fig. 4b are examples with some mismatch. These results show that the attention-based encoder is able to learn effective audio and visual representations based on features extracted at different resolutions, even from complex datasets that have multiple visual objects and audio mixed with multiple sound sources. Furthermore, the attention model trained with cross-modal contrastive learning is able to improve the recommendation performance on the Gameplay dataset, even though the model was trained on the less noisy VGG-Sound dataset. This shows the generalizability of the cross-modal contrastive learning approach. As future work, we plan to improve the Gameplay recommendations further by using a contrastive learning model trained on the Gameplay dataset.

6   Conclusions

We presented self-supervised approaches that combine a novel attention-based encoder with a projection module to learn audio and visual representations based on their correspondence, by training on unlabeled videos. The attention encoder extracts local and global audio-visual features at different resolutions and attends to them based on their relative importance. This helps in disentangling latent features extracted from videos having multiple objects and sound sources, without using explicit object detection or audio source separation. The model projects correlated audio and visual inputs closer in the latent space compared to uncorrelated audio-visual pairs. Our results show that when trained with cross-modal contrastive learning, the attention encoder is able to learn better audio and visual representations even without data augmentation and significantly improve the sound recommendation accuracy on video datasets with different complexities. The generated representations can be used for unimodal and multi-modal similarity and multimodal content creation tasks, such as creative video editing using recommended sound effects based on the objects and context in the visual scenes.

Acknowledgments. The author would like to thank Norihiro Nagai, Isamu Terasaka, Kiyoto Shibuya, and Saket Kumar for the feedback and support they provided.

References

1. Arandjelovic, R., Zisserman, A.: Look, listen, and learn. In: Proceedings of ICCV (2017)
2. Arandjelović, R., Zisserman, A.: Objects that sound. In: Ferrari, V., Hebert, M., Sminchisescu, C., Weiss, Y. (eds.) ECCV 2018. LNCS, vol. 11205, pp. 451–466. Springer, Cham (2018). https://doi.org/10.1007/978-3-030-01246-5_27
3. Chen, H., Xie, W., Vedaldi, A., Zisserman, A.: VGG-sound: a large-scale audio-visual dataset. In: Proceedings of ICASSP (2020)
4. Chen, T., Kornblith, S., Norouzi, M., Hinton, G.: A simple framework for contrastive learning of visual representations. In: Proceedings of ICML (2020)
5. Chen, T., Kornblith, S., Swersky, K., Norouzi, M., Hinton, G.: Big self-supervised models are strong semi-supervised learners. In: Proceedings of NeurIPS (2020)
6. Chen, X., Fan, H., Girshick, R., He, K.: Improved baselines with momentum contrastive learning. arxiv (2020)
7. Gao, R., Feris, R., Grauman, K.: Learning to separate object sounds by watching unlabeled video. In: Ferrari, V., Hebert, M., Sminchisescu, C., Weiss, Y. (eds.) ECCV 2018. LNCS, vol. 11207, pp. 36–54. Springer, Cham (2018). https://doi.org/10.1007/978-3-030-01219-9_3
8. Grill, J., et al.: Bootstrap your own latent: a new approach to self-supervised learning. arxiv (2020)
9. Hadsell, R., Chopra, S., LeCun, Y.: Dimensionality reduction by learning an invariant mapping. In: Proceedings of CVPR (2006)
10. He, K., Fan, H., Wu, Y., Xie, S., Girshick, R.: Momentum contrast for unsupervised visual representation learning. In: Proceedings of CVPR (2020)
11. Jetley, S., Lord, N., Lee, N., Torr, P.: Learn to pay attention. In: Proceedings of International Conference on Learning Representations (ICLR) (2018)
12. McFee, B., Raffel, C., Ellis, D., McVicar, M., Battenberg, E., Nieto, O.: librosa: audio and music signal analysis in Python. In: Proceedings of the 14th Python in Science Conference (2015)
13. Misra, I., Maaten, L.: Self-supervised learning of pretext-invariant representations. In: Proceedings of CVPR (2020)
14. Oord, A., Li, Y., Vinyals, O.: Representation learning with contrastive predictive coding. In: Proceedings of CVPR (2019)

15. Owens, A., Efros, A.A.: Audio-visual scene analysis with self-supervised multisensory features. In: Ferrari, V., Hebert, M., Sminchisescu, C., Weiss, Y. (eds.) ECCV 2018. LNCS, vol. 11210, pp. 639–658. Springer, Cham (2018). https://doi.org/10.1007/978-3-030-01231-1_39
16. Owens, A., Isola, P., McDermott, J.: Visually indicated sounds. In: Proceedings of the CVPR (2016)
17. Senocak, A., Oh, T., Kim, J., Yang, M., Kweon, I.: Learning to localize sound source in visual scenes. In: Proceedings of the CVPR (2018)
18. Zhao, H., Gan, C., Rouditchenko, A., Vondrick, C., McDermott, J., Torralba, A.: The sound of pixels. In: Ferrari, V., Hebert, M., Sminchisescu, C., Weiss, Y. (eds.) ECCV 2018. LNCS, vol. 11205, pp. 587–604. Springer, Cham (2018). https://doi.org/10.1007/978-3-030-01246-5_35

Poster

Security Automation Through a Multi-processing Real-Time System for the Re-identification of Persons

Andre Coleiro and Daren Scerri[✉]

Institute of Information and Communication Technology, Malta College or Arts, Science and Technology, Paola, Malta
{andre.coleiro,daren.scerri}@mcast.edu.mt
http://mcast.edu.mt

Abstract. Security personnel frequently require to tediously review multiple camera feeds to track activity. An intelligent re-identification system can solve this problem by re-identifying the same person or object from multiple camera feeds. This study proposes a test-case and solution to accurately track vehicle occupants at a car-park and re-identify them entering/exiting the premises from another feed. Such solution can also be re-purposed to implement a non-ticket based controlled parking system. Our solution utilizes a multi-threaded three-phase approach to provide a dynamic low-cost solution for re-identification. An innovative combination of techniques including human body segmentation, clothes type detection, color features and histogram comparisons are used together to identify a person, saving the feature attributes as tuples within a temporal data structure. Real-time comparisons of feature attributes obtained from two camera process threads are made to perform re-identification. Given the challenge of non-overlapping cameras, it was still possible to re-identify the same person using a combination of extracted features, like clothes type, clothes color features and refined histogram profiles. Standard short-range (10–15 m) and long-range (>15 m) low-resolution car park camera feeds were used to test the performance of our solution. Short-range re-identification achieved an impressive average accuracy of 95.66% with long-range lower-resolution feeds achieving 51.33% accuracy. Most inaccuracies were due to false positives due to low-quality imagery when person was highly distant.

Keywords: Computer vision · Artificial intelligence · Feature extraction

1 Introduction

In recent years, security in private and public spaces has increased in its importance and necessity. Technologies like IoT (Internet of Things) and Computer Vision are being increasingly utilized by video surveillance system manufacturers and operators to automate observations that normally require manual

© Springer Nature Switzerland AG 2021
G. Bebis et al. (Eds.): ISVC 2021, LNCS 13018, pp. 141–153, 2021.
https://doi.org/10.1007/978-3-030-90436-4_11

observations and interventions. However, research and development of intelligent systems like the re-identification of persons or objects appearing in different camera feeds is a challenging task [9]. [20] and [8] emphasise the importance of such systems, but highlight their limitation and unresolved issues mainly concerning costs and accuracy. The process of re-identification has always imposed challenges due to changes in the appearance of the person or object caused by environmental lighting, picture quality, occlusions, camera angles and posture [10]. All aforementioned elements cause problems in the re-identification algorithm when re-identifying the same person or object. Several systems use feature extraction to eliminate such issues when re-identifying a person; however, it is not an easy task; in fact, a state-of-the-art system performed less than 30% accuracy when performing re-identification using feature extraction [2,11].

The aim of this experimental study is develop a low-cost, lightweight solution for detecting and re-identifying persons from multiple non-overlapping CCTV live feeds within a car-park. Each person that parks in the parking lot can be re-identified using a re-identification system to help security personnel to track vehicle owners and other persons within the premises, without the need of going through the different feeds manually. Accuracy of detection is the dependent variable for this study, with camera distance and lighting being the independent variables. Given the ethical implications of most facial recognition systems, the challenge is to perform an on-the-fly re-identification of person without requiring prior storage of any personal data like facial photos or contact details. The proposed solution can also serve to generate an ID for a vehicle, assign it to person/s, and persist this connection only until required. Hence, the hypothesis of this study is that by using multiple CCTV live feeds, it is possible to accurately re-identify a person from one camera to an other in real-time without the need of intrusive facial recognition.

2   Background

2.1   Person Detection and Tracking

Detection and tracking of a person are two challenging tasks to achieve, especially in such scenarios where multiple people and obstacles are in the camera perspective. Some human detection systems can quickly accomplish the detection of a human even in complex scenarios such as in crowded areas; however, false positives still occur regularly [3]. Multiple cameras are convenient when tracking a person in a video since a single camera's perspective might not cover the whole area. To mitigate this problem, a paper written by [13] presents a system that can detect and track multiple persons from multiple cameras that overlap each other in complex environments with different lighting and obstacles that might block the person from the camera perspective. The multi-person tracking presented by [13] is performed using a volumetric 3D reconstruction of the footage measured from the segmented foreground of the camera's overlapping view. Banks, airports, shopping centers and sports can use this system since various conditions, as discussed before, can occur that might interfere with tracking a particular person when using a single stationary camera [19]. The authors approach this method by implementing a minimum of three to four cameras with different bird-eyes view overlapping perspective from each other to cover a more broad area of the detection. Implementing the detection and tracking system by this method can eliminate various problems since the persons being identified in the surveillance cameras are detected from different angles, as shown in Fig. 1. Other studies also use the multiple camera technique to track people in cluttered scenes to eliminate the lack of visibility [14,18].

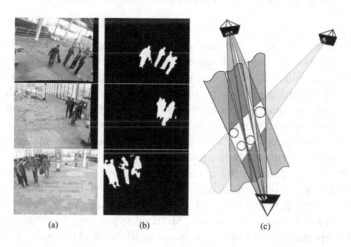

Fig. 1. [13] (a) Three images captured from three cameras with different angles, (b) Corresponding foreground segmentation images, (c) The cameras perspectives capturing the people in the scene.

2.2   Person Re-identification

Person re-identification has been attempted several times to be solved; however, it is still a very challenging task since the person appearance can frequently change as it relies on the camera angle, human pose and illumination. A person re-identification system usually will consist of two full-body person images and compare them to output a similarity score to decide whether the two images consists of the same person [17]. A system with multiple cameras installed can detect different persons throughout the camera perspectives. However, without any computer vision algorithm, manual observation is required to identify a person from a camera to another. [10] proposed a research study to retrieve trajectories of multiple persons by using non-overlapping surveillance cameras as shown in Fig. 2.

The authors define the word "trajectory" as the order of the camera perspectives that a single person has visited. To re-identify the same person throughout multiple cameras, some challenges are expected. The person features are highly

Fig. 2. [10] Multiple camera setup that do not overlap.

affected by direct lighting to the camera and the camera angle. The authors also stated that the person detected appearance is essential in this process to not change with time since it could easily cause the tracking and re-identification process to fail. To mitigate this problem, the system will compare the person detected in a single camera with more than one camera to see different appearances of the person in different camera views; however, it can still cause failure due to an increase of people [10]. The cluttered background presents another challenge when re-identifying an individual from one camera to another. This makes it more difficult for the algorithm to calculate discriminative biometrics cues involving facial and gait features [16]. In some scenarios, the person appearance can look dissimilar in multiple camera views because of the non-rigid nature of the human body, as mentioned before. Multiple supervised learning approaches and Novel deep learning-based methods are available and can solve these problems with ease [1,6,12]. The Novel deep learning methods perform better than the supervised learning approaches; however, they require a lot of time to be trained [21].

3   Research Methodology

This research aims to develop an intelligent multi-processing real-time system to re-identify multiple persons present in different CCTV live feeds through computer vision and image processing techniques. The re-identification process is made possible by comparing the three main attributes extracted from the detected person images, including histogram comparison, clothes type detection, and clothing color.

3.1   Prototype Pipeline

For the initial stage of the prototype, the pre-trained YOLOv5 (You-Only-Look-Once) model is used to detect various object classes illustrated in the live-feed footage from the CCTV camera. In the first camera located in a parking lot, the YOLOv5 model is specifically filtered to detect the person and the vehicle classes only; meanwhile, only the person class is required in the other cameras

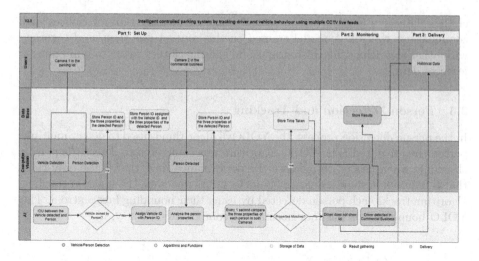

Fig. 3. Research pipeline

since they are located in an entrance or an exit of the premises. Once the person is detected from the footage, a cropped image of the person of that particular frame is stored in a variable to extract the three main attributes. In addition, an IoU (Intersection over Union) value between the vehicle and the person bounding box in the first camera is calculated to identify if that person is the vehicle owner (Fig, 3).

For the clothing type attribute, the data-set is trained by evaluating and detecting multiple clothing articles from multiple fed images. The prototype can then specifically identify the type of clothing from the person detected in the initial stage from the original image.

The other two main attributes are to determine the color of the clothes and the histogram of the person. The multiple cameras covering different perspectives store the vehicle ID linked with a specific person represented with a random unique ID, the clothing type and their color and the histogram that plots the general intensity distribution of the image, all in a data structure linked to a specific camera. The system uses these data structures to detect and re-identify the same person by comparing the attributes amongst different camera perspectives. The re-identification process of this system is successfully performed if the attributes of the person detected in multiple cameras match with each other, and the histogram comparison resulted in greater than 45%. The final segment of this system calculates the time taken of the detected person to maneuver between the different cameras covering different perspectives.

3.2   Datasets

A modified COCO dataset was constructed to identify persons and cars. Other classes within the COCO were removed to maximize performance. A custom clothes dataset was used in the second stage to identify type of clothes and combinations thereof. A model trained on this dataset was then used together with other algorithms, like histograms and specific clothes colors to build person features data.

3.3   Person Detection and Tracking

In the person detection process, the YOLOv5 algorithm is used to detect multiple persons in a live feed. The YOLO algorithm was configured to detect the person class only when needed to increase the performance since that is the only class that is required in some scenarios (Camera 1). As reviewed, the centroid tracking algorithm tracks each person detected by using their bounding box centroid. The YOLO bounding box has four normalized components (x, y, w, h).

$$\overline{x} = \frac{x_{MIN} + x_{MAX}}{2} \qquad (1) \qquad\qquad \overline{y} = \frac{y_{MIN} + y_{MAX}}{2} \qquad (2)$$

Finally, the centroid tracking algorithm uses the denormalized coordinates to find the centroid of the bounding box by using the above formulas [5]. After detecting and tracking the person, the person bounding box is cropped and saved as a numpy array to be used in other processes.

3.4   Vehicle Detection and Assignment

In the vehicle detection process, the YOLOv5 algorithm is used to detect multiple vehicles shown in camera one. This process aims to perform a bounding box with a unique ID for each car and calculates the IoU value with the person bounding box shown in the camera. Camera one has the perspective of two or three parking spaces. If a person is detected in the camera, an IoU value between each car and the person is calculated to determine which car belongs to the detected person.

3.5   Clothes Detection

In the clothes detection process, a flattened array that includes the image of the detected person is fed to the detector. A threshold of 0.2 was set for this algorithm to accurately predict and detect the correct clothing type even if the person in the frame is distant. As mentioned in the clothes model training section, a model is trained to classify and detect different clothing articles using the YOLOv5 algorithm. Since this process uses the same object detection algorithm (YOLOv5) to detect the persons and vehicles, the process is very similar to each other, and the model is the only distinction between them.

3.6   Clothes Color Detection

One of the attributes mentioned in the research pipeline was the clothes color. The clothes color is detected by first reading the numpy array of the person detected and cropping a small area from the upper clothing article. These cropped areas are brightened so that even if the image is in a dark area, the actual color of the clothes is achieved. The human eye can see over a million different colors [15]. To simplify and lower processing overhead, seven colors were chosen from where the algorithm can compare and select the closest color of the RGB value provided in the parameter of the function. For further accuracy, clothes segmentation was considered instead of the cropping areas method. However, machine learning based segmentation algorithms like Mask-RCNN have a high processing overhead. Hence, given one of the aims of this study is to develop the lightest possible implementation, such a solution was not acceptable.

3.7   Histogram Processing and Correlation Metrics

In this process, the person AOI (Area of Interest) identified by the person detector, is converted into HSV, normalized, and background removed to create a histogram of the person features. Together with the other attributes, each histogram property is compared with other person AOIs, to indicate the degree of similarity between different persons and produce a correlation metric.

3.8   Final Stage - Re-identification Using Multiple Features

The detectors mentioned above are executed for every person detected in each camera and attributes saved in a tuple data structure. Every second, a function that compares the data structure of both cameras is executed. The clothing type, clothes color, and histograms from different feeds are compared with each other. For a successful re-identification clothes type and color feature aggregations need to match, followed by valid histograms comparison on segmented persons. The time person took to maneuver from a camera to another is then calculated. If the person was linked to a vehicle, the vehicle ID is also displayed.

3.9   Ethical Considerations

To safeguard the identity of the participants, no personal data was collected prior to their participation. The findings required for this study, which provides information related to the participants, will be stored in a CSV format and consists of random person unique ID generated from the tracking algorithm, clothing type, clothing color, histogram, and the assigned car's ID.

4   Findings and Discussion of Results

The final prototype was tested using four different scenarios. Each scenario includes two video feeds captured from two different cameras. To successfully fulfill the aims of this study and directly address the key issue of developing security systems, it is ideal to have the live feeds captured within the parking lot and the other in areas where re-identification upon entrance or existing premises is required. For testing purpose camera 1 is located in a parking lot to extract the detected person attributes and assign the car to the person with the highest IoU. Meanwhile, camera 2 is located in an exit to re-identify the same person. The histogram of each following test is generated with a *no-background* detection to remove any cluttered background that can affect the histogram visualisation.

(a) Camera 1   (b) Camera 2

(c) Camera 1 Person Attributes   (d) Camera 2 Person Attributes

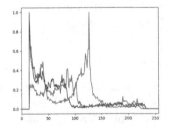
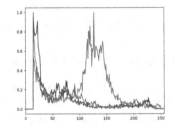

(e) Person Histogram Detected in   (f) Person Histogram Detected in
Camera 1   Camera 2

Fig. 4. Single person re-identification

4.1 Single Person Comparison from 2 Separate Feeds

As shown in Fig. 4f, the results of the person attributes detected in Fig. 4a and b match with the human observed ground truth. Since both cameras have a clear visibility and adequate lighting, the detection is highly accurate.

(a) Image A   (b) Image A

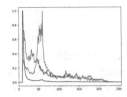

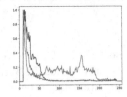

(c) Person A Attributes in Camera 1   (d) Person A Attributes in Camera 2

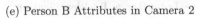

(e) Person B Attributes in Camera 2

(f) Person A Histogram in   (g) Person A Histogram in   (h) Person B Histogram in
Camera 1   Camera 2   Camera 2

Fig. 5. Comparison between three person through two feeds

4.2   Multiple Persons Comparison from 2 Separate Feeds

As presented in Fig. 5, Person A and Person B were detected. This scenario also tests the simultaneous detection of more than one person as showcased in camera 2 were both persons are detected. The attributes detected in Fig. 5a and b matched each other and the ground truth observation. Person B, was detected only in Fig. 5b, with the only attribute that did not match with the ground truth results being the clothes type color. Lighting in parking lots can vary, especially lighter colors, including white, which, despite image pre-processing, can be easily conflicted with the color grey in areas with poor lighting. However, given the multiple attribute and temporal approaches a single attribute mismatch was mitigated by the other attributes and temporal aggregation.

Ground-Truth Test Results: Accuracy was calculated for short-range and long-range re-identifications in different car-park scenarios. The short-range re-identification achieved an impressive result of an average of 95.66% and in long-range the system achieved 51.33% accuracy. From the results documented in Table 1 our system managed to achieve a high level of accuracy compared with other studies. The results show that accuracy is based on re-identification by using feature extraction from the detected person similar to other studies, with the advantage that in this study, the re-identification is done by identifying the person and extracting their features from the live feed in real-time and by using a low-cost system using computer vision.

Table 1. Accuracy comparison with other studies

	Accuracy (rank-1)
This study: YOLOv5 + Short Range Re-Identification	**95.66%**
Other study: Re-ID based on CAM to CAM topology [4]	92.35%
Other study: Re-Identification using Radio Signals [7]	83.6%
This study: YOLOv5 + Long Range Re-Identification	**51.33%**
Other study: Salient Color Names for Person Re-identification [22]	37.80%

Approach Limitations: While the short-range results were highly satisfactory, the long-range (>15 m) re-identification 51.33% accuracy was mainly due to false positives due to the segmented image being low in quality. The longer the distance the more a person's features were likely to be classified incorrectly. In the case of the short-range re-identification, the small number of false positives occurred due to different lighting conditions between the cameras that might affect the detected person feature attributes since in camera 1 the videos are captured indoors, and camera 2 videos are captured outdoors with better lighting. Although the solution was tested in different scenarios and thresholds adjusted to account for similarly dressed persons, the probability of identifying similarly dressed persons as same increases especially at long range. Temporal aggregation of data and a higher threshold for a valid histogram comparison match was found to reduce false positive matches. The best histogram comparison score threshold was found to be 45%. This threshold was established following a series of ground-truth tests in different scenarios.

5   Conclusion

This study aimed to successfully process a re-identification of detected persons using two cameras running simultaneously in real-time and calculate the time taken by a person to maneuver from one camera one to another. This was achieved by; first, persons or objects are detected using YOLOv5, feature attributes of the person are extracted and saved, with the data structure compared with other persons detected in another camera. Various studies aim to find matches with the given query image of a person from different datasets that consists of numerous person images. The majority of the systems take a significant amount of time to re-identify the person using this method since the datasets consist of large amounts of images. We found that re-identification can be successfully done by extracting the person features attributes. We also used an IoU metric to assign a vehicle to a person and persist the connection only as required. The elapsed time calculation between appearance in different feeds is useful for car park control and emergencies. The re-identification results show that most feature attributes were correctly identified since a high re-identification accuracy was achieved, especially in short-range detections. Most of the false positives that occurred were when the person detected was distant, and the image was of poor quality. Another observed limitation was lighting quality. In very low-light cases we witnessed a negative impact on feature extraction accuracy. Hardware requirements were kept low, with a standard 6 GB Nvidia GTX GPU able to adequately handle two camera processes and the re-identification algorithm in separate processing threads.

Although the proposed solution achieved impressive results, especially in short-range live feeds, the final re-identification formula can be improved by considering other features like, for example, shoes and head-wear. Further tests and improvement through the integration of our prototype solution with a professional CCTV system are also suggested.

References

1. Ahmed, E., Jones, M., Marks, T.K.: An improved deep learning architecture for person re-identification. In: Proceedings of the IEEE Conference on Computer Vision and Pattern Recognition, pp. 3908–3916 (2015)
2. An, L., Chen, X., Kafai, M., Yang, S., Bhanu, B.: Improving person re-identification by soft biometrics based reranking. In: 2013 7th International Conference on Distributed Smart Cameras (ICDSC), pp. 1–6. IEEE (2013)

3. Andriluka, M., Roth, S., Schiele, B.: People-tracking-by-detection and people-detection-by-tracking. In: 2008 IEEE Conference on Computer Vision and Pattern Recognition, pp. 1–8. IEEE (2008)
4. Cho, Y.J., Kim, S.A., Park, J.H., Lee, K., Yoon, K.J.: Joint person re-identification and camera network topology inference in multiple cameras. Comput. Vis. Image Underst. **180**, 34–46 (2019)
5. Deakin, R., Bird, S., Grenfell, R.: The centroid? Where would you like it to be be? Cartography **31**(2), 153–167 (2002)
6. Dikmen, M., Akbas, E., Huang, T.S., Ahuja, N.: Pedestrian recognition with a learned metric. In: Kimmel, R., Klette, R., Sugimoto, A. (eds.) ACCV 2010. LNCS, vol. 6495, pp. 501–512. Springer, Heidelberg (2011). https://doi.org/10.1007/978-3-642-19282-1_40
7. Fan, L., Li, T., Fang, R., Hristov, R., Yuan, Y., Katabi, D.: Learning longterm representations for person re-identification using radio signals. In: Proceedings of the IEEE/CVF Conference on Computer Vision and Pattern Recognition, pp. 10699–10709 (2020)
8. Gong, S., Cristani, M., Loy, C.C., Hospedales, T.M.: The re-identification challenge. In: Gong, S., Cristani, M., Yan, S., Loy, C.C. (eds.) Person Re-Identification. ACVPR, pp. 1–20. Springer, London (2014). https://doi.org/10.1007/978-1-4471-6296-4_1
9. Hou, L., Wan, W., Hwang, J.-N., Muhammad, R., Yang, M., Han, K.: Human tracking over camera networks: a review. EURASIP J. Adv. Sig. Process. **2017**(1), 1–20 (2017). https://doi.org/10.1186/s13634-017-0482-z
10. Kawanishi, Y., Deguchi, D., Ide, I., Murase, H.: Trajectory ensemble: multiple persons consensus tracking across non-overlapping multiple cameras over randomly dropped camera networks. In: Proceedings of the IEEE Conference on Computer Vision and Pattern Recognition Workshops, pp. 56–62 (2017)
11. Li, W., Wang, X.: Locally aligned feature transforms across views. In: Proceedings of the IEEE Conference on Computer Vision and Pattern Recognition, pp. 3594–3601 (2013)
12. Li, W., Zhao, R., Xiao, T., Wang, X.: DeepReID: deep filter pairing neural network for person re-identification. In: Proceedings of the IEEE Conference on Computer Vision and Pattern Recognition, pp. 152–159 (2014)
13. Liem, M.C., Gavrila, D.M.: Joint multi-person detection and tracking from overlapping cameras. Comput. Vis. Image Underst. **128**, 36–50 (2014)
14. Mittal, A., Davis, L.S.: M2Tracker: a multi-view approach to segmenting and tracking people in a cluttered scene. Int. J. Comput. Vis. **51**(3), 189–203 (2003)
15. Papineau, D.: Can we really see a million colors (2015)
16. Perwaiz, N., Fraz, M.M., Shahzad, M.: Person re-identification using hybrid representation reinforced by metric learning. IEEE Access **6**, 77334–77349 (2018)
17. Rahimpour, A., Liu, L., Taalimi, A., Song, Y., Qi, H.: Person re-identification using visual attention. In: 2017 IEEE International Conference on Image Processing (ICIP), pp. 4242–4246. IEEE (2017)
18. Ristani, E., Solera, F., Zou, R., Cucchiara, R., Tomasi, C.: Performance measures and a data set for multi-target, multi-camera tracking. In: Hua, G., Jégou, H. (eds.) ECCV 2016. LNCS, vol. 9914, pp. 17–35. Springer, Cham (2016). https://doi.org/10.1007/978-3-319-48881-3_2
19. Rout, R.K.: A survey on object detection and tracking algorithms. Ph.D. thesis, National Institute of Technology Rourkela (2013)
20. Saghafi, M.A., Hussain, A., Zaman, H.B., Saad, M.H.M.: Review of person re-identification techniques. IET Comput. Vis. **8**(6), 455–474 (2014)

21. Wang, X., Zheng, W.S., Li, X., Zhang, J.: Cross-scenario transfer person reidentification. IEEE Trans. Circ. Syst. Video Technol. **26**(8), 1447–1460 (2015)
22. Yang, Y., Yang, J., Yan, J., Liao, S., Yi, D., Li, S.Z.: Salient color names for person re-identification. In: Fleet, D., Pajdla, T., Schiele, B., Tuytelaars, T. (eds.) ECCV 2014. LNCS, vol. 8689, pp. 536–551. Springer, Cham (2014). https://doi.org/10.1007/978-3-319-10590-1_35

A Method for Transferring Robot Motion Parameters Using Functional Attributes of Parts

Takahiro Suzuki$^{(\boxtimes)}$ and Manabu Hashimoto

Chukyo University, 101-2 Yagoto-honmachi Showa-ku, Nagoya, Aichi, Japan
{suzuki,mana}@isl.sist.chukyo-u.ac.jp

Abstract. We propose a method for automatically transferring robot motion parameters among parts. Various parts are used for assembly in factories, for example, "connecting rods", "gears", and "links". During robotic assembly, operators have to assign robot motion parameters for each assembly part, which is time-consuming. Many assembly parts often have the same name and similar functionality but different shapes and sizes. For example, all connecting rods have two ring-shaped holes and a long rod-shaped part that connects them. Therefore, if the parts are in the same category, each part has a common "function". We focus on such "functions". The robot motion parameters are transferred among parts using these "functions". We conducted experiments to evaluate the proposed method involving two types of parts, connecting rods and links. The component-insertion success rate of approximately 80% or more was obtained. With this method, the time required for an operator to transfer robot motion parameters is reduced.

Keywords: Robot motion transferring · Functional-attribute recognition · Physical simulation

1 Introduction

Various parts are used for assembly in factories, for example, "connecting rods", "gears", "links". When manufacturers want to use industrial robots for automated lines, operators have to assign detailed motion parameters to the robots such as grasping point, approaching angle, and smooth trajectory of the robot hand. However, some parts have different shapes and sizes but categorized under the same name. For example, there are many types of connecting rods, but they all have two ring-shaped elements and a bar-shape element. Also, "bolts", all have a threaded rod-shaped part and a part that comes into contacts with a wrench. Such groups of parts are defined as "categories".

Assembly-robot operators used to assign robot motion parameters for each part even if in the same category. However, this is time-consuming. Current methods address this problem by automatically detecting the grasping point. For example, Zhao et al. [1] and Kumra et al. [2] automatically detected a "grasping

© Springer Nature Switzerland AG 2021
G. Bebis et al. (Eds.): ISVC 2021, LNCS 13018, pp. 154–165, 2021.
https://doi.org/10.1007/978-3-030-90436-4_12

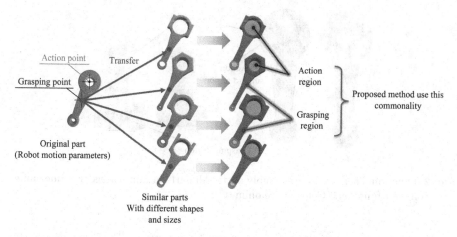

Fig. 1. With proposed method, grasping and action points are transferred from original part to similar parts, during which commonality of "function" is used. This reduces time required for manually assigning such parameters.

point" using a convolutional neural network. Quillen et al. [3] proposed a method for enabling robots to grasp using reinforcement learning. Pattern et al. [4], Liu et al. [5], Chen et al. [6], and Kevinet et al. [7] automatically detected robot motion parameters of target objects on the basis of the experience of successfully grasping the object in the past. Yang et al. [8] detected a grasping point using object attributes. However, these methods detect robot motion parameters required for pick&place work in which a robot grasps an object and places it at another. That is, this parameter does not take into account the motion after grasping. Therefore, during assembly, this work may not be executed due to the grasping point of the object. Ruinian et al. [9] detected the grasping points of everyday objects and how to handle them by deep learning. However, since this method was developed for everyday objects, it is unclear whether it can be applied to assembly in factories.

We propose a method for automatically transferring robot motion parameters after grasping an object during assembly. Parts used in factories have "functions", and all parts in the same category always have a common function. The proposed method uses the commonality of functions between parts. The robot motion parameters assigned by assembly-robot operators for part A are automatically transferred to part B in the same category on the basis of the common function (Fig. 1). The main contributions of this paper are as follows.

- Automatically transfer robot motion parameters during assembly.
- Minimize manual assigning by assembly-robot operators during assembly.

2   Problem Formulation

The robot motion parameter assignment reduction problem is formulated as follows:

Fig. 2. Functional attributes of assembly parts. All parts in same category (same name) have common function. (Color figure online)

Definition. Given point clouds of the robot motion parameters manually assigned to part A and unknown part B, which are in the same category, the goal is to automatically transfer the robot motion parameters of part A to part B.

The following are assumptions in this study.

Assumption. 1) Assembly parts are stably placed, and there is only one object in the scene. 2) The viewpoint of the camera is from above the parts. 3) Parts A and B are in the same category (same name). 4) The robot motion parameters assigned by operators are accurate.

3   Parts Function

3.1   "Part Functions" of Industrial Parts

Figure 2 shows an example of the parts used during assembly. The parts have "functions". We defined three functions for this study.

The first function is "grasping". The blue region in Fig. 2 is defined as the grasping region. When a human or robot inserts a connecting rod into a shaft, they grasp the bar-shaped region between two ring-shaped regions. When they insert a bolt into the screw hole, they grasp a part that comes into contact with a wrench. Therefore, the grasping region includes the points at which humans and robots grasp.

The second function is "action". The red region in Fig. 2 is defined as the action region. In a connecting rod, a ring-shaped region is inserted into the shaft. For bolts, a threaded rod-shaped part is inserted in the screw hole. Therefore, a part has a point (action point) at which it can be connected to other parts.

The third function is "action support". The yellow region in Fig. 2 is defined as the action support region. Certain parts, such as connecting rods and links, have holes in the action region. In this case, there is a region that surrounds the action region, i.e., a region that creates the action region. This region is the

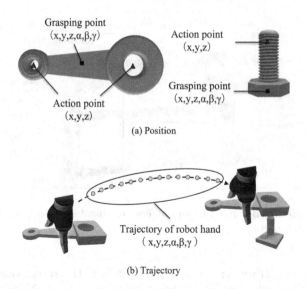

(a) Position

(b) Trajectory

Fig. 3. Robot motion parameter required for robot to assemble object. If this parameter can be recognized, robot can assemble object.

action support region. Parts that do not have holes in the action region (e.g., connectors, bolts, etc.) do not have an action support region.

All parts in the same category have a common function.

3.2 Robot Motion Parameters for Assembly

There are two robot motion parameters that an operator must assign to a robot for assembly.

The first parameter is related to the position such as the grasping and action points (Fig. 3(a)). Assembly consists of two motions: a robot grasping a part and connecting it to other parts. That is, an object can be assembled if two points are known: 1) at which the part is grasped (grasping point) and 2) at which it is connected to another part (action point). A grasping point consists of **x,y,z** in three-dimensional (3D) space and α, β, γ, which are the grasping angles. An action point consists of **x,y,z** in 3D space.

The second parameter is related to the trajectory of the robot hand (Fig. 3(b)). During assembly, it is necessary to move a part between grasping the part and connecting it to another part. The trajectory of the robot hand when moving a part is the parameters related to it. This parameter consists of a sequence of points. These points consist of **x,y,z** in 3D space. During assembly, an object can be assembled by matching the action-point of the grasping part (e.g., connecting rod) with the position of the part (e.g., shaft) to be connected. For example, when inserting a connecting rod into a shaft, the ring-shaped region is matched to the shaft. In other words, if there is no obstacle to the robot's movement during connection from the grasping point, it is not necessary to uniquely

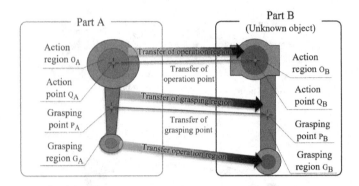

Fig. 4. Basic idea Robot motion parameters are transferred on basis of functional attributes between parts.

determine the trajectory on the way. By matching the start point of the 3D vector **v** from the action point to the grasping point with the position of the part to be connected (e.g., shaft), the end point of **v** becomes the position of the robot hand when connecting to another part. That is, the position of the robot hand during assembly is determined from the positional relationship between the grasping and action points.

3.3 Basic Idea of Proposed Method Regarding Functional Attributes of Parts

The basic idea of the proposed method is shown in Fig. 4. When transferring the grasping and action points from part A to part B, the major obstacle is the difference in shape and size between the parts. Parts A and B have different shapes and sizes. For example, part B is larger than part A and the head of part A is circular, but the head of part B is a mixture of circles and squares. Therefore, it is difficult to directly transfer robot motion parameters from part A to part B. A common function between parts is used to transfer such parameters from part A to part B while avoiding differences in shape and size.

The flow of the proposed method is as follows and show in Fig. 5. Grasping region of part A G_A and that of part B G_B are first matched. Next, on the basis of this correspondence, grasping point P_A is transferred to grasping point P_B. The action point is also transferred in the same manner. Finally, the operating pattern is transferred from the positional relationship between the grasping and action points.

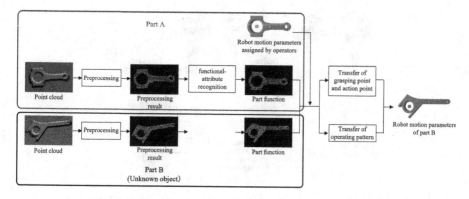

Fig. 5. Flow of proposed method. First, determine and match functional attributes of parts A and B. Next, transfer grasping and action points. Finally, transfer operating pattern.

4 Proposed Method for Transferring Robot Motion Parameters

The proposed method consists of three modules.

4.1 Module for Functional-Attribute Recognition

In this module, the input point cloud is segmented into functional attributes consisting of a grasping region, action region, and action support region. For preprocessing, the plane and noise are removed from the input point cloud. Next, this point cloud is input to PointNet++ [10] and segmented into functional attributes. If the action region has holes, the region is extracted from the action support region. PointNet++ is a deep neural network that performs classification and segmentation of point clouds and has spatial transformer networks (STN) [11] for robustness against geometric transformation of a point cloud. In factories, parts are placed in various orientations, so robustness geometric transformation is required.

4.2 Module for Transferring of Grasping and Action Points

This module transfers the grasping point(action point) of part A assigned by operators to part B. The grasping and action points are transferred using the same algorithm. The flow of transferring grasping and action points is shown in Fig. 6.

A local reference frame is first set for the center-of-gravity points of the functional region of parts A and B. The first axis of the local reference frame is a vector from the center of gravity to that of the other region. The second axis is the normal vector of the plane detected from the point cloud around the center of gravity. The first and second axes are orthogonalized by Gram-Schmidt

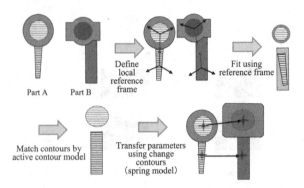

Fig. 6. Details of transferring grasping and action points.

orthonormalization. The third axis is calculated from the outer product of the first and second axes.

Each point cloud of the functional region is then coarse fitted on the basis of the calculated local reference frame.

Next, the contours of the coarse fitted point cloud are matched using an active contour model [12]. With the proposed method, the contour (initial position) of part A is moved to match that (optimal position) of part B. The objective function ($\fallingdotseq$ energy function of the active contour model) is, the overlap rate of the region surrounded by the contours of point cloud of parts A and B. Intersection over Union is used to calculate this rate. The optimal position is the contour position when the overlap rate exceeds the set threshold.

Finally, on the basis of the deformation of the contour, the grasping and action points are transferred from part A to part B. A simple physics-simulation method using a spring model is applied to the transferring of points. The insides of the grasping and action regions of part A are discretized into mass points to construct a spring model. The displacement of the contour part (result of the previous stage processing) is regarded as the external force of the spring model, and the displacement inside the region is calculated. The transfer result is the point after moving the mass point nearest the grasping point(action point) assigned by the operator.

4.3   Transferring Operating Pattern

The operating pattern is the trajectory of the robot hand until the robot grasps a part and connects it to other parts. Therefore, as described in Sect. 3, the trajectory of the robot hand is determined only from the grasping point of the part and the connecting point to other parts. The vector **v** between the grasping and action points is calculated, and the operating pattern is determined from **v**.

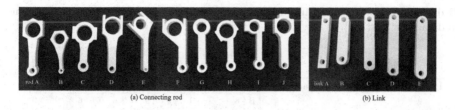

(a) Connecting rod   (b) Link

Fig. 7. Parts used in experiments.

5   Experiments on Transferring Robot Motion Parameters

5.1   Setup

The experimental setup was as follows. The OS was Ubuntu 18.04, CPU was Intel CORE i9, GPU was GeForce GTX1660Ti, robot operating system (ROS) was Melodic, robot was UR5, and robot hand was Robotiq 2F-85. A connecting rod was inserted into the shaft, and the grasping and action points of a link were transferred. The parts used in the experiments are shown in Fig. 7. We used ten types of connecting rods and five types of links. These parts were fabricated by printing a model created using 3D-CAD software with a 3D printer. The sizes of the connecting rods were 15 to 22 cm in length, 5 to 10 cm in width, and 4 or 6 cm in hole diameter. The sizes of the links were 18 to 24 cm in length, 3 or 4 cm in width, and 2 cm in hole diameter.

In the learning of PointNet++ used for functional-attribute recognition, 3D models of the various connecting rods and links were created, and humans annotated the functional- attributes. Next, the data were converted into a point cloud of 2.5D data viewed from certain viewpoints. The learning parameters of Point-Net++ are 300 epochs, batch size of 16, 2048 points per data, and the number of data is 8400 The termination condition in a model, such as the active contour model is when the overlap rate is higher than 0.93. The parameters of the spring model are a spring constant of 300, damped constant of 30, viscous resistance of 0.2, mass of mass points of 0.2, step time of 0.001, and iteration count of 5000.

In the experiment involving connecting rods, the robot inserted a connecting rod into a shaft on the basis of the transfer result of the robot motion parameters with the proposed method. The shaft diameters were 3.5 and 5.5 cm, and the tolerance between the connecting rod and shaft was 0.5 cm. The motion procedure of the robot was as follows. It first, moved over the connecting rod and obtained the point cloud. It then, grasped the grasping point of the connecting rod transferred with the proposed method. Next, it moved the connecting rod so that the action point was on the shaft. The position of the shaft was assigned in advance. Finally, it inserted the connecting rod into the shaft.

We created pairs of a connecting rod, to which an operator assign robot motion parameters, and an unknown type of connecting rod from ten parts to show in Fig. 7. We operated the robot for ten trials for each connecting rod pair and determined the success or failure on whether the robot was able to insert

Table 1. Number of successful robot motions using connecting rods (Each connecting rod pair for 10 trials).

		Transfer destination									
		A	B	C	D	E	F	G	H	I	J
Part with operator-assigned parameters	A	–	9	10	7	10	10	7	10	10	10
	B	8	–	9	9	9	9	9	6	9	9
	C	9	10	–	7	10	8	7	9	8	9
Average (Proposed)		8.5	9.5	9.5	7.7	9.7	9.0	7.7	8.3	9.0	9.3
Without transferring		10	1	0	8	0	0	9	2	0	1

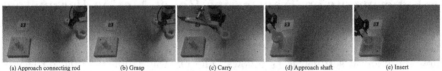

(a) Approach connecting rod   (b) Grasp   (c) Carry   (d) Approach shaft   (e) Insert

Fig. 8. Motions of robot inserting connecting rod into shaft.

the connecting rod into the shaft. An operator assigned robot motion parameters for three types of connecting rods. We used a method of detecting the grasping and action points with a common algorithm as a comparison method. With this method, the grasping point is the center of gravity of the part., a hole is detected from the point cloud of that part, and the center of gravity is action point. In other words, the comparison method does not transfer but only recognizes the grasping and action points.

In the experiment involving links, we fabricated five types of links; thus, 20 pairs were used. We created pairs of a link, to which an operator assign robot motion parameters, and an unknown link from ten parts to show in Fig. 7. This experiment involved 10 trials per pair, and it was visually confirmed whether robot motion parameters were successful.

5.2   Experimental Results

The results from the experiment using connecting rods are listed in Table 1, and the motions of the robot inserting a connecting rod into a shaft are shown in Fig. 8. The rows of the table show the IDs of the connecting rods to which an operator assigned the robot motion parameters, and the columns show the IDs of the connecting rod for which the robot motion parameters were transferred. The IDs correspond to those in Fig. 6. The table also shows the number of successful robot motions in the ten trials. For example, the number of successful robot motions was nine out of ten when the motion parameters of part A were transferred to part B with the proposed method. When the connecting rods were the same in the pair, it was not necessary to transfer the robot motion parameters. The second line from the bottom shows the average number of successful robot motions with the proposed method, the bottom line shows the average

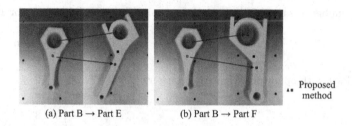

(a) Part B → Part E   (b) Part B → Part F   Proposed method

Fig. 9. Transferred robot motion parameters. Green points are those assigned by operator, red points are those transferred with proposed method, and the blue points are those detected with comparison method. (Color figure online)

number of successful robot motions with the comparison method. For example, for part A, the average number of successful robot motions with the proposed method was 8.5, and that with the comparison method was 10. The average success rate of robot motions with the proposed method was 87.8%, and that with the comparison method was 31%. Compared with the comparison method, the proposed method had a higher number of successful robot motions in seven of the ten parts.

The transferred robot motion parameters are shown in Fig. 9. Because the comparison method detects the grasping point on the basis of rule (grasping point is the center of gravity of the part and hole of the center of gravity is action point.), it is not always possible to detect an optimal point for grasping. When the robot attempted to grasp the blue point (with comparison method), the grasping was unstable due to the shape of the surrounding part. With the proposed method, the robot grasped a part stably because the region where it can be stably grasped was extracted on the basis on by the functional attributes. There were a few failures in robot motion (connecting rods failed to be inserted in the shaft) with the proposed method. The causes of the failure are that the action point was transferred to an incorrect position, and that the parts moved when the robot grasped it, causing the action point to shift. This is because the termination condition was set to 0.93 (overlap rate) and the contours did not match, causing a shift between the grasping and action points. However, if the termination condition is too large, the number of calculations will be enormous, and the processing time will be long. Therefore, the termination condition should be determined while considering the processing time and success rate of the robot motion.

The results from the experiment involving links are shown in Table 2. The reading of this table is the same as in Table 1. The IDs correspond to those in Fig. 6. The table shows the number of successful robot motions out of ten trials. The transferred robot motion parameters are shown in Fig. 10. The average success rate of robot motions with the proposed method was 86.5% One of the causes of transfer failure was misrecognition of functional attributes. Because there is no change in shape between the grasping region and action support region, it is difficult to clearly segment the functional attribute of the link.

Table 2. Number of successful robot motions using links (each link pair for 10 trials)

		Transfer destination				
		A	B	C	D	E
Part with operator-assigned parameters	A	–	7	10	8	9
	B	7	–	8	8	7
	C	9	8	–	9	8
	D	10	8	10	–	9
	E	10	8	10	10	–

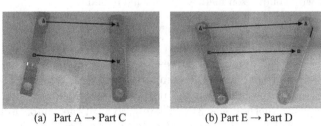

(a) Part A → Part C   (b) Part E → Part D

Fig. 10. Transferred robot motion parameters.

One solution to this problem is to use an algorithm that revises the result of functional-attribute recognition by PointNet++ from statistical information on the functional attribute.

6   Conclusion

We focused on the common functions between two different parts and proposed a method of automatically transferring robot motion parameters among parts. By introducing this method to factories, manually assigning such parameters during assembly can be reduced. In the experiment using connecting rods, the average success rate of robot motions with the proposed method was 87.8% and that of the comparison method was 31%. In the experiment using links, the average success rate of robot motion with the proposed method was 86.5% Parts are randomly stacked in factories, so we will investigate a method that can be applied to such situations for future work. Since one object is created from multiple parts in actual assembly, we will also investigate a method that can be applied to such assembly.

Acknowledgements. This paper is based on results obtained from a project, JPNP20006, commissioned by the New Energy and Industrial Technology Development Organization (NEDO).

References

1. Zhao, J., Liang, J., Kroemer, O.: Towards precise robotic grasping by probabilistic post-grasp displacement estimation. In: FSR (2019)
2. Kumra, S., Kanan, C.: Robotic grasp detection using deep convolutional neural networks. In: IROS (2017)
3. Quillen, D., Jang, E., Nachum, O., Finn, C., Ibarz, J., Levine, S.: Deep reinforcement learning for vision-based robotic grasping: a simulated comparative evaluation of off-policy methods. In: ICRA (2018)
4. Pattern, T., Park, K., Vincze, M.: DGCM-Net: dense geometrical correspondence matching network for incremental experience-based robotic grasping. Front. Rob. AI **7**(120), 1–18 (2020)
5. Liu, C., Li, W., Sun, F., Zhang, J.: Grasp planning by human experience on a variety of objects with complex geometry. In: IROS (2015)
6. Chen, X., Ghadirzadeh, A., Bhorkman, M., Jensfelt, P.: Adversarial feature training for generalizable robotic visuomotor control. In: ICRA (2020)
7. Kevin, Z., Andy, Z., Johnny, L., Shuran, S.: Form2Fit: learning shape priors for generalizable assembly from disassembly. In: ICRA (2020)
8. Yang, Y., Liu, Y., Liang, H., Lou, X., Choi, C.: Attribute-based robotic grasping with one-grasp adaptation. In: ICRA (2021)
9. Ruinian, X., Fu-jen, C., Chao, T., Weiyu, L., Patricio, A.: An affordance keypoint detection network for robot manipulation. In: ICRA (2021)
10. Charles, R. Qi., Li, Y., Hao, S., Leonidas, J. Guibas.: PointNet++: deep hierarchical feature learning on point sets in a metric space. In: NIPS (2017)
11. Jaderberg, M., Simonyan, K., Zisserman, A., Kavukcuoglu, K.: Spatial transformer networks. In: NIPS (2015)
12. Kass, M., Witkin, A., Terzopoulos, D.: Snakes: active contour models. Int. J. Comput. Vis. **1**(4), 321–331 (1988)

Uncooperative Satellite 6D Pose Estimation with Relative Depth Information

Jingrui Song[1,2(✉)], Shuling Hao[2], and Kefeng Xu[2]

[1] University of Chinese Academy of Sciences, Beijing, China
songjingrui18@mails.ucas.ac.cn
[2] Institute of Software, Chinese Academy of Sciences, Beijing, China
{shuling,kefeng}@iscas.ac.cn

Abstract. The pose estimation of satellites or non-cooperative space targets is of great significance for evaluating their operating conditions, threatness and so on. With the development of ground-based Adaptive Optics (AO) systems, the imaging quality of optical systems for space targets has been greatly improved. We can estimate the space target pose in these AO images with computer vision algorithms. However, the image degradation during the imaging process of AO systems complicates the problem. This paper takes the Tiangong-1 satellite as an example to solve the simulation problem of ground-based optical imaging and the single-shot 6D pose estimation problem. We first propose a satellite image rendering pipeline based on the influence of atmospheric turbulence, built on Tiangong-1, which is used to generate spacecraft pose annotated data. Through this method, we obtain image data similar to the real image, that can be used to train and evaluate neural networks. Secondly, we propose a deep learning framework based on YOLO-6D, providing fast and accurate pose estimation. In particular, we introduce a relative depth prediction branch, which predicts the relative depth while estimating the satellite pose. Preliminary experimental results indicate that this method is suitable for the Tiangong-1 dataset and has achieved good performance.

Keywords: Uncooperative satellites · Image simulation · 6D pose estimation · Convolutional neural networks · Depth information

1 Introduction

As human space activities continue to be active, there are more and more inactive satellites and space fragments in low-earth orbit, resulting in an increasingly complex space environment. Many institutions in academia and industry are committed to predicting the posture of these space objects in order to solve problems such as on-orbit proximity operations in space rendezvous, docking, and debris removal [6–8]. Many academic projects have been carried out, including the Phoenix program by DARPA [13], the RemoveDEBRIS program mission

© Springer Nature Switzerland AG 2021
G. Bebis et al. (Eds.): ISVC 2021, LNCS 13018, pp. 166–177, 2021.
https://doi.org/10.1007/978-3-030-90436-4_13

by Surrey Space Center [12], and the Restore-L mission by NASA [14]. According to the different observation carriers, we divide the space target image into two types, ground-based observation image and space-based observation image. Space-based observation images are mainly taken by the camera carried by the satellite itself. Due to the limitations of the satellite's own resources and energy, this type of camera is usually a monocular camera and does not have particularly superior performance. Ground-based observation images are mainly obtained by ground-based optical telescopes. Due to the complex light environment in space and the lack of real data, the two are more challenging. For space-based imagery, it faces more serious backlighting and no-light environment and the interference of the earth background. The projects mentioned above is mainly based on space-based observation pictures. For ground-based images, there are more problems with the degradation of objects after long-distance imaging through the telescope, such as the inability to distinguish the relative distance of the objects in the image. Unlike space-based images, there is still a lack of relevant research on ground-based optical load imaging. Tiangong-1 was China's prototype space station, serving as a crewed laboratory and an experimental testbed from September 2011 to April 2018. At around 8:15 on April 2, 2018, it reentered the atmosphere and plunged into the central area of the South Pacific. This paper takes the Tiangong-1 satellite as an example to estimate the pose of single-view images under ground-based observation.

6D pose estimation is a traditional computer vision problem. The development of deep learning has played an important role in promoting the 6D pose estimation problem. More and more solutions based on deep learning have achieved good results [19–22]. An important feature of deep learning is to rely on large annotated datasets. Although there is a lot of open-source 3D annotated data such as LINEMOD [23] and YCB-Video [24], there is still a pressing need for space target pose estimation to build usable datasets. And also annotating 3D datasets is expensive and time-consuming work. So, most jobs will use simulation data to solve problems. The work of this paper continues the traditional approach. However, rendering the generated data directly through the CAD model will result in a large "gap" between generated "real" images and real-world images. In order to address these difficulties, we proposed a pipeline based on Blender that simulates ground-based optical telescope imaging.

Another problem of uncooperative satellite pose estimation is that the CCD (Charge-Coupled Device) imaging system of the ground-based optical telescope will be affected by various factors during the imaging process, atmospheric turbulence, noise in the imaging process, and optical diffraction, resulting in blur and degradation. Besides, compared with depth images, single-view RGB images exhibit inherent depth ambiguity, which makes satellite 6D pose estimation more challenging. In this paper, we propose a novel deep learning pose estimation framework based on YOLO-6D. Which can not only provides shape constraints but also provide relative depth information.

The rest of the paper is organized as follows. Sections 2 details some outstanding 6D pose estimation approaches and simulation frameworks. Image simulation pipeline and network architecture are in Sect. 3. And in Sect. 4, We did a detailed comparative experiment. Finally, Sect. 5 concludes this paper.

2   Related Works

For a long time, the lack of 6D pose datasets has always plagued the application of deep learning to 6D pose estimation. And with the advent of deep learning, the demand for accurately annotated training images increased a lot, resulting in some large real and synthetic datasets such as LINEMOD dataset [23] and YCB Video dataset [24]. However for specific tasks (special domain like space targets) annotated data is still lacking. To address this, many methods have been proposed to generate high-quality images, which can be used for training. NVIDIA Deep Learning Dataset Synthesizer (NDDS) [15], VisII-A VIrtual Scene Interface [16], AI Habitat [17], Stilleben [18] are all excellent simulation frameworks. Meanwhile, these methods have a flaw. They do not generalize well to real image datasets of satellite due to the domain shift between image features. In other words, there is a gap between real images and simulated images.

Due to the lack of depth information, single-view 6D pose estimation is more challenging. The main methods to solve monocular 6D pose estimation are template-matching and feature-matching. The main features of template-based method are that the algorithm is very robust when the object is well textured, but it is difficult to deal with low-resolution weakly textured objected. Traditional feature-matching mainly calculates six parameters by establishing the relationship between the 3D model and the 2D pixel location, then using the perspective-n-Point algorithm to recover the pose. They mostly rely on hand-crafted features, but it is easy to fail for our images, because of the instability of feature points during imaging processing. Recent years, inspired by the significant improvement of CNN networks, many approaches therefore focus on improving this problem. One type of the method is to directly predict 6D pose from the image [9,25], but this scheme has poor generalization ability, because it is not clear whether the network structure can effectively learn the feature representation of the pose space. Thus, many approaches turned to the two-stage method, using a specific representation as an intermediate representation (keypoints, heatmap, vector, etc.). First, predict the intermediate representation, then use the PNP algorithm to predict the 6D pose. A single-shot CNN architecture is proposed without posterior refinement [1]. By predicting 3D bounding box vertices and then using PNP algorithm to recover 6D pose, the prediction results can be obtained at a faster speed. [26] proposed a heatmap-based approach for a more robust prediction of occluded objects. In order to solve the prediction problem of occluded objects, many approaches turned to dense method from sparse method. Peng Sida et al. [27] proposed an intermediate representation based on vector-filed, and then voted for the keypoint locations through RANSAC, which not only provides more abundant location information but also be an ideal representation for occluded objects.

In this paper, we focus on 6D pose estimation from monocular RGB images, with depth information supervised, unlike in RGBD-based methods. The advantage of this is that we provide more constraint information for the model through the weak supervision of depth. At the same time, our network trained based on simulation data can easily migrate to real images without depth images.

3 Approach

Given an image observed by a ground-based optical telescope, our purpose is to estimate the 6D pose, 3D rotation R and 3D translation t of the object in camera coordinates. Just like other methods, We assume that the 3D model of the satellite is available. In order to solve the problem of lacking of real images and difficulty in calibrating, we propose a simulating image pipeline, using Blender to render multi-angle satellite images, and apply the degradation process of the telescope observation process to generate training data for reducing the gap between real data and simulated data. Secondly, inspired by YOLO-6D, we propose a framework based on depth supervision. One branch of the network predicts the 2D projection of the predefined keypoints, and the other branch predicts the relative depth of the 3D model projection. Through this scheme, the network can learn depth constraints and shape constraints. And compared to the depth-based 6D pose estimation method, it can easily migrate to real data without providing additional depth images. As a drawback, our network does not handle multiple objects.

Figure 1 depicts the corresponding workflow. In the remainder of this section, we will introduce our two-stream network architecture.

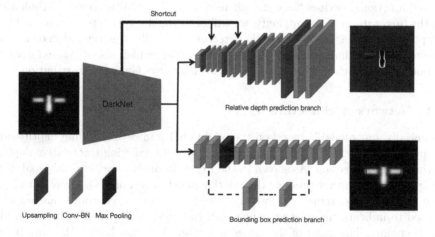

Fig. 1. The architecture of our approach. The input to the network is a single RGB image. The Darknet is used as an encoder to extract the features, while the two branches are used as the decoder.

3.1   Image Simulation

We propose a rendering pipeline to simulate the observation image of optical telescope, as shown in Fig. 2. BlenderProc [2] is a modular procedural pipeline that helps in generating real looking images for the training of convolutional neural networks. First, we made a CAD model of Tiangong-1 based on public data. Then we uniformly take a certain number of observation points on the surface of a sphere with a fixed radius around the CAD model, and use BlenderProc to render the image and its depth map at the corresponding angle. Of course, we randomly simulate the changes of the sun's rays. In practice, because the back-light can not get effective pictures, we randomly place the sun's light source near the camera. Besides, the satellite is a symmetrical object, which means the same rendered picture may correspond to more than one angle. In order to overcome such symmetry ambiguity, this paper adopts the method of [9], and only selects half of the observation points.

Affected by various factors including atmospheric turbulence, various noises, and optical diffraction, the imaging process of the CCD imaging system of the ground-based optical telescope will produce blurred and degraded images. The obtained image is the result of all the degradation processes, and the degradation process is linear for most imaging systems. Therefore, the image degradation process can be formulated as

$$g(x, y) = f(x, y) \otimes h(x, y) + n(x, y) \qquad (x, y) \in \Omega. \qquad (1)$$

In the formula, $g(x, y)$ represents the image collected by the CCD; $f(x, y)$ is the original image; $h(x, y)$ is the Point Spread Function(PSF); $n(x, y)$ represents the noise function. Ω is the image area, $\otimes$ is the convolution symbol. The point spread function describes the comprehensive influence of atmospheric turbulence on the target image. For simplicity, we will omit the derivation process here. The adaptive optics system uses a CCD detector. Normally, this type of detector is affected by two kinds of noise: one is photon noise, which obeys Poisson distribution, and the other is electronic noise, which obeys Gaussian distribution.

3.2   Network Architecture

Essentially, our model is based on the YOLO-6D framework, adding depth and shape constraints to the prediction of 6D pose, by predicting the relative depth of the model projection. As shown in the Fig. 1, in order to achieve this goal, we designed a stream that predicts the relative depth based on YOLO-6D, forming an encoder-decoder structure. Two branches have a common encoder, one branch is used to indicate the relative depth, and the other indicates 2D projection of the keypoints. The input of the model is a single full-color image, the output of branch 1 is a two-dimensional prediction projection of predefined keypoints, and the output of branch 2 is a relative depth map of the same size. The predefined keypoints are defined as 8 corners of the tight 3D bounding box fitted to the object's 3D model, and the ninth point is the center of the 3D model. Of course,

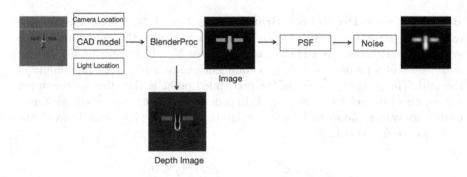

Fig. 2. The pipeline to simulate the observation image of optical telescope

you can also have other definitions, but the definition of 8 corners is universal and applies to all rigid bodies.

For the public encoder, we continue to use the darknet of YOLO-6D as the backbone, consisting of 15 convolutional layers and pooling layers. Through the encoder at the front of the network, a $416 \times 416 \times 3$ RGB image is extracted as a vector $26 \times 26 \times 256$. The two branches decode the vector and obtain the relative depth map and 2D projection of the key points. Since the two tasks belong to different branches, the relative depth prediction can provide certain parameter constraints for pose estimation. In order to train our model end-to-end, we define a loss function

$$Loss = \alpha L_{pos} + \beta L_{depth}. \tag{2}$$

It combines the loss functions of the two tasks and weighs them through two hyper-parameters α and β. We now turn to their individual descriptions.

Depth Prediction Branch. The purpose of the branch is mainly to decode the feature maps extracted by the encoder and generate the relative depth projection of the 3D models. Through decoding, the relative depth information of the monocular picture and its 2D more accurate contour can be obtained. Not only can the depth ambiguity be reduced, but it also produces a certain constraint on image noise. The branch is composed of 4 up-sampling layers, 13 convolutional layers with batch normalization and 3 shortcuts. After that, we use the Sigmoid function as activation function in the last convolutional layer. Let (I, D) denote a training sample, and I is a 2D rendering image of the 3D model under a certain viewing angle, D is the corresponding depth map, we normalize D to D_n:

$$D_n = \sum_{i,j} \frac{d_{max} - d_{i,j}}{d_{range}}. \tag{3}$$

To train the depth branch, we adopt the L1 norm to minimize the difference between the generated depth image $\widehat{D}$ and the corresponding ground truth D_n:

$$L_{depth} = L1_{loss}(\widehat{D}, D_n). \tag{4}$$

Bounding Box Prediction Branch. The Bound box prediction branch extends the structure of YOLO-6D. This branch divides the images into $S \times S$ grids. Each grid contains a D dimensional vector V, which consists of 2 coordinate values of 9 predefined points, a confidence value and a class probability of the grid. The predicted value of the predefined point is the offset of the upper left corner of the selected centre grid. In order to predict the location with high confidence values and avoid higher computational complexity, as in [1], we define a confidence function instead:

$$c(x) = \begin{cases} e^{\alpha(1-\frac{D_T(x)}{d_{th}})}, & \text{if } D_T(x) < d_{th} \\ 0, & \text{otherwise} \end{cases} \tag{5}$$

The function L_{pt} is based on the 2D Euclidean distance in the image space between the predicted coordinate value and the ground truth of the control points. Since it is almost impossible to have multiple targets in the field of view of the observation satellite, this network only considers the posture estimation of a single object. The L_{id} only needs to distinguish background and object. Therefore, the loss of this branch is:

$$L_{pos} = \lambda_{pt} L_{pt} + \lambda_{conf} L_{conf} + \lambda_{id} L_{id}. \tag{6}$$

4   Experiment

Dataset. We create our dataset Tiangong-1 Dataset by the pipeline proposed in Sect. 3. The camera position setting is shown in formula [7–9]. The light source is set to a random sun light source on the same side of the camera. A total of 15,000 images and their depth maps are rendered as Fig. 3.

$$z_n = (2n/N - 1) \cdot distance \tag{7}$$

$$x_n = (\sqrt{1 - z_n^2} \cdot cos(2\pi n\phi)) \cdot distance \tag{8}$$

$$y_n = (\sqrt{1 - z_n^2} \cdot sin(2\pi n\phi)) \cdot distance \tag{9}$$

Here, N represents twice the total number of samples, $n \in [N//2, N]$. The 3D model is located at the centre of the world coordinate system, and $distance$ represents the distance from the camera to the origin of the coordinate system. And $\phi = (\sqrt{5} - 1)/2$.

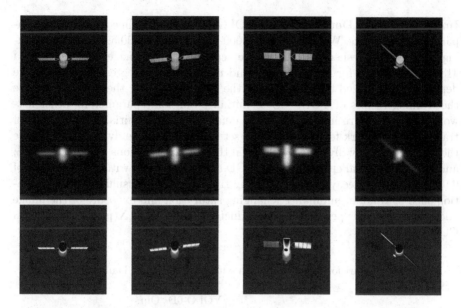

Fig. 3. The simulated image is rendered by our pipeline, the first line is raw images rendered by BlenderProc, the second and third lines are the degraded images and the relative depth images, respectively.

Evaluation Metrics. We use five metrics to evaluate our model, namely—2D projection metric [11], average 3D distance of model points (ADD) metric [10], Mean Angle Error, Mean Corner Error and Mean Translation Error.

The 2D projection metric computes the mean distance between the projections of 3D model points given the estimated and the ground truth pose. The pose estimation is considered as correct only if the 2D distance is less than 5 pixels. The ADD metric computes the distance between the ground truth points cloud and the estimated points cloud. We use 10%, 30%, and 50% of the object's diameter as the threshold, and the proportion of less than the threshold is used as the measure of pose estimation.

$$\textbf{ADD Metric} = avg_{x \in M} ||(R_{gt}\mathbf{x} + t_{gt}) - (R_{est}\mathbf{x} + t_{est})||_2 \qquad (10)$$

where, M is a set of vertices of the model, R_{gt}, t_{gt} and R_{est}, t_{gt} represent ground truth matrix and estimate matrix, respectively.

Mean Angle Error is used to calculate the average angle error of R_{est} and R_{gt}:

$$2cos(|\alpha|) = trace(R_{gt}^{-1}R_{est}) - 1. \qquad (11)$$

Mean Corner Error and Mean Translation Error represent the projection error of the keypoints and the error of t_{est} and t_{gt}, respectively.

Implementation Details. We use YOLO-6D as the baseline and also for comparing our networks. We divides the 15000 images into 12000 and 3000 for training and testing, respectively. Then we scale the input image and depth to a 418 * 418 solution for both training and testing. When regressing the relative depth, we normalized the depth using the formula (3). For the network, we use the training results of YOLO-6D to initialize our some parameters, other network parameters are initialized in the default way. The initial learning rate of training the network for 300 epochs is set to 0.001, and we dynamically reduce the learning rate by dividing by 10 when the num of iterations are at 60%, 80%, and 90% of the total epochs. We use SGD as our optimizer with a momentum of 0.9 and a weight decay of 5e−4. During training, we use usual data augmentation such as random luminance, changing saturation and exposure of the image and so on. All the experiments are conducted on one Titan X(pascal) GPU with CUDA 10.1.

Table 1. Comparision of our approach with YOLO-6D On Tiangong-1 dataset

	YOLO-6D	Ours
2D projection metric	91.21%	95.07%
ADD metric (10%)	75.23%	81.76%
ADD metric (30%)	76.40%	83.66%
ADD metric (50%)	77.02%	83.79%
Mean angle error	5.24	4.89
Mean corner error	2.40	2.23
Mean translation error	2.51	2.38

Object Pose Estimation. We set the comparison to verify whether the depth information of the object and relative depth loss can improve network performance. In Table 1, we use YOLO-6D as a baseline. Our method outperforms YOLO-6D 4% for the 2D projection metric, around 6% for the ADD metric(10%, 30%, 50%). For the Mean Angle Error, Mean Corner Error and Mean Translation Error, Our methods have achieved better performance. It means that the depth prediction branch provides more constraints. In Fig. 4, we show some visualizations results of our method for the Tiangong-1 pose estimation.

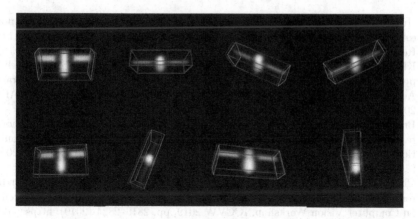

Fig. 4. Pose estimation results of our method. The green boxes are the ground truth poses, and the red boxes are the predicted poses. (Color figure online)

5   Conclusion and Future Work

In this paper, we are committed to solving the problem of pose estimation of observation images of ground-based optical telescopes. Taking Tiangong-1 as an example, we propose a method of rendering degraded images and our rendering dataset Tiangong-1 dataset. And then, we propose a novel pose estimation framework, which uses simulation data for weakly supervised training of deep images to provide more constraints for the network, so that it has the potential to judge relative depth. At the same time, it can be easily transferred to real data. In preliminary experiments, this method has achieved good performance.

Uncooperative satellite attitude estimation is a complicated problem. Due to the symmetry of satellites and the complexity of the space environment, there are many situations where our model cannot be applied well, such as satellite occlusion (partially visible) and satellite symmetry ambiguity problem. In the future, we can try to make further explorations through dense methods, at the same time, the cost of the algorithm also needs to be traded off.

References

1. Tekin, B., Sinha, S.N., Fua, P.: Real-time seamless single shot 6D object pose prediction. In: Computer Vision and Pattern Recognition (2018)
2. Denninger, M., et al.: BlenderProc. arXiv preprint arXiv:1911.01911 (2019)
3. Cai, Y., Ge, L., Cai, J., Yuan, J.: Weakly-supervised 3D hand pose estimation from monocular RGB images. In: Ferrari, V., Hebert, M., Sminchisescu, C., Weiss, Y. (eds.) ECCV 2018. LNCS, vol. 11210, pp. 678–694. Springer, Cham (2018). https://doi.org/10.1007/978-3-030-01231-1_41
4. Kang, J., Liu, W., Tu, W., Yang, L.: YOLO-6D+: single shot 6D pose estimation using privileged silhouette information. In: 2020 International Conference on Image Processing and Robotics (ICIP) (2020)

5. Hu, Y., Hugonot, J., Fua, P., Salzmann, M.: Segmentation-driven 6d object pose estimation. In: 2019 IEEE/CVF Conference on Computer Vision and Pattern Recognition (CVPR) (2019)
6. Kisantal, M., Sharma, S., Park, T.H., Izzo, D., Märtens, M., D'Amico, S.: Satellite pose estimation challenge: dataset, competition design, and results. IEEE Trans. Aerosp. Electron. Syst. **56**(5), 4083–4098 (2020). https://doi.org/10.1109/TAES. 2020.2989063
7. Proença, P.F., Gao, Y.: Deep learning for spacecraft pose estimation from photo-realistic rendering. In: IEEE International Conference on Robotics and Automation, ICRA 2020, pp. 6007–6013 (2020). https://doi.org/10.1109/ICRA40945.2020. 9197244
8. Chen, B., Cao, J., Parra, A., Chin, T.: Satellite pose estimation with deep landmark regression and nonlinear pose refinement. In: IEEE/CVF International Conference on Computer Vision Workshop, ICCVW 2019, pp. 2816–2824 (2019). https://doi. org/10.1109/ICCVW.2019.00343
9. Kehl, W., Manhardt, F., Tombari, F., Ilic, S., Navab, N.: SSD-6D: making RGB-based 3D detection and 6D pose estimation great again. In: 2017 IEEE International Conference on Computer Vision (ICCV) (2017)
10. Hinterstoisser, S., et al.: Model based training, detection and pose estimation of texture-less 3D objects in heavily cluttered scenes. In: Asian Conference on Computer Vision (2012)
11. Brachmann, E., Michel, F., Krull, A., Yang, M.Y., Gumhold, S., Rother, C.: Uncertainty-driven 6D pose estimation of objects and scenes from a single RGB image. In: Computer Vision and Pattern Recognition (2016)
12. Forshaw, J.L., et al.: RemoveDEBRIS: an in-orbit active debris removal demonstration mission. Acta Astronaut. **127**, 448463 (2016)
13. Sullivan, B., et al.: DARPA Phoenix payload orbital delivery system (PODs): FedEx to GEO. In: AIAA SPACE 2013 Conference and Exposition (2013)
14. Reed, B.B., Smith, R.C., Naasz, B.J., Pellegrino, J.F., Bacon, C.E.: The restore-l servicing mission. In: AIAA SPACE 2016 (2016)
15. To, T., et al.: NDDS: NVIDIA deep learning dataset synthesizer (2018). https:// github.com/NVIDIA/DatasetSynthesizer
16. Morrical, N.V.: ViSII - A Virtual Scene Imaging Interface (2020). https://github. com/owl-project/ViSII
17. Savva, M., et al.: Habitat: a platform for embodied AI research. In: Proceedings of the IEEE/CVF International Conference on Computer Vision (ICCV) (V)
18. Schwarz, M., Behnke, S.: Stillleben: realistic scene synthesis for deep learning in robotics. In: IEEE International Conference on Robotics and Automation (ICRA), May 2020 (2020)
19. Brachmann, E., Krull, A., Michel, F., Gumhold, S., Shotton, J., Rother, C.: Learning 6D object pose estimation using 3D object coordinates. In: Fleet, D., Pajdla, T., Schiele, B., Tuytelaars, T. (eds.) ECCV 2014. LNCS, vol. 8690, pp. 536–551. Springer, Cham (2014). https://doi.org/10.1007/978-3-319-10605-2_35
20. Choi, C., Christensen, H.I.: RGB-D object pose estimation in un- structured environments. J. Robot. Autonom. Syst. **75**, 595–613 (2016)
21. Lai, K. Bo, L., Ren, L., Fox, D.: A scalable tree-based approach for joint object and pose recognition. In: National Conference on Artificial Intelligence (2011)
22. Zhang, H., Cao, Q.: Combined holistic and local patches for recovering 6D object pose. In: International Conference on Computer Vision (2017)

23. Hinterstoißer, S., et al.: Model based training, detection and pose estimation of texture-less 3D objects in heavily cluttered scenes. In: Asian Conference on Computer Vision (2012)
24. Xiang, Y., Schmidt, T., Narayanan, V., Fox, D.: PoseCNN: a convolutional neural network for 6D object pose estimation in cluttered scenes. science and systems. In: Robotics (2018)
25. Xiang, Y., Schmidt, T., Narayanan, V., Fox, D.: PoseCNN: a convolutional neural network for 6D object pose estimation in cluttered scenes. arXiv:abs/1711.00199 (2018)
26. Oberweger, M., Rad, M., Lepetit, V.: Making deep heatmaps robust to partial occlusions for 3D object pose estimation. arXiv:abs/1804.03959 (2018)
27. Peng, S., et al.: PVNet: pixel-wise voting network for 6DoF pose estimation. In: 2019 IEEE/CVF Conference on Computer Vision and Pattern Recognition (CVPR), pp. 4556–4565 (2019)

Non-homogeneous Haze Removal Through a Multiple Attention Module Architecture

Patricia L. Suárez[1(✉)], Dario Carpio[1], and Angel D. Sappa[1,2]

[1] ESPOL Polytechnic University, FIEC, CIDIS, Guayaquil, Ecuador
{plsuarez,dncarpio,asappa}@espol.edu.ec
[2] Computer Vision Center, 08193 Bellaterra, Barcelona, Spain
asappa@cvc.uab.es

Abstract. This paper presents a novel attention based architecture to remove non-homogeneous haze. The proposed model is focused on obtaining the most representative characteristics of the image, at each learning cycle, by means of adaptive attention modules coupled with a residual learning convolutional network. The latter is based on the Res2Net model. The proposed architecture is trained with just a few set of images. Its performance is evaluated on a public benchmark—images from the non-homogeneous haze NTIRE 2021 challenge—and compared with state of the art approaches reaching the best result.

Keywords: Spatial attention · Adaptive · Residual learning · Instance normalization

1 Introduction

In recent years outdoor computer vision applications have increased enormously due to, on the one hand the reduction on the price of cameras on the other hand the technological advancements in processing capabilities (i.e., hardware and deep learning based approaches). This increase on applications can be appreciated in the video surveillance field, where global industry shipments are expected to exceed 100 million units by 2025 [17], remote sensing, driving assistance, just to mention a few. Applications developed for these fields show interesting results in clear scenarios, where sharp and well focused images are captured. However, in spite of the wide acceptance of these applications, their performance drops considerably in poor visibility scenarios. Poor visibility could be due to the lack of light or bad weather conditions (e.g., natural phenomena such as dust, mist, rain, fog or snow). This drop in performance become a challenge and an opportunity to do research on this topics (e.g., high dynamic range cameras for poor lighting conditions, image dehazing/deraining approaches). The current work tackle the dehazing problem, which is focused on removing haze from the given image.

Haze removal is a challenging task due to the complexity of the parameters that can affect the sharpness of the image. During last decades different approaches have been proposed in the literature to the homogeneous haze removal (e.g., [2,3,13,16,19]). The problem become even more complex when the non-homogeneous haze is considered. Actually, most of the approaches in the literature have been proposed by assuming

© Springer Nature Switzerland AG 2021
G. Bebis et al. (Eds.): ISVC 2021, LNCS 13018, pp. 178–190, 2021.
https://doi.org/10.1007/978-3-030-90436-4_14

that the haze is equally distributed all over the image. This assumption is based on the atmospheric scattering model that describes the formation of hazy images. This model has been proposed by McCartney et al. [18] and can be expressed as:

$$\mathbf{H}(p) = \mathbf{t}(p)\mathbf{DH}(p) + (1 - \mathbf{t}(p))\mathbf{A}, \tag{1}$$

where $\mathbf{H}$ is the hazy image, p is the pixel location in the image, $t(p)$ is the medium transmission map, $\mathbf{DH}(p)$ is the dehazed image, and $\mathbf{A}$ is the atmospheric light. The first term is the direct attenuation and the second term is the atmospheric light. According to Eq. 1, $DH(p)$ is recover by:

$$\mathbf{DH}(p) = \frac{\mathbf{H}(\mathbf{p}) - \mathbf{A}}{\mathbf{t}(\mathbf{p})} + \mathbf{A}. \tag{2}$$

However, Eq. 2 has a problem in its definition, because it works with assumptions for $\mathbf{t}(p)$ and $\mathbf{A}$ since they are variables that can take any value depending on the distribution of the haze in the image. Although there are some approaches that relies on this mathematical model (e.g., [3,6,9]), some failure in the haze removal process can be appreciated in these cases. In recent year, with the rise of deep learning based approaches some architectures have been proposed to capture image features and decide which region requires more attention according to the processing criteria. These models that allows to adjust the focus to the different regions of the images are an interesting option to tackle the non-homogeneous haze removal problem. The non-homogeneous haze removal has become a quite active research topic in recent years. As a proof of that it can be mentioned the NTIRE challenge regularly organized since 2017 [1] starting focused on Single Image Super-Resolution, until 2018 when the organizers start several challenges one of them related to single image dehazing and since NTIRE 2020 focus on non-homogeneous image dehazing. This challenge proposes to develop approaches to remove non-homogeneous haze by providing just a small set of images to be used for training. Removing non-homogeneous haze is a difficult problem since the effect of haze in the image causes an uncontrolled scattering of light in different regions of the images. In the current work this challenging problem is addressed by means of a novel architecture that relies on attention modules to detect and focus those regions of the image that require haze removal. In the case of haze removal, the useful information is the regions of the image with the greatest activation values that you want to preserve and locate spatially in the regions of interest on images. The proposed approach uses a feature fusion network proposed by [19], which has been modified to support a spatial attention block, with the aim of adaptively learning the spatial regions of the image that have greater representation and use them to improve the process of haze removal. Additionally, the learning transfer network from [25] has been adapted, including a residual layer of skip connections, to improve the quality of the images, and replacing the batch normalization by instance normalization, to improve image stylization. The manuscript is organized as follows. Related works are presented in Sect. 2. Then, the proposed approach is detailed in Sect. 3. Experimental results are presented in Sect. 4. Finally, conclusions are given in Sect. 5.

2 Related Work

During the last decades different haze removal approaches have been proposed in the literature. Initial approaches were mainly focused on the transmission map (see Eq. 1), while more recent ones are based on the usage of deep learning schemes. One of the approaches tackling the transmission map estimation has been presented by Berman et al. [3]. In this work, the authors propose a non-local prior-based approach. It is based on non-local prior knowledge, which assumes that the colors of a clear image are well projected by hundreds of different colors in the RGB space. These colors are grouped together and, being non-local, can be located throughout the image plane depending on the distance from the RGB sensor. In images with haze varying camera distances are converted into different transmission coefficients. Therefore, each group of colors in the image without haze is called a line in RGB space. With these lines the algorithm calculates the distance map of the image and therefore the image can be obtained without haze. This algorithm requires no training and works with a wide range of images. The algorithm is based on the grouping of the colors present in an image without haze, these groups are converted into lines in RGB space and the authors have called them haze lines, with which the distance map is calculated and it is possible to remove the haze in the images. Another technique, presented in [2], is based on a fusion resulting from a process of applying white balance and contrast enhancement. The method uses the pyramidal Laplacian representation to minimize artifacts. According to the authors, the results are comparable to other similar techniques. On the contrary to previous approaches, Long et al. [16] propose to use a dark channel prior to haze removal. In order to avoid artifacts, the authors use a low-pass Gaussian filter to change the coarse atmospheric estimation. They modified the transmission to prevent color distortion. Experimental results achieve good results showing very fine details in the recovered image. Another method for the haze removal is proposed in [7]; it is based on the minimization of two fused energy functions. As a result of these optimized combined functions, a set of saturation difference maps is obtained that allows to remove the haze from the images. Experimental results show that the image's structures are very well preserved.

In recent years several deep learning based approaches have been proposed; for instance Li et al. [13] presents a semi-supervised approach to image haze removal based on a CNN network with multiple losses. Also, gradient information is used as a prior to facilitate the haze removal process. This approach has been evaluated in real and synthetic images presenting results comparable to other deep learning based approaches Following the line of convolutional networks, Li et al. [12] proposes an adaptive regional network (RATNet) that performs a regular global filtering, and the restoration of lighting and details, separately, which at the end are concatenated to obtain the image without haze. The obtained results are similar to other adaptive learning convolutional but it has not been tested with synthetic images like previous approach. Qin et al. [19] present an interesting approach based on a Feature Attention (FA) module that uses channel and pixel attention to extract the most important characteristics from images and contributes to taking this information proportionally, because the haze is not proportionally distributed in the image. This architecture defines a local residual learning that inhibits the characteristics of the image. It corresponds to the haze from being considered in the learning. The results that have been obtained for the non-homogeneous haze removal process are very efficient and one of the most important in the state of the art. Given these results, in our approach we have decided to include this attention block, but it has been modified to include spatial attention, to improve the removal of the haze, taking into account the most representative characteristics, respecting their spatial location within the image. Another technique presented in the literature [20] is a method also based on deep learning, in this case the authors address the removal of haze in synthetic images. However, they apply a prior bidirectional domain transfer process so that the synthetic images can better generalize in the training process. Then these enhanced images are used as input of two simultaneous haze removal networks with consistency constraint, which are trained and then merged to obtain the resulting clear image. According to the authors, the proposed approached is robust to remove haze in both real and synthetic images. Another method to remove the haze is presented in [5], where a network with two modules is proposed; one of them performs the color correction for each channel to balance the image with haze and the second module to improve the visibility of the images based on attention blocks. The obtained results show that the proposed approach restores hazy images whether these are real or synthetically generated.

3 Proposed Approach

This section presents the approach proposed to perform image haze removal. It is based on the usage of an improved version of a channel adaptive residual learning deep network, which has been initially presented in [26]. According to the authors, the attention blocks allows the network to adaptively learn relevant, versus non-relevant information present in the image, by using the features extracted from each channel of the image. This adaptive process is especially interesting when the image does not have the evenly distributed haze.

3.1 Architecture

As mentioned above, the proposed architecture is based on the combination of a characteristic attention scheme and a stylized transfer learning that allow to eliminate the non-homogeneous haze present in the images. Figure 1 illustrates each of the model components. First, the "Pre-trained general feature extractor" is modeled inspired by [25]. This extractor has been created based on a wide data domain learning which helps during the training with few samples, as is our case, for which the weights of the Res2Net model have been loaded to accelerate the convergence and avoid overfitting, so as not to start learning from scratch. The architecture, also includes multiple skip connections, residual learning and a combination of spatial and channel attention maps to help extract high frequency data. Also, the other component named as "Non-Homogeneous Dehaze Feature Extractor" of the hazy images is modeled, refined by means of attention modules. This component is in charge of the extraction of the most representative characteristics of the hazy images. It is made up of learning groups that contains a stack of attention blocks that focus on extracting spatial descriptors, per channel and per pixel.

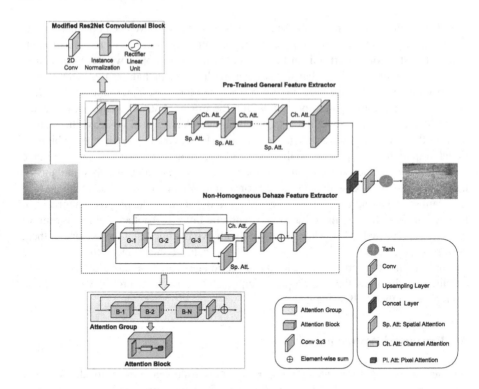

Fig. 1. Proposed dehaze architecture.

The depth of block stacking allows for further refinement of the resulting descriptor characteristics. After the grouping of blocks, the model proposes to apply spatial and channel attention to stylize the information obtained from the stacking of blocks; this is additionally combined with multiple skip connections and residual learning. The final result of the descriptor component of the images with non-homogeneous haze is concatenated with the final result of the global feature extractor. The final result of the descriptor component is concatenated with the last result of the global feature extractor. An hyperbolic tangential activation function has been applied to obtain the reconstruction of the image without haze and be able to estimate the convergence of the model applying gradients and backpropagation.

The proposed model has been designed to work with attention modules combined with residual learning to improve the transfer of characteristics through the learning layers. Regarding the attention modules used in the proposed architecture, the attention modules spatial, channel and pixel are combined to help the haze elimination process inspired by the work presented in [19]. The main contribution of the proposed architecture to improve the haze elimination process is the introduction of the spatial attention module inspired by [24] that allows local focus on the most representative features of the haze image and mapping them with the fundamental truth, to refine the feature descriptor. It is important to emphasize that in the "Non-Homogeneous Dehaze Feature

Extractor" a residual connections have been applied in the model in conjunction with the spatial attention modules to accelerate the convergence of the model and improve the haze elimination process. It is important to highlight that in the learning transfer network based on a Res2Net network, the normalization of the model data has been modified by substituting batch normalization for instances normalization (see Fig. 3), as suggested by Ulyanov et al. [21], in order to improve the stylization of image details and reduce the fading of gradients to speed up model convergence, see Sect. 3.3 for more detail. Additionally, in the general feature extractor of prior knowledge transfer network, a spatial and channel attention layer has been included. Besides, multiple skip connections and residual learning to refine the high-frequency characteristics of the pre-trained model.

This model can be as deep as the non-homogeneous distribution of the haze is complex, which is why it is a parameter of the model. The attention modules applied in the model are explained in detail below.

Attention Modules
Continuing with the evolution of deep learning models, we now have the so-called attention modules that have emerged from some previous works such as [14] and [10], where they were implemented to make the selection of areas of interest for a specific purpose. Nowadays, with the improvements in computer equipment, complex problems can be addressed with deep learning architectures [4, 19]. This technology has evolved in such a way that simple models are now designed to detect relevant features, but with

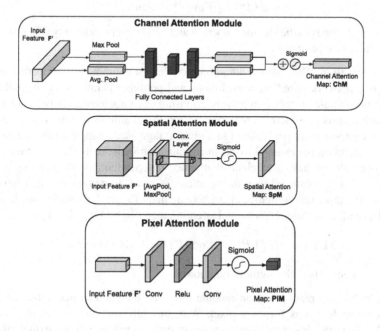

Fig. 2. Attention modules implemented.

multiple levels of learning. These models include attention modules used to generate blocks of attention grouped at various levels so that they can focus their learning on the most representative information and not consider useless low frequency information present in the given image. In the case of haze removal, the useful information are the patterns that best fit in the network activation functions. Our approach uses three levels of attention modules (spatial, channel and pixel) grouped in the learning layers of the proposed model. The main idea is to detect the existing correlation in the characteristic maps of each layer of the model to determine the best attention mechanism that is capable of learning where is the most relevant information finding the mapping between the input and the ground truth using the descending gradient and the back propagation during the learning process. The different attention modules are detailed below.

Spatial Attention: it consists of a convolutional network to generate a map to extract the inter-spatial relationship of characteristics. The spatial attention map (SpM) is characterized by the inter-spatial relationship of image characteristics. In addition, this map focuses on where the most representative part is located, which is complementary to the attention of the channel. This spatial attention is computed by means of average grouping and maximum grouping operations along the channel axis and the outputs are concatenated to generate an efficient characteristic descriptor. A convolution layer is applied to the resulting feature descriptor to generate a spatial attention map using a sigmoid activation function that encodes where to emphasize or suppress. Figure 2 shows the implemented spatial attention module. The spatial attention map can be expressed as:

$$
\begin{aligned}
\mathbf{SpM}(\mathbf{F}) &= \sigma\left(f^{m \times m}([\text{AvgPool}(\mathbf{F}); \text{MaxPool}(\mathbf{F})])\right) \\
&= \sigma\left(f^{n \times n}\left([\mathbf{F}\text{avg}^{\,\text{spm}}; \mathbf{F}\text{max}^{\text{spm}}]\right)\right),
\end{aligned}
\tag{3}
$$

where σ corresponds to the sigmoid function and ($f^{n \times n}$) represents a pooling operation with the filter size of $m \times m$

Channel Attention. The channel attention module is a combination of operations performed in a network based on convolutions and pooling operations. A channel attention map is computed by obtaining the relationship of characteristics between channels. Since each map is considered a feature detector, the channel's attention is focused on "what" is representative per channel in a given image used as input to the model. This module of attention per channel works in combination with the module of spatial attention. In our case, we have used channel attention independently in the learning transfer network and in a combined way in the attention block to extract the descriptor that represents the most representative characteristic map. Figure 2 shows the implemented channel attention module. The channel attention map can be formulated as:

$$
\mathbf{ChM}(\mathbf{F}) = \sigma(MLP(\text{AvgPool}(\mathbf{F})) + MLP(\text{MaxPool}(\mathbf{F})),
\tag{4}
$$

where σ corresponds to the sigmoid function.

Pixel Attention. A pixel attention module has been included to maximize the learning of context locations for each pixel. With this information, a pixel map is constructed, which weights correspond to relevant features mapped to contextual information. Figure 2 shows the implemented pixel attention module. This contributes maintain uniformly the removing process despite a non-homogeneous haze. The pixel attention map can be formulated as:

$$\mathbf{PiM(F)} = \sigma\left(\text{Conv}\left(\delta\left(\text{Conv}\left(F^*\right)\right)\right)\right), \tag{5}$$

where σ corresponds to the sigmoid function and δ correspond to RELU function.

3.2 Loss Functions

The loss functions used to optimize the proposed image de-hazing architecture are as follow. Firstly, an L1 loss is considered to minimize the outliers in a better way. This loss function can be formulated as:

$$\mathcal{L}_{l1} = \frac{1}{N}\sum_{j}^{N} \text{l1}\left(gt_j - f_\gamma\left(hz_j\right)\right), \tag{6}$$

where hz_j corresponds to hazy image and gt_j refers to ground truth at pixel j. $f_\alpha(gt)$ denotes our model parameterized by α. N is the number of pixels evaluated. In order to address the limitations of the l1 loss function, the usage of a reference-based measure is proposed. One of the reference-based index is the structural similarity index [23], which evaluates images accounting for the fact that the human visual perception system is sensitive to changes in the local structure; the idea behind this loss function is to help the learning model to produce a visually improved image. The structural similarity loss is defined as:

$$\mathcal{L}_{SSIM} = \frac{1}{B}\sum_{i=1}^{B} 1 - SSIM(i), \tag{7}$$

where SSIM(i) is the Structural Similarity Index (see [23] for more details) of each image i of the batch size B.

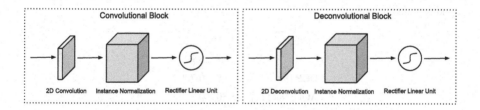

Fig. 3. Instance Normalization applied in Res2Net block.

In addition to the previous terms, the perceptual loss [27] is also applied to extract high-level features to enhanced the restoring image process. We use the Res2Net pre-trained loss network θ. The loss function is described as:

$$\mathcal{L}_{\text{percep}} = \frac{1}{C_l H_l W_l} \left\|\phi_{lj}\left(f_\theta(h)\right) - \phi_l(gt)\right\|_2^2, \tag{8}$$

where hz and gt are hazy inputs and ground truth images, respectively. $f_\theta(hz)$ is the dehazed images. $\phi_l(gt)$ denotes the feature map with size $C_l \times H_l \times W_l$. The feature restoration loss is the L_2 loss.

3.3   Instance Normalization

Another field of analysis has emerged around the style of an image is evaluated by the statistics of convolutional neural network filters, a renewed interest in the texture generation and image stylization problems in order to obtain qualitative improvement in the generated image, discarding the instance-specific contrast information from an image during style transfer.

Ulyanov et al. [21] introduce a method named *instance normalization* for a better stylization and texture synthesis, that derive entropy loss which improves samples diversity. The instance normalization layer is applied at test time as well as at training time. According to [22] the generator network should discard contrast information in the content image to learn a highly nonlinear contrast normalization function as a combination of such layers. Let $x \in \mathbb{R}^{N \times C \times W \times H}$ an input tensor containing a batch of N images, where C, W and H are the depth, width and high respectively of the image tensor and let x_{tijk} denote its $tijk$-th element of x image tensor, where k and j span spatial dimensions, t is the index of the image in the batch, i is the feature channel (in the case of an RGB image being used as an input, it would represent a color channel), a simple version of instance normalization is defined as:

$$ y_{tijk} = \frac{x_{tijk}}{\sum_{l=1}^{W} \sum_{m=1}^{H} x_{tilm}}. \tag{9} $$

A small change in the stylization architecture proposed by [22] is a qualitative improvement in the generated images. The change is limited to swapping batch normalization with instance normalization, and to apply the latter both at training and testing times. The resulting method can be used to train high-performance architectures for real-time image generation.

Table 1. Results from the NH-Haze 2021 validation dataset. The best results are in **bold**, and the second best are underlined.

Methods	NH-Haze 2021	
	PSNR	SSIM
DCP [8]	11.68	0.7090
AOD-Net [11]	13.30	0.4693
GCANet [4]	18.79	0.7729
FFA [19]	20.45	0.8043
TDN [15]	20.23	0.7622
TBD [25]	21.66	0.8430
Ours	**22.42**	**0.8546**

4   Experimental Results

This section starts by describing the datasets; then training details are provided and next the evaluation metrics are introduced; finally, results from the proposed approach

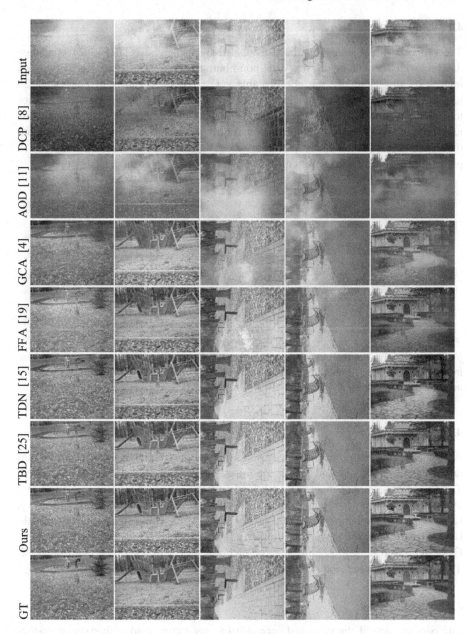

Fig. 4. Experimental results: 1st. row shows the validation images; 2nd. to 7th. row correspond to results from state of the art techniques; 8th. row presents results from the proposed approach; 9th. row depicts ground truth images from NH-Haze 2021 dataset.

are presented and compared with the state-of-the-art dehazing algorithms, both quantitatively and qualitatively.

4.1 Datasets

The proposed architecture has been evaluated by using the NTIRE 2021 challenge dataset, which contains images with non-homogeneous haze. Since the validation images for this challenge are not available yet, a group of 5 pairs of images 21–25 has been selected from the provided set of images and used to compute the metrics to evaluate results. The NTIRE 2021 challenge dataset contains 30 non-homogeneous haze images and their corresponding ground truth. From the group of data to carry out the experiments, 20 pairs of images have been selected for training. Additionally, 5 pairs of images have been selected for testing and 5 images for model validation.

Fig. 5. Results from the proposed approach on the NH-Haze 2021 validation images—note these images have been used as benchmark at the NTIRE 2021 challenge, hence the ground truth are not provided yet and just qualitative results can be presented.

4.2 Training Settings

A data augmentation process has been performed on the training set. It consists on random rotation of 90, 180 and 270 °C; additionally, an horizontal flip has been applied. The hazy-clean pairs of images are randomly cropped in patches of 256×256. Adam optimizer has been used, where β_1 and β_2 take the default values of 0.9 and 0.999, respectively. For quantitative evaluation, we adopt the Peak Signal to Noise Ratio (PSNR) metric and the Structural Similarity Index (SSIM) metric. Two NVIDIA A100 GPU were used during training, with a batch size of 8 and a learning rate of 0.0002. The train process takes about 72 h.

4.3 Comparisons

The performance of the proposed approach has been compared with six state-of-the-art dehazing algorithms, which are: DCP [8], AOD-Net [11], GCA-Net [4], FFA-Net [19], TDN [15] and TBD [25]. Table 1 presents the obtained results from all the approaches. Figure 4, shows the qualitative results obtained with the validation set with all approaches compared with the ground truth images. It can be appreciated that our approach presents better results when compared with all other approaches. Results from the 5 images in the validation set of the NTIRE 2021 dehazing challenge are provided in Fig. 5 for a qualitative evaluation.

5   Conclusions

This paper presents a deep learning network based on three-level attention modules (spatial, channel and pixel) with the aim of extracting the most relevant information to maintain from the image to which the haze elimination is being applied. In particular our contribution is the spatial attention that has been applied. It focuses on the characteristics of the most relevant locally presented in the image and not considering those characteristics that do not contribute to the clarification of the image. Additionally, the learning transfer of the pre-trained Res2Net model has been applied to take the learning of the network and not start from scratch, taking into account that the dataset is very limited. In this way, the Res2Net block has also been modified to work with normalization by instance, in order to facilitate the stylization of the details of the images and accelerate the convergence of the model. Our method presents improved results if we compare it with other methods of the state of the art.

Acknowledgements. This work has been partially supported by the ESPOL Polytechnic University; the Spanish Government under Project TIN2017-89723-P; and the "CERCA Programme/Generalitat de Catalunya". The authors gratefully acknowledge the support of the CYTED Network: "Ibero-American Thematic Network on ICT Applications for Smart Cities" (REF-518RT0559) and the NVIDIA Corporation with the donation of the Titan Xp GPU used for this research.

References

1. Agustsson, E., Timofte, R.: Ntire 2017 challenge on single image super-resolution: dataset and study. In: Proceedings of the IEEE Conference on Computer Vision and Pattern Recognition Workshops, pp. 126–135 (2017)
2. Ancuti, C.O., Ancuti, C.: Single image dehazing by multi-scale fusion. IEEE Trans. Image Process. **22**(8), 3271–3282 (2013)
3. Berman, D., Avidan, S., et al.: Non-local image dehazing. In: Proceedings of the IEEE Conference on Computer Vision and Pattern Recognition, pp. 1674–1682 (2016)
4. Chen, D., He, M., Fan, Q., Liao, J., Zhang, L., Hou, D., Yuan, L., Hua, G.: Gated context aggregation network for image dehazing and deraining. In: 2019 IEEE Winter Conference on Applications of Computer Vision (WACV), pp. 1375–1383. IEEE (2019)
5. Dudhane, A., Biradar, K.M., Patil, P.W., Hambarde, P., Murala, S.: Varicolored image dehazing. In: proceedings of the IEEE/CVF Conference on Computer Vision and Pattern Recognition, pp. 4564–4573 (2020)
6. Fattal, R.: Dehazing using color-lines. ACM Trans. Graph. (TOG) **34**(1), 1–14 (2014)
7. Galdran, A., Vazquez-Corral, J., Pardo, D., Bertalmio, M.: Fusion-based variational image dehazing. IEEE Sig. Process. Lett. **24**(2), 151–155 (2016)
8. He, K., Sun, J., Tang, X.: Single image haze removal using dark channel prior. In: 2009 IEEE Conference on Computer Vision and Pattern Recognition, pp. 1956–1963 (2009)
9. Ju, M., Ding, C., Ren, W., Yang, Y., Zhang, D., Guo, Y.J.: Ide: Image dehazing and exposure using an enhanced atmospheric scattering model. IEEE Trans. Image Process. **30**, 2180–2192 (2021)
10. Lee, M., Ban, S.-W.: Incremental knowledge representation based on visual selective attention. In: Ishikawa, M., Doya, K., Miyamoto, H., Yamakawa, T. (eds.) ICONIP 2007. LNCS, vol. 4985, pp. 940–949. Springer, Heidelberg (2008). https://doi.org/10.1007/978-3-540-69162-4_98

11. Li, B., Peng, X., Wang, Z., Xu, J., Feng, D.: AOD-Net: all-in-one dehazing network. In: 2017 IEEE International Conference on Computer Vision (ICCV), pp. 4780–4788 (2017)

12. Li, H., Wu, Q., Ngan, K.N., Li, H., Meng, F.: Region adaptive two-shot network for single image dehazing. In: 2020 IEEE International Conference on Multimedia and Expo (ICME), pp. 1–6. IEEE (2020)

13. Li, L., Dong, Y., Ren, W., Pan, J., Gao, C., Sang, N., Yang, M.H.: Semi-supervised image dehazing. IEEE Trans. Image Process. **29**, 2766–2779 (2019)

14. Liew, S.H., Low, Y.F., Lim, K.C., Choo, Y.H., Farghaly, M.R.M.: Performance evaluation of convolutional neural network in classification of EEG signals based on attention task. ARPN J. Eng. Appl. Sci. **13**, 3400–3404 (2006)

15. Liu, J., Wu, H., Xie, Y., Qu, Y., Ma, L.: Trident dehazing network. In: 2020 IEEE/CVF Conference on Computer Vision and Pattern Recognition Workshops (CVPRW), pp. 1732–1741 (2020)

16. Long, J., Shi, Z., Tang, W., Zhang, C.: Single remote sensing image dehazing. IEEE Geosci. Remote Sens. Lett. **11**(1), 59–63 (2013)

17. Markets and Markets, Inc.: Video Surveillance Market. https://www.marketsandmarkets.com/Market-Reports/video-surveillance-market-645.html

18. McCartney, E.J.: Optics of the Atmosphere: Scattering by Molecules and Particles. Wiley, New York (1976)

19. Qin, X., Wang, Z., Bai, Y., Xie, X., Jia, H.: FFA-Net: feature fusion attention network for single image dehazing. In: Proceedings of the AAAI Conference on Artificial Intelligence, pp. 11908–11915 (2020)

20. Shao, Y., Li, L., Ren, W., Gao, C., Sang, N.: Domain adaptation for image dehazing. In: Proceedings of the IEEE/CVF Conference on Computer Vision and Pattern Recognition, pp. 2808–2817 (2020)

21. Ulyanov, D., Vedaldi, A., Lempitsky, V.: Instance normalization: the missing ingredient for fast stylization. arXiv preprint arXiv:1607.08022 (2016)

22. Ulyanov, D., Vedaldi, A., Lempitsky, V.: Improved texture networks: maximizing quality and diversity in feed-forward stylization and texture synthesis. In: Proceedings of the IEEE Conference on Computer Vision and Pattern Recognition, pp. 6924–6932 (2017)

23. Wang, Z., Bovik, A.C., Sheikh, H.R., Simoncelli, E.P.: Image quality assessment: from error visibility to structural similarity. IEEE Trans. Image Process. **13**(4), 600–612 (2004)

24. Woo, S., Park, J., Lee, J.-Y., Kweon, I.S.: CBAM: convolutional block attention module. In: Ferrari, V., Hebert, M., Sminchisescu, C., Weiss, Y. (eds.) ECCV 2018. LNCS, vol. 11211, pp. 3–19. Springer, Cham (2018). https://doi.org/10.1007/978-3-030-01234-2_1

25. Yu, Y., Liu, H., Fu, M., Chen, J., Wang, X., Wang, K.: A two-branch neural network for non-homogeneous dehazing via ensemble learning. In: Proceedings of the IEEE/CVF Conference on Computer Vision and Pattern Recognition, pp. 193–202 (2021)

26. Zhang, Y., Li, K., Li, K., Wang, L., Zhong, B., Fu, Y.: Image super-resolution using very deep residual channel attention networks. In: Ferrari, V., Hebert, M., Sminchisescu, C., Weiss, Y. (eds.) ECCV 2018. LNCS, vol. 11211, pp. 294–310. Springer, Cham (2018). https://doi.org/10.1007/978-3-030-01234-2_18

27. Zhu, J.Y., Park, T., Isola, P., Efros, A.A.: Unpaired image-to-image translation using cycle-consistent adversarial networks. In: Proceedings of the IEEE International Conference on Computer Vision, pp. 2223–2232 (2017)

Vehicle Detection and Tracking from Surveillance Cameras in Urban Scenes

Oumayma Messoussi[1]([✉]), Felipe Gohring de Magalhães[1], Francois Lamarre[2], Francis Perreault[2], Ibrahima Sogoba[2], Guillaume-Alexandre Bilodeau[1], and Gabriela Nicolescu[1]

[1] Polytechnique Montreal, Montreal, QC H3T 1J4, Canada
{oumayma.messoussi,felipe.gohring-de-magalhaes,
guillaume-alexandre.bilodeau,gabriela.nicolescu}@polymtl.ca
[2] Cysca Technologies, Montreal, QC H2Y 1N9, Canada
{francois.lamarre,francis.perreault,ibrahima.sogoba}@cysca.ca,
https://www.cysca.ca/

Abstract. Detecting and tracking vehicles in urban scenes is a crucial step in many traffic-related applications as it helps to improve road user safety among other benefits. Various challenges remain unresolved in multi-object tracking (MOT) including target information description, long-term occlusions and fast motion. We propose a multi-vehicle detection and tracking system following the tracking-by-detection paradigm that tackles the previously mentioned challenges. Our MOT method extends an Intersection-over-Union (IOU)-based tracker with vehicle re-identification features. This allows us to utilize appearance information to better match objects after long occlusion phases and/or when object location is significantly shifted due to fast motion. We outperform our baseline MOT method on the UA-DETRAC benchmark while maintaining a total processing speed suitable for online use cases.

Keywords: Multi-object tracking · Tracking-by-detection · Object re-identification

1 Introduction

In smart cities, intelligent transportation systems that rely on cameras and other sensors play a critical role in ensuring road users safety. Autonomous vehicles, for example, require superior computer vision algorithms to comprehend their surroundings and to have the ability to interact with them. In order to navigate between two points, they must be able to recognize road signs, traffic signals, people, and automobiles. Detecting traffic violations and managing parking spaces are illustrations of other applications. Automated parking management, for example, necessitates recognizing when vehicles enter the parking area and following their path until they reach the parking place. This aids in saving expenses and eliminating manual work. The ability to describe a vehicle

© Springer Nature Switzerland AG 2021
G. Bebis et al. (Eds.): ISVC 2021, LNCS 13018, pp. 191–202, 2021.
https://doi.org/10.1007/978-3-030-90436-4_15

trajectory is also important for the user's safety because it tracks their movement and, as a result, can detect how it interacts with surrounding moving objects in order to avoid crashes. Therefore, video monitoring has several advantages for both road users and those in charge of them.

When tracking vehicles, a surveillance system can offer information about an object category, location, and trajectory utilizing multi-target detection and tracking algorithms. We aim to develop a method to detect and track multiple vehicles in single-camera views in an online use case. We also tackle challenges like motion-related displacements and long-term occlusions.

To solve this, there are numerous approaches to this problem, which we review in Sect. 2. We approach this problem from a tracking-by-detection perspective, in which detection and tracking are performed in two steps. The first task, known as multi-object detection, identifies and locates vehicles in a video frame. Multi-object tracking is the next phase, which assigns unique identifiers to detected objects, extracts information describing them, and connects detections in each frame to create trajectories.

Within this approach, some methods use the IOU metric to match detections through time by measuring the overlap between candidate bounding boxes [1,2,17]. The main appeal of this approach is its low execution time. These methods can process a high number of frames per second making them well suited for real-time or online use cases. Yet there is still room for improvement by incorporating other types of features to describe the candidate objects. Therefore, in our work, we build upon V-IOU [2] and add an appearance feature component from a vehicle re-identification model [3] thus yielding more robust results in challenging scenes with large displacements due to fast motion and long-term occlusions.

Our contributions in this work are the following:

– Performance improvement in terms of multi-object tracking metrics by extending data association with re-identification features.
– Online/fast end-to-end detection and tracking achieved through the choice of models as well as the design of the data association step.

2   Background and Related Works

Challenges in MOT

Multi-object tracking is an active topic in computer vision research, owing to the numerous challenges it presents. A tracking model faces difficulties due to potential crossing tracks, which can alter identities or produce gaps in tracks, similar to how a human struggles to keep track of multiple things in a video sequence. The following are some of the most significant issues encountered:

– **Occlusion:** Another target or a background item can partially or completely obscure a target's view. During the occlusion phase, the object features become erroneous or outdated. The features of the front target interfere with those of the occluded target when partial occlusion is used. Full occlusion, on the other hand, renders the features of the target irreversible.

- **Fast motion:** When an object moves at a high speed in a video, its position changes notably between frames. As a result, spatial data about a target becomes unreliable. Fast movement can also lead to motion blur, causing appearance descriptors to be inaccurate.
- **Scale changes:** When a target travels closer or further away from the camera, its scale changes, and its size changes as well. As a result, the tracking technique must react to these changes and update the target bounding box in order to prevent losing information about the whole object or accidentally adding background data.
- **Illumination variations:** Changes in illumination surrounding the targets, such as those caused by the weather, might affect the look of the objects. A hazy sky or a night setting may also drastically alter the appearance of objects. In the dark, for example, a vehicle headlights seem like spotlights on the camera, preventing it from properly capturing the vehicle. These flaws make tracking more difficult and make identity switches more frequent.
- **Target similarity:** Because of the significant resemblance in appearance, tracking several items of the same category increases the complexity of the task. This makes distinguishing between two or more targets and maintaining their individual identities difficult.

Object detection algorithms have improved dramatically in recent years owing to advances in deep learning and sophisticated CNN architectures [7–11]. To take advantage of the excellent detection results, the majority of top-performing MOT techniques employ the tracking-by-detection approach. In this method, an object detector is applied to each frame, and the MOT method is then used to find the best match between objects.

As opposed to batch tracking methods like IHTLS [12], revisited JPDA [13] and GOG [14], which process a number of frames or a whole video sequence before giving results, online MOT techniques process one frame at a time without having visibility or knowledge about future frames. As a result, online MOT techniques are more naturally suited to real-time systems, yet not all online MOT algorithms are real-time. Due to access to information from previous and future frames, offline MOT techniques naturally perform better in terms of MOT performance measures. Offline techniques can use this information to link/fill gaps in fragmented tracks, for example. Consequently, online MOT is a more difficult task by definition.

Optimization Approaches
Detection-based tracking method frequently present the following four components: object detection, object state propagation, data association, and track lifespan management. SORT [17], an early online tracking method, proposed a simple approach for enhancing frame-to-frame association. They accomplish so by employing the Faster R-CNN object detection model, then modeling the target state by spatial and motion information. The IOU metric is used to associate detections to tracks by measuring the amount of overlap between bounding

boxes. When a match is made, the target state is updated using the detection information and a Kalman [15] motion model. The Hungarian algorithm [16] is applied to solve the cost matrix computed with the IOU scores, with a minimum overlap threshold to select assignments. While this approach has been reported to analyze video sequences at a speed of up to 260 frames per second (FPS), it struggles with long-term occlusions, resulting in an increase in the number of ID change errors. DeepSORT [18] was later proposed as an improvement by adding appearance information extracted from a person re-identification (ReID) model. This combination of spatial cues from the IOU score and the ReID features, give results in terms of tracking metrics that are more robust.

Similarly to SORT, the data association component of the IOU tracker [1] is reduced to a simple IOU between detected bounding boxes in frame pairs. The authors argue that having strong high-accuracy detections enables for simpler tracking techniques to reach greater processing rates while still competing with more complex MOT approaches in terms of tracking performance, without relying on visual or motion characteristics. Yet, a small number of missed detections can dramatically increase the number of ID switches and fragmentation errors. Hence, the IOU tracker was improved later by adding visual object tracking in V-IOU [2]. Forward visual tracking predicts a target location when detections are not matched, for a fixed number frames TTL (time to live). When new tracks are created, backward visual tracking is used to see if they can be linked to previously terminated tracks. V-IOU tracker achieves a good trade-off between speed and tracking performance with inference speeds of over 200 FPS, thus maintaining its primary selling feature. However, this technique does not include appearance elements for full occlusion circumstances when the visual tracker fails, therefore there is still space for development. The IOU-based association cost is also greatly affected by displacements caused by fast motion. When an item travels quickly between two frames, the bounding boxes may be widely apart, resulting in little or no overlap. This lowers the IOU score which in turn raises the association cost, making it impossible to link the boxes even if they represent the same target.

Neural Network Approaches

While previous approaches represented data association as an optimization problem, works like DAN [19] and DMAN [20] use end-to-end neural networks to tackle the challenge. DAN (Deep Affinity Network) learns the appearance cues of objects and their affinities at different abstraction levels and then computes correlations between pairs of features vectors. DMAN (Dual Matching Attention Networks) proposes the use of a cost-sensitive loss function, as well as temporal and spatial attentions, in a single object tracker for each candidate detection in a frame. While these methods achieve comparable performances with top performers on some MOT benchmarks, they significantly compromise on speed, with around 6 FPS for DAN and 0.3 FPS for DMAN.

Recurrent neural networks are also used in other works [21,22] to describe temporal relationships between targets. Recurrent networks are used to combine detections into tracks based on different features (spatial, appearance or motion cues). The initial findings in [21] reveal that this technique has a significant rate of false positives and ID switches, thus the authors recommend using ReID cues for occluded objects.

Braso et al. [23] suggested a graph-based method that makes use of the MOT usual network flow. Instead of estimating pairwise costs, the neural solver for the MOT approach learns to predict final trajectories directly from graphs. To accomplish so, a message passing network (MPN) that employs appearance and geometry characteristics is used to train on the MOT graph domain. Lee et al. suggested FPSN [24], or Feature Pyramid Siamese Network, that employed a Feature Pyramid Network to extract target features from multiple levels, resulting in a multi-level discriminative feature. FPSN-MOT adds spatio-temporal motion characteristics to address the absence of motion information in traditional Siamese networks. Osep et al. presented Track, then Decide: Category-Agnostic Vision-based Multi-Object Tracking [25], a tracking by segmentation approach based on pixel-level information. To create object segmentations, this technique is model-free and employs category-agnostic picture segmentation. Objects are then tracked by using semantic information to conduct mask-based association on pixels.

3   Proposed Solution

We present the approaches we used for both the object detection and multiple object tracking components of our system in this section. An overview of our tracker is presented in Fig. 1.

This work focuses on identifying vehicles in surveillance video sequences, then assigning unique IDs to each target and keeping track of them throughout the video stream. Given the good performance of such approaches in terms of MOT metrics and speed on numerous MOT challenges and benchmarks, as well as their modularity/adaptability to diverse applications, we chose a tracking-by-detection scheme to solve this problem. This means that our work is built around two key components: an object detection model for predicting vehicle locations and a multi-object tracker for linking detections across frames.

Object Detection
We focused on selecting a model that can identify vehicles in urban scenes with a variety of constraints, such as occlusions and changing weather. As a result of these difficulties, object detection is a difficult task that necessitates ongoing study and the usage of relevant datasets tailored to the application. Our work confirms the idea that robust object detection, which enables effective object localization in difficult settings, is critical to the object tracking method overall performance.

For a good balance of speed and precision, we chose SpotNet [11] as our vehicle detection model to recognize vehicles in video frames. Perreault et al. have

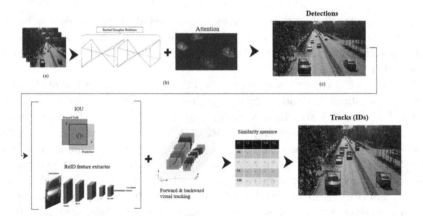

Fig. 1. Overall pipeline: (a) Our method takes as input RGB video frames. (b) Our detector of choice SpotNet [11] generates candidate detections (bounding boxes, class labels and confidences) in each frame. (c) Detections are then passed to both the feature extractor and the association step. (d) Association costs are computed using the cosine similarity for each pair of ReID feature vectors and the IOU scores between bounding boxes. Visual object tracking is also employed forward and backward for unmatched tracks. (e) The final output is the established trajectories with their unique IDs.

proposed a model that utilises a CNN backbone, regression, and segmentation heads to create a simple and efficient detector. This model uses a dual Hourglass network composed of down-sampling and up-sampling layers to construct a rich feature map. The inclusion of a self-attention mechanism in this detector is its novelty, represented by multi-task learning, with object segmentation being learned as an additional task to guide the model. The segmentation branch was trained with semi-supervised segmentations obtained using PAWCS [27] for background subtraction for fixed camera configurations, and Farneback optical flow [28] for moving camera settings. On two object detection benchmarks with traffic scenarios, SpotNet outperformed the competition.

Base MOT Method

We build on the V-IOU tracker [2] that follows the tracking-by-detection scheme in which the tracking method input is the object detection model bounding boxes, which supports our choice of a robust detector. This technique, like its predecessor [1], uses the IOU metric to assess the degree of overlap between previously detected bounding boxes and the predicted bounding boxes in the current frame to connect detections between frames. Then, it solves a linear assignment problem with a configurable minimum IOU threshold σ_{IOU}. When no association is detected, it reverts to visual object tracking to predict the next locations of a target within a time window defined by a parameter TTL, both forward and backward. We resort to MedianFlow [33] in our pipeline to temporarily track each unmatched target. The authors' findings show that V-IOU lowers fragmentation and ID switch rates compared to the base IOU tracker.

However, this model has two flaws: it generates a moderately high number of false positives, which is likely due to the visual object tracker predictions, and it only uses spatial information from bounding boxes to make the association, which suggests a vulnerability in urban settings where vehicle appearances can change after being occluded.

Proposed ReID Extension

To address the problems above, we extend the matching process of the chosen V-IOU tracker with information characterizing the vehicle visual appearance to deal with long-term occlusions and large spatial displacements due to fast motion in order to develop a more efficient and robust MOT system. By minimizing fragmentation and ID switches, appearance cues have been shown to increase association outcomes.

Particularly, we chose to enhance the data association component of our MOT technique with vehicle ReID elements based on Miah et al.'s comprehensive analysis of different appearance features for MOT in urban scenarios [30]. We utilize the feature extraction module from [3], which has been trained on three vehicle ReID datasets. The CNN feature extractor is trained using Triplet loss and cross-entropy loss on a ResNet [31] architecture with 50 layers. When training using classification annotations, cross-entropy was utilized so that the CNN could learn to minimize the classification loss amongst vehicle models, resulting in the acquisition of robust discriminative features. An adaptive feature learning approach presented in the same publication is also used to fine-tune the feature extraction model. From unlabeled video sequences, this method tries to extract positive and training examples to better adapt the visual domain to test sequences.

We include the ReID feature in our tracker in the following way. Vehicle bounding boxes are output from the object detector and supplied to the feature extractor model, which generates feature vectors of size 2048 describing object appearances, as well as to the MOT method, which performs the data association step. Our new cost function is as follows:

$$cost(d_i, t_j) = 1 - \alpha * IOU(d_i, t_j) - \beta * cosine(R_{d_i}, R_{t_j}) \tag{1}$$

for a detection d_i and a track t_j, with R_{d_i}, R_{t_j} respectively their 2048-dimensional ReID feature vectors, and $\alpha + \beta = 1$. The association cost of the bounding boxes is evaluated with the IOU, while the ReID feature vectors are compared with the cosine similarity.

While visual object tracking can aid with short-term occlusions, ReID features are invariant to viewing angle and orientation change problems since they are derived from a CNN trained on numerous pictures of the same item with varied orientations and illumination conditions. The new association function will compute the spatial and appearance similarity between the anticipated bounding boxes and candidate detections when an item is occluded for a long duration. As a result, the object is more likely to be recovered after longer occlusions when utilizing the ReID model rather than simply employing IOU for matching. The anticipated locations and candidate detections would be far apart in cases where the vehicles travel at comparatively higher speeds, resulting in an IOU score near to zero. Because it helps minimize association costs, the ReID extension plays a key role in enhancing the chance of accurately matching predictions to detections in rapid motion scenarios. Backward predictions are also matched to terminated tracks using ReID vectors to generate more cohesive trajectories with fewer gaps. Finally, mismatched detections start new tracks, which are visually monitored until they are linked to fresh detections in the following TTL frames, at which point they are terminated. Tracks shorter than t_{min} are also eliminated. We include a custom cosine similarity function written in Python and accelerated using a package called Numba to keep the overall processing time of our system as low as feasible. This decreases the cosine affinity execution time to about $1/36th$ when compared to a conventional implementation.

4   Results and Discussion

Dataset and Evaluation

For all our fine-tuning and tests, we used the UA-DETRAC [29] dataset and benchmark suite. It provides around 10 h of video collected from real-world traffic settings at a frame rate of 25 FPS and a 960 × 540 pixels resolution. This results in more than 140,000 frames and a total of 1.21 million bounding boxes from 8250 vehicles. This dataset presents 4 vehicle classes (Car, Bus, Van, Other) and 4 weather conditions (Sunny, Cloudy, Rain, Night).

To examine the influence of the detection model on tracking, the evaluation procedure of UA-DETRAC processes detection and tracking data for each threshold in the range 0.0 to 1.0 with a step of 0.1. This implies that the detections with confidence scores less than or equal to the current threshold are chosen for each iteration, and the MOT technique is then assessed for this subset. The benchmark proposes a set of metrics called DETRAC-MOT which are PR-MOTA (MOT accuracy), PR-MOTP (MOT precision), PR-MT (mostly tracked), PR-ML (mostly lost), PR-IDS (ID switches), PR-FM (fragmentation), PR-FP (false positives) and PR-FN (false negatives). All of these metrics are based on the detector precision-recall curve.

We fine-tuned our proposed MOT method on the UA-DETRAC train split of 60 sequences. The best parameter values we obtained are:

$$\sigma_{IOU} : 0.6, \alpha : 0.7, \beta : 0.3, TTL : 15 \text{ and } t_{min} : 3$$

Results

During our tests, we observed that SpotNet is rather safe with its confidence scores. It rarely outputs confidences higher than 90%. So we multiplied the scores for the top 50 detections per frame by 1.25 and clipped them to 100% to spread out the confidence score distribution between 0 and 1 to be compatible with the test procedure of UA-DETRAC. Finally, the results of our tracker shown in Table 2 confirm that our proposed method outperforms our baseline on the UA-DETRAC tracking benchmark, V-IOU with Mask R-CNN, particularly in terms of PR-MOTP with a 13.9% increase. We also score a marginal improvement for PR-MOTA with a 0.5% increase. Thus, we get state-of-the-art results of 31.2% PR-MOTA and 50.9% PR-MOTP. While the base V-IOU method still has the lead in terms of PR-MT, PR-IDS, PR-FM, we outperform it in terms of PR-ML, PR-FP and PR-FN. Altogether, our method is more consistent and better performing on most PR-MOT metrics. Our approach produces approximately three times less false positives than V-IOU with Mask R-CNN. This illustrates the considerable gain achieved by upgrading the object detector to SpotNet, a far more robust model capable of handling a variety of demanding circumstances. We also see a slight reduction in the number of false negatives.

On PR-ML, we see a noticeable improvement from 22.6 to 18.5. This measure quantifies the proportion of ground truth tracks that are tracked 20% or less of the time. This supports the concept that integrating visual object tracking with ReID cues is a better method for improved trajectory maintenance, resulting in more consistent tracks overall. Nonetheless, we leave opportunity for additional studies with alternative values to fine-tune the weights of the spatial and appearance criteria α and β (Table 1).

Table 1. DETRAC-MOT results on the UA-DETRAC test set with top 50 SpotNet detections. **Bold**: best result in each metric. Results * taken from [29]. Results & taken from [2]. Results # taken from [32]. The last line presents results of our method.

Detector	Tracker	PR-MOTA	PR-MOTP	PR-MT	PR-ML	PR-IDS	PR-FM	PR-FP	PR-FN
DPM	GOG*	5.5	28.2	4.1	27.7	1873.9	1988.5	38957.6	230126.6
EB	KIOU*	21.1	28.6	21.9	**17.6**	462.2	712.1	19046.9	**159178.3**
M-RCNN	V-IOU&	30.7	37.0	**32.0**	22.6	**162.6**	**286.2**	18046.2	179191.2
SpotNet	Kalman +IOU#	30.6	42.7	–	–	3634	–	–	–
SpotNet	**V-IOU+ReID**	**31.2**	**50.9**	28.1	18.5	252.6	329.1	**6036.4**	170700.6

In Table 2, we give a more detailed view about the impact of each step with an ablation study. When compared to utilizing SpotNet with the standard version of V-IOU, adding the ReID features substantially reduces the frequency of ID switches and fragmentation. Adding the ReID component results in the highest increase in PR-MOTA and PR-MOTP, while utilizing spotNet results in the biggest improvement in PR-FP. Through the design of our cost function, we interpret the gain in terms of PR-MOTP. Our cost is responsible for 30% of the ReID feature similarity. The more we visually track an item using Medianflow [33] in circumstances with relatively long occlusions, the more inaccuracies are incorporated into the predicted boxes. As a result, IOU would assign low scores between the anticipated vehicle position and candidate detections. By lowering the association cost, the ReID scores will appropriately compensate for the IOU, allowing our technique to fill gaps in trajectories. It also helps in a similar way for detections that are spatially distant for smaller objects moving at fast speeds. This would result in extremely short tracks of length one, which would be rejected by the assessment process using the base V-IOU tracker. We can link these detections despite the displacement when ReID features are implemented.

Table 2. Ablation study on the UA-DETRAC test set. Bold: best result in each metric. Results & taken from [2].

Detector	Tracker	PR-MOTA	PR-MOTP	PR-MT	PR-ML	PR-IDS	PR-FM	PR-FP	PR-FN
M-RCNN	V-IOU&	30.7	37.0	**32.0**	22.6	**162.6**	**286.2**	18046.2	179191.2
SpotNet	V-IOU	27.6	39.8	23.6	20.9	293.1	382.4	**4783.9**	194784.4
SpotNet	V-IOU+ReID	**31.2**	**50.9**	28.1	**18.5**	252.6	329.1	6036.4	**170700.6**

Finally, we present the processing speed values for each component of our system on the RTX 6000, with a detection threshold of 0.7. (yielding up to 20–25 candidates per frame). For the detection step, SpotNet can process up to 9 FPS, while our V-IOU with ReID and cosine extension can process up to **60 FPS**, resulting in a total end-to-end speed of up to 6 FPS.

5   Conclusion

Our work adopts the popular tracking-by-detection paradigm to propose an MOT method that combines spatial information with re-identification features to track vehicles in urban scenes in online use cases. Our data association function design shows solid performance on the UA-DETRAC benchmark for long-term occlusions and large shifts due to fast motion. This work enables further improvement in terms of speed as well as adding more information to further improvement tracking performance.

References

1. Bochinski, E.: High-speed tracking-by-detection without using image information. In: International Workshop on Traffic and Street Surveillance for Safety and Security at IEEE AVSS 2017 (2017)
2. Bochinski, E.: Extending IOU Based multi-object tracking by visual information. In: IEEE International Conference on Advanced Video and Signals-Based Surveillance, pp. 441–446 (2018)
3. Wu, C., Liu, C., Chiang, C., Tu, W., Chien, S.: Vehicle re-identification with the space-time prior. In: 2018 IEEE/CVF Conference on Computer Vision and Pattern Recognition Workshops (CVPRW) (2018)
4. Szeliski, R.: Computer Vision: Algorithms and Applications. Springer, London (2011). https://doi.org/10.1007/978-1-84882-935-0
5. Fiaz, M.: Handcrafted and deep trackers: recent visual object tracking approaches. ACM Comput. Survey **52**, 1–44 (2019)
6. Li, W.: Multiple object tracking with motion and appearance cues. In: IEEE/CVF International Conference on Computer Vision Workshop (ICCVW), pp. 161–169 (2019)
7. Ren, S.: Faster R-CNN: towards real-time object detection with region proposal networks. IEEE Trans. Patt. Anal. Mach. Intell. **39**, 1137–1149 (2017)
8. He, K.: Mask R-CNN. In: 2017 IEEE International Conference on Computer Vision (ICCV), pp. 2980–2988 (2017)

9. Redmon, J.: You only look once: unified, real-time object detection. In: 2016 IEEE Conference on Computer Vision and Pattern Recognition (CVPR), pp. 779–788 (2016)
10. Zhou, X.: Objects as Points. ArXiv, abs/1904.07850 (2019)
11. Perreault, H.: SpotNet: self-attention multi-task network for object detection. In: 2020 17th Conference on Computer and Robot Vision (CRV), pp. 230–237 (2020)
12. Dicle, C.: The way they move: tracking multiple targets with similar appearance. In: 2013 IEEE International Conference on Computer Vision (ICCV), pp. 2304–2311 (2013)
13. Rezatofighi, S.: Joint probabilistic data association revisited. In: 2015 IEEE International Conference on Computer Vision (ICCV), pp. 3047–3055 (2015)
14. Pirsiavash, H.: Globally-optimal greedy algorithms for tracking a variable number of objects. CVPR **2011**, 1201–1208 (2011)
15. Kalman, E.: A new approach to linear filtering and prediction problems. J. Basic Eng. **82**, 35–45 (1960)
16. Kuhn, H. W.: The Hungarian method for the assignment problem. Naval Res. Logis. Q. **2**, 83–97 (1955)
17. Bewley, A.: Simple online and realtime tracking. In: 2016 IEEE International Conference on Image Processing (ICIP), pp. 3464–3468 (2016)
18. Wojke, N.: Simple online and realtime tracking with a deep association metric. In: 2017 IEEE International Conference on Image Processing (ICIP), pp. 3645–3649 (2017)
19. Sun, S.: Deep affinity network for multiple object tracking. IEEE Trans. Patt. Anal. Mach. Intell. **43**, 104–119 (2021)
20. Zhu, J., Yang, H., Liu, N., Kim, M., Zhang, W., Yang, M.-H.: Online multi-object tracking with dual matching attention networks. In: Ferrari, V., Hebert, M., Sminchisescu, C., Weiss, Y. (eds.) ECCV 2018. LNCS, vol. 11209, pp. 379–396. Springer, Cham (2018). https://doi.org/10.1007/978-3-030-01228-1_23
21. Kieritz, H.: Joint detection and online multi-object tracking. In: 2018 IEEE Conference on Computer Vision and Pattern Recognition Workshops (CVPR), pp. 1459–1467 (2018)
22. Milan, A.: Online multi-target tracking using recurrent neural networks. In: Proceedings of the Thirty-First AAAI Conference on Artificial Intelligence, pp. 4225–4232 (2017)
23. Braso, G.: Learning a neural solver for multiple object tracking. In: 2020 IEEE/CVF Conference on Computer Vision and Pattern Recognition (CVPR), pp. 6246–6256 (2020)
24. Lee, S.: multiple object tracking via feature pyramid Siamese networks. IEEE Access **7**, 8181–8194 (2019)
25. Osep, A.: Track, then decide: category-agnostic vision-based multi-object tracking. In: 2018 IEEE International Conference on Robotics and Automation (ICRA), pp. 3494–3501 (2018)
26. Newell, A.: Stacked Hourglass networks for human pose estimation. ECCV (2016)
27. St-Charles, P.-L.: A self-adjusting approach to change detection based on background word consensus. In: 2015 IEEE Winter Conference on Applications of Computer Vision, pp. 990–997 (2015)
28. Farnebäck, G.: Two-frame motion estimation based on polynomial expansion. In: Bigun, J., Gustavsson, T. (eds.) SCIA 2003. LNCS, vol. 2749, pp. 363–370. Springer, Heidelberg (2003). https://doi.org/10.1007/3-540-45103-X_50
29. Wen, L.: UA-DETRAC: a new benchmark and protocol for multi-object detection and tracking. Comput. Vis. Image Underst **193**, 102907 (2020)

30. Miah, M.: An empirical analysis of visual features for multiple object tracking in urban scenes. In: International Conference on Pattern Recognition (ICPR) (2020)
31. He, K.: Deep residual learning for image recognition. In: 2016 IEEE Conference on Computer Vision and Pattern Recognition (CVPR), pp. 770–778 (2016)
32. Kang, Z.: Multiple Object Tracking in Videos. Master's thesis, Department of computer engineering, École Polytechnique de Montréal (2021)
33. Kalal, Z.: Forward-backward error: automatic detection of tracking failures. In: Proceedings of the 2010 20th International Conference on Pattern Recognition, pp. 2756–2759 (2010)

Towards the Creation of Spontaneous Datasets Based on Youtube Reaction Videos

Vitor Miguel Xavier Peres[✉] and Soraia Raupp Musse[✉]

School of Technology, Pontifical Catholic University of Rio Grande do Sul,
6681, Ipiranga Avenue, Porto Alegre 90520-08, Brazil
vitor.peres@edu.pucrs.br, soraia.musse@pucrs.br

Abstract. Reaction videos from YouTube provide a range of possibilities when looking to investigate human behavior. This research aims to present a method of creating a spontaneous facial expression dataset from YouTube reaction videos. In this work, we use Convolutional Neural Networks to classify emotions in facial expressions, as well as feature extraction tools to support this classification. To understand the behavior of faces that react to a given trailer, we firstly select automatically interest moments in the video where reactions were more intense and then we present two metrics: Agreement and Continuity rates, which aim to help to identify spontaneous emotions, that cannot be classified by Neural Networks with high assertiveness. Using our metrics, we found an average of 71% of the faces that present similarity of classified emotions, in the most intense moments in the video. Our proposal is to use our metrics jointly with the Neural Network accuracy, which can be lower than usual, in order to find spontaneous expressions. Finally, we show an example of generated dataset.

Keywords: Facial expression · Video reaction · YouTube · Spontaneous emotion

1 Introduction

The perception of human faces is a very studied research area in the psychology literature, encompassing topics as diverse as the visual information our brains can interpret when we look at faces [3], if prejudicial attitudes can affect how we see faces, or how people with neuro-developmental disorders (Alzheimer, Parkinson, CVA, Attention Deficit Disorder) see human faces [5]. Nowadays, each time more we have datasets for training situations that exist in real life, and such training exists in order to help detection and classification techniques. This is the specific case of facial emotion classification. While there are many datasets with posed and trained facial expressions [15,18], the classification of spontaneous faces is still a issue.

© Springer Nature Switzerland AG 2021
G. Bebis et al. (Eds.): ISVC 2021, LNCS 13018, pp. 203–215, 2021.
https://doi.org/10.1007/978-3-030-90436-4_16

The main challenge of creating spontaneous dataset of faces, main goal of this work, is to find specific stimuli for each emotion and the best reaction for those stimuli [8], given the difficulty of identifying the attenuation of the emotional impact caused by the stimulus [16]. In this work, we propose a technique for automatically creating spontaneous dataset, based on YouTube reaction videos. Reaction videos are sequences in which people are filmed, showing their emotional reactions, while watching them. This kind of content on YouTube has been expanding in popularity, and shows the distinct emotions and expressions from viewers with respect to movie trailers, politicians' speeches, sports highlights, music live shows and others.

Carvalho et al. [6] uses YouTube video reactions to study emotions and attention. The authors compare their method with the International Affective Picture System (IAPS) [4], that aims to provide a set of normative emotional stimuli for experimental investigations of emotion and attention from static images. According to Carvalho et al. [6], their analysis provide an effective process that can be sustained over longer periods, both at the subjective and physiological levels. In addition, YouTube video reactions facilitates and approximates the process of exposure of the reaction actors in a potential real-world scenario, without ethical and behavioral restrictions [20].

Our methodology includes the automatic identification of stimulus-generating target moments. Here we use the hypothesis that the most intense time is when most people react in a more intense way. Therefore, we also studied the most intense moments that contains more similarity among the subjects. Once we have the most interest moments in the video, we can classify the expressed emotions using a Convolutional Neural Network. In addition, we present two metrics: Agreement and Continuity rates, which aim to help to identify spontaneous emotions, that cannot be classified by Neural Networks with high assertiveness. Our ultimate goal is to provide a methodology for extracting spontaneous facial expressions from YouTube reactions that includes selecting the best reaction frame(s) and include the generation of genuine facial behaviors. The main contribution of this work is the study of hypotheses of video reactions and the detection of most intense emotions, which are used as target in the emotions classification.

2   Related Work

Affectiva [18] presents a comprehensively labeled dataset of valid spontaneous facial responses recorded in a wild environment. This dataset includes 242 facial videos (over 168,000 frames) recorded under real-world conditions. It uses FACS [7], which is a anatomically based system used to describe visually the facial movements, through a individual components of muscle movement, called Action Unit (AU). The dataset is comprehensively labeled for the following [18]: i) frame-by-frame labels for the presence of 10 symmetrical FACS Action Unit, 4 asymmetric FACS Action Unit, 2 head movements, smile, general expressiveness, feature tracker fails and gender; ii) the location of 22 automatically detected landmark points; iii) self-report responses of familiarity with, liking of, and desire to watch again for the stimuli videos and iv) baseline performance of detection algorithms on this dataset. Disfa [17] contains approximately 130,000 annotated frames from 27 subjects. For every frame, the intensity of 12 Action Unit was manually annotated on a six-point ordinal scale (0 and 5 increasing levels of intensity).

In Aff-Wild2 [15], whose key factor is an extension of the Aff-Wild [21], it contains 1,413,000 video frames containing over 260 people. Initially, the collection of videos was aimed only at large scale, even considering large variations in pose, age, lighting conditions and ethnicities. In this research, 4 specialist note-takers with extensive experience in facial analysis and functional understanding of facial expressions were used. And in the process of classification of emotions, the Convolutional Neural Networks VGGFace [19], ResNet-50 [11] and DenseNet-121 [12] were used, pre-trained by the VGGFace datasets, VGGFace2 and ImageNet. Aff-Wild2 has the same collection focus as our research, which seeks the use of reaction video images. The main limitation of the annotation process is the dependence on an expert, who follows a document for guidance to carry out the task. This document contains suggested Excitement and Valence (*Arousal* and *Valence*) patterns for emotions, which facilitates the annotation process. In our case, the primary aim is to create a dataset previously annotated automatically.

Patnaik [10], also features a dataset with spontaneous facial expressions, using the same process of inducing emotions as emotional videos. The dataset comprises of 428 videos of spontaneous facial expressions from 50 participants, which through related work [6] were used to elicit 4 emotions: Happiness, Surprise, Sadness and Disgust. The face collection method is very similar to the posed face collection method, where a controlled environment with a specific camera, lighting, and position are defined in advance.

3   Proposed Method

The proposed method consists of 6 steps: 1) collect and video convert (detailed in Sect. 3.1); 2) pre-processing data and frames extraction (detailed in Sect. 3.2); 3) faces and facial landmarks (AUs) detection (detailed in Section 3.3) 4) Most Intense Moment detection (detailed in Sect. 3.4); 5) facial emotion recognition and 6) validation using the two proposed metrics (detailed in Sect. 3.5 and Sect. 3.6). Figure 1, illustrates the framework of our method. Next sections details the various parts of the pipeline.

3.1   Obtaining Data

In this work, we propose to create a new dataset from the capture of facial expressions from YouTube reaction videos. This content was proposed because it is widely created and disseminated on various social networks and because it presents a vast and diversified behavior when analyzing the facial expressions

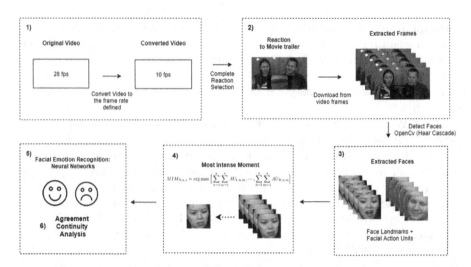

Fig. 1. Overview of our method: 1) video collection, 2) pre-processing data and frame extraction, 3) faces and facial landmarks extraction, 4) the computation of Most Intense Moment (MIM), 5) facial emotion recognition and 6) execution of validation metrics.

(reactions) of viewers in relation to movie trailers, political discourse, sports highlights, live shows, etc. A similar approach can be found in DISFA (Denver Intensity of Spontaneous Facial Action) [17] and Affectiva-MIT Facial Expressions [18], mentioned in Sect. 2, in which spontaneous facial expressions are collected from participants while they watch videos that stimulated genuine emotions.

The main difference with our research is related to the way the authors collect the facial expressions. In general, YouTube videos do not have a controlled environment, e.g., brightness control, camera position or configuration, captured frames per second captured and scenery (may contain faces that do not represent the focus of the study). With the huge variety of formats and transmission rates that content creators send to the platform, as well as the frame rate intervals available within the platform (24, 25, 30, 48, 50, 60 frames per second), it is clear that some data processing is needed in order to prepare them for analyse. So, in this part of our pipeline, we extract the interested videos and in next phase we specify how we process our data.

3.2   Pre-processing and Frames Extraction

In our work, we normalize the video framerate, so we obtain the same number of frames per second for the video reactions. It is important because it allows us to synchronize all videos from people who react to the same trailer, and later compare their reactions. We define that the *framerate*[1] of the collection

---

[1] Framerate or FPS (Frames Per Second).

will be fixed at 10 FPS, through the **PyTube**[2] and **MoviePy**[3], where the first downloads the best quality YouTube video, and the second converts the original rate of FPS for that defined in the scope of work.

3.3   Faces and Facial Landmarks Extraction

The OpenCV Haar Classifier [13] was used to extract Faces from each generated frame, which returns the location and radius of the detected faces. During the process, the need to discard the area where the video to react (trailer) is located in the image, since, in many of the initial tests, faces from the original trailer were detected. In order to avoid capturing faces which are not from the reacting people, we use OpenCV's Template Matching feature to blur or erase the trailer frames within the reaction video.

Once the faces are detected, we use OpenFace [1], which is an open source facial recognition software that uses deep learning, to determine facial landmarks, head poses and Action Unit (AU) facials. These data compose the information we use as quantitative data, for each face, at each frame.

3.4   Most Intense Moment (MIM)

Once we have data for each frame, we proposed a first analysis to find out the most intense moments of the video trailer. It is going to be useful as it provides the time of the trailer, where subjects reacted emotionally. We propose that MIM, the most intense moment, should present high values of the sum of the intensity of the Action Unit, activated for each analyzed face. Equation 1 describes how we found the frame of the video, from a certain interval of time, in which the subjects s showed higher expressiveness regarding the activation of the facial Action Unit:

$$MIM_{N,a,s} = \arg\max \left[\sum_{n=1}^{a} \sum_{m=1}^{s} AU_{1,n,m}, \cdots, \sum_{n=1}^{a} \sum_{m=1}^{s} AU_{N,n,m} \right], \qquad (1)$$

where N is the number of frames, a is the number of analyzed AUs (we have used 16), and s is the number of subjects (faces) at each frame. The *Most Intense Moment MIM* of a certain video is the frame which obtained the higher value for $MIM_{N,a,s}$. We processed MIM for each second in the movie, extracting the most intense frame at each second.

3.5   Facial Emotion Recognition

For the recognition of emotions in facial expressions, we used Convolutional Neural Networks at Keras API, which has pre-trained Deep Learning models

---

[2] https://github.com tools). /pytube/pytube.
[3] https://zulko.github.io/moviepy/.

available. We used the VGG16 model, trained using Fer2013 [9] dataset, which is widely used in the literature for classification of Emotions or Genders with the use of Convolutional Neural Networks [2] and face recognition [14]. This dataset was composed from a series of challenges available on the *Kaggle*[4] platform , with the objective of promoting the learning of posed facial expressions. Fer2013 contains approximately 30,000 RGB images of different facial expressions with a restricted size of 48×48, and having the division into 7 main classes: Angry, Disgust, Fear, Happy, Sad, Surprise and Neutral. The VGG16 model returns the classified classes for each tested face and the percentage of accuracy. In this work, we opted to select the emotion with higher % of accuracy, having as minimum threshold the accuracy of 30%. Our goal is to include more spontaneous reactions. However, as one can expect, only having such rule (using classification of emotion with minimum accuracy of 30%) we can incorrectly classify many faces. So, we propose two metrics to help such analysis, as discussed in next sections.

3.6   Emotion Recognition Analysis

For the experiment discussed in this paper, 11 videos were collected from YouTube, as mentioned before, having groups of people perceiving, containing 23 people reacting, and 12 individual videos. All these videos were part of the reaction to the Official Trailer of the Marvel WandaVision[5] series, with a duration of 1 m 20 s (80 s). Although we are interested about to finding spontaneous reactions, in this work, we hypothesize that the used platform (VGG16) works well as a primary to classify posed emotions and that spontaneous emotions are going to be classified with less accuracy.

We propose two metrics with the purpose of contributing to the reliability of the classification of spontaneous facial emotions by the Neural Networks. The first metric seeks to identify if people agree with the same emotion at the same time (same frame), while reacting to the trailer they are watching. The idea here is to use the group behavior as a way to validate the most probable emotion in the analysed time. It is important to notice here that when we say groups, we are not talking only about videos with groups of people reacting, but instead considering all video reactions together, once they are fully synchronized.

While the first analysis occurs in a specific frame, in the second metric, we enlarge the analysed time by including some frames before and after the target time. The hypothesis is that when enlarging the analysis time, we can find more frames that can have the expected emotion, as in the target moment. The two metrics are detailed in next sections.

Emotional Agreement Metric. In order to propose this metric, we firstly observed the similarities of the intensity curves of the faces, both in group and individual reactions, as illustrated in Fig. 3. It is important to notice here that we only use data extracted from faces of one MMI per second, as discussed

---

[4] Described and available at https://www.kaggle.com/msambare/fer2013.

[5] Official Trailer - https://www.youtube.com/watch?v=sj9J2ecsSpo.

in Sect. 3.4. In (a) it is interesting to see that, approximately in times 25, 50 and 60 s, we can visually observe some peaks of intensity of face 3, for instance. Our proposal aims to compute the mean, in Fig. 3(b), and standard deviation (c) of the facial AUs intensity values. Separated into 4 equal intervals, basically aligned to the y axis, we selected the smallest standard deviation values with the highest mean intensity values, thus proposing a methodology to find frames in the video, where people reacting to the videos presented more similar and intense emotional reaction. Therefore, we order the list of mean intensity (from higher to lower values) together with the values of standard deviation (from lower to higher values) and select the N first values in this list. In this experiment, 5 moments were selected of the analyzed trailer: 3, 38, 46, 68 and 71 s, as presented in Table 1.

Table 1. Facial emotion recognition results for each face in Group video, obtaining using Neural Network VGG16, trained by Fer2013 [9]. Also includes the agreement rate percentual index between face in the same video.

Video - Face	Moment 1	Moment 2	Moment 3	Moment 4	Moment 5	Agreement
	3 s	38 s	46 s	68 s	71 s	
Y1 - Face 1	Sad	Happy	Sad	Happy	Happy	53%
Y1 - Face 2	Happy	Happy	Happy	Happy	Neutral	
Y1 - Face 3	Sad	Fear	Sad	Sad	Sad	
Y2 - Face 1	Neutral	Happy	Sad	Disgust	Angry	0
Y2 - Face 2	Angry	Sad	Happy	Sad	Sad	
Y3 - Face 1	Neutral	Happy	Happy	Happy	Happy	0
Y3 - Face 2	Sad	Fear	Angry	Fear	Angry	
Y4 - Face 1	Happy	Surprise	Happy	Happy	Neutral	20%
Y4 - Face 2	Angry	Angry	Happy	Angry	Angry	
Y5 - Face 1	Angry	Angry	Angry	Angry	Angry	60%
Y5 - Face 2	Sad	Sad	Angry	Angry	Angry	
Y6 - Face 1	Happy	Happy	Happy	Angry	Happy	60%
Y6 - Face 2	Happy	Sad	Happy	Happy	Happy	
Y7 - Face 1	Sad	Sad	Happy	Sad	Sad	0
Y7 - Face 2	Happy	Angry	Disgust	Angry	Disgust	
Y8 - Face 1	Neutral	Neutral	Happy	Happy	Neutral	20%
Y8 - Face 2	Happy	Angry	Happy	Angry	Happy	
Y9 - Face 1	Sad	Sad	Sad	Sad	Sad	0
Y9 - Face 2	Happy	Neutral	Happy	Fear	Happy	
Y10 - Face 1	Sad	Sad	Neutral	Neutral	Neutral	0
Y10 - Face 2	Angry	Surprise	Fear	Angry	Fear	
Y11 - Face 1	Neutral	Happy	Happy	Happy	Happy	80%
Y11 - Face 2	Sad	Happy	Happy	Happy	Happy	

Analyzing the results of Table 1, one can see a low agreement of emotions between the faces of the groups at each analyzed frame. For instance, taking the first line of Table 1, we can see that 3 faces of video $Y1$ presents an average agreement of 53%. The best agreement is observed in video $Y11$, but almost half of videos did not present any agreement. This analysis confirms what Barrett [3] infers in the literature, where different reactions (or emotions) are likely to occur in the same situation perceived by different observers.

Another analysis performed was in relation to the agreement between all faces in a certain moment, as presented in Table 2. Among the analyzed moments, moment 3 (46 s) had the higher average of 51% of agreement between all the analysed faces. Due to the fact that this metric presented lower agreement values, we proposed a lightly change in such metric, assuming that emotions do not change so rapidly and can persist for more time, or even start before our analysis time, as discussed in next section.

Emotional Continuity Metric. In contrast to the first analysis, which sought agreement between the distinct faces of the same group reacting to the pre-determined moment, we verified whether there is continuity of emotions before and after the frame found as having more similarity between faces. Our intention is to improve the possibility of finding spontaneous reactions, providing more flexibility in the time analysis. Figure 2 illustrates the simple process, where t is the selected frame by previous metric, we extend the analyses from frame $t - K$ to $t + K$, where K is a chosen constant. In this work, we use $K = 2$.

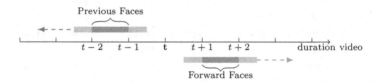

Fig. 2. Representation of frame t asn the most similar and intense frame extended by $K = 2$.

Table 2. Emotions and their respective percentage of occurrence at each moment, of the videos in groups and individuals. In the last column, we present the average agreement rate of each moment, in the total analyzed faces set.

	Group	Individual	Agreement
Moment 1	Sad - 35%/Happy - 30%	Sad - 50%/Happy - 25%	15%
Moment 2	Sad - 26%/Happy - 30%	Angry - 25%/Happy - 25%	15%
Moment 3	Happy - 57%	Happy - 25%/Surprise - 25%	51%
Moment 4	Angry - 30%/Happy - 35%	Sad - 42%/Surprise - 25%	24%
Moment 5	Angry - 22%/Happy - 35%	Angry - 25%/Sad - 33%	27%

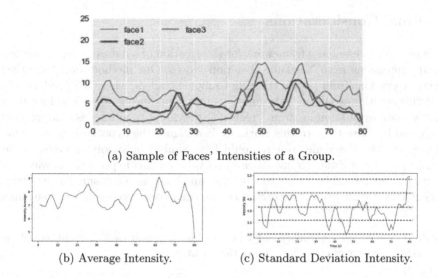

(a) Sample of Faces' Intensities of a Group.

(b) Average Intensity.   (c) Standard Deviation Intensity.

Fig. 3. Representation of differences in action unit intensities of group (Fig. 3a), during the entire reaction. And graphs representing the average of the sums of the action unit intensities (Fig. 3b) among all the analyzed faces of the videos in groups, as well as the standard deviation (Fig. 3c).

In Table 3, we provide the percentages of correct classification of emotions when using our continuity metric. This table can be compared with Table 1, and one can see that percentages of correct classification has increased. In the general analysis, on average, each face maintained in 71% the continuity of emotions during the target moments. This rate can confirm the questioning regarding the constancy of facial emotions, using $K = 2$.

3.7 Dataset Generated

The dataset creation is the last phase of our pipeline. Once we know the percentage of correctness of expected emotion, according to metrics presented in previous sections, we selected only to include images of faces that obtained at least 80% of emotion continuity agreement. So, from 18,400 images (frames) extracted from the YouTube reaction videos, we used 30% as threshold minimum in the VGG16 accuracy and 80% minimum of our proposed similarity metric. It results in a total of 373 images, with an aspect ratio of 125 × 125 pixels, organized in the following classes: 46 = *Angry*, 15 = *Fear*, 113 = *Happy*, 15 = *Neutral*, 98 = *Sad* and 23 = *Surprise*. In Fig. 4 we present some faces present in the dataset, reproduced from the *"Creative Commons BY-NC"* license. For more information about the dataset, please contact.

4 Final Considerations

This research presented a framework for the creation of a dataset of spontaneous facial expressions from YouTube Reaction videos. Our method aims to gather facial expressions from people reacting to movie trailers, where it is understood that this reaction would include emotions in a spontaneous tone. The idea is to have variations of stimulus from "real life" providing spontaneous emotions, as suggested by Barret [3]. In this work, we investigate the hypothesis that people who reacted to the same trailer, would have similar behaviors or emotions in similar periods of time. To investigate and validate this hypothesis, it was necessary to understand how the faces behave, and using as a measure the intensity of the Action Unit present in each face, we calculated the average of the sums

Table 3. Percentage Continuity index of each face, given at each moment as well as the percent average of each face, during the 5 moments.

Video - Face	Moment 1	Moment 2	Moment 3	Moment 4	Moment 5	Average
	3 s	38 s	46 s	68 s	71 s	
Y1 - Face 1	80%	80%	80%	100%	80%	84%
Y1 - Face 2	60%	60%	80%	60%	60%	65%
Y1 - Face 3	50%	–	80%	60%	80%	54%
Y2 - Face 1	100%	100%	80%	60%	60%	80%
Y2 - Face 2	60%	100%	80%	60%	–	60%
Y3 - Face 1	60%	80%	100%	100%	80%	84%
Y3 - Face 2	100%	80%	60%	80%	60%	76%
Y4 - Face 1	60%	60%	80%	80%	60%	64%
Y4 - Face 2	–	–	100%	80%	60%	48%
Y5 - Face 1	100%	80%	100%	100%	100%	96%
Y5 - Face 2	60%	–	60%	80%	60%	52%
Y6 - Face 1	100%	100%	100%	80%	60%	88%
Y6 - Face 2	100%	–	80%	100%	100%	76%
Y7 - Face 1	60%	100%	60%	80%	–	60%
Y7 - Face 2	60%	–	60%	100%	–	44%
Y8 - Face 1	60%	60%	60%	80%	60%	64%
Y8 - Face 2	80%	60%	80%	60%	80%	72%
Y9 - Face 1	100%	100%	100%	100%	100%	100%
Y9 - Face 2	60%	60%	60%	–	80%	52%
Y10 - Face 1	100%	60%	–	80%	60%	60%
Y10 - Face 2	60%	80%	–	60%	80%	56%
Y11 - Face 1	60%	100%	100%	80%	100%	88%
Y11 - Face 2	100%	100%	100%	100%	100%	100%

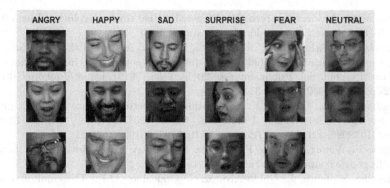

Fig. 4. Dataset samples generated from the continuity metric. The 5 main emotions (angry, fear, surprise, happy, sad) and neutral that were obtained in this research, reproduced under the creative commons BY-NC license. In this analysis, no face was found that corresponds to Disgust's emotion.

of the intensities of all the faces together with the standard deviations, in order to find moments of interest in the studied trailer time. The proposed metrics evaluate the similarity of emotions in the faces, in one specific frame as well as in its neighbors frames. So, we generate a rate of similarity of emotions as a second factor to be used together with the emotion accuracy, as classified by VGG16. In our tests, we found an average of 71% of similarity in our metric, using at least 30% of accuracy of the specific emotion, as classified by VGG16. From those images, we selected the faces with at least 80% of similarity rate in order to compose the final dataset.

Among the limitations of this research, it is important to notice that we used VGG16 as a ground truth of emotions classification, but we are aware that we need to perform evaluations with subjects. Another limitation is the detection of most intense moments, given the subjectivity perceived by each person, it certainly has to be evaluated by subjects as well. Another limitation is the number of trailers tested, once we based our studies, for the moment, in one only trailer. As next steps in the research, in addition to deal with our limitations, we seek to identify different styles of emotions that can categorize spontaneous facial expressions and perform a deep analysis in order to understand the differences between the spontaneous datasets generated with posed datasets.

Acknowledgment. The authors would like to thank CNPq and CAPES for partially funding this work.

References

1. Amos, B., Ludwiczuk, B., Satyanarayanan, M.: OpenFace: a general-purpose face recognition library with mobile applications. Technical report, CMU-CS-16-118, CMU School of Computer Science (2016)

2. Arriaga, O., Valdenegro-Toro, M., Plöger, P.: Real-time convolutional neural networks for emotion and gender classification (2017)
3. Barrett, L.F., Adolphs, R., Marsella, S., Martinez, A.M., Pollak, S.D.: Emotional expressions reconsidered: challenges to inferring emotion from human facial movements. Psychol. Sci. Public Interest **20**(1), 1–68 (2019). https://doi.org/10.1177/1529100619832930, pMID: 31313636
4. Bradley, M.M., Lang, P.J.: International Affective Picture System, pp. 1–4. Springer International Publishing, Cham (2017). https://doi.org/10.1007/9783319280998421, https://doi.org/10.1007/9783319280998421
5. Bruce, V., Young, A.: Face Perception. Psychology Press, Hove (2012). https://books.google.com.br/books?id=aJjVW1eYebUC
6. Carvalho, S., Leite, J., Galdo-Álvarez, S., Gonçalves, O.F.: The emotional movie database (EMDB): a self-report and psychophysiological study. Appl. Psychophysiol. Biofeedback **37**(4), 279–294 (2012)
7. EKMAN, P.: Facial action coding system (FACS). A Human Face (2002). https://ci.nii.ac.jp/naid/10025007347/en/
8. Ekman, P., Rosenberg, E.: What the Face Reveals: Basic and Applied Studies of Spontaneous Expression Using the Facial Action Coding System (FACS). Series in Affective Science. Oxford University Press, Oxford (2005). https://books.google.com.br/books?id=UXapcWqtO-sC
9. Goodfellow, I.J., et al.: Challenges in representation learning: a report on three machine learning contests (2013)
10. Happy, S.L., Patnaik, P., Routray, A., Guha, R.: The Indian spontaneous expression database for emotion recognition. IEEE Trans. Affect. Comput. **8**(1), 131–142 (2017). https://doi.org/10.1109/TAFFC.2015.2498174
11. He, K., Zhang, X., Ren, S., Sun, J.: Deep residual learning for image recognition. CoRR abs/1512.03385 (2015). http://arxiv.org/abs/1512.03385
12. Iandola, F.N., Moskewicz, M.W., Karayev, S., Girshick, R.B., Darrell, T., Keutzer, K.: Densenet: Implementing efficient convnet descriptor pyramids. CoRR abs/1404.1869 (2014). http://arxiv.org/abs/1404.1869
13. Khan, M., Chakraborty, S., Astya, R., Khepra, S.: Face detection and recognition using OpenCV. In: 2019 International Conference on Computing, Communication, and Intelligent Systems (ICCCIS), pp. 116–119 (2019)
14. Khanzada, A., Bai, C., Celepcikay, F.T.: Facial expression recognition with deep learning. CoRR abs/2004.11823 (2020). https://arxiv.org/abs/2004.11823
15. Kollias, D., Zafeiriou, S.: Aff-Wild2: extending the Aff-wild database for affect recognition (2019)
16. Koukounas, E., Over, R.: Changes in the magnitude of the eyeblink startle response during habituation of sexual arousal. Behav. Res.Therapy **38**(6), 573–584 (2000). https://doi.org/10.1016/S0005-7967(99)00075-3, https://www.sciencedirect.com/science/article/pii/S0005796799000753
17. Mavadati, S.M., Mahoor, M.H., Bartlett, K., Trinh, P., Cohn, J.F.: DISFA: a spontaneous facial action intensity database. IEEE Trans. Affect. Comput. **4**(2), 151–160 (2013)
18. McDuff, D., el Kaliouby, R., Senechal, T., Amr, M., Cohn, J.F., Picard, R.: Affectiva-MIT facial expression dataset (am-fed): naturalistic and spontaneous facial expressions collected "in-the-wild". In: Proceedings of the 2013 IEEE Conference on Computer Vision and Pattern Recognition Workshops, pp. 881–888. CVPRW 2013, IEEE Computer Society, USA (2013). https://doi.org/10.1109/CVPRW.2013.130, https://doi.org/10.1109/CVPRW.2013.130

19. Parkhi, O.M., Vedaldi, A., Zisserman, A.: Deep face recognition. In: Proceedings of the British Machine Vision Conference (BMVC). pp. 41.1-41.12. BMVA Press, September 2015. https://doi.org/10.5244/C.29.41, https://dx.doi.org/10.5244/C. 29.41

20. Schaefer, A., Nils, F., Sanchez, X., Philippot, P.: Assessing the effectiveness of a large database of emotion-eliciting films: a new tool for emotion researchers. Cogn. Emot. **24**(7), 1153–1172 (2010). https://doi.org/10.1080/02699930903274322

21. Zafeiriou, S., Kollias, D., Nicolaou, M.A., Papaioannou, A., Zhao, G., Kotsia, I.: Aff-wild: valence and arousal 'in-the-wild' challenge. In: 2017 IEEE Conference on Computer Vision and Pattern Recognition Workshops (CVPRW), pp. 1980–1987 (2017). https://doi.org/10.1109/CVPRW.2017.248

Automated Bite-block Detection to Distinguish Colonoscopy from Upper Endoscopy Using Deep Learning

Md Marufi Rahman[1], JungHwan Oh[1(✉)], Wallapak Tavanapong[2], Johnny Wong[2], and Piet C. de Groen[3]

[1] Department of Computer Science and Engineering, University of North Texas, Denton, TX 76203, USA
Junghwan.Oh@unt.edu
[2] Computer Science Department, Iowa State University, Ames, IA 50011, USA
tavanapo@iastate.edu
[3] Division of Gastroenterology Hepatology and Nutrition, University of Minnesota, Minnesota, MN 55455, USA
degroen@umn.edu

Abstract. Colonoscopy is currently the gold standard procedure for colorectal cancer (CRC) screening. However, the dominant explanations for the continued incidence of CRC are endoscopist-related factors. To address this, we have been investigating an automated feedback system which measures quality of colonoscopy automatically to assist the endoscopist to improve the quality of the actual procedure being performed. One of the fundamental steps for the automated quality feedback system is to distinguish a colonoscopy from an upper endoscopy since upper endoscopy and colonoscopy procedures are performed in the same room at different times, and it is necessary to distinguish the type of a procedure prior to execution of any quality measurement method to evaluate the procedure. In upper endoscopy, a bite-block is inserted for patient protection. By detecting this bite-block appearance, we can distinguish colonoscopy from upper endoscopy. However, there are various colors (i.e., blue, green, white, etc.) of bite-blocks. Our solution utilizes analyses of Hue and Saturation values and two Convolutional Neural Networks (CNNs). One CNN detects image patches of a bite-block regardless of its colors. The other CNN detects image patches of the tongue. The experimental results show that the proposed solution is highly promising.

Keywords: Object detection · Bite-block · Image processing · Convolutional neural network · Upper endoscopy · Colonoscopy

1 Introduction

Colorectal cancer (CRC), despite being a preventable cancer, is still expected to cause about 53,200 deaths in the U.S. in 2020 [1]. Colonoscopy allows for detailed examination

© Springer Nature Switzerland AG 2021
G. Bebis et al. (Eds.): ISVC 2021, LNCS 13018, pp. 216–228, 2021.
https://doi.org/10.1007/978-3-030-90436-4_17

of the entire colon and removal of all premalignant lesions during the procedure. Currently, the dominant explanations for the continued incidence of CRC are endoscopist-related factors, such as choice of suboptimal equipment, not removing remaining debris, not reaching the cecum, too fast withdrawal, no effort at inspection of areas behind folds and angulations, and an inadequate polyp removal technique [2].

Since 2003, we have developed software (Endoscopic Multimedia Information System or EMIS) for automated measurements of quality and feedback during colonoscopy [3]. EMIS measures and provides feedbacks for multiple intra-procedure quality metrics (e.g., clear withdrawal time without blurry frames, amount of stool during insertion and withdrawal, and Boston Bowel Preparation Scale score estimates).

Typically, upper endoscopy and colonoscopy procedures are performed in the same room at different times. It is necessary to distinguish the type of a procedure prior to execution of any quality measurement method to evaluate the procedure. For instance, stool detection generates useful information only for colonoscopy, but not for upper endoscopy. We need to develop a method detecting the procedure type at the beginning of the procedure so that only colonoscopy related modules run on the procedure. In upper endoscopy, a bite-block (Fig. 1) is inserted for patient protection. By detecting bite-block appearance, we can distinguish colonoscopy from upper endoscopy.

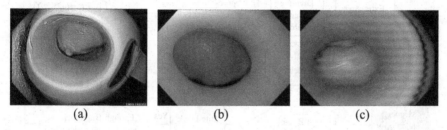

(a)   (b)   (c)

Fig. 1. Examples of Bite-blocks: (a) Blue Bite-block, (b) White Bite-block, (c) Green Bite-block. (Color figure online)

Since bite-block colors are the most distinguishable characteristics, we used color feature in our previous work [4], in which we could detect a green bite block only. However, hospitals may use bite blocks with different colors as seen in Fig. 1. The performance of our previous method drops when a bite-block is not green.

In this paper, we propose a method to distinguish colonoscopy from upper endoscopy by detecting bite-block regardless of its colors in a video. A brief description of the proposed method is as follows. For a given video, several frames are extracted from the beginning part of the video since a bite-block is appearing at the start of upper endoscopy. Each frame is divided to a number of small patches with the patch size of 32 × 32 pixels in our case. We use patches instead of a whole image since the image has complex contents, but a patch is more homogenous. We determined the patch size by experiments. After all these patches are preprocessed, only informative patches are used for the next step. Each patch is fed into two Convolutional Neural Networks (CNNs) called Bite-block CNN and Tongue CNN hereafter. Bite-block CNN is trained using many patches from bite-block and non-bite-block areas. To detect the bite-block patches regardless of their colors, bite-block and non-bite-block patches are converted to grayscale from color. Then, the grayscale patches are used for training Bite-block CNN. Tongue CNN is trained using many patches from tongue and non-tongue areas. In this case, we do not covert to grayscale, just use color patches since the color variation of tongues is small. Bite-block CNN classifies an input patch to either bite-block patch or not. Tongue CNN classifies an input patch to either tongue patch or not. Since the classification accuracy of Bite-block CNN is not good enough as will be seen later on, we developed additional algorithms using Hue and Saturation values to improve the accuracy. If the number of bite-block patches in a frame exceeds a certain threshold, and if the number of tongue patches in the same frame exceeds a certain threshold too, this frame is called a bite-block frame. These two conditions need to be satisfied together since a bite-block is inserted in front of the tongue, so bite-block and tongue are seen together. If the number of consecutive bite-block frames in each video is exceeding a certain threshold, the input video is considered as an upper endoscopy video. The overall procedure of the proposed method is shown in Fig. 2. Our contribution is the new method that discriminates upper endoscopy from colonoscopy effectively regardless of the color of the bite block used during upper endoscopy.

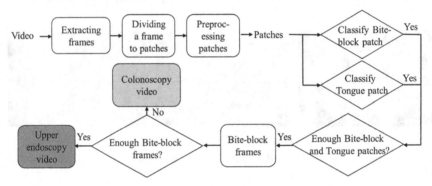

Fig. 2. Overall procedure of the proposed method.

The rest of the paper is organized as follows. Section 2 discusses the related work. Section 3 describes the proposed methodology. Section 4 shows our experimental results. Finally, Sect. 5 summarizes our concluding remarks.

2 Related Work

To the best of our knowledge, the most recent and relevant work for discriminating upper endoscopy from colonoscopy is our previous work [4] based on detection of green bite-block regions. The main idea was to partition very large positive examples (pixel values of a green bite-block) into a number of groups, in which each group is called 'positive plane.' Each positive plane is modeled as a separate entity for that group of positive examples. We used a 'convex hull' to represent a positive plane to enable fast detection. Overall, our experimental results showed very good accuracy. However, the method only detects green bite-blocks.

3 Methodology

Our proposed method decides whether a given video is an upper endoscopy video or not. An upper endoscopy video should have enough frames with a bite-block. A bite-block frame should have a sufficiently large bite-block area. To detect a bite block area, we use Bite-block CNN and Tongue CNN as well as Hue and Saturation analyses.

3.1 Image Preprocessing

For a given video, a number of frames are extracted from the start of the video since a bite-block appears at the start of the video. We use our previous method [5] to remove water bubble, or blurry frames (Fig. 3). Each of the remaining frames is divided into non-overlapping patches. The patch size is 32×32 pixels, which was empirically determined. We use patches instead of whole images for analysis because images are more likely to have complex contents whereas patches are more likely to show homogenous content. The latter enhances CNN speed and accuracy.

(a)   (b)

Fig. 3. Examples of frames with (a) water and bubble, or (b) blurriness.

The frame size for our upper endoscopy and colonoscopy videos is 720×480 pixels. After discarding border pixels, each frame has 330 patches. Then, too dark or too bright patches (Fig. 4) are eliminated as follows. First, Gaussian blur filter is applied to remove high frequency noises [6]. Next, the ratios, R_{bright} and R_{dark}, are computed for each patch. If these ratios are larger than a certain threshold ($TH_{non\text{-}informative}$), the patch is considered as non-informative, and discarded.

$$R_{bright} = \frac{\text{Number of too bright pixels}}{\text{Total number of pixels}} \quad R_{dark} = \frac{\text{Number of too dark pixels}}{\text{Total number of pixels}}$$

A pixel is too bright if its grayscale value is larger than a certain threshold (TH_{bright}), and it is too dark if its grayscale value is lower than a certain threshold (TH_{dark}).

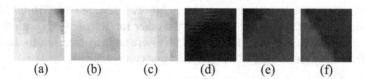

(a)   (b)   (c)   (d)   (e)   (f)

Fig. 4. Examples of non-informative patches: (a), (b), (c) too bright, and (d), (e), (f) too dark.

3.2 Bite-block CNN and Tongue CNN

We train Bite-block CNN using many informative patches of bite-block and non-bite-block areas. To detect the bite-block patches regardless of their colors, we use OpenCV library [7] to convert RGB values of pixels to gray scale. These grayscale patches are used for training Bite-block CNN to classify an input patch to either bite-block or not. We train Tongue CNN using many informative patches from tongue and non-tongue areas. We use color patches directly due to a small color variation of the tongue. Tongue CNN classifies an input patch to either tongue patch or not. We investigated three different CNN architectures for Bite-block CNN and Tongue CNN: our own CNN called 'Simple CNN' built from scratch, VGG16 [8], and Resnet50 [9].

Implementation with Simple CNN

Simple CNN was made up from scratch for our experiments. It has four convolution layers (with the number of kernels of 16, 32, 64, 128, respectively), each of them is followed by a pooling layer. One fully connected layer is at the end. Each convolution layer has kernels of size 3×3. Max-pooling of 2×2 sliding with a stride of 1 is used for pooling operation. We use RELU activation function after each convolution layer. The output layer is a softmax layer generating a class along with the class probability of the input patch. Learning rate was 0.0001. For optimization, we used 'Adam' optimizer and the loss function of 'sparse categorical cross entropy' as it is a two-class classification. The training and validation data were split to 80% and 20%, respectively. The validation loss was computed after five iterations. We used the 'early stopping' method, which stops the training when the validation loss does not improve further. We set the total number of epochs to 50. Two separate Simple CNNs were implemented, one for Bite-block CNN and the other for Tongue CNN with the same configurations.

Implementation with VGG16 and Resnet50

We used the pre-trained networks such as VGG16 and ResNet50 with the fine-tuning to implement CNNs for the patch classification. Fine-tuning a pre-trained network is popular as it has the advantage of decreased need of data and compute time. As mentioned in [10], the learned kernels from the pre-trained CNNs on ImageNet are useful for medical image classification tasks even though they were trained on completely different image domains. The pretrained VGG16 has 16 layers and Resnet50 has 50 layers with the output layer for 1000 classes. For our classification purposes, we fine-tuned the pretrain networks by changing the number of classes from 1,000 to two. We changed the input image size to 32×32 for a fair comparison among the Simple CNN, VGG16, and Resnet50 models. The training and validation data were split to 80% and 20%, respectively. The validation loss was computed after five iterations. We used the 'early stopping' method, which stops the training when the validation loss does not improve further. We set the total number of epochs to 50. Two separate VGG16 CNNs were implemented, one for Bite-block CNN and the other for Tongue CNN with the same configurations. And two separate Resnet50 CNNs were implemented, one for Bite-block CNN and the other for Tongue CNN with the same configurations.

3.3   Classifications of Bite-block and Tongue Patches

Figure 5(a), (b) and (c) show correctly detected white, blue, and green bite-block patches, respectively. Figure 5(d) shows a correctly detected tongue patch.

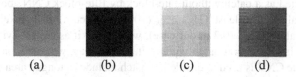

(a)   (b)   (c)   (d)

Fig. 5. Examples of correctly detected patches. (Color figure online)

However, in the test results of Bite-block CNN, many white bite-block patches are classified as non bite-block patches. Some examples of the incorrectly detected patches are shown in Fig. 6. Figure 6(a) and (b) show two white bite-block patches which are incorrectly detected as non bite-block patches. Figure 6(c) and (d) show two non bite-block patches which are incorrectly detected as bite-block patches.

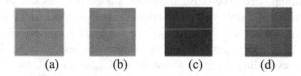

(a)   (b)   (c)   (d)

Fig. 6. Examples of incorrectly detected patches.

We need an additional algorithm to compensate the lower accuracy of Bite-block CNN. To find a better solution, we selected 90 frames from 45 different upper endoscopy videos, in which there are 15 frames with green bite-blocks, 15 frames with blue bite-blocks, 15 frames with white bite-blocks, and 45 frames with no bite-block. From these frames, we generated 1,532 patches with green bite-blocks, 2,011 patches with blue bite-blocks, 2,379 patches with white bite-blocks, and 19,663 patches with no bite-block. We examined Hue and Saturation values of all the pixels in these patches (25,585). We found that a patch with green or blue bite-blocks has at least a certain percentage (TH$_{Hue\ pixels}$: 30% in our case) of pixels that their Hue values are larger than a certain value (TH$_{Hue}$: 60° in our case). However, a patch with white or no bite-blocks has less than a certain percentage (TH$_{Hue\ pixels}$: 30% in our case) of pixels that their Hue values are larger than a certain value (TH$_{Hue}$: 60° in our case). There is no clear distinction between the patches with white bite-blocks and those with no bite-block. We also found that a patch with white or no bite-blocks has at least a certain percentage (TH$_{Sat\ pixels}$: 70% in our case) of pixels that their Saturation values are smaller than a certain value (TH$_{Sat}$: 0.2 in our case). However, a patch with green or blue bite-blocks has less than a certain percentage (TH$_{Sat\ pixels}$: 70% in our case) of pixels that their Saturation values are smaller than a certain value (TH$_{Sat}$: 0.2 in our case).

By combining the results of Bite-block CNN, and the values of Hue and Saturation, we can classify the patches more accurately. There are many different possible combinations of how to apply these three, Bite-block CNN result, the values of Hue, and the values of Saturation. After testing, we decided that we apply Bite-block CNN first. If it is predicted as a patch with bite-block, we check its Hue values. If at least $TH_{Hue\ pixels}$ (30% in our case) of its pixels are larger than a certain value, TH_{Hue} (60° in our case), we classify it as a patch with bite-block. Otherwise, we classify it as a patch without it. If it is predicted as a patch without bite-block by Bite-block CNN above, we check its Saturation values. If at least $TH_{Sat\ pixels}$ (70% in our case) of its pixels are smaller than a certain value, TH_{Sat} (0.2 in our case), we classify it as a patch with bite-block, otherwise, we classify it as a patch without it. In this way, we can achieve very high accuracy. Tongue CNN is used to decide if a patch includes a tongue area or not. We do not use any other additional algorithm since Tongue CNN itself generated a reasonable accuracy. We discuss more experimental results in Sect. 4.

3.4 Detection of Upper Endoscopy Video

As discussed in Introduction, if the number of bite-block patches in a frame exceeds a certain threshold ($TH_{Bite-block\ patch}$), and if the number of tongue patches in the same frame exceeds a certain threshold ($TH_{Tongue\ patch}$), this frame is called a bite-block frame. These two conditions need to be satisfied together since a bite-block is inserted in front of the tongue (which is visible within the opening), so bite-block and tongue are seen together. $TH_{Bite-block\ patch}$, and $TH_{Tongue\ patch}$ are 5% and 7%, respectively in our case, which were determined by experiments. If the number of consecutive bite block frames in each video is exceeding a certain threshold ($TH_{Bite-block\ frame}$), the input video is considered as an upper endoscopy video. To decide this threshold ($TH_{Bite-block\ frame}$), we examined 140 upper endoscopy videos, and found that a bite-block appeared at least 0.5 s. Since we extracted the frames at 10 frames per second, the value of $TH_{Bite-block\ frame}$ was 5 in our case.

4 Experiments and Results

In this section, we discuss the datasets, the performance metrics, the various experiments conducted, and their results and analyses. We used a workstation with Intel(R) Core(TM) i7–10700 CPU @ 2.9 GHz 8 Core(s), 16 Logical Processor(s), and NVIDIA Geforce RTX 2070 Super with 8GB RAM. We implemented the proposed CNNs using Keras [11].

4.1 Datasets

Our dataset has a total 234 upper endoscopy videos in which 78 videos have blue bite-blocks, 78 videos have green bite-blocks, and 78 videos have white bite-blocks. We used 174 and 60 of these videos for training and testing, respectively. In addition, we included 60 colonoscopy videos for testing. The videos do not have any patient identifiable information. ImageDatagenerator of Keras [12] was used to augment the patches by Zooming, Shearing, and Horizontal Flipping. Zooming factor of 0.2 was used, which means 20% larger (or closer). The zooming amount was uniformly applied for each dimension (width and height) separately. Shearing factor of 20.0 was used, which means 20 degree slanting in a counter-clockwise direction. In Horizontal Flipping, all the rows in an image are reversed. Tables 1 and 2 show upper endoscopy datasets for training of Bite-block CNNs and Tongue CNNs, respectively. Table 3 shows the details of upper endoscopy and colonoscopy datasets for testing of the proposed methods. Training and testing datasets are completely different and there is no overlap between them.

Table 1. Description of the upper endoscopy dataset for training of Bite-block CNNs (Numbers of Patches after Augmentation).

Color of bite-block	Number of videos	Number of frames	Number of patches	Number of bite-block patches	Number of non-bite-block patches
Blue	58	1,300	1,098,676	527,368	571,308
Green	58	1,300	1,009,292	484,464	526,428
white	58	1,300	1,012,368	485,940	131,607
Total	**174**	**3,900**	**3,120,336**	**1,497,772**	**1,622,564**

Table 2. Description of the upper endoscopy dataset for training of Tongue CNNs (Numbers of Patches after Augmentation).

Color of bite-block	Number of videos	Number of frames	Number of patches	Number of tongue patches	Number of non-tongue patches
Blue	58	440	443,890	244,433	199,457
Green	58	425	442,777	239,967	202,810
white	58	435	443,333	242,200	201,133
Total	**174**	**1,300**	**1,330,000**	**726,600**	**603,400**

Table 3. Description of the upper endoscopy and colonoscopy datasets for testing.

Type of video	Color of bite-block	Number of videos	Number of frames	Numberof patches
Upper endoscopy	Blue	20	1,400	4,619,354
Upper endoscopy	White	20	1,400	4,568,734
Upper endoscopy	Green	20	1,400	4,483,412
Colonoscopy	None	60	4,200	12,600,335
Total		**120**	**8,400**	**26,271,835**

4.2   Training and Testing

We implemented three different CNN architectures: Simple CNN, VGG16 [8], and Resnet50 [9] for Bite-block CNN and Tongue CNN as discussed in Sect. 3.2. When we trained three different CNN architectures for Tongue CNN, we used all those Tongue and Non-Tongue patches together in Table 2. For convenience, we call these three CNNs as 'Simple-Tongue', 'VGG16-Tongue', and 'Resnet50-Tongue'. When we trained and tested three different CNN architectures for Bite-block CNN, we used different options to select images from the training and testing datasets. For example, when we trained Simple CNN for Bite-block CNN, we used all patches in Table 1, and tested all patches in Table 3. For convenience, we call this option 'Simple-Bite-WGB' (W means white, G means green, and B means Blue). One other option is to use the patches from the upper endoscopy videos with white and green bite-blocks for training, and to use the patches from the upper endoscopy videos with blue bite-blocks for testing. For convenience, we call this option 'Simple-Bite-WG'. In this way, we can resemble more realistic circumstance in hospitals in which they may use a bite-block with different colors. All the options that we experimented are summarized in Table 4. When we did testing, we utilized all Hue and Saturation values as discussed in Sect. 3.3. For convenience and simplicity, we did not include the words 'Hue' or "Saturation' in the names of options, but all of them consider Hue and Saturation values.

Table 4. Options for training and testing Bite-block CNNs + Tongue CNNs (white: upper endoscopy videos with white bite-block, green: upper endoscopy videos with green bite-block, blue: upper endoscopy videos with blue bite-block, colon: colonoscopy videos. The information of all these videos is in Tables 1, 2 and 3).

Names of options	CNN architecture	Training videos for bite-block CNN	Testing videos
Resnet50-Bite-WGB + Resnet50-Tongue	Resnet50	blue, white, green	blue, white, green, colon
VGG16-Bite-WGB + VGG16-Tongue	VGG16	blue, white, green	blue, white, green, colon
Simple-Bite-WGB + Simple-Tongue	Simple CNN (from scratch)	blue, white, green	blue, white, green, colon
Resnet50-Bite-WG + Resnet50-Tongue	Resnet50	white, green	blue, colon
VGG16-Bite-WG + VGG16-Tongue	VGG16	white, green	blue, colon
Simple-Bite-WG + Simple-Tongue	Simple CNN (from scratch)	white, green	blue, colon

(*continued*)

Table 4. (*continued*)

Names of options	CNN architecture	Training videos for bite-block CNN	Testing videos
Resnet50-Bite-WB + Resnet50-Tongue	Resnet50	white, blue	green, colon
VGG16-Bite-WB + VGG16-Tongue	VGG16	white, blue	green, colon
Simple-Bite-WB + Simple-Tongue	Simple CNN (from scratch)	white, blue	green, colon
Resnet50-Bite-GB + Resnet50-Tongue	Resnet50	green, blue	white, colon
VGG16-Bite-GB + VGG16-Tongue	VGG16	Green, blue	white, colon
Simple-Bite-GB + Simple-Tongue	Simple CNN (from scratch)	Green, blue	white, colon

4.3 Performance Metrics and Accuracy Comparison

The performance evaluation metrics are Sensitivity (or Recall), Precision, and F1-score. To calculate these metrics, we consider the following terms. We measured accuracy both on the frame level and the video level. At the frame level, True Positive (TP) means a correctly detected Bite-block frame, False Positive (FP) means an incorrectly detected Bite-block frame. True Negative (TN) means a correctly detected non Bite-block frame, and False Negative (FN) means an incorrectly detected non Bite-block frame. At the video level, a correctly detected upper endoscopy video will be considered as True Positive, and a correctly detected colonoscopy video will be counted as True Negative. An incorrectly detected upper endoscopy video will be False Positive (FP), and an incorrectly detected colonoscopy video will be counted as False Negative (FN). Using these terms, the performance metrics are defined as follows:

$$\text{Sensitivity} = \frac{TP}{TP+FN} \quad \text{Precision} = \frac{TP}{TP+FP} \quad F1 - \text{score} = \frac{2*precision*recall}{precision+recall}$$

Table 5 shows the accuracy results of the options in Table 4 at the frame level. All these results were generated by applying Hue and Saturation values discussed in Sect. 3.3. For this test, we used 60 endoscopy videos in Table 3. Before the testing, we expected that the first three options in Table 4 might generate better accuracies than the remaining options since these three options have the endoscopy videos with same color bite-blocks in the training and testing sets. However, all the options provided very similar and high accuracies as seen in Table 5. It can be interpreted that we can distinguish endoscopy videos with a bite-block with the colors not included in the training. As expected, VGG16 [8] or Resnet50 [9] based CNNs generated better accuracy compared to the Simple CNNs built from scratch since they have more layers.

Table 6 represents the accuracy results in the video level for 120 videos (60 colonoscopy and 60 upper endoscopy videos) in Table 3. These results were obtained by

Table 5. Accuracy results of the options in Table 4 at the frame level.

Names of options	Precision	Sensitivity	F1-score
Resnet50-Bite-WGB + Resnet50-Tongue	**0.713**	**0.957**	**0.817**
VGG16-Bite-WGB + VGG16-Tongue	0.691	0.947	0.799
Simple-Bite-WGB + Simple-Tongue	0.662	0.875	0.753
Resnet50-Bite-WG + Resnet50-Tongue	0.710	0.968	0.805
VGG16-Bite-WG + VGG16-Tongue	0.690	0.964	0.793
Simple-Bite-WG + Simple-Tongue	0.658	0.899	0.743
Resnet50-Bite-WB + Resnet50-Tongue	0.683	0.982	0.794
VGG16-Bite-WB + VGG16-Tongue	0.674	0.971	0.793
Simple-Bite-WB + Simple-Tongue	0.681	0.955	0.790
Resnet50-Bite-GB + Resnet50-Tongue	0.679	0.935	0.782
VGG16-Bite-GB + VGG16-Tongue	0.670	0.932	0.775
Simple-Bite-GB + Simple-Tongue	0.624	0.748	0.670

applying the methods discussed in Sect. 3.4. The first three options in Table 4 generated slightly better accuracies than the remaining options at the video level, but we can see the similar result patterns in the video level as in the frame level.

Table 6. Accuracy results of the options in Table 4 in the video level.

Names of options	Precision	Sensitivity	F1-score
Resnet50-Bite-WGB + Resnet50-Tongue	**0.909**	1	**0.952**
VGG16-Bite-WGB + VGG16-Tongue	**0.909**	1	**0.952**
Simple-Bite-WGB + Simple-Tongue	0.934	0.950	0.942
Resnet50-Bite-WG + Resnet50-Tongue	0.771	1	0.871
VGG16-Bite-WG + VGG16-Tongue	0.771	1	0.871
Simple-Bite-WG + Simple-Tongue	0.783	0.900	0.837
Resnet50-Bite-WB + Resnet50-Tongue	0.771	1	0.871
VGG16-Bite-WB + VGG16-Tongue	0.771	1	0.871
Simple-Bite-WB + Simple-Tongue	0.800	1	0.889
Resnet50-Bite-GB + Resnet50-Tongue	0.771	1	0.871
VGG16-Bite-GB + VGG16-Tongue	0.771	1	0.871
Simple-Bite-GB + Simple-Tongue	0.792	0.950	0.864

4.4 Effects of Hue and Saturation

As discussed in Sect. 3.3, we improve the accuracy of patch classification by considering the values of Hue and Saturation additionally. To evaluate how much it can be improved, we implemented three modules ('Bite-block CNN only', 'Hue-Saturation only', and 'Bite-block CNN with Hue-Saturation') in which Bite-block CNN was implemented using Simple CNN discussed in Sect. 3.2. The module of 'Hue-Saturation only' used the all the threshold values only discussed in Sect. 3.3. To test them, we selected 45 frames (15 of white, 15 of green and 15 of blue bite-blocks) and 45 frames without bite-block. They generated a total of 19,663 patches (5,922 patches with bite-blocks and 13,741 patches without bite-block). Using these patches, we compare the results of classification of patches with or without bite-block. As seen in Table 7, 'Bite-Block CNN only' or Hue-Saturation only' generated low and unbalanced Precision (0.53) and Sensitivity (0.68) while 'Bite-Block CNN with Hue-Saturation' generated high and balanced Precision (0.78) and Sensitivity (0.81).

5 Conclusion

To distinguish a colonoscopy from an upper endoscopy, we propose and test a novel automated method to detect bite-block appearances. There are various colors (i.e., blue, green, white, etc.) of bite-blocks. To detect these bite-blocks regardless of their colors, the proposed method uses two CNNs and Hue and Saturation features. As seen in the experimental results, the proposed method achieved excellent accuracy that warrants use in endoscopic practice. In the current experiments, we used the upper endoscopy videos which have three different colors (White, Green, and Blue) of bite-blocks. In the future, we will incorporate upper endoscopy videos with bite-blocks of additional, different colors to enhance the proposed method.

Table 7. Accuracy comparison of three modules at the frame level.

Modules	Precision	Sensitivity	F1-score
Bite-block CNN only	0.525	0.869	0.663
Hue-Saturation only	0.767	0.684	0.712
Bite-block CNN with Hue-Saturation	**0.784**	**0.812**	**0.793**

References

1. American Cancer Society: Colorectum Cancer Statistics (2020). https://cancerstatisticscenter.cancer.org/?_ga=2.95264916.902125337.1581945528-1873365005.1581945528#!/cancer-site/Colorectum

2. Xirasagar, S., Wu, Y., Tsai, M.-H., Zhang, J., Chiodini, S., de Groen, P.C.: Colorectal cancer prevention by a CLEAR principles-based colonoscopy protocol: an observational study. Gastrointest. Endosc. **91**, 905-916.e4 (2020)
3. Tavanapong, W., Oh, J., Kijkul, G., Pratt, J., Wong, J., de Groen, P.C.: Real-time feedback for colonoscopy in a multi-center clinical trial. In: IEEE 33rd International Symposium on Computer Based Medical Systems (CBMS), Mayo Clinic, Rochester, MN, 28–30 July 2020, pp. 13–18 (2020)
4. Muthukudage, J., JungHwan, O., Nawarathna, R., Tavanapong, W., Wong, J., de Groen, P.: Fast object detection using color features for colonoscopy quality measurements. In: El-Baz, A.S., Saba, L., Suri, J. (eds.) Abdomen and Thoracic Imaging, pp. 365–388. Springer US, Boston (2014). https://doi.org/10.1007/978-1-4614-8498-1_14
5. Islam, A.B.M.R., Alammari, A., Oh, J., Tavanapong, W., Wong, J., de Groen, P.C.: Non-informative frame classification in colonoscopy videos using CNNs. In: Proceedings of the 2018 3rd International Conference on BIOMEDICAL Imaging, Signal Processing, pp. 53–60 (2018)
6. Fan, L., Zhang, F., Fan, H., Zhang, C.: Brief review of image denoising techniques. Visual Comput. Ind Biomed. Art **2**(1), 1–12 (2019). https://doi.org/10.1186/s42492-019-0016-7
7. Bradski, G.: The openCV library. Dobb's J. Softw. Tools Prof. Progr. **25**, 120–123 (2000)
8. Simonyan, K., Zisserman, A.: Very deep convolutional networks for large-scale image recognition (2014). arXiv preprint arXiv:1409.1556
9. He, K., Zhang, X., Ren, S., Sun, J.: Deep residual learning for image recognition. In: 2016 IEEE Conference on Computer Vision and Pattern Recognition (CVPR), pp. 770–778 (2016)
10. Tajbakhsh, N., et al.: Convolutional neural networks for medical image analysis: Full training or fine tuning? IEEE Trans. Med. Imaging **35**, 1299–1312 (2016)
11. Ramasubramanian, K., Singh, A.: Deep learning using keras and tensorflow. In: Ramasubramanian, K., Singh, A. (eds.) Machine Learning Using R: With Time Series and Industry-Based Use Cases in R, pp. 667–688. Apress, Berkeley (2019). https://doi.org/10.1007/978-1-4842-4215-5_11
12. Gulli, A., Pal, S.: Deep Learning with Keras. Packt Publishing Ltd., Birmingham (2017)

How Does Heterogeneous Label Noise Impact Generalization in Neural Nets?

Bidur Khanal[1]([✉]) and Christopher Kanan[1,2,3]

[1] Rochester Institute of Technology, Rochester, USA
{bk9618,kanan}@rit.edu
[2] Paige, New York, USA
[3] Cornell Tech, New York, USA

Abstract. Incorrectly labeled examples, or label noise, is common in real-world computer vision datasets. While the impact of label noise on learning in deep neural networks has been studied in prior work, these studies have exclusively focused on homogeneous label noise, i.e., the degree of label noise is the same across all categories. However, in the real-world, label noise is often heterogeneous, with some categories being affected to a greater extent than others. Here, we address this gap in the literature. We hypothesized that heterogeneous label noise would only affect the classes that had label noise unless there was transfer from those classes to the classes without label noise. To test this hypothesis, we designed a series of computer vision studies using MNIST, CIFAR-10, CIFAR-100, and MS-COCO where we imposed heterogeneous label noise during the training of multi-class, multi-task, and multi-label systems. Our results provide evidence in support of our hypothesis: label noise only affects the class affected by it unless there is transfer.

Keywords: Multi-class · Multi-task · Multi-label · Heterogeneous label noise

1 Introduction

Supervised deep learning models have been successful in various tasks such as large-scale image classification, object detection, semantic segmentation, and many more [16,24,26]. One of the significant contributions behind the success of supervised deep learning is the availability of well-labeled large datasets. However, such well-labeled datasets are only available for a handful of problems [8,19]. Often tools like Amazon Mechanical Turk [6] and Computer Vision Annotation Tool (CVAT) [3] are used to label them. The problem with these tools is that they are expensive and require significant time and human effort to label. To circumvent that, many datasets in the real world are either incompletely labeled or extracted from sources that inherently contain label noise [9].

Label noise is detrimental to the training of any deep learning model as it directly impacts the model's learning ability [37]. Vision tasks learned with

© Springer Nature Switzerland AG 2021
G. Bebis et al. (Eds.): ISVC 2021, LNCS 13018, pp. 229–241, 2021.
https://doi.org/10.1007/978-3-030-90436-4_18

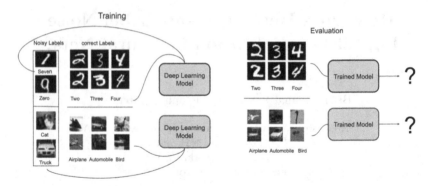

Fig. 1. An example of how class-dependent heterogeneous label noise is introduced by corrupting the labels of CIFAR10 and MNIST Dataset. We investigated the impact of noisy labels (red) on the model's performance on clean labels (green). (Color figure online)

noisy labels don't generalize well, resulting in poor test performance [33]. It is essential to thoroughly study the impact of noisy labels to understand how they are associated with poor performance. This knowledge can be used to improve the current methods that learn with noisy labels [18]. However, to the best of our knowledge, most of the works studied up to now have mainly focused on examining the performance of the deep learning model under the influence of homogeneous noisy labels imposed by corrupting all the true labels with the same degree [4,27].

We know that the noise may not always be homogeneous and can depend on various heterogeneous sources [35]. Some of the labels might be affected to a greater extent than others because of which the label noise is heterogeneous in nature. The previous studies have not thoroughly investigated the heterogeneous case in supervised vision tasks. Therefore, some open questions still exist. For example: what is the impact of heterogeneous noisy labels of certain classes on the performance of a class with clean labels (as shown in Fig. 1) when they are trained together in a naive classification setting? We want to examine to what extent the noise-free class is affected by class-dependent noisy labels. We further extended the question to study the impact in other classification settings, such as multi-task and multi-label learning.

Multi-task learning [1] is an approach where a single network is trained to perform two or more tasks. While training a multi-task network, the tasks could positively or negatively interfere resulting in positive or negative transfer respectively. Positive transfer improves the performance of another task, while negative transfer impacts its performance. We hypothesized that if there is a positive transfer between two or more tasks, then training with noisy tasks should impact the performance of clean tasks. The transferred benefit obtained by training tasks together should drop with an increase in label noise in helping tasks. In this work, we verified our hypothesis with experiments.

Finally, we also investigated the impact of label-dependent noisy labels in multi-label learning, in which noise is present only in a certain group of labels, and examined the impact on the group with clean labels. In summary, the key contributions of our work are:

- Using the popular vision datasets: MNIST, CIFAR10, CIFAR100, and MS-COCO dataset, we assessed the impact of class-dependent, task-dependent, and label-dependent heterogeneous noisy labels on multi-class classification, multi-task learning, and multi-label learning settings, respectively with an attempt to the fill gap that previous studies didn't cover.
- By investigating task-dependent heterogeneous noisy labels, we showed that if there is a positive transfer from one task to another, inducing label noise in helping task should also impact the performance of other tasks that have clean labels. The drop in task transfer benefit is proportional to the number of noisy labels in helping tasks, i.e., the higher the noisy labels, the higher the transfer drop.

2 Related Works

Label Noise is a topic of interest in the deep learning fraternity with a large number of published works. Several surveys provide comprehensive literature reviews on its impact. Song et al. [13] discussed the generalization problems introduced by label noise in supervised learning methods. They categorically reviewed the state-of-the-art methods used to improve the robustness against label noise. Zhu et al. [37] categorized noise into attribute noise and class noise (label noise) to study their impacts separately and highlighted the class noise to be more harmful. Frenay et al. [9] further investigated the source of label noise and its consequences in learning. Algan et al. [4] discussed various noise model-free methods and noise model-based methods to train deep neural networks for the image classification tasks efficiently. These studies highlight the growing interest in developing algorithms that can learn with noisy labels.

Nowadays, several approaches have been used to improve the existing methods for robust noisy label learning. Some methods used techniques to reduce the influence of incorrect labels in learning [11], while some modified the loss function [29]. The possible negative influence of noisy labels can be predicted with reliable techniques. Yao et al. [31] investigated the quality of the feature embedding that can be used to identify how well the noisy labels could be trusted. Ghosh et al. [10] initialized the network with embeddings learned from contrastive learning to improve the supervised network for classification under noisy conditions. Zhang et al. [34] and Yi et al. [32] used the label correction method to improve the model's robustness. While Song et al. [28], Harutyunyan et al. [12] and Lyu et al. [21] focused on improving the model's generalization ability itself. Nishi et al. [23] used a combination of weak augmentation and strong augmentation techniques to obtain the best performance in the dataset under noisy labels.

Every year, there is a growing number of papers that uniquely approach this problem. Most of these methods test the robustness of their method by introducing the noise through instance-independent homogeneous corruption of labels in clean data. Lui et al. [20] highlight the challenges introduced by instance-dependent label noise and showed that existing methods that learn from noisy labels fail at instance labels. In their analysis, they discussed the problem of memorizing instance-dependent noisy labels. Cheng et al. [7] and Xia et al. [30] proposed methods to deal with bounded-instance and label-dependent noisy labels. Though we see emerging interest in this area, we haven't found works that thoroughly studied the impact of heterogeneous and dependent noisy labels, as a function of noise strength, in different learning settings. With this works, we have tried to fill the gap in that direction, presenting some insights and verifying our hypothesis that label noise only affects certain classes if there is transfer.

3   Problem Setup

We designed some methods to systematically corrupt the labels and introduce heterogeneous label noise. We studied in three major classification settings: multi-class classification, multi-task learning, and multi-label learning.

3.1   Multi-class Classification

In a multi-class classification problem, we have inputs $[\mathbf{X_1}, \mathbf{X_2}, .., \mathbf{X_N}]$ and our goal is to assign correct target label to each inputs. Let us suppose there are four possible target labels such that an input only corresponds to a particular label $t \in [t_1, t_2, t_3, t_4]$. To introduce label noise, we first select a label (say t_1), which won't be corrupted (we term this *uncorrupted* or *uncorrupt* label). The other remaining labels $[t_2, t_3, t_4]$ (grouped into a list termed as corrupt list) are corrupted based on a probability value p, which determines the strength of corruption, i.e. 0 means that a label will never be changed, while 1 means the label is always replaced with other labels. We maintain a corrupt target list that contains all the possible labels that a corrupted label can take. While corrupting certain labels, we replace them with a randomly chosen value from the corrupt target list.

There are two possible ways to create a corrupt target list: include the uncorrupt label t_1 along with all other labels or just include labels from the corrupt list. For instance, to corrupt a label t_2, we might randomly replace it with a label from a target label list $[t_1, t_3, t_4]$ (**strategy 1**) or from $[t_3, t_4]$ (**strategy 2**). We have used both strategies in our experiments and separately studied them. At the end of the training, we examined the test classification accuracy in both corrupted and uncorrupted label. Our primary interest is in the uncorrupted label because we want to measure the impact on its performance while training with noisy labels (corrupted).

3.2   Multi-task Learning

In multi-task learning, we aim to boost the performance in some tasks by training tasks together. Let T_1 and T_2 be any arbitrary tasks that a joint network should learn together. In this setup, we first find a task T_1 that benefits by training together with the other task T_2. The overall performance of task T_1, when there is positive transfer, should be higher than that when task T_1 is trained alone. Our hypothesis says that inducing label noise in a helping task, i.e. T_2 should impact the performance of task T_1, resulting in a drop in its test performance. First, task T_1 is trained independently to establish a single task performance baseline. Then, a shared network is trained jointly on tasks T_1 and T_2, such that positive transfer benefit is obtained in task T_1.

After the transfer benefit is seen in task T_1, the labels of task T_2 are corrupted by randomly changing the labels within the task. The labels of task T_1 shouldn't be changed as we are interested in studying the impact in a clean task on introducing noise in the helping task. The labels are corrupted in a similar manner described in multi-class classification. In both the clean and corrupted tasks, the test performance is measured as a function of label corruption strength in helping tasks. We only used two tasks to make our experiments simpler and tractable.

3.3 Multi-label Learning

Unlike the multi-class classification problem, in multi-label learning problem, the inputs $[\mathbf{X_1}, \mathbf{X_2}, .., \mathbf{X_N}]$ can belong to one or more target labels $[t_1, t_2, ...t_M]$, where N is the total number of input samples and M is the total number of possible labels. The labels are no more treated as mutually exclusive targets, and the input-output mapping can be one-to-many. We are interested in seeing how the label noise in a certain category impacts the prediction performance in a group of clean labels.

Let L_1, L_2, L_3 and L_4 be any four arbitrary labels. We can divide the labels into two categories, i.e., uncorrupted and corrupted lists. For instance, the uncorrupted list may contain label L_1 and L_2, and corrupted list may contain other two labels L_3 and L_4. The labels can be grouped in any combination. We corrupted labels in the corrupted list of training data by randomly swapping the labels within the list with some probability as described in previous setups.After training, the test performance of both uncorrupted and corrupted labels is evaluated as a function of corruption strength.

4   Experiments and Datasets

We now describe the three categories of experiments designed to study the impact of heterogeneous noisy labels. The datasets and network architecture selection are made based on the requirements and design of the experiments.

4.1   Multi-class Classification

Multi-class classification is a well-studied problem; therefore, there are many open-source datasets available on the web. In our study, we have used two popular datasets: MNIST [17] and CIFAR10 [14]. MNIST contains 60,000 training

Fig. 2. Overview of Multi-Task learning Architecture that was used in our experiment. CIFAR100 was split into two tasks each containing 50 classes. The CNN features of ResNet18 with twice the original width were used as the shared features.

images and 10,000 testing images of handwritten digits. Each image is a gray-scaled image with 28×28 dimensions and represents one of ten digits. CIFAR10 contains 50000 training and 10000 test RGB images of dimension 32×32 categorized into ten classes. To classify the MNIST, we have used a basic LeNet-5 CNN architecture with dropout, ReLU activation in the hidden layer, and a final softmax layer. For CIFAR10, we have used a ResNet18 based architecture.

Using the method discussed in the setup Sect. 3.1, we corrupted any nine out of ten classes in training sets of MNIST and CIFAR10 with a certain probability value while keeping the tenth class as it is. The mean classification accuracy of each corrupted class and the uncorrupted class was evaluated at each corruption probability. We chose eight corruption probability values from 0 to 1 to experiment with, and at each probability, we performed ten sets of experiments, using a different uncorrupted class at each for robustness. There were 80 sets of training experiments combining eight corruption probability and ten sets of experiments. In all of these eighty experiments, we didn't include the uncorrupted class in any of the corrupt target lists. We also performed another 80 sets of experiments with the exact setting, but this time, including the uncorrupted class in the corrupt target lists. For the final result, we averaged the values at each corruption probability.

4.2   Multi-task Learning

We used two tasks to study the impact of task-specific label noise in a multi-task learning scenario. We split 100 classes of the CIFAR100 [15] into two 50-class classification tasks: Task1 and Task2 and trained multi-task network. We monitored the validation loss in Task1 to save the best model for testing.

In our experiment, we tried three random splits for robustness. Each split had different classes assigned to the tasks. After the splits, we also trained a single task network for task T_1 of each three splits, which provided us the baseline to compare multi-task performance. We averaged the single task performance of all the splits to get a mean single-task performance. Similarly, we also averaged the multi-task performance of all the splits across respective tasks and corruption probability to find respective mean values.

As shown in Fig. 2, we used a 2-head classification network with a shared ResNet18 backbone. We doubled the width of the ResNet18 architecture to obtain a higher transfer benefit than its single-task counterpart with the same width. Further, we used Mish activation function [22] instead of ReLU because of

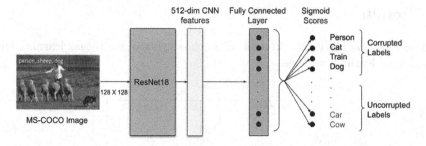

Fig. 3. Overview of Multi-Label Classification Architecture that was used in our experiment. The last CNN layer of ResNet18 was connected to an 80-dimensional fully connected layer having sigmoid activation function. We corrupted a group of labels (corrupted labels) by randomly changing their values to other values within the group and trained them with the unchanged (uncorrupted) group of labels.

its higher performance [22]. The images from two tasks were fed to the network alternatively while training. The categorical cross-entropy loss was computed separately for each output head and then summed and back-propagated. We then introduced label noise in Task2 by corrupting the labels of 50 classes with some probability as done in multi-class classification. The test classification accuracy in both the tasks at that particular corruption probability was evaluated. For this experiment, we chose 12 different probability values in the range from 0 to 1. At each corruption probability, we trained three times and averaged the test accuracy for robustness.

4.3   Multi-label Learning

For multi-label learning, we used a small subset of MS-COCO dataset; we call it mini MS-COCO [2]. This version contains randomly selected 20% MS-COCO training images such that datasets' statistics match that of the original dataset. We downsampled all the images to the fixed size of 128 × 128. An image can contain one or more labels out of 80 labels.

We modified the Resnet18 for multi-label classification by changing the softmax activation function in the last layer into a sigmoid function for each output node (Fig. 3). Instead of outputting a probability value for each node, the network outputs a one-hot encoded vector. We induced label noise in the training examples by corrupting the class labels. We divided the 80 labels into two categories: **category 1**, which contained corrupted labels and **category 2** which contained uncorrupted labels. The labels in **category 1** were corrupted by randomly changing the true labels to other labels within the category using a certain probability, while **category 2** was not changed at all. Corruption can be done in two ways: either the number of corrupted labels is greater or less than the number of uncorrupted labels. For both the case, we experimented with 12 different probability values in the range from 0 to 1 and measured mean average precision for each.

5   Results

We now analyze the results in multi-class classification, multi-task learning and multi-label learning settings.

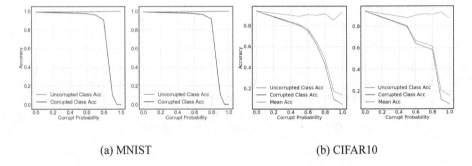

(a) MNIST   (b) CIFAR10

Fig. 4. Result of multi-class classification in MNIST and CIFAR10: Average classification accuracy in corrupted class and uncorrupted class as a function of corruption probability (strength). In the **left** plot of (**a**) and (**b**), the corrupted label can take the label of uncorrupted class while in the **right** plot of (**a**) and (**b**), the corrupted label can not take the label of uncorrupted class. In both datasets, the classification accuracy of the uncorrupted class is not affected by the noisy labels of corrupted classes.

5.1   Multi-class Classification

We present the classification accuracies of corrupted and uncorrupted classes as a function of corruption probability in Fig. 4. The trend lines start at zero corruption baseline and end horizontally at full corruption probability.

As expected, the performance of corrupted classes in both MNIST and CIFAR10 datasets dropped with the increase in corruption probability as shown by Fig. 4. But, the performance drop was not seen until a large number of labels were corrupted, which highlights that neural networks are inherently robust to a certain level of noisy labels. In MNIST, the corrupted class performance didn't drop off until 80% corruption. Similar behavior is shown by the bigger network (ResNet18) in CIFAR10 dataset. The model's performance in corrupted classes started to drop off after 60% label corruption. We also saw that bigger networks start to memorize the noisy labels if overtrained. In contrast to LeNet-5, the ResNet18 architecture was able to overfit even the noisy labels at later epochs of training. This behavior is similar to what the [33] paper discusses. These plots in Fig. 4 also underline that the performance of the uncorrupted class remained almost consistent and didn't drop with an increase in the corruption probability. This behavior is consistent in both datasets. These experiments were done in two settings in which the corrupted label can either take the label of uncorrupted class or not. In both settings, we observed a similar trend in the accuracy of uncorrupted classes. The results strongly suggest that the class-dependent label noise of corrupted classes do not perturb the feature learning of the uncorrupted class.

5.2   Multi-task Learning

As described in the experiment section, Task1 (50 classes of CIFAR100) benefits from training together with Task2 (other 50 classes of CIFAR100) in hard parameter sharing configuration. In single-task learning, the average accuracy of Task1 was about 75.63 %. When Task1 was trained with Task2 in a multi-task learning setting, the average accuracy improved to 79.50%, which is about 3.87 raw improvement (equivalently 5.11% improvement).

The average classification accuracy in Task2 was 80.9% at zero corruption. As shown in Fig. 5, the blue trend line starts at high accuracy and falls with an increase in corruption probability. The line falls slowly at first but drops drastically later, approaching close to zero. The trend line of Task1 (red) is of greater importance to us than the trend in Task2. Initially, the line starts with a positive offset from the STL line due to the task transfer benefit achieved by training with Task2. Interestingly we start to lose the transfer benefit as Task2 is corrupted. At full corruption, the task transfer benefit completely vanishes and the multi-task learning performance in Task1 is almost the same as single-task performance. This result validates the hypothesis we proposed that the task-specific noisy labels impact the task transfer benefit. It is important to note that multi-task test performance does not fall far below the single task test performance line. It suggests that task-specific corruption doesn't introduce negative interference but only reduces the task transfer benefit achieved from multi-task learning.

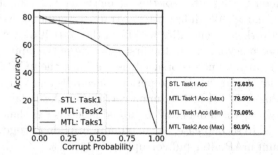

Fig. 5. Average classification accuracy in two tasks as a function of label corruption in one of the tasks. Task1 represents the classification task of 50 classes of CIFAR100, while Task2 represents the classification task of the other 50 classes. Task2 labels are corrupted incrementally, while Task1 labels are not changed at all. STL (green line) is the single task learning baseline performance in Task1. MTL (blue line) and MTL (red line) are the performance of Task2 and Task1, respectively, in a multi-task learning setting. This plot shows the average value across three experiments (that used differently split 100 classes into two 50–50 class tasks) across each probability value. (Color figure online)

5.3 Multi-label Learning

After the experiments in Sect. 4.3, we analyzed the impact of label-dependent noisy labels in the performance of clean labels in the multi-label classification setting. Figure 6 shows the mean average precision (mAP) as trend lines, which are functions of corruption probability in **category 1**.

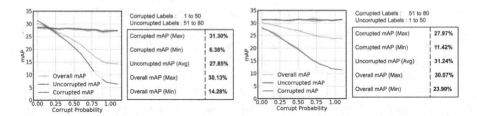

Fig. 6. Results in Multi-Label Classification of mini MS-COCO dataset in two cases where the number of corrupted labels is either greater (**left** figure) or less (**right** figure) than the number of uncorrupted labels. Three trend lines: Uncorrupted mAP, Corrupt mAP, and Overall mAP, show the mean average precision as a function of corruption probability (strength) in labels belonging to the corrupted category. mAP of corrupted category and the overall dataset falls with increase in corruption probability. The consistent trend line of uncorrupted labels shows that their mAP isn't affected by label corruption in the other category. The shades in the line show the standard deviation across multiple experiments with random weight initialization.

Our baseline, even at no corruption, starts with a lesser mAP than compared to the state-of-the-art methods for multi-label classification because we have used a smaller architecture ResNet18 in a naive configuration, without any hyperparameter tuning. State-of-the-art methods [5,25,36] obtained higher mAP using larger model. We didn't use pre-trained weights as we are interested in finding if a network can generalize well from the start if we train with dependent heterogeneous noisy labels. In the first case where the number of corrupted labels is greater than the uncorrupted labels, initially, the mAP in **category 1** is 31.30%. With label corruption, the performance falls and ultimately drops to the minimum value of 6.38% at maximum corruption. A similar trend is seen in the second case, where the number of corrupted labels is less than the number of uncorrupted labels. In second case, the maximum mAP in **category 1** is 27.97% while the minimum mAP after full corruption is 11.42%.

The trend line of the uncorrupted category (blue, **category 2**) shows that the corrupted labels didn't impact its performance at all. The line stays consistent throughout the horizontal axis. It is important to note that the corrupted mAP and uncorrupted mAP start at different offsets because the mean average precision across the two categories isn't the same. We also showed the overall mAP trend line follows the dominant category with more samples. Our work shows that in a naive setup, the label-dependent noisy labels do not affect the performance of clean labels even on training together.

6 Discussion

Both the multi-class and the multi-label classification showed that the corrupted labels do not affect the network's performance in classifying clean labels. This behavior strongly hints that noisy labels don't impact the learning of low-level features much, otherwise, the network wouldn't have performed well in clean labels either. An interesting future work could be to investigate how the heterogeneous noisy labels impact the features learned at each layer in a deeper network.

In multi-task learning, we found that the performance in a clean task drops if the helping task is corrupted. While training, we also observed that the overfitting of label noise is an issue in a multi-task setting as well, which can be prevented by a properly tuned regularizer. But if the model somehow overfits, the performance in both the corrupted task and uncorrupted task drops no matter whether there is a positive or negative transfer between tasks. In such a case, we saw that the test performance in the clean task decreased below the single-task performance baseline, at high corruption in the helping task. However, if the overfitting was avoided, the corruption in helping task affected the clean task but the performance in the clean task didn't drop below its single task performance even at full corruption in helping task.

All our experiments investigated the classification case. However, in the real world, the heterogeneous label noise can appear in regression tasks as well. In future work, we are interested in investigating how the label noise in a certain range affects the overall generalization of the regression task.

7 Conclusion

In this work, we investigated the impact of heterogeneous noisy labels in three supervised classification settings. In multi-class classification, we found that training with the class-dependent noisy labels of certain classes doesn't affect the model's performance on classes with clean labels. On examining the multi-task learning, we observed that task transfer benefit is affected by task-dependent noise in helping tasks. The transferred benefit decreases with the increase in label corruption in helping tasks and reaches a minimum at full corruption where multi-task performance is approximately the same as single-task performance. Finally, we showed that label noise in certain categories of labels in the multi-label classification also doesn't affect the performance in clean labels when trained together.

Acknowledgements. This work was supported in part by the DARPA/SRI Lifelong Learning Machines program [HR0011-18-C-0051], AFOSR grant [FA9550-18-1-0121], and NSF award #1909696. The views and conclusions contained herein are those of the authors and should not be interpreted as representing the official policies or endorsements of any sponsor.

References

1. An Overview of Multi-Task Learning for Deep Learning. https://ruder.io/multi-task, https://ruder.io/multi-task/. Accessed 1 Mar 2021
2. giddyyupp/coco-minitrain, https://github.com/giddyyupp/coco-minitrain. Accessed 1 Mar 2021
3. openvinotoolkit/cvat. https://github.com/openvinotoolkit/cvat. Accessed 1 Mar 2021
4. Algan, G., Ulusoy, I.: Image classification with deep learning in the presence of noisy labels: a survey. Knowl.-Based Syst. **215**, 106771 (2021)
5. Ben-Baruch, E., et al.: Asymmetric loss for multi-label classification (2021)
6. Buhrmester, M., Kwang, T., Gosling, S.: Amazon's Mechanical Turk: A new source of inexpensive yet high-quality, data? (2011)
7. Cheng, H., Zhu, Z., Li, X., Gong, Y., Sun, X., Liu, Y.: Learning with instance-dependent label noise: a sample sieve approach (2021)
8. Deng, J., Dong, W., Socher, R., Li, L.J., Li, K., Fei-Fei, L.: ImageNet: a large-scale hierarchical image database. In: CVPR09 (2009)
9. Frenay, B., Verleysen, M.: Classification in the presence of label noise: a survey. IEEE Trans. Neural Netw. Learn. Syst. **25**(5), 845–869 (2014)
10. Ghosh, A., Lan, A.: Contrastive learning improves model robustness under label noise (2021)
11. Han, B., et al.: Co-teaching: robust training of deep neural networks with extremely noisy labels. In: Advances in Neural Information Processing Systems, vol. 31. Curran Associates, Inc. (2018)
12. Harutyunyan, H., Reing, K., Steeg, G.V., Galstyan, A.: Improving generalization by controlling label-noise information in neural network weights (2020)
13. Song, H., Kim, M., Park, D., Lee, J.-G.: Learning from noisy labels with deep neural networks: a survey Accessed on Mon, 1 March 2021
14. Krizhevsky, A., Nair, V., Hinton, G.: CIFAR-10 (Canadian institute for advanced research)
15. Krizhevsky, A., Nair, V., Hinton, G.: CIFAR-100 (Canadian institute for advanced research)
16. Krizhevsky, A., Sutskever, I., Hinton, G.E.: ImageNet classification with deep convolutional neural networks. In: Advances in Neural Information Processing Systems, vol. 25. Curran Associates, Inc. (2012)
17. LeCun, Y., Cortes, C.: MNIST handwritten digit database (2010). http://yann.lecun.com/exdb/mnist/
18. Li, J., Wong, Y., Zhao, Q., Kankanhalli, M.S.: Learning to learn from noisy labeled data. In: 2019 IEEE/CVF Conference on Computer Vision and Pattern Recognition (CVPR)
19. Lin, T.Y., et al.: Microsoft coco: common objects in context (2014)
20. Liu, Y.: The importance of understanding instance-level noisy labels (2021)
21. Lyu, Y., Tsang, I.W.: Curriculum loss: robust learning and generalization against label corruption (2020)
22. Misra, D.: Mish: A self regularized non-monotonic activation function (2020)
23. Nishi, K., Ding, Y., Rich, A., Höllerer, T.: Augmentation strategies for learning with noisy labels (2021)
24. Ren, S., He, K., Girshick, R., Sun, J.: Faster R-CNN: towards real-time object detection with region proposal networks. In: Advances in Neural Information Processing Systems, vol. 28. Curran Associates, Inc. (2015)

25. Ridnik, T., Ben-Baruch, E., Noy, A., Zelnik-Manor, L.: ImageNet-21k pretraining for the masses (2021)
26. Ronneberger, O., Fischer, P., Brox, T.: U-Net: convolutional networks for biomedical image segmentation (2015)
27. Sanchez, G., Guis, V., Marxer, R., Bouchara, F.: Deep learning classification with noisy labels. In: 2020 IEEE International Conference on Multimedia & Expo Workshops (ICMEW)
28. Song, H., Kim, M., Park, D., Lee, J.: Prestopping: how does early stopping help generalization against label noise? (2019)
29. Wang, Y., Ma, X., Chen, Z., Luo, Y., Yi, J., Bailey, J.: Symmetric cross entropy for robust learning with noisy labels. In: 2019 IEEE/CVF International Conference on Computer Vision (ICCV). IEEE, October 2019. https://doi.org/10.1109/iccv.2019.00041
30. Xia, X., et al.: Part-dependent label noise: towards instance-dependent label noise (2020)
31. Yao, J., Wang, J., Tsang, I., Zhang, Y., Sun, J., Zhang, C., Zhang, R.: Deep learning from noisy image labels with quality embedding (2017)
32. Yi, K., Wu, J.: Probabilistic end-to-end noise correction for learning with noisy labels. In: 2019 IEEE/CVF Conference on Computer Vision and Pattern Recognition (CVPR)
33. Zhang, C., Bengio, S., Hardt, M., Recht, B., Vinyals, O.: Understanding deep learning (still) requires rethinking generalization. Commun. ACM **64**(3), 107–115 (2021)
34. Zhang, Q., Lee, F., Wang, Y.G., Miao, R., Chen, L., Chen, Q.: An improved noise loss correction algorithm for learning from noisy labels. J. Vis. Commun. Image Represent. **72**, 102930 (2020)
35. Zhang, Y., Zheng, S., Wu, P., Goswami, M., Chen, C.: Learning with feature-dependent label noise: a progressive approach. In: International Conference on Learning Representations (2021)
36. Zhu, F., Li, H., Ouyang, W., Yu, N., Wang, X.: Learning spatial regularization with image-level supervisions for multi-label image classification (2017)
37. Zhu, X., Wu, X.: Class Noise vs. Attribute Noise: a quantitative study. Artif. Intell. Rev. **22**(3), 177–210 (2004). https://doi.org/10.1007/s10462-004-0751-8

A Simple Generative Network

Daniel N. Nissani (Nissensohn)[✉]

Independent Researcher, Tel Aviv, Israel
dnissani@post.bgu.ac.il

Abstract. Generative neural networks are able to mimic intricate probability distributions such as those representing handwritten text, natural images, etc. Since their inception several models were proposed. The most successful of these were based on adversarial (GAN), auto-encoding (VAE) and maximum mean discrepancy (MMD) relatively complex architectures and schemes. Surprisingly, a very simple architecture (a single feed-forward neural network) in conjunction with an obvious optimization goal (Kullback–Leibler divergence) was apparently overlooked. This paper demonstrates that such a model (denoted SGN for its simplicity) is able to generate samples visually and quantitatively competitive as compared with the fore-mentioned state of the art methods.

1 Introduction

This work is about generative neural networks. When fed by input samples from some (typically simple) distribution, these networks are able to generate output samples which mimic data obeying arbitrary probability distributions, such as those representing natural images, handwritten text, etc. Since the publication of Variational Autoencoders (VAE, Kingma and Welling 2014) several other similarly capable models have been proposed. These include Generative Adversarial Networks (GAN, Goodfellow et al. 2014), Maximum Mean Discrepancy networks (MMD, Li et al. 2015; Dziugaite et al. 2015) and Normalizing Flows networks (Rezende and Mohamed 2015). For a comparative exhaustive survey (and even more exhaustive references list) the reader may refer to (Mohamed and Lakshminarayanan 2017; Bond-Taylor et al. 2021).

With such a variety of schemes it is curious and surprising that a most simple architecture and direct approach seems to have been overlooked. It is the modest purpose of this paper to fill this gap.

Amongst the approaches cited above the one conceptually closest to our work is the MMD network (Li et al. 2015). The architecture of this model is very simple and consists of a single feed-forward multi-layer neural net. This stands in contrast to the popular fore-mentioned GANs which are based on two competing networks, a generator and a discriminator, and to the VAEs which are based on an auto-encoding scheme. GANs are capable of generating high quality samples, but are known to suffer from delicate convergence issues; and VAEs on the other hand have apparently not been able so far to generate high fidelity samples. The MMD (a.k.a. GMMN; Li et al. 2015)

D. N. Nissani—Independent Researcher.

© Springer Nature Switzerland AG 2021
G. Bebis et al. (Eds.): ISVC 2021, LNCS 13018, pp. 242–250, 2021.
https://doi.org/10.1007/978-3-030-90436-4_19

model is based on the well known principle (e.g. Mnatsakanov 2008) which states that, under relatively mild conditions, two distributions which are equal in all their moments are themselves equal. This principle led the authors to adopt a (Gaussian) kernel functions based optimization goal. This choice in turn yielded poor generated samples, both in terms of visual quality and in terms of Mean Log Likelihood (MLL), a popular quantitative measure. As result of this the authors of this work shifted their focus to a modified variant of MMD networks (denoted GMMN + AE), based on a more complex auto-encoding architecture.

We adopt in our present work the single network simple architecture and will demonstrate in the sequel that it is possible to generate high quality samples by a proper, different choice of optimization goal, namely the Kullback–Leibler divergence. Due to its simplicity we baptize our model SGN.

The proposed SGN model is presented in the next Section. In Sect. 3 we present simulation results; in Sect. 4 we summarize our work and make a few concluding remarks.

2 SGN Proposed Model

Figure 1 describes our proposed architecture. Samples of a random vector $\mathbf{z} \in R^D$ are generated by a multivariate 'simple' (i.e. easily synthesized, typically Gaussian, Uniform, etc.) distribution $p_z(\mathbf{z})$. The generated samples are mapped by means of a parameterized function $F(\mathbf{z}; \mathbf{w})$ into $\mathbf{y} \in R^d$, where D and d are the function F domain and range spaces dimensions respectively, and $\mathbf{w}$ is its parameters vector. The map F: $R^D \rightarrow R^d$ induces a corresponding implicit mapping between the distributions $p_z(\mathbf{z})$ and $p_y(\mathbf{y})$[1].

The system has also access to the data $\mathbf{x} \in R^d$ with same dimensionality as the generated samples $\mathbf{y}$. The parameterized function F naturally lends itself to a simple multi-layer feed forward neural network implementation. The network may be trained to solve the optimization problem:

$$w* = \underset{w}{\operatorname{argmin}} \, d\Big(p_y(x; \, w), \, p_x(x)\Big) \tag{1}$$

where $d(.,.)$ is a suitable measure of discrepancy between both distributions, and where we made explicit, for clarity, the implicit effect of w upon $p_y(\mathbf{x})$. As it turns out the well known Kullback–Leibler divergence (a.k.a. KL-divergence)

$$D_{KL} = E_x\left[\log\left(\frac{p_x(x)}{p_y(x)}\right) \right] \tag{2}$$

may well serve such a measure. In conjunction with an appropriate density estimator it can be readily adapted to a stochastic gradient descent (SGD) scheme.

---

[1] This mapping can in some cases be explicitly calculated and manipulated; in fact this precisely is what the fore-mentioned Normalizing Flows approach (Rezende and Mohamed 2015) do.

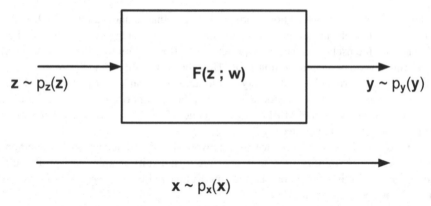

Fig. 1. Proposed model architecture

More significantly, and in contrast with e.g. the popular log-likelihood optimization criterion, the KL-divergence is a bounded (from below) goal and thus provides a solid minimization convergence target. The expectation operator $E_x[.]$ (w.r.t. the data x) can be approximated by application of the frequentist interpretation

$$D_{KL} \cong \frac{1}{M} \sum_{i=1}^{M} \log \frac{p_x(x_i)}{p_y(x_i)} \equiv \frac{1}{M} \sum_{i=1}^{M} D_{KL}^i \tag{3}$$

where $\{x_i\}, i = 1, 2, \ldots M$ is our data sample and D_{KL}^i is *defined* as our SGD optimization goal.

Of course we do not have direct access to the densities p_x and p_y and we should estimate them. Of the available non-parametric estimators those based on the k-Nearest Neighbor (kNN ahead) method are especially suitable: they provide good quality density estimates of multivariate random vectors at both high and low density regions; they have a single not too sensitive parameter (k); and they are compactly differentiable. These kNN based estimators have been considerably studied (Wang et al. 2006; Wang et al. 2009).

A naïve implementation of the k-th nearest neighbor calculation (which is required for these estimators) conducts exhaustive (i.e. O(N)) search over a set such as $\{x_l\}, l = 1, 2, \ldots N$ of vectors and may become prohibitive for large samples such as those required by e.g. ImageNet (Deng et al. 2009). Many approximate kNN calculation methods exist, however; see e.g. (Li et al. 2016) for a comprehensive survey. Those of interest to us exhibit high performance, with an achievable average recall ratio of 0.8 (recall ratio is defined as the mean ratio between the number of found *true* nearest neighbors and k). And, more importantly, they incur O(log(N)) computational complexity for vectors of high dimensionality (e.g. Malkov and Yashunin 2016). These methods potentially open the way to real life applications.

Following these considerations we pick (Wang et al. 2006) density estimator resulting in

$$\hat{p}_x(\mathbf{x_i}) = \frac{k}{(N-1)\,c(d)\rho_k^d(\mathbf{x_i})} \qquad (4a)$$

and

$$\hat{p}_y(\mathbf{x_i}) = \frac{k}{N\,c(d)v_k^d(\mathbf{x_i})} \qquad (4b)$$

where $\rho_k(\mathbf{x_i})$ is the L^2 distance between $\mathbf{x_i}$ and its k-nearest neighbor in the data sample $\{\mathbf{x_l}\}\backslash\mathbf{x_i}$, denoted $\mathbf{x_n}$, $v_k(\mathbf{x_i})$ is the L^2 distance between $\mathbf{x_i}$ and its k-nearest neighbor in the generated sample $\{\mathbf{y_l}\}$, denoted $\mathbf{y_m}$, $c(d) = \pi^{d/2}/\Gamma(d/2+1)$ is the d-dimensional unit ball volume, and $\Gamma(.)$ is the gamma function. The decrease of the densities in Eqs. (4a) and (4b) above with the increase of the distances $\rho_k(\mathbf{x_i})$ and $v_k(\mathbf{x_i})$ is of course intuitive. The difference between the 'N factors' in the equations reflects the fact that the search set $\{\mathbf{x_l}\}$ in (4a) should exclude $\mathbf{x_i}$ itself.

Applying Eqs. (4a) and (4b) into (3) we immediately get

$$D_{KL}^i = d\log\frac{v_k(\mathbf{x_i})}{\rho_k(\mathbf{x_i})} + \log\frac{N}{(N-1)} = \frac{d}{2}\log\frac{||\mathbf{x_i}-\mathbf{y_m}||^2}{||\mathbf{x_i}-\mathbf{x_n}||^2} + \log\frac{N}{(N-1)} \qquad (5)$$

where $||.||$ denotes the L^2 norm; note that the dependence of D_{KL}^i on k is now implicit through its impact on these norms. For our minimization purpose we may ignore the first factor and the last term in the right hand sides of (5), and provide an explicit expression for our simplified sample-wise SGD goal D^i

$$D^i = \log\frac{\sum_1^d(y_m^j - x_i^j)^2}{\sum_1^d(x_n^j - x_i^j)^2} \qquad (6)$$

where $j = 1,2,\ldots d$, and $i = 1,2,\ldots N$.

We may notice by differentiating our goal D^i that its derivative does not depend on $\mathbf{x_n}$, the k-nearest neighbor in $\{\mathbf{x_l}\}\backslash\mathbf{x_i}$ to the current sample $\mathbf{x_i}$ and so its calculation maybe skipped (in practice however we may wish to follow D^i convergence plot; in such case $\mathbf{x_n}$ should obviously be required and calculated).

Following common practice we update the $\mathbf{w}$ parameter vector after processing a mini-batch comprised of B $\mathbf{x_i}$ samples. After each such $\mathbf{w}$ update a feed-forward operation of a full $\mathbf{y_l} = F(\mathbf{z_l}; \mathbf{w})$, $l = 1,2,\ldots N$ sample (using the updated $\mathbf{w}$ value) should be executed. This is required in order that further k nearest neighbor calculations be up-to-date. This creates a processing overhead. To maintain this overhead reasonably small the ratio N/B should be moderately small; since feed forward execution is much faster than back-propagation (e.g. $\sim \times 400$ faster on a Matlab based platform) a ratio N/B < 400 should apparently suffice.

Finally we note that contrary to 'conventional' neural nets (e.g. Classifiers) where differentiation of the goal function at sample $\mathbf{x_i}$ is executed w.r.t. the output at same corresponding sample (i.e. $\mathbf{y_i}$), in our case differentiation of the goal at data sample $\mathbf{x_i}$ is performed w.r.t. the network output $\mathbf{y_m}$ (that is the point in the set $\{\mathbf{y_l}\}$ k-nearest to $\mathbf{x_i}$).

3 Simulation Results

In order to probe and demonstrate the capabilities of this simple model a Matlab based platform was coded and tested over the MNIST dataset (LeCun et al. 1998). We built a small neural network with a single hidden layer of dimension 300. The generating random vector z was of dimension $D = 100$ and the output generated vector y, compatible with the MNIST data x, of dimension $d = 28^2 = 784$.

We experimented with both Uniform noise $z \sim U[0, 1]^D$ and a Gaussian Mixture source (GM ahead) $z \sim \sum_1^C p_i.N(\mu_i, \sigma I)$ with $C = 32$, equal priors $p_i = 1/C$, means μ_i drawn at setup from a binary random vector (of dimension D), $i = 1,2,...C$, $\sigma = 0.1$, and where I is the identity matrix.

The hidden layer activation function was a.tanh(.) with $a = 5$. Smaller values of a as well as use of ReLU activation (instead of tanh) resulted in generated samples with degraded contrast.

Random permutation of the MNIST training set was executed at the end of every training epoch (60000 characters).

We worked mainly with sample size $N = 1e3$ and mini-batch size $B = 1e3$ (the fore-mentioned ratio N/B was thus 1). We also performed experiments with $N = 5e3$ (and $B = 5e3$ too); since the larger the sample size N the better it reflects the actual data distribution this yielded as expected better MLL values (see ahead).

We used $k = 1$ as our kNN parameter; testing with $k = 2$ actually worsened our results. We used an exact exhaustive search scheme (of O(N) computational and memory complexity) for kNN; as mentioned above good quality approximate kNN methods of O(log(N)) computational complexity exist, such as (Malkov and Yashunin 2016) and should be used with larger datasets maintaining an N/B ratio < 400; for example $N = 1e5$, $B = 1e3$, with $N/B = 100$ could possibly work out well on ImageNet.

We used SGD with no acceleration methods, with constant learning step $\eta = 0.2$ and with normalized goal function derivative.

Following the steps of many (Goodfellow et al. 2014; Li et al. 2015; Bengio et al. 2014; etc.) we use a protocol based upon a Gaussian Parzen Window density estimator in order to quantitatively evaluate our results and be able to compare them with other works. The estimator comprises 1e4 generated y points; the Gaussian Parzen Window 'bandwidth' parameter was fine tuned by line search using a validation set of 5e3 points extracted from the MNIST training dataset. The empirical MLL of the 1e4 MNIST test dataset x points was calculated and reported. This method has been shown to yield unreliable results in some cases (Theis et al. 2016; Wu et al. 2017) but no better quantitative method seems to have been generally adopted.

Please refer to Table 1 which describes MNIST MLL values of our work as compared with several generative models, all calculated using the above sketched methodology. SGN Uniform and GM noise sources parameters values are as described above. Simulation conditions at the cited works, such as source noise class and dimension, are either missing (e.g. GAN, Goodfellow et al. 2014) or incomplete (e.g. MMD, Li et al. 2015); hence we should treat the results in Table 1 as indicative rather than definitive. We notice that SGN yields competitive MLL values re cited state of the art methods. In particular SGN with Uniform source yields much better results (244) than GAN (225), and it is also strikingly superior to 'plain' (i.e. GMMN) MMD (147). This is, as mentioned above,

Table 1. Mean log-likelihood figures of merit

MODEL	MLL	BY
Deep GSN	214	Bengio et al. 2014
GAN	225	Goodfellow et al. 2014
MMD (GMMN)	147	Li et al. 2015
MMD (GMMN+AE)	282	"
SGN ($z \sim$ U$[0,1]^D$, N = 5e3)	244	This work
SGN ($z \sim$ U$[0,1]^D$, N = 1e3)	238	"
SGN ($z \sim$ GM, N = 5e3)	232	"
SGN ($z \sim$ GM, N = 1e3)	225	"

the MMD scheme which shares with us a simple single neural net architecture. It might be of interest to implement an 'enhanced' SGN scheme (i.e. SGN + AE as the analog to the GMMN + AE variant (Li et al. 2015)) and check whether a significant quality boost is achieved, as in their case. We observe as expected, somewhat degraded MLL results as we decrease the sample size from N = 5e3 to N = 1e3 in both Uniform and GM sources.

We refer now to Fig. 2, which shows a convergence plot of averaged D^i (Eq. (6) above) for a Gaussian Mixture source and sample size N = 1e3, with parameters values as described above. We can see that while initial convergence is rapid, final stages exhibit a 'long tail': it took approximately 2000 epochs to achieve the results shown in Table 1 and Fig. 3b.

While true KL-divergence is bounded from below by 0 we notice convergence of our averaged D^i to approximately -0.35. This is not to be attributed to our simplification from D^i_{KL} (Eq. (5) above) to D^i (Eq. (3)) but rather to the KL-divergence estimator bias under finite sample size (this estimator bias is known to only *asymptotically* vanish, see Wang et al. 2009). In fact we have experienced as expected a clear bias (absolute value) decrease (to about -0.16) upon increasing sample size to N = 1e4.

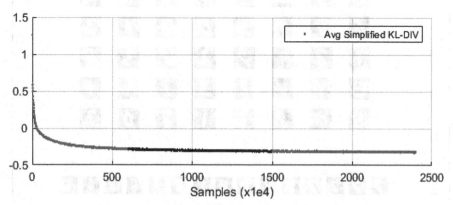

Fig. 2. Averaged D^i Convergence plot, GM source, N = 1e3; plot colors illustrate initial, interim and final convergence stages

Figure 3a provides visual samples of the MNIST data **x** for reference. Figure 3b shows a random set of samples generated by a GM distribution source and sample size N = 1e3 (all other parameters as described above). It may be verified that all digits

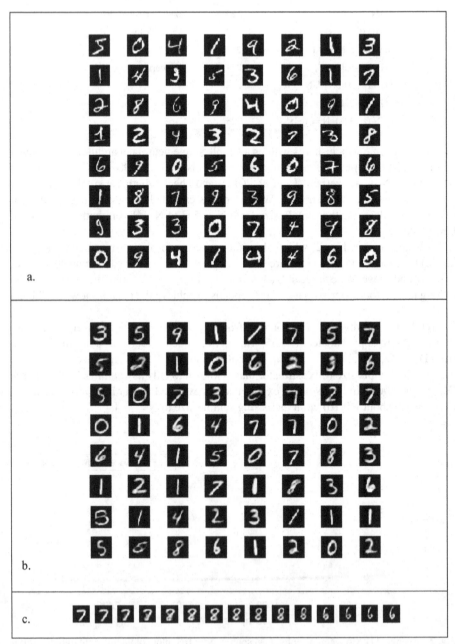

Fig. 3. a. MNIST samples; b. GM, N = 1e3 generated samples; c. U[0,1]^D, N = 1e3 Latent space interpolated samples

classes are represented. We leave for the reader to judge their visual quality. Similar visual quality is achieved by $U[0,1]^D$ with N = 1e3. Samples generated by GM and $U[0,1]^D$ sources with N = 5e3, appear to exhibit, again as expected, somewhat better visual quality.

Figure 3c shows the result of interpolating, in latent space, from a randomly selected corner point of the $U[0,1]^D$ hypercube to the opposite corner along a major diagonal; near one corner the digit '7' predominates, smoothly passing through '8' at the center region of the hypercube and ending at '6' at the opposite corner.

It is interesting to generate samples from a Gaussian or Uniform Mixture source, with the number of modes at least equal to the number of distinct classes and with sufficiently separated modes (i.e. small mode dispersion relative to the intermodal distances). One might intuitively expect in such a case that each mode will generate samples belonging to one and only one class. Interpolation results such as those shown in Fig. 3c seem to intuitively support this idea. Should this be the case it would be perhaps possible to achieve good (that is linearly separable) unsupervisedly learned representations, by means of e.g. complementing SGN to an auto-encoding scheme. This is work in progress, and no results to report yet.

4   Concluding Remarks

A generative network model, denoted SGN, consisting of a multi-layer feed-forward neural net along with a kNN based KL-divergence goal function was presented. Given its (practically trivial) simplicity it is surprising that such a model appears to have been overlooked. When tested on MNIST data it was shown to generate visually appealing samples with competitive mean log-likelihood metrics relative to state of the art methods.

To extend its applicability to more realistic datasets (such as ImageNet) a more computationally efficient kNN method should be implemented than the one, of complexity O(N), used herein. A significant variety of such methods, suitable to high dimensionality spaces, have been studied with approximate but impressive performance. Some of them exhibit O(log(N)) complexity. The integration of such a method within the SGN concept, as well as the assessment of the impact of its approximate nature upon the quality of the generated samples (relative to the exact kNN method) is left for future work.

Due to the poor results of the MMD (GMMN) method with a simple architecture (like ours), the authors turned their focus to a more complex, auto-encoding enhanced scheme, and achieved an impressive performance boost, both in terms of visual quality and MLL. It would be interesting to test whether such combined architecture has a similar boosting effect on SGN.

A Matlab based SGN software package will be provided upon request.

References

Bengio, Y., Thibodeau-Laufer, E., Alain, G.: Deep generative stochastic networks trainable by Backprop. ICML (2014)

Bond-Taylor, S., Leach, A., Long, Y., Willcoks, C.G.: Deep generative modeling: a comparative review of VAEs, GANs, normalized flows, energy-based and autoregressive models. arXiv: 2103.04922 (2021)

Deng, J. Dong, W., Socher, R., Li, L., Li, K., Fei-Fei, L.: ImageNet: a large-scale hierarchical image database. CVPR (2009)

Dziugaite, K.D., Roy, D.M., Ghahramani, Z.: Training generative neural networks via maximum mean discrepancy optimization. UAI (2015)

Goodfellow, I., et al.: Generative adversarial networks. NIPS (2014)

Kingma, D.P., Welling, M.: Auto-encoding variational Bayes. ICLR (2014)

LeCun, Y., Bottou, L., Bengio, Y., Haffner, P.: Gradient-based learning applied to document recognition. Proc. IEEE 86(11), 2278–2324 (1998)

Li, Y. Swersky, K., Zemel, R.: Generative moment matching networks. ICML (2015)

Li, W., Zhang, Y., Sun, Y., Wang, W., Zhang, W., Lin, X.: Approximate nearest neighbor search on high dimensional data—experiments, analyses, and improvement. IEEE Trans. Knowl. Data Eng. 32(8), 1475–1488 (2020)

Malkov, Y.A., Yashunin, D.A.: Efficient and robust approximate nearest neighborr search using hierarchical navigable small world graphs. IEEE Trans. PAMI 42(4), 824–83 (2016)

Mnatsakanov, R.M.: Hausdorff moment problem: reconstruction of probability density functions. Stat. Probab. Lett. 78(12), 1612–1618 (2008)

Mohamed, S., Lakshminarayanan, B.: Learning in implicit generative models. ICLR 2017 (2017)

Rezende, D.J., Mohamed, S.: Variational inference with normalizing flows. ICML (2015)

Theis, L., van den Oord, A., Bethge, M.: A note on the evaluation of generative models. ICLR (2016)

Wang, Q., Kulkarni, S.R., Verdu, S.: A nearest-neighbor approach to estimating divergence between continuous random vectors. ISIT (2006)

Wang, Q., Kulkarni, S.R., Verdu, S.: Divergence estimation for multidiimensional densities via k-nearest-neighbor distances. IEEE Trans. IT 55(5), 2392–2405 (2009)

Wu, Y., Burda, Y., Salakhutdinov, R., Grosse, R.: On the quantitative analysis of decoder-based generative models. ICLR (2017)

Hyperspectral Video Super-Resolution Using Beta Process and Bayesian Dictionary Learning

Vahid Khorasani Ghassab[(✉)] [iD] and Nizar Bouguila [iD]

Concordia University, Montreal, QC H3G 1M8, Canada
{vahid.khorasani,nizar.bouguila}@concordia.ca

Abstract. In this paper, we present an algorithm to super-resolve the acquired frames in a hyperspectral video using sparse coding and applying a Beta process. For this purpose, we apply Beta process in Bayesian dictionary learning and we will generate a sparse coding regarding the hyperspectral video super-resolution. The spatial super-resolution was followed by a spectral video restoration process using two different dictionaries which one of them is trained for spatial super-resolution and the other one is trained for the spectral restoration. We have experimented our proposed strategy over a large public hyperspectral video database including a 31-frame hyperspectral video (each frame has 33 bands from 400 nm to 720 nm wavelength with a 10 nm step) and compared the outcome with other state of the art methodologies. The proposed method is evaluated on RMSE, PSNR, SSIM and VSNR metrics. The comparison results prove that our proposed method outperforms other state of the art techniques.

Keywords: Hyperspectral video · Super-resolution · Beta process · Bayesian dictionary learning · Sparse coding

1 Introduction

Spectroscopy is a field which studies over the interactions of matter and electromagnetic radiations. The electromagnetic radiations are considered as the wavelength of the radiation. The measurement of the spectral information at multiple spatial points is denominated as imaging spectroscopy or hyperspectral imaging. A hyperspectral image displays a narrow wavelength range of the electromagnetic spectrum which is considered as a spectral band. Such images are three-dimensional hyperspectral data cubes with two spatial and one spectral dimensions. There are four different ways to sample the hyperspectral cubes using sensors which are spatial scanning, spectral scanning, snapshot imaging, and spatio-spectral scanning.

In hyperspectral video acquisition, multiple cubes will be recorded and each cube is recognized as a video frame. The hyperspectral data cube which is

© Springer Nature Switzerland AG 2021
G. Bebis et al. (Eds.): ISVC 2021, LNCS 13018, pp. 251–262, 2021.
https://doi.org/10.1007/978-3-030-90436-4_20

acquired at time instant t is considered as a hyperspectral frame and every single 2D image from a scene which is recorded in particular wavelength is considered as a *band*. In fact, in hyperspectral video acquisition, we provide a trade-off between temporal and spectral resolution.

Hyperspectral sensors are popular in remote sensing [4]. The motivation behind hyperspectral image and video super-resolution is due to difficulty and trickiness of obtaining high resolution hyperspectral images and videos using satellites sensors [13]. The sensitivity of human vision to luminance has been analyzed in [2] and [5], and the luminance components in images have been mixed up with hyperspectral components. On the other hand, hyperspectral unmixing has been utilized for hyperspectral imaging super-resolution [21,32]. In another approach, the proposed method fuses a low-resolution HSI (LR-HSI) with a high-resolution multispectral image (HR-MSI) to get high-resolution HSI (HR-HSI) [29]. In addition, Chang *et al.* [6], proposed weighted low-rank tensor recovery for hyperspectral image restoration.

In this work, in order to consider the scene material reflectance spectra, we use a set of Bernoulli distributions, each one representing a proportion in the video frame. The sparse code for producing the high resolution video frames will be generated using the Bernoulli distributions and the transformed dictionary. Accordingly, a Bayesian sparse coding method is applied with the first dictionary which is learned using a Beta process [22] and applied for the spatial super-resolution of the video frames. In addition, the second dictionary will be estimated using a Bayesian dictionary learning process and will be transformed based on the spectral quantization of the video frame and for the purpose of spectral restoration. This model will be able to restore and super-resolve the dense hyperspectral cubes in all the frames.

1.1 Scene Geometry in Hyperspectral Imaging

Remote sensing is used in hyperspectral imaging. Remote imaging devices concentrate on the reflected luminance from the adjacent areas on the surface of the scene which is planned for imaging. Many hyperspectral cameras measure sequential small areas in geometric shapes when the camera sensor moves. The geometric patterns need to be assembled together using a processing method. The details in a hyperspectral image or a video frame depend on the spatial resolution of the sensor. Spatial resolution of the sensor relies on Instantaneous Field of View (IFOV) which is the sensor angular cone of visibility. Considering the ground distance to sensor as d, the size of the viewed area can be calculated as $A = IFOV \times d$. The area on the ground is denominated as *resolution cell* which represents maximum spatial resolution of the sensor. The angular field of view presents the width of imaged objects and is considered as the scan mirror. Spectrum is a light array or a band of colors which is produced by separation of the light components in the order of wavelength. Furthermore, dispersing elements are the optical elements which disperse the light into its spectrum and can be categorized into two groups, *1) Prism, 2) Diffraction grating*. The scene geometry is described in Fig. 1, in which the light from a single ground-resolution cell, scan mirror, dispersing elements, imaging optics and wavelength bands are presented.

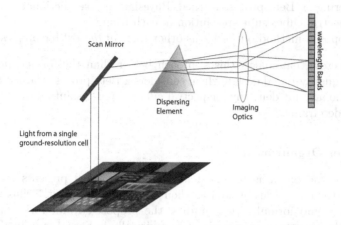

Fig. 1. Description of scene geometry in hyperspectral imaging considering the light from a single ground-resolution cell, scan mirror, dispersing elements, imaging optics and wavelength bands.

1.2 Hyperspectral Video Registration

We consider a model in hyperspectral video frame registration in which 5 bands are obtained in each frame, and there is a 10 nm frame offset for 5 bands of the subsequent frame. Optical flow is applied for frame registration in order to capture the minimum vertical and horizontal pixel displacements, (γ_x, γ_y) as follows

$$(\gamma_x, \gamma_y) = \min \sum_{x,y} \|I_{(x,y)} - I_{(x+\gamma_x, y+\gamma_y)}\|_2^2, \tag{1}$$

where γ_x and γ_y are the horizontal and vertical pixel displacements, respectively, $I_{(x,y)}$ is the hyperspectral video frame corresponding to pixel (x, y).

1.3 Contribution

In order to improve the visual quality and spatial super-resolving performance and reducing the reconstruction error in hyperspectral video frames, we apply a set of Bernoulli distributions, each one representing a proportion in the video frame. We used a Bayesian dictionary learning process for spectral restoration of the video. Moreover, a Bayesian sparse dictionary is considered for dense hyperspectral cubes super-resolution in each frame. This dictionary was learned using a Beta process. The importance of our contribution can be described as follows

- The hyperspectral video spatial and visual quality improvement.
- Applying a Bayesian dictionary learning process for spectral restoration of the video.
- Considering a Beta-process-learned Bayesian sparse dictionary for dense hyperspectral cubes super-resolution in each frame.
- The proposed method outperforms other *state of the art* techniques.

The key factor, that makes this approach better than the former methods is the robust quality-based design which considers a Beta process learned Bayesian sparse dictionary for dense hyperspectral cubes super-resolution in each hyperspectral video frame.

1.4 Paper Organization

The rest of the paper is arranged as follows. Section 2 presents the related works and their novelties as well as their disadvantages, Sect. 3 illustrates the methodology and formulation regarding the proposed framework. The represented methodology has been evaluated empirically in Sect. 4, and finally a conclusion has been provided in Sect. 5.

2 Related Works

2.1 Super-Resolution

Image Super-Resolution
Single image super resolution concentrates on restoring a high spatial-resolution image from a degraded low resolution image sample by increasing the high frequency contents in the corrupted areas. Many computer vision and machine learning techniques have tried to address this problem. Ahmadi et al. [1] have proposed a multi-dimensional reconstruction of internal defects in additively manufactured steel using photothermal super resolution combined with virtual wave based image processing. In this work, three different methods are integrated to improve the defect reconstruction ability of active thermographic testing. In another approach, Ren et al. have proposed a Fringe pattern improvement super-resolution model [23] which considers a deep-learning-based approach which is able to super-resolve the holograms by training a convolutional neural network using large-scale data. Recently, a convolutional-neural-network-based method is proposed by Fu et al. [10], in which IoT applications are considered on both image classification and single image super-resolution. In another research work, Romano et al. have discussed a single image super-resolution method which amplifies the speed and accuracy [24]. This approach leveraged the global filter learning, refining the cheap upscaling kernel and a hash-based learning and upscaling for super-resolving the single images.

Multi-Frame Super-Resolution

Multi-frame super-resolution methods work on restoring the complementary information from several low-resolution frames. Such algorithms can be applied on single-image super-resolution as well as video and lightfield super-resolution. In this regard, a robust multi-frame super-resolution is proposed by Köhler *et al.* which considers iteratively re-weighted minimization and spatially adaptive Bayesian modeling [16]. In another approach, Duo *et al.* have proposed a method using industrial Internet of Things (IIoT) paradigm which is able to overcome the reduction in original video resolution after transmission [9]. Video super-resolusion has been discussed in another work in which convolutional-neural-network is used for the enhancement of video spatial resolution by training the video on spatial and the temporal dimensions [14].

Spectral and Spatio-Spectral Super-Resolution

Spectral and spatio-spectral super-resolution concentrate on improving the resolution of images or video frames which use multiple bands across the electromagnetic spectrum. Liu *et al.* [19] have proposed a spectral imaging resolution-enhancement method which considers total variation (TV) constraints for the degraded Fourier transform IR (FTIR) spectrum for noise degradation in robot vision sensing. In another approach, Dai *et al.* have discussed spatio-spectral representation of X-ray fluorescence image super-resolution [7]. This method addresses the tradeoff between signal to noise ratio of pixel spectrum and the spatial resolution of an XRF scan.

2.2 Hyperspectral Image Analysis

Similar as spectral imaging, hyperspectral imaging also obtains and analyzes the information from electromagnetic spectrum. The application of clustered differential pulse code modulation for lossless hyperspectral image compression is proposed by Li *et al.* [18]. In another approach, a hierarchical Bayesian model accounting is presented by Thouvenin *et al.* for endmember variability and abrupt spectral changes to unmix multi-temporal hyperspectral images [25]. Recently, deep spatio-spectral representation learning is used for 3D hyperspectral image denoising [8]. In this work, a 3D U-net architecture is applied for encoding rich multi-scale information of hyperspectral images. In [11], a hyperspectral and multi-spectral image fusion is performed by Guilloteau *et al.* for spectrally varying spatial blurs as an application to high dimensional infrared astronomical imaging.

2.3 Hyperspectral Image and Video Super-Resolution

The motivation behind performing hyperspectral image and video super-resolution is the difficulty and trickiness of obtaining high resolution hyperspectral images and videos using satellites sensors [13]. Hyperspectral unmixing has been utilized for hyperspectral imaging super-resolution in [21] and [32].

Recently, a deep recursive network has been presented by Wei *et al.* for hyperspectral image super-resolution [27]. In this approach, a deep neural network is implicitly used as a prior and the original unified optimization problem is reformulated into three sub-problems in which recursive residual networks are leveraged for these sub-optimization problems. In another work, band attention through adversarial learning has been used for hyperspectral super-resolution [17]. In this research, the super-resolution process is put in generative adversarial network (GAN) framework for keeping more texture details in the hyperspectral images. Wang *et al.* have proposed a hyperspectral super-resolution method [26] using spectrum and feature context, in which a dual-channel network is designed through 2D and 3D convolution for information extraction from different wavelength bands. Moreover, in a recent approach, Hu *et al.* applied intrafusion network for hyperspectral image super-resolution [12]. The intrafusion network is made of three modules which are parallel convolution module, intrafusion module, and spectral difference module which apply spectral and spatial information for hyperspectral image super-resolution. Using degeneration estimation into hyperspectral image super-resolution is proposed in [31], which explains an unsupervised deep framework for blind hyperspectral super-resolution.

3   Methodology

3.1   Spatial Super-Resolution for a Hyperspectral Video

We consider $V^{low} \in \mathbb{R}^{m \times n \times L \times D}$ as the low resolution four dimensional hyperspectral video, where m, n, L and D are width, height, spectral dimension and the number of frames. Our objective is to super-resolve V^{low} and obtain a high resolution hyperspectral video, $V^{high} \in \mathbb{R}^{M \times N \times L \times D}$, where $M > m$, $N > n$. We define $S_{i,j}^{low} \in \mathbb{R}^{m \times n}$ and $S_{i,j}^{high} \in \mathbb{R}^{M \times N}$ as spectral frames for V^{low} and V^{high} respectively, where i represents the spectral band value and j is the frame number. Let $\Phi \in \mathbb{R}^{L \times |\mathcal{K}|}$ be a dictionary matrix with columns ϕ_k where $k \in \mathcal{K} = 1, 2, \ldots, K$. We consider $s_{i,j,\gamma}^{low} \in \mathbb{R}^L$ as the γth pixel in $S_{i,j}^{low}$ which shows a sparse representation $\alpha_{\gamma}^{low} \in \mathbb{R}^{|\mathcal{K}|}$ over the dictionary Φ. Accordingly, $s_{i,j,\gamma}^{low} = \Phi \alpha_{\gamma}^{low} + \epsilon_{\gamma}^{low}$. In order to learn the dictionary, we apply *beta process Bayesian model* as follows

$$s_{i,j,\gamma}^{low} = \Phi \alpha_{\gamma}^{low} + \epsilon_{\gamma}^{low},$$

$$\alpha_{\gamma}^{low} = z_{\gamma} \odot p_{\gamma},$$

$$\phi_k \sim \mathcal{N}(\phi_k | \mu_{k^*}, \Lambda_{k^*}^{-1}) \quad \forall k \in \mathcal{K},$$

$$z_{\gamma k} \sim Bern(z_{\gamma k} | \pi_{k^*}),$$

$$\pi_k \sim Beta(\pi_k | \frac{a^*}{K}, \frac{b^*(K-1)}{K}),$$

$$p_{\gamma k} \sim \mathcal{N}(p_{\gamma k} | \mu_{p^*}, \lambda_{p^*}^{-1}),$$

$$\epsilon_{\gamma} \sim \mathcal{N}(\epsilon_{\gamma} | 0, \Lambda_{\epsilon^*}^{-1}), \tag{2}$$

where $\odot$ denotes Hadamard product, $\mathcal{N}$ describes the normal distribution, $\sim$ represents a draw ($i.i.d.$) from a distribution, $*$ notation describes the parameters of the prior distributions, and $Bern$ and $Beta$ illustrate Bernoulli and Beta distributions, respectively. $z_\gamma \in \mathbb{R}^{|\mathcal{K}|}$ is a binary vector whose kth element has been computed based on Bernoulli distribution with parameter π_{k^*}. In addition, a^* and b^* are hyper-parameters of $Beta$ distribution. $p_\gamma \in \mathbb{R}^{|\mathcal{K}|}$ includes $p_{\gamma k}$ elements which are weight vectors from the Normal distribution. Λ_{k^*} is defined as the precision matrix of the prior distribution whose components are $\lambda_{k^*} I_L$, where $\lambda_{k^*} \in \mathbb{R}$ is a predefined constant and $I_L \in \mathbb{R}^{L \times L}$ represents the identity matrix. $\mu_{k^*} \in \mathbb{R}^L$ denotes the mean parameter, $\Lambda_{\epsilon^*} = \lambda_{\epsilon^*} I_L$ ($\lambda_{\epsilon^*} \in \mathbb{R}^L$) and $\mu_{p^*} = 0$.

Considering the mentioned inferencing, a set of posterior distributions will be obtained which are:

- Distributions over the dictionary matrix columns which are denominated as *atoms*. Gaussian priors have been placed over the dictionary atoms. Accordingly, by estimating ϕ_ks, Φ will be estimated.
- Bernoulli distributions over π_k which has been calculated using beta distribution.

After estimation of the dictionary, Φ will be used for V^{low} sparse code computation. The goal is to obtain the high resolution video frames and use them with $\hat{\Phi}$ (which indicates the estimated dictionary) to estimate V^{high}. We consider a sparse code θ such that $s_{i,j,\gamma}^{low} = \Phi\theta$. The best estimate of $s_{i,j,\gamma}$ in a mean square sense will be given by $\tilde{\theta}_{opt} = \mathbb{E}[\mathbb{E}[\theta|z]]$, where $\mathbb{E}$ represents the mathematical expectation.

3.2   Spectral Video Restoration

In order to extract the spectral domain of the hyperspectral video frames, we extract and measure 5 reliable wavelength bands out of 33 wavelength bands in each frame. This 5 reliable wavelength bands are the ones in which video frame are registered using optical flow. For this purpose, an over complete dictionary, D_γ is generated using the whole available wavelength bands in each frame which are super-resolved using spatial super-resolution discussed in Subsect. 3.1, and the spectral domain is calculated as follows

$$S_{ij} = D_\gamma \hat{\psi}_{ij}, \tag{3}$$

where S_{ij} is the extracted spectral frame pixel, i, j is the coordinate pixel location in the frame, and $\hat{\psi}_{ij}$ is the predicted sparse coefficient which is computed as

$$\hat{\psi}_{ij} = \arg\min_{\psi_{ij}}\{\|W(D_\gamma\psi_{ij} - \tilde{k}_{ij})\|_2^2 + \lambda_1\|\psi_{ij}\|_1\}, \tag{4}$$

where λ_1 is the sparsity regularizer, k_{ij} is the optical response in pixel location i, j from 33 wavelength bands in a hyperspectral frame which is achieved from

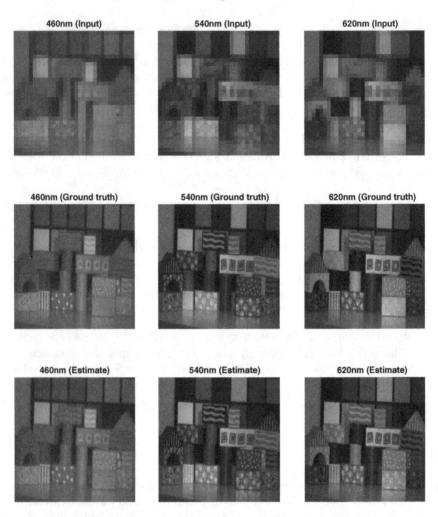

Fig. 2. Super-resolution performance over hyperspectral video sample in comparison with the ground truth and the degraded input on three different hyperspectral band wavelength, 460 nm, 540 nm and 620 nm.

optical flow registration and $\tilde{k}_{ij} = (1 - \lambda_2)k_{ij} + \lambda_2\bar{k}_{ij}$, where $\bar{k}_{ij}$ is the median of k_{ij} in eight neighboring pixels and λ_2 is a mixing constant which is used for regularization of the significance of k_{ij} and $\bar{k}_{ij}$. Moreover, W is a diagonal weight matrix which is used for computation of the vicinity of the frames based on the estimated optical flow and the highest credit is given to the closest frames. The restored spectral video frame, S is obtained by concatenation of extracted spectral pixels, S_{ij}.

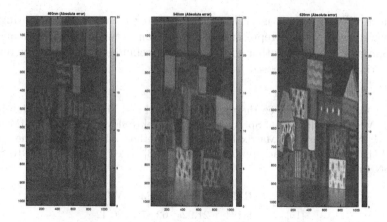

Fig. 3. The corresponding errors in super-resolving a hyperspectral video over three different hyperspectral band wavelengths, 460 nm, 540 nm and 620 nm. It is visible that the error increases when the band wavelength increases.

4 Experiments

4.1 Experimental Settings

The experiments are performed using MATLAB (R2018a) on Windows 7 Enterprise edition with 3.5 GHz processor and 32 GB RAM. We have used a hyperspectral video database including a 31 frame hyperspectral video. Each frame has 33 bands from 400 nm to 720 nm wavelength with a 10 nm step [20]. In order to benchmark the proposed method, we have compared the outcomes with Matrix Factorization based method (MF) [15], the Spatial Spectral Fusion Model (SSFM) [13], the ADMM based approach [28], the Coupled Matrix Factorization method (CMF) [30] and the spatio-spectral sparse representation approach, GSOMP [3]. We consider the video frames from the database as the ground truth and in RGB format. We apply root mean squared error (RMSE), peak signal-to-noise ratio (PSNR), structural similarity index measure (SSIM), and wavelet-Based Visual Signal-to-Noise Ratio (VSNR) as the comparison metrics to evaluate the quality of different methods.

4.2 Emperical Results

In this section, the super-resolving performance of the proposed model over the mentioned databased is experimented and the results are described. In Fig. 2, the super-resolution performance over hyperspectral video sample in comparison with the ground truth and the degraded input on three different hyperspectral band wavelength, 460 nm, 540 nm and 620 nm is represented. It is obvious that using the proposed model, the quality of video frames are significantly increased. In Fig. 3, the corresponding errors in super-resolving a hyperspectral video over three different hyperspectral band wavelengths, 460 nm, 540 nm and

620 nm are illustrated. It is visible that the error increases by increasing the band wavelength. Table 1 represents a comparison between the performance of the proposed method and other state of the art techniques. The outcome reveals the superiority of the proposed framework.

Table 1. Comparison between the proposed method and Matrix Factorization based method (MF) [15], the Spatial Spectral Fusion Model (SSFM) [13], the ADMM based approach [28], the Coupled Matrix Factorization method (CMF) [30] and the spatio-spectral sparse representation approach, GSOMP [3] based on RMSE, PSNR, SSIM and VSNR metrics.

	RMSE	PSNR	SSIM	VSNR
[15]	8.17	21.92	62.87%	20.42
[13]	9.18	19.51	51.30%	18.44
[28]	6.12	29.27	83.96%	27.27
[30]	6.62	27.06	71.16%	25.58
[3]	6.09	29.42	84.4%	27.42
Proposed	**5.41**	**33.12**	**87.1%**	**31.32**

5   Conclusion

In this paper, we have presented a method regarding hyperspectral video super-resolution. For this purpose, we applied a Beta process in Bayesian dictionary learning and we generated a sparse coding regarding the hyperspectral video super-resolution. We have used a hyperspectral video database including a 31 frame hyperspectral video for evaluation of the proposed model, and we compared the outcome with Matrix Factorization based method (MF) [15], the Spatial Spectral Fusion Model (SSFM) [13], the ADMM based approach [28], the Coupled Matrix Factorization method (CMF) [30] and the spatio-spectral sparse representation approach, GSOMP [3] based on RMSE, PSNR, SSIM and VSNR metrics. The comparison results prove that our proposed method outperforms other state of the art techniques.

Acknowledgment. This research was made possible thanks to Natural Sciences and Engineering Research Council of Canada (NSERC).

References

1. Ahmadi, S., et al.: Multi-dimensional reconstruction of internal defects in additively manufactured steel using photothermal super resolution combined with virtual wave based image processing. IEEE Trans. Ind. Inform. **17**, 7368–7378 (2021)

2. Aiazzi, B., Baronti, S., Selva, M.: Improving component substitution pansharpening through multivariate regression of MS + Pan data. IEEE Trans. Geosci. Remote Sens. 45(10), 3230–3239 (2007)

3. Akhtar, N., Shafait, F., Mian, A.: Sparse spatio-spectral representation for hyperspectral image super-resolution. In: Fleet, D., Pajdla, T., Schiele, B., Tuytelaars, T. (eds.) ECCV 2014. LNCS, vol. 8695, pp. 63–78. Springer, Cham (2014). https://doi.org/10.1007/978-3-319-10584-0_5

4. Bioucas-Dias, J.M., Plaza, A., Camps-Valls, G., Scheunders, P., Nasrabadi, N., Chanussot, J.: Hyperspectral remote sensing data analysis and future challenges. IEEE Geosci. Remote Sens. Mag. 1(2), 6–36 (2013)

5. Carper, W., Lillesand, T., Kiefer, R.: The use of intensity-hue-saturation transformations for merging spot panchromatic and multispectral image data. Photogramm. Eng. Remote. Sens. 56(4), 459–467 (1990)

6. Chang, Y., Yan, L., Zhao, X.L., Fang, H., Zhang, Z., Zhong, S.: Weighted low-rank tensor recovery for hyperspectral image restoration. IEEE Trans. Cybern. 50(11), 4558–4572 (2020)

7. Dai, Q., Pouyet, E., Cossairt, O., Walton, M., Katsaggelos, A.K.: Spatial-spectral representation for x-ray fluorescence image super-resolution. IEEE Trans. Comput. Imaging 3(3), 432–444 (2017)

8. Dong, W., Wang, H., Wu, F., Shi, G., Li, X.: Deep spatial-spectral representation learning for hyperspectral image denoising. IEEE Trans. Comput. Imaging 5(4), 635–648 (2019)

9. Dou, W., Zhao, X., Yin, X., Wang, H., Luo, Y., Qi, L.: Edge computing-enabled deep learning for real-time video optimization in IIoT. IEEE Trans. Ind. Informat. 17(4), 2842–2851 (2020)

10. Fu, S., Li, Z., Liu, K., Din, S., Imran, M., Yang, X.: Model compression for IoT applications in industry 4.0 via multiscale knowledge transfer. IEEE Trans. Ind. Informat. 16(9), 6013–6022 (2019)

11. Guilloteau, C., Oberlin, T., Berné, O., Dobigeon, N.: Hyperspectral and multispectral image fusion under spectrally varying spatial blurs-application to high dimensional infrared astronomical imaging. IEEE Trans. Comput. Imaging 6, 1362–1374 (2020)

12. Hu, J., Jia, X., Li, Y., He, G., Zhao, M.: Hyperspectral image super-resolution via intrafusion network. IEEE Trans. Geosci. Remote Sens. 58(10), 7459–7471 (2020)

13. Huang, B., Song, H., Cui, H., Peng, J., Xu, Z.: Spatial and spectral image fusion using sparse matrix factorization. IEEE Trans. Geosci. Remote Sens. 52(3), 1693–1704 (2013)

14. Kappeler, A., Yoo, S., Dai, Q., Katsaggelos, A.K.: Video super-resolution with convolutional neural networks. IEEE Trans. Comput. Imaging 2(2), 109–122 (2016)

15. Kawakami, R., Matsushita, Y., Wright, J., Ben-Ezra, M., Tai, Y.W., Ikeuchi, K.: High-resolution hyperspectral imaging via matrix factorization. In: CVPR 2011, pp. 2329–2336. IEEE (2011)

16. Köhler, T., Huang, X., Schebesch, F., Aichert, A., Maier, A., Hornegger, J.: Robust multiframe super-resolution employing iteratively re-weighted minimization. IEEE Trans. Comput. Imaging 2(1), 42–58 (2016)

17. Li, J., et al.: Hyperspectral image super-resolution by band attention through adversarial learning. IEEE Trans. Geosci. Remote Sens. 58(6), 4304–4318 (2020)

18. Li, J., Wu, J., Jeon, G.: GPU acceleration of clustered DPCM for lossless compression of hyperspectral images. IEEE Trans. Ind. Informat. 16(5), 2906–2916 (2019)

19. Liu, T., Liu, H., Li, Y.F., Chen, Z., Zhang, Z., Liu, S.: Flexible FTIR spectral imaging enhancement for industrial robot infrared vision sensing. IEEE Trans. Ind. Informat. **16**(1), 544–554 (2019)

20. Mian, A., Hartley, R.: Hyperspectral video restoration using optical flow and sparse coding. Opt. Express **20**(10), 10658–10673 (2012)

21. Minghelli-Roman, A., Polidori, L., Mathieu-Blanc, S., Loubersac, L., Cauneau, F.: Spatial resolution improvement by merging MERIS-ETM images for coastal water monitoring. IEEE Geosci. Remote Sens. Lett. **3**(2), 227–231 (2006)

22. Ren, L., Wang, Y., Carin, L., Dunson, D.: The Kernel beta process. Adv. Neural. Inf. Process. Syst. **24**, 963–971 (2011)

23. Ren, Z., So, H.K.H., Lam, E.Y.: Fringe pattern improvement and super-resolution using deep learning in digital holography. IEEE Trans. Ind. Inf. **15**(11), 6179–6186 (2019)

24. Romano, Y., Isidoro, J., Milanfar, P.: RAISR: rapid and accurate image super resolution. IEEE Trans. Comput. Imaging **3**(1), 110–125 (2016)

25. Thouvenin, P.A., Dobigeon, N., Tourneret, J.Y.: A hierarchical Bayesian model accounting for endmember variability and abrupt spectral changes to Unmix multi-temporal hyperspectral images. IEEE Trans. Comput. Imaging **4**(1), 32–45 (2017)

26. Wang, Q., Li, Q., Li, X.: Hyperspectral image super-resolution using spectrum and feature context. IEEE Trans. Ind. Electron. 11276–11285 (2020)

27. Wei, W., Nie, J., Li, Y., Zhang, L., Zhang, Y.: Deep recursive network for hyperspectral image super-resolution. IEEE Trans. Comput. Imaging **6**, 1233–1244 (2020)

28. Wycoff, E., Chan, T.H., Jia, K., Ma, W.K., Ma, Y.: A non-negative sparse promoting algorithm for high resolution hyperspectral imaging. In: 2013 IEEE International Conference on Acoustics, Speech and Signal Processing, pp. 1409–1413. IEEE (2013)

29. Xu, Y., Wu, Z., Chanussot, J., Wei, Z.: Nonlocal patch tensor sparse representation for hyperspectral image super-resolution. IEEE Trans. Image Process. **28**(6), 3034–3047 (2019)

30. Yokoya, N., Yairi, T., Iwasaki, A.: Coupled nonnegative matrix factorization Unmixing for hyperspectral and multispectral data fusion. IEEE Trans. Geosci. Remote Sens. **50**(2), 528–537 (2011)

31. Zhang, L., Nie, J., Wei, W., Li, Y., Zhang, Y.: Deep blind hyperspectral image super-resolution. IEEE Trans. Neural Netw. Learn. Syst. 2388–2400 (2020)

32. Zhukov, B., Oertel, D., Lanzl, F., Reinhackel, G.: Unmixing-based multisensor multiresolution image fusion. IEEE Trans. Geosci. Remote Sens. **37**(3), 1212–1226 (1999)

Adding Color Information to Spatially-Enhanced, Bag-of-Visual-Words Models

Robert Laurenson and Clark F. Olson[✉]

University of Washington, Bothell, WA 98011, USA
{laurer22,cfolson}@uw.edu

Abstract. A late-fusing method, based on the HoNC (Histogram of Normalized Colors) descriptor, is provided for combining color with shape in spatially-enhanced-BOVW models to improve predictive accuracy for image classification. The HoNC descriptor is a pure color descriptor that has several useful properties, including the ability to differentiate achromatic colors (e.g., white, grey, black), which are prevalent in real-world images, and to provide illumination intensity invariance. The method is distinguishable from prior late-fusing methods that utilize alternative descriptors, e.g., hue and color names descriptors, that are lacking with respect to one or both of these properties. The method is shown to boost the predictive accuracy by between about 1.9%–3.2% for three different spatially-enhanced BOVW model types, selected for their suitability for real-time use cases, when tested against two datasets (i.e., Caltech101, Caltech256), across a range of vocabulary sizes. The method adds between about 150–190 mS to the model's total inference time.

Keywords: Bag of visual words model · Spatial histogram · Late-fusing · Color descriptor · HoNC · Image classification

1 Introduction

The Bag-of-Visual-Words (BOVW) model is one of the most successful approaches for image classification available [1–3]. Despite the emergence of other machine learning models such as convolutional neural networks (CNN), the BOVW model remains relevant for real-time applications, such as traffic sign recognition and home intruder detection, where there is a need to generate inferences in real time.

In Abdi et al. [5], for example, a real-time traffic sign detector based on a spatially-enhanced BOVW model is reported as having a 90.48% recognition accuracy and 100 mS inference time when tested against the GTSRB dataset of German traffic sign images. By comparison, R-FCN, a CNN-based real-time object detector currently ranked #2 on the Facebook AI leaderboard for real-time object detection using the PASCAL VOC 2007 dataset[1], is reported in [6] as having a mAP (mean average precision) of 80.5%

---

[1] https://paperswithcode.com/task/real-time-object-detection.

© Springer Nature Switzerland AG 2021
G. Bebis et al. (Eds.): ISVC 2021, LNCS 13018, pp. 263–275, 2021.
https://doi.org/10.1007/978-3-030-90436-4_21

and 9 FPS throughput (equivalent to a 111.11 mS inference time) when tested against the PASCAL VOC 2007 dataset.

The traditional BOVW model represents an image with a histogram encoding the frequency of occurrence of quantized versions of object features called visual words [2, 8]. A significant drawback of traditional BOVW models is that they lack spatial information depicting the spatial distribution of object features in the image plane [1, 4]. The lack of spatial information limits the predictive accuracy provided by such models for image classification.

To overcome this limitation, SE-BOVW (spatially-enhanced BOVW) models were introduced, e.g., [2, 4, 5, 9]. SE-BOVW models add spatial information to the frequency information encoded by the traditional BOVW histogram for the purpose of improving predictive accuracy.

The inclusion of color offers yet another possibility for improving the predictive accuracy of SE-BOVW models. However, color has not been consistently treated in SE-BOVW models, included in some [1] while excluded in others [4, 5], leading Khan et al. [4] to call out the need for additional research regarding how to best use color and shape to improve performance of SE-BOVW models.

In light of the foregoing, there is a need for a method of using color to improve the predictive accuracy of spatially-enhanced BOVW models for image classification that is generalizable to many of the models in this class. A primary application of the method is the image classification phase of object detection [10].

2 Literature Review

Color has been shown to yield excellent results when combined with shape for image classification [10, 12]. Van de Weijer and Khan [8] compare and contrast early- and late-fusing methods for combining color and shape in BOVW models. With early fusing, the color and shape descriptors used for feature description and extraction are combined into multi-cue descriptors that are thereafter quantized and encoded into a histogram, while, with late fusing, the color and shape descriptors are separately quantized and encoded into distinct histograms that are thereafter combined.

Elfiky et al. [1] describe a late-fusing method for introducing color to a specialized (compact) variant of a SE-BOVW model that features the use of a color names (CN) descriptor. With a CN descriptor, RGB values are mapped to real-world color names using a mapping that is learned from Internet search results [13], rather than the specific dataset at hand.

Mansoori et al. [11] report good results from using a hue descriptor in a late-fusing method for including hue in a BOVW model for content-based image retrieval. Van de Weijer and Schmid [14] as well recommend the use of a hue descriptor in the case when the dataset colors are saturated.

Kopf et al. [15] describe an approach for enhancing the traditional BOVW model that does not explicitly use a hue or color descriptor. In this approach, an image is divided into sub-groups, each associated with a unique range of pixel hues, using hue-based masking. A histogram is formed for each sub-group from the shape descriptors in that sub-group, and then all these histograms are concatenated to form the final histogram for the image.

Olson et al. [16] and Olson and Zhang [17] describe a color descriptor, Histogram of Normalized Colors (HoNC), and a combination descriptor, formed by combining the HoNC descriptor with a SIFT descriptor, that performs well in the area of keypoint recognition.

The work described herein builds upon the foregoing work to develop a novel late-fusing method, featuring the HoNC descriptor [16, 17], for adding color to SE-BOVW models to improve image classification performance. The use of the HoNC descriptor distinguishes the method from prior late-fusing methods [1, 11] that employ a CN and hue descriptor, respectively. Compared to a hue descriptor, the HoNC descriptor better handles achromatic colors, e.g., white, grey, and black, which are prevalent in real-world images. Compared to a CN descriptor, the HoNC descriptor includes a formal mechanism, color normalization, for achieving illumination intensity invariance, which mechanism is lacking in the CN descriptor [20].

3 Method

For our method, rather than rely on color alone, we elected to join color with shape based on preliminary testing showing that such models outperform models that rely on color alone. For our shape descriptor, we elected to use the SIFT descriptor given its excellent performance and invariance properties, as reported in [14]. The major decision points for our method were: 1) whether to use early- or late-fusing; and 2) which color descriptor to use.

3.1 Early vs. Late Fusing

In choosing between early and late fusing for our method, we balanced design simplification considerations with performance. We found that, while early fusing results is a simpler, more efficient and more scalable design, late fusing significantly outperforms early fusing due to the large quantization error that is introduced with early fusing, as explained in the next section. Accordingly, we adopted late fusing for our method despite the additional complexity involved.

3.2 Quantization Error Considerations

We tested early fusing with several descriptors, but found in each case that early fusing caused the model performance to drop. We also found in each case that the quantization error, as measured by the MSE (Mean-Squared Error) between the descriptors and the visual codewords they are mapped to increased. For example, when early fusing of HoNC and SIFT descriptors was used with a "single-level" spatial pyramiding SE-BOVW model [9], the model's predictive accuracy dropped about 5%, from 52% to 47.01%, and the MSE jumped from 78,579 to 140,591. We conjecture from this data that the quantization error introduced by early fusing introduces error into the final image histogram, which in turn reduces the predictive accuracy of the model.

We further found this increase in quantization error could not be mitigated by modest increases in the vocabulary size. In fact, using parametric modeling of the inverse relationship that has been found to exist between the vocabulary size and the MSE at that vocabulary size [18], we estimate that the vocabulary size in this example would have to be increased from 200 to roughly 55,000 in order to reduce the MSE to the original level of 78,579, which is not feasible.

We also considered the use of portmanteau vocabularies [8, 19] as a potential solution. With portmanteau vocabularies, the joint probability distribution of color and shape is empirically estimated, and used to construct a compact vocabulary of multi-cue words that has far fewer entries than implied by enumerating every possible combination of the two individual vocabularies [19]. However, we ultimately rejected this approach because the performance gains that were reported, 2.8% and 5.4%, were insufficient to overcome the 5% deficit in performance that we experienced with early fusing of HoNC and SIFT descriptors, and add a reasonable boost.

For all the foregoing reasons, we rejected an early-fusing approach for joining the HoNC and SIFT descriptors, and opted for a late-fusing approach.

3.3 Choice of Color Descriptor

In choosing a color descriptor for our method, we considered the HoNC descriptor, given the successful use of that descriptor for keypoint recognition as reported in [16, 17]; the Histogram of Weighted Hues (HoWH) descriptor, given the use of hue descriptors for content-based image retrieval as reported in [11]; and the CN descriptor, given the use of that descriptor for image classification as reported in [1, 10].

While HoWH, like HoNC, utilizes a normalization procedure to achieve illumination intensity invariance, HoWH weights hue with saturation, to achieve robustness with respect to achromatic colors, which have an undefined hue [14]. However, this also causes achromatic colors to be ignored because these colors have low saturation [14]. Since achromatic colors are prevalent in real-world images, accounting for up to 44% of all pixels according to some estimates [20], we were concerned that selection of the HoWH descriptor would unduly limit the generalizability of our method.

The CN descriptor is able to distinguish between achromatic colors, but it does so at the expense of achieving illumination intensity invariance [20]. No such tradeoff is required by the HoNC descriptor. The CN descriptor also utilizes a universal mapping, learned from Internet search results, to map RGB values into pre-selected categories of generic color names [10, 13, 20]. We were concerned that this universal mapping, not tied to the specific dataset at issue, could introduce error and subjectivity into the image classification process.

Based on the foregoing, we ultimately selected HoNC because it seemed to do the best job at balancing illumination intensity invariance and ability to distinguish achromatic colors, two desirable properties for a color descriptor that, according to [20], are often at cross-purposes.

3.4 Final Design

Our final design, as configured for testing, is illustrated in Fig. 1. The testing set that forms the input consists of randomly selected images from each class that are independent of the training set. For each image in the testing set, feature extraction and description of both color and shape are performed using a dense detector. The color descriptors follow the upper processing path shown in the figure, while the shape descriptors follow the lower path.

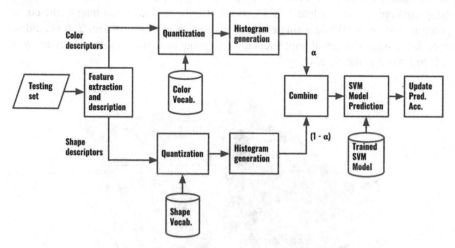

Fig. 1. Block diagram of testing stage of final design

The color descriptors are quantized using color vocabulary, previously determined in a training stage, by mapping each color descriptor to the closest color visual word. The color visual words for each image are then encoded into a spatially enhanced color histogram using a selected SE-BOVW model. Similarly, the shape descriptors are quantized using a shape vocabulary, also previously determined in a training stage, by mapping each shape descriptor to the closest shape visual word. The shape visual words for each image are then encoded into a spatially enhanced shape histogram using the same SE-BOVW model used above.

The color and shape histograms for each image are then weighted, respectively, with the values α and $(1 - \alpha)$, and the weighted histograms concatenated to form the histogram for the image. In our final design, we set α to 0.20, after determining that value optimized performance relative to alternative values in the range 0.10–0.40. The histogram for the image is then input to a previously-trained SVM model, which generates a prediction for the image.

3.5 Representative Examples of Spatially-Enhanced BOVW Models

In this section, we describe three representative examples of SE-BOVW models, appropriate for real-time use cases, with which to test our method. In these descriptions, it is important to distinguish between the image histogram, which represents the entire image, and a spatial histogram, which is a component of the image histogram associated with a particular codeword.

Single-Level SPR

Our first model is the "single-level" variant of the spatial pyramiding representation described in [9]. The image histogram generated for each image associates a single spatial histogram with each visual codeword in the vocabulary. An example of this spatial histogram, suitable for a 300 × 300-pixel image, is shown in Fig. 2. The spatial histogram depicts the absolute X-Y locations of the descriptors that map to the corresponding codeword. While a single spatial histogram is shown in Fig. 2, it should be appreciated that, in an actual implementation, a spatial histogram will be associated with each codeword in the vocabulary.

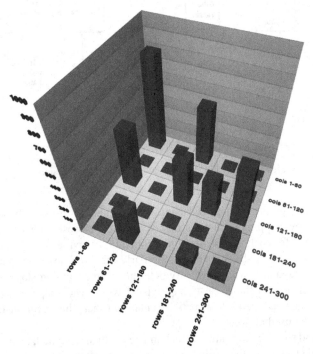

Fig. 2. Example of spatial histogram for Single-Level SPR model

As shown, the base of the spatial histogram is a 5 ×5 two-dimensional grid, where the horizontal, or X, dimension of the base grid represents rows of the image plane, and the vertical, or Y, dimension of the base grid represents columns of the image plane. Each cell of the grid corresponds to a range of spatial (X-Y) locations on the image plane and the height of the spatial histogram at that cell indicates a count of the number of descriptors located at or within these spatial locations that map to the visual word corresponding to the spatial histogram.

To populate the image histogram, each descriptor for the image is quantized by mapping it to its closest visual word. The spatial histogram for that visual word is then located, and the frequency count of the cell corresponding to the X- and Y-locations of the descriptor on the image plane is incremented.

The complexity of the algorithm for generating the histogram is $O(n)$, where n is the number of descriptors for the image. The dimensionality of the histogram is $25m$, where m is the size of the vocabulary in terms of number of visual words. Hereinafter, this model type will be referred to as "Single-Level SPR" where SPR stands for "Spatial Pyramid Representation".

Single-Level-SPR/HPS-Lite

Our second model combines the foregoing Single-Level SPR representation with a modification of the HPS_{ad}^{intra} representation described in Khan et al. [4], which will hereinafter be referred to as "HPS-Lite", where HPS stands for "Hard Pairwise Similarity."[2] The combination will be referred to as Single-Layer SPR/HPS-Lite.

As shown in Fig. 3, the image histogram generated for each image associates two spatial histograms with each visual word in the vocabulary, the Single-Level SPR spatial histogram shown in blue and the HPS-Lite spatial histogram shown in red. The structure and manner of populating the Single-Level SPR spatial histogram was described in the previous section and will not be repeated here. Instead, we focus our attention on the HPS-Lite spatial histogram.

The HPS-Lite spatial histogram is generated from a pairwise comparison of all the descriptors that map to the visual codeword to which the spatial histogram corresponds. It depicts the relative locations (i.e., in terms of distance and angle) between these pairs of descriptors, and is intended to complement the information represented by the Single-Level SPR histogram, i.e., absolute X-Y locations of the descriptors that map to the visual codeword to which the spatial histogram corresponds.

The base of the HPS-Lite spatial histogram consists of a 5×5 two-dimensional grid, where the horizontal (or X) dimension represents the distance between pairs of descriptors that both map to the visual word to which the spatial histogram corresponds, and the vertical (or Y) dimension represents the angle between such pairs of descriptors.

The process for populating the HPS-Lite spatial histograms begins by mapping each descriptor to its closest visual word, ordering the descriptors, and then comparing each descriptor d_i with all descriptors d_j ahead of it in the ordered list (i.e., all d_j, where $j > i$).

If two such descriptors match, i.e., both map to the same visual word, the Euclidean distance D_{ij} between the pair in image space is calculated, as well as the angle A_{ij} between the pair relative to the horizontal. These distance and angle values are calculated by "constructing" a vector between the pair and then taking D_{ij} as the length of this vector, and A_{ij} as the angle of this vector relative to the horizontal. The HPS-Lite spatial histogram corresponding to the visual word to which the pair of descriptors match is retrieved, and then the count in the cell corresponding to these distance and angle values is incremented.

---

[2] The modification consists of the elimination of a hard Gaussian weighting step described in Khan et al. [4] that we considered unnecessary and to detract from real-time performance.

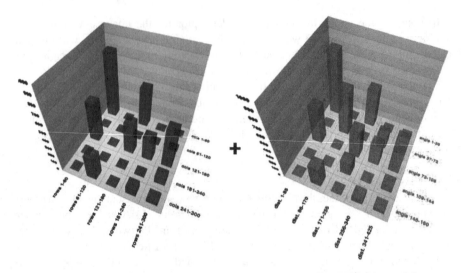

Fig. 3. Concatenated spatial histogram for Single-Level-SPR/HPS-Lite model

After an HPS-Lite spatial histogram corresponding to a visual codeword has been populated, it is normalized, as described in Khan et al. [4]. The complexity of the algorithm for generating the image histogram is $O(n^2)$, where n is the number of descriptors for the image. The dimensionality of the final histogram is $50m$, where m is the vocabulary size in terms of number of visual words.

Multi-level SPR

Our third model is the Multi-Level Spatial Pyramiding Representation of [9], where the parameter L, indicating the number of levels beyond the base level, is set to 2, for a total of 3 levels. At this setting, an image histogram is generated that associates each visual word in the vocabulary with three spatial histograms, a 1×1 spatial histogram, corresponding to level 0, a 2×2 spatial histogram, corresponding to level 1, and a 4×4 spatial histogram, corresponding to level 2. Through this association between visual words and spatial histograms, a total of 21 bins are allocated in the image histogram for each visual word.

An example of the three-level spatial pyramiding representation depicting this association between visual words and spatial histograms is shown in Fig. 4. In this example, there are three visual words, indicated by circles, diamonds, and crosses, respectively. At the bottom left, three 1×1 spatial histograms are depicted corresponding, respectively, to the circle, diamond, and cross visual words. At the bottom center, three 2×2 spatial histograms are depicted corresponding, respectively, to the circle, diamond, and cross visual words. Lastly, at the bottom right, three 4×4 spatial histograms are depicted corresponding, respectively, to the circle, diamond, and cross visual words.

To populate the image histogram, each descriptor from the image is quantized by mapping it to its closest visual word, and then all three of the spatial histograms corresponding to that visual word are located. Next, the appropriate cell in each of these spatial histograms is incremented.

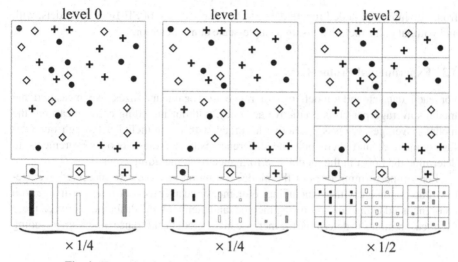

Fig. 4. Example of a three-level spatial pyramid (reproduced from [9])

As a result of the foregoing, an image histogram representing the image is generated that is infused with the absolute locations of the descriptors in the image plane, at multiple levels of granularity. The complexity of the algorithm for generating this histogram is $O(n)$, where n is the number of descriptors for the image. The dimensionality of the resulting histogram is $21m$, where m is the vocabulary size in terms of number of visual words. Hereinafter, this model type will be referred to as "Multi-Level SPR".

4   Experiments

In this section, we discuss the datasets used for testing, our platform, and our experimental protocol.

4.1   The Datasets

We used Caltech101 and Caltech256 for our testing having 102 and 257 classes, respectively. Compared to PASCAL VOC 2007 and COCO, which are currently being used for benchmarking by Facebook AI in the field of real-time object detection, we considered Caltech101 and Caltech256 to be better suited to the problem at hand, which is image classification not object detection per se, while still having a similar, modest number of classes.

4.2   Platform

Our software platform is based on an OpenCV 4.1.1 library including the extra modules for SIFT and SURF. To this library, we added several color descriptor code modules, e.g., HoNC, HoWH, and several utility code modules, as obtained from GitHub. For our testing software, we started with C++ code for testing the traditional BOVW model obtained from GitHub[3], and added functionality to facilitate testing of SE-BOVW models, with and without color included, using a single-scale dense detector.

4.3 Experimental Protocol

For each dataset and model, over a range of vocabulary sizes, we measured the model's average-per-class predictive accuracy, without including color, measured the model's average-per-class predictive accuracy with color included through our late-fusing method, and then took the difference between these two measurements to determine the boost in the model's performance from including color.

For top-performing ones of the model configurations, we also measured average-test-time-per image without including color, measured average-test-time-per-image with color included using our late-fusing method, and then took the difference between these two measurements to determine the increase in the model's inference time from including color.

5 Results

5.1 Boost in Performance

Table 1 shows the boost in average-per-class-predictive accuracy that results from using our late-fusing method to include color in each of the three-representative SE-BOVW models. The test results show the boost in performance in each case ranges between about 1.9–3.2%.

Table 1. Summary of boost test results

Dataset	Vocab. Size	Single-Level SPR	Single-Level SPR/HPS-Lite	Multi-Level SPR
Caltech101*	100	2.80	2.28	2.02
	200	2.84	1.95	2.45
	400	2.08	2.05	1.93
Caltech256[†]	50	2.69	2.41	2.61
	100	2.69	2.23	3.21
	400	2.12	1.88	2.80

*Based on 10 runs
[†]Based on a single run.

---

[3] https://github.com/hkhojasteh/Bag-of-Visual-Words.

5.2 Comparison with Alternative Color Descriptors

Table 2 shows that, for Caltech101, when a hue descriptor, HoWH, is substituted for HoNC in our late-fusing method, or when color normalization in HoNC is disabled, the mean boost in performance for each of the models drops by statistically significant amounts, where "statistical significance" is assessed using a two-sample t-test.

Table 2. Test results for alternative descriptors – Caltech101

Dataset	Model	Performance	
Caltech101		Mean Boost from HoWH	Mean Boost from HoNC-none
	Single-Level SPR	0.82* [drop from 2.24‡, p < .01]	0.89† [drop from 2.24‡, p < .01]
	Single-Level SPR/HPS-Lite	0.77* [drop from 1.99‡, p < .01]	1.05† [drop from 1.99‡, p < .05]
	Multi-Level SPR	0.65* [drop from 2.46‡, p < .01]	1.75† [drop from 2.46‡, p < .10]

*Computed over three independent runs at $N = 200$ with α set to 0.05
†Computed over three independent runs at $N = 200$ with α set to 0.20
‡Computed over seven independent runs at $N = 200$ with α set to 0.20

Similar, although less pronounced, drops in performance occur when these same substitutions are made for Caltech256. Together, these results confirm that HoNC significantly outperforms HoWH in our method and also that the illumination intensity invariance provided by color normalization in HoNC significantly boosts performance.

5.3 Comparison with State-of-the-Art

Table 3 shows that the increase in inference time from using our late-fusing method to include color in the highest performing SE-BOVW models ranges between about 150–190 mS.

The second stage of the detector of [5] is a SE-BOVW model that is based on [4] and is similar to the SE-BOVW models described in Sect. 3.5 and tested herein. If that model were to be modified to include color using the subject method, it can reasonably be assumed that the predictive accuracy would jump by about 2.55%, and the inference time would jump by about 170 mS, which are the midpoints of the ranges we measured for our method. Table 4 compares the performance of this modified detector with that of NAS-FPN AmoebaNet [7], a CNN-based detector that is currently ranked #6 on the Facebook AI leaderboard for real time object detection using the COCO dataset.

Table 3. Summary of increase in inference time (mS) test results

Dataset	Vocab. Size	Single-Level SPR	Single-Level SPR/HPS-Lite	Multi-Level SPR
Caltech101*	100	–	152.25	–
	200	150.56	–	181.73
	400	147.08	–	165.87
Caltech256[†]	50	–	–	–
	100	190.54	–	174.46
	400	–	–	192.50

*Based on 10 runs
[†]Based on a single run

Table 4. Comparison with state-of-the-art models

Model	Perf	Inf. Time (mS)	Dataset	No. of classes	Date
Modified detector	93.03% (Pred. Acc.)	270	GTSRB	43	NA
NAS-FPN AmoebaNet	48.3% (mAP)	278.9	COCO	80	2019 [7]

6   Conclusion

In conclusion, we have provided a novel, generalizable method for joining color with shape, featuring the HoNC descriptor, to improve the predictive accuracy of SE-BOVW models for image classification.

References

1. Elfiky, N.M., Shahbaz Khan, F., van de Weijer, J., Gonzàlez, J.: Discriminative compact pyramids for object and scene recognition. Pattern Recogn. **45**(4), 1627–1636 (2012). https://doi.org/10.1016/j.patcog.2011.09.020
2. Khan, R., Barat, C., Muselet, D., Ducottet, C.: Spatial orientations of visual word pairs to improve bag-of-visual-words model. In: Proceedings of the British Machine Vision Conference 2012, Surrey, pp. 89.1–89.11 (2012). https://doi.org/10.5244/C.26.89
3. Vigo, D.A.R., Khan, F.S., van de Weijer, J., Gevers, T.: The impact of color on bag-of-words based object recognition. In: 2010 20th International Conference on Pattern Recognition, pp. 1549–1553 (2010). https://doi.org/10.1109/ICPR.2010.383
4. Khan, R., Barat, C., Muselet, D., Ducottet, C.: Spatial histograms of soft pairwise similar patches to improve the bag-of-visual-words model. Comput. Vis. Image Understand. **132**, 102–112 (2015). https://doi.org/10.1016/j.cviu.2014.09.005
5. Abdi, L., Meddeb, A.: Spatially enhanced bags of visual words representation to improve traffic signs recognition. J. Signal Process. Syst. **90**(12), 1729–1741 (2017). https://doi.org/10.1007/s11265-017-1324-9

6. Dai, J., Li, Y., He, K., Sun, J.: R-FCN: object detection via region-based fully convolutional networks. arXiv:1605.06409 [cs]. (2016). http://arxiv.org/abs/1605.06409. Accessed 9 May 2021

7. Ghiasi, G., Lin, T.-Y., Pang, R., Le, Q.V.: NAS-FPN: learning scalable feature pyramid architecture for object detection. arXiv:1904.07392 [cs], Apr 2019. http://arxiv.org/abs/1904.07392. Accessed 9 May 2021

8. van de Weijer, J., Khan, F.S.: Fusing color and shape for bag-of-words based object recognition. In: Tominaga, S., Schettini, R., Trémeau, A. (eds.) CCIW 2013. LNCS, vol. 7786, pp. 25–34. Springer, Heidelberg (2013). https://doi.org/10.1007/978-3-642-36700-7_3

9. Lazebnik, S., Schmid, C., Ponce, J.: Spatial pyramid matching. In: Dickinson, S.J., Leonardis, A., Schiele, B., Tarr, M.J. (eds.) Object Categorization, pp. 401–415. Cambridge University Press, Cambridge (2009)

10. Khan, F., Anwer, R., Weijer, J., Bagdanov, A., Vanrell, M., López, A.: Color attributes for object detection. In: Proceedings/CVPR, IEEE Computer Society Conference on Computer Vision and Pattern Recognition, June 2012. https://doi.org/10.1109/CVPR.2012.6248068

11. Mansoori, N.S., Nejati, M., Razzaghi, P., Samavi, S.: Bag of visual words approach for image retrieval using color information. In: 2013 21st Iranian Conference on Electrical Engineering (ICEE), Mashhad, Iran, pp. 1–6, May 2013. https://doi.org/10.1109/IranianCEE.2013.6599562

12. van de Sande, K.E.A., Gevers, T., Snoek, C.G.M.: Evaluating color descriptors for object and scene recognition. IEEE Trans. Pattern Anal. Mach. Intell. 32(9), 1582–1596 (2010). https://doi.org/10.1109/TPAMI.2009.154

13. van de Weijer, J., Schmid, C., Verbeek, J., Larlus, D.: Learning color names for real-world applications. IEEE Trans. Image Process. 18(7), 1512–1523 (2009). https://doi.org/10.1109/TIP.2009.2019809

14. van de Weijer, J., Schmid, C.: Coloring local feature extraction. In: Computer Vision – ECCV 2006, Berlin, Heidelberg, pp. 334–348 (2006). https://doi.org/10.1007/11744047_26

15. Kopf, S., et al.: Enhancing bag of visual words with color information for iconic image classification. In: IPCV 2016 : Proceedings of the 2016 International Conference on Image Processing, Computer Vision, and Pattern Recognition : WORLDCOMP 2016, July 25–28, 2016, Las Vegas, Nevada, USA, pp. 206–209 (2017). https://madoc.bib.uni-mannheim.de/42193/

16. Olson, C.F., Hoover, S.A., Soltman, J.L., Zhang, S.: Complementary keypoint descriptors. In: Bebis, G., et al. (eds.) ISVC 2016. LNCS, vol. 10072, pp. 341–352. Springer, Cham (2016). https://doi.org/10.1007/978-3-319-50835-1_32

17. Olson, C.F., Zhang, S.: Keypoint recognition with histograms of normalized colors. In: 2016 13th Conference on Computer and Robot Vision (CRV), Victoria, BC, Canada, pp. 311–318, June 2016. https://doi.org/10.1109/CRV.2016.37

18. Kolesnikov, A., Trichina, E., Kauranne, T.: Estimating the number of clusters in a numerical data set via quantization error modeling. Pattern Recogn. 48(3), 941–952 (2015). https://doi.org/10.1016/j.patcog.2014.09.017

19. Khan, F.S., van de Weijer, J., Bagdanov, A.D., Vanrell, M.: Portmanteau vocabularies for multi-cue image representation. In: Proceedings of the 24th International Conference on Neural Information Processing Systems, Red Hook, NY, USA, pp. 1323–1331 (2011). Accessed 14 Feb 2021

20. van de Weijer, J., Schmid, C.: Applying color names to image description. In: 2007 IEEE International Conference on Image Processing, San Antonio, TX, USA, pp. III-493–III-496 (2007). https://doi.org/10.1109/ICIP.2007.4379354

A Novel Similarity Measure for Retinal Optical Coherence Tomography Images

Tae Hong[1], Farnaz Mohammadi[2], Rohan Chatterjee[1], Eric Chan[1],
Mohammad Pourhomayoun[1], Vahid Mohammadzadeh[2], Kouros Nouri-Mahdavi[2],
and Navid Amini[1,2(✉)]

[1] California State University Los Angeles, Los Angeles, CA 90032, USA
namini@calstatela.edu
[2] University of California Los Angeles, Los Angeles, CA 90095, USA

Abstract. Optical coherence tomography (OCT) has become an essential tool for imaging of the retina to perform diagnosis and management of ocular and non-ocular diseases. In this paper, we evaluate the performance of structural similarity (SSIM) and multiscale structural similarity (MS-SSIM) metrics in comparing cross-sectional OCT images of the retina. We will then propose new metrics that only consider areas with a high signal-to-noise ratio in retinal OCT images. Our experimental comparisons demonstrate that, as opposed to SSIM and MS-SSIM measurements, the proposed metrics, called ROI-SSIM and ROI-MS-SSIM, more effectively extract structural information from OCT images and hence, yield similarity values more reflective of human visual perception.

Keywords: OCT · Structural similarity · Region of interest · Multiscale structural similarity · Retinal segmentation

1 Introduction

Optical coherence tomography (OCT) is a non-invasive, micrometer-scale, and cross-sectional imaging technology for biological tissue [1]. It has been widely used for retinal imaging in ophthalmology as it provides high resolution structural information of the retina. In OCT, many one-dimensional scans (A-scans) are performed at several depths to create a two-dimensional cross-sectional image called a B-scan. B-scans, if acquired closely and rapidly, can be translated into a volumetric image of a retina.

As the most common form of output data from OCT devices, B-scans are widely used to qualitatively and quantitatively evaluate retinal morphology to confirm the presence of ocular diseases such as glaucoma [2–6] age related macular degeneration (AMD) [7–9], and diabetic retinopathy (DR) [10–13], as well as non-ocular diseases, such as multiple sclerosis (MS) [14–17], Parkinson disease (PD) [18–21], and Alzheimer's disease (AD) [22–25]. Accordingly, there is a great deal of studies that measure similarity between OCT B-scans for the purpose of diagnosis and management of these diseases [26–32].

Since OCT B-scans are affected by speckle noise, a large group of studies have presented methods of denoising, or otherwise enhancing these images for better detection of

© Springer Nature Switzerland AG 2021

G. Bebis et al. (Eds.): ISVC 2021, LNCS 13018, pp. 276–286, 2021.
https://doi.org/10.1007/978-3-030-90436-4_22

retinal abnormalities [28, 33–37]. Another group of studies have aimed to generate OCT B-scans using neural networks as a substitute for when patients were unavailable for in-person office visits and image capturing sessions [31, 38–41]. A third group of studies develop registration techniques for OCT B-scans for a variety of purposes such as longi-tudinal evaluation of retinal structures [42–44]. These studies inspect the correspondence between OCT B-scans in order to quantify the accuracy of image registration.

The three groups of studies mentioned above along with numerous others rely on mean squared error (MSE), peak signal to noise ratio (PSNR), or the structural similarity index measure (SSIM) as methods that produce a quantitative evaluation of the similarity between two B-scans for quantitatively analyzing the quality of denoised, generated, or registered B-scans. However, all of these metrics have limitations in how noise is handled [45, 46]. Furthermore, they take into consideration the regions of an OCT B-scan that contain unreliable information (i.e., areas with a low signal-to-noise ratio) [47].

The metrics, MSE and PSNR, only provide pixel-wise comparisons and do not concern the constituent structures of an image, deviating from the human perception of structural information within an image. On the other hand, SSIM is perceptually correlated, i.e., its calculation assumes that the human visual system is adapted to extract structural information from images.

In this paper, a new method of similarity measurement is proposed, where the retina is extracted as the region of interest before similarity is measured using SSIM or its enhanced version, multi-scale SSIM (MS-SSIM) [48]. We rely on the fact that OCT devices yield low signal-to-noise ratio in the areas above (i.e., vitreous) and below (i.e., choroid and sclera) the retina. Accordingly, the top and bottom boundaries of the retina, namely, the internal limiting membrane (ILM) and the outer boundary of Bruch's membrane (BM) are detected.

To the best of our knowledge, the proposed similarity measure is the first instance of a measure that is calculated in accordance with the image acquisition properties of OCT devices. Our proposed similarity measure can break the tradition of using PNSR, MSE, or SSIM as similarity measures for retinal OCT images. Based on promising results from experimental comparisons on 2010 pairs of OCT B-scans from 101 glau-coma patients, we expect the proposed similarity measure will significantly improve the accuracy of comparisons between OCT B-scans, which will potentially lead to more precise diagnosis and management of ocular and non-ocular diseases.

The rest of this paper is organized as follows. Section 2 describes the related work. Section 3 focuses on the main ideas underlying our proposed similarity measure for retinal OCT images. Section 4 covers the experimental results and corresponding discussions. Finally, the conclusions of this study are presented Sect. 4.

2 Related Work

As of the writing of this manuscript, there is no study reporting a similarity measure customized or designed for optical coherence tomography B-scans. Nevertheless, there are several studies that use MSE, PSNR, or SSIM and its variations in order to produce a quantitative evaluation of the similarity between two B-scans. We divide these studies into three groups based on their primary objective:

(1) **Noise reduction on OCT images:** A large body of research studies present noise reduction methods for OCT images; Chen et al. [33] aim at denoising OCT B-scans and present a denoising generative adversarial network, called a DN-GAN, which they train using high-noise and low-noise B-scans. Once trained, the generator of the DN-GAN accepts a high-noise OCT B-scan and outputs the denoised image. The investigators compare the output denoised image against the low-noise B-scan using PNSR and SSIM as comparison metrics in order to demonstrate denoising effectiveness of the DN-GAN. Another study by Akter and associates [34] uses a neural network with U-Net architecture to remove vitreoretinal interface, opacity artifacts, and speckle noise from OCT B-scans. Comparisons are made, through MSE, PNSR, and SSIM, between the outputs of the U-Net model against ground-truth images that manually had artifacts removed. A deep learning network with an enhanced loss function is proposed by Qiu and colleagues [28], where they use SSIM and MS-SSIM for quantitative evaluation of their denoised B-scans. Halupka et al. introduce two novel convolutional neural networks for removing speckle noise, an MSE- trained CNN and a CNN with a GAN architecture. They gauge performance using PSNR, SSIM, MS-SSIM, and MSE.

(2) **Synthetic OCT image generation:** There are studies aiming at generating OCT B-scans using neural networks from prior B-scans. For instance, Hassan and co-investigators build a generative deep learning model using the conditional GAN architecture to predict glaucoma progression over time. The patient's OCT B-scans are predicted from three or two prior measurements. The predicted images demonstrate high similarity with the ground truth images based on the SSIM metric.

(3) **Registration of OCT images:** Studies with the main focus on registration of OCT images form another group of studies that need to measure the similarity between B-scans. As an example, Kurokawa et al. [49] propose and develope a registration algorithm for OCT B-scans aiming at compensating for eye-motion artifacts that occur during the acquisition of the retinal OCT images. The investigators quantify the effectiveness of image registration using MSE and demonstrate that the corrected scans permit proper analysis of the retinal tissue.

There are numerous other studies aiming to modify or construct OCT B-scans that rely largely on these similarity measurements for their quantitative analysis [9].

3   Methods

3.1   Structural Similarity Index Measure

Similarity measures, MSE and PSNR. only provide pixel-wise comparisons and do not concern the constituent structures of an image, deviating from the human perception of structural information within an image. On the other hand, SSIM is perceptually correlated, i.e., its calculation is based on the assumption that the human visual system is adapted to extract structural information from images. The system compares images x and y by separating the index into three separate measurements of luminance, contrast, and structure, and calculating their product as shown in (1).

$$\text{SSIM}(x, y) = l(x, y) \cdot c(x, y) \cdot s(x, y) \tag{1}$$

Measurements are taken in an 11×11 Gaussian weighted window that is passed over the image pixel by pixel to generate a score. The mean, standard deviation, and covariance are defined with a weight w_i in the respective manners shown in (2), (3), and (4):

$$\mu_x = \sum_{i=1}^{N} w_i x \tag{2}$$

$$\sigma_x = \left(\sum_{i=1}^{N} w_i (x_i - \mu_x)^2 \right)^{\frac{1}{2}} \tag{3}$$

$$\sigma_{xy} = \sum_{i=1}^{N} w_i (x_i - \mu_x)(y_i - \mu_y) \tag{4}$$

Luminance, contrast, and structure are then respectively defined as formulated in (5), (6), and (7):

$$l(x, y) = \frac{2\mu_x \mu_y + C_1}{\mu_x^2 + \mu_y^2 + C_1} \tag{5}$$

$$c(x, y) = \frac{2\sigma_x \sigma_y + C_2}{\sigma_x^2 + \sigma_y^2 + C_2} \tag{6}$$

$$s(x, y) = \frac{\sigma_{xy} + C_3}{\sigma_x \sigma_y + C_3} \tag{7}$$

The three measurements are finally brought together to form SSIM:

$$\text{SSIM}(x, y) = \frac{(2\mu_x \mu_y + C_1)(2\sigma_{xy} + C_2)}{(\mu_x^2 + \mu_y^2 + C_1)(\sigma_x^2 + \sigma_y^2 + C_2)} \tag{8}$$

C_1, C_2, and C_3 are constants used for stabilization when the mean and standard deviation values are very close to zero [50].

3.2 Multi-scale Structural Similarity Index Measure

MS-SSIM is an extension of SSIM that takes measurements at different scales of the images being compared. Starting with the original image pair as index 1 of the scale, a low-pass filter is applied to the images, which are then downsampled by a factor of 2. This process is iteratively repeated four times to form a total of 5 scales. Contrast and structure are measured at each scale while luminance is measured only at the last scale. The calculation for MS-SSIM is defined as follows:

$$\text{MS - SSIM}(\mathbf{x}, \mathbf{y}) = l_M(x, y) \prod_{j=1}^{M} \left[c_j(x, y) \cdot s_j(x, y) \right] \tag{9}$$

where M is the total number of scales [3].

By taking several measurements at different scales, MS-SSIM allows the comparison to combat the effects of speckle noise more effectively than SSIM. It should be noted that the speckle noise is caused by multiple forward and backward scattering of light waves due to the large number of scattering particles within ocular tissues.

3.3 Boundary Extraction

B-scans acquired by OCT have brought us much closer to an accurate tissue diagnosis than ever before. Nevertheless, these B-scans contain information that is not reliably captured. Specifically, posterior and anterior to the retinal layers are regions respectively known as the vitreous and the choroid/sclera. The point of maximum sensitivity when scanning the retina with an OCT device is known as the zero-delay line and it typically sits inside of the vitreous. As an OCT device scans deeper into the layers of the eye, the signals captured are reduced and details are lost. This results in the information in the choroid being captured unreliably and appearing as a hazy membrane that contains no valuable information [47]. While the zero-delay line sits within the vitreous, the fluid nature of the material within this region causes inconsistencies when imaged, and serves no meaningful purpose during inspection of a B-scan. Sezer and colleagues [51] introduces a technique known as EDI-OCT, where the zero delay line is positioned closer to the choroid to capture a reproducible and high resolution image of the choroid. However, this methodology is severely limited by the lack of an automated process in SD-OCT devices, as well as difficulty in obtaining clear images in the choroidoscleral junction.

Based on the above, we aim to remove the vitreous and choroid/sclera from out B-scans and designate the retinal layers as our region of interest (ROI), effectively setting the retinal layers as the only region to be considered for image comparison. We call this method ROI-SSIM or ROI-MS-SSIM depending on whether we use SSIM or MS-SSIM for comparing the retinal layers. An example of a B-scan that has gone through this process can be seen in Fig. 1.

To extract the ROI within the OCT B-scans, we use a segmentation approach introduced in [52]. The process starts with the identification of a line within the outer nuclear layer (See the yellow line segment in Fig. 1(b)). This line splits the image into two sections, the inner segment of the retina and the outer segment of the retina.

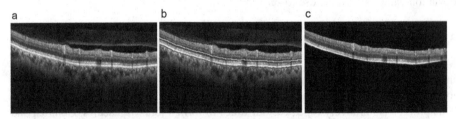

Fig. 1. (a) Raw OCT B-scan. (b) OCT B-scan with yellow line through outer nuclear layer, red line marking the upper boundary, and blue line marking the lower boundary. (c) ROI extracted OCT B-scan. (Color figure online)

The inner segment consists of all pixels above the line within the outer nuclear layer, while the outer segment consists of all pixels below it. Briefly put, in the inner segment, the point of the greatest contrast rise in each column of pixels are connected to form a line and is designated as the upper boundary of the retinal layers known as the inner limiting membrane (ILM) represented by the red line segment in Fig. 1(b). In the outer segment, the points of the greatest contrast drop are found in each vertical column of pixels and are connected to form a line that is the lower boundary known as the outer boundary of Bruch's membrane (BM) shown with the blue line segment in Fig. 1(b). Both lines are smoothed out by removing distant or disconnected segments and closing gaps using linear interpolation.

Once the boundaries have been determined, the intensity values of each column of pixels are set into a vector. Each intensity value in a position before the upper boundary or after the lower boundary is set to 0 representing black resulting in a masked B-scan such as the one illustrated in Fig. 1(c). Figure 2 shows a diagram of the comparison process of a pair of B-scans. After extracting the ROI for one of the B-scans, the corresponding region is extracted in the other B-scan in the pair to keep the ROI consistent between the two images. The two images then have their similarity measured using SSIM and MS-SSIM.

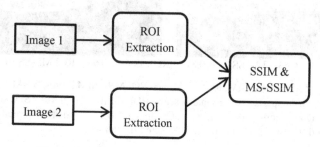

Fig. 2. Overview of similarity measurement process.

4 Experimental Results and Discussions

Similarity measurements were taken using original OCT B-scans against B-scans that were predicted and generated by a Conditional Generative Adversarial Network (cGAN) developed in [38]. The original scans were acquired from glaucomatous eyes of 101 patients using the Posterior Pole Algorithm of the Spectralis Spectral-Domain OCT (SD-OCT), which acquires 61 horizontal B-scans at approximately 120 μm apart, extending across a 30° × 25° area of the macula. Each B-scan consists of 768 A-scans, with the acquisition process being repeated 9–11 times to decrease speckle noise [5]. The generator of the cGAN used for prediction of B-scans was trained using two older OCT examinations of these patients. For each original B-scan used in our comparison, the cGAN used two or three B-scans from previous visits to predict how the patient's B-scan would appear at the same time-point as the original B-scan [38]. The original and predicted B-scans formed the pair that was used to measure similarity using our proposed method.

For each pair, four different measurements were made: SSIM, MS-SSIM, ROI-SSIM, and ROI-MS-SSIM. The first two measurements used SSIM and MS-SSIM without making any adjustments to the scans. The ROI labeled measurements extracted the ROI of the predicted scan using the method described in this paper, then extracted same region from the original scans. It then used SSIM and MS-SSIM to make the similarity measurement of this pair of images. An Example of similarity measurements with and without the ROI extracted can be seen in Fig. 3.

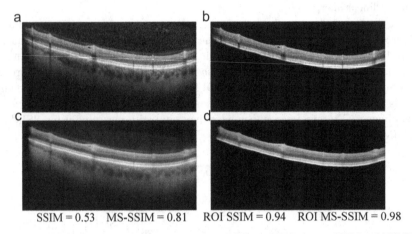

SSIM = 0.53   MS-SSIM = 0.81   ROI SSIM = 0.94   ROI MS-SSIM = 0.98

Fig. 3. Example SSIM, MS-SSIM, ROI SSIM, and ROI MS-SSIM scores. SSIM and MS-SSIM scores derived from comparison of original B-scans. ROI SSIM and ROI MS-SSIM scores derived from ROI extracted versions of the images. (a) Original raw B-scan. (b) original predicted B-scan. (c) ROI extracted B-scan. (d) ROI extracted predicted B-scan.

Table 1. Comparison of similarity scores.

Comparison method	Median score
SSIM	0.477
MS-SSIM	0.724
ROI SSIM	0.922
ROI MS-SSIM	0.970

A total of 2010 pairs of original and cGAN-generated B-scans stored in JPEG format were used in our experimental comparisons, where four measurements were made for all pairs. Table 1 summarizes the median similarity score for each comparison method. The SSIM measurements result in a median score of 0.477 indicating moderate similarity between a pair of B-scans. Given the high level of similarity in appearance of the retinal layers, scores of 0.922 and 0.970 are a more accurate representation of how the B-scans appear and these scores are better aligned with our visual perception. Another observation is that MS-SSIM's ability to handle noise by taking measurements at different scales makes it a superior form of similarity measurement over SSIM when analyzing OCT scans.

The distribution of the results can be seen in the box plot depicted in Fig. 4. The box plots for measurements taken without ROI extraction have a shorter range than those taken with ROI extraction. This can be attributed to the fact that pixels with low levels of signal-to-noise ratio within the vitreous and choroid/sclera are taken into consideration when comparing the images, resulting in a greater range of scores. Additionally, MS-SSIM's ability to handle noise more effectively than base SSIM results in average scores that are ultimately the highest with ROI MS-SSIM.

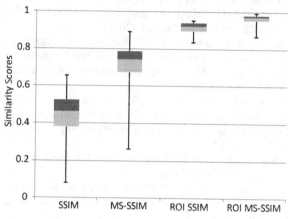

Fig. 4. Box plots of similarity scores.

With this new approach of similarity measurement, we are able to generate vastly improved similarity scores when comparing OCT B-scans that are perceptually similar.

5 Conclusions

In this paper, we introduce a novel method of measuring similarity between OCT B-scans. Due to the unreliable information that is captured in the vitreous and choroid/sclera areas, we focus only on the sections of B-scans that were captured with a high signal-to-noise ratio. An algorithm detecting changes in intensities along the axial depth profile of OCT signals was utilized to find the inner limiting membrane and the outer boundary of Bruch's membrane. These two boundaries defined the region of interest consisting of the retinal layers. All pixels outside of this region are masked and SSIM and MS-SSIM were used for quantitative comparisons. In order to evaluate the proposed ROI-SSIM and ROI-MS-SSIM metrics in the context of OCT imaging, we assembled a dataset containing 2010 pairs of OCT B-scans from 101 glaucoma patients. Original B-scans were compared against artificially constructed B-scans and the median ROI-MS-SSIM score of 0.97 is achieved, which is more reflective of the human visual system as opposed to SSIM or MS-SSIM measurements alone. It is expected that the proposed similarity measure will significantly improve the accuracy of comparisons between OCT B-scans, which will potentially lead to more precise diagnosis and management of ocular and non-ocular diseases.

References

1. Huang, D., et al.: Optical coherence tomography. Science **254**(5035), 1178–1181 (1991)
2. Miraftabi, A.: et al.: Local variability of macular thickness measurements with SD-OCT and influencing factors. Transl. Vis. Sci. Technol. (2016)
3. Amini, N., et al.: The relationship of the clinical disc margin and Bruch's membrane opening in normal and glaucoma subjects. Investig. Ophthalmol. Vis. Sci. (2016)
4. Amini, N., et al.: Influence of the disc–fovea angle on limits of RNFL variability and glaucoma discrimination. Investig. Ophthalmol. Vis. Sci. (2014)
5. Mahmoudinezhad, G., et al.: Detection of longitudinal GCIPL change: comparison of two spectral domain optical coherence tomography devices. Am. J. Ophthalmol. (2021)
6. Mohammadzadeh, V., et al.: Macular imaging with optical coherence tomography in glaucoma. Surv. Ophthalmol. (2020)
7. Thakoor, K., Bordbar, D., Yao, J., Moussa, O., Chen, R., Sajda, P.: Hybrid 3D-2D deep learning for detection of neovascularage-related macular degeneration using optical coherence tomography B-scans and angiography volumes. In: Proceedings - International Symposium on Biomedical Imaging (2021)
8. Corvi, F., et al.: Reproducibility of qualitative assessment of drusen volume in eyes with age related macular degeneration. Eye (2020)
9. Chen, Z., Li, D., Shen, H., Mo, H., Zeng, Z., Wei, H.: Automated segmentation of fluid regions in optical coherence tomography B-scan images of age-related macular degeneration. Opt. Laser Technol. (2020)
10. Vujosevic, S., et al.: Hyperreflective retinal spots in normal and diabetic eyes: b-scan and en face spectral domain optical coherence tomography evaluation. Retina (2016)
11. Khansari, M.M., et al.: Automated deformation-based analysis of 3D optical coherence tomography in diabetic retinopathy. IEEE Trans. Med. Imaging (2020)
12. Schwartz, R., et al.: Objective evaluation of proliferative diabetic retinopathy using OCT. Ophthalmol. Retina (2020)
13. Amini, N., Vahdatpour, A., Dabiri, F., Noshadi, H., Sarrafzadeh, M.: Joint consideration of energy-efficiency and coverage-preservation in microsensor networks. Wirel. Commun. Mob. Comput. (2011)
14. He, Y., et al.: Segmenting retinal OCT images with inter-B-scan and longitudinal information. (2020)
15. He, Y., Carass, A., Solomon, S.D., Saidha, S., Calabresi, P.A., Prince, J.L.: Retinal layer parcellation of optical coherence tomography images: data resource for multiple sclerosis and healthy controls. Data Br. (2019)
16. Graves, J.S.: Optical coherence tomography in multiple sclerosis. Semin. Neurol. (2019)
17. Amini, N., Javaherian, A.: A MATLAB-based frequency-domain finite-difference package for solving 2D visco-acoustic wave equation. Waves in Random and Complex Media (2011)
18. Uchida, A., et al.: Outer retinal assessment using spectral-domain optical coherence tomography in patients with Alzheimer's and Parkinson's disease. Investig. Ophthalmol. Vis. Sci. (2018)
19. Pilat, A., et al.: In vivo morphology of the optic nerve and retina in patients with Parkinson's disease. Investig. Ophthalmol. Vis. Sci. (2016)
20. Chorostecki, J., et al.: Characterization of retinal architecture in Parkinson's disease. J. Neurol. Sci. (2015)
21. Saeedi, R., Amini, N., Ghasemzadeh, H: Patient-centric on-body sensor localization in smart health systems. In: Conference Record - Asilomar Conference on Signals, Systems and Computers (2015)

22. den Haan, J., Janssen, S.F., van de Kreeke, J.A., Scheltens, P., Verbraak, F.D., Bouwman, F.H.: Retinal thickness correlates with parietal cortical atrophy in early-onset Alzheimer's disease and controls. Alzheimer's Dement. Diagnosis, Assess. Dis. Monit. (2018)

23. Alber, J., et al.: A recommended 'minimum data set' framework for SD-OCT retinal image acquisition and analysis from the Atlas of Retinal Imaging in Alzheimer's Study (ARIAS). Alzheimer's Dement. Diagnosis, Assess. Dis. Monit. (2020)

24. Marziani, E., et al.: Evaluation of retinal nerve fiber layer and ganglion cell layer thickness in Alzheimer's disease using spectral- domain optical coherence tomography. Investig. Ophthalmol. Vis. Sci. (2013)

25. Ghasemzadeh, H., Amini, N., Sarrafzadeh, M.: Energy-efficient signal processing in wearable embedded systems. (2012)

26. Sahu, S., Singh, H.V., Kumar, B., Singh, A.K., Kumar, P.: Enhancement and de-noising of OCT image by adaptive wavelet thresholding method. In: Handbook of Multimedia Information Security: Techniques and Applications (2019)

27. Devalla, S.K., et al.: A deep learning approach to denoise optical coherence tomography images of the optic nerve head. Sci. Rep. (2019)

28. Qiu, B., et al.: Noise reduction in optical coherence tomography images using a deep neural network with perceptually-sensitive loss function. Biomed. Opt. Express (2020)

29. Saya Nandini Devi, M., Santhi, S.: Improved edge detection methods in OCT images using a hybrid framework based on CGWO algorithm. In: Proceedings of the 2019 IEEE International Conference on Communication and Signal Processing, ICCSP 2019 (2019)

30. Das, V., Dandapat, S., Bora, P.K.: Unsupervised super-resolution of OCT images using generative adversarial network for improved age-related macular degeneration diagnosis. IEEE Sens. J. (2020)

31. Lazaridis, G., Lorenzi, M., Ourselin, S., Garway-Heath, D.: Improving statistical power of glaucoma clinical trials using an ensemble of cyclical generative adversarial networks. Med. Image Anal. (2021)

32. Kande, N.A., Dakhane, R., Dukkipati, A., Yalavarthy, P.K.: SiameseGAN: a generative model for denoising of spectral domain optical coherence tomography images. IEEE Trans. Med. Imaging (2021)

33. Chen, Z., Zeng, Z., Shen, H., Zheng, X., Dai, P., Ouyang, P.: DN-GAN: denoising generative adversarial networks for speckle noise reduction in optical coherence tomography images. Biomed. Signal Process. Control **55**, 101632 (2020)

34. Akter, N., Perry, S., Fletcher, J., Simunovic, M., Roy, M.: Automated artifacts and noise removal from optical coherence tomography images using deep learning technique. In: 2020 IEEE Symposium Series on Computational Intelligence SSCI 2020, pp. 2536–2542 (2020)

35. Halupka, K.J., et al.: Retinal optical coherence tomography image enhancement via deep learning. Biomed. Opt. Express **9**(12), 6205 (2018)

36. Amini, N., Miremadi, S.G., Fazeli, M.: A hierarchical routing protocol for energy load balancing in wireless sensor networks. In: Canadian Conference on Electrical and Computer Engineering (2007)

37. Amini, N., et al.: Design and evaluation of a wearable assistive technology for hemianopic stroke patients. In: Proceedings of the 2020 International Symposium on Wearable Computers, pp. 7–11 (2020)

38. Hassan, O.N., et al.: Conditional GAN for prediction of glaucoma progression with macular optical coherence tomography. In: Bebis, G., et al. (eds.) ISVC 2020. LNCS, vol. 12510, pp. 761–772. Springer, Cham (2020). https://doi.org/10.1007/978-3-030-64559-5_61

39. Kaiser, W.X., et al.: Method of assessing human fall risk using mobile system. **8**(823), 526 (2014)

40. Raof, R.A.A., et al.: Color thresholding method for image segmentation algorithm of Ziehl-Neelsen sputum slide images. In: 2008 5th International Conference on Electrical Engineering, Computing Science and Automatic Control, CCE 2008 (2008)
41. Forero, M.G., Sroubek, F., Cristóbal, G.: Identification of tuberculosis bacteria based on shape and color. Real-Time Imaging (2004)
42. Gabriele, M.L., et al.: Optical coherence tomography scan circle location and mean retinal nerve fiber layer measurement variability. Investig. Ophthalmol. Vis. Sci. (2008)
43. Lang, A., et al.: Combined registration and motion correction of longitudinal retinal OCT data. In: Medical Imaging 2016: Image Processing (2016)
44. Zhang, X., Xu, W., Huang, M.C., Amini, N., Ren, F.: See UV on your skin: An ultraviolet sensing and visualization system. In: BODYNETS 2013 - 8th International Conference on Body Area Networks (2013)
45. Wang, Z., Bovik, A.C.: A universal image quality index. IEEE Signal Process. Lett. **9**(3), 81–84 (2002)
46. Rehman, A., Wang, Z.: SSIM-based non-local means image denoising. In: Proceedings - International Conference on Image Processing, ICIP (2011)
47. Barteselli, G., Bartsch, D.U., Freeman, W.R.: Combined depth imaging using optical coherence tomography as a novel imaging technique to visualize vitreoretinal choroidal structures. Retina (2013)
48. Wang, Z., Simoncelli, E.P., Bovik, A.C.: Multi-scale structural similarity for image quality assessment
49. Kurokawa, K., Crowell, J.A., Do, N., Lee, J.J., Miller, D.T.: Multi-reference global registration of individual A-lines in adaptive optics optical coherence tomography retinal images. J. Biomed. Opt. (2021)
50. Wang, Z., Bovik, A.C., Sheikh, H.R., Simoncelli, E.P.: Image quality assessment: from error visibility to structural similarity. IEEE Trans. Image Process. **13**(4), 600–612 (2004)
51. Sezer, T., Altınışık, M., Koytak, İ.A., Özdemir, M.H.: The choroid and optical coherence tomography. Turk Oftalmoloiji Dergisi (2016)
52. Mayer, M.A., Hornegger, J., Mardin, C.Y., Tornow, R.P.: Retinal nerve fiber layer segmentation on FD-OCT scans of normal subjects and glaucoma patients. Biomed. Opt. Express **1**(5), 1358 (2010)

Subspace Discrimination Method for Images Using Singular Value Decomposition

Eri Mochizuki[1], Haruka Sone[1], Hayato Itoh[2], and Atsushi Imiya[3(✉)]

[1] School of Science and Engineering, Chiba University, Yayoi-cho 1-33, Inage-ku, Chiba 263-8522, Japan
[2] Graduate School of Informatics, Nagoya University, Furo-cho, Chikusa-ku, Nagoya 464-8601, Japan
[3] Institute of Management and Information Technologies, Chiba University, Yayoi-cho 1-33, Inage-ku, Chiba 263-8522, Japan
imiya@faculty.chiba-u.jp

Abstract. In this paper, we introduce the linear subspace method for the second-order tensor. The subspace method based on the principal component analysis for vector data is a conventional and established method for pattern recognition and classification. A pair of orthonormal vector sets derived by the singular value decomposition of matrices provides a pair of linear spaces to express images. The application of the subspace method to a pair of linear subspaces provides recognition methodologies for images through tensor analysis.

1 Introduction

The subspace method based on the principal component analysis (PCA) for vector data is a conventional and established method for pattern recognition and classification[1]. In this paper, we extend the subspace method for the vector spaces [1–3] to a pair of linear spaces, which we call the bilinear space, derived by image singular decomposition (image SVD). We also define the geodesic distance between bilinear spaces for discrimination and identification. Furthermore, we construct orthogonal canonical projections to the bilinear spaces for the classification of images. These methods provide recognition methodologies for images through tensor analysis without embedding images in vector spaces.

The optical flow field, which is the motion field on the retina, is a fundamental query for motion perception and recognition [4–6]. Two-dimensional vectors are equivalent to complex numbers. Using this correspondence, optical flow fields are expressed as complex two-way arrays. Then, extending image SVD to complex images, the subspace method of the bilinear space is applied to the classification of optical flow fields. Using orthogonal canonical projections [1,2], which define a

---

[1] Mathematical tools in the linear subspace method related to this work are summarised in Appendix.

© Springer Nature Switzerland AG 2021
G. Bebis et al. (Eds.): ISVC 2021, LNCS 13018, pp. 287–298, 2021.
https://doi.org/10.1007/978-3-030-90436-4_23

common linear subspace of pattern categories, we extract the static background motion in a sequence of images. The motion fields orthogonal to this bilinear subspace express additional motion fields to the static motion. Therefore, these additional motion fields correspond to the dynamic motion fields in a scene.

In refs. [7–9], optical flow fields are embedded into an appropriate vector space to employ the classical PCA for classification and recognition. The extension of PCA from real data to complex data is called complex PCA [10,11]. Complex PCA extracts the principal components from analytical signals constructed from real observations through the Hilbert transform. In climatology and geophysics, the complex PCA of time series extracts the spatiotemporal oscillations and delay in a travelling wave of the wind flow on earth and ocean currents.

2   Mathematical Preliminaries

For a pair of matrices F and G in $\mathbf{C}^{m \times n}$, the inner product $\langle F, G \rangle = \mathrm{tr} G^* F = (\mathrm{vec} G)^* \mathrm{vec} F$ introduces the Frobenius norm $|F|_F = \sqrt{\langle F, F \rangle} = \sqrt{\mathrm{tr} F^* F}$. Then, for elements in $\mathbf{C}^{m \times n}$,

$$d_{\ell_2}(F, G) = |F - G|_F \tag{1}$$

defines distance. Here, $F^* = ((\overline{f_{nm}}))$ denotes the conjugate of $F = ((f_{mn}))$. If $F = ((f_{mn}))$ is a real matrix, F^* is equivalent to the transpose $F^\top = ((f_{nm}))$ of F. The angle between $X \in \mathbf{C}^{m \times n}$ and $Y \in \mathbf{C}^{m \times n}$ is

$$\angle[X, Y] = \cos^{-1} \frac{|\langle X, Y \rangle|}{|X|_F |Y|_F}. \tag{2}$$

For $F \in \mathbf{C}^{m \times n}$, image SVD derives the form

$$F = U \Sigma V^*, \quad U^* U = I, \quad V^* V = I, \tag{3}$$

where $U = (u_1, u_2, \cdots, u_m)$ and $V = (v_1, v_2, \cdots, v_n)$ are eigenmatrices of $F^* F$ and $F F^*$, respectively, and Σ is the diagonal matrix in the main diagonal of $m \times n$ matrix with the eigenvalues $\{\sigma_l\}_{l=1}^L$, for $L \leq \min(m, n)$, of $F^* F$ and $F F^*$. Since both U and V are orthogonal matrices, the column vectors $\{u_i\}_{i=1}^m$ and $\{v_j\}_{j=1}^n$ of U and V define orthonormal bases of the linear spaces spanned by the column and row vectors of the image array, respectively. For $\mathbf{L}_c = \mathcal{L}(\{u_i\}_{i=1}^m)$ and $\mathbf{L}_r = \mathcal{L}(\{v_j\}_{j=1}^n)$, we call $\mathbf{L}_c \times \mathbf{L}_r$ the bilinear space. The geodesic distance between bilinear spaces $\mathcal{L}(\{u_i^A\}_{i=1}^m) \times \mathcal{L}(\{v_j^A\}_{j=1}^n)$ and $\mathcal{L}(\{u_i^B\}_{i=1}^m) \times \mathcal{L}(\{v_j^B\}_{j=1}^n)$ is

$$d_{G_2}(A, B) = \sqrt{\sum_{i=1}^m (\angle[u_i^A, u_i^B])^2 + \sum_{j=1}^n (\angle[v_j^A, v_j^B])^2}. \tag{4}$$

Next, we define orthogonal projections

$$P_k = \sum_{i=1}^k u_i u_i^*, \quad Q_k = \sum_{j=1}^k v_j v_j^*. \tag{5}$$

for $k \leq \mathrm{rank} F \leq \min(m, n)$. If an input image $X \in \mathbf{C}^{m \times n}$ satisfies the relation

$$\frac{|P_k X Q_k^*|_F}{|X|_F} = \frac{|(Q_k \otimes P_k)\mathrm{vec} X|}{|\mathrm{vec} X|} = \cos \angle [(Q_k \otimes P_k)\mathrm{vec} X, \mathrm{vec} X] > 1 - \varepsilon \quad (6)$$

for a small positive constant $0 < \varepsilon \ll 1$, then, for a small positive constant δ, the relation $|P_k X Q_k^* - X|_F < \delta$, is satisfied. Furthermore, Eq. (6) implies that there exists $Y \in \mathbf{L}_c^k \times \mathbf{L}_r^k = \mathcal{L}(\{u_i\}_{i=1}^k) \times \mathcal{L}(\{v_j\}_{j=1}^k)$ which satisfies the inequality $|X - Y|_F \leq \mu$ for a small positive constant μ. These geometrical properties imply that F is compressed as

$$F_k = P_k F Q_k^* = U \Sigma_k V^* = \sum_{i=1}^{k} \sigma_k u_i v_i^*, \quad (7)$$

where Σ_k is the diagonal matrix with the leading k elements of Σ.

For a sequence of image $F(t)$, for $t = 1, 2, \cdots, T$, we obtain the temporal sequence of decompositions

$$F(t) = U(t) \Sigma(t) V(t)^*, \quad (8)$$

and the temporal bilinear space $\mathbf{L}_c(t) \times \mathbf{L}_r(t)$, where $\mathbf{L}_c(t) = \mathcal{L}(\{u_i(t)\}_{i=1}^m)$ and $\mathbf{L}_r(t) = \mathcal{L}(\{v_j(t)\}_{j=1}^n)$. Furthermore, for a set of images $\{F(\alpha)\}_{\alpha=1}^P$, we can compute image SVD of the average $\overline{F}$ of $\{F(\alpha)\}_{\alpha=1}^P$.

3   Numerical Examples

3.1   Discrimination of Still Images

Table 1 shows the parameters of image data for the performance evaluation of the image discrimination. We use twenty one categories of images, such that, six car sets four fruit sets six pack sets and seven vegetable sets. Each image set in each category contains 40 images captured from every $9°$ from $0°$ to $360°$. The original images are captured by a hyperspectral camera with 400 channels. Then, monochrome images are generated from hyperspectral images. Fruits and vegetables are prepared on a white dish. For image data $F(c, s, (\pi/40)d)$, c, s and d stand for the category, set and direction, respectively.

For the object identification and direction estimation, the averages

$$\overline{F}(c, s) = \frac{1}{40} \sum_{d=0}^{39} F(c, s, \frac{\pi}{20} d), \quad \overline{F}(c, d) = \frac{1}{T} \sum_{s=1}^{S} F(c, s, \frac{\pi}{20} d) \quad (9)$$

are computed as reference data sets. $\overline{F}(c, s)$ is the average over the directions. Furthermore, $\overline{F}(c, d)$ is the average of images in the same category with the same direction. Figures 1(a), 1(b), 1(c) and 1(d) show the averages $\overline{F}(c, t)$. Furthermore, Figs. 1(e), 1(f), 1(g) and 1(h) show the averages $\overline{F}(c, d)$.

For object identification and direction estimation, we compute

$$t^* = \arg\min_t D(\overline{\boldsymbol{F}}(c,t), \boldsymbol{X}), \quad d^* = \arg\min_d D(\overline{\boldsymbol{F}}(c,d), \boldsymbol{X}). \tag{10}$$

In object identification the category and set are recognised. Furthermore, in direction estimation the category and direction are recognised.

When $\angle[\boldsymbol{u}_i^A, \boldsymbol{u}_i^B] \ll \pi/6$, $\angle[\boldsymbol{u}_i^A, \boldsymbol{u}_i^B] \approx |\boldsymbol{u}_i^A - \boldsymbol{u}_i^B|$, we have an approximation

$$d_{G_2}(\boldsymbol{A}, \boldsymbol{B}) \approx \sqrt{\sum_{i=1}^m |\boldsymbol{u}_i^A - \boldsymbol{u}_i^B|^2 + \sum_{j=1}^n |\boldsymbol{v}_j^A - \boldsymbol{v}_j^B|^2}$$
$$= \sqrt{|\boldsymbol{U}_A - \boldsymbol{U}_B|_F^2 + |\boldsymbol{V}_A - \boldsymbol{V}_B|_F^2}. \tag{11}$$

For the performance comparisons of discrimination and identification, we adopt the Frobenius distance, ℓ_1 matrix distance and ℓ_1-Grassmann distance between the input and data, such that

$$d_{\ell_1}(\boldsymbol{A}, \boldsymbol{B}) = |\boldsymbol{A} - \boldsymbol{B}|_1 = \sum_{i=1}^m \sum_{j=1}^n |a_{ij} - b_{ij}|, \tag{12}$$

$$d_{G_1}(\boldsymbol{A}, \boldsymbol{B}) = \sum_{i=1}^k \angle[\boldsymbol{u}_i^A, \boldsymbol{u}_i^B] + \sum_{j=1}^k \angle[\boldsymbol{v}_j^A, \boldsymbol{v}_j^B]$$
$$\approx \sum_{i=1}^m |\boldsymbol{u}_i^A - \boldsymbol{u}_i^B|_1 + \sum_{j=1}^n |\boldsymbol{v}_j^A - \boldsymbol{v}_j^B|_1$$
$$= |\boldsymbol{U}_A - \boldsymbol{U}_B|_1 + |\boldsymbol{V}_A - \boldsymbol{V}_B|_1. \tag{13}$$

Equation (13) is defined as the ℓ_1 analogous of Eq. (11).

Table 2 shows the results for object identification and direction estimation. To evaluate the ability of the Grassmann distance for object identification, an image from a fixed category in each direction is used as the query. Furthermore, to evaluate the ability of the Grassmann distance for direction estimation, an image from a fixed direction in each category is used as the query. Therefore, recognition of a direction of an image of a car in a category, six categories of cars are generated. Then, an image of a category is used as query. In the Table 1, the distance for the correct identification of the category is listed. These results show that by the Grassmann distance for the bilinear spaces produces better results both for object identification and direction estimation. Therefore, these results demonstrate the advantages of the bilinear subspace method for image pattern recognition.

For both identification problems, the principal angles between bilinear subspaces of the target image and reference categories are essential since bilinear spaces define the distribution of target and object images in image data space. The Frobenius distance computes differences between images in the image data space although the Grassmann distance computes principal angles between of bilinear subspaces of images derived by image SVD. These results show the advantages of the subspace method for bilinear spaces both problems.

Table 3 evaluates the performance of the Grassmann and Frobenius distances for both problems with respect to the dimensions of bilinear spaces. For both problems, the principal angles between bilinear subspaces of the target image and reference categories are essential since bilinear spaces define the distribution of target and object images in image data space.

Table 1. Properties of data set. We use twenty three categories of images; six car sets, four fruit sets, six pack sets, and seven vegetable sets from 0° to 360°. The original images are captured by a hyperspectral camera with 400 channels. Then, monochrome images are generated from hyperspectral images.

Category (c)	Set (s)	Direction (d)	Size (pixels)	Trimming
Car	6	40	560 × 300	None
Fruit	4	40	560 × 300	None
Pack	6	40	560 × 300	None
Vegetable	7	40	560 × 300	None

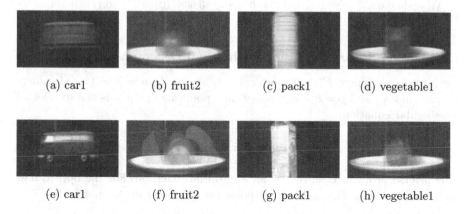

(a) car1   (b) fruit2   (c) pack1   (d) vegetable1

(e) car1   (f) fruit2   (g) pack1   (h) vegetable1

Fig. 1. Examples of average images. (a), (b), (c) and (d) are average images for object identification. (e), (f), (g) and (h) are average images for direction estimation. From left to right averages of six car sets, four fruit sets , six paper-pack sets and seven vegetables sets are presented. Each category contains 40 images captured from every 9° from 0° to 360°. The original images are captured by a hyperspectral camera with 400 channels. Then, monochrome images are generated from hyperspectral images. Each image is the average over the directions.

Table 2. Performance evaluation for object identification and direction estimation. To evaluate the ability of the Grassmann distance for object identification, an image from a fixed category in each direction is used as the query.

	Object identification				Direction estimation			
	d_{ℓ_1}	d_{ℓ_2}	d_{G1}	d_{G2}	d_{ℓ_1}	d_{ℓ_2}	d_{G1}	d_{G2}
Car	0.842	0.833	0.446	**0.346**	0.958	0.900	0.988	**0.842**
Fruit	1.000	1.000	0.738	**0.631**	0.744	0.613	0.988	**0.901**
Pack	0.755	0.815	0.490	**0.350**	0.930	0.885	0.985	**0.855**
Vegetable	0.957	0.964	0.696	**0.500**	0.489	0.364	0.732	**0.489**

Table 3. Performance evaluation for object identification and direction estimation. The Grassmann and Frobenius distances are computed for $k = 10$ and $k = \text{rank}F$.

	Object identification				Direction estimation			
	Grassmann dist.		Frobenius dist.		Grassmann dist.		Frobenius dist.	
k	10	rank$F$	10	rank$F$	10	rank$F$	10	rank$F$
Car	0.842	0.842	0.833	0.833	0.192	0.842	0.875	0.900
Fruit	1.000	1.000	1.00	1.000	0.106	0.906	0.350	0.613
Pack	0.735	0.755	0.810	0.815	0.140	0.855	0.750	0.885
Vegetable	0.957	0.957	0.964	0.964	0.068	0.489	0.171	0.364

3.2   Motion Separation Using Orthogonal Decomposition

For a temporal image $F(t)$, the optical flow vector [5] $u = \dot{x} = (\dot{x}, \dot{y})^\top$, where $\dot{x} = u = u(x, y)$ and $\dot{y} = v = v(x, y)$, of each point $x = (x, y)^\top$ is the solution of the singular equation

$$\frac{D}{Dt} a(x, y, t) = f_x \dot{x} + f_y \dot{y} + a_t = 0. \tag{14}$$

This inverse problem is solved by an appropriate method. For the optical flow vector $u_{mn} = (\dot{x}_{mn}(t), \dot{y}_{mn})^\top$ of the point $(m, n)^\top$, we call the matrix

$$F(t) = ((f_{mn}(t))), \quad f_{mn}(t) = \dot{x}_{mn}(t), +i\dot{y}_{mn}(t) \tag{15}$$

the flow matrix of the image sequence.

We evaluate the reconstruction performance of the bilinear subspace method. For the kth-order reconstruction $F_k(t) = ((f^k_{mn}(t)))$, where $f^k_{mn}(t) = \dot{x}^k_{mn}(t) + \dot{y}^k_{mn}(t)$, of the flow matrix $F(t) = ((f_{mn}(t)))$, we define

$$d^1_{mn}(t) = |\dot{x}_{mn}(t) - \dot{x}^k_{mn}(t)| + |\dot{y}_{mn}(t) - \dot{y}^k_{mn}(t)|, \tag{16}$$
$$d^2_{mn}(t) = |\dot{x}_{mn}(t) - \dot{x}^k_{mn}(t)|^2 + |\dot{y}_{mn}(t) - \dot{y}^k_{mn}(t)|^2, \tag{17}$$
$$\Theta_{mn}(t) = |\theta_{mn} - \theta^k_{mn}|, \tag{18}$$
$$\Phi_{mn}(t) = |\phi_{mn}(t) - \phi^k_{mn}(t)|, \tag{19}$$

where

$$\theta_{mn}(t) = \angle(f_{mn}(t), f_{mn}^k(t)) = \angle(\dot{x}_{mn}(t), \dot{y}_{mn}(t))^\top, (\dot{x}_{mn}^k(t), \dot{y}_{mn}^k(t))^\top), \quad (20)$$
$$\phi_{mn} = \angle((\dot{x}_{mn}(t), \dot{y}_{mn}(t), 1)^\top, (\dot{x}_{mn}^k(t), \dot{y}_{mn}^k(t), 1)^\top). \quad (21)$$

We evaluate the trajectories of the averages and variances of $d_{mn}^1(t)$, $d_{mn}^2(t)$, $a_{mn}(t)$ and $b_{mn}(t)$. The results are shown in Fig. 2. The results for $k = 1, 3, 6,$ 10, 15, 36, 66 and 251 are indicated by the blue, yellow, green, red, purple, brown, orange and black curves, respectively. These statistical analyses imply that accurate and stable optical flow fields are reconstructed for $k \geq 10$. The dimension k is selected as $k = \frac{n(n+1)}{2}$, where n is the number of the nth-order partial derivatives for two-dimensional images. The orders of the partial derivatives of two-dimensional images define the local dimensionalities of images. Therefore, for the accurate and stable reconstruction of optical flow fields from the image SVD of optical flow, the same number of bases with local smoothness order of the topographic map of the grey scale image are required.

We define the projections

$$P_k(t) = U_k(t)U_k(t)^*, \quad Q_k(t) = V_k(t)V_k(t)^*, \quad (22)$$

where $U_k(t)$ and $V_k(t)$ are the matrices constructed from the leading k columns of $U(t)$ and $V(t)$, respectively, and thier summations are

$$P_k = \sum_{t=1}^T P_k(t), \quad Q_k = \sum_{t=1}^T Q_k(t). \quad (23)$$

For the eigenmatrices X and Y of P_k and Q_k, such that

$$P_k X = X\Lambda, \quad Q_k Y = Y\Sigma, \quad (24)$$

the matrices

$$P_X = XX^*, \quad Q_Y = YY^* \quad (25)$$

are the orthogonal canonical projections to the bilinear subspaces[2] defined by $\{P_k(t)\}_{t=1}^T$ and $\{Q_k(t)\}_{t=1}^T$, respectively.

The transforms

$$F_k(t) = P_X F(t)Q_Y^*, \quad (26)$$
$$\hat{F}_k(t) = (I - P_X)F(t)(I - Q_Y^*) = P_X^\perp F(t)(Q_Y^\perp)^*, \quad (27)$$

extract common flow fields on $t = 1, 2, \cdots T$ and the removes the common flow fields from a sequence of flow fields, respectively, since the relations[3] $P_X^* P_X^\perp = O$

---

[2] Each orthogonal projection in a linear space defines the corresponding linear subspace. We call this linear subspace the linear subspace defined by the orthogonal projection.

[3] If $\langle F, G \rangle = 0$, then F and G are orthogonal. Since

$$\langle P_X F(t)Q_Y^*, P_X^\perp F(t)(Q_Y^\perp)^* \rangle = \langle F(t), P_X^* P_X^\perp F(t)(Q_Y^\perp)^* Q_Y) \rangle = \langle F(t), O F(t) O \rangle,$$

$P_X F(t)Q_Y^*$ and $P_X^\perp F(t)(Q_Y^\perp)^*$ are orthogonal and $P_X^\perp F(t)(Q_Y^\perp)^*$ is an element in the bilinear space $\Pi_X^\perp \times \Pi_Y^\perp$.

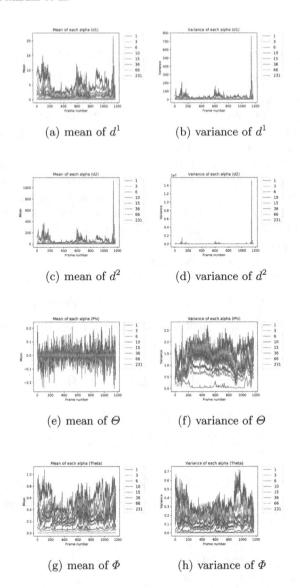

(a) mean of d^1 (b) variance of d^1

(c) mean of d^2 (d) variance of d^2

(e) mean of Θ (f) variance of Θ

(g) mean of Φ (h) variance of Φ

Fig. 2. Time trajectory of averages and variances of features. From top to bottom d^1, d^2, Θ and Φ are shown, and left and right columns shows averages and variances, respectively. for the image sequence of Fig. 3. For $k = 1, 3, 6, 10, 15, 36, 66$ and 251, are indicated by blue, yellow, green, red, purple, brown, orange and black curves, respectively. These statistical analyses imply that accurate and stable optical flow fields are reconstructed for $k \geq 10$. (Color figure online)

and $\boldsymbol{Q}_Y^* \boldsymbol{Q}_Y^\perp = \boldsymbol{O}$ imply the property $\langle \boldsymbol{P}_X \boldsymbol{F}(t) \boldsymbol{Q}_Y^*, \boldsymbol{P}_X^\perp \boldsymbol{F}(t)(\boldsymbol{Q}_Y^\perp)^* \rangle = 0$. Since the bilinear space $\boldsymbol{\Pi}_X \times \boldsymbol{\Pi}_Y$ defined by the projections $\boldsymbol{P}_X$ and $\boldsymbol{Q}_X$ is the common

(a) frame0014

(b) frame0364

(c) frame0465

(d) frame0888

Fig. 3. Temporal trajectory motion separation. From top to bottom, $\hat{F}_{36}$ for frames 0014, 0364, 0465 and 0888 are presented. Optical flow vectors generated by sign boards, passing cars, and trees on the side of street are extracted. Furthermore, in the image on the top optical flow field generated by turning motion of the car is extracted. Dominant motion field vectors which correspond to optical flow vectors generated by the ego-motion of the car are removed, since the optical flow field generated by the ego-motion defines the common bilinear subspace for a number of frames in an image sequence.

bilinear subspace through a sequence, the optical flow fields $\hat{F}_k(t)$, which is the projection of $F(t)$ to the bilinear space $\Pi_X^\perp \times \Pi_Y^\perp$ defined by the projections $P_X^\perp$ and $Q_X^\perp$, excludes the optical flow fields which are common through frames in a sequence.

Figure 3 shows temporal trajectory of motion separation by $\hat{F}_{36}$. In this example, dominant motion field vectors which correspond to optical flow vectors generated by the ego-motion of the car are removed and additional motion on each frames are extracted since the optical flow field generated by the ego-motion defines the common bilinear subspace for a number of frames in an image sequence. Furthermore, significant motion field vectors corresponding to irregular motions in the background, optical flow vectors on the sign boards and optical flow vectors on cars from side roads are extracted. These examples show that the dominant motion is removed and that motions depending on frames are extracted.

4   Conclusions

A pair of orthonormal vector sets derived by image SVD of a matrix provides a pair of linear spaces to an express image. We directly applied the subspace-based pattern recognition method to image arrays using image SVD although the vectorisation of image arrays allows us to accept the conventional pattern recognition methodologies for image array analysis.

We also extended image SVD to complex-valued images [10,11]. This extension of image SVD derived the linear-subspace-based classification and analysis methods for optical flow fields in temporal image sequences. The complex image SVD for optical flow fields extracts common and abnormal motions in a temporal image sequence for the longitudinal analysis of optical flow fields.

This research was supported by the Grants-in-Aid for Scientific Research funded by the Japan Society for the Promotion of Science under 20K11881.

Appendix

Let P_1 and P_2 be the orthogonal projections to the linear subspaces Π_1 and Π_2, respectively. Setting σ_i to be the singular values of $P_1 P_2$ and $P_2 P_1$ such that $0 \le \sigma_1 < \sigma_2 < \cdots < \sigma_k$, the principal angles between Π_1 and Π_2 are $\cos^{-1}\sigma_1 > \cos^{-1}\sigma_2 > \cdots > \cos^{-1}\sigma_k$, and the Grassmann distance along the geodesic between Π_1 and Π_2 is

$$d(\Pi_1, \Pi_2) = \sqrt{\sum_{i=1}^{k} \theta_i^2}$$

for $\theta_i = \cos^{-1}\sigma_i$. For orthonormal bases $\{u_{1i}\}_{i=1}^m$ and $\{u_{2j}\}_{j=1}^n$,

$$P_1 = \sum_{i=1}^{m} u_{1i} u_{1i}^*, \quad P_2 = \sum_{i=1}^{n} u_{2i} u_{2i}^*$$

are the orthogonal projections to linear subspaces $\mathbf{\Pi}_1 = \mathcal{L}(\{\boldsymbol{u}_{1i}\}_{i=1}^m)$ and $\mathbf{\Pi}_2 = \mathcal{L}(\{\boldsymbol{u}_{2i}\}_{j=1}^n)$, respectively. Since

$$\boldsymbol{P}_1\boldsymbol{P}_2\boldsymbol{u}_{2i} = (\boldsymbol{u}_{1i}^*\boldsymbol{u}_{2i})\boldsymbol{u}_{1i}, \quad \boldsymbol{P}_2\boldsymbol{P}_1\boldsymbol{u}_{1i} = (\boldsymbol{u}_{2i}^*\boldsymbol{u}_{1i})\boldsymbol{u}_{2i},$$

that is,

$$\boldsymbol{P}_1\boldsymbol{P}_2\boldsymbol{P}_1\boldsymbol{u}_{1i} = |(\boldsymbol{u}_{1i}^*\boldsymbol{u}_{1i})|^2\boldsymbol{u}_{1i}, \quad \boldsymbol{P}_2\boldsymbol{P}_1\boldsymbol{P}_2\boldsymbol{u}_{2i} = |(\boldsymbol{u}_{2i}^*\boldsymbol{u}_{1i})|^2\boldsymbol{u}_{2i},$$

the principal angles between $\mathbf{\Pi}_1$ and $\mathbf{\Pi}_2$ are $\angle[\boldsymbol{u}_{1i}, \boldsymbol{u}_{2i}] = \cos^{-1}\sqrt{|(\boldsymbol{u}_{1i}^*\boldsymbol{u}_{2i})|^2}$.

Let $\{\boldsymbol{u}_{ji}\}_{i=1}^{k(j)}$ be orthogonal base sets of linear subspaces $\mathbf{\Pi}_j$ and $\boldsymbol{P}_j$ be the orthogonal projection to $\mathbf{\Pi}_j$ fro $j = 1, 2, \cdots, m$. If $\boldsymbol{w} \in \mathbf{\Pi}_j$, $\boldsymbol{P}_j\boldsymbol{w} = \boldsymbol{w}$ for $j = 1, 2, \cdots, m$. Therefore, if $|\boldsymbol{P}_j\boldsymbol{w} - \boldsymbol{w}|^2 \ll \epsilon^2$, then $\boldsymbol{w}$ lies in a space close to all of $\{\mathbf{\Pi}_j\}_{j=1}^m$. These geometric conditions imply that the minimiser of

$$J(\boldsymbol{w}) = \sum_{j=1}^m |\boldsymbol{P}_j\boldsymbol{w} - \boldsymbol{w}|^2$$

is close to all $\{\mathbf{\Pi}_j\}_{j=1}^m$. The minimiser of $J(\boldsymbol{w})$ with respect to $|\boldsymbol{w}| = 1$ derives the eigenvalue equation

$$\sum_{j=1}^m \boldsymbol{P}_j^*\boldsymbol{P}_j\boldsymbol{w} = \lambda\boldsymbol{w}, \quad \boldsymbol{P}_j = \sum_{i=1}^{k(j)} \boldsymbol{u}_{ji}\boldsymbol{u}_{ji}^*.$$

Since

$$\boldsymbol{P}_j^* = \sum_{i=1}^{k(j)} (\boldsymbol{u}_{ji}\boldsymbol{u}_{ji}^*)^* = \sum_{i=1}^{k(j)} \boldsymbol{u}_{ji}\boldsymbol{u}_{ji}^*,$$

the relations

$$\boldsymbol{P}_j^* = \boldsymbol{P}_j, \quad \boldsymbol{P}_i^*\boldsymbol{P}_i = \left(\sum_{i=1}^{k(j)} (\boldsymbol{u}_{ji}\boldsymbol{u}_{ji}^*)^*\right)\left(\sum_{i=1}^{k(j)} \boldsymbol{u}_{ji}\boldsymbol{u}_{ji}^*\right) = \sum_{i=1}^{k(j)} \boldsymbol{u}_{ji}\boldsymbol{u}_{ji}^*$$

are satisfied. Therefore, the eigenvectors of $\boldsymbol{A} = \sum_{j=1}^m \boldsymbol{P}_j$ for different eigenvalues are mutually orthogonal and all eigenvalues are nonnegative. Therefore, setting

$$0 = \lambda_1 \leq \cdots \leq \lambda_k < \lambda_{k+1} < \cdots < \lambda_n,$$

for $k + 1 = \min\{k(1), k(2), \cdots, k(m)\}$,

$$\boldsymbol{P}_\wedge = \sum_{k=1}^l \boldsymbol{w}_k\boldsymbol{w}_k^*$$

is the orthogonal projection to the linear subspace

$$\mathbf{\Pi}_\wedge = \{\boldsymbol{x} \,|\, |\boldsymbol{P}_j\boldsymbol{x} - \boldsymbol{x}| \ll \epsilon^2, \, j = 1, 2, \cdots, m\}$$

for $0 < \epsilon \ll 1$. The orthogonal projection $P_\wedge$ is the canonical projection to the common linear subspace of $\{\Pi_j\}_{j=1}^m$. Therefore, for $x \in \Pi_j$, $\Pi_\wedge$ excludes $y = (I - P_\wedge)x$.

Let Π and Ω be a pair of linear subspace in $\mathbf{C}^n$ with the condition $\Pi \cap \Omega = \{o\}$. For $\forall p \in \Pi$ such that $p \neq o$ and $\forall q \in \Omega$ such that $q \neq o$, if $p^*q = 0$, Π and Ω are orthogonal complement each other. Therefore, the relations $p \neq \Omega$ and $q \neq \Pi$ are satisfied if $p \in \Pi$ and $q \in \Omega$. We set $\Omega^\perp := \Pi$ and $\Pi^\perp := \Omega$. Assuming $\Pi \cup \Omega = \mathbf{C}^n$, $x \in \mathbf{R}^n$ is uniquely expressed as $x = p + q$ for $p \in \Pi$ and $q \in \Omega$. Therefore, using the orthogonal projections P_Π and $P_\Omega = I - P_\Pi = P_\Pi^\perp$ to Π and Ω, respectively, $x \in \mathbf{C}^n$ is uniquely decomposed into $P_\Pi x$ and $P_\Omega x$.

References

1. Iijima, T.: Pattern Recognition, Corona-sha (1974)
2. Fukui, K., Maki, A.: Difference subspace and its generalization for subspace-based methods. IEEE Pattern Anal. Mach. Intell. **37**, 2164–2177 (2015)
3. Oja, E.: Subspace Methods of Pattern Recognition. Research Studies Press (1983)
4. Gibson, J.J.: The Ecological Approach to Visual Perception, Houghton Mifflin (1979)
5. Lucas, B.D., Kanade, T.: An iterative image registration technique with an application to stereo vision. In: Proceedings of IJCAI1981, pp. 674–679 (1981)
6. Farnebäck, G.: Two-frame motion estimation based on polynomial expansion. In: Bigun, J., Gustavsson, T. (eds.) SCIA 2003. LNCS, vol. 2749, pp. 363–370. Springer, Heidelberg (2003). https://doi.org/10.1007/3-540-45103-X_50
7. Ohnishi, N., Imiya, A.: Independent component analysis of optical flow for robot navigation. Neurocomputing **71**, 2140–2163 (2008)
8. Wulff, J., Black, M.J.: Efficient sparse-to-dense optical flow estimation using a learned basis and layers. In: CVPR, pp. 120–130 (2015)
9. Fan, S., Zhang, Y., Zhang, Y., Fang, Z.: Motion process monitoring using optical flow-based principal component analysis-independent component analysis method. Adv. Mech. Eng. **9**, 1–12 (2017)
10. Horel, J.D.: Complex principal component analysis: theory and examples. J. Appl. Meteorology Climatology **23**, 1660–1672 (1984)
11. Camiz, S., Creta, S.: Principal component analysis of complex data and application to climatology. In: Mola, F., Conversano, C., Vichi, M. (eds.) Classification, (Big) Data Analysis and Statistical Learning. SCDAKO, pp. 77–85. Springer, Cham (2018). https://doi.org/10.1007/978-3-319-55708-3_9

Cervical Cancer Detection and Classification in Cytology Images Using a Hybrid Approach

Eduardo L. Silva[1,2(✉)], Ana Filipa Sampaio[1], Luís F. Teixeira[2,3], and Maria João M. Vasconcelos[1]

[1] Fraunhofer Portugal AICOS, 4200-135 Porto, Portugal
eduardo.silva@fraunhofer.pt
[2] Faculty of Engineering of the University of Porto, Porto, Portugal
[3] INESC TEC, Porto, Portugal

Abstract. The high incidence of cervical cancer in women has prompted the research of automatic screening methods. This work focuses on two of the steps present in such systems, more precisely, the identification of cervical lesions and their respective classification. The development of automatic methods for these tasks is associated with some shortcomings, such as acquiring sufficient and representative clinical data. These limitations are addressed through a hybrid pipeline based on a deep learning model (RetinaNet) for the detection of abnormal regions, combined with random forest and SVM classifiers for their categorization, and complemented by the use of domain knowledge in its design. Additionally, the nuclei in each detected region are segmented, providing a set of nuclei-specific features whose impact on the classification result is also studied. Each module is individually assessed in addition to the complete system, with the latter achieving a precision, recall and F1 score of 0.04, 0.20 and 0.07, respectively. Despite the low precision, the system demonstrates potential as an analysis support tool with the capability of increasing the overall sensitivity of the human examination process.

Keywords: Cervical cancer · Classification · Computer-aided diagnosis · Deep learning · Detection · Machine learning

1 Introduction

Cervical cancer is the fourth most common type of cancer in women worldwide, despite being one of the more easily treatable types of cancer when detected early on [1]. Owing partially to this, there has been a significant research effort into effective screening methods over the last decades. The Papanicolau (or Pap) test is one of the most widely used, and it consists of analysing cells scraped from the squamocolumnar junction in the cervix [2] for malignant or pre-malignant signs. When performed manually, this is a very demanding task that requires highly

© The Author(s) 2021
G. Bebis et al. (Eds.): ISVC 2021, LNCS 13018, pp. 299–312, 2021.
https://doi.org/10.1007/978-3-030-90436-4_24

specialised resources. Therefore, automated systems have gained a particular interest in more recent decades.

These computer-aided diagnosis (CAD) systems usually consider different steps in order to analyze each microscopic image from a sample: focus and adequacy assessment, region of interest (ROI) identification and respective classification [3]. Currently, there are still limitations associated with the last two stages, namely the acquisition of adequate clinical data in sufficient amounts.

In order to overcome these challenges, this work explores the combination of deep learning (DL) and conventional machine learning (ML) algorithms in hybrid pipelines for the detection and classification of abnormal regions in liquid-based cytology (LBC) images. While hybrid approaches have been investigated before in similar settings, most of these studies do not explicitly employ both types of algorithms for the detection and classification stages, using them instead for related tasks, such as feature extraction. Furthermore, the proposed system incorporates specific domain knowledge in its design, assessing the impact of clinically relevant features, such as those of the nuclei, in the algorithms' discerning ability between different cervical lesions. In this manner, the present work provides a fresh perspective in terms of the architecture of CAD systems.

2 Related Work

With the technological advances in computer hardware and slide preparation techniques over the years, numerous approaches for the automatic analysis of cervical cytology images have been proposed [3]. When it comes to detect and isolate regions of interest in these images, the approaches more frequently encountered are based on conventional computer vision (CV) techniques aiming to segment an image's cells and their inner structures.

The International Symposium on Biomedical Imaging (ISBI) challenges focus precisely on this issue, with some innovative works being produced within this scope. For example, the submission ranked first in the 2014 challenge by Ushizima, Bianchi and Carneiro [4] used a graph-based algorithm to identify cellular clumps (aggregates of partially overlapping cells), merging regions based on pixel adjacency and intensity similarity. As for the winners of the 2015 version of the challenge, Phoulady et al. [5] used iterative thresholding to detect cell's nuclei. In [6], the authors also employed a classical approach to analyse Pap smear slides, namely using a sliding window strategy followed by the cells segmentation through a mini-batch k-means algorithm, which allows for the generation of 33 features that are later used for classification purposes.

Despite the major significance of the features that can be extracted from an adequately segmented image, this task is not easy to accomplish. Subsequently, deep learning techniques have emerged as alternatives for the detection and classification of abnormal regions. As an example, Du et al. [7] proposed a Faster R-CNN based system for the detection and classification of cervical cells from LBC samples, obtaining the best performance with a ResNet101 backbone when compared with other convolutional neural network (CNN) backbones. Zhou et al. [8]

also performed several experiments for detecting abnormal cells in cervical pathology images with deep learning models, testing multiple architectures from which the RetinaNet achieved the highest average precision.

Regarding the classification of cervical cells, this task has had a bigger focus than their detection, partially because of the larger amount of available data directed towards it. Some of the aforementioned works [6–8] resort to deep neural networks for the classification of the cells or regions previously located. Similarly, Zhang et al. [9] and Kwon et al. [10] also used DL methods to tackle this task, more specifically through the use of custom networks, obtaining an accuracy of 98.2% and 84.5%, respectively. Ghoneim, Muhammad and Hossain [11] also performed several experiments with DL methods in which three separate networks were compared as feature extractors matched with three types of classifiers, with the best combination obtained being with a CaffeNet and an extreme learning machine. In the work of Su et al. [12], a more traditional approach used a C4.5 decision tree and a logistic regression algorithm to classify the cells, achieving results comparable to the deep learning approaches. Prum, Handayani and Boursier [13] also proposed a conventional system using a support vector machine (SVM) to classify the cells based on the histogram of gradients of each image, after centering and cropping them around the respective nucleus.

Concerning hybrid methodologies, the explicit use of both deep and conventional machine learning to detect and classify cervical cells is scarce, however, some approaches use both types of algorithms for other related tasks. For instance, Jia, Li and Zhang [14] proposed a novel system to classify cervical cells using a modified LeNet-5 CNN for feature extraction and an SVM as the final classifier, achieving better results than when using only CNN for both tasks. In a more exploratory study, Khamparia et al. [15] developed a framework for the classification of cervical cells in which several CNN and ML algorithms were tested as feature extraction mechanisms and classifiers, respectively. From the experiments performed, the combination of the ResNet50 with the random forest (RF) ensemble achieved the highest accuracy. Sarwar, Sharma and Gupta [16] also proposed a hybrid ensemble method which combined the output of 15 conventional ML and DL algorithms, consistently achieving the highest accuracy when compared to the individual use of each algorithm. Gautam et al. [17] used a different approach in which the cervical cells' nuclei were segmented using conventional CV methods and classified in a hierarchical fashion using an AlexNet.

In a truly hybrid approach, Zhu et al. [18] proposed a system composed of a YOLOv3 network to detect the cervical lesions, followed by a more accurate reclassification of the detected targets using an Xception model. The final classification was performed according to The Bethesda System (TBS) [19] through two ensembled XGboost models, obtaining a specificity and sensitivity comparable to human cytologists. Furthermore, the system's area under the receiver operating characteristic curve tended to increase with the number of models used, suggesting that their combination in hybrid pipelines is a step in the right direction.

3   Methodology

The proposed hybrid system, outlined in Fig. 1, follows a deep learning and a traditional machine learning approach for the detection and classification stages, respectively. Its design takes into consideration current domain knowledge by discerning between lesions with similar severity levels in the detection phase and using additional nuclei-specific features in the final classification.

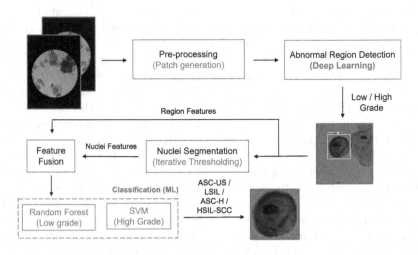

Fig. 1. Overview of the proposed hybrid system's pipeline composed of DL and traditional ML modules to detect and classify cervical lesions.

3.1   Dataset

Due to the lack of public annotated data aimed at both detecting and classifying cervical lesions with the intended detail level, this work was developed using a private dataset comprehending images of microscopic fields of view of LBC samples with a resolution of 1920×2560 pixels, acquired with a μSmartScope [20] - a portable device based on a smartphone for the automatic acquisition of microscopic images. These were obtained from 21 samples and annotated by a specialist from Hospital Fernando Fonseca (HFF). The annotations are bounding boxes surrounding the regions of interest (individual or clumps of squamous cells) and the respective class according to TBS [19]: atypical squamous cells of undetermined significance (ASC-US), low-grade squamous intraepithelial lesion (LSIL), atypical squamous cells, cannot rule out high-grade squamous intraepithelial lesion (ASC-H), high-grade squamous intraepithelial lesion (HSIL) and squamous cell carcinoma (SCC). A few examples of these classes can be seen in Fig. 2 and their distribution in Table 1, for both the entire dataset and the training set (after balancing operations).

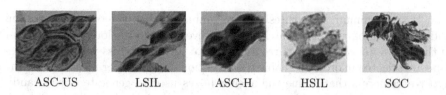

ASC-US   LSIL   ASC-H   HSIL   SCC

Fig. 2. Examples of different classes of HFF dataset.

Table 1. Dataset class distribution (*after balancing).

Class	No. of patches	No. of training patches*
ASC-US	724	544
LSIL	112	523
ASC-H	152	585
HSIL	273	496
SCC	26	58

Data Preparation. The samples are first divided, based on their diagnosis outcome, into an overall training and a test set (80% and 20%, respectively) to guarantee that images from the same patient are kept in the same set. The overall training set is further divided into several training and validation subsets by applying a stratified 5-fold cross-validation procedure to the images of each sample. The balancing of this subset is achieved through data augmentation techniques, more specifically rotations of 90, 180 and 270°, vertical and horizontal flipping, and blurring and sharpening of the patches containing the under-represented classes. Despite this, considering the extremely low number of examples of the SCC class, we opted to merge it with the HSIL class due to their similarity. In addition to these operations, a random down-sampling is applied on the empty patches, i.e., patches without annotations, to ensure the inclusion for each image of at least one empty patch.

3.2 Experimental Pipeline

The system's input consists of separate images which undergo a pre-processing stage where they are cropped around the optic disk and split into multiple 320 × 320 pixels non-overlapping patches. Then, to minimize the number of ROIs that are divided between patches, the training and validation patches are adjusted: depending on the ROI's size, either the patch is enlarged to capture it entirely, or the fraction of the ROI is only considered if its area is equal to 10% or more of the entire ROI.

Afterwards, the detection of the abnormal cervical lesions is performed through a RetinaNet with a ResNet50 backbone pre-trained on the COCO dataset [21]. In order to optimize the network's performance, a random hyperparameter search process was conducted in which several settings were tuned, namely the minimum score threshold, maximum number of detections, warm-up and base learning rate, and batch size. However, due to the long training times of the neural networks, only three iterations of the 5-fold cross-validation procedure are selected in order to enable the execution of more experiments. As for the hyper-parameters that define the anchor boxes used to generate object candidates, these were modified based on the k-means clustering of the ground-truth bounding boxes' scales and aspect ratios for the overall training set. A maximum intersection over union (IoU) threshold of 0.4 was also set since abnormal regions do not have a high degree of overlap. These experiments were performed in a Linux Server featuring one NVIDIA T4 GPU with 16 GB of RAM over approximately 300 epochs and made use of the Adam optimizer together with the smooth L1 loss for the regions' localization, and the focal cross-entropy loss for their classification in two groups: low-grade lesions, composed of the LSIL and ASC-US classes, and high-grade lesions, composed of the HSIL-SCC and ASC-H classes. This first classification takes into account the direct dependence between the class composition and the severity level of the labels in each group, embedding clinical knowledge in the development of the pipeline.

The nuclei in these detected regions are segmented through an iterative thresholding algorithm based on the work of Phoulady et al. [5] which comprises the application of global thresholds of increasing value to the image in an iterative manner, accepting or discarding new regions based on their solidity and bounding box area. In this context, the solidity of a region refers to the measure of its concavity and is calculated by dividing its area by the area of its convex hull.

From the region and the segmented nuclei, a total of 17 geometrical, 10 colour and 34 texture features are extracted, partially inspired by the work of [22] and also due to their relevance to the clinical diagnosis. The geometrical features are composed of specific properties of the nuclei, more specifically their segmented, bounding box and convex hull areas, bounding box aspect ratio, maximum and minimum diameters, equivalent diameter, solidity, extent, minimum enclosing circle area ratio, elliptical symmetry, compactness index, principal axis ratio, eccentricity and irregularity index, the latter characterized by the difference between the maximum and minimum diameters. The colour features are extracted from the CIELCh colour space and are composed of the energy, mean, standard deviation, skewness and range of the chroma and hue channels. Lastly, the texture features are based on the dissimilarity, homogeneity, energy and correlation of the grey level co-occurrence matrices.

These features are then fed to two classifiers, one for each abnormality level detected in the previous phase. Two model types were tested for this stage: SVM and random forest. Both types underwent a process of hyper-parameter optimization, namely a grid search for the SVM and a random search for the RF (the difference between the methods stems from the longer training times of the RF models, making a grid search unfeasible). To assess the influence of the properties of the nuclei structures in the developed models, two types of feature sets were used in the experiments: one with only features extracted from the detected region as a whole - the baseline set -, and another with added nuclei features. These experiments were also repeated for the subset of the regions containing at least one nucleus to investigate if the cases in which these were absent from the region significantly impacted the performance of the algorithms. All experiments were performed using a 5-fold cross-validation procedure. It is also worth noting that the features used by the random forest algorithms remained unchanged while the ones provided to the SVM were normalized since this algorithm is based around the distance between the data points from different classes, thus not being scale-invariant.

Finally, the output of this stage (and the pipeline) is the label not only of the detected regions but of the respective patches, source images and samples as well. The diagnosis outcome of a sample is determined as the most severe lesion level found in the objects detected in all the patches extracted from the multiple source images of that sample.

4 Results

This section provides a performance evaluation of the experiments previously detailed for the lesion detection and classification modules individually and the complete system.

4.1 Lesion Detection

The system's performance for the detection task was assessed through the COCO competition metrics [21]. From the hyper-parameter combinations tested at this stage, the best-performing one obtained a mean average precision (mAP@0.5 IoU) of 0.15 and an average recall (AR@10) of 0.42, with a base and warm-up learning rates of 0.00003 and 0.00001, correspondingly, and a minimum score, maximum detections and batch size of 0, 10 and 16, respectively, during the adapted 5-fold cross-validation. The analysis of the detections performed by RetinaNet (a couple of which are present in Figs. 3a and 3b) provides some insights regarding how certain dataset properties influenced the apparent overall low performance obtained. In particular, the high number of false positives, even in situations where the falsely detected region presented characteristics similar to the ones found in abnormal regions, may be due to the fact that abnormal regions that do not belong to a clear lesion level are not annotated in the dataset, as the specialists cannot accurately propose a classification for them.

Another possible cause is the presence of squamous cells of different types that possess similar abnormality characteristics, as illustrated in Fig. 4, making them difficult to differentiate. This difficulty extends to the annotation process as well, further increasing its subjectivity. Moreover, there can be a substantial morphological variety between cells of the same type (Fig. 5), hindering the learning process by the network, especially when considering the limited amount of available data.

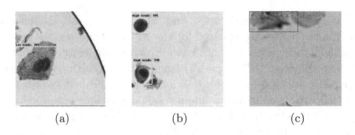

(a)   (b)   (c)

Fig. 3. Validation set detection results: correct (a) low and (b) high grade detections, and (c) uninformative ground truth bounding box fragment in the test set.

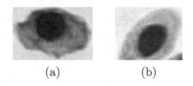

(a)   (b)

Fig. 4. Similar (a) low-grade (LSIL) and (b) high-grade (HSIL) lesions.

The high number of false negatives is also related to the presence of uninformative fractions of bounding boxes, such as the one displayed in Fig. 3c. These can be generated during the partitioning of the image into patches since our method does not take into account the image's characteristics. This is especially noticeable in the test set, where the patches are not pre-adjusted as in the overall training set, leading to an increased number of uninformative regions and consequently to a lower mAP@0.5 IoU of 1% and an AR@10 of 27%.

4.2   Lesion Classification

The results of the classification module were first calculated for each class (pertinent to each type of classifier and at the ROI level) and then averaged together. These are displayed in Table 2 for each feature set and classifier.

Table 2. Results obtained for the classification task by the high-grade (HG) and low-grade (LG) models using the regions (R) and nuclei (N) features. Each metric was averaged over the five cross-validation iterations.

Algorithm	Classifier	Features	Accuracy	Precision	Recall	F1
SVM	LG	R	0.74 ± 0.08	0.75 ± 0.05	0.73 ± 0.05	0.72 ± 0.07
SVM	LG	R + N	0.74 ± 0.07	0.73 ± 0.05	0.73 ± 0.05	0.72 ± 0.06
RF	LG	R	0.74 ± 0.09	0.76 ± 0.06	0.73 ± 0.06	0.72 ± 0.08
RF	LG	R + N	0.76 ± 0.01	0.77 ± 0.06	0.76 ± 0.06	**0.75** ± 0.01
SVM	HG	R	0.80 ± 0.04	0.80 ± 0.06	0.80 ± 0.07	**0.79** ± 0.06
SVM	HG	R + N	0.80 ± 0.05	0.80 ± 0.07	0.79 ± 0.08	0.78 ± 0.07
RF	HG	R	0.78 ± 0.03	0.79 ± 0.03	0.78 ± 0.03	0.77 ± 0.03
RF	HG	R + N	0.79 ± 0.05	0.78 ± 0.07	0.79 ± 0.07	0.77 ± 0.07

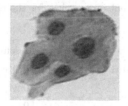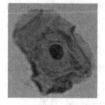

Fig. 5. Morphologically different lesions of the same class (ASC-US).

It is possible to observe that the use of nuclei features had a greater influence on the low-grade regions than on the high-grade ones, where the performance of the SVM classifiers using the entire feature set was even lower than the models using only the region features. Consequently, the best-performing classifiers for each lesion level used different sets of features, with the low-grade model (RF) using both region and nuclei features, while the high-grade model (SVM) only made use of the former. These variations can be linked to the intrinsic morphological differences between the regions of each type. Although not presented in detail here, this pattern was also noticed in the experiments with only the nuclei-possessing regions, indicating that it was not derived from the absence of nuclei in certain ones.

As such, the models that obtained the highest cross-validation performance were used as the system's final classifiers, with the low and high-grade classifiers obtaining an accuracy, precision, recall and F1 score of 0.79, 0.56, 0.50 and 0.46, and of 0.53, 0.75, 0.55 and 0.42, respectively, on the test set. Much like in the previous detection stage, the decreased performance here is also partially related to the presence of uninformative ground truth bounding boxes. Still, the possibility of overfitting having occurred cannot be ruled out due to the considerable performance difference between the cross-validation and test sets.

From Table 3 it is possible to observe that the proposed system's classifiers are still distant from the best performing methods accuracy-wise even though it achieved similar results to the hybrid approach proposed by Sarwar, Sharma and Gupta [16] while also outperforming the most realistic configuration by Prum, Handayani and Boursier [13]. However, it is difficult to directly compare our work to the others due to the use of different datasets.

4.3   Complete System

The complete pipeline was evaluated at four different levels: regions of interest, patches, source images and samples. This is accomplished by assigning the most severe label detected in a given level to the level immediately above in the same image hierarchy. The reasoning behind this method is to try to mimic (to some extent) the evaluation process performed by the specialists since their final diagnosis relies on the analysis of multiple fields of view and specific regions within them for each patient. With this in mind, the results obtained on the test set are presented in Table 4 for each level.

Table 3. Performance comparison of different approaches for the classification of cervical cells.

Method	Accuracy
Ghoneim, Muhammad and Hossain [11]	**0.98**
Jia, Li and Zhang [14]	0.94
Gautam et al. [17]	0.94
Proposed system's low-grade classifier	0.79
Sarwar, Sharma and Gupta [16]	0.79
Proposed system's high-grade classifier	0.53
Prum, Handayani and Boursier [13]	0.46

As evidenced by the results, the general performance improves from the region level up to the source image evaluation (except for a slight decrease in F1 from the patch to the source image level), as the individual errors pertaining to the ROIs cease to have such a substantial impact. However, there is a performance decrease from the source image to the sample level. The analysis of the final, sample-wise outputs of the system (Table 5) reveals that there is a clear tendency to assign samples with severity labels higher than their respective ground truth. This is linked to the method described above in which a level's classifications are passed up in the image hierarchy since it only takes one example with a severity higher than the other ones for the following level to be classified with that more severe label. Even though this method is similar to the one used by the human specialists, this drawback is not as evident in that case since they usually need multiple instances of a class (or a clear example of one) before attributing a final diagnosis.

Table 4. System test results per image hierarchy level (*only considering regions correctly identified by the detection module)

Level	Precision	Recall	F1	Precision*	Recall*	F1*
ROI	0.01	0.02	0.01	0.44	0.67	0.50
Patch	0.20	0.21	0.21	0.55	0.75	0.58
Source Image	0.20	0.24	0.20	0.45	0.60	0.49
Sample	0.04	0.20	0.07	0.17	0.50	0.25

Furthermore, over half of the samples were misclassified or falsely signalled as abnormal in the detection stage. As the exclusion of the examples incorrectly classified by the detection model enables a substantial performance increase of the system (Table 4), it becomes clear that the main performance bottleneck occurs during the detection of the abnormal regions. Even though there can be multiple reasons for this, as in the classification stage, the most limiting factor is

Table 5. Sample labels predicted by the system (test set) and respective ground truth values. High-grade (HG), low-grade (LG).

Sample	Predicted grade	Grade ground truth	Final classification	Ground truth
1	HG	LG	HSIL-SCC	ASC-US
2	LG	Normal	ASC-US	Normal
3	HG	HG	ASC-H	HSIL-SCC
4	HG	Normal	ASC-H	Normal
5	HG	LG	ASC-H	LSIL
6	HG	HG	ASC-H	HSIL-SCC
7	HG	HG	ASC-H	ASC-H

probably the dataset itself. The relatively low number of original examples, allied to the subjective annotation process, make this a challenging task, hindering not only the training of the algorithms but their proper evaluation as well, further reinforcing the need for innovative strategies, such as hybrid approaches, to overcome these challenges.

Nonetheless, despite the system's limitations (such as the low mAP obtained during the detection phase) that prevent its deployment as a fully automated tool, the higher recall levels achieved in the cross-validation demonstrate its potential for usage as a tool to support the analysis of the medical specialists, possibly increasing the sensitivity of their process.

5   Conclusions

In this work, a hybrid system for the examination of cervical cytology images was proposed as a way of overcoming the limitations of a private dataset and integrating clinical knowledge in the pipeline design. A RetinaNet model was used for the detection of abnormal regions and their separation in low and high-grade lesions, with random forest and SVM classifiers being applied to each of the detected regions for the specification of the final lesion class. These classification algorithms were trained using geometrical, colour and texture features extracted from each region and from the nuclei within them, which were previously segmented through an iterative thresholding algorithm.

The detection and classification modules were first evaluated separately, followed by the assessment of the complete system. While the detection module only achieved a mAP@0.5 IoU of 0.15 and an AR@10 of 0.42, the classification models were able to attain F1 scores of 0.75 and 0.79 for the low and high-grade lesions, respectively, during the 5-fold cross-validation. Moreover, the use of nuclei features during this stage resulted in a performance boost of the low-grade lesions' classifier. Despite this, both modules' performance dropped significantly in the test set, likely due to the substantial presence of uninformative bounding boxes derived from the partitioning of each image into patches, indicating a need for additional constraints to accept or discard fragments of bounding boxes, such as a textural analysis of the region.

As for the performance of the complete system, it generally increases with the hierarchy level. However, a noticeable decrease occurs from the source image to the sample level due to misclassifications with high severity labels occurring in the previous levels. As such, alternative strategies to aggregate the results of previous levels should be explored, potentially leading to a more reliable system.

An analysis of the system's outputs also revealed that a significant portion of the misclassifications resulted from the erroneous identification of the lesion level by the detection module, indicating that this represents the main performance bottleneck. In this manner, hybrid approaches, such as the one proposed, reveal increased potential to tackle challenges of this nature, especially in environments where the drawbacks of the DL-only methods are not so easily overcome. Additionally, despite its limitations, the proposed system demonstrated that it can still prove helpful as a support tool for the inspection of cervical samples by medical specialists, potentially increasing the sensitivity of their analysis process.

Acknowledgments. This work was done under the scope of project "CLARE: Computer-Aided Cervical Cancer Screening" and financially supported by FEDER through Operational Competitiveness Program – COMPETE 2020 and by National Funds through Foundation for Science and Technology FCT/MCTES (POCI-01-0145-FEDER-028857). The authors would also like to thank Hospital Fernando Fonseca's and Portuguese Oncology Institute's Pathology Anatomy Services.

References

1. World Health Organization. Cervical Cancer. https://www.who.int/health-topics/cervical-cancer. Accessed 29 June 2021
2. Bengtsson, E., Malm, P.: Screening for cervical cancer using automated analysis of pap-smears. Computational and mathematical methods in medicine 2014 (2014)
3. Conceição, T., Braga, C., Rosado, L., Vasconcelos, M.J.M.: A review of computational methods for cervical cells segmentation and abnormality classification. Int. J. Mol. Sci. **20**(20), 5114 (2019)
4. Ushizima, D.M., Bianchi, A.G., Carneiro, C.M.: Segmentation of subcellular compartments combining superpixel representation with voronoi diagrams. Technical report, Lawrence Berkeley National Lab. (LBNL), Berkeley, CA (United States) (2015)
5. Phoulady, H.A., Goldgof, D.B., Hall, L.O., Mouton, P.R.: An approach for overlapping cell segmentation in multi-layer cervical cell volumes. The second overlapping cervical cytology image segmentation challenge-IEEE ISBI (2015)
6. Kuko, M., Pourhomayoun, M.: Single and clustered cervical cell classification with ensemble and deep learning methods. Inf. Syst. Front. **22**(5), 1039–1051 (2020)
7. Du, J., Li, X., Li, Q.: Detection and classification of cervical exfoliated cells based on faster R-CNN. In: 2019 IEEE 11th International Conference on Advanced Infocomm Technology, ICAIT 2019, pp. 52–57. Institute of Electrical and Electronics Engineers Inc., October 2019

8. Zhou, M., Zhang, L., Du, X., Ouyang, X., Zhang, X., Shen, Q., Wang, Q.: Hierarchical and Robust Pathology Image Reading for High-Throughput Cervical Abnormality Screening. In: Liu, M., Yan, P., Lian, C., Cao, X. (eds.) MLMI 2020. LNCS, vol. 12436, pp. 414–422. Springer, Cham (2020). https://doi.org/10.1007/978-3-030-59861-7_42

9. Zhang, L., Lu, L., Nogues, I., Summers, R.M., Liu, S., Yao, J.: DeepPap: deep convolutional networks for cervical cell classification. IEEE J. Biomed. Health Inf. **21**(6), 1633–1643 (2017)

10. Kwon, M., Kuko, M., Pourhomayoun, M., Martin, V., Kim, T., Martin, S.: Multi-label Classification of Single and Clustered Cervical Cells Using Deep Convolutional Networks. California State University, Los Angeles (2018)

11. Ghoneim, A., Muhammad, G., Hossain, M.S.: Cervical cancer classification using convolutional neural networks and extreme learning machines. Futur. Gener. Comput. Syst. **102**, 643–649 (2020)

12. Su, J., Xu, X., He, Y., Song, J.: Automatic detection of cervical cancer cells by a two-level cascade classification system. Analytical Cellular Pathology 2016 (2016)

13. Sophea, P., Handayani, D.O.D., Boursier, P.: Abnormal cervical cell detection using hog descriptor and SVM classifier. In: 2018 Fourth International Conference on Advances in Computing, Communication & Automation (ICACCA), pp. 1–6. IEEE (2018)

14. Jia, A.D., Li, B.Z., Zhang, C.C.: Detection of cervical cancer cells based on strong feature CNN-SVM network. Neurocomputing **411**, 112–127 (2020)

15. Khamparia, A., Gupta, D., de Albuquerque, V.H.C., Sangaiah, A.K., Jhaveri, R.H.: Internet of health things-driven deep learning system for detection and classification of cervical cells using transfer learning. The Journal of Supercomputing **76**(11), 8590–8608 (2020). https://doi.org/10.1007/s11227-020-03159-4

16. Sarwar, A., Sharma, V., Gupta, R.: Hybrid ensemble learning technique for screening of cervical cancer using papanicolaou smear image analysis. Personalized Med. Universe **4**, 54–62 (2015)

17. Gautam, S., Jith, N., Sao, A.K., Bhavsar, A., Natarajan, A., et al.: Considerations for a pap smear image analysis system with CNN features. arXiv preprint arXiv:1806.09025 (2018)

18. Zhu, X., et al.: Hybrid AI-assistive diagnostic model permits rapid TBS classification of cervical liquid-based thin-layer cell smears. Nat. Commun. **12**(1), 1–12 (2021)

19. Birdsong, G.G., Davey, D.D.: The bethesda system for reporting cervical cytology. In: The Bethesda System for Reporting Cervical Cytology: Definitions, Criteria, and Explanatory Notes, pp. 1–28. Springer International Publishing, January 2015

20. Rosado, L., et al.: Smartscope: towards a fully automated 3d-printed smartphone microscope with motorized stage. In: International Joint Conference on Biomedical Engineering Systems and Technologies, pp. 19–44. Springer (2017)

21. COCO - Common Objects in Context. https://cocodataset.org/. Accessed 16 May 2021

22. Rosado, L., Da Costa, J.M.C., Elias, D., Cardoso, J.S.: Mobile-based analysis of malaria-infected thin blood smears: automated species and life cycle stage determination. Sensors **17**(10), 2167 (2017)

Open Access This chapter is licensed under the terms of the Creative Commons Attribution 4.0 International License (http://creativecommons.org/licenses/by/4.0/), which permits use, sharing, adaptation, distribution and reproduction in any medium or format, as long as you give appropriate credit to the original author(s) and the source, provide a link to the Creative Commons license and indicate if changes were made.

The images or other third party material in this chapter are included in the chapter's Creative Commons license, unless indicated otherwise in a credit line to the material. If material is not included in the chapter's Creative Commons license and your intended use is not permitted by statutory regulation or exceeds the permitted use, you will need to obtain permission directly from the copyright holder.

Ensemble Learning to Perform Instance Segmentation over Synthetic Data

Alonso Cerpa[(⊠)] , Graciela Meza-Lovon ,
and Manuel E. Loaiza Fernández

Department of Computer Science, Universidad Católica San Pablo, Arequipa, Peru
{alonso.cerpa,gmezal,meloaiza}@ucsp.edu.pe

Abstract. Recently, deep neural networks have led the progress of instance segmentation. There are several models of neural networks, such as the Mask R-CNN network, that perform this task with good results. However, it is possible to improve the results of the Mask R-CNN network if several models of it are combined, and their results are merged using Ensemble Learning. We propose the algorithm "Simple Instance Segmentation Ensemble" that is capable of assembling the results of two Mask R-CNN networks to produce better results. In our experiments, we train several Mask R-CNN networks with synthetic images of machinery objects. In addition, these Mask R-CNN networks have different backbones and different sizes of kernels for the Gaussian Blur filter applied to the synthetic machinery images used during training. We tested the performance of these networks by predicting real images of machinery. Besides, we propose the SISE algorithm to assemble the predictions of two previously trained Mask R-CNN networks, and we obtained better results than those of the individual Mask R-CNN networks. In particular, our best result is an ensemble that has one Mask R-CNN trained with synthetic images smoothed by Gaussian Blur filter with a kernel size of 7×7, and another network with a kernel size of 3×3. Both networks have as backbone a ResNeXt 101 with FPN (Feature Pyramid Network). This ensemble has a bounding box mAP of 89.42% and a segmentation mAP of 88.34% in the real machinery test images.

Keywords: Ensemble learning · Instance segmentation · Object segmentation · Mask R-CNN · Object detection · Ensemble methods

1 Introduction

In the context of machine learning, Ensemble Learning is an approach that combines the predictions of two or more learning models to produce better results than those obtained individually by the models that make up the ensemble. Those models can belong to the same type or different types of models, e.g., an ensemble can be composed of a support vector machine, a linear regression classifier, and a decision tree; or an ensemble can be composed of support vector machines with different setups. Moreover, in Ensemble Learning, predictions

© Springer Nature Switzerland AG 2021
G. Bebis et al. (Eds.): ISVC 2021, LNCS 13018, pp. 313–324, 2021.
https://doi.org/10.1007/978-3-030-90436-4_25

obtained from the ensemble's members can be combined using statistics, such as the mode, the mean, among others. For example, simple classifiers such as decision trees, support vector machines, random forest, usually employ ensemble techniques based on the mode such as the voting mechanism, while ensembles that perform regression tasks, e.g., those composed by linear regression models, use the average technique for combining results. However, when the tasks are more complex, as in the case of object segmentation, it is necessary to use more sophisticated strategies for merging the results.

On the other hand, deep learning is revolutionizing day-to-day technology in tasks such as automatic text translation, automatic speech-to-text transformation, image classification, object detection, and segmentation. In particular, for object segmentation, also known as instance segmentation, there exist several deep learning models, such as TensorMask [1], SpineNet [2], Mask R-CNN [3], which perform properly and consequently provide good results. However, this research holds the hypothesis that if we apply Ensemble Learning techniques to instance segmentation models, such as Mask R-CNN, and merge their results, it is possible to improve the results provided by the individual members.

Furthermore, the training of instance segmentation models requires a great deal of data to obtain good results. However, obtaining and labeling the data can be time-consuming and costly. An alternative to overcome this problem is training the models with synthetic data generated by a synthetic image renderer. This alternative not only allows you to generate unlimited data but also allows the automatic labeling of it. There exists a disadvantage of training using synthetic data. It is the trained model is not always able to generalize and predict properly when tested with real data. In the context of instance segmentation, Hinterstoisser et al. [4] and Cerpa et al. [5] address this problem by applying Gaussian Blur to synthetic training images, which reduces the overfitting and allows the network to perform correctly not only with synthetic data but also with real data.

This research aims to propose an Ensemble Learning algorithm to improve the results of two Mask R-CNN networks trained with synthetic images generated by a renderer and subsequently smoothed with a Gaussian Blur filter. After training, these networks have different weights as we trained them using different images to which we applied Gaussian Blur of different sizes of kernels. The synthetic and real images we use correspond to pieces of machinery.

This paper is organized as follows: In Sect. 2, recent works where Ensemble Learning is successfully applied in various tasks are discussed. In Sect. 3, the architecture of our technique along with our proposed algorithm called Simple Instance Segmentation Ensemble (SISE) is presented. In Sect. 4, we show the results obtained from experimenting with individual mask R-CNN models and also the results of these models merged using the proposed SISE algorithm. Finally, we draw the conclusions of the application of our algorithm in Sect. 5.

2   Related Works

In the context of classification techniques, Mera et al. [6] made a comparison of many classifier models for spill detection in satellite images. For this purpose, they use a variety of Ensemble Learning methods such as Random Forest, Rotation Forest [7], etc., and also classification models such as Multilayer Perceptron, Support Vector Machines, Decision Trees, among others. Of all these, Rotation Forest with various Multilayer Perceptron models gave the best results. Similarly, in the area of intrusion detection, Gao et al. [8] made two proposals for Ensemble Learning. First, they proposed an Ensemble Learning algorithm called MultiTree that uses multiple decision trees. Secondly, they built an ensemble of various classification models such as Deep Neural Networks, Decision Trees, Random Forests, K-Nearest-Neighbors, and then they employed an adaptive voting algorithm.

In the context of Ensemble Learning techniques for segmentation, Gaonkar et al. [9] presented an ensemble of models for the segmentation of heterogeneous medical magnetic resonance images. The ensemble allowed them to overcome the problem of heterogeneity in magnetic resonance images and provide robustness to the method. In this context, heterogeneous means that magnetic resonance can be performed with different scanning protocols and different parameters, in such a way that the images obtained will vary. Similarly, Zuo and Drummond [10] proposed the combination of Random Forests with Convolutional Neural Networks (CNNs) to improve the performance of individual CNNs in semantic segmentation. The authors claimed that their algorithm is appropriated when there are little training data and when training time is short. For example, it is ideal for robots that navigate through scenarios and need to learn from the data they receive at the time. On the other hand, in the area of instance segmentation, Kang et al. [11] propose the ensemble of 2 Mask R-CNN [3] instance segmentation models for the segmentation of polyps in colonoscopy images. One of the models has a ResNet50 [12] as a backbone and the other a ResNet101 [12], in such a way that the merged results of both models significantly exceed the state of the art in the area of polyp segmentation.

Finally, commenting on the techniques that train their instance segmentation models with synthetic data, Hinterstoisser et al. [4] generated their own synthetic data consisting of toys and tableware to perform instance segmentation. They found that applying Gaussian Blur (G.B.) to synthetic training images improved the test results with real images, so they considered it essential. Also in their experiments with a Mask R-CNN network they decided to freeze the feature extractor backbone network and only train the other layers to further improve their results. In a similar work, Cerpa et al. [5] generated their own synthetic data consisting of 3 objects of machinery. Then, they applied various levels of Gaussian Blur to the synthetic data and trained a Mask R-CNN network with that data. They concluded that applying Gaussian Blur to the synthetic data was essential so that their trained network does not suffer from overfitting at the moment to test with real data.

3   Proposal of the Ensemble Technique

In this paper, we propose an algorithm for ensembling the predictions of two Mask R-CNN models [3] called Simple Instance Segmentation Ensamble (SISE). For the training of each model, we use synthetic images, and subsequently, we apply a Gaussian Blur filter with different sizes of kernels. It is important to mention that the reason for applying Gaussian Blur is to soften the synthetic images so that the objects that appear in them blend harmoniously with the image's background and thus favor the prediction using real images. The difference between the two Mask R-CNN models that make up the ensemble is that we train the first model using Gaussian Blur images with a kernel of size $Y \times Y$, and we train the second model with synthetic Gaussian Blur images with a kernel of size $Z \times Z$.

The dataset we use consists of synthetic and real images of 3 pieces of machinery as shown in Fig. 1. This dataset is the same as the one used by Cerpa et al. [5].

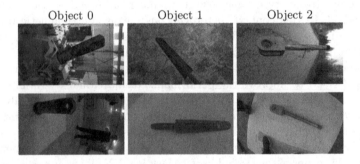

Fig. 1. The first row shows the synthetic training images for objects 0, 1 and 2. The second row shows the real test images for objects 0, 1 and 2.

3.1   Overview of the Proposed Technique

This subsection provides an overview of our proposal, which has two phases: 1) the training phase in which we train two Mask R-CNN models, and 2) the testing phase that merges the results of the two trained models, using the Simple Instance Segmentation Ensemble.

We show the training phase in Fig. 2. This figure shows an ensemble made up of two deep learning networks specialized in object detection and segmentation, namely, Mask R-CNN networks. Model 1 is trained using synthetic images with a Gaussian Blur filter whose kernel is 5×5, while Model 2 uses synthetic images with 7×7 Gaussian Blur filter. Furthermore, both models have as backbone a ResNet. Both the Gaussian Blur size and the backbone type are adjustable, i.e., their values change when performing our experiments in order to obtain the ensembles with the best settings. In Fig. 2, we show an ensemble composed of two Mask R-CNNs whose backbones are ResNet 50. As a result of the training, we obtain two Mask R-CNN models with different weights, which we use to carry out the prediction fusion process.

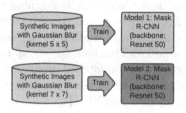

Fig. 2. Pipeline of the training phase of the Ensemble Learning.

The testing phase is shown in Fig. 3. The upper part of the figure shows that the real images are entered into a trained Model 1, which, subsequently, provides a prediction for each image entered. Similarly, Model 2 receives the same real images and outputs a set of predictions, which could be coincident with the results of Model 1, but at the same time, dissimilar; since both models have different setups of weights. It is important to mention that this model returns predictions for each test image. These predictions consist of 4 elements: 1) the class, 2) the probability of the detected object, 3) the mask of the object, and 4) the bounding box of the object. On the right side of Fig. 3, we observe that both sets of predictions are the input for the SISE algorithm, which integrates the previous predictions and produces a new set of them that reflect the strengths of the models and whose result provide better performance than the models evaluated individually.

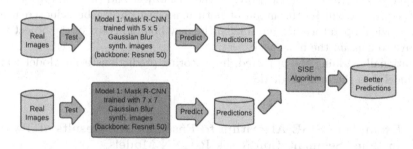

Fig. 3. Pipeline of the testing phase of the Ensemble Learning.

3.2 Ensemble Algorithm for Instance Segmentation: SISE (*Simple Instance Segmentation Ensemble*)

This section explains the algorithm proposed for merging the predictions of two instance segmentation models, namely, Mask R-CNNs [3]. We name this algorithm as Simple Instance Segmentation Ensemble (SISE). This algorithm receives Model 1's predictions ($Pred1$) and Model 2's predictions ($Pred2$) for the same input image. The predictions $Pred1$ are of size N, where N is the number of objects in the image recognized by Model 1. The predictions $Pred2$, have M objects recognized in the image. N is not necessarily equal to M. This is because Models 1 and 2 are different, and could provide a different number of object predictions for the same image. Besides $Pred1$ and $Pred2$, the algorithm receives a boolean $AddUnmatch$. This boolean allows the algorithm to include in the final predictions $PredN$ the unmatched predictions that have high scores. The result of the SISE algorithm for a given image is a new set of predictions $PredN$, with a maximum size of $min(N, M)$.

The idea of the algorithm is to create a new prediction for a particular test image under the following guidelines:

- Choosing from all pairs of predicted objects (i, j) (where i is the i-th recognized object of $Pred1$ and j is the j-th recognized object of $Pred2$) those that have the same class prediction and the highest Intersection over Union IoUs, i.e., those that exceed the threshold of 0.5, since we assume that those pairs that have the highest IoUs refer to the same object. The IoU is the ratio between the intersection area of the bounding boxes of the objects i and j and the union area of their bounding boxes. IoU is defined as:

$$IoU(i, j) = \frac{\text{Intersection area of } i \text{ and } j}{\text{Union area of } i \text{ and } j} \tag{1}$$

- Ordering and keeping the best pairs i and j.
- Creating the new prediction for which we define four items: the class, the score, the mask, and the bounding box of the object. The class of the final prediction for that object is the class of the i object. The new score will be equal to the average of the scores of the i-th object and the j-th object. The object mask will be the union of both masks which can be achieved using the logical operator OR, and finally, the new bounding box of the object will have to contain the new mask.
- Optionally, adding the unpaired, high-scoring predictions from Model 1 and Model 2 to the final prediction.

3.3 Example of SISE Algorithm to Ensemble the Results of Two Instance Segmentation Mask R-CNN Models

In Fig. 4, we illustrate the merging procedure of the SISE algorithm using the results of two R-CNN mask models corresponding to ensemble 1 of Table 2. In the first row of Fig. 4, we observe that Model 2's prediction is closer to the ground trough and helps to improve the result of the final prediction, while in the second row of Fig. 4, the opposite occurs, Model 1's prediction helps to improve the result of the final prediction.

Data: Predictions from Model 1 $Pred1$ of size N and predictions from Model 2 $Pred2$ of size M. $AddUnmatch$ is a boolean that indicates if the algorithm should add predictions that are unmatched and with a big score.

Result: New predictions $PredN$

1   $ListIdxsIoU \leftarrow []$
2   **for** $i \leftarrow 0$ **to** $N - 1$ **do**
3   **for** $j \leftarrow 0$ **to** $M - 1$ **do**
4       $iou \longleftarrow IoU(Pred1[i].bbox, Pred2[j].bbox)$
5   **if** $iou > 0.5$ **and** $Pred1[i].class = Pred2[j].class$ **then**
6         $tuple \leftarrow (iou, i, j)$
7         $ListIdxsIoU.append(tuple)$
8   **end**
9   **end**
10 **end**
11 Sort $ListIdxsIoU$ from hightest to lowest by the iou value of each tuple
12 $ListIdxs \leftarrow []$
13 $List1 \leftarrow [0, ..., N - 1]$
14 $List2 \leftarrow [0, ..., M - 1]$
15 **for** $tuple \in ListIdxsIoU$ **do**
16   **if** $tuple[1] \in List1$ **and** $tuple[2] \in List2$ **then**
17       $List1.remove(tuple[1])$
18       $List2.remove(tuple[2])$
19       $tupleX \leftarrow (tuple[1], tuple[2])$
20       $ListIdxs.append(tupleX)$
21   **end**
22 **end**
23 $PredN \leftarrow []$
24 **for** $tuple \in ListIdxs$ **do**
25     $Pred \leftarrow None$
26     $idx1 \leftarrow tuple[0]$
27     $idx2 \leftarrow tuple[1]$
28     $Pred.class \leftarrow Pred1[idx1].class$
29     $Pred.score \leftarrow avg(Pred1[idx1].score, Pred2[idx2].score)$
30     $Pred.mask \leftarrow LogicOr(Pred1[idx1].mask, Pred2[idx2].mask)$
31     $Pred.bbox \leftarrow createBbox(Pred.mask)$
32     $PredN.append(Pred)$
33 **end**
34 **if** $AddUnmatch$ **then**
35   Add all predictions from $Pred1$ and $Pred2$ to $PredN$ that have not already been matched and that have their score greater than 0.9
36 **end**
37 **return** $PredN$

Algorithm 1: SISE (Simple Instance Segmentation Ensemble) Algorithm: Ensembles results from two instance segmentation models (Mask R-CNN) applied over one image.

Prediction - Model 1   Prediction - Model 2   Prediction - Ensemble

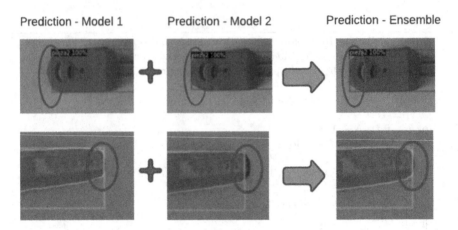

Fig. 4. Example of the application of the SISE algorithm on the predictions of real images.

4 Experiments and Results

To implement the training and testing of the Mask R-CNN network [3], the detection and segmentation algorithm library *Detectron 2* [13] was used. This library is based on *PyTorch*. In addition, we use the pre-trained weights of Mask R-CNN offered by the Detectron 2 library. Such weights are obtained training with the data set *Common Objects in Context* (COCO) [14]. During our training we fine-tune the weights provided by *Detectron 2*, using the data set of objects of machinery that was used in the work of Cerpa et al. [5]. Such data set consists of 3069 synthetic images used for training and 108 real images used for testing, divided evenly between 3 pieces, which are shown in Fig. 1. An 8GB Nvidia GeForce RTX 3070 GPU and an AMD Ryzen 5 5600X processor were used for training and testing.

Table 1. Results of testing on real data with synthetically trained Mask R-CNN models. G.B. is an abbreviation of Gaussian Blur.

#	Backbone	G.B.	mAP bbox	mAP segm
1	ResNet-50-FPN	7	81.37	81.19
2	ResNet-50-FPN	5	84.87	82.61
3	ResNet-50-FPN	3	75.80	76.13
4	ResNet-101-FPN	7	70.54	73.02
5	ResNet-101-FPN	5	72.75	72.76
6	ResNet-101-FPN	3	70.45	71.11
7	ResNeXt-101-FPN	7	87.37	87.22
8	ResNeXt-101-FPN	5	83.11	84.31
9	ResNeXt-101-FPN	3	**87.56**	**88.22**

Table 2. Ensemble of the results of testing on real data with synthetically trained Mask R-CNN models. G.B. is an abbreviation of Gaussian Blur.

#	Backbone	G.B.	Add unmatched pred.	mAP bbox	mAP segm
1	M1: ResNet-50-FPN M2: ResNet-50-FPN	M1: 7 M2: 5	No	87.71	85.21
2	M1: ResNet-50-FPN M2: ResNet-101-FPN	M1: 3 M2: 5	No	79.96	80.00
3	M1: ResNeXt-101-FPN M2: ResNeXt-101-FPN	M1: 7 M2: 3	Yes	**89.42**	**88.34**

About the experiments, several Mask R-CNN models were first trained on the basis of the pre-trained weights with the COCO data set. In these models, the following backbones were used: ResNet-50-FPN (*Residual Network* [12] with 50 layers with *Feature Pyramid Network* [15]), ResNet-101-FPN, and ResNeXt-101-FPN (ResNeXt [16] of 101 layers with FPN). In addition, the following Gaussian Blur (G.B.) kernel sizes were used: 7, 5 and 3, for their application in the synthetic training images. The results of training these solitary Mask R-CNN models are shown in Table 1. When applying our SISE algorithm (*Simple Instance Segmentation Ensemble*) to perform the ensemble of results, two of the models obtained with the previous parameters were used, but only the results of the best ensembles are shown in Table 2. All these ensembles improve the mAPs of the solitary models that compose them, both in detection and segmentation.

Analyzing the results of the experiments with the solitary models of Table 1, in the first row we have the description of each column, where the symbol # is the model number, backbone means the network backbone feature extractor, G.B. stands for Gaussian Blur, mAP bbox is the mAP of the bounding box, and mAP segm is the mAP of object segmentation. Considering only these solitary models, model #9 is the best, which corresponds to a Mask R-CNN network with a backbone of ResNeXt-101-FPN and with a Gaussian Blur of 3 × 3, obtaining the best bounding box mAP with 87.56% and also the best segmentation mAP with 88.22%.

On the other hand, taking into account only the models ensembled in Table 2, in the first row there is the description of each column that is similar to the description of Table 1, however, the only difference is that there is a column named *Add unmatched pred* which means to add unmatched predictions with a high score of prediction, in particular it is a boolean that corresponds to the input of our SISE algorithm. Analyzing the obtained mAPs, the best ensemble is #3, which corresponds when we have as modelo 1 a Mask R-CNN network with backbone ResNeXt-101-FPN and a 7 × 7 Gaussian Blur, and have as model 2 a Mask R-CNN network with backbone ResNeXt-101-FPN and a 3 × 3 Gaussian Blur, obtaining the best bounding box mAP with 89.42% and also the best object segmentation mAP with 88.34%. This ensemble #3 from Table 2 is also better than all solitary models, beating the best solitary model #9 from Table 1.

In the bounding box, the solitary model #9 has a box mAP of 87.56% while the ensemble #3 has a box mAP of 89.42%, having a difference of approximately 2%. On the segmentation side, the solitary model #9 has a mAP of 88.22% while the ensemble #3 has a mAP of 88.34%, which gives us a difference of approximately 0.1%.

Another observation worth noting is that for all the ensembles in Table 2, the mAP of each ensemble exceeds the mAP of each of the models that make up the ensemble, both in bounding box mAP and segmentation mAP. For example, choosing ensemble #1 from Table 2, you have 2 ResNet-50-FPN models, but model 1 has Gaussian Blur kernel (G.B.) of 7×7 and model 2 has a G.B. kernel of 5×5. This ensemble #1 has a bbox mAP of 87.71% while its model 1 that composes it has a bbox mAP of 81.37% and model 2 a bbox mAP of 84.87%, in this way the ensemble increases the bbox mAP of the best model by around 3%. On the segmentation side, the ensemble has a segm mAP of 85.21%, while model 1 has a segm mAP of 81.19% and model 2 has a segm mAP of 82.61%, thus the ensemble improves by approximately 2.5% the segm mAP of the best model that composes it.

Observing qualitative results, Fig. 5 shows the predictions on real data of the best ensemble #3 (from Table 2) by means of the SISE algorithm that performs the ensemble of results. This ensemble has as model 1 a Mask R-CNN network with backbone ResNeXt-101-FPN and a Gaussian Blur kernel of 7×7, and as model 2 a Mask R-CNN network with backbone ResNeXt-101-FPN and a Gaussian Blur kernel of 3×3.

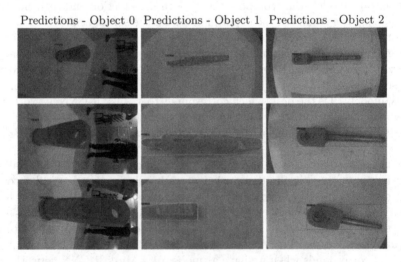

Predictions - Object 0   Predictions - Object 1   Predictions - Object 2

Fig. 5. Predictions of the SISE algorithm over real images, having as model 1 a Mask R-CNN (ResNeXt-101-FPN) with Gaussian Blur of 7×7, and as model 2 a Mask R-CNN (ResNeXt-101-FPN) with Gaussian Blur of 3×3.

5   Conclusions

In conclusion, an algorithm called SISE (*Simple Instance Segmentation Ensemble*) has been presented that performs an ensemble or fusion of the results of 2 Mask R-CNN models. In addition, the effectiveness of the SISE algorithm has been proven using synthetic images of machinery as training data and real machinery images as test data. In particular, we have synthetically trained several Mask R-CNN models and then tested their performance with real data. We then use the SISE algorithm to ensemble the results of several pairs of chosen models. And so we achieved our best results, having as model 1 a Mask R-CNN network with backbone ResNeXt-101-FPN and a Gaussian Blur kernel of 7 × 7 for the synthetic training data, and as model 2 a Mask R-CNN network with backbone ResNeXt-101-FPN and a Gaussian Blur kernel of 3 × 3 for the synthetic training data. This ensemble has a bounding box mAP of 89.42% and an object segmentation mAP of 88.34%, and as expected, the ensemble produces better results than each of the models 1 and 2 that compose such ensemble.

Acknowledgment. M. E. LOAIZA acknowledges the financial support of the CONCYTEC – BANCO MUNDIAL Project "Mejoramiento y Ampliación de los Servicios del Sistema Nacional de Ciencia Tecnología e Innovación Tecnológica" 8682-PE, through its executing unit PROCIENCIA, within the framework of the call E041-01, Contract No. 038-2018-FONDECYT-BM-IADT-AV.

References

1. Chen, X., Girshick, R., He, K., Dollár, P.: Tensormask: a foundation for dense object segmentation. In: Proceedings of the IEEE/CVF International Conference on Computer Vision, pp. 2061–2069 (2019)
2. Du, X., et al.: Spinenet: learning scale-permuted backbone for recognition and localization. In: Proceedings of the IEEE/CVF Conference on Computer Vision and Pattern Recognition, pp. 11 592–11 601 (2020)
3. He, K., Gkioxari, G., Dollár, P., Girshick, R.: Mask R-CNN. In: Proceedings of the IEEE International Conference on Computer Vision, pp. 2961–2969 (2017)
4. Hinterstoisser, S., Lepetit, V., Wohlhart, P., Konolige, K.: On pre-trained image features and synthetic images for deep learning. In: Proceedings of the European Conference on Computer Vision (ECCV) (2018)
5. Salas, A.J.C., Meza-Lovon, G., Fernández, M.E.L., Raposo, A.: Training with synthetic images for object detection and segmentation in real machinery images. In: 2020 33rd SIBGRAPI Conference on Graphics, Patterns and Images (SIBGRAPI). IEEE, pp. 226–233 (2020)
6. Mera, D., Fernández-Delgado, M., Cotos, J.M., Viqueira, J.R.R., Barro, S.: Comparison of a massive and diverse collection of ensembles and other classifiers for oil spill detection in sar satellite images. Neural Comput. Appl. **28**(1), 1101–1117 (2017)
7. Rodriguez, J.J., Kuncheva, L.I., Alonso, C.J.: Rotation forest: A new classifier ensemble method. IEEE transactions on pattern analysis and machine intelligence **28**(10), 1619–1630 (2006)

8. Gao, X., Shan, C., Hu, C., Niu, Z., Liu, Z.: An adaptive ensemble machine learning model for intrusion detection. IEEE Access 7, 82 512–82 521 (2019)
9. Gaonkar, B., et al.: Multi-parameter ensemble learning for automated vertebral body segmentation in heterogeneously acquired clinical mr images. IEEE J. Trans. Eng. Health Med. **5**, 1–12 (2017)
10. Zuo, Y., Drummond, T.: Fast residual forests: rapid ensemble learning for semantic segmentation. In: Conference on Robot Learning. PMLR, pp. 27–36 (2017)
11. Kang, J., Gwak, J.: Ensemble of instance segmentation models for polyp segmentation in colonoscopy images. IEEE Access, vol. 7, pp. 26 440–26 447 (2019)
12. He, K., Zhang, X., Ren, S., Sun, J.: Deep residual learning for image recognition. In: Proceedings of the IEEE Conference on Computer Vision and Pattern Recognition, pp. 770–778 (2016)
13. Wu, Y., Kirillov, A., Massa, F., Lo, W.-Y., Girshick, R.: Detectron2 (2019). https://github.com/facebookresearch/detectron2
14. Lin, T.-Y., et al.: Microsoft COCO: common objects in context. In: Fleet, D., Pajdla, T., Schiele, B., Tuytelaars, T. (eds.) ECCV 2014. LNCS, vol. 8693, pp. 740–755. Springer, Cham (2014). https://doi.org/10.1007/978-3-319-10602-1_48
15. Lin, T.-Y., et al.: Feature pyramid networks for object detection. In: Proceedings of the IEEE Conference on Computer Vision and Pattern Recognition, pp. 2117–2125 (2017)
16. Xie, S., Girshick, R., Dollár, P., Tu, Z., He, K.: Aggregated residual transformations for deep neural networks. In: Proceedings of the IEEE Conference on Computer Vision and Pattern Recognition, pp. 1492–1500 (2017)

Improving Efficient Semantic Segmentation Networks by Enhancing Multi-scale Feature Representation via Resolution Path Based Knowledge Distillation and Pixel Shuffle

Biao Yang[✉][iD], Fanghui Xue[iD], Yingyong Qi[iD], and Jack Xin[iD]

Department of Mathematics, University of California, Irvine, CA 92697, USA
biaoy1@uci.edu

Abstract. Multi-resolution paths and multi-scale feature representation are key elements of semantic segmentation networks. We develop two techniques for efficient networks based on the recent FasterSeg network architecture. One is to use a state-of-the-art high resolution network (e.g. HRNet) as a teacher to distill a light weight student network. Due to dissimilar structures in the teacher and student networks, distillation is not effective to be carried out directly in a standard way. To solve this problem, we introduce a tutor network with an added high resolution path to help distill a student network which improves FasterSeg student while maintaining its parameter/FLOPs counts. The other finding is to replace standard bilinear interpolation in the upscaling module of FasterSeg student net by a depth-wise separable convolution and a Pixel Shuffle module which leads to 1.9% (1.4%) mIoU improvements on low (high) input image sizes without increasing model size. A combination of these techniques will be pursued in future works.

Keywords: Multi-resolution paths · Distillation · Pixel shuffle

1 Introduction

Semantic segmentation is concerned with pixel-wise classification of images and has been studied as a long-standing problem in computer vision, see [7,14] and references therein. Predictions are first made at a range of scales, and are then combined with averaging/pooling or an attention layer. A class of efficient networks (called FasterSeg) have been recently constructed [2] based on differentiable neural architecture search [8] of a supernet and a subsequent knowledge distillation [5] to generate a smaller student net with 3.4M parameters and 27G FLOPs on full resolution (1024 × 2048) image input[1].

---

[1] This model was searched on our machine based on source code from FasterSeg [2].

© Springer Nature Switzerland AG 2021
G. Bebis et al. (Eds.): ISVC 2021, LNCS 13018, pp. 325–336, 2021.
https://doi.org/10.1007/978-3-030-90436-4_26

We are interested in distilling such a light weight Student Net from a high performance Teacher Net which we choose as HRNet-OCR [17] in this work. Our motivation is to improve the FasterSeg Student Net while maintaining its size and FLOPs by enhancing the resolutions of its multi-scale feature maps and their combinations for better prediction. The HRNet has about 10% higher accuracy than the FasterSeg Teacher Net on Cityscapes dataset [4]. Specifically, we first add a higher resolution path to the FasterSeg Student Net architecture and train it through distilling HRNet predictions. Then we let this high resolution path guide the prediction of the lower resolution paths in FasterSeg Student Net through a feature affinity (FA) matrix. At inference, the high resolution path is absent hence its role is virtual and does not add computational overheads on the Student Net. Though knowledge distillation at intermediate level was known in FitNets [10], the knowledge passing across multi-resolution paths for semantic segmentation appears new. In addition, we improve the inaccurate interpolation treatment in FasterSeg's feature fusion module by a combination of depth-wise separable convolutions and Pixel Shuffle (PS) technique [11], resembling the efficient operations in Shufflenets [9,18] for regular image classification task.

Our main contributions are:

1) introducing a novel *teacher-tutor-student framework* to enhance multi-resolution paths by path-wise knowledge distillation with application to Faster-Seg Student Net while keeping computational costs invariant, which utilizes the intermediate feature information from the tutor model;
2) improving multi-scale feature map fusion by depth-wise separable convolution and Pixel Shuffle techniques to gain 1.9% (1.4%) validation accuracy in mIoU on low (high) resolution input images from Cityscapes dataset, at reduced computational costs.

The rest of the paper is organized as follows. Sect. 2 is a summary of related works. Sect. 3 presents our teacher-tutor-student distillation framework. Sect. 4 shows improved semantic segmentation results by our student network with virtual high resolution path on Cityscapes data sets, and their analysis. Sect. 5 describes the Pixel Shuffle technique for multi-scale feature fusion and supporting experimental results. The concluding remarks are in Sect. 6.

2   Related Works

2.1   Overview

Semantic segmentation has been studied for decades. Recent lines of research include hierarchical architecture search, knowledge distillation (introduced in [5] for standard classification), and two-stream methods. Among large capacity models are Autodeeplabs ([7] and references therein), high resolution net (HRNet [17]), zigzag net [6] and hierarchical multi-scale attention network [14]. Among the light weight models are FasterSeg [2], and BiSenet [16]. In Gated-SCNN [13], a high level stream on region masks guides the low level stream on shape features for better segmentation. A gated structure connects the intermediate layers of the two streams, and resulted in 2% mask (mIoU) gain over DeepLabV3+ [1] on Cityscapes dataset [4]. In [15], a dual super-resolution learning framework is introduced to produce high resolution representation on low resolution input. A 2% gain in mIoU over various baseline models is accomplished on Cityscapes data. A feature affinity function is used to promote cooperation of the two super-resolution networks, one on semantic segmentation, the other on single image super-resolution.

Though knowledge distillation at an intermediate level [10] has been known conceptually, how to set it up in the multi-resolution paths for semantic segmentation networks is not much studied. In part, a choice of corresponding locations in the Teacher Net and Student Net depends on network architecture. This is what we set out to do on FasterSeg Student Net.

Besides the conventional upscaling methods like bilinear interpolation, Pixel Shuffle (PS) is widely adopted in various multi-resolution image processing tasks. In the super-resolution task [11], an artful PS operator has been applied to the output of the convolutional layer in the low resolution, and hence has reduced the computational complexity. This technique is inherited by [15] for the super-resolution semantic segmentation, boosting the performance of the model with low resolution input.

2.2   Search and Training in FasterSeg

The FasterSeg search space [2] consists of multi-resolution branches with searchable down-sampling-path from high resolution to low resolution, and searchable operations in the cells (layers) of the branches. Each cell (layer) contains 5 operations: skip connect, 3×3 Conv, 3×3 Conv $\times 2$, Zoomed 3×3 Conv and Zoomed 3×3 Conv $\times 2$. The "Zoomed Conv" contains bilinear down-sampling, 3×3 Conv and bi-linear up-sampling.

Below we recall FasterSeg's architecture search and training procedure [2] in order to introduce our proposed path-wise distillation. In the search stage, the overall optimization objective is:

$$L = L_{seg}(M) + \lambda \, Lat(M) \tag{1}$$

where $Lat(M)$ is the latency loss of the supernet M; L_{seg} is the supernet loss containing cross-entropy of logits and targets from different branches. Note that the branches come from resolutions: 1/8, 1/16, 1/32, 1/8+1/32 and 1/16+1/32, as well as losses from different expansion ratios (max, min, random and architecture parameter ratio).

The architecture parameters (α, β, γ) are in a differentiable computation graph, and optimized by gradient descent. The α is for operations in each cell, β for down-sampling weight, and γ for expansion ratio. Following [8], the training dataset is randomly half-split into two disjoint sets Train-1 and Train-2. Then the search follows the first order DARTS [8]:

1) Update network weights W on Train-1 by gradient: $\nabla_w L_{seg}(M|W, \alpha, \beta, \gamma)$.

2) Update architecture α, β, γ on Train-2 by gradient:

$$\nabla_{\alpha,\beta,\gamma} L_{seg}(M|W,\alpha,\beta,\gamma) + \lambda \cdot \nabla_{\alpha,\beta,\gamma} LAT(M|W,\alpha,\beta,\gamma).$$

For teacher-student co-searching with two sets of architectures (α_T, β_T) and $(\alpha_S, \beta_S, \gamma_S)$, the first order DARTS [8] becomes:

1) Update network weights W by $\nabla_w L_{seg}(M|W,\alpha_T,\beta_T)$ on Train-1,
2) Update network weights W by $\nabla_w L_{seg}(M|W,\alpha_S,\beta_S,\gamma_S)$ on Train-1,
3) Update architecture α_T, β_T by $\nabla_{\alpha,\beta,\gamma} L_{seg}(M|W,\alpha_T,\beta_T)$ on Train-2,
4) Update architecture α_S, β_S, γ_S by $\nabla_{\alpha,\beta,\gamma} L_{seg}(M|W,\alpha_S,\beta_S,\gamma_S)$ $+\lambda\nabla_{\alpha,\beta,\gamma} LAT(M|W,\alpha_S,\beta_S,\gamma_S)$ on Train-2.

The next step is to train the weights to obtain final models.

Step 1): train Teacher Net by cross-entropy to compute the losses between logits of different resolutions and targets.

$$loss_T = CE(pred8_T, target) + \lambda CE(pred16_T, target) + \lambda CE(pred32_T, target) \tag{2}$$

where $predn_T$ is the prediction of the $1/n$ resolution path of the Teacher Net.

Step 2): train Student Net with an extra distillation loss between logits of resolution 1/8 from Teacher Net and logits of resolution 1/8 from Student Net.

$$\begin{aligned} Loss_S = &CE(pred8_S, target) + \lambda CE(pred16_S, target) \\ &+ \lambda CE(pred32_S, target) + KL(pred8_T, pred8_S). \end{aligned} \tag{3}$$

Here $predn_S$ is the prediction of $1/n$ resolution path of the Student Net.

3   Resolution Path Based Distillation

In Sect. 3.1, we first show how to build a FasterSeg Student Net with 1/4 resolution path. Then we introduce feature affinity loss in Sect. 3.2, with search and training details in Sect. 3.3.

3.1   Tutor Model with 1/4 Resolution Path

We build a FasterSeg Student Net ("student tutor") with 1/4 resolution path, see in Fig. 1. The 1/4 resolution path follows the 1/4 resolution stem and contains 2 basic residual 2× layers also used in other stems. The 1/4 path then merges with the 1/8 resolution path by interpolating output of the 1/8 resolution path to the 1/4 resolution size, refining and adding. The model is trained with HRNet-OCR as the Teacher Net.

In Fig. 1, the stem is a layer made up of Conv and Batch normalization and ReLU. The cell is mentioned in Sect. 2.2. And the head is to fuse outputs of different resolution paths together. In 1/4 path, its output is directly added to the output of 1/8 path. While for the other paths, the outputs are concatenated with up-sampled output of lower resolution paths, and then go through a 3×3 Conv.

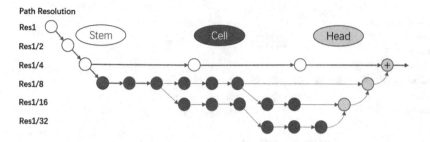

Fig. 1. Tutor net: a FasterSeg form of Student Net with 1/4 resolution path added.

3.2 Feature Affinity Loss

Feature Affinity (FA) loss [15] is a measure to overcome dimension inconsistency in comparing two feature maps by aggregating information from all channels. Consider a feature map with dimensions (H, W, C), which contains $H \times W$ vectors (in pixel direction) of length C. A pixel of a feature map F is denoted by F_i, where $1 \leq i \leq H \times W$. The affinity of two pixels is reflected in the affinity matrix with entries being the pairwise normalized inner product:

$$S_{ij} = (\frac{F_i}{\|F_i\|_p})^T \cdot (\frac{F_j}{\|F_j\|_p}). \tag{4}$$

In other words, the affinity matrix consists of cosine similarities of all pixel-pairs. In order to make sure their consistency in the spacial dimension, we need to interpolate the student affinity matrix to the same dimensional size of the teacher affinity matrix. Let the two affinity matrices for the Teacher and Student Nets be denoted by S_{ij}^t and S_{ij}^s. Then the Feature Affinity (FA) loss is defined as [15]:

$$L_{fa} = \frac{1}{H^2 W^2} \sum_{i=1}^{HW} \sum_{j=1}^{HW} \|S_{ij}^t - S_{ij}^s\|_q. \tag{5}$$

where q is not necessarily the dual of p. Here we choose $p = 2, q = 1$, and consider adding the FA loss (5) to the distillation objective for gradient descent.

Let $S^{1/n}$ be the output of the $1/n$ resolution path of Student Net after passing to ConvNorm layers, $T^{1/n}$ be the output of the $1/n$ resolution path of Teacher Net. We introduce a path-wise FA loss as:

$$FA\_loss = L_{fa}(S^{1/8}, T^{1/4}) + \lambda L_{fa}(S^{1/16}, T^{1/16}) + \lambda L_{fa}(S^{1/32}, T^{1/32}), \tag{6}$$

where λ balances the FA losses on different paths. In our experiment, $\lambda = 0.8$ is chosen to weigh a little more on the first term for the 1/8 path of the student net to mimic the 1/4 path of the tutor net. Figure 2 illustrates how our path-wise FA loss is constructed for distillation learning in the training process.

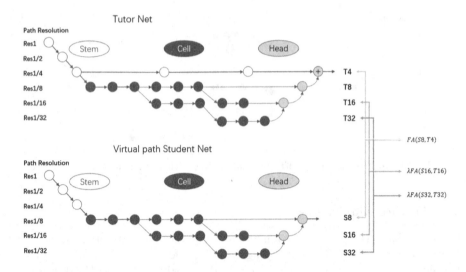

Fig. 2. Student Net with virtual 1/4 path (lower) distilled from tutor net (upper).

3.3   Teacher Net Guided Student Net Search and Training

We summarize our search and training steps below.

Search:
FasterSeg searches its own teacher model, which takes time and may not be most ideal. Instead, we opt for a state-of-the-art model as teacher to guide the search of a light weight Student Net. In our experiments, the Teacher Net is HRNet-OCR [14]. To shorten inference time, we set it back to the original HRNet [12]. The search objective is:

$$L = L_{seg}(M) + \lambda_1 \, Lat(M) + \lambda_2 \, Dist(M, HR). \tag{7}$$

The $L_{seg}(M)$ and $Lat(M)$ are same as in Eq. (1) of FasterSeg, with the added third term to narrow the distance between Student Net and the Teacher Net HR.

By first order DARTS [8] on the randomly half split training datasets (Train-1 and Train-2), we have:

1) Update network weights W by $\nabla_w L_{seg}(M|W, \alpha, \beta, \gamma)$ on Train-1
2) Update architecture α, β, γ by $\nabla_{\alpha,\beta,\gamma} L(M|W, \alpha, \beta, \gamma)$ on Train-2.

Training:

1) The baseline model is a FasterSeg student model distilled from HRNet. The training objective is:

$$Loss_S = CE(pred8_S, target) + \lambda \, CE(pred16_S, target)$$
$$+ \lambda \, CE(pred32_S, target) + KL(pred_{HR}, pred8_S). \tag{8}$$

Here $pred_{HR}$ is the prediction of the HRNet and $predn_S$ is the same notation as in FasterSeg training.

2) For the Student Net with virtual 1/4 path, we first train a FasterSeg Student Net with additional 1/4 resolution path as in Sect. 3.1. This more accurate yet also heavier temporary Student Net serves as a "tutor" for the final Student Net.

Similar to FasterSeg, we only use the outputs of the 1/4, 1/16 and 1/32 resolution paths. The output of the 1/8 path is fused with that of the 1/4 path for computational efficiency and memory savings. The resulting loss is:

$$Loss_{Tu} = CE(pred4_{Tu}, target) + \lambda\, CE(pred16_{Tu}, target)$$
$$+ \lambda\, CE(pred32_{Tu}, target) + KL(pred_{HR}, pred4_{Tu}). \tag{9}$$

Here Tu stands for the "tutor" model with 1/4 resolution path.

Next we distill the true Student Net from the "tutor net" by minimizing the loss function:

$$Loss_S = c\, FA\_loss + CE(pred8_S, target) + \lambda\, CE(pred16_{Tu}, target)$$
$$+ \lambda\, CE(pred32_{Tu}, target) + KL(pred4_{Tu}, pred8_S), \tag{10}$$

where $predn_{Tu}$ is the prediction of the tutor model.

4 Experiments

In Sect. 4.1, we introduce the dataset and our computing environment. We present experimental results and analysis in Sect. 4.2, and analyze FA loss in Sect. 4.3.

4.1 Dataset and Implementations

We use the Cityscapes [4] dataset for training and validation. There are 2975 images for training, 500 images for evaluation, and 1525 images for testing. The class mIoU (mean Intersection over Union) is the accuracy metric.

Our experiments are conducted on Quadro RTX 8000. Our environment is CUDA 11.2 and CUDNN 7.6.5, implemented on Pytorch.

4.2 Experimental Results and Analysis

We perform our method on both low resolution (256×512) input and high resolution (512×1024) input. The different resolution here means the cropping size of the raw image input. The evaluation is on the original image resolution of 1024×2048. And we use only the train dataset for training and perform validation on validation (Val) dataset.

During the search process, we set pretrain epochs as 20, number of epochs as 30, batch size as 6, learning rate as 0.01, weight decay as 5.e−4, initial latency weight λ_1 as 1.e−2, distillation coefficient λ_2 as 1.

We first train a baseline student model with total epochs as 500, batch size as 10, learning rate as 0.012, learning rate decay as 0.990, weight decay as 1.e−3. The baseline model is comparable to FasterSeg's student [2] in performance.

Then we train our 1/4 path tutor model for low (high) resolution input as a student initialized from the baseline model above with HRNet as teacher. The total number of epochs is 350 (400 for high), batch size is 10, learning rate is 0.0026 (0.003 for high), learning rate decay is 0.99, and weight decay is 1.e−3.

Finally, we distill the student model with virtual 1/4 path from the 1/4 path tutor model with 400 epochs, batch size 10, learning rate 0.003, learning rate decay 0.99, weight decay 1.e−3 and coefficient c for FA loss as 1.

The results are in Table 1 where the baseline Student Net has 60.1% (71.1%) mIoU for low (high) resolution input. The tutor net with 1/4 path has 63.6% (73.03%) mIoU for low (high) resolution input. The Student Net with virtual 1/4 path increases the accuracy of the baseline Student Net to 62.2% (72.3%) mIoU for low (high) resolution input. While we have trained the Student Net for different input sizes (256×512 and 512×1024), the inferences are made on the full resolution (1024×2048). For all of our experiments, FLOPs is also computed on the full resolution (1024×2048) images, regardless of the training input size. The improvement by the student net with virtual 1/4 path over the baseline student net are illustrated through images in Fig. 3. In the rectangular regions marked by dashed red lines, more pixels are correctly labeled by the student net with virtual 1/4 path. On test dataset, the baseline Student Net has 57.7% (69.3%) mIoU for low (high) resolution input, and the virtual 1/4 path Student Net has 60.2% (69.7%) mIoU for low (high) resolution input.

We show ablation experimental results for low resolution input in Table 2. It contains student nets with virtual 1/4 path trained from scratch and different coefficient c settings for the FA loss in Eq. (10). Both fine tuning and FA loss contribute to the improvement of the accuracy.

To further understand our teacher-tutor-student distillation framework, we studied direct student net distillation from HRNet with the help of FA loss. However, the mIoU is lower than that from the above teacher-tutor-student distillation framework. This might be due to the more disparate architectural structures between the teacher model and the FasterSeg form of the student net. We notice that our improvement is lower for the high resolution input. This may be due to reaching the maximal capability of the student net. In our experiment, we only have 2 layers in the 1/4 resolution path of the student net. For more gain in mIoU, adding more layers in the path is a viable approach to be explored in the future.

4.3   Analysis of FA Loss

In [15], the authors added a ConvNorm layer right after the extraction of feature maps to adjust their distributions before computing FA loss. We found that it

Table 1. Tutor/student net with virtual 1/4 path for low/high image input sizes on Cityscapes Val dataset.

Input size	256×512	512×1024	Param/FLOPs
Baseline student net	60.1	71.1	3.4M/27G
Tutor net w. 1/4-path	63.6	73.0	3.9M/100G
Student net (w. virtual 1/4-path)	62.2	72.3	3.4M/27G

Table 2. Student nets with virtual 1/4 path on low input size images of Val dataset.

Input size	256×512
Baseline student net	60.1
Student net (w. virtual 1/4-path) from scratch	59.9
Student net (w. virtual 1/4-path) $c = 0$	60.9
Student net (w. virtual 1/4-path) $c = 1$	62.2

would be better not add extra layers to the tutor model in our case as the tutor model is already fixed. By checking the affinity matrices with and without ConvNorm layers, we observed that given the tutor model, adding such extra layers to both student and tutor models before computing FA loss forces the entries of affinity matrices all close to 1 (a trivial way to reduce FA loss). This phenomenon is illustrated in Fig. 4. And we also find that enlarging the coefficient c in FA loss will help the model converge faster but might cause overfitting.

5   Pixel Shuffle Prediction Module

In this section, we develop a specific technique for FasterSeg student prediction module, see Fig. 5. FasterSeg [2] uses Feature Fusion Module (FFM) to fuse two feature maps from different branches, with the outcome of size $C \times H \times W$, which is passed through the Head Module to generate the prediction map of size $19 \times H \times W$. Afterward, a direct interpolation by a factor of 8 up-scales the prediction map to the original input size. This treatment makes FasterSeg fast however at an expense of accuracy.

We discovered an efficient improvement by generating a larger prediction map without introducing too many parameters and operations. The idea is to adopt depth-wise separable convolution [3] to replace certain convolution operations in FasterSeg. First, we reduce the channel number of FFM by half and then use Refine Module (group-wise convolution) to raise the channel number. Finally, we apply Pixel Shuffle on the feature map to give us a feature map of size $C/2 \times 2H \times 2W$. Let us estimate the parameters and operations of FFM and Heads focusing on the convolution operations. The FFM is a 1×1 convolution with C^2 parameters and $C^2 HW$ operations. The Head contains a 3×3 Conv and a 1×1 Conv, whose parameters are $9C^2 + CN$ and the operations are $9C^2 HW + CNHW$. In

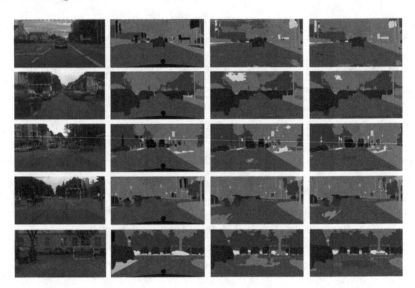

Fig. 3. Baseline student net improved by student net with virtual 1/4-path (pixels in rectangular regions). The 4 columns (left to right) display input images, true labels, output labels of the baseline net and the student net with virtual 1/4-path resp. The 5 example images are taken from the validation dataset.

Table 3. Comparison of validation mIoUs of our proposed up-scaling method with depth-wise separable convolution (dep. sep. conv) and Pixel Shuffle (PS) on low/high input image sizes vs. those of the FasterSeg student (original net) [2] implemented on our local machine.

Input size	256×512	512×1024	Param/FLOPs
Original net	60.1	71.1	3.4 MB/27 GB
Our net with dep. sep. conv & PS	62.0	72.5	3.3 MB/27 GB

total, there are $10\,C^2HW + NCHW$ and $10\,C^2 + NC$ operations. Similarly in our structure, FFM consumes $C^2/2$ parameters and $(C^2/2)HW$ operations, Refine costs $50C$ parameters and $50CHW$ operations, the Head takes $9\,(C/2)^2 + (C/2)N$ parameters and $9(C/2)^2 2H2W + (C/2)N2H2W$ operations. In total, there are $(11/4)\,C^2 + NC/2 + 50\,C$ parameters and $9.5\,C^2HW + 2\,CNHW + 50\,CHW$ operations. If C is large enough, our proposed structure has fewer parameters and operations to produce a larger prediction map.

In our experiments, we replace the Prediction Module of FasterSeg model with our Pixel Shuffle Prediction Module, keeping all the other choices in training the same. As shown in Table 3, our proposed model has 0.1 MB fewer parameters, yet has achieved 1.9 % (1.4 %) mIoU improvement for low (high) resolution input images.

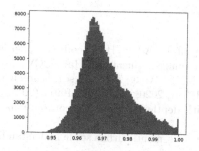 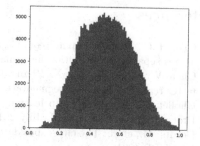

(a) Histogram of S_{ij} with ConvNorm layers added to feature maps prior to computing FA loss from Eq. (10). (b) Histogram of S_{ij} from Eq. (10).

Fig. 4. Histograms of affinity matrix entries in tutor-student distillation learning.

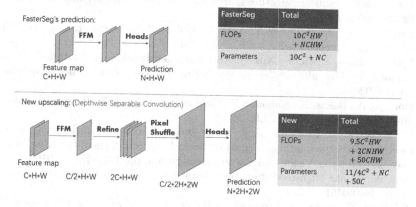

Fig. 5. Proposed pixel shuffle prediction module vs. that of FasterSeg [2].

6 Conclusion

We presented a teacher-tutor-student resolution path based knowledge distillation framework and applied it to FasterSeg Student Net [2] guided by HRnet. While preserving parameter sizes and FLOPs counts, our method improves mIoU by 2.1% (1.2%) on low (high) input image sizes on Cityscapes dataset. We designed a depth-wise separable convolution and Pixel Shuffle technique in the resolution upscaling module which improved FastserSeg's Student Net by 1.9% (1.4%) on low (high) input image sizes with slightly lower (same) parameter (FLOPs) count. In future work, we plan to add more cells on the 1/4 resolution path, combine the two methods developed here for further improvements.

Acknowledgements. The work was partially supported by NSF grants DMS-1854434, DMS-1952644, and a Qualcomm Faculty Award. The authors would like to thank Dr. Shuai Zhang and Dr. Jiancheng Lyu for helpful and enlightening discussions, and ISVC2021 reviewers for their constructive comments.

References

1. Chen, L.C., Zhu, Y., Papandreou, G., Schroff, F., Adam, H.: Encoder-decoder with atrous separable convolution for semantic image segmentation. In: ECCV (2018)
2. Chen, W., Gong, X., Liu, X., Zhang, Q., Li, Y., Wang, Z.: Fasterseg: Searching for faster real-time semantic segmentation. ICLR, 2020; arXiv 1912.10917 (2019)
3. Chollet, F.: Xception: Deep learning with depthwise separable convolutions. In: Proceedings of IEEE CVPR, July 2017
4. Cordts, M., et al.: The cityscapes dataset for semantic urban scene understanding. In: CVPR (2016)
5. Hinton, H., Vinyals, O., Dean, J.: Distilling the knowledge in a neural network. In: NeurIPS-Workshop (2014)
6. Lin, D., Shen, D., Shen, S., Ji, Y., Lischinski, D., Cohen-Or, D., Huang, H.: Zigzag-net: fusing top-down/bottom-up context for object segmentation. In: CVPR (2019)
7. Liu, C., Chen, L., Schroff, F., Adam, H., Wei, H., Yuille, A., Li, F.: Auto-deeplab: Hierarchical neural architecture search for semantic image segmentation. CVPR (2019). arXiv:1901.02985v2 (2019)
8. Liu, H., Simonyan, K., Yang, Y.: DARTS: Differentiable architecture search. ICLR (2019). arXiv preprint arXiv:1806.09055 (2018)
9. Lyu, J., Zhang, S., Qi, Y., Xin, J.: Autoshufflenet: Learning permutation matrices via an exact Lipschitz continuous penalty in deep convolutional neural networks. KDD (2020)
10. Romero, A., Ballas, N., Kahou, S.E., Chassang, A., Gatta, C., Bengio, Y.: Fitnets: Hints for thin deep nets (ICLR, 2015)
11. C Shi, W., et al.: Real-time single image and video super-resolution using an efficient sub-pixel convolutional neural network. In: Proceedings of the IEEE conference on Computer Vision and Pattern Recognition, pp. 1874–1883 (2016)
12. Sun, K., et al.: High-resolution representations for labeling pixels and regions. arXiv: 1904.04514 (2019)
13. Takikawa, T., Acuna, D., Jampani, V., Fidler, S.: Gated-SCNN: gated shape CNNs for semantic segmentation. In: Proceedings of the IEEE/CVF International Conference on Computer Vision, pp. 5229–5238 (2019)
14. Tao, A., Sapra, K., Catanzaro, B.: Hierarchical multi-scale attention for semantic segmentation. arXiv: 2005.10821 (2020)
15. Wang, L., Li, D., Zhu, Y., Tian, L., Shan, Y.: Dual super-resolution learning for semantic segmentation. In: Proceedings of the IEEE/CVF Conference on Computer Vision and Pattern Recognition, pp. 3774–3783 (2020)
16. Yu, C., Wang, J., Peng, C., Gao, C., Yu, G., Sang, N.: BiSenet: Bilateral segmentation network for real-time semantic segmentation (ECCV, 2018)
17. Yuan, Y., Chen, X., Wang, J.: Object-contextual representations for semantic segmentation. arXiv preprint arXiv:1909.11065v5 (ECCV, 2020)
18. Zhang, X., Zhou, X., Lin, M., Sun, J.: Shufflenet: an extremely efficient convolutional neural network for mobile devices. In: CVPR (2017)

Towards Stereoscopic Video Deblurring Using Deep Convolutional Networks

Hassan Imani and Md Baharul Islam[✉]

Department of Computer Engineering, Bahcesehir University, Istanbul, Turkey

Abstract. These days stereoscopic cameras are commonly used in daily life, such as the new smartphones and emerging technologies. The quality of the stereo video can be affected by various factors (e.g., blur artifact due to camera/object motion). For solving this issue, several methods are proposed for monocular deblurring, and there are some limited proposed works for stereo content deblurring. This paper presents a novel stereoscopic video deblurring model considering the consecutive left and right video frames. To compensate for the motion in stereoscopic video, we feed consecutive frames from the previous and next frames to the 3D CNN networks, which can help for further deblurring. Also, our proposed model uses the stereoscopic other view information to help for deblurring. Specifically, to deblur the stereo frames, our model takes the left and right stereoscopic frames and some neighboring left and right frames as the inputs. Then, after compensation for the transformation between consecutive frames, a 3D Convolutional Neural Network (CNN) is applied to the left and right batches of frames to extract their features. This model consists of the modified 3D U-Net networks. To aggregate the left and right features, the Parallax Attention Module (PAM) is modified to fuse the left and right features and create the output deblurred frames. The experimental results on the recently proposed Stereo Blur dataset show that the proposed method can effectively deblur the blurry stereoscopic videos.

Keywords: Stereoscopic video · Image deblurring · Convolutional neural networks · Motion · Disparity · PAM

1 Introduction

Recently, many works of literature have been published for 2D image deblurring utilizing the power of deep learning. For example, [1,2] used CNNs to estimate the blur kernels in the case of the non-uniform blur. Also, there were proposed many CNN-based models for image deblurring such as [3,4]. Seungjun et al. [3] proposed a blind deblurring model for deblurring the videos with motion blur. This model is a multi-scale CNN-based network that tries to restore sharp frames. The method in [4] proposed based on the coarse-to-fine method, which is progressively restoring the sharp image on different resolutions to offer a technique that is less complex than the previous methods, and its results are better

© Springer Nature Switzerland AG 2021
G. Bebis et al. (Eds.): ISVC 2021, LNCS 13018, pp. 337–348, 2021.
https://doi.org/10.1007/978-3-030-90436-4_27

than the previous ones. The proposed model is also a multi-scale network. Zhang et al. [5] proposed a method that is designed to cope with the spatially variant blur when there is a camera motion. They used three CNNs and an RNN.

Motion plays an essential role in video processing tasks [6]. When the aim is to deblur a video, motion information can be used. It is because most of the blur in video frames is due to motion. This motion can be the camera motion or the movement of the objects in the video causing the blur. Most of the video-related methods, firstly, calculate the motion between the consecutive frames, and secondly, use a processing step including the transformation to the frames [7,8]. As a result, the accuracy of the motion estimation directly influences the performance of the overall method. However, accurate motion estimation is complex and slow [6]. Most methods assume that the brightness is constant, but this assumption may not be valid because of the inevitable change in lighting and pose and the motion blur and occlusion. Besides, most of the motion estimation methods solve an optimization problem, making the motion estimation slow.

Because of the change in the disparity and wanted or unwanted movement of the camera, calculation and compensation for the spatial blur using the spatial data from one view seems complicated. The amount of the information appears to be insufficient. However, some of the deep learning-based models, such as [9], reached an acceptable performance for 2D image deblurring. However, their performance drops when the amount of the blur is not scattered in the image uniformly. For stereoscopic video deblurring, [10] utilized the information from the left and right views for deblurring, where a coarse depth or piecewise rigid 3D scene flow is utilized to estimate blur kernels in a hierarchical or iterative framework. However, they have a complicated optimization method, and it makes these methods challenging to use everywhere.

Some literature used the stereo disparity and video motion for stereoscopic image and video deblurring. The authors in [11] estimated the depth layers and layer-specific point spread functions and used them to deblur the images. They firstly calculated the disparity utilizing the information from the left and right blur images, and then they proposed a region tree scheme to calculate the point spread functions. Sellent et al. [12] considered scene flow and stereo video deblurring as a mutual task. They used local homographs to create blur kernels using scene flow estimation. They used a weighting method in the boundaries of the objects with a motion to spot the degradations accurately. In this work, the scene flow and deblurring are considered separately, and the previously computed scene flow is used. Recently, DAVANet [13] is proposed, which consists of three parts: an encoder-decoder network architecture, a disparity estimation network, and a fusion model to combine the two models and create the deblurred images. They also proposed a new dataset named Stereo Blur dataset. We used this dataset for the experiments in this paper.

Motivation. Our motivation for proposing a new model for stereoscopic video deblurring is based on two facts: (1) Aggregating the information from the consecutive frames of one view can help to spot the artifacts in pixels of the middle frame using the motion information between the successive frames. In other

Fig. 1. Five left frames from the Stereo Blur Dataset [13]. As can be seen from these consecutive frames, some blur regions in the target middle frame are not blurred in the surrounding frames, and these frames can help deblur the middle frame.

words, because of the small motion between the limited number of consecutive frames, for deblurring one frame of a video, the neighboring frames can help to deblur the target frame. For example, as shown in Fig. 1, suppose that we want to deblur the middle frame. Some regions are blurred in the middle frame but not in the neighboring 1, 2, 4, or 5 frames. After compensating for motion, we can use them to deblur the middle target frame. (ii) In stereo vision, two views from one scene are available. We believe that with the disparity information, the corresponding pixels in one view can help remove the blur from the other view. In most cases, the blur in the left and right frames is not the same.

Contributions. This paper proposes a new deep learning-based stereoscopic video deblurring model to cope with the motion blur in dynamic scenes. This model uses the neighboring frames and the information from the other stereo view to deblur one frame. Specifically, we first find the keypoints and descriptors for the middle frame and the neighbouring frames, and then match the features among the two images using the Brute Force method. Then, we calculate the homography matrix to transform the neighbouring frame to the middle frame to consider for the camera rotation and translation. Then, we extract the features from the main frame and the transformed neighboring frames using some modified 2D U-Net [14] networks that using 3D CNNs. Finally, we aggregate the extracted features from the left and right views using a modified PAM [15] model and create the deblurred middle frame. The main contributions of this paper are as follows:

1. We propose a new stereoscopic video deblurring model. The proposed model uses the information from the other stereo view and the neighboring frames to deblur the middle frame.
2. To fuse the left and right videos features, the PAM module is modified to make it suitable for aggregating features from the stereo videos.
3. The 2D U-Net model is modified to make it suitable for extracting features from the 3D input as the batch of the consecutive frames.

2   Proposed Method

The architecture of the proposed method is shown in Fig. 2. As can be seen from this Figure, for each view, we select the middle frame from the consecutive

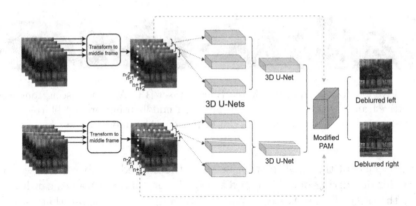

Fig. 2. Overview of the proposed stereoscopic video deblurring architecture. In this architecture, firstly, 4 left and right neighboring frames are transformed to the corresponding middle frames. Then, eight 3D U-Net models are used to extract features from the left and right neighboring frames, and a modified PAM module is used to fuse the left and right features and create the deblurred frames.

frames as the frame that we want to deblur. Let us say frame number n is selected from the left and right videos as the middle frames that we want to deblur. Two previous and two next frames $(n-1, n-2, n+1, n+2)$ are also selected. The motion between the middle frame and these four frames is calculated, and based on this motion, the frames $(n-1, n-2, n+1, n+2)$ are transposed to the middle frame n to have different representations of the target frame. Then, the resulting five frames are used as input to the modified U-Net networks to extract their features. Three modified U-Net networks are used to extract features from the five frames from each view. In [16,17] the authors discussed that how multi-scale networks similar to the 2D U-Net can help to learn the misalignments. Besides, in [18] the experimental results show that the cascaded framework can further improve the ability to handle the movements which are used for video denoising. Therefore, based on their impressive results for different tasks, we designed our model based on the cascaded architecture. Frames n, $n-1$, and $n-2$ to the first, frames $n+1$, n, and n-1 to the second, and frames $n, n+1$, and $n+2$ are feed to the third modified U-Net networks. The layers of the modified U-Net networks use 3D convolutional layers and are suitable to accept a stack of frames. The output of the U-Net in the first stage is used as input to another U-Net. The second stage U-Net is applied to the output features of the first stage U-Nets.

After extracting features from the left and right batches of frames, they are used as input to the modified PAM module. The modified PAM module is used to fuse the left and right features and consider the disparity between the left and right views. Finally, the signals from the output of the modified PAM module are fed to a convolutional layer to create the deblurred version of the input middle left and right frames. We added two 2D convolutional layers at the output of the modified PAM module, each followed by a ReLU activation function. In between the 3D convolutional layers, we added a Batch Normalization (BN) layer to standardize the input features. The final convolutional layer's output has just one filter to make the whole network have an output with the same size as the middle input frame.

As can be seen from Fig. 3, the neighboring frames are transformed to the middle frame before applying to the model. As shown in this figure, we first convert both the middle frame (number 3) and the neighbouring frame to a grayscale image. Then, we use the keypoint detector and descriptor method named Oriented fast and Rotated BRIEF (ORB) [19] to extract their descriptors. In this method, a binary descriptor based on BRIEF [20] which is rotation invariant and resistant to noise, is used. ORB is two times faster than SIFT [21]. To match the extracted features, we use the Brute-Force matcher [22]. It takes the descriptor of one feature in the first set and matches it with all other features in the second set using the distance between them. The closest feature is identified as the matching feature. Finally, the homography matrix calculated from the matched features is used to transform the colored frame number 2 to the middle frame number 3. This process is used to transform all other three frames to the middle frame to make them ready to use as the inputs to our deblurring model.

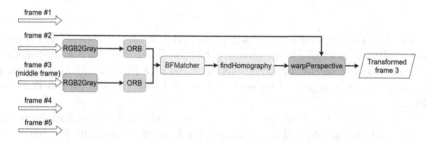

Fig. 3. Transformation of the neighbouring frames to the middle frame. Here we transform the neighbouring frame number 2 to the middle frame number 3. After RGB to grayscale image conversion, we apply the Oriented Rotated BRIEF (ORB) to each frame. Then, using the Brute-Force matcher, we match the features among the two frames and find the homography matrix (findHomography). Finally, the homography matrix is used to transform the colored frame number 2 to the middle frame 3.

2.1   3D U-Net Architecture

The original U-Net [14] model includes one contracting path to catch the context and one symmetric expanding path that allows accurate localization and uses 2D convolutions and other 2D max-pooling which its input is a 2D image. To utilize the U-Net architecture when the inputs are multiple images, we modified the original U-Net architecture. The architecture of the modified U-Net is depicted in Fig. 4. In this Figure, the contracting path consists of 3D convolutional layers. This path includes two $5 \times 5 \times 5$ convolutions, followed by a ReLU activation function. A 3D $2 \times 2 \times 2$ max-pooling with a stride of 2 is added to downsample the features. In the expansive path, the contracting path is done in an inverse

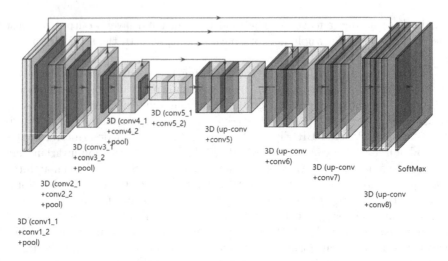

Fig. 4. The architecture of the modified U-Net. We used 3D CNNs and 3D max-pooling layers to make the modified U-Net suitable for the input stack of the frames. Every 3D convolution is followed by a ReLU.

manner. The feature maps are up-sampled, and a $2 \times 2 \times 2$ convolution is used to reduce the number of feature channels to 50%. Then, we add a concatenation layer and two $5 \times 5 \times 5$ convolutions, each followed by a ReLU activation function. This architecture is repeated for each of the 3D U-Nets in our proposed model in Fig. 2.

In the modified U-Net architecture, we changed the 2D convolutions to 3D and used 3D max-pooling. These changes can help to compensate for motion in the videos too. In the 3D convolutions, consecutive frames instead of just one frame are included. Therefore, using 3D convolution and 3D max-pooling has the advantage of considering the motion in the video implicitly.

2.2   Modified PAM Architecture

Based on the self-attention mechanisms [23,24], Wang et al. in [15] proposed 2D PAM to calculate global correspondence in stereoscopic images. PAM effectively fuses the data from the stereo image pairs. The original PAM architecture is modified to make it suitable for our inputs which have the time dimension added. We also converted the residual block to 3D. The architecture of the modified PAM is shown in Fig. 5. "L" and "R" show the left and right features, which are input to the modified PAM module. They are fed to the 3D residual blocks. The output is fed into a $1 \times 1 \times 1$ 3D convolutional layer. Then, batch-wised matrix multiplication is applied, and the resulted feature maps are passed to a SoftMax layer to create the parallax attention maps M_{RtoL} and M_{LtoR}. Then, the weighted sum of features at all disparity values is fused with their input left features. Finally, the features are fused to create the output features for the left

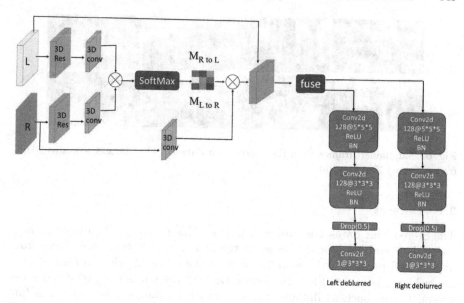

Fig. 5. The modified PAM module. The input features are fed to a transition residual block, and the output is the integration of the input features. 2D convolutions are converted to 3D.

feature map. For the fusion of the right features, the process is the same, and just the left feature fusion is shown in Fig. 5.

We added three convolutional layers followed by a ReLU activation and batch normalization to make rich features suitable for deblurring. The first 2D convolution has 128 filters and followed by a ReLU activation function and a batch normalization layer. The size of the kernel for this convolution is 5×5. The second convolutional layer is similar to the first one with a kernel size of 3×3. Next, a dropout layer with a rate = 0.5 is applied. Using a dropout layer is one way to avoid overfitting. This layer forces the activation values of random neurons to zero. This layer help to design larger models with more nodes per layer, since it probabilistically decreases the capacity of the network and prevents the model from overfitting. The last layer is a convolutional layer with 64 filters and a kernel size of 3×3 (Fig. 5).

3 Dataset and Experimental Setup

Because of the unavailability of the datasets for stereoscopic video deblurring, we trained and tested our model on just one dataset.

Fig. 6. Sample left frames from the Stereo Blur dataset. This dataset contains 20,637 frames from 135 stereo videos.

3.1 Dataset

The Stereo Blur dataset is proposed in [13]. This dataset includes comprehensive indoor and outdoor scenarios. In the indoor videos, there are videos from objects and persons with small disparities. The outdoor videos consist of people, vehicles, boats, and natural scenes. Besides, the dataset is variegated using several factors such as illumination and weather changes. The dataset is further extended to cover various motion scenarios using three different types of photography fashions: handheld, fixed, and onboard shots.

For the creation of the dataset, the authors used the ZED stereo camera [25], which has a frame rate of 60 Frames Per Second (FPS). They expanded the final video frame rate to 480 FPS using a frame interpolation method in [26]. Both the left and right views of the stereo video are with the same configurations. Moreover, this dataset consists of the disparity between the left and right views and the mask map for rejecting the inaccurate values in disparity ground truth and occluded parts of the images, which are calculated by bidirectional consistency check [27]. Overall, the dataset contains sequences of 135 stereo videos from dynamic scenes. The videos are converted to frames, and a total of 20,637 blurred and reference stereo frame pairs together with their corresponding disparities are included in the dataset. The dataset is split into 98 training and 37 testing sequences.

3.2 Experimental Setup

We train the proposed stereo deblurring model on the Stereo Blur dataset. Firstly, we center-cropped all the frames in the dataset with a size of 256×256 and created another dataset. In the created dataset, for each middle left and right frame (number n), we created a folder containing the middle frame n and four other frames $(n-2, n-1, n+1, n+2)$. Frame number n folder contains 5 left, 5 right, and 2 ground truth frames called in the training process.

We use Stochastic Gradient Descent (SGD) with momentum to train our network. For doing faster convergence, SGD drives gradients in the right direction. The random division of the dataset is done in [13] and that division is used here. The batch size for training is selected as 1 on NVIDIA GTX 2080 ti. The proposed model is implemented and trained using PyTorch 1.8.1. The weight decay

Table 1. Performance evaluation of the proposed stereo deblur model and comparison with the image-based deblurring methods on Stereo Blur Dataset, in terms of PSNR, SSIM, running time, and parameter number. A "−" indicates that the result is not available. The best results are in **bold**.

Image-based methods	PSNR	SSIM	Time (sec)	Params (M)
Whyte [28]	24.48	0.8410	700	–
Sun [1]	26.13	0.8830	1200	**7.26**
Gong [2]	26.51	0.8902	1500	10.29
Nah [3]	30.35	0.9294	4.78	11.71
Kupyn [9]	27.81	0.8895	**0.22**	11.38
Zhang [5]	30.46	0.9367	1.40	9.22
Tao [4]	31.65	0.9479	2.52	8.06
DAVANet [13]	**33.19**	**0.9586**	0.31/pair	8.68
Video-based method (**ours**)	30.56	0.9221	0.57/pair	19.9

is 0.001, and the Nesterov momentum is 0.9. The initial learning rate is set to 0.0001 and divided by 10 after the validation loss saturates. Mean Squared Error (MSE) is used as our loss function. We initialized the parameters randomly and trained them by the online error Back Propagation (BP) algorithm.

4 Results and Discussions

Due to the not publicly available stereoscopic video deblurring dataset, we conduct our experiments on the stereo blur dataset [13] which is initially developed for stereoscopic image deblurring. This dataset contains stereo image sequences which are the frames of the stereo videos. Besides, to the best of our knowledge, no stereoscopic video deblurring method reported its results on this dataset. For this reason, we compare our results with the stereoscopic image deblurring methods and use the frame-based average for comparison.

We compare our stereo video deblurring results regarding Structural SIMilarity index (SSIM) and Peak Signal-to-Noise Ratio (PSNR) to the deep learning-based and traditional methods. The networks of the CNN-based methods of [3–5,9] are fine-tuned on the Stereo Blur dataset in [13]. Table 1 shows the results of the comparison between image and video-based deblurring methods. It can be seen that no stereo video deblurring method is reported their results on the Stereo Blur dataset. The table also shows that the proposed method perform better than the following image-based methods: Whyte et al. [28], Sun et al. [1], Gong et al. [2], Nah et al. [3], Kupyn et al. [9], and Zhang et al. [5]. Tao et al. [4] and DAVANet [13] are performing better than our method. Comparing the 2D or 3D image-based deblurring methods with our stereo video deblurring method may be misleading. To the best of knowledge, there are two stereo video deblurring method in the literature [10,12]. These methods are not open-source,

Fig. 7. Four sample qualitative test results from the Stereo Blur dataset. (Left to right) left blur frame, deblurred frame using our model, and ground truth.

and they have not reported their results on the Stereo Blur dataset. The reason is that the Stereo Blur dataset is proposed after these methods. They did their experiments on some stereo videos that they generated for their usage. Sellent et al. [12] proposed a small-scale dataset which is stereo image-based. We could not use this dataset since it is not based on the consecutive frames which our algorithm needs at least 5 consecutive frames. Besides, it is small-scale and can not be used to train our deep learning-based model. The method in [10] created the blurred stereo images with synthetically blurring the stereo images in the KITTI [29] and Sellent et al. [12] datasets, and we could not compare our results with this method either. Therefore, we could not compare our method's performance with these methods.

Figure 7 shows the qualitative performance of our method on four test videos from the Stereo Blur dataset. As can be seen from this Figure, the motion blur is enhanced in most cases. It is the effect of using the neighboring frames for strengthening the central frame. It is because the motion blur is not appearing in all the consecutive frames. Consider a specific region in a frame. When there is a motion blur in the central frame, some neighboring frames are not blurred within that particular region. Therefore, fewer or non-blurred frames can be used to deblur the other frames, and our method effectively utilizes this information. This Figure indicates that the proposed method can deblur the stereo video with acceptable performance.

5   Conclusions and Future Works

This paper proposed a new stereoscopic video deblurring model that uses the stereo information and the neighboring frames to deblur the middle frame. Due to the slight motion in consecutive frames of a video, the past and previous frames carry information about the main frame. Instead of the blur frame itself, the information from the neighboring previous and past frames is used to deblur the target frame. The network architecture has two parts: the first part extracts features from the middle frame and the neighboring frames of each view, and the second part fuses the left and right features and creates the deblurred frames. Quantitative and qualitative experimental results on the Stereo Blur dataset show that the proposed method can deblur the stereo videos with acceptable performance. From the experiments, it is noticeable that there is a need for a very big dataset to develop deep learning-based methods for stereoscopic video deblurring. In the future, we will train deep learning-based methods on the combination of several datasets, and create blurry frames synthetically and extend the dataset to avoid overfitting. Tao et al. [4] and DAVANet [13] are performing better than our method. In the future, we will adapt our model to use an encoder-decoder-like architecture similar to DAVANet [13], or we will design a new model based on the Transformers to get the state-of-the-art results.

References

1. Sun, J., Cao, W., Xu, Z., Ponce, J.: Learning a convolutional neural network for non-uniform motion blur removal. In: Proceedings of the IEEE Conference on Computer Vision and Pattern Recognition, pp. 769–777 (2015)
2. Gong, D., et al.: From motion blur to motion flow: a deep learning solution for removing heterogeneous motion blur. In: Proceedings of the IEEE Conference on Computer Vision and Pattern Recognition, pp. 2319–2328 (2017)
3. Nah, S., Hyun Kim, T., Mu Lee, K.: Deep multi-scale convolutional neural network for dynamic scene deblurring. In: Proceedings of the IEEE Conference on Computer Vision and Pattern Recognition, pp. 3883–3891 (2017)
4. Tao, X., Gao, H., Shen, X., Wang, J., Jia, J.: Scale-recurrent network for deep image deblurring. In: Proceedings of the IEEE Conference on Computer Vision and Pattern Recognition, pp. 8174–8182 (2018)
5. Zhang, J., et al.: Dynamic scene deblurring using spatially variant recurrent neural networks. In: Proceedings of the IEEE Conference on Computer Vision and Pattern Recognition, pp. 2521–2529 (2018)
6. Xue, T., Chen, B., Wu, J., Wei, D., Freeman, W.T.: Video enhancement with task-oriented flow. Int. J. Comput. Vision **127**(8), 1106–1125 (2019)
7. Liu, C., Sun, D.: A bayesian approach to adaptive video super resolution. In: CVPR 2011. IEEE, pp. 209–216 (2011)
8. Baker, S., Scharstein, D., Lewis, J., Roth, S., Black, M.J., Szeliski, R.: A database and evaluation methodology for optical flow. Int. J. Comput. Vision **92**(1), 1–31 (2011)
9. Kupyn, O., Budzan, V., Mykhailych, M., Mishkin, D., Matas, J.: Deblurgan: blind motion deblurring using conditional adversarial networks. In: Proceedings of the IEEE Conference on Computer Vision and Pattern Recognition, pp. 8183–8192 (2018)
10. Pan, L., Dai, Y., Liu, M., Porikli, F.: Simultaneous stereo video deblurring and scene flow estimation. In: Proceedings of the IEEE Conference on Computer Vision and Pattern Recognition, pp. 4382–4391 (2017)
11. Xu, L., Jia, J.: Depth-aware motion deblurring. In: 2012 IEEE International Conference on Computational Photography (ICCP). IEEE, pp. 1–8 (2012)

12. Sellent, A., Rother, C., Roth, S.: Stereo video deblurring. In: European Conference on Computer Vision, pp. 558–575. Springer (2016)
13. Zhou, S., Zhang, J., Zuo, W., Xie, H., Pan, J., Ren, J.S.: Davanet: stereo deblurring with view aggregation. In: Proceedings of the IEEE/CVF Conference on Computer Vision and Pattern Recognition, pp. 10 996–11 005 (2019)
14. Ronneberger, O., Fischer, P., Brox, T.: U-Net: convolutional networks for biomedical image segmentation. In: Navab, N., Hornegger, J., Wells, W.M., Frangi, A.F. (eds.) MICCAI 2015. LNCS, vol. 9351, pp. 234–241. Springer, Cham (2015). https://doi.org/10.1007/978-3-319-24574-4_28
15. Wang, L., et al.: Learning parallax attention for stereo image super-resolution. In: Proceedings of the IEEE/CVF Conference on Computer Vision and Pattern Recognition, pp. 12 250–12 259 (2019)
16. Dosovitskiy, A., et al.: Flownet: learning optical flow with convolutional networks. In: Proceedings of the IEEE International Conference on Computer Vision, pp. 2758–2766 (2015)
17. Wu, S., Xu, J., Tai, Y.-W., Tang, C.-K.: Deep high dynamic range imaging with large foreground motions. In: Proceedings of the European Conference on Computer Vision (ECCV), pp. 117–132 (2018)
18. Tassano, M., Delon, J., Veit, T.: Fastdvdnet: towards real-time deep video denoising without flow estimation. In: Proceedings of the IEEE/CVF Conference on Computer Vision and Pattern Recognition, pp. 1354–1363 (2020)
19. Rublee, E., Rabaud, V., Konolige, K., Bradski, G.: Orb: an efficient alternative to sift or surf. In: 2011 International Conference on Computer Vision. IEEE, pp. 2564–2571 (2011)
20. Calonder, M., Lepetit, V., Strecha, C., Fua, P.: BRIEF: Binary Robust Independent Elementary Features. In: Daniilidis, K., Maragos, P., Paragios, N. (eds.) ECCV 2010. LNCS, vol. 6314, pp. 778–792. Springer, Heidelberg (2010). https://doi.org/10.1007/978-3-642-15561-1_56
21. Lowe, D.G.: Distinctive image features from scale-invariant keypoints. Int. J. Comput. Vision 60(2), 91–110 (2004)
22. Middelkamp, A.: Online. Praktische Huisartsgeneeskunde 3(4), 3–3 (2017). https://doi.org/10.1007/s41045-017-0040-y
23. Zhang, H., Goodfellow, I., Metaxas, D., Odena, A.: Self-attention generative adversarial networks. In: International Conference on Machine Learning. PMLR, pp. 7354–7363 (2019)
24. Fu, J., et al.: Dual attention network for scene segmentation. In: Proceedings of the IEEE/CVF Conference on Computer Vision and Pattern Recognition, pp. 3146–3154 (2019)
25. Capture the world in 3d., Stereolabs. (n.d.). https://www.stereolabs.com/
26. Niklaus, S., Mai, L., Liu, F.: Video frame interpolation via adaptive separable convolution. In: Proceedings of the IEEE International Conference on Computer Vision, pp. 261–270 (2017)
27. Sundaram, N., Brox, T., Keutzer, K.: Dense point trajectories by GPU-accelerated large displacement optical flow. In: Daniilidis, K., Maragos, P., Paragios, N. (eds.) ECCV 2010. LNCS, vol. 6311, pp. 438–451. Springer, Heidelberg (2010). https://doi.org/10.1007/978-3-642-15549-9_32
28. Whyte, O., Sivic, J., Zisserman, A., Ponce, J.: Non-uniform deblurring for shaken images. Int. J. Comput. Vision 98(2), 168–186 (2012)
29. Geiger, A., Lenz, P., Stiller, C., Urtasun, R.: Vision meets robotics: the kitti dataset. Int. J. Robot. Res. 32(11), 1231–1237 (2013)

Color Point Pair Feature Light

Luis Ronald Istaña Chipana[1,2][(✉)] [iD] and Manuel Eduardo Loaiza Fernández[2] [iD]

[1] Universidad Nacional San Agustín, Arequipa, Peru
listana@unsa.edu.pe
[2] Department of Computer Science, Universidad Católica San Pablo, Arequipa, Peru
{luis.istana,meloaiza}@ucsp.edu.pe
http://www.unsa.edu.pe, http://www.ucsp.edu.pe

Abstract. Object recognition in the field of computer vision is a constant challenge to achieve better precision in less time. In this research, is proposed a new 3D descriptor, to work with depth cameras called CPPFL, based on the PPF descriptor from [1]. This proposed descriptor takes advantage of color information and groups it more effectively and lightly than the CPPF descriptor from [2], which uses the color information too. Also, it is proposed as an alternative descriptor called CPPFL+, which differs in the construction taking advantage of the same concept of grouping colors, so it gains a "plus" in speed. This change makes the descriptor more efficient compared to PPF and CPPF descriptors. Optimizing the object recognition process [3], it can reach a rate of ten frames per second or more depending on the size of the object. The proposed descriptor is more tolerant to illuminations changes since the hue of a color is more relevant than the other components.

Keywords: 3D descriptor · Object recognition · RGB-D cameras

1 Introduction

In the area of computer vision, a basic task is the recognition of objects in different scenarios with the aim of understanding that is in the environment. With both information, it can be explored with different applications in the fields of medicine, mechanics, safety, etc. [4]. Taking advantage of the recent technology described as RGB-D cameras, which provide more information than an ordinary camera, it opens up a world of possibilities for the development of new techniques of object recognition in a 3D scenario.

Currently, there are techniques to apply in different cases to the recognition of 3D objects. We can briefly mention 2D descriptors based on image recognition techniques. Which extends the recognition of RGB images to RGB-D images, or add an extra value to the image matrix. We have "Speed up Robust Features" (SURF) [5], "Pyramid histogram of oriented gradient" (PHOG) [6]. These techniques can be easily adapted to using learning networks as applied in unsupervised learning [7] or deep learning implementation [8].

© Springer Nature Switzerland AG 2021
G. Bebis et al. (Eds.): ISVC 2021, LNCS 13018, pp. 349–361, 2021.
https://doi.org/10.1007/978-3-030-90436-4_28

Another approach to solving the problem is 3D descriptors, which have as input to clouds of 3D points or meshes. We have as an example the implementation of "Fast Point Feature Histograms" (FPFH) [9], "Signature of Histograms of OrienTations" (SHOT) [10], or Viewpoint-oriented Color Shape Histogram (VCSH) [11]. But, a technique that stands out among this type of descriptor is the Point Pair Features (PPF) presented by B. Dros et al. [1], which shows great potential due to two factors, the first factor is the relationships between 3D points which is a form of interpretation of the surface. To take advantage of existing color information, a variant called Color Point Pair Features (CPPF) was proposed by [2], this extends the original descriptor by increasing the color information to create a new descriptor.

2   3D Descriptors

2.1   Point Pair Feature (PPF) Descriptor

A type of 3D descriptor is the PPF descriptor presented by [1], which is based on the geometric relationships of distances and angles that have the pairs of 3D points that are part of an object. While in the recognition phase it uses the pairs relative to each evaluated point belonging to the stage where the recognition of an object is desired. It describes in detail the data that this descriptor uses, the properties that it has, the processes that this method uses to achieve object recognition, and then a color-based variant. The set of features have been taken from the geometric relationships that have the points of an object, such as distance or existing angles. With two 3D points, m1 and m2, 4 different values are obtained, a Euclidean distance and 3 different angles as can be seen in Fig. 1. All of these values will be used for the creation of the CPPFL descriptor and are very important because they will be used to calculate the position and orientation of the object sought.

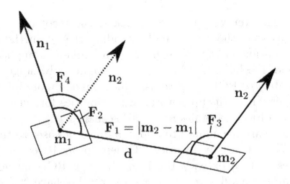

Fig. 1. Point Pair Feature (PPF) descriptor components by [1].

2.2   Color Point Pair Feature (CPPF) Descriptor

As an extension of the PPF method, we have the CPPF descriptor [2]. This 3D descriptor adds 6 values, using 3 values per color, to represent the color information corresponding to each pair of 3D points, extending the vector from 4 to 10 values. We see the descriptor in [3] CPPF, which it is created from the values of two points taking into account its positions p_i and p_j, its normal n_i and n_j, finally, its colors c_i and c_j. This result in the Eq. 1. This allows pairs of points with similar color values to be compared in addition to the original information proposed by the PPF method.

$$F_{CPPF} = CPPF(p_i, p_j, n_i, n_j, c_i, c_j) \tag{1}$$

3   CPPFL Proposed Descriptor

The Color Point Pair Feature Light (CPPFL) descriptor is based on the PPF descriptor and adds the color components. Unlike the CPPF descriptor, which also adds the color value, the proposed descriptor encapsulates the color value efficiently for use in object recognition. This difference improves recognition times as well as accuracy. first, it covers the creation of this descriptor and then the results obtained by comparing it with its predecessors.

3.1   Color Point Pair Feature (PPF) Descriptor

As mentioned above, our descriptor will use the PPF descriptor as a base, the next step is to see the transformation of a color input to a representative and divisor value. That is a function that receives all 3 parameters of the RGB color space and returns a single one as in Eq. 2.

$$F(R, G, B) = C_1 \tag{2}$$

The result of this transformation will be used directly as the key of the hash table without further calculation or operations on it. The first step is to split the RGB color space using the color hue used by HSV and HSL. The R, G, and B values correspond to the components of the RGB color space. While the MAX and MIN values are equivalent to the largest and smallest of these components respectively. Equation 3 converts an input in RGB format to an identifier of a primary or secondary color.

$$C = \begin{cases} floor(\frac{G-B}{MAX-MIN} + 5.5) & \mod 6 \ si \ MAX = R \\ floor(\frac{B-R}{MAX-MIN} + 1.5) & si \ MAX = G \\ floor(\frac{R-G}{MAX-MIN} + 3.5) & si \ MAX = B \end{cases} \tag{3}$$

Applying 3 to the RGB color space yields a division as seen in Fig. 2. A uniform division can be observed for the 6 main and secondary colors. At this point, there is an ambiguity regarding the area that belongs to the color white, and in counterpart to the color black.

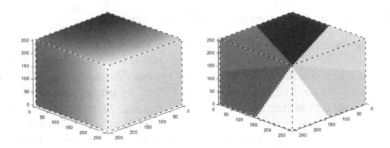

Fig. 2. Division of the RGB color space into color groups according to the proposal.

To resolve this ambiguity, an additional division can be performed taking into account monochromatic colors. Consequently, three values are defined: (α, β, γ) that will serve to limit monochromatic color spaces. Depending on the value, they will have different sizes as can be seen in Fig. 3. Joining all, we get the next rules:

1. If the largest value is less than α, the color is very dark and can be considered black with a code equal to 6.
2. If the smallest value is greater than $255 - \beta$, the color is very clear and can be considered white with a code equal to 7.
3. If the difference of these 2 values is less than γ, there is neutrality in terms of color and can be considered gray with a code equal to 8.
4. If not in the above cases, the corresponding code is calculated using Eq. 3.

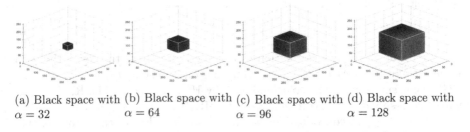

(a) Black space with $\alpha = 32$ (b) Black space with $\alpha = 64$ (c) Black space with $\alpha = 96$ (d) Black space with $\alpha = 128$

Fig. 3. Space reserved for the color black with different values of α.

To summarize, the function that returns an identifier or code for a color in RGB format or Eq. 2 will return a value depending on the most representative color to the input. All the keys that are obtained are integers, which can be used as part of the key in a hash table. The colors recognized with their corresponding code can be seen in Table 1.

This value will be the new representative in the descriptor structure, which can be used directly as the key of the hash table. The value of the unknown α

Table 1. Colors and their corresponding key for use in a hash table.

Principal color	Key	Secondary color	Key	Monochromatic color	Key
Green	1	Yellow	0	Black	6
Blue	3	Magenta	4	Gray	7
Red	5	Cyan	2	White	8

must be a low number, because achromatic colors are common, but do not have a wide range. Being a lighter version in terms of colors and even starting from the PPF descriptor, it will be called CPPFL.

3.2 Creating the CPPFL+ Variant

Based on the CPPFL descriptor, and its strategy of dividing the color space into 9 different groups, there is also the possibility of increasing the speed by taking advantage of this information. If each 3D point has a color, these can be grouped according to the proposed division. If two points end up grouped under the same color, they usually belong to the same space and do not provide much descriptive information. On the other hand, if two points differ in color, they generally have a prudent distance between them and also tend to have more discriminating information since it is very likely that they belong to different surfaces. This idea extends to the creation of a new descriptor, which will be a subset of the CPPFL descriptor. This descriptor will have the name CPPFL+, which follows the same procedures with the difference that points of the same color are not used for its creation. With this, the number of points evaluated is much lower but maintains a similar descriptive capacity.

4 Test with Database Captured with a Kinect Device

To test the effectiveness of our proposal to the state of the art. Testing has been done on the database provided by [12] which consists of 17 scenes with 27 models divided into 6 classes. In this stage, we will have two phases, one for learning for the creation of the 3D descriptor, and another for the recognition of the object using the 3D descriptor. Both phases are from the original PPF descriptor, the process is adapted to work with color information. During the learning phase, only the times are measured.

4.1 Learning Phase Using the Proposed 3D Descriptors

To test the creation time of the descriptors using the 3D models in the Kinect database, the models can be seen in Fig. 4. We first create the descriptor for each model using the following descriptors: PPF, CPPF, CPPFL, and CPPFL+. In all four types, we use the same data settings: the size of voxels and the same 3D point cloud of the model with color information. This process of creating each 3D descriptor is repeated and we obtain as a result an average value for each type of descriptor.

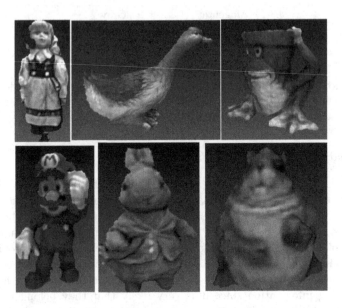

Fig. 4. Models captured with a Kinect camera, belonging to the Kinect database [12].

As noted in Fig. 5, each model has its own descriptor creation time for the 4 mentioned. The lowest values are always obtained by CPPFL+ and as a second place to the CPPFL descriptor. The values obtained are linked to the number of points that each model has after it has been reduced by a Voxel filter.

4.2 Recognition Phase Using the Proposed 3D Descriptors

For this part, the new descriptor is tested compared to the other 3D descriptors. We first evaluate the effectiveness and then the efficiency of the different descriptors. The values of correctly hit of the position in different scenarios are shown in Table 2. Each row represents a count of the correctly successful models using the PPF, CPPF, CPPFL, and CPPFL+ descriptors, while each column represents the count by a specific type of model for valid combinations of that model.

It is noted that the PPF descriptor is always below the descriptors that use color. As for the three descriptors that are supported by the color information have similar performance, this is because this task is to locate the object in the presented environment. Where it is observed that the proposed descriptors have a better percentage of recognition.

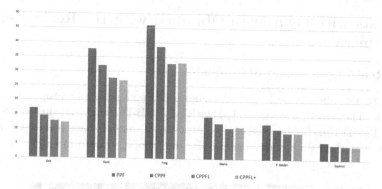

Fig. 5. Time required to create the PPF, CPPF, CPPFL, and CPPFL+ descriptors for kinect database models.

Table 2. Accuracy of 3D descriptors for translation and orientation.

Own dataset	Doll	Duck	Frog	Mario	P. Rabbit	Squirrel
ppf	0.28	0.0	0.12	0.15	0.39	0.56
cppf	0.28	0.0	0.15	0.15	0.37	0.48
cppfl	0.28	0.66	0.32	0.23	0.49	0.41
cppfl+	0.43	0.66	0.32	0.23	0.49	0.33

To verify that the proposed descriptor recognizes in real-time, the time it takes for each recognition is displayed, even if it fails. These times are seen in Table 3. We have the average recognition time values between the original and proposed descriptors applying the optimized process. These times allow the execution of several frames per second. In addition, it is noted that the CPPFL+ descriptor offers better times in all cases.

Table 3. Recognition time in seconds

Descriptor	Doll	Duck	Frog	Mario	P. Rabbit	Squirrel
ppf	2.395	5.023	4.427	1.370	1.485	0.538
cppf	0.405	0.599	0.426	0.298	0.280	0.146
cppfl	0.506	0.833	0.839	0.244	0.263	0.102
cppfl+	0.317	0.510	0.370	0.202	0.193	0.086

5   Tests with Own Data Obtained with the RealSense Camera

5.1   RealSense Camera 3D Models

To verify the effectiveness and efficiency obtained with the proposal of this research. The descriptor was tested with an RGB-D image stream, as detailed below. To test the effectiveness of the proposal, 3D models have been used taking into account their difference in color, size and shape, as seen in Fig. 6.

Fig. 6. Models captured with a RealSense camera.

The values of the models used are fixed, so they can be compared between the descriptors: CPPF, CPPFL, and CPPFL+. Resulting in the values in Table 4. Each row represents a model, while each column represents the descriptor used, except the last one, which is the number of 3D points characteristic of the models to observe the time-quantity relationship. Because the objects are relatively smaller than the models in the Kinect database, they have a much shorter processing time than those obtained with the Kinect database because after being reduced it does not have more than 100 characteristic 3D points.

5.2   Recognition with Own Data Captured with the RealSense Camera

For this part, the same camera with which the models were captured was used. When testing with a data stream that varies by test, these are not directly comparable between descriptors because each frame of the video stream represents a unique scenario.

Table 4. Time required for model creation using CPPF, CPPFL, CPPFL+ descriptors for models captured with a RealSense. Adding the number of 3D points for each model after being processed.

Own dataset	CPPF(ms)	CPPFL(ms)	CPPFL+(ms)	Points
Yellow car	1	1	1	17
Blue car	1	1	1	21
Coffee	2	1	1	50
Blue box	4	3	2	71
Red box	2	2	2	66
Green box	3	3	2	69

We have 3 different sets of scenarios tested. The first is two small vehicles of similar shape, but different colors as seen in Fig. 7a. A similar shape makes it necessary to use color to differentiate those, this could be very important in real applications. The second is of a bottle of coffee being clogged with other objects as in Fig. 7b. It is important to have a tolerance to interference because the environment does not always provide all the information about the object. The third is three boxes of equal shapes, but of different colors, as seen in Fig. 7c. For these tests, geometrically similar objects are used, being boxes almost all the values on position and normal are very similar. The colors of the boxes are red, green, and blue. They are not entirely that color and they are affected by different illuminations.

 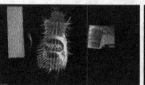 

(a) Models of cars being recognized.   (b) Recognition of a bottle of coffee.   (c) Models of boxes being recognized.

Fig. 7. Video captures of the tests. (Color figure online)

Table 5. Performance of the CPPFL descriptor with an RGB-D camera.

Video	Precision %	CPPFL (ms)	CPPFL+(ms)
2 cars	95	100–200	75–150
Clogged coffee bottle	80	250–800	200–600
3 different color boxes	85	350–900	270–650

The results of object recognition are presented in Table 5, where each row corresponds to a video. The Precision column indicates a value relative to the number of correct positionings of 3D models across the set of scenarios. As for the other columns they represent the milliseconds required for such a process. These values are displayed as ranges because it is not always the same time that each frame, or RGB-D image, of the video, is rendered.

6   Testing with Lighting Changes

To verify the tolerance to lighting changes in the recognition of 3D objects is that some tests were performed with the proposed descriptor CPPFL. The two most extreme cases are when there is no lighting, and when there is too much lighting to the point of seeing everything white. Consequently, two more practical cases can be raised, when the scenario is dark or clear.

In Fig. 8c shows a scenario of three models of aircraft with low lighting and Fig. 8d shows the same scenario, but with better lighting. These models are created to have a lighting level close to the lighting ends.

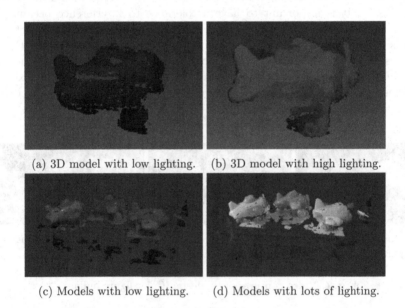

(a) 3D model with low lighting.   (b) 3D model with high lighting.

(c) Models with low lighting.   (d) Models with lots of lighting.

Fig. 8. Models of 3 aircraft.

From these scenarios, the 3D models for each aircraft are extracted. Figure 8a has a model with low lighting and Fig. 8b has the same model with good lighting. As it can be seen the dark model is more difficult to notice because the low lighting makes the different colors less light. In the model with better lighting, it is easier to distinguish the colors present and that will be used by the CPPFL descriptor.

Two test cases are created with these models using the CPPF and CPPFL descriptors because both handle color and the models are geometrically similar. In each case, the descriptors of these models are used to recognize them on a stage with different lighting. That is, the descriptors of low-light models are used to recognize objects on a stage with good lighting, while the descriptors of models with good lighting are used to recognize these same 3D objects on a stage with bad lighting. It should be noted that the tests are done on a video stream captured by the RGB-D RealSense camera.

In the first test case in Fig. 9 the detection and alignment of the descriptors of the light models on a dark environment are observed. As for performance, it is observed in Fig. 9a a misalignment and detection of the models using the CPPF descriptor. However, in Fig. 9b it can be seen that there is a better positioning of the models using the proposed CPPFL descriptor, this recognition remains stable for most of the frames in the video.

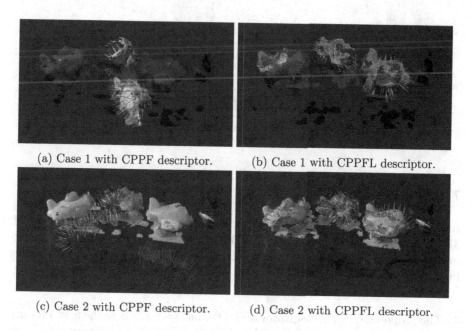

(a) Case 1 with CPPF descriptor.   (b) Case 1 with CPPFL descriptor.

(c) Case 2 with CPPF descriptor.   (d) Case 2 with CPPFL descriptor.

Fig. 9. (a) Recognition in case 1 with CPPF. (b)Recognition in case 1 with CPPFL. (c) Recognition in case 2 with CPPF. (d) Recognition in case 2 with CPPFL

In the second test case in Fig. 9 the detection and alignment of the descriptors of the dark models on a light environment are observed. Figure 9c , it is shown that the CPPF descriptor suffers from same detection and alignment problem as in the first case. Even in cases where the overlay seems correct, it is more due to a coincidence because the original colors are no longer present. In contrast, the proposed CPPFL descriptor obtains good detection and alignment of the models.

Then the tolerance that the descriptor has to light changes is highlighted, which is something that happens as the hours of the day change.

To quantify these results, we selected 100 frames from a one-minute RGB-D video. These 100 frames will be processed using the CPPF and CPPFL descriptors. From each video, the models detected and aligned correctly using each descriptor are counted, and in Fig. 10 the results are shown by comparing both descriptors. As can be seen, the CPPFL descriptor finds in a greater number of frames the 3D models of the objects that are present in the video, showing better performance than the CPPF descriptor in scenarios with variable lighting.

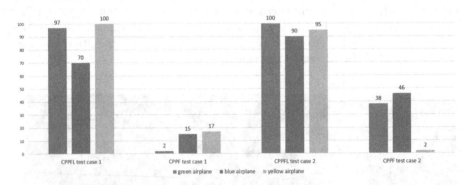

Fig. 10. Test results in different lighting conditions for CPPF and CPPFL descriptors.

7   Conclusions

In this academic article, a new descriptor has been proposed for the recognition of 3D objects using depth cameras (RGB-D), which demonstrates an improvement in the detection and alignment of the position and orientation of an object sought in a 3D scenario. Based on the results obtained in this article, the following conclusions were reached:

1. The proposed CPPFL descriptor uses a 6-value vector, where the first 4 retain geometry information and the other 2 stores color-related information.
2. In the process of creation and recognition of 3D objects, different factors are observed to take into account such as the minimum space between points, the maximum number of neighbors to be analyzed, the number of pairs of points used to optimize the result.
3. The CPPFL descriptor works in the RGB color space using segmentation of 9 base colors, 6 chromatic, and 3 achromatic.
4. After optimizing the process, the CPPF descriptor can process the data in almost real-time with good results.
5. The proposed descriptor use segmentation of the principal colors to make it tolerant to lighting changes

As for the accuracy of the CPPFL descriptor in the evaluation of the detection of a 3D object in a scenario, there is an improvement of 8having a significant improvement over the CPPF descriptor.

Aknowledgement. M. E. LOAIZA acknowledges the financial support of the CONCYTEC – BANCO MUNDIAL Project "Mejoramiento y Ampliación de los Servicios del Sistema Nacional de Ciencia Tecnología e Innovación Tecnológica" 8682-PE, through its executing unit PROCIENCIA, within the framework of the call E041-01, Contract No. 038-2018-FONDECYT-BM-IADT-AV.

References

1. Drost, B., Ulrich, M., Navab, N., Ilic, S.: Model globally, match locally: efficient and robust 3D object recognition. In: Proceedings of the IEEE International Conference on Computer Vision. IEEE, pp. 998–1005 (2010)
2. Choi, C., Christensen, H.I.: RGB-D object pose estimation in unstructured environments. Robot. Auton. Syst. **75**, 595–613 (2016)
3. Hinterstoisser, S., Lepetit, V., Rajkumar, N., Konolige, K.: Going further with point pair features. In: Leibe, B., Matas, J., Sebe, N., Welling, M. (eds.) ECCV 2016. LNCS, vol. 9907, pp. 834–848. Springer, Cham (2016). https://doi.org/10.1007/978-3-319-46487-9_51
4. Szeliski, R.: Computer Vision: Algorithms and Applications. Springer Science & Business Media (2010). https://doi.org/10.1007/978-1-84882-935-0
5. Bay, H., Tuytelaars, T., Van Gool, L.: SURF: speeded up robust features. In: Leonardis, A., Bischof, H., Pinz, A. (eds.) ECCV 2006. LNCS, vol. 3951, pp. 404–417. Springer, Heidelberg (2006). https://doi.org/10.1007/11744023_32
6. Saïdani, A., Echi, A.K.: Pyramid histogram of oriented gradient for machine-printed/handwritten and Arabic/Latin word discrimination. In: 2014 6th International Conference of Soft Computing and Pattern Recognition (SoCPaR). IEEE, pp. 267–272 (2014)
7. Bo, L., Ren, X., Fox, D.: Unsupervised feature learning for RGB-D based object recognition. In: Experimental Robotics. Springer, pp. 387–402 (2013). https://doi.org/10.1007/978-3-319-00065-7_27
8. Lenz, I., Lee, H., Saxena, A.: Deep learning for detecting robotic grasps. Int. J. Rob. Res. **34**(4–5), 705–724 (2015)
9. Rusu, R.B., Blodow, N., Beetz, M.: Fast point feature histograms (FPFH) for 3D registration. In: IEEE International Conference on Robotics and Automation, 2009. ICRA 2009. Citeseer, pp. 3212–3217 (2009)
10. Salti, S., Tombari, F., Di Stefano, L.: Shot: unique signatures of histograms for surface and texture description. Comput. Vis. Image Underst. **125**, 251–264 (2014)
11. Wang, W., Chen, L., Liu, Z., Kühnlenz, K., Burschka, D.: Textured/textureless object recognition and pose estimation using RGB-D image. J. Real-Time Image Proc. **10**(4), 667–682 (2015)
12. Tombari, F., Salti, S.: 3D keypoint detection benchmark. https://vision.deis.unibo.it/keypoints3d/ (2011) [updated 2018-12-15]

Semi Automatic Hand Pose Annotation Using a Single Depth Camera

Marnim Galib$^{(\boxtimes)}$, Giffy Jerald Chris, and Vassilis Athitsos

Department of Computer Science and Engineering, University of Texas at Arlington, Arlington, TX, USA
{marnim.galib,giffy.chris}@mavs.uta.edu, athitsos@uta.edu

Abstract. This paper addresses the problem of 3D hand pose annotation using a single depth camera. While hand pose annotations are critically important for training deep neural networks, creating such reliable training data is challenging and manual labor intensive. We propose a semi-automatic pipeline for efficiently and accurately labeling the 3D hand poses in a depth video containing single hand images. The process starts by selecting a subset of frames that are representative of all the frames in the dataset and the user only provides an estimate of the 2D hand key-points in these selected frames. We use this information to infer the 3D location of the hand joints for all the frames by enforcing appearance, temporal and distance constraints. Finally, we demonstrate that our method can generate 3D hand pose training data more accurately using less manual intervention and offering more flexibility in comparison to other state-of-the-art methods.

Keywords: Hand pose annotation · 3D hand pose · Semi automatic hand pose

1 Introduction

Recent works on hand pose estimation [6,13,15,16,18,22] have increasingly used more and more training data to infer more accurate hand pose estimation results. However, generating this huge amount of training data is a very difficult task and requires handling a lot of challenges. Human hand has a complex structure with many degrees of freedom which allows it to perform dexterous movements such as touching, grasping or performing different sign language gestures. Creating a large dataset that contains these different gestures is a huge task in itself. The problem becomes even more challenging when two hands are interacting with each other as hands contain self-similar parts (fingers) which are hard to differentiate. While we can infer the pose and location of occluded rigid objects from non-occluded parts, that is not possible for highly articulated human hands. Lighting conditions and background clutter may also create problems for accurate hand pose estimation and therefore we need a large amount of training data to tackle these issues.

© Springer Nature Switzerland AG 2021
G. Bebis et al. (Eds.): ISVC 2021, LNCS 13018, pp. 362–373, 2021.
https://doi.org/10.1007/978-3-030-90436-4_29

Pioneering works [2,20] in the field of hand pose estimation have used RGB datasets to estimate 3D hand poses. However, 3D hand pose estimation from RGB images suffer from depth ambiguity since any given 2D point in the image plane can correspond to multiple 3D points in the world space. To tackle this issue, recent works [6,13,23] have used multiple RGB camera based methods where, 31–140 RGB cameras have been used to capture the hand pose from different viewpoints. These methods detect the hand keypoints from easy views to triangulate the 3D position of the keypoints and use them to annotate the hand pose in difficult, occluded views. However, these setups are very complex, requires significant resources and proper synchronization to work correctly.

With the introduction of RGB-D sensors, we can get the depth information accurately without using multiple cameras. By combining an RGB camera with a depth camera, it provides not only the color and light intensity, but also the distance of each observed pixel. Intel's Creative Interactive Gesture Camera and PrimeSense Carmine 1.09 Depth Camera have been used to create several benchmark hand pose datasets [10,15,16,18]. Some of these hand pose datasets use generative approaches [10,17] to fit a pre-defined hand model to the input depth map by minimizing some hand-crafted cost functions. Discriminative approaches, which directly localizes hand joints from an input depth map, have also been proposed. However, both of these methods still fail when there is a good amount of occlusion in the image such as Fig. 1.

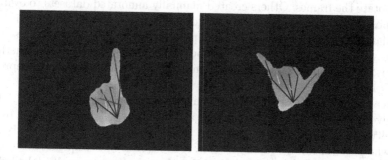

Fig. 1. Annotations errors in the MSRA15 dataset [15]

To overcome these annotation errors, semi-automatic methods have been introduced in recent years [9,12] that uses manual annotation of a small subset of frames to infer the annotations of the remaining frames. Oberweger *et al.* [9] proposed a semi-automatic pipeline where 10% of the frames are annotated in 2D by a human annotator and using these 2D annotations they estimate the 3D hand pose in all the frames. We propose an improvement over the existing pipeline by selecting a more optimized set of frames to be annotated and generate 3D hand pose for all the frames with more accuracy. Firstly, given a hand depth video, we select a small number of frames that are representative of all the frames in the depth sequence. The frames are automatically selected using a distance function and we refer these representative frames as reference frames. We then annotate the 2D hand joint locations in reference frames and find the corresponding 3D hand pose by maintaining the hand joint constraints. We generate the 3D hand pose of the remaining frames by initializing with it's closest reference frame and optimize the 3D hand poses of all the frames by enforcing appearance, distance and temporal constraints.

In summary, the main contributions of this work are:

1. We propose a simple yet effective improvement over recently introduced semi-automatic hand pose annotation methods [9,12], using which we can select the reference frames more efficiently based on a cosine distance threshold.
2. We demonstrate that using our improved reference frame selection combined with optimization of the non-reference frames based on [9] achieves better results on a depth hand pose dataset.
3. We also show that using a much smaller number of manual annotations our results are comparable with Oberweger *et al.* [9], and when we use similar number of annotations, our results are better than [9].

2   Related Work

In this section, we present a brief overview of different hand pose annotation methods. Recent works using depth cameras have used tracking based methods to annotate the frames. Others created manually annotated datasets to evaluate hand pose estimation methods against ground-truth annotations. Synthetic hand pose datasets and marker-based hand pose datasets have also been used for dealing with challenging hand articulations. Semi-automatic annotation methods have also been proposed that uses some manual supervision to generate improved annotations.

Creating datasets using manual annotation is a challenging and labor-intensive approach. These benchmarks are generally small in size due to the difficulty of annotating them. MSRA14 [10] dataset was created using six subjects who perform various rapid gestures. A 400-frame video sequence is recorded for each subject and the ground truth hand poses were manually labelled for all 2400 frames. Other datasets such as Dexter+Object [14] contains 3k frames with ground truth annotations while the EgoDexter [8] consists of 1485 frames of ground truth 2D and 3D fingertip positions. These datasets were mainly created for evaluation purposes and creating a large dataset using manual annotations is just not feasible.

Hand pose datasets that capture real hand images are limited in quantity and coverage. Therefore, additional synthetic data has been used to increase the accuracy of 3D pose estimation. Compared to real datasets, it is easier to acquire synthetic data and these annotations are more accurate in case of occlusions [5]. For these reasons, multiple synthetic image datasets have been introduced in recent years [5,7] that contain 300k to five million frames. However, synthetic hand images exhibit a certain level of deviation from real images as these do not capture the sensor characteristics such as noise and missing data that are present in real images. Also, synthetically generated images sometime produce kinematically implausible and unnatural hand poses.

Additional sensors such as data-gloves or magnetic sensors can aid automatic capture of human hands [21,22], but sometimes these methods restrict the natural motion of human hand. Less intrusive magnetic sensors [19] have been proposed, however, the sensitivity of magnetic sensors increases with their size, meaning small sensors lack in precision and are easier to be disturbed by external magnetic fields [1]. Also, some data glove annotations are not very accurate and sometimes the gloves are visible in training images which biases the learning algorithm.

Tracking based methods have been used to create popular hand pose datasets. The ICVL dataset [16] is one of the first benchmark datasets on depth images that uses 3D skeletal tracking followed by manual refinement. The dataset contains 180k training images from 10 different subjects, however the limitations of annotation accuracy have been noted in literature [9]. MSRA15 [15] is one of the more complex datasets in the field that consists of 76,500 depth images captured from 9 subjects that perform 17 different poses. It was annotated in an iterative way where an optimization method [10] and manual re-adjustment procedure alternate until convergence. These annotations are also reported to contain annotation errors such as missing finger and thumb annotations [9]. Tompson et al. [18] used 3 RGBD sensors at viewpoints separated by approximately 45 degrees surrounding the user from the front to create the NYU hand pose dataset. They used a predefined 3D hand model that was manually readjusted for poses that failed to fit perfectly. The dataset contains 80k depth frames and regarded as one of the most popular benchmarks for 3D hand pose estimation. However, this method also drifts to wrong poses, where manual correction is needed [22].

Semi-automatic methods for annotating hand poses in depth video are relatively rare. Rogez et al. [12] proposed a semi-automatic method for hand pose estimation from egocentric viewpoints. They used a chest-mounted RGB-D sensor to collect egocentric hand-object interactions and propose a semi-automatic labelling tool to annotate partially occluded hands and fingers in 3D. Oberweger et al. [9] extended this work by creating a semi-automatic pipeline for generating 3D hand pose annotations for all the frames using manual 2D annotations of a small subset of frames. Compared to this work, we propose a method that selects the number of frames to be annotated in an automatic manner, offers flexibility in terms of how many reference frames to annotate and provides more accurate 3D annotation compared with other state-of-the-art methods.

3   Creating Training Data Efficiently

Given a sequence of depth frames $\{D_i\}_{i=0}^{N}$ capturing a hand in motion, our goal is to estimate the 3D hand joints in the depth maps while eliminating as much manual effort as possible. Our approach is based on the common observation that not all the frames in a hand depth video vary significantly from each other. Therefore, if we annotate the hand joints in some frames and propagate this information to the similar frames, that should lead to better accuracy. We discuss this process in more detail in this section:

3.1   Selecting the Reference Frames

First, we want to select some reference frames to do manual annotation. A simple way to select the reference frames would be to regularly sample the video after a regular time interval, for example every n-th frame can be selected as a reference frame. However, this type of selection process might not be optimal since hand movement can be fast or slow in different part of the video. On the other hand, users tend to keep their hand still in between poses and there could be a lot of consecutive frames that are almost same.

Instead of temporal sampling, we would like to select the reference frames such that for each unannotated frame, there is a minimum degree of similarity with one of the annotated frames and select as few reference frames as possible. In other words, we need to find groups or clusters in the dataset frames so that frames belonging to each group are similar and we can select one of similar frames for doing manual annotation work. TSNE [4] is used to visualize very high dimensional dataset in a low-dimensional space where similar objects in high dimensional space are grouped together in the low-dimensional space. We show the TSNE plot for a synthetic hand pose dataset called Blender [11],

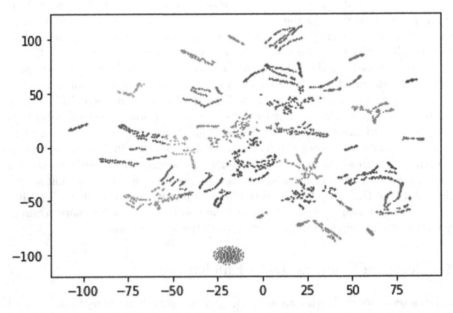

Fig. 2. TSNE plot for Blender Dataset where each dot represents a hand frame and colors encode the temporal order. Consecutive dots in the TSNE plot represents similar hand poses, and we can identify temporal changes in hand articulation as all blue dots do not belong to the same cluster. (Color figure online)

which contains 3040 depth frames of single hand articulation in Fig. 2 and frames belonging to a single TSNE cluster are shown in Fig. 3.

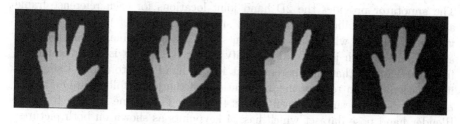

Fig. 3. Visualization of consecutive dots that belong to the same TSNE cluster

Although the TSNE plot validates our assumption that some of the hand poses in the dataset are indeed similar, we can not use the centroid of the visualized clusters as reference frames because sometimes TSNE moves far away points close to each other. Also, we can not assume the relative size of clusters from the TSNE plot as TSNE tends to expand dense clusters and shrink sparse ones.

To find the similarity between frames, we define a distance function on the depth frames. We use cosine distance to measure the similarity between frames and use ρ as a threshold.

$$\forall i \ \forall j \ s.t. \ i \neq j, d(D_i, D_j) = cos(\theta) = \frac{D_i . D_j}{||D_i||||D_j||} \tag{1}$$

Here, D_i and D_j are two depth maps, and they are considered similar if $d(D_i, D_j) < \rho$. We start by selecting the first frame as a reference frame and iterate over the whole set of frames. Every time the distance of the next frame is greater than the threshold ρ, the next frame is considered as the reference frame. We then find the closest frame of the newly added reference frame and based on the threshold we either add it to the list of reference frames or discard it for doing manual annotation. If we find frames within ρ distance of a reference frame then we know that these frames are significantly similar to the selected reference frame and therefore we do not need manual annotation for these frames. This reference frame selection process is illustrated in Eq. 2, where, D_{i-1} is the previous reference frame and D_i is the current frame being compared.

$$R = \begin{cases} 1 \ if \ d(D_{i-1}, D_i) > \rho \\ 0 \ else \end{cases} \tag{2}$$

Selecting the reference frames in this way has more flexibility as we can change the ρ threshold to select different number of reference frames. A low distance threshold would increase the number of reference frames, this would not harm the accuracy of the annotations per say but would drastically increase manual annotation work. On the other hand, a high distance threshold would pick far too less frames which would not be representative of the entire dataset and could yield sub-par results.

3.2 Initializing the 3D Joint Location in the Reference Frames

After selecting the reference frames we need to label them by a human annotator. The annotator provides the 2D hand joint locations for each reference frame alongside the visibility information as shown in Fig. 4 (left). Joints that are visible are marked with dots, while joints that are not visible are marked with a triangle. For each joint we also specify whether the joint is closer or farther from the camera than the parent joint in the hand skeleton tree. Using this information we can recover the 3D locations of the joints following Oberweger et al. [9] and the result is shown in Fig. 4 (right). This frame is taken from the Blender hand pose dataset which has 24 keypoints as shown on both pictures. The annotation tool can be easily modified to annotate 21 or 16 joints as needed.

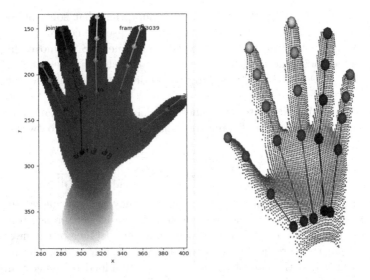

Fig. 4. Initialization of the 3D hand joint locations in Reference frames

3.3 Initializing the 3D Joint Locations in the Remaining Frames

The previous section computes the 3D location of hand joints in the reference frames. Now we need to propagate this information to the remaining frames to infer the 3D hand keypoints in all the frames. I is the set of reference frames for which the 3D location of the joints have been initialized in the previous section. So, we check for a frame $\hat{c}$ not initialized yet and find it's closest reference frame $\hat{a} \in I$. D_c and D_a are depth maps for a non-reference frame and a reference frame respectively.

$$\begin{bmatrix} \hat{c} \\ \hat{a} \end{bmatrix} = \underset{c \in [1;N]; a \in I}{argmin} \; d(D_c, D_a) \tag{3}$$

To align the an unannotated frame with it's closest reference frame we use SIFT-Flow [3]. SIFT-Flow aligns an image to it's nearest neighbor by comparing pixel-wise SIFT features between two images. For each pixel in the reference frame, SIFT-Flow divides it's neighborhood into a 4X4 cell array, quantizes the orientation into 8 bins in each cell and obtains a 4X4X8 = 128-dimensional vector as the SIFT representation. Using this 128-dimensional SIFT vector, we map the 2D hand keypoints in frame $\hat{a}$ to 2D hand keypoints in unannotated frame $\hat{c}$. We backproject these 2D keypoints on the Depth map, D_c to get an initial estimate of the location of 3D hand keypoints.

Fig. 5. SIFTFlow optimization of a non-reference frame in the Blender Dataset; on the left the initialization is wrong for the thumb finger, and by using it's closest reference frame the annotation is corrected on the right picture

We refine the 3D hand keypoints further by minimizing the appearance difference to it's closest reference frame while maintaining the known hand bone constraints. As the closest reference frames were annotated by a human annotator, using this manual supervision we can resolve some ambiguities in the closest unannotated frames as shown in Fig. 5. Thus, we can refine the 3D hand keypoints in the remaining frames using 3D hand keypoints of reference frames following the works of [3,9].

3.4   Global Optimization

The previous step already optimizes the remaining frames based on their closest reference frames. However, each frame is processed independently and the optimized keypoints may have appearance difference with the next frame in hand depth video. In this step, we need to make sure that consecutive frames have some degree of continuity between them while maintaining consistency with closest reference frames. Also, the 3D hand keypoints of reference frames must remain consistent with their manual 2D annotations. So, we perform a global optimization over all the 3D joint locations for all the frames following the pipeline of Oberweger *et al.* [9] to optimize the keypoints further.

4   Evaluations

We implement our improved semi-automatic method on a synthetic hand pose dataset called Blender and compare our results with the results of Oberweger *et al.* [9] on the same dataset. We show quantitative comparison in the next section by calculating the mean, median and maximum keypoint error in millimeter (mm). Finally, we show that our semi-automatic hand pose annotation pipeline achieves similar results as [9] while using half as many reference frames, and surpasses the accuracy of [9] while using few less reference frames.

4.1   Evaluation on Synthetic Data

The Blender dataset contains 3040 frames of single hand movement from a starting position. We apply our proposed reference frame selection method based on cosine distance with a distance threshold ρ. Using $\rho = 0.045$, we selected 141 reference frames from the 3040 frames of the Blender dataset. We plot the TSNE diagram with the selected reference frames in Fig. 6. The TSNE embedding for all the frames in the Blender dataset are shown in 'Blue' and the selected reference frames are marked in 'Orange'.

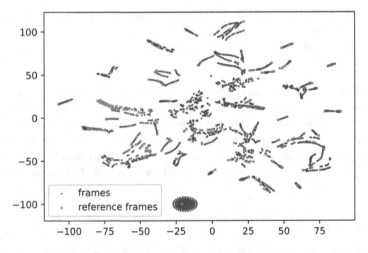

Fig. 6. Reference frames selected using our improved method, are plotted on the TSNE diagram where most of the clusters (made of consecutive blue dots) have at least one reference frame (orange dots) in them. Using the manual annotation of these reference frames (orange dots), nearby frames with blue dots can be annotated more accurately. (Color figure online)

From the TSNE plot, it is evident that by selecting only a small percentage of frames as reference frames ($141/3040 \approx 5\%$) we have managed to select at least one reference frame from most of the clusters in the TSNE plot. So, we can reliably say that our selected reference frames are representative of all the frames of the Blender dataset. By selecting more reference frames, we can cover the sparsely represented clusters more densely, which should result in improved accuracy at the expense of extra annotations.

After selecting the reference frames, we only use the 2D annotation of the reference frames and estimate the 3D joint locations of all the frames in the dataset. Then, we compare our estimated 3D keypoints with the ground truth 3D keypoints and calculate the mean, median and maximum error. We also compare the results for similar number of reference frames (we use 288 reference frames compared with 10% or 304 reference frames used by [9]) and show the results on Table 1. We achieve mean error of 4.69 mm and median error of 3.35 mm compared with 4.91 mm and 3.68 mm achieved by [9] and therefore we can say that our improved reference selection has lead to better accuracy as shown in Table 1.

Table 1. Comparison of final results on the Blender Dataset

	Our method	Oberweger *et al.* [9]
Mean error (mm)	4.69	4.91
Max error (mm)	84.33	73.65
Median error (mm)	3.35	3.68

4.2 Evaluation on Different Number of Reference Frame Selection

One of the advantages of using a distance threshold based reference frame selection is that, we can select a variable number of reference frames using a different cosine distance threshold ρ. To demonstrate our results with different distance thresholds, we have selected 3 different ρ thresholds such as 0.05, 0.045 and 0.035 on the Blender datasets, which results in 73, 141, 288 reference frames consecutively. We compare our results of different reference frame selection with 10% reference frames selected based on [9] in Table 2.

As we can see from the table, the annotation results improved with the selection of more reference frames, i.e. with more human annotation work we can always get better results. However, we got comparably good results with Oberweger *et al.* [9] while selecting approximately 5% of the frames as reference frames and our results are better than [9] while using a few less reference frames.

Table 2. Evaluation on blender dataset for different number of reference frames

	~2% frames (73 frames)	~5% frames (141 frames)	~10% frames (288 frames)	Oberweger *et al.* [9] (304 frames)
Mean error (mm)	5.79	5.50	4.69	4.91
Max error (mm)	76.79	78.98	84.33	73.65
Median error (mm)	4.60	4.17	3.35	3.68

5   Conclusion and Future Work

Training data is the backbone of the deep learning methods being used for hand pose estimation. Our method with improved reference frame selection can be used to annotate all the frames in a depth video with reliable accuracy. This saves time compared to manually annotating all the frames and provides better accuracy than inferring the annotations without any manual supervision. Moreover, this pipeline of annotating frames using a representative subset can be applied for other articulated structures such as human bodies. Finally, we have demonstrated our semi-automatic method on a hand pose dataset containing single hand images and where hand segmentation was easy. As a future work, it remains to be seen whether this method can be extended to the more challenging double-handed poses or for annotating hand-object interactions.

References

1. Chen, W., et al.: A survey on hand pose estimation with wearable sensors and computer-vision-based methods. Sensors **20**(4), 1074 (2020)
2. de La Gorce, M., Fleet, D.J., Paragios, N.: Model-based 3D hand pose estimation from monocular video. IEEE Trans. Pattern Anal. Mach. Intell. **33**(9), 1793–1805 (2011)
3. Liu, C., Yuen, J., Torralba, A.: Sift flow: dense correspondence across scenes and its applications. IEEE Trans. Pattern Anal. Mach. Intell. **33**(5), 978–994 (2010)
4. Maaten, L.v.d., Hinton, G.: Visualizing data using t-SNE. J. Mach. Learn. Res. **9**, 2579–2605 (2008)
5. Malik, J., et al.: DeepHPS: end-to-end estimation of 3D hand pose and shape by learning from synthetic depth. In: 2018 International Conference on 3D Vision (3DV), pp. 110–119. IEEE (2018)
6. Moon, G., Yu, S.I., Wen, H., Shiratori, T., Lee, K.M.: InterHand2. 6M: a dataset and baseline for 3D interacting hand pose estimation from a single RGB image. arXiv preprint arXiv:2008.09309 (2020)
7. Mueller, F., et al.: GANerated hands for real-time 3D hand tracking from monocular RGB. In: Proceedings of the IEEE Conference on Computer Vision and Pattern Recognition, pp. 49–59 (2018)
8. Mueller, F., Mehta, D., Sotnychenko, O., Sridhar, S., Casas, D., Theobalt, C.: Real-time hand tracking under occlusion from an egocentric RGB-D sensor. In: Proceedings of the IEEE International Conference on Computer Vision Workshops, pp. 1284–1293 (2017)
9. Oberweger, M., Riegler, G., Wohlhart, P., Lepetit, V.: Efficiently creating 3D training data for fine hand pose estimation. In: Proceedings of the IEEE Conference on Computer Vision and Pattern Recognition, pp. 4957–4965 (2016)
10. Qian, C., Sun, X., Wei, Y., Tang, X., Sun, J.: Realtime and robust hand tracking from depth. In: Proceedings of the IEEE Conference on Computer Vision and Pattern Recognition, pp. 1106–1113 (2014)
11. Riegler, G., Ferstl, D., Rüther, M., Bischof, H.: A framework for articulated hand pose estimation and evaluation. In: Paulsen, R.R., Pedersen, K.S. (eds.) SCIA 2015. LNCS, vol. 9127, pp. 41–52. Springer, Cham (2015). https://doi.org/10.1007/978-3-319-19665-7_4

12. Rogez, G., Khademi, M., Supančič III, J.S., Montiel, J.M.M., Ramanan, D.: 3D hand pose detection in egocentric RGB-D images. In: Agapito, L., Bronstein, M.M., Rother, C. (eds.) ECCV 2014. LNCS, vol. 8925, pp. 356–371. Springer, Cham (2015). https://doi.org/10.1007/978-3-319-16178-5_25

13. Simon, T., Joo, H., Matthews, I., Sheikh, Y.: Hand keypoint detection in single images using multiview bootstrapping. In: Proceedings of the IEEE Conference on Computer Vision and Pattern Recognition, pp. 1145–1153 (2017)

14. Sridhar, S., Mueller, F., Zollhöfer, M., Casas, D., Oulasvirta, A., Theobalt, C.: Real-time joint tracking of a hand manipulating an object from RGB-D input. In: Leibe, B., Matas, J., Sebe, N., Welling, M. (eds.) ECCV 2016. LNCS, vol. 9906, pp. 294–310. Springer, Cham (2016). https://doi.org/10.1007/978-3-319-46475-6_19

15. Sun, X., Wei, Y., Liang, S., Tang, X., Sun, J.: Cascaded hand pose regression. In: Proceedings of the IEEE Conference on Computer Vision and Pattern Recognition, pp. 824–832 (2015)

16. Tang, D., Jin Chang, H., Tejani, A., Kim, T.K.: Latent regression forest: structured estimation of 3D articulated hand posture. In: Proceedings of the IEEE Conference on Computer Vision and Pattern Recognition, pp. 3786–3793 (2014)

17. Taylor, J., et al.: Efficient and precise interactive hand tracking through joint, continuous optimization of pose and correspondences. ACM Trans. Graph. (TOG) 35(4), 1–12 (2016)

18. Tompson, J., Stein, M., Lecun, Y., Perlin, K.: Real-time continuous pose recovery of human hands using convolutional networks. ACM Trans. Graph. (ToG) 33(5), 1–10 (2014)

19. Wetzler, A., Slossberg, R., Kimmel, R.: Rule of thumb: deep derotation for improved fingertip detection. arXiv preprint arXiv:1507.05726 (2015)

20. Wu, Y., Lin, J., Huang, T.S.: Analyzing and capturing articulated hand motion in image sequences. IEEE Trans. Pattern Anal. Mach. Intell. 27(12), 1910–1922 (2005)

21. Xu, C., Nanjappa, A., Zhang, X., Cheng, L.: Estimate hand poses efficiently from single depth images. Int. J. Comput. Vis. 116(1), 21–45 (2016)

22. Yuan, S., Ye, Q., Stenger, B., Jain, S., Kim, T.K.: BigHand2. 2M benchmark: hand pose dataset and state of the art analysis. In: Proceedings of the IEEE Conference on Computer Vision and Pattern Recognition, pp. 4866–4874 (2017)

23. Zimmermann, C., Ceylan, D., Yang, J., Russell, B., Argus, M., Brox, T.: Freihand: a dataset for markerless capture of hand pose and shape from single RGB images. In: Proceedings of the IEEE/CVF International Conference on Computer Vision, pp. 813–822 (2019)

FamSearch: Visual Analysis
of Genealogical Data

Michael Burch[1,3]($\boxtimes$) (ID), Günter Wallner[2,3] (ID), Huub van de Wetering[3] (ID),
Shahrukh Tufail[3], Linda Zandt-Sloot[3], Stasius Gladkis[3], Minji Hong[3],
and Carlo Lepelaars[3]

[1] University of Applied Sciences of the Grisons, Chur, Switzerland
michael.burch@fhgr.ch
[2] Johannes Kepler University Linz, Linz, Austria
guenter.wallner@jku.at
[3] Eindhoven University of Technology, Eindhoven, The Netherlands
{h.v.d.wetering,s.tufail,l.zandt-sloot,s.gladkis,
m.hong,c.lepelaars}@tue.nl

Abstract. This paper describes an interactive visualization tool consisting of several views offering different perspectives on genealogical data that is stored and maintained by the Brabants Historical Information Center (BHIC). The dataset consists of several attributes, static as well as dynamic ones, containing information about several million people having lived in the Netherlands. With the tool, we can gain insights in family histories and build, confirm, and reject hypotheses, or search for one's own relatives having lived in that region. Genealogical, temporal, and geographical relations can be investigated and linked to each other to identify correlations. Moreover, family events such as marriages, divorces, births, deaths, and similar can be explored. To support these tasks the tool provides several algorithms and interactive visualizations that enable data exploration. Visualizations include, amongst others, timeline diagrams, pedigree trees, population pyramids, sunbursts, and word clouds. We illustrate the usefulness of the tool by showcasing which and how patterns and anomalies can be found.

Keywords: Genealogical data · Information visualization ·
Interactions · Diagrammatic representations

1 Introduction

This paper discusses the development and application of *FamSearch*, an interactive visualization tool for genealogical data. To test the tool we applied it to a large dataset consisting of several million records of people having lived in *Brabant*, a region in the Netherlands. The data is publicly available and is stored and maintained by BHIC, Brabants' Historical Information Center [1]. The BHIC dataset is a collection of genealogical registers of people in the region

© Springer Nature Switzerland AG 2021
G. Bebis et al. (Eds.): ISVC 2021, LNCS 13018, pp. 374–385, 2021.
https://doi.org/10.1007/978-3-030-90436-4_30

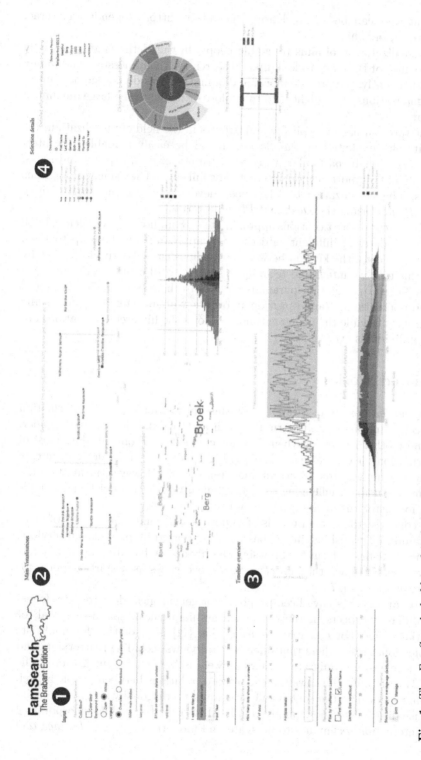

Fig. 1. The *FamSearch* dashboard including the input window (1), visualizations window (2), a timeline window (3), and a selection details window (4). The main visualizations include the scatterplot family overview, word cloud, and population pyramid.

of Brabant that can be accessed from the website https://opendata.picturae. com/organization/bhic.

The visualization tool aims to enable people in the Netherlands, especially in the province of Brabant, to look up and search for their ancestors and family histories. Currently, the provided local and online services do not support interactive visualizations that might help to explore or navigate the large amount of family data.

As the target users are typically non-experts in the field of visualization, the visual variables exploited by *FamSearch* should be easily readable and interpretable [7,19,20]. In particular, to cover a variety of data aspects and tasks, the tool should support several interactively linked and well-known diagrams and plots. The visualization tool has been developed using the programming language *Python* using the *Dash* and *Plotly* libraries.

As of now, the dataset contains approximately 18 million records such as birth and marriage dates of different subjects from approximately 1700 up to 1900. Using these records, the kinship between individuals can be derived. To visually support this task we integrated techniques such as word clouds [4,15], pedigree timelines [9], and population pyramids [10], and others (see Fig. 1). The word cloud and population pyramid provide an overview about name frequencies and age distributions while the pedigree timeline shows the hierarchical relationships between individuals over time.

2   Related Work

Genealogical data exists in a variety of forms but the major one is information about people and associated attributes such as birth and death dates, gender, father and mother names, or when they got married [5]. From this data most of the information for generating a family tree or pedigree can be derived, in case the data is complete, free of errors, and linkable [8]. However, in most of the situations it remains challenging to algorithmically present a quick and reliable solution for historians or the general public.

Consequently, the human user is of importance to guide the process of identifying family relationships, in the best case supported by professional services, either in a text-based form for browsing the history or based on an interactive graphical user interface that provides visual overviews as a starting point for further explorations [17].

Several approaches have been proposed for genealogical data to date, focusing on different aspects in the data such as hierarchical, spatio-temporal, or multivariate ones. For example, *GenealogyVis* [11] is a solution for hobbyists and professional researchers that offers several views including scatterplots and matrix-, stream-, and migration views as well as hierarchy visualizations. The *TimeNets* technique [9] shows the evolution of relations between people as well as special events. The *GeneaQuilts* [3] system uses a diagonally arranged matrix-based visualization to show family relationships over time while incorporating several interaction techniques to navigate and filter the data. The *Lineage* tool supports tree-like multivariate visualizations [13] for examining diseases based on genealogical data. Ball [2] introduced a family-centric perspective that also focuses on communities. While the temporal aspect is a crucial concept in this approach, it does not provide a view on population distributions based on certain attribute characteristics. *Shakespear* [16], on the other hand, also takes into account the migration behavior of ancestors and relatives.

The pedigree timeline [9] can verify and show ancestors whereas the traditional family tree [12] can help to define parent-child relationships. A pedigree chart [6] is a form of node-link diagram that presents family information in the form of an easily readable chart of ancestors from one generation to the next. Nonetheless, a pedigree chart does not tell the whole story as many features about the individuals are missing. For instance, it does not show how many marriages a person had. As a consequence, we support a sunburst-like diagram [18,22] to show the person under investigation as a focus-and-context representation. Population pyramids [10] are useful for showing changes or differences in population patterns. This can be seen as two histograms, one for each gender, joined back-to-back.

3   FamSearch Visualization Tool

This section describes the interactive visualization tool and typical user tasks.

3.1   Graphical User Interface

Figure 1 shows the dashboard of *FamSearch* which makes it possible to filter the data and reconfigure the dashboard (1 - input window), provides different visualizations based on the input (2 - visualization window), offers a timeline giving an overview of the investigated period (3 - timeline window), and has a window displaying details about the selected user (4 - selection details window).

The input window (1) offers, among others, the option to change the color scheme of the dashboard from a standard white background to a dark one [14]. The users can also choose a color-blind variant.

The visualization window (2) includes three types of diagrams: an overview scatterplot, a word cloud, and a population pyramid. Users can choose which one of these visualizations should be displayed as large main visualization.

The timeline window (3) shows two graphs: The upper one displays the most frequent first/last names over time. Below, a histogram shows all births and deaths over time split on gender. The selected period is highlighted.

The selection details window (4) shows more specific information about the selected birth/death dates, and to whom the persons are married. Furthermore, a sunburst and a pedigree timeline visualize the family relationships.

The dashboard has been designed to support two common tasks as follows:

Task 1 - Finding Ancestors. To assist users in finding their ancestors, the data can be filtered on last name or the first or last name of their known ancestor. It is also possible to filter on parts of a name only. Users can also filter the data using the birth and death dates of their relatives by selecting the respective year range for the visualizations. The scatterplot will then show all the possible individuals who were born or have died within this period. The number of displayed labels is adjusted based on the amount of data points to keep them legible.

By clicking on a data point in the scatterplot more detailed information about that individual is displayed in the selection details window. As the selection details show information about family members (mother, father, children), the users are supported in tracing their ancestors. The word cloud visualization displays the most frequently occurring names that fit the search of the users which can be helpful for recognizing a name and, in turn, narrow the search.

Task 2 - History of Family Name. The *FamSearch* dashboard offers multiple options for exploring the history of a family name. First, the users can select a family name in the input panel specifying that they only want to see names that match the input precisely.

For the distribution of a family or first name in a specific year, the users can select the population pyramid and a year of interest. Moreover, the users can opt for the population pyramid to show the marriage-age distribution instead. By selecting the first name option for the word cloud, users can see what the most common first names for a selected surname are. The line plot in the timeline window shows the top 10 most popular first names for the family name and its occurrence frequency over time. Note, that these ten names may not match with the information presented in the word cloud as the word cloud shows the most common names of the specified year range whereas the timeline plot shows the information over the whole timeline.

3.2 Visualizations

The tool includes eight types of interactively linked visualizations.

Scatterplot. This visualization provides an overview of the individuals based on the input selection provided by the users. It shows the birth years/months (diamond-shaped for women and cross-shaped for men). The x-axis represents the year of birth or death and the y-axis represents the month of birth or death (Fig. 2). When an individual is selected by clicking on a data point, the parents or children of this person are highlighted.

Fig. 2. A scatterplot for the time period of 1811–1887. The selected individual ("Geertrui Berg") is highlighted in green, her mother in pink, her father in blue, and her children in yellow. (Color figure online)

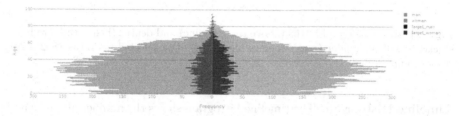

Fig. 3. A population pyramid showing the age distribution of individuals whose name starts with a 'B' for the year 1852. Women are shown on the left (pink in general, red for target name), men on the right (blue for general, black for target name). (Color figure online)

Population Pyramid. The population pyramid shows the age and gender distribution of the individuals in the dataset in a specific year (i.e. the first year of the selected period). The population pyramid displays two histograms side-by-side, one for women and one for men, with the age (group) on the y-axis and the frequency on the x-axis (see Fig. 3). This plot can show the age distribution of the input name on top of the age distribution of the general population. This enables the user to observe the proportion of the dataset that is selected by using an input name. By deselecting the distribution of the general population the distribution of the input name can be examined in more detail.

Word Cloud. This visualization gives an overview about the frequency of occurrence of either first and/or last names within a selected period. Specific inputs for the word cloud include the option to display solely first and/or last names and the number of words.

Timeline Name Frequency. The timeline name frequency shows the frequency of occurrence of a name over time (see Fig. 4). Users can deselect one or more names to make the plot more readable. This view is similar to the *Baby Name Voyager* [21] which uses a stacked area chart instead of a line graph.

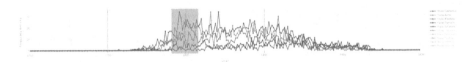

Fig. 4. Timeline overview of name frequency showing the top 5 most occurring first names starting with "Maria", therefore also including double first names. The selected period is 1791–1808.

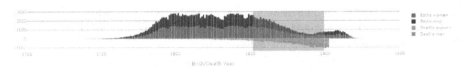

Fig. 5. Histograms for all births (above the zero line) and deaths (below the zero line), stacked based on gender (pink/women, blue/men). The selected period is 1852–1899. (Color figure online)

Timeline Histogram. The timeline histogram shows the number of births and deaths (color-coded by gender, binned by age) per year from the1700 s up to 1900s. The currently selected years are highlighted. From this visualization the population trend can be roughly observed. Besides, it also shows the distribution of the available data in the database (Fig. 5).

Detailed Information Table. The detailed information table shows the person's ID, first name, last name, gender, birth year, death year, whom they were married to, and when their wedding took place.

Sunburst Diagram. The sunburst diagram (cf. Fig. 7) shows the hierarchical information in a radial structure, with the top of the hierarchy (the selected person) at the center and deeper levels farther away from the center (children and grandchildren).

Pedigree Chart. In the pedigree chart (Fig. 6), the hierarchical information is represented with lines over time. In the center the selected person is shown. Above the selected person their paternal maternal ancestors (mother and grandparents on the mother's side) are shown and below the paternal ancestors (father and grandparents on the father's side). The main aim of this plot is to show parent-child relationships.

3.3 Interaction Techniques

Apart from basic interactions such as zooming and panning, the following interactions have been implemented in *FamSearch*.

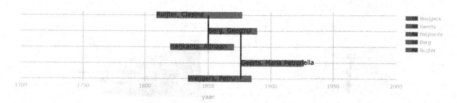

Fig. 6. A pedigree chart for the selected person "Maria Petronella Geerts" showing both parents and her maternal grandparents.

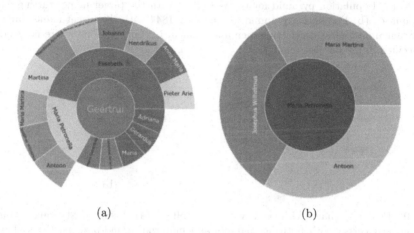

(a)   (b)

Fig. 7. (a) Sunburst for "Geertrui Berg" (1850), showing her children and grand-children. (b) Sunburst after selecting the daughter "Maria Petronella Geerts" (1876) of "Geertrui Berg", showing only the daughter and her children.

Select and Reconfigure. Users can select single data points of interest and can reconfigure the spatial arrangement of the visualizations. Selection can be performed based on name, year, single data points, people, and the layout.

Encoding. *FamSearch* offers possibilities to change the encoding of the data. This includes three color modes (white, dark, and color-blind). In addition, the dashboard gives the users the option to choose which of the visualizations should be shown as the largest plot. The size of the main panel can be altered in preset steps from "really small" to "large". Likewise, the font size of labels can be increased or decreased.

Tooltips. When hovering over the diagrams, tooltips display the coordinates and the ID of an element. Moreover, a click on an element generates a table, a sunburst diagram, and a pedigree chart on the right side of the dashboard which show more detailed information about the selected person. The population pyramid shows the frequency of an age group when hovering over the bars. The timeline name frequency plot shows the year that the user hovers over and

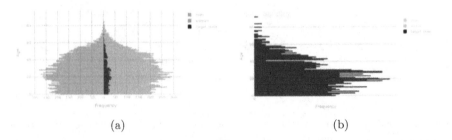

(a)   (b)

Fig. 8. (a) Population pyramid for the year 1844 with the target name starting with "Johannes". (b) Population pyramid for the year 1844 with the target name starting with "Johannes" after deselecting men and women, i.e. only persons where no gender is specified in the dataset remain.

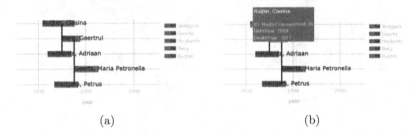

(a)   (b)

Fig. 9. Pedigree chart with and without tooltip: (a) Pedigree showing "Maria Petronella Geerts" with both her parents and maternal grand-parents. (b) Pedigree showing "Maria Petronella Geerts" and both her parents and maternal grand-parents, while hovering over her grandmother "Clasina Ruijter".

the exact amount of births with the selected name in that year. The timeline histogram shows the year the user is currently hovering over to make it easier to precisely select a time period. The sunburst shows the last name and year of birth on hovering while only the first name is displayed in the chart itself. Lastly, the pedigree shows the ID as well as birth and death year to make it easier to locate someone in the plot (see Fig. 9).

4   Application Examples

In this section, small application examples of *FamSearch* are discussed which also relate to some extent to the tasks defined earlier.

4.1   Popularity of a Name over Time

In this use case we will show how the tool can be applied to investigate the popularity of a name over time. In our case we have chosen "Johannes" – a very popular name throughout the time period covered by the database. The three most frequent spelling variations of the name are "Johannes", "Joannes",

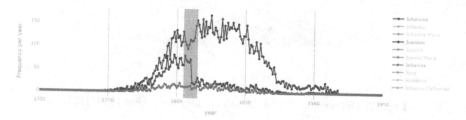

Fig. 10. Frequency of the names "Johannes", "Joannes", and "Johannis" over the years, with the highlighted period 1805–1815 showing the sudden drop in popularity of the spelling "Johannis".

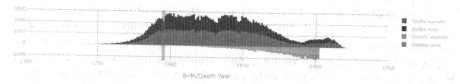

Fig. 11. Overview of the births and deaths with the selected time period of 1794–1796.

and "Johannis" as identified through a word cloud. As we can see from Fig. 10, the name went a bit out of fashion around 1805, only to become even more popular after approximately 5 years. The frequency of occurrence of the spelling "Joannes" dropped around 1810 (cf. Fig. 12). The spelling "Johannis" was never as popular as the two other variants, it stayed quite constant initially but almost completely died out after 1873, with only one more entry in 1894.

4.2 Dips in the Birth Frequency

Looking closer at the birth-death timeline visualization as shown in Fig. 11 we can witness several dips in the number of births (1795, 1828–1832, 1844–1845). The first dip at 1795 aligns with when the Austrians were driven out of the Netherlands by the French in 1794 at the Battle of Fleurus. The second dip between 1828 and 1832 (Fig. 12) aligns with the 'July Revolution' taking place in France in 1830. This revolution, in turn, led to the start of the 'Belgian Revolution' on August 25th of the same year, ending with the independence of Brussels from the United Kingdom of the Netherlands.

4.3 French First Names

At the start of the dataset (approximately 1750) French names such as "Jean", "Pierre", and "Antoine" are quite common but their popularity drops around the time that France gets into financial and political problems (1787). In 1787 the French minister of Finance is fired, France is basically bankrupt. Two years later the French revolution starts on the 14th of July. The names almost disappear after the French revolution. We hypothesize that French names got less popular due to these reasons.

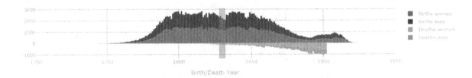

Fig. 12. Overview of births/deaths in the time period 1828–1832.

5 Conclusion and Future Work

In this paper, we presented a tool for visualizing the hierarchical relationships and features of genealogical data. The main purposes of the tool are to search for ancestors, explore family histories, and to visually analyze the popularity of names over time. Towards this end, different visualizations and interaction techniques were included to provide a certain number of perspectives on the data. However, some improvements can be made. Also a user evaluation is planned to investigate whether our interactive visualization tool is useful and understandable. Such an evaluation might be conducted for experts and non-experts from both fields, i.e. genealogy and visualization.

References

1. Brabants' historisch informatie centrum (2020). https://www.bhic.nl/english
2. Ball, R.: Visualizing genealogy through a family-centric perspective. Inf. Vis. **16**(1), 74–89 (2017)
3. Bezerianos, A., Dragicevic, P., Fekete, J., Bae, J., Watson, B.: GeneaQuilts: a system for exploring large genealogies. IEEE Trans. Vis. Comput. Graph. **16**(6), 1073–1081 (2010)
4. Burch, M., Lohmann, S., Pompe, D., Weiskopf, D.: Prefix tag clouds. In: Banissi, E., et al. (eds.) Proceedings of 17th International Conference on Information Visualisation, IV, pp. 45–50. IEEE Computer Society (2013)
5. Chen, Y.-L., Lu, J.-T.: Mining inheritance rules from genealogical data. In: Li, Q., Wang, G., Feng, L. (eds.) WAIM 2004. LNCS, vol. 3129, pp. 569–578. Springer, Heidelberg (2004). https://doi.org/10.1007/978-3-540-27772-9_57
6. Garcia-Giordano, L., Paraiso-Medina, S., Alonso-Calvo, R., Fernández-Martínez, F.J., Maojo, V.: genoDraw: a web tool for developing pedigree diagrams using the standardized human pedigree nomenclature integrated with biomedical vocabularies. In: Proceedings of the American Medical Informatics Association Annual Symposium, AMIA. AMIA (2019)
7. Healey, C.G., Enns, J.T.: Attention and visual memory in visualization and computer graphics. IEEE Trans. Vis. Comput. Graph. **18**(7), 1170–1188 (2012)
8. Ivie, S., Pixton, B., Giraud-Carrier, C.G.: Metric-based data mining model for genealogical record linkage. In: Proceedings of the IEEE International Conference on Information Reuse and Integration, IRI, pp. 538–543. IEEE Systems, Man, and Cybernetics Society (2007)
9. Kim, N.W., Card, S.K., Heer, J.: Tracing genealogical data with TimeNets. In: Santucci, G. (ed.) Proceedings of the International Conference on Advanced Visual Interfaces, AVI, pp. 241–248. ACM Press (2010)

10. Korenjak-Cerne, S., Kejzar, N., Batagelj, V.: Clustering of population pyramids. Informatica (Slovenia) **32**(2), 157–167 (2008)
11. Liu, Y., Dai, S., Wang, C., Zhou, Z., Qu, H.: GenealogyVis: a system for visual analysis of multidimensional genealogical data. IEEE Trans. Hum.-Mach. Syst. **47**(6), 873–885 (2017)
12. de Moura Borges, J.L.C.: A contextual family tree visualization design. Inf. Vis. **18**(4), 439–454 (2019)
13. Nobre, C., Gehlenborg, N., Coon, H., Lex, A.: Lineage: visualizing multivariate clinical data in genealogy graphs. IEEE Trans. Vis. Comput. Graph. **25**(3), 1543–1558 (2019)
14. Pedersen, L.A., Einarsson, S.S., Rikheim, F.A., Sandnes, F.E.: User interfaces in dark mode during daytime – improved productivity or just cool-looking? In: Antona, M., Stephanidis, C. (eds.) HCII 2020. LNCS, vol. 12188, pp. 178–187. Springer, Cham (2020). https://doi.org/10.1007/978-3-030-49282-3_13
15. Seifert, C., Kump, B., Kienreich, W., Granitzer, G., Granitzer, M.: On the beauty and usability of tag clouds. In: Proceedings of 12th International Conference on Information Visualisation, IV, pp. 17–25. IEEE Computer Society (2008)
16. Shakespear, D.: Interactive genealogy explorer: visualization of migration of ancestors and relatives. In: Braake, S.T., Fokkens, A., Sluijter, R., Declerck, T., Wandl-Vogt, E. (eds.) Proceedings of the First Conference on Biographical Data in a Digital World. CEUR Workshop Proceedings, vol. 1399, pp. 94–100. CEUR-WS.org (2015)
17. Spence, R.: Information Visualization: Design for Interaction, 2 edn. Pearson/Prentice Hall, Harlow, Essex (2007)
18. Stasko, J.T., Zhang, E.: Focus+context display and navigation techniques for enhancing radial, space-filling hierarchy visualizations. In: Mackinlay, J.D., Roth, S.F., Keim, D.A. (eds.) Proceedings of the IEEE Symposium on Information Visualization (INFOVIS 2000), pp. 57–65. IEEE Computer Society (2000)
19. Ware, C.: Information Visualization: Perception for Design. Morgan Kaufmann, Burlington (2004)
20. Ware, C.: Visual Thinking: for Design. Morgan Kaufmann Series in Interactive Technologies, Paperback (2008)
21. Wild Sky Media: Baby name voyager (2021). https://www.babynamewizard.com/voyager. Accessed Sep 2021
22. Yang, J., Ward, M.O., Rundensteiner, E.A., Patro, A.: Interring: a visual interface for navigating and manipulating hierarchies. Inf. Vis. **2**(1), 16–30 (2003)

Hierarchical Sankey Diagram: Design and Evaluation

William P. Porter$^{(\boxtimes)}$, Conor P. Murphy, Dane R. Williams,
Brendan J. O'Handley, and Chaoli Wang

University of Notre Dame, Notre Dame, USA
wporter2@nd.edu

Abstract. We present the hierarchical Sankey diagram that aims to augment the original Sankey diagram by enabling users to examine inflow links and levels of detail through four different variants. We provide the details of our design along with results on a student course performance dataset. Finally, the effectiveness of the four variants for the hierarchical Sankey diagram is evaluated via a user study.

Keywords: Hierarchical Sankey diagram · Inflow · Level-of-detail

1 Introduction

Sankey diagrams and their variants [1,4,8,9,11–15] have been an area of significant research in data visualization and utilized to study different applications [2,3,5–7,10]. An important question researchers have studied along this topic is how to convey more information concerning data flow. Existing layouts attempt to improve the original Sankey diagram through various modifications. Riehmann et al. [8] presented several concepts for improving a static Sankey diagram with interactive features. Among these concepts is the ability to adjust grouping and level of detail on nodes, making it possible to drill down on a node to see how the flows pass through the subnodes contained in the hierarchy. Furthermore, their system enhances the Sankey diagram by introducing *flow tracing*, enabling users to select a node so that the contributing links are highlighted and moved to the foreground. Another interactive modification to Sankey diagrams was given by Kosara et al. [4], where a parallel sets layout is utilized and then improved by interactive queries. To facilitate hierarchical analysis, they grouped nodes into a single combined node. This design works similarly to the example given in [8], except that instead of breaking down a hierarchy into more specific nodes, the specific nodes can be combined into a larger node in the hierarchy. Sankey diagrams have also been modified to visualize data flows better without an interactive system. In one case, this is achieved by modifying the color of flows as exhibited in Lupton and Allwood [6]. For example, by adjusting the coloring of flows to correspond with the source node, they demonstrated how to convey information regarding the context of the data.

© Springer Nature Switzerland AG 2021
G. Bebis et al. (Eds.): ISVC 2021, LNCS 13018, pp. 386–397, 2021.
https://doi.org/10.1007/978-3-030-90436-4_31

While the original Sankey diagram is helpful for quick summarization of prominent trends of data, there exist two main limitations. First, the original Sankey diagram does not preserve the history of links. Thus, when viewing the outflow links from a node, it is impossible to identify which inflow links comprise that particular link and to what degree. Second, the original Sankey diagram cannot visualize the hierarchical structure within a particular node. Although the modifications to the Sankey diagram mentioned above improve the demonstration of data flow, there is still no solution that allows users to dynamically visualize the context of a data flow and change the specificity of nodes.

In this paper, we present the *hierarchical Sankey diagram*. Our hierarchical version of the Sankey diagram expands upon a standard Sankey diagram by addressing these limitations while preserving the core ability of the diagram to visualize data flow quickly. To make a Sankey diagram visually appealing and easy to understand, we usually avoid showing a large number of nodes when enabling level-of-detail exploration. Often, these nodes, which are essentially groupings of individual data points, serve as a general category for data. Within these categories may exist several subcategories, which may contain their distinct trends of data flow. We advocate an *in-place* approach by presenting two types of variants: *inflow* and *level-of-detail*. By "in-place", we mean modifying the original Sankey diagram rather than supplementing it with another separate view. These variants are built upon the fundamental idea of splitting nodes and merging them to enable more dimensions of comparison and generate more insight.

The contributions of our work are the following. First, our work offers an in-place solution to extending the capabilities of the Sankey diagram by splitting nodes dynamically. Second, unlike previous approaches that are practically limited to a single column [6], we present a new solution (i.e., vertical separation) to visualizing the inflow history across multiple columns. Third, previous works show that Sankey diagrams can either only depict change among groups over columns or break down the flow of a hierarchical relationship. By splitting nodes with our level-of-detail variants, we enable the Sankey diagram to communicate both dimensions: level-of-detail and change among groups over columns. Fourth, we conduct a user study to evaluate the effectiveness of the variants and assess user preference.

2 Design

2.1 Inflow Variants

We design two variants for inflow links: vertical separation (i.e., splitting the original node based on the inflow links) and color distinction (i.e., coloring the outflow links based on the inflow links). Note that neither variant affects nodes with no inflow links. In the following discussion, let us consider a Sankey diagram with four nodes in each column and four outflow links from each node.

The first variant, vertical separation, replaces the original node with four copies corresponding to the inflow links. As shown in Fig. 1, the four nodes still represent the same data category as the original node, and together, they contain the same data points as the original one. However, these data points are split based on the source node. This variant has the advantage of quickly summarizing the distribution of outflow links based on inflow links (i.e., which node did data points go to next based on where the data points previously were) and comparing these distributions to the other inflow separations. However, if many nodes are split apart, the diagram may appear cluttered and lose the advantage of rapidly assessing information trends.

The second variant, color distinction, colors the outflow links based on the inflow links. This is similar to partitioning bundles of flows [6]. If a node contains four inflow links, each outflow link will show four partitioned color bands corresponding to the respective colors of the inflow links. The size (i.e., bandwidth) of the original outflow link will remain the same, and the sizes of color bands that comprise it are proportional to their contributions to the outflow link. Refer to Fig. 2 for an example. We point out that color distinction does not scale to multiple columns as vertical separation does. Moreover, it does not work well for a thin outflow link associated with many inflow links.

2.2   Level-of-Detail Variants

We design two variants to show the level-of-detail node information: horizontal split and vertical split. Data points can be grouped into categories differently: numerical data can be categorized by the specific numbers as well as intervals of varying sizes, and categorical data can be grouped based on similarities between data points. Regardless of whether a dataset is numerical, categorical, or a combination of both, there are often subcategories generalized by nodes.

The first variant, horizontal split, adds a new column of the subcategories to the right side of the column where the original node belongs, as shown in Fig. 3. While the original node and inflow links are preserved, the original node now has new outflow links to each subcategory. The advantage of this variant is that the original node is kept, and it is easier to see its breakdown. However, chaining together subcategories by applying this variant to more subcategories could significantly increase the diagram's horizontal space. Furthermore, the columns of the Sankey diagram are usually distinctive and naturally represent different groupings. Therefore, adding a new column for subcategories may confuse users.

The second variant, vertical split, means replacing the original node with new nodes of further specificity based on subcategories. These subcategorical nodes can be further split into their subcategories, replacing the node being broken down. Note that vertical split replaces a node with its child nodes showing the next level of detail, while vertical separation duplicates the same node based on the inflow links. Refer to Fig. 4 for an example. The advantage of replacing the original node is that it allows users to identify each subcategories' inflow and outflow. Subcategories of a node may have their own trends, and this variant is useful for identifying them. However, it can be more difficult to quickly assess the size and trend of the original category as users would need to recombine the inflow and outflow links of these subcategories mentally. Adding marks to the

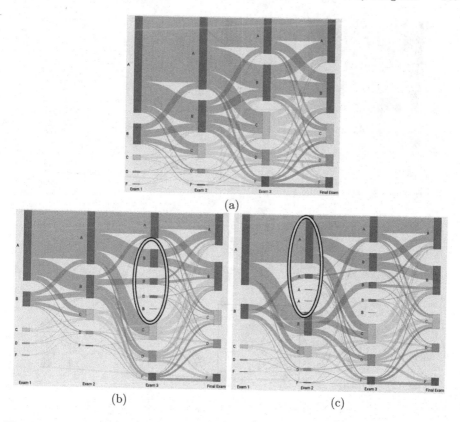

(a)

(b)   (c)

Fig. 1. Inflow: vertical separation. (a) shows the original Sankey diagram. (b) separating B on Exam 3 column. (c) continuing on (b) and separating A on Exam 2 column.

visualization indicating that certain nodes belong to the same initial node (e.g., dashed vertical lines connecting them or a bounding box around the split nodes in a group) would help. Still, it may lead to visual clutter with multiple such instances.

3   Results

3.1   Dataset and Web Application

The dataset was collected from student performance data of a course. The performance data include student grades in three exams and the final exam. The grades are quantitative (0 to 100), and we used standard groupings for letter grades. A, B, C, D, and F represent the groupings [90-100], [80-90), [70-80), [60-70), and [0-60), respectively. A '+' indicates a grade that the ones-digit is ≥ 7, and a '-' indicates a grade that the ones-digit is ≤ 3. B, C, and D all have both '+' and '-' while A only has '-' and F has neither. We created a web application by

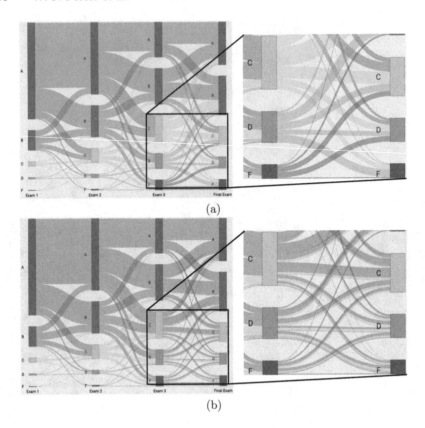

Fig. 2. Inflow: color distinction. (a) and (b) show the results before and after applying this variant to all nodes on Exam 3 column.

implementing the four variants of the hierarchical Sankey diagram using D3.js. We have released the application at https://www.nd.edu/~cwang11/hsd/. The figures shown in the paper are screenshots of this web application. We added highlights in Figs. 1, 3, and 4 and zoom-in views in Fig. 2 to show the intended changes, which are easy to observe when interacting with the application.

3.2   Visualization Results

As depicted in Fig. 1(b), the vertical separation variant to inflow links grants us further insight. Before splitting node B on Exam 3 (refer to Fig. 1(a)), users cannot identify the relation between inflow and outflow links. After the split, B is broken down into four new nodes: one from each of the Exam 2 nodes (A, B, C, and D). Note that F is not shown as there is no inflow from it. The ability to relate the outflow and inflow links dramatically extends the capabilities of a Sankey diagram, which is premised on the relationship between nodes. This variant allows users to draw considerable more insight into the data quickly. By also splitting another node from another column (e.g., A on Exam 2), Fig. 1(c)

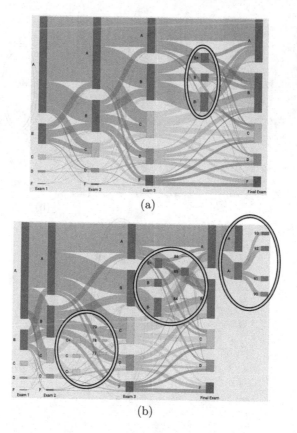

(a)

(b)

Fig. 3. Level-of-detail: horizontal split. (a) splitting B on Exam 3 column. (b) splitting C on Exam 2 column then further splitting C+, B on Exam 3 column then further splitting B, and A on Final Exam column then further splitting A−.

demonstrates how multiple nodes can be split to extend the capabilities of inflow history even further. Figure 2 depicts another variant to this idea using color distinction. Rather than create a new node, this variant simply colors the outflow link according to the contribution of the inflow links. While the result may appear more challenging to read, it has the advantage of not creating new nodes to avoid overcrowding. Consequently, as shown in Fig. 2(b), where this hierarchy is applied to all nodes on the Exam 3 column, it is possible to quickly assess and compare inflow history across all nodes of a particular column.

As shown in Fig. 3(a), the horizontal split for level-of-detail creates a new column to represent the breakdown of specificity. Here, we split the general category of B into their subcategories of B+, B, and B−. Figure 3(b) demonstrates this successive breakdown into a different level of detail. Notice how new columns are created for new levels of detail, and the inflow to each hierarchy is its parent. In Fig. 4, (a) and (b) show the same breakdowns using vertical split rather than horizontal split. As depicted, the original node is replaced by the new categories.

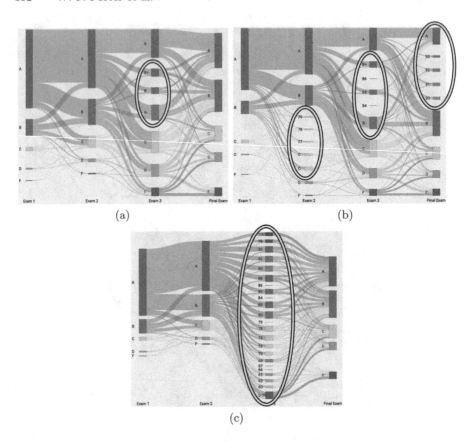

Fig. 4. Level-of-detail: vertical split. (a) and (b) show the same breakdowns as in Fig. 3 (a) and (b), respectively. (c) applying this variant to all nodes on Exam 3 column to the finest level of detail.

However, the Sankey diagram may begin to lose its readability as the number of nodes increases due to constant expansions of the level-of-detail hierarchy of nodes. Such a result is shown in Fig. 4(c).

4   Evaluation

We conducted an uncontrolled user study to evaluate the effectiveness of each of the variants in communicating inflow or level-of-detail information to users and gauge which variant users prefer to use. We did not include the original Sankey diagram in the study because it only supports the examination of inflow. We recruited students from the Department of Computer Science and Engineering at our university who responded to a department-wide email soliciting paid volunteers. A total of 19 participants completed the study, and each was compensated $20 for a session that lasted less than one hour. The majority of the

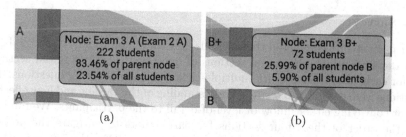

(a)   (b)

Fig. 5. Tooltips when hovering over nodes in the hierarchical Sankey diagram.

participants are juniors and seniors (nine juniors and seven seniors). In terms of demographic breakdown, four are Asian, 11 are Caucasian, one is Hispanic, and three are other ethnicities. We hosted our implementation as a web application and distributed the URL to participants on the day they chose to complete the study. Participants completed the study using their personal computers. One of the student co-authors of this work was available via a Zoom link at all times to answer questions from the participants or help troubleshoot the application.

4.1   Tutorial

As the first step of the study, we provided a tutorial that introduces participants to the variants and helps them understand how to use the variants to gain a particular type of insight from the dataset. In addition, the tutorial prepares participants for the format of questions that will be asked in the next phase. The tutorial is divided into four sections, one for each variant. Participants were instructed to use the application to select a variant and then interact with the diagram for that variant. For example, in the Inflow: Vertical Separation section, participants separated node Exam 3 A and were told how one of the new nodes, Exam 3 A (Exam 2 A), represents students that received an A on Exam 2 and an A on Exam 3. The instructions also describe the corresponding tooltip as shown in Fig. 5(a) that appears when the Exam 3 A (Exam 2 A) node is hovered. The tooltip includes title, number of students corresponding to the node, percentage of the parent node (Exam 3 A) the previous number represents, and percentage of all scores from Exam 3. In the Level-of-Detail: Horizontal Split section, participants clicked on node Exam 3 B and took note of the three resultant nodes: Exam 3 B+, Exam 3 B, and Exam 3 B−. The instructions describe the corresponding tooltip as shown in Fig. 5(b) that appears when the Exam 3 B+ node is hovered. The tooltip includes title, number of students, percentage of the source node (all B grades), and percentage of all grades for Exam 3. Participants completed the tutorial by following a Google Form and checking a checkbox after finishing each section. The purpose is to dissuade them from skimming through the tutorial without thoroughly reading it. More than two-thirds of the participants agreed that the tutorial was sufficient to learn how to use and interpret the hierarchical Sankey diagram.

4.2 Survey

After participants completed the tutorial, they moved on to a new Google Form with the survey including seven sections of questions. The four initial sections, one for each variant, come with multiple-choice and short-answer questions. The questions were designed to test the understanding of the variant and how effective it is at conveying either inflow or level-of-detail to the participants. We randomized the order of these four sections for participants to mitigate the possible accumulation of learning effects in answering questions. For the inflow variants, participants were asked to identify the most common score from Exam 1 received by students who also received the specified scores on the following two exams and state the number of students who received these scores on the three exams. This question assesses the ability of the variants to allow a user to compare the outflows of a given node, separated by the inflow to that node, to a specified target node. They were also asked to answer the number of students who received a given grade on Exam 3 with specified grades on Exam 1 and Exam 2. This question assesses the ability of the variants to convey to a user how a path can be created between three nodes using inflow information. For the level-of-detail variants, participants were asked to identify the number of students who received a specific letter grade (A- or B-) on Exam 3 and state the percentage of the overall letter grade those students represent. These questions assess the ability of the variants to convey the size of a node's subcategories.

The fifth section of the survey asks two questions that can be answered with an inflow variant and two questions that can be answered with a level-of-detail variant. In this section, there is no guidance on which variant to use in answering a question. Participants were asked to give the answer to the question and also state which variant was used to come up with the answer. In this way, we can examine whether users understand the differences between the variants and which one is optimal for a given task. The sixth section of questions asks participants to describe the usage of a Sankey diagram to assess their baseline knowledge of the diagram. We also asked various questions that require comparing and contrasting the inflow and level-of-detail variants against each other, stating the advantages and disadvantages of each variant and stating the preferred choice between each pair of variants. These questions were asked to assess further the participant's understanding and preference of the variants. The seventh section asks participants to rate on a scale of 1-5 how strongly they feel that (1) the variants, in general, provide additional use beyond the standard Sankey diagram and (2) the pair of inflow and pair of level-of-detail variants, are effective in understanding the prior grades of students that comprise nodes and the more specific grades that can be revealed by breaking down nodes. These questions were asked to understand the participant's judgment of the effectiveness of our in-place approaches to the hierarchical Sankey diagram.

Table 1. Participant performance for the four variants of the hierarchical Sankey diagram, corresponding to the first four sections of the survey.

Type	Variant	# questions	Aggregate score	Percentage
Inflow	Vertical separation	3	37/57	64.91%
Inflow	Color distinction	3	46/57	80.70%
Level-of-detail	Horizontal split	2	37/38	96.37%
Level-of-detail	Vertical split	2	37/38	96.37%

4.3 User Study Results

Table 1 reports the aggregate scores of participants for the first four sections of the survey, which evaluates how effective each variant is in helping the participants answer the questions correctly. Participants were more accurate in their responses when using color distinction to answer questions in the first and second sections of the survey, which measure the performance of the inflow variants. Only 11 students were able to correctly answer *"Of the students who scored a B on Exam 2 and an A on Exam 1, how many students received an A on Exam 3?"* using vertical separation, whereas 17 students correctly answered *"Of the students who scored an A on Exam 2 and a B on Exam 1, how many students received a B on Exam 3?"* using color distinction. Both variants saw 18 correct responses to the questions *"How did most of the students perform on Exam 1 who scored a C on Exam 2 and a C on Exam 3?"* (vertical separation) and *"How did most of the students perform on Exam 1 who scored a B on Exam 2 and a B on Exam 3?"* (color distinction). However, only seven participants correctly identified how many students the group contained using vertical separation, compared to 13 correct answers using color distinction.

Performance was relatively similar when using the level of detail variants. Using horizontal split, all participants correctly answered *"How many students received an A- on Exam 3?"* and 17 correctly answered *"What percentage of all students who scored an A on Exam 3 does this make up?"*. Using vertical split, all participants correctly answered *"How many students received a B- on Exam 3?"* and 16 correctly answered *"What percentage of all students who scored a B on Exam 3 does this make up?"*. The concept of hierarchical subcategories that make up the level-of-detail variants is perhaps very straightforward to users, explaining the high level of correctness in participant responses to these questions. On the other hand, the inflow variants attempt to solve a problem that potentially requires more thought from users, even with an effective visual tool. In this case, we can see a more apparent separation in understanding between the two inflow variants for the questions asked, suggesting that color distinction is more effective at creating a continuous path between nodes that a user can interpret.

We found that participants preferred color distinction over vertical separation when asked to choose a variant to answer an inflow-related question about the data. Still, the results were reversed when asked directly to select a preference between the two. Of the two questions that require a participant to choose an inflow variant without guidance, the question, *"How many students received an A on Exam 1, a B on Exam 2, and a C on Exam 3?"* was answered by ten participants using the color distinction variant and eight participants using vertical separation (one student chose horizontal split). The other question of this type, *"Of the students who scored a C on Exam 3 and a B on Final Exam, how did most of these students perform on Exam 2?"* was answered by 11 participants using color distinction and eight participants using vertical separation. However, when asked to select their preference between the two variants, 14 participants picked vertical separation, and only five preferred color distinction. A similar outcome occurred in the comparison of preference between level-of-detail variants. *"How many students scored 78/100 on Exam 3?"* was answered by ten participants using horizontal split and nine using vertical split, and *"How many students received a B+ on Exam 3 and an A on Final Exam?"* was answered by ten participants using horizontal split and seven using vertical split (two participants used vertical separation). When asked directly which of the two variants they preferred, 11 participants selected vertical split, while eight picked horizontal split.

5   Conclusions and Future Work

We have presented the design and evaluation of the hierarchical Sankey diagram, which includes inflow support via vertical separation or color distinction and level-of-detail support via horizontal split or vertical split. The evaluation results show that color distinction is more effective than vertical separation for inflow-related questions, although vertical separation was preferred in use. We note that these results may not indicate the efficacy of both variants as color distinction is limited to a single column, but vertical separation can scale to multiple columns. Thus, the survey could only assess questions related to a single column for comparison. Furthermore, horizontal split and vertical split perform similarly for level-of-detail-related questions, and there is no clear preference over horizontal split and vertical split. We believe that the general in-place approach presented for augmenting the standard Sankey diagram can be helpful in many cases. Therefore, besides making the current code open source, we will generalize our implementation as a library to benefit others.

Acknowledgments. This research was supported in part by the U.S. National Science Foundation through grants IIS-1455886, DUE-1833129, IIS-1955395, IIS-2101696, and OAC-2104158. The authors would like to thank the anonymous reviewers for their helpful comments.

References

1. Burch, M., Timmermans, N.: Sankeye: a visualization technique for AOI transitions. In: Proceedings of ACM Symposium on Eye Tracking Research and Applications (Short Papers), pp. 48:1–48:5 (2020)

2. Chou, J.K., Wang, Y., Ma, K.L.: Privacy preserving event sequence data visualization using a Sankey diagram-like representation. In: Proceedings of ACM SIGGRAPH Asia Symposium on Visualization, pp. 1:1–1:8 (2016)
3. Huang, C.W., Lu, R., Iqbal, U., et al.: A richly interactive exploratory data analysis and visualization tool using electronic medical records. BMC Med. Inf. Decis. Mak. 15, 92:1-92:14 (2015)
4. Kosara, R., Bendix, F., Hauser, H.: Parallel sets: interactive exploration and visual analysis of categorical data. IEEE Trans. Vis. Comput. Graph. 12(4), 558–568 (2006)
5. Lehrman, B.: Visualizing water infrastructure with Sankey maps: a case study of mapping the Los Angeles aqueduct, California. J. Maps 14(1), 52–64 (2018)
6. Lupton, R.C., Allwood, J.M.: Hybrid Sankey diagrams: visual analysis of multidimensional data for understanding resource use. Resour. Conserv. Recycl. 124, 141–151 (2017)
7. Müller, G., Sugiyama, H., Stocker, S., Schmidt, R.: Reducing energy consumption in pharmaceutical production processes: framework and case study. J. Pharm. Innov. 9, 212–226 (2014)
8. Riehmann, P., Hanfler, M., Froehlich, B.: Interactive Sankey diagrams. In: Proceedings of IEEE Symposium on Information Visualization, pp. 233–240 (2005)
9. Sansen, J., Lalanne, F., Auber, D., Bourqui, R.: Adjasankey: visualization of huge hierarchical weighted and directed graphs. In: Proceedings of International Conference on Information Visualisation, pp. 211–216 (2015)
10. Verma, J., Luo, H., Hu, J., Zhang, P.: DrugPathSeeker: interactive UI for exploring drug-ADR relation via pathways. In: Proceedings of IEEE Pacific Visualization Symposium, pp. 260–264 (2017)
11. Vosough, Z., Hogräfer, M., Royer, L.A., Groh, R., Schulz, H.J.: Parallel hierarchies: a visualization for cross-tabulating hierarchical categories. Comput. Graph. 76, 1–17 (2018)
12. Vosough, Z., Kammer, D., Keck, M., Groh, R.: Mirroring Sankey diagrams for visual comparison tasks. In: Proceedings of International Conference on Information Visualization Theory and Applications, pp. 349–355 (2018)
13. Xia, M., Velumani, R., Wang, Y., Qu, H., Ma, X.: QLens: visual analytics of MUlti-step problem-solving behaviors for improving question design. IEEE Trans. Vis. Comput. Graph. 27(2), 870–880 (2021)
14. Zarate, D.C., Bodic, P.L., Dwyer, T., Gange, G., Stuckey, P.: Optimal Sankey diagrams via integer programming. In: Proceedings of IEEE Pacific Visualization Symposium, pp. 135–139 (2018)
15. Zhou, K., Wu, W., Zhao, J., Li, M., Qian, Z., Chen, Y.: Click or not: different mouseover effects may affect clicking-through rate while browsing interactive information visualization. J. Vis. 23(1), 157–170 (2020)

Dynamic Antenna Pattern Visualization for Aviation Safety Incorporating Multipath and Situational Awareness

Chad Mourning[✉] and Simbo Odunaiya

Ohio University, Athens, USA
mourning@ohio.edu

Abstract. The Ohio University Navaid Performance Prediction Model (OUNPPM) is a widely used tool for certification of navigational aid compliance and safety at commercial, private, and military airports. The main purpose of OUNPPM is to calculate multipath errors from structures near the navigational aids and generate traditional error plots expected by certifying authorities, but users often leverage the rapid situational awareness provided by OUNPPM's virtual world component to aid in engineering judgements before running a complete analysis. This paper introduces a new isosurface-based approach of visualizing useful aspects of the OUNPPM output, focusing on the localizer array, with examples such as: nominal antenna array patterns, antenna array patterns deformed by hardware fault, antenna array patterns deformed by scatterer-induced multipath error, as well as scattered field visualization by itself. These new visualization capabilities can expedite the development of a new user's intuition into the nature of antenna array multipath in professional work or as a teaching aid. The paper concludes with recommendations for future work to improve the overall usefulness for users.

Keywords: Visualization · Isosurface · Real-time graphics · Antenna pattern

1 Introduction

Navigational aids (navaids) are a critical piece of aviation safety infrastructure, but their accuracy is directly impacted by the multipath produced from entities within the airport environment. The Ohio University Navaid Performance Prediction Model [9] is a freely available software package, developed since the 1960s, used to certify airports in over 20 countries. Until now, OUNPPM modelled the effects of the navaid antenna array, but there was no way to directly visualize the array antenna pattern or the effects surrounding multipath had on that pattern-in-space within the tool. This paper introduces a new antenna pattern visualization capability for OUNPPM which incorporates deformations in the field caused by multipath in surrounding objects. These patterns respond to changes in the simulated environment quickly, and will render in real time

© Springer Nature Switzerland AG 2021
G. Bebis et al. (Eds.): ISVC 2021, LNCS 13018, pp. 398–407, 2021.
https://doi.org/10.1007/978-3-030-90436-4_32

allowing a user to diagnose alterations to the pattern caused by changes to the antenna array or nearby scatterers. The contributions of this paper are as follows: a new isosurface-based approach for visualizing antenna patterns deformed by multipath, discussions on effective techniques for leveraging isosurface antenna pattern visualization to convey useful information to users, and recommendations for future work.

2   Background

In order for aircraft to safely land at airports a series of landing aids have been developed, which include features such as lighting systems and, relevant to this paper, electromagnetic navigational aids. The feature presented in this paper will focus on one particular navigational aid, the instrument landing system (ILS) localizer, a large antenna array, which provides a deviation from centerline indication for pilots. OUNPPM has been in development since the 1960s as a tool for the simulation and modelling of multipath error [2] in these navigational aids by entities in the surrounding airport environments. Multipath [1] arises when the direct signal combines at the intended target with other signals via reflection or diffraction from surfaces, including the terrain, buildings, telephones wires, wind turbines, and even passing vehicles, such as other airplanes. Even though OUNPPM has had the ability to calculate the field strength of the combined pattern-in-space for decades, only now has the ability to visualize those patterns been added. OUNPPM is widely used by the FAA, international civil aviation authorities, and their contractors to ensure the safe operation of their airports, primarily by modelling, in advance, planned changes to airports. Additionally, antenna array manufactures use OUNPPM and similar tools to ensure the safety of their new designs.

Computational tools have been used to visualize antenna patterns since the 1980s, starting with parameterized wireframes for single elements [11] and quickly moving on to entire arrays of antennas by the 1990s [3,4]. Due to the complicated electromagnetic interactions of the antenna pattern with the scatterers, the pattern-in-space of the nominal plus multipath signals cannot be cleanly parameterized, however it can be approximated using techniques such as Geometric Theory of Diffraction [7], Physical Optics [13], or Method of Moments [6]. Using one of these techniques, the pattern can be discretely sampled as a three-dimensional scalar field, or, more precisely, a normalized complex field, $|E|(v)$, and an isosurface based approach for visualization was selected to model this field. The isosurface(s) of the pattern is generated via marching cubes [8] in the normal way.

3   Motivation

OUNPPM is used in over twenty countries to certify the safety of airports with some users having several decades of experience with the program. Elder users have developed an intuition about the effects that placement of a new scatterer will have on the pattern, but novice users can take a long time to develop that same skill. This new feature will provide novice users an opportunity to learn about the effects of scatterers on the pattern at an accelerated rate in a manner more amenable to their visual processing capabilities.

Additionally, automated orthoimagery acquisition was recently added to the model as well. While that is a not a particularly novel feature on its own, when used in tandem with antenna pattern visualization it provides increased situational awareness for the user to aid in decision making and understanding, particularly when using non-trivial scatterers such as wind turbines.

4   Methodology

As an intermediate step between scenario specification and output plotting, OUNPPM calculates field strengths at user defined inspection points in a 3D Cartesian space around a navigational aid, typically following one of three standard inspection flighpaths mandated by the FAA [5]. In order to visualize the antenna pattern, including off-nominal deformations because of multipath from nearby scatterers, this new feature generates a custom "flightpath" of a regular, rectilinear grid of inspection points and processes it through the OUNPPM multipath modelling backend. A marching cubes [8] pass is run on the resulting grid of field strengths to create one of two effects for the user:

- A fixed antenna pattern isosurface for a specific field strength.
- An animated antenna pattern sweeping multiple field strengths.

There are two ways the field strengths can change when running the application: changes to the antenna array elements or changes to a scatterer size, position, or material. When antenna pattern visualization is enabled in the application and the user saves their current simulation, changes to the antenna array or scatterers are forwarded to the 3D accelerated context and processed in a background thread. Once the results are generated, and the marching cubes pass is run on the data, the isosurface representing the current antenna pattern is visualized in the world. This antenna pattern visualization is placed within the context of a coordinate system relative to the threshold of the runway-navaid system as well as optional orthoimagery providing increased situational awareness.

Isosurface coloration is based on the normal of that face of the discretized isosurface. The red channel corresponds to the contribution of the x, green channel for y and blue channel for z.

5   Examples

5.1   Case 1: Nominal Antenna Patterns

The standard service volume for a localizer consists of a longer (18 nautical mile), narrower ($\pm 10°$) sector and a shorter (10 nautical mile), wider ($\pm 35°$)

sector. In order to provide optimal coverage over both sectors, the localizer array typically consists of both a *course* and a *clearance* array. The array distributions are specified as amplitudes and phases for both a Carrier + Side Band (CSB) signal and a Side Band Only (SBO) signal. This means, that, for a given array, OUNPPM will have four patterns to visualize:

– Course CSB
– Course SBO
– Clearance CSB
– Clearance SBO

Figure 1 shows the nominal antenna patterns for the Wilcox 14–10 antenna array as viewed from 1500 ft above the localizer, consisting of, from left to right, the Course CSB, the Course SBO, the Clearance CSB, and the Clearance SBO.

Fig. 1. A nominal antenna pattern from the back.

Figure 2 shows the nominal antenna patterns for the Wilcox 14–10 antenna array as viewed from the side, consisting of, from left to right, the Course CSB, the Course SBO, the Clearance CSB, and the Clearance SBO.

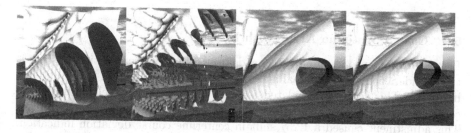

Fig. 2. A nominal antenna pattern from the side.

5.2   Case 2: Animated Antenna Pattern

The first, obvious extension of rendering a field strength-in-space isosurface is sweeping multiple field strengths in rapid succession to generate an apparent motion. The signal does modulate at frequency, but that is not what is being captured here, rather, Fig. 3 conveys the attenuation of field strength as it travels from the array over a distance. The value in this visualization is that the field does not attenuate evenly since it is a complicated summation of multiple signals (14 or 10, for the Wilcox 14–10 course and clearance arrays, respectively).

Figure 3 shows the field strength isosurfaces for the Course CSB at increasing field strengths. The image captures eight isosurfaces that, if played back in sequence, gives an apparent motion of the pattern moving towards the array as the field strengths will attenuate with distance from the array. The selected field strengths were 1×10^{-5}, 1.25×10^{-5}, 1.5×10^{-5}, 1.75×10^{-5}, 2×10^{-5}, 2.25×10^{-5}, 2.5×10^{-5}, and 2.75×10^{-5} μA.

Fig. 3. A sequence of 8 swept field strength isosurfaces. From left to right, top to bottom: 1×10^{-5}, 1.25×10^{-5}, 1.5×10^{-5}, 1.75×10^{-5}, 2×10^{-5}, 2.25×10^{-5}, 2.5×10^{-5}, and 2.75×10^{-5} μA.

5.3   Case 3: Antenna Array with Bend

Before moving on to antenna patterns deformed by scatterer multipath, there is the consideration of off nominal antenna patterns due to defects in the antenna hardware. This scenario simulated a phase fault in the first element right of center in the localizer which added a 90° phase offset in the SBO distribution. This adjustment caused a 1.25° shift in centerline course deviation indication. Figure 4 shows, on the left, the nominal pattern, and the pattern with the faulty element on the right. The pattern is now clearly asymmetric, with fewer lobes on the lefthand side and almost flat on the right. An examination of the bottom leaves a lingering question; since the isosurface is discrete, can a user distinguish if the peaks are absent on the right because the signal strength is higher or lower? It is not clear from this image; however, if the coloration scheme were changed predicated on the gradient of the signal strength field, $\nabla|E|(\boldsymbol{v})$, in the user's viewing direction, this could be inferred. The isosurface is not guaranteed to be closed in the region of space visualized, so view-dependent dynamic coloring of the same face would be necessary to achieve this effect. This is considered future work.

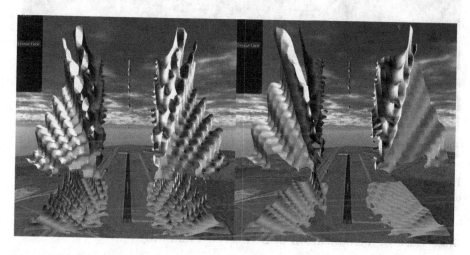

Fig. 4. The same localizer array, but the righthand image has a 90° fault added to the innermost righthand element.

Similarly, amplitude faults in the localizer distribution units can be also be modelled in OUNPPM which would cause deviations in the antenna pattern; however, that scenario has not been modelled and captured for this paper.

5.4 Case 4: Deformed Antenna Pattern by Scatterer

In this example a scatterer, representing a 100 ft tall building, 1000 ft long, approximating an airport terminal, is placed 500 ft to the left side of the runway, from the perspective of the antenna array, and perfectly parallel to the runway's direction. It can be seen as the red quadrilateral in the lower left of Fig. 5.

In Fig. 5, the top of the signal is excluded because there is no change. The localizer is set 4 ft above the ground and the top of the building is 100 ft, so there is no expected change more than 196 ft above the ground. Because the scatterer is on the left, the scattered field is reflected to the right, with the areas circled in red being the change in pattern. The change is very slight and hard to detect in stills, but OUNPPM has the ability to toggle quickly between the current and previous isosurface for rapid optical change detection. Improved change detection by, for instance, extracting the difference in two isosurfaces (or the isosurface of the difference in two fields) is considered future work.

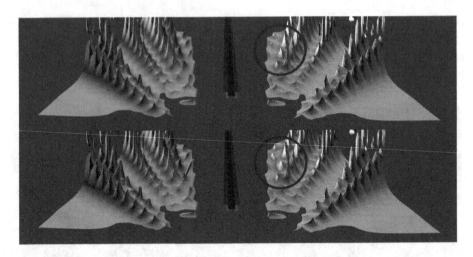

Fig. 5. Deformation in an antenna pattern caused by a scatterer. Nominal signal shown on top, deformed signal shown on bottom. (Color figure online)

5.5   Case 5: Visualization of Scattered Field only

In addition to calculating the total combined field of the direct+incident signal and multipath, OUNPPM has the ability to output the intermediate values individually. The direct+incident field is trivial, since it is identical to running the scenario without scatterers; however, separating out the scattered field, and visualizing its isosurface allows a user to see the effected geographic regions impacted by that scatterer.

Figure 6 shows the isosurface of the scattered field reflected from the scatterer. An observer will notice that the field terminates at the scatterer plate, and reflects back towards the array. For Fig. 6 a strong field strength was selected, so the isosurface is close to the ground near the center of the reflection; weaker field isosurfaces correlated with increasing elevation angles.

OUNPPM also supports pseudo-diffraction of the signal behind scatterer plates. Figure 7 shows the isosurface of the scattered field reflected from the scatterer as well as the diffracted field. An observer will notice a "seam" in the isosurface in the plane of the scatterer plate. Note: the test flightpath only sampled a $3000 \times 3000 \times 3000$ foot area, the pattern to the left continues outwards in reality.

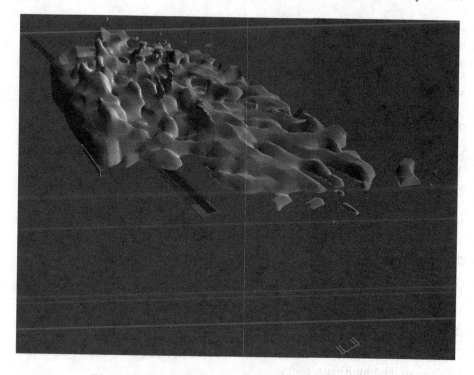

Fig. 6. Reflected scattered field from a scatterer plate.

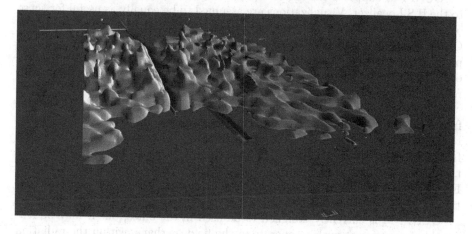

Fig. 7. Reflected and diffracted field from a scatterer plate.

6   Conclusions

The addition of pattern visualization to OUNPPM successfully allows the user to interactively modify a scenario and visualize the output in real-time. This has useful application in engineering analysis and in developing an intuition about effects on the pattern by scatterers. Similarly, design of the layout of airports may be accelerated and engineering costs may be reduced by increases in speed an accuracy of OUNPPM users. The addition of these features may also be useful for teaching concepts of Physical Optics and Antenna Theory in educational settings.

The scattered field visualizations are particularly useful since they clearly outline regions of space where a scatterer will interfere with the direct+incident signal. However, since users currently have to specify the field strength, it might be more useful to show, for instance, the field of similar strength to the nominal direct+incident field on centerline. Further research is necessary.

Similarly, change detection techniques will further accelerate analysis by highlighting only relevant areas in the output. Current method of direct examination may also be error prone, defeating the purpose of the technology.

7   Future Work

Currently, OUNPPM calculates the multipath effects of scatterers, but not terrain, on the antenna pattern. A sister project, the Ohio University Glideslope Model (OUGS), calculates multipath effects of terrain deviations on the antenna pattern, but not scatterers; this visualization feature can be added to OUGS. In the further future the functionality of the OUNPPM and OUGS can be combined into one unified multipath tool.

OUNPPM supports ILS Glideslope, VOR, and DME modelling in addition to the ILS Localizer. Visualizations are assumed to be equally as useful for these other navigational aids, but tests should be conducted to confirm. Similarly, OUNPPM supports modelling for wire scatterers, which was not explored in this paper. It is expected that the scattered field from wires may look significantly different than the scattered field from plates, since the field is mostly diffraction rather than reflection.

High-resolution isosurface generation can take several seconds, so another future area of research will be to immediately present a low resolution isosurface to the user and incorporate background processing to iteratively refine the isosurface resolution. Similarly, isosurface generation is currently accomplished using the traditional marching cubes approach [8], so a more modern approach like Flying Edge [12] may be implemented to determine if there are any construction-time or rendering-time benefits .

OUNPPM is currently designed to be used in the office, but it may be reasonable for a user to wish to operate in the field, perhaps, within the radiation pattern itself. [10] has introduced an augmented reality method for visualization of antenna patterns, and a similar technique could be applied for OUNPPM in the field.

As mentioned in the body of the paper, an immediate area for further research is change detection between the isosurfaces. This should enhance the user's ability to rapidly determine the effects on the system.

References

1. Braasch, M.S.: Multipath. In: Teunissen, P.J.G., Montenbruck, O. (eds.) Springer Handbook of Global Navigation Satellite Systems. SH, pp. 443–468. Springer, Cham (2017). https://doi.org/10.1007/978-3-319-42928-1_15
2. Corrington, M.S.: Frequency-modulation distortion caused by multipath transmission. Proc. IRE **33**(12), 878–891 (1945)
3. Elbinger, S., Routier, R.: 3d visualization applied to electromagnetic engineering. Naval Eng. J. **109**(5), 31–46 (1997)
4. Elsherbeni, A.Z., Taylor, C.: Visualization of two and three dimensional antenna patterns. In: Proceedings of SOUTHEASTCON'94, pp. 270–272. IEEE (1994)
5. FAA, O.: United statues standard flight inspection manual. FAA Order 8200 (2005)
6. Harrington, R.F.: Field Computation by Moment Methods. Wiley-IEEE Press, Hoboken (1968)
7. Keller, J.B.: Geometrical theory of diffraction. JOSA **52**(2), 116–130 (1962)
8. Lorensen, W.E., Cline, H.E.: Marching cubes: a high resolution 3d surface construction algorithm. ACM Siggraph Comput. Graph. **21**(4), 163–169 (1987)
9. Luebbers, R., Mitchel, L., Ungvichian, V., Mroz, M.: The ohio university ils modeling center. Technical report, Technical Memorandum S-46, Avionics Engineering Center, Ohio University (1977)
10. Nguyen, D.H., et al.: Beamviewer: visualization of dynamic antenna radiation patterns using augmented reality. In: 2016 IEEE Conference on Computer Communications Workshops (INFOCOM WKSHPS), pp. 794–795. IEEE (2016)
11. Ruhlmann, G., McKeeman, J.: Displaying three dimensional antenna patterns on personal computers. In: Proceedings, IEEE Energy and Information Technologies in the Southeast', pp. 48–51. IEEE (1989)
12. Schroeder, W., Maynard, R., Geveci, B.: Flying edges: a high-performance scalable isocontouring algorithm. In: 2015 IEEE 5th Symposium on Large Data Analysis and Visualization (LDAV), pp. 33–40. IEEE (2015)
13. Wood, R.W.: Physical Optics. Macmillan, London (1905)

Computer-Assisted Heuristic Evaluation
of Data Visualization

Ying Zhu[1]([✉])(iD) and Julia A. Gumieniak[2]

[1] Georgia State University, Atlanta, USA
yzhu@gsu.edu
[2] Binghamton University, Binghamton, USA
jgumien1@binghamton.edu

Abstract. Heuristic evaluation has been an important part of data visualization. Many heuristic rules and guidelines for evaluating data visualization have been proposed and reviewed. However, applying heuristic evaluation in practice is not trivial. First, the heuristic rules are discussed in different publications across different disciplines. There is no central repository of heuristic rules for data visualization. There are no consistent guidelines on how to apply them. Second, it is difficult to find multiple experts who are knowledgeable about the heuristic rules, their pitfalls, and counterpoints. To address this issue, we present a computer-assisted heuristic evaluation method for data visualization. Based on this method, we developed a Python-based tool for evaluating plots created by the visualization tool Plotly. Recent advances in declarative data visualization libraries have made it feasible to create such a tool. By providing advice, critiques, and recommendations, this tool serves as a knowledgeable virtual assistant to help data visualization developers evaluate their visualizations as they code.

Keywords: Data visualization · Evaluation · Heuristic rules

1 Introduction

Evaluation is an important part of data visualization [11,18,21], and heuristic evaluation is one of several commonly used evaluation methods. In heuristic evaluation, a small group of evaluators review and critique a data visualization plot based on heuristic rules or guidelines. The heuristic rules and guidelines are proposed by data visualization experts based on their experience. Many heuristic rules have been proposed, tested, and challenged [5,7,10,12–15,17,19,22,28,30–32,36,37,39,41,42,44–46,48]. Heuristic evaluation is a type of formative evaluation that can guide visualization developers to improve visualization design, such as visual encoding and interactions [24]. In addition, some researchers have argued that visualization criticism can be used to great effect in visualization teaching and research [10,20].

Supported in part by NSF Award #1852516.

© Springer Nature Switzerland AG 2021
G. Bebis et al. (Eds.): ISVC 2021, LNCS 13018, pp. 408–420, 2021.
https://doi.org/10.1007/978-3-030-90436-4_33

In theory, heuristic evaluation is considered easy to learn and apply and requires little time and other resources [15], but applying heuristic rules in practice is not trivial. First, the heuristic rules are presented in many different research papers and books, often across different disciplines such as computer science, statistics, psychology, and other fields [28,29]. There is no well-curated central repository of these heuristic rules.

Second, heuristic evaluation is generally difficult for a single individual [25,27]. Ideally, heuristic evaluations should be conducted by a small number of experts who are knowledgeable about the heuristic rules as well as the pitfalls and contexts of these rules [26]. In reality, it is not easy to find such an expert, let alone several of them. Therefore, data visualization developers are usually responsible for evaluating their own data visualizations without external help. In addition, data visualization developers generally lack knowledge about evaluating data visualizations because they work in a wide range of fields (e.g., business, physical science, social science, economy, medicine), and most of them are not formally trained in data visualization. As a result, there are many poorly designed data visualizations on the web, in various publications, and in student works.

To address this issue, we propose a computer-assisted heuristic evaluation method and tool to help data visualization developers conduct heuristic evaluations to improve their designs (Fig. 1). This method is made feasible by the recent advances in declarative data visualization libraries [16,33–35], such as Plotly [3], Altair [1], and d3.js [2,9]. In a declarative data visualization library (e.g., Plotly or Altair), plots are stored in a JSON file (Fig. 3), which can be processed by the proposed computer-assisted heuristic evaluation tool. Based on the characteristics of each plot, the evaluation tool will retrieve a set of internally stored heuristic rules and use them to evaluate the plot (Fig. 1). Since declarative tools like Plotly supports a wide variety of data visualizations, such as statistical charts, maps, graphs, parallel coordinates, and 3D plots, our evaluation tool can be used to evaluate many types of data visualizations.

This tool can provide two types of assistance. For heuristic rules that are too abstract or sophisticated for automatic checking, the tool will display these rules to help the developer conduct heuristic evaluation. In this case, the tool serves as a knowledgeable virtual assistant that reminds developers of the heuristic rules and reduces their mental workload. For heuristic rules that are specifically defined, the proposed tool can automatically check the visualization design and provide specific warnings and recommendations.

Our target audience is data visualization developers who create plots through coding. This API-based tool is easy to use and fully integrated with the current data visualization programming environments such as Jupyter Notebook and Google Colab. For example, a developer only needs to import a Python library and make one API call to start the evaluation. It is particularly useful for individual data visualization developers conducting heuristic evaluations on their own. As far as we know, this is the first computer-based heuristic evaluation tool for data visualization.

2   Background and Related Work

Heuristic evaluation was first proposed by Jacob Nielsen [25–27] for usability inspection of user interfaces, and it has become popular in the field of human-computer interaction (HCI). According to Nielsen and Molich [27], "Heuristic evaluation is an informal method of usability analysis where a number of evaluators are presented with an interface design and asked to comment on it." Their experiments showed that individual evaluators were less effective than a small group of evaluators in finding usability issues [27]. Nielsen [26] also showed that usability specialists were better than non-specialists at performing the heuristic evaluation. Our work directly addresses the issues identified by Nielsen. Our computer-assisted heuristic evaluation tool is designed to help individual data visualization developers who are not experts in data visualization evaluation.

The standard evaluation method for data visualization is controlled user studies, but such studies are complex and time-consuming [4, 23]. Many researchers have advocated using heuristic evaluation as a valuable alternative or supplement to the controlled user studies. Tory and Moller [40] argued that expert review could generate valuable feedback on visualization tools, and they recommended developing heuristics based on visualization guidelines and usability guidelines. Munzner [24] proposed a nested model for visualization design and validation, and classified heuristic evaluation as a type of formative evaluation. She further pointed out that heuristic evaluation and expert review are helpful for improving the design of visual encoding and interaction techniques. Lam et al. [21] identified seven guiding scenarios for information visualization evaluation. They pointed out that heuristic evaluation is a useful tool for the design stage and for evaluating collaborative data analysis. Kosara, et al. [20] and Brath and Banissi [10] argued that the visualization design and education could benefit from using more and better critiques. All the previous works assumed that the heuristic evaluations were carried out by human evaluators. However, our work showed that a computer program could be a virtual evaluator for some heuristic evaluation tasks.

Many heuristic rules and guidelines have been proposed for data visualization. Seminal works by Bertin [7], Cleveland and McGill [13], Chambers, et al. [12], Tufte [41, 42], and Shneiderman [38] are highly influential in the data visualization field. In 1990s, Senay and Ignatius [37] collected many heuristic rules and principles for the purpose of developing a visualization tool assistant to help scientists and engineers in selecting and creating effective data visualizations. Many scholars continued to develop, analyze, and classify heuristic rules for data visualization [5, 6, 8, 14, 15, 28, 30–32, 36, 39, 44–46, 48].

Some researchers have tried to develop software tools to assist the evaluation of data visualizations [4, 23]. However, these tools were primarily for assisting user studies, not heuristic analysis. Our evaluation assistant tool is different from the previous work in that our tool focuses on heuristic analysis through code and data analysis.

3   Methodology

3.1   Overview

Figure 1 shows the workflow of computer-assisted heuristic evaluation. A data visualization developer creates a visualization plot using a declarative visualization library, such as Plotly, Altair, or d3.js. The plot is internally stored in a JSON file (see Fig. 3), which is passed to the heuristic evaluation program via a single API call. The heuristic evaluation program processes the JSON file and analyzes the plots based on selected heuristic rules. The outputs of the evaluation program are a set of rules, analyses, warnings, and recommendations. Based on this information, the developer continues to revise and evaluate the visualization plots.

The heuristic evaluation library can be loaded as an external package in a standard programming environment such as Jupyter Notebook, Google Colab, or Observable. The developer only needs to make one API call to start the heuristic evaluation. Therefore, the evaluation tool is easy to use and integrates seamlessly with the current visualization programming practice. This workflow is similar to a writer using a tool like Grammarly to help detect grammar errors and improve the quality of writing.

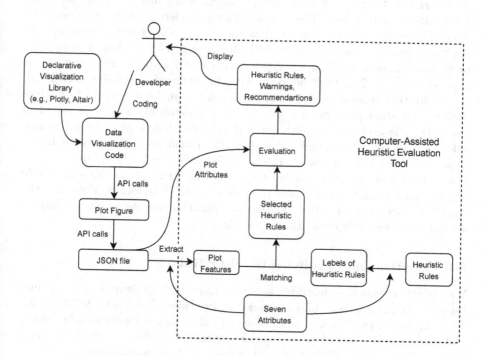

Fig. 1. Computer-assisted heuristic evaluation of data visualization

3.2   Declarative Visualization Libraries

Declarative programming is a programming paradigm in which a developer specifies the logic of a computation without describing its control flow. On the other hand, in imperative programming, a developer implements the control flow to create the desired outcome. One of the best-known examples of declarative programming is the JavaScript library React.

Data visualization libraries can also be divided into imperative libraries and declarative libraries. Imperative libraries include Matplotlib, Seaborn, Bokeh, R/ggplot, Google Charts, etc. Declarative libraries include Plotly [3], Altair [1], d3.js [2], etc. Altair and d3.js are based on the declarative language and visualization grammar research by Heer's lab [16, 33–35]. Their visualization grammars Vega and Vega Lite provide a declarative JSON syntax to create an expressive range of data visualizations. The Plotly library is based on d3.js and uses a similar JSON syntax to store its plots. Plotly also includes a set of imperative API called Plotly Express. Therefore, Plotly developers can choose to use either the declarative Plotly API, the imperative Plotly Express API, or both. In this paper, we will use Plotly in our examples.

In Plotly, a developer creates a plot figure by assigning values to some attributes of a JSON data structure, such as specifying chart type, mapping data variables to X and Y axes, adding labels, etc. Many more attributes are filled with default values. The internal Plotly rendering engine processes the JSON file to draw the plot figure. A developer can also create a figure by calling the imperative Plotly Express APIs in a way similar to that of Matplotlib or Seaborn. Even if the figure is created with Plotly Express, the figure is still expressed in a JSON data structure and can be retrieved with a simple API call.

Declarative libraries such as Plotly and Altair make it feasible to analyze data visualization plots in their entirety. Every detail of the plot is stored in the JSON file and can be retrieved and analyzed based on certain heuristic rules. In contrast, it is much more difficult to analyze a plot created by an imperative visualization library (such as Matplotlib or Seaborn) because one has to write a static code analyzer to process the API calls in the source code and the many default attributes of the plot are difficult to locate. Therefore, the recent advances in declarative visualization libraries provide an opportunity to apply certain heuristic evaluations algorithmically.

3.3   Selecting and Classifying Heuristic Rules

We collected over one hundred heuristic rules and guidelines by searching through various academic papers, books, and websites [5–8, 12–15, 28, 30–32, 36–39, 41, 42, 44–46, 48]. While some rules are specific, many rules are loosely defined and difficult to be checked by a computer program. Therefore, we divide the rules into three categories: *difficult-to-check, advice, and automatic-check.*

The rules in the *difficult-to-check* category are considered too difficult to be checked by a computer program for various reasons, such as too general, too abstract, or too short. For example, the rules "expose uncertainty" [5], "relate"

[38], "flexibility" [15] would fall into this category. We do not include these rules in our program.

The rules in the *advice* category are more specific but still not specific enough to be checked automatically. In this category, a rule might be associated with a specific plot (e.g., a line chart) or a specific feature of the plot (e.g., axis), but it is difficult to conduct a specific evaluation. This type of heuristic rules will be presented to the developer so the developer can conduct the heuristic evaluation herself. In this case, our program would serve as a virtual assistant that advises the developer with heuristic rules relevant to the current plot.

Due to the space limit, we will only list a few examples of the rules in the *advice* category here.

- Maximizing data-ink ratio, but within reason.
- Remove the extraneous ink.
- Choose colormaps that match the nature of the data

The rules in the *automatic-check* category are mostly low-level, specific rules that can be automatically checked by a program. Table 1 shows 20 rules in the *Automatic-Check* category. Additional rules are implemented in our program, and we continue to add more rules.

3.4   Codifying Heuristic Rules

Given a particular plot, how does our program select the relevant heuristic rules for evaluation? We have developed a novel mechanism to match heuristic rules with visualization plots. The basic idea is to label each heuristic rule based on seven attributes. Similarly, each plot is also labeled based on the seven attributes. The heuristic rules with the same or similar labels as the plot are selected for evaluation. We will describe this mechanism in this section and the next two sections.

Each rule in the *advice* and *automatic-check* category is classified based on its connections to the following seven attributes: visual frames, visual structures, visual unities, visual primitives, labeling, interaction, and data attributes. A visualization plot can also be classified based on these attributes. The following list shows the attributes and their possible values.

- Visual Frames: single or multiple visual structures
- Visual Structures: scatter plot, line plot, bar plot, pie chart, map, graph, and other chart types supported by the visualization libraries
- Visual Unities: points, lines, 2D shapes, texts, tooltips, etc.
- Visual Primitives: X or Y position, shape, size, color, and orientation
- Labeling: chart title, X or Y-axis label, ticks on axes, labels, legend, background color, and other style or layout features supported by the visualization libraries
- Interaction: tooltip, zoom, pan, filter, etc.
- Data Attributes: range, dimension, multivariant, categorical, ordinal, nominal, numerical, continuous, etc.

Table 1. Examples of heuristic rules and their classifications

Heuristic rules	Classification
A plot should have a title	Labeling (title)
Each axis should have a label	Visual Primitives (color)
Avoid using more than four different colors	Visual Primitives (color)
Avoid using color to encode ordinal data	Visual Primitives (color)
Local contrast affects color and gray perception	Visual Primitives (color)
Color perception varies with the size of the colored item	Visual Primitives (color, size)
Use color blind friendly palettes	Visual Primitives (color)
Use a lighter color for secondary elements such as frames, grids, and axes	Visual Primitives (color)
A reasonable number of reference values on a coordinate axis might be between four and twelve	Labeling (axis)
If data squeezes toward zero, use a log scale	Labeling (axis), Data (range)
Zoom, filter, and details on demand	Visual Unities (text), Interaction (zoom, filter, tooltip)
Ensure visual variable has sufficient length. For example, it is difficult to tell small differences in size	Visual Primitives (all)
Quantitative assessment requires position or size variation	Visual Primitives (position, size)
Preserve data to graphic dimensionality. For example, avoid representing one or two-dimensional data in 3D visualizations	Visual Structure (3D), Data (dimension)
In general, the position is the most accurate and effective visual variable. Use position for visual encoding when possible	Visual Primitive (position)
Integrate text wherever relevant	Visual Unities (text)
Consider replacing a pie chart with a bar chart	Visual Structure (pie chart)
Do not use line plots if wild points are at all common	Visual Structure (line plot)
Multivariate data calls for multivariate representation. One implication is to consider replacing a stacked bar chart with multiple bar charts or replacing a grouped bar chart with a scatter plot with color-coding	Visual Frame (multiple views), Visual Structure (scatter plot, bar chart), Data (multivariate)
A line plot can only be used to express a continuous function	Visual Structure (line plot), Data (continuous)

The seven attributes are partially based on the visual hierarchy and visual actions proposed by Zhou and Feiner [47]. We removed the visual object "visual discourse" from Zhou and Feiner's original visual hierarchy because it is too abstract for a computer program to check, and we added labeling and data. Visual frame, visual structure, visual unit, and visual primitives are primarily related to visual perception. Labeling and interaction are primarily related to usability. Therefore, the focus of our heuristic analysis is on visual perception or usability, depending on the specific rules.

Table 1 shows the classification of the rules discussed in Sect. 3.3 based on the seven attributes.

3.5 Extracting Plot Features

With declarative visualization library Plotly (or Altair), every attribute of a plot is stored in a JSON file. Our program will parse the JSON file and retrieve relevant information based on the seven attributes discussed in Sect. 3.4. For example, from the JSON file (Fig. 3), our program can identify whether the plot is a single frame or multi-frame plot (Visual Frames), the chart type (Visual Structures), what Visual Units are used, how different data variables are mapped to different Visual Primitives, and whether the plot has titles and labels. Since the JSON file for the figure created by Plotly contains the data, it is also possible to retrieve and analyze data attributes based on the JSON file. Therefore, each plot can be labeled based on the values for the seven attributes. Several examples will be discussed in Sect. 4.

3.6 Computer-Assisted Evaluation

Since both the heuristic rules and plots are labeled based on the same seven attributes, it is now possible to match them by the labels. For a particular plot, our program searches for the heuristic rules with labels that match the labels of the plot. Once the heuristic rules are selected for a particular plot, the nature of the assistance provided to the developer depends on the type of rules. For the rules in the *advice* category, our program displays the rules and lets the developer evaluate the plot. Our program can also display a more detailed description of the rules, such as the sources of the rules, context, potential pitfalls, and counterpoints. In this case, our program serves as a knowledgeable assistant that advises the developer in evaluating the visualization design.

For the rules in the *automatic-check* category, our program will analyze the plot based on the values extracted from the JSON file. Since the logic of the evaluation varies from rule to rule, each heuristic rule is implemented separately in a function. The output of the automatic evaluation is a set of rules, analyses, warnings, and recommendations.

We implemented this computer-assisted evaluation tool in Python for Plotly-generated charts. This is an API-based tool with no graphical user interface. Our goal is to make it integrate seamlessly with the existing coding workflow. It can work in any Python programming environment such as Jupyter Notebook and Google Colab.

4 Case Studies

Figure 2 shows four plots created with Plotly. All four examples are taken from the official Plotly programming guide [3], which unfortunately contains many data visualizations that need improvement.

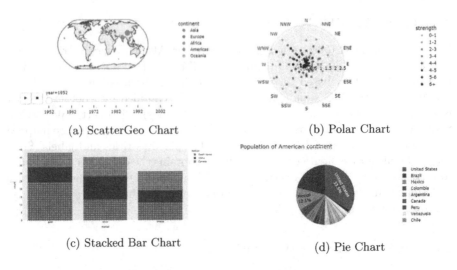

(a) ScatterGeo Chart

(b) Polar Chart

(c) Stacked Bar Chart

(d) Pie Chart

Fig. 2. Charts created with Plotly

For each chart (or figure), a program calls the Plotly API fig.to_json() or fig.to_plotly_json() to retrieve the JSON file (see Fig. 3) and call our API heustic_eval(fig.to_json()) to start the heuristic evaluation.

For Fig. 2(a), from the JSON file, our program detects five *geo* traces, each with two markers: *color* and *size*. Based on the heuristic rules, a warning will be displayed to inform the developer that he or she used more than four colors. Our program also detects *buttons* with 'method': 'animate' in the JSON file. This means the plot has an animation button. Based on this information, the heuristic rule about animation will be displayed, advising the developer about the pros and cons of animation [17,43].

For Fig. 2(b), from the JSON file, our program detects eight *scatterpolar* type traces, each with two markers: *color* and *symbol*. Based on the heuristic rules, two warnings will be displayed. The first one warns the developer that too many colors are used. The second one warns the developer about the drawbacks of using shapes as visual variables [7].

For Fig. 2(c), from the JSON file, our program detects three *bar* traces, each with two markers: *color* and *pattern*. Based on the heuristic rules, two warnings will be displayed. One warns the developer about the drawbacks of stacked bar charts and suggests an alternative: a grouped bar chart. The second warns about the pitfalls of using patterns as a visual variable [7].

For Fig. 2(d), from the JSON file, our program detects a *pie* chart with 25 *values* and *labels*. A warning will be displayed to remind the developer about the drawbacks of pie charts and suggest an alternative: bar chart.

Our program also detects the missing *title* property in the JSON files of Figs. 2(a), 2(b), and 2(c) and generates warnings.

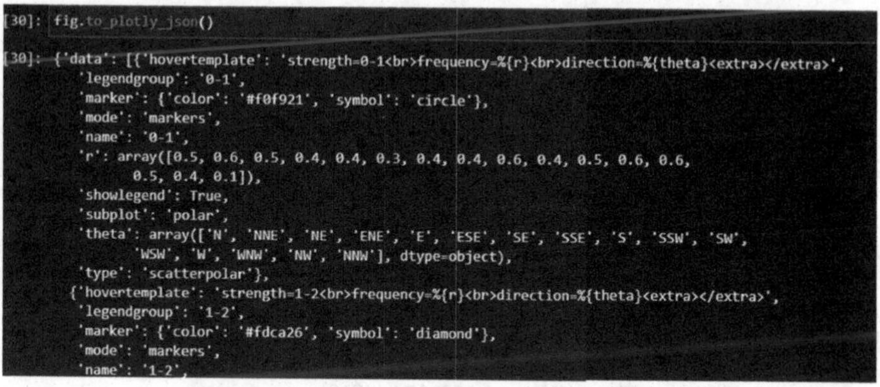

```
[30]: fig.to_plotly_json()

[30]: {'data': [{'hovertemplate': 'strength=0-1<br>frequency=%{r}<br>direction=%{theta}<extra></extra>',
        'legendgroup': '0-1',
        'marker': {'color': '#f0f921', 'symbol': 'circle'},
        'mode': 'markers',
        'name': '0-1',
        'r': array([0.5, 0.6, 0.5, 0.4, 0.4, 0.3, 0.4, 0.4, 0.6, 0.4, 0.5, 0.6, 0.6,
               0.5, 0.4, 0.1]),
        'showlegend': True,
        'subplot': 'polar',
        'theta': array(['N', 'NNE', 'NE', 'ENE', 'E', 'ESE', 'SE', 'SSE', 'S', 'SSW', 'SW',
               'WSW', 'W', 'WNW', 'NW', 'NNW'], dtype=object),
        'type': 'scatterpolar'},
       {'hovertemplate': 'strength=1-2<br>frequency=%{r}<br>direction=%{theta}<extra></extra>',
        'legendgroup': '1-2',
        'marker': {'color': '#fdca26', 'symbol': 'diamond'},
        'mode': 'markers',
        'name': '1-2',
```

Fig. 3. Part of the JSON file for the Polar Chart in Fig. 2(b)

5 Limitations

This computer-assisted heuristic evaluation method has its limitations. First, it only works for heuristic rules that are more specific. Many heuristic rules are too abstract to be checked automatically. This tool can help visualization developers find some design flaws, but much of the evaluation still needs to be done by a human. Second, this tool works with declarative visualization libraries such as Plotly, Altair, d3.js, or d3.js based tools. It does not work with imperative visualization libraries such as Matplotlib, Seaborn, Bokeh, or R/ggplot. So far, we have only implemented this tool in Python for Plotly, but it can be adapted to support Altair and d3.js.

6 Conclusion and Future Work

We have presented a method and tool for computer-assisted heuristic evaluation of data visualization. Heuristic evaluation is a valuable method for improving visualization designs. However, heuristic evaluation is often difficult for individual visualization developers who are often unfamiliar with the wide range of heuristic rules and their pitfalls. The proposed tool addresses this issue by providing virtual assistance during the coding process, informing developers of the relevant heuristic rules, and in some cases, automatically checking the visualization plots for possible design flaws or improvements. Although the tool is still limited to certain specifically defined heuristic rules and only works for declarative visualization libraries, it is a step toward AI-enabled automatic evaluation of data visualizations.

We are improving the tool by adding and testing more heuristic rules and adding support for Altair and d3.js based visualization libraries.

References

1. Altair: Declarative visualization in python. https://altair-viz.github.io/, Accessed 07 Aug 2021
2. d3.js. https://d3js.org/, Accessed 07 Aug 2021
3. Plotly graphing libraries. https://plotly.com/python/, Accessed 07 Aug 2021
4. Aigner, W., Hoffmann, S., Rind, A.: Evalbench: a software library for visualization evaluation. Comput. Graph. Forum 32, 41–50 (2013)
5. Amar, R., Stasko, J.: A knowledge task-based framework for design and evaluation of information visualizations. In: Proceedings of the IEEE Symposium on Information Visualization, pp. 143–149 (2004)
6. Barcellos, R., Viterbo, J., Bernardini, F., Trevisan, D.: An instrument for evaluating the quality of data visualizations. In: 2018 22nd International Conference Information Visualisation (IV), pp. 169–174 (2018)
7. Bertin, J.: Semiology of Graphics, 1st edn. ESRI Press, Noida (2010)
8. Borland, D., Taylor, R.M., II.: Rainbow color map (still) considered harmful. IEEE Comput. Graph. Appl. 27(02), 14–17 (2007)
9. Bostock, M., Ogievetsky, V., Heer, J.: D3 data-driven documents. IEEE Trans. Vis. Comput. Graph. 17, 2301–2309 (2011)
10. Brath, R., Banissi, E.: Evaluation of visualization by critiques. In: Proceedings of the Sixth Workshop on Beyond Time and Errors on Novel Evaluation Methods for Visualization (BELIV), pp. 19–26. ACM (2016)
11. Carpendale, S.: Evaluating information visualizations. In: Kerren, A., Stasko, J.T., Fekete, J.-D., North, C. (eds.) Information Visualization. LNCS, vol. 4950, pp. 19–45. Springer, Heidelberg (2008). https://doi.org/10.1007/978-3-540-70956-5_2
12. Chambers, J.M., Cleveland, W.S., Tukey, P.A., Kleiner, B.: Graphical Methods for Data Analysis. Duxbury Press, Pacific Grove (1983)
13. Cleveland, W.S., McGill, R.: Graphical perception: theory, experimentation, and application to the development of graphical methods. J. Am. Stat. Assoc. 79, 531–554 (1984)
14. Forsell, C.: Evaluation in information visualization: Heuristic evaluation. In: Proceedings of the International Conference on Information Visualisation, pp. 136–142. IEEE (2012)
15. Forsell, C., Johansson, J.: An heuristic set for evaluation in information visualization. In: Proceedings of the International Conference on Advanced Visual Interfaces, pp. 199–206. ACM (2010)
16. Heer, J., Bostock, M.: Declarative language design for interactive visualization. IEEE Trans. Vis. Comput. Graph. 16(6), 1149–1156 (2010)
17. Hullman, J., Adar, E., Shah, P.: Benefitting infovis with visual difficulties. IEEE Trans. Vis. Comput. Graph. 17, 2213–2222 (2011)
18. Isenberg, T., Isenberg, P., Chen, J., Sedlmair, M., Moller, T.: A systematic review on the practice of evaluating visualization. IEEE Trans. Vis. Comput. Graph. 19, 2818–2827 (2013)
19. Kosara, R.: An empire built on sand: reexamining what we think we know about visualization. In: Proceedings of the Sixth Workshop on Beyond Time and Errors on Novel Evaluation Methods in Visualization, pp. 162–168. ACM (2016)
20. Kosara, R., Drury, F., Holmquist, L.E., Laidlaw, D.H.: Visualization criticism. IEEE Comput. Graph. Appl 28, 13–15 (2008)
21. Lam, H., Bertini, E., Isenberg, P., Plaisant, C., Carpendale, S.: Empirical studies in information visualization: seven scenarios. IEEE Trans. Vis. Comput. Graph. 18, 1520–1536 (2012)

22. Larkin, J.H., Simon, H.A.: Why a diagram is (sometimes) worth ten thousand words. Cogn. Sci. **11**, 65–100 (1987)

23. Lücke-Tieke, H., Beuth, M., Schader, P., May, T., Bernard, J., Kohlhammer, J.: Lowering the barrier for successful replication and evaluation. In: 2018 IEEE Evaluation and Beyond - Methodological Approaches for Visualization (BELIV), pp. 60–68 (2018)

24. Munzner, T.: A nested model for visualization design and validation. IEEE Trans. Vis. Comput. Graph. **15**, 921–928 (2009)

25. Nielsen, J.: Heuristic evaluation. In: Nielsen, J., Mack, R.L. (eds.) Usability Inspection Methods. Wiley, Hoboken (1994)

26. Nielsen, J.: Finding usability problems through heuristic evaluation. In: Proceedings of the SIGCHI Conference on Human Factors in Computing Systems, pp. 373–380. ACM (1992)

27. Nielsen, J., Molich, R.: Heuristic evaluation of user interfaces. In: Proceedings of the SIGCHI Conference on Human Factors in Computing Systems, pp. 249–256. ACM (1990)

28. Parish, C.M., Edmondson, P.D.: Data visualization heuristics for the physical sciences. Mater. Des. **179**, 107868 (2019)

29. Rougier, N.P., Droettboom, M., Bourne, P.E.: Ten simple rules for better figures. PLOS Comput. Biol. **10**(9), 1–7 (2014)

30. Santos, B.S., Ferreira, B.Q., Dias, P.: Heuristic evaluation in information visualization using three sets of heuristics: an exploratory study. In: Kurosu, M. (ed.) HCI 2015. LNCS, vol. 9169, pp. 259–270. Springer, Cham (2015). https://doi.org/10.1007/978-3-319-20901-2_24

31. Santos, B.S., Ferreira, B.Q., Dias, P.: Using heuristic evaluation to foster visualization analysis and design skills. IEEE Comput. Graph. Appl **36**, 86–90 (2016)

32. Santos, B.S., Silva, S., Dias, P.: Heuristic evaluation in visualization: an empirical study. In: 2018 IEEE Evaluation and Beyond - Methodological Approaches for Visualization (BELIV), pp. 78–85 (2018)

33. Satyanarayan, A., Moritz, D., Wongsuphasawat, K., Heer, J.: Vega-lite: a grammar of interactive graphics. IEEE Trans. Vis. Comput. Graph. **23**(1), 341–350 (2017)

34. Satyanarayan, A., Russell, R., Hoffswell, J., Heer, J.: Reactive vega: a streaming dataflow architecture for declarative interactive visualization. IEEE Trans. Vis. Comput. Graph. **22**, 659–668 (2016)

35. Satyanarayan, A., Wongsuphasawat, K., Heer, J.: Declarative interaction design for data visualization. In: Proceedings of the 27th Annual ACM Symposium on User Interface Software and Technology, pp. 669–678. ACM (2014)

36. Scholtz, J.: Developing guidelines for assessing visual analytics environments. Inf. Vis. **10**, 212–231 (2011)

37. Senay, H., Ignatius, E.: Rules and principles of scientific visualization. Technical report, Department of Electrical Engineering and Computer Science, George Washington University (1990). http://www6.uniovi.es/hypvis/percept/visrules.htm, Accessed 07 Aug 2021

38. Shneiderman, B.: The eyes have it: a task by data type taxonomy for information visualizations. In: Proceedings of IEEE Symposium on Visual Languages, pp. 336–343 (1996)

39. Tarrell, A., Forsell, C., Fruhling, A., Grinstein, G., Borgo, R., Scholtz, J.: Toward visualization-specific heuristic evaluation. In: Proceedings of the Fifth Workshop on Beyond Time and Errors: Novel Evaluation Methods for Visualization. ACM (2014)

40. Tory, M., Möller, T.: Evaluating visualizations: do expert reviews work? IEEE Comput. Graph. Appl. **25**, 8–11 (2005)
41. Tufte, E.R.: Visual Explanations: Images and Quantities, Evidence and Narrative. Graphics Press, Cheshire (1997)
42. Tufte, E.R.: The Visual Display of Quantitative Information, 2nd edn. Graphics Press, Cheshire (2011)
43. Tversky, B., Morrison, J.B., Betrancourt, M.: Animation: can it facilitate? Int. J. Hum.-Comput. Stud. **57**, 247–262 (2002)
44. Väätäjä, H., et al.: Information visualization heuristics in practical expert evaluation. In: Proceedings of the Sixth Workshop on Beyond Time and Errors on Novel Evaluation Methods for Visualization, pp. 36–43. ACM (2016)
45. Wall, E.: A heuristic approach to value-driven evaluation of visualizations. IEEE Trans. Vis. Comput. Graph. **25**, 491–500 (2019)
46. Williams, R., Scholtz, J., Blaha, L.M., Franklin, L., Huang, Z.: Evaluation of visualization heuristics. In: Kurosu, M. (ed.) HCI 2018. LNCS, vol. 10901, pp. 208–224. Springer, Cham (2018). https://doi.org/10.1007/978-3-319-91238-7_18
47. Zhou, M.X., Feiner, S.K.: Top-down hierarchical planning of coherent visual discourse. In: Proceedings of the International Conference on Intelligent User Interface (IUI), pp. 129–136. ACM (1997)
48. Zuk, T., Schlesier, L., Neumann, P., Hancock, M., Carpendale, S.: Heuristics for information visualization evaluation. In: Proceedings of the 2006 AVI Workshop on Beyond Time and Errors: Novel Evaluation Methods for Information Visualization, pp. 1–6 (2006)

Frame Fields for CAD Models

David Desobry[✉], François Protais, Nicolas Ray, Etienne Corman,
and Dmitry Sokolov

Université de Lorraine, CNRS, Inria, LORIA, 54000 Nancy, France
david.desobry@inria.fr

Abstract. Given a triangulated surface, a unit length tangent vector field can be used to orient entities located on the surface, such as glyphs or strokes. When these entities are invariant under a $\pi/2$ rotation (squares, or curvature hatching), the orientation can be represented by a frame field *i.e.* four orthogonal tangent unit vectors at each point of the surface. The generation of such fields is a key component of recent quad meshing algorithms based on global parameterization as it defines the orientation of the final facets. State-of-the-art methods are able to generate smooth frame fields subject to some hard constraints (direction and topology) or smooth constraints (matching the curvature direction). When we have a surface triangular mesh, and a vector defined on each facet, we cannot directly know if all the vectors are colinear. We first have to define the (so called) parallel transport of every edge to compare the vectors on a common plan.

When dealing with CAD models, the field must be aligned with feature edges. A problem occurs when there is an acute angle corner formed by two colliding feature edges. Our solution not only defines the parallel transport to obtain smoothed frame fields on a surface triangular mesh, it also redefines the parallel transport wherever there is a low angle corner, to smooth a frame field as if these corners' angles were $\pi/2$.

Keywords: Frame fields · CAD models · Geometry processing

1 Introduction

State-of-the-art quandrangular mesh generation proceeds in two steps: first a guiding frame field is computed, second a parametrization representing the quads is extracted. The frame field defines the orientation of the quads at each point of the domain, whereas the parameterization step determines the vertex positions of the quads. So, frame fields are an intermediate result in the pipeline of quad mesh generation. A high quality quad mesh typically has low distortion and few singular vertices (valence $\neq$ 4). Frame fields are produced by a numerical optimization that maximizes the smoothness of the field, naturally preventing creation of singularities: in the vicinity of a singular point a field has a high curvature that is penalized by the optimization (Fig. 1).

© Springer Nature Switzerland AG 2021
G. Bebis et al. (Eds.): ISVC 2021, LNCS 13018, pp. 421–434, 2021.
https://doi.org/10.1007/978-3-030-90436-4_34

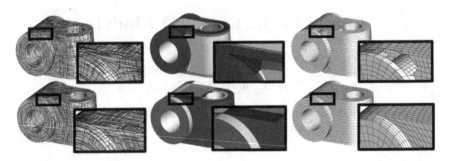

Fig. 1. Producing a frame field with minimal rotation on a CAD model is not sufficient for quad meshing (upper row). Our algorithm allows to handle those sharp edges configurations.

CAD models are particular surfaces because they have a network of feature edges that must be preserved during the remeshing process. Thus, a feature edge of the input triangle mesh must be a feature edge of the output quandrangular mesh. Unfortunately, these edges can meet with acute angle making it impossible to fit a perfect quadrangle in such a sharp corner, as illustrated in Fig. 2. As a consequence, the guiding frame field computed as an intermediate step cannot be turned into a quad mesh and the standard quad meshing method fails. Typical failure cases are shown in Fig. 9.

These problematic sharp corners are omnipresent in CAD models as they appear naturally from fillets and chamfers – common designs for mechanical pieces. In the ABC dataset [12] (a collection of one million Computer-Aided Design models) we found that more than 65% of the models have potentially problematic sharp corners. In Thingi10k [22], which is not specialized in CAD models, around 35% of the dataset present at least one sharp corner. This is why non-orthogonality and metric deformation has been a common subject of research recently. In this paper, we propose an easier and much faster way to deal with these problematic cases than previous works.

Fig. 2. If two colliding feature edges produce a low angle corner constraint, a classical frame field will align with both feature edge as if they were parallel. It produces a 1/2 singularity that can't be meshed with valid quads.

1.1 Contribution

Our solution automatically produces high quality orthogonal frame field aligned with feature edges with a topology compatible with quad meshing on CAD models. It then relaxes the orthogonality of the frame field to match even more the feature edges configurations that require non-orthogonality.

These two steps are performed by solving two linear systems, so the impact on performances compared to standard orthogonal frame field generation is very low. Previous works [5,7,9] are providing some solutions to solve these problems, but they are much harder to implement, require non-linear optimizations that highly impact performances, and need fine parameter tuning to results close to ours.

The rest of the paper is organized as follows: after a review of related work, we formalize the problem in Sect. 2, recall the mathematical background for orthogonal frame field generation Sect. 3.3, and present our first contribution to avoid degenerate fields Sect. 3. In Sect. 4, we further optimize the field curvature by relaxing its orthogonality. We evaluate the quality of our field in Sect. 5 for producing quad meshes.

1.2 Related Work

Frame field generation has been an active research area during the last decade [21]. They were introduced in computer graphics to place hatches in non photo-realistic rendering [6]. However, the main application is quad meshing by global parameterization that was discovered a few years later [17], and improved in [2,10]. Frame fields are usually produced by numerical optimization. The objective is to minimize the field smoothness, with some minor application dependent modifications like following the surface curvature [17], or better represent a 3D field projected in 2D [7]. Most works are contributing to better optimize the smoothness or to add geometric and topological constraints. The main challenge of frame field generation comes from the field topology (mostly the position and type of field singularities), which requires adding integer constraints in the optimization problem.

The first solution was to use periodic functions where the field topology was "encoded" in the modulus of the function. The idea comes from the observation that if the kth direction of a frame have an angle of $\alpha + k\pi/2$ with a fixed vector, then $\cos(4(\alpha + k\pi/2))$ is the same for all directions. Therefore Hertzmann et al. [6] encode a frame by a cosine and minimizes the L^2-norm between adjacent samples. It is, however, more efficient to optimize the field with both the sine and the cosine [17], that is usually referred as representation vector or complex representation. The problem when working with these variables is to preserve the constraint that $\cos^2(4\alpha) + \sin^2(4\alpha) = 1$, making the problem highly non linear. Forcing the norm of the frame field [1,11] improves the results but seriously impacts performances.

In some cases, control over the field topology is desirable. For instance, to reduce the number of singularities, change their types, or enforce the field behavior along non contractible loops. Complete control over the field topology can be obtained directly [20], or by modification of an existing field [15]. The problem is that the topology is defined by a large set of integers (a bit more than the index of each point of the surface that can be a singularity), that are very hard to set. In [2,7], these integers variables are automatically optimized, but could probably be constrained to force some of the topological degrees of freedom.

In practice, automatically generated field topology is not always the best, but it is difficult to choose a topology before generating the frame field. One can fix the topology of an existing frame field [15] as a post-processing. Another possibility is to modify the optimization problem in a way that will favor locally high field curvature against producing singularities on geometric details [19]. Our method is inspired by this work to control the impact of sharp corners.

Non orthogonal frame fields were introduced in [14] for generating planar quad meshes, where directions must be conjugate instead of orthogonal. Changing the metric of the surface [9,16] naturally stretches the crosses, that loose their orthogonality. However, setting the metric prior to the cross constraints makes it hard to support alignment with feature edges, and the optimization becomes more challenging. Representing the field as root of a complex polynomial [3,4] also supports non orthogonal frames, but introduces non-linear optimization problems and requires fine parameter tuning. In [7], the 2D frame field is the projection of a frame field defined on a surface, leading to non orthogonal frame fields, obtained by minimizing a different objective function. It should be possible to adapt it for our case, but it makes the solution dependent of a non trivial implementation of their mixed-integer solver. We instead solve the topology with orthogonal frames, then further optimize its geometry by relaxing the orthogonality. It should be possible to produce frame fields similar to ours using these methods, but it requires to adapt complex optimizations framework, whereas our method only requires to solve a couple of linear systems. Moreover, we support extreme distortions on sharp corners that would challenge the solvers.

2   Formalization and Our Approach Overview

Our pipeline takes as input a triangle mesh with identified feature edges, and computes a non-orthogonal, per-triangle constant frame field aligned with the feature edges. The goal is to compute a frame field with the lowest total rotation; the field must not have index $1/2$ singularities at sharp corners. In practice, we relax the orthogonality of the field at the very last step, therefore in this section we give formal definitions for the total rotation and the singularity indices both for orthogonal and non-orthogonal fields.

N.B. Our frame field will be represented on faces of a triangulated surface. It makes frames independent across feature edges, thus we can cut the mesh along feature edges without loss of generality. From now on, **feature edges will be considered as boundaries**; it considerably simplifies the notations.

Orthogonal Frame Fields: a frame on a triangle consists of a set of four tangent unit vectors $\{v, v^{\perp}, -v, -v^{\perp}\}$. It is common to endow each triangle i with a reference vector b_i and describe the frame as a rotation angle α_i of the reference vector b_i around the normal. Thus, a frame field can be represented by the set of angles $\{\alpha_i, \alpha_i + \pi/2, \alpha_i + 2\pi/2, \alpha_i + 3\pi/2\}$, refer to Fig. 5–left.

The rotation of an orthogonal frame field is usually measured by the rotation r_{ij} between frames of two adjacent triangles i, j:

$$r_{ij} = -\alpha_i + \alpha_j + c_{ij} + p_{ij}\pi/2, \tag{1}$$

where c_{ij} accounts for the change (once both triangles rotated into a common plane) between the reference vectors b_i and b_j, therefore $-\alpha_i + \alpha_j + c_{ij}$ is the rotation between two adjacent frames. Since the frame is invariant under $\pi/2$ rotation, the integer p_{ij} reflects the matching between the branches of the frames (see Fig. 3). In most cases, p_{ij} is chosen to minimize the rotation.

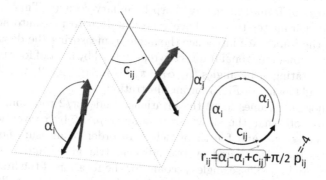

Fig. 3. (α_i) are frame angles, c_{ij} is the rotation between reference vectors of triangles i and j. Integer p_{ij} disambiguates the modulo $\pi/2$.

The problem to generate the smoothest orthogonal frame field can be formulated as the minimization of the total field rotation:

$$\arg\min \sum_{ij} r_{ij}^2 \text{ subject to boundary constraints.} \tag{2}$$

The last thing we need to define for orthogonal frame fields is the frame field index. For a vertex v we define the index as follows:

$$\mathcal{I}(v) := \frac{1}{2\pi}\left(\sum_{ij \in E(v)} r_{ij} - \theta_v\right) + 1 - \frac{\mathbb{1}_{\partial\Omega}(v)}{2}, \tag{3}$$

where $\mathbb{1}_{\partial\Omega}(v) \in \{0, 1\}$ is the indicator variable telling us whether it is a boundary vertex or not, $E(v)$ denotes the set of dual edges over the 1-ring of the vertex v, and θ_v is the sum of all mesh angles at the vertex (all the triangle corners incident to the vertex). Most common indices are illustrated in Fig. 4, they follow the convention used in [13].

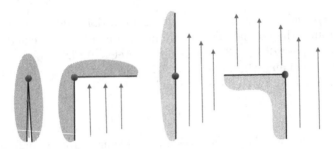

Fig. 4. Index for boundary vertices with a constant field. From left to right: indices $1/2, 1/4, 0, -1/4$.

Non Orthogonal Frame Fields: We want to relax the orthogonality constraint so non-orthogonal frames fit neatly sharp boundary corners. Thus, we need to add an extra parameter to the above representation to take into account the skewness of the frame. We introduce the angle ρ_i measuring the deviation from orthogonality; non-orthogonal frames are represented by a set of four unit vectors obtained by rotating b_i by angles $(\alpha_i, \alpha_i + \pi/2 + \rho_i, \alpha_i + 2\pi/2, \alpha_i + 3\pi/2 + \rho_i)$, refer to the right panel of Fig. 5 for an illustration.

Non-orthogonal frames loose the invariance under $\pi/2$ rotation. Thus, it is important to note that the skewness parameter ρ_i is, by convention, always applied to the second and fourth branches. In order to measure how a frame rotates across the edge shared by two adjacent triangles i and j, we need to define two r_{ij}^0 and r_{ij}^1. These angles account for the rotation of the first and third branches and the skew second and fourth branches respectively as illustrated in Fig. 6.

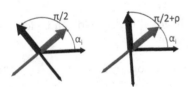

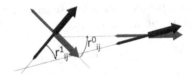

Fig. 5. A non-orthogonal frame (right) has an extra degree of freedom ρ_i pulling the second branch away from orthogonality.

Fig. 6. Non orthogonal frame fields have two angular differences r_{ij}^0 and r_{ij}^1, one for each pair of vectors.

Imagine that the first branch of the frame on triangle i is matched with the first (or third) branch of the frame on triangle j (i.e. $p_{ij} = 0 \bmod 2$) then r_{ij}^0 is given by Eq. (1). In this case the second branch matches on i the second (or fourth) branch on j and r_{ij}^1 is computed by reapplying Eq. (1) with angles $\alpha_i + \rho_i$ and $\alpha_j + \rho_j$.

When $p_{ij} \mod 2 = 1$, the first branch of the frame on triangle i is matched with the second (or fourth) branch of the frame on triangle j then r_{ij}^0 is obtained by replacing α_j by $\alpha_j + \rho_j$ in Eq. (1).

The overall formula can be summarized by:

$$\begin{cases} r_{ij}^0 = -\alpha_i + \alpha_j + c_{ij} + p_{ij}\frac{\pi}{2} + (p_{ij} \mod 2)\rho_j \\ r_{ij}^1 = -\alpha_i - \rho_i + \alpha_j + c_{ij} + p_{ij}\frac{\pi}{2} + (1 - (p_{ij} \mod 2))\rho_j \end{cases} \tag{4}$$

Then the smoothest non orthogonal frame field is the one minimizing the total rotation:

$$\arg\min \sum_{ij} \left(r_{ij}^0\right)^2 + \left(r_{ij}^1\right)^2 \text{ subject to boundary constraints.} \tag{5}$$

Our Approach Overview: as explained in Sect. 3.1, one daunting challenge for quad meshing a CAD model is the omnipresence of sharp corners. It forces index 1/2 boundary singularities to appear in the smoothest frame fields, making it impossible to extract a valid quad-mesh. To avoid this situation the main idea is to trade some smoothness against the appearance of acceptable singularities on sharp corners. More precisely, we alter the notion of smoothness to ban unmeshable configurations.

So, given a triangle mesh with boundary (recall that all feature edges are considered as a boundary), our algorithm computes two tangent directions per triangle by following the steps described in the subsequent sections:

- Section 3: compute an **orthogonal** frame field without index 1/2 singularities at sharp corners. The idea is to change the objective rotation ω (Sect. 3.2) and then to compute the smoothest frame field with respect to ω (Sect. 3.3)
- Section 4: compute a **non-orthogonal** field that reduces the field rotation w.r.t the orthogonal field. In other words, we relax the orthogonality constraint.

3   Compute a Meshable Orthogonal Frame Field

A standard way to compute the smoothest (orthogonal) frame field is to minimize the total field rotation $\sum_{ij} r_{ij}^2$ under boundary constraints. The problem, however, is that this approach often leads to unmeshable frame fields (Sect. 3.1). To avoid this pitfall, we do not generate frame fields whose rotation is the smallest possible, but rather the closest to a prescribed rotation ω that prevents sharp corner collapses (Sect. 3.2). We represent ω by a rotation angle ω_{ij} between each pair of adjacent triangles i and j. Once this target rotation has been obtained, the frame field is simply computed by minimizing the distance to the target $\sum_{ij}(r_{ij} - \omega_{ij})^2$, Sect. 3.3 provides all necessary details.

3.1 Problem Characterization

A frame field becomes non quad meshable whenever there is a boundary vertex with index of 1/2 (see Fig. 2 and Fig. 8 left).

Let v be a boundary vertex with a small total angle θ_v. The frame field minimizing the rotation is very likely to be such that $\sum_{ij \in E(v)} r_{ij} = \theta_v$ i.e. placing an index of 1/2 on vertex v. Note that Eq. (3) provides a way to detect potential problematic configurations. Indeed, if the total angle at a boundary vertex is $\theta_v < \pi/4$, minimizing the rotations of the frames around this vertex leads to the problematic index 1/2 singularity, with a total field rotation of θ_v. This case can be avoided by forcing the frame rotation to be as close as possible to a target rotation field ω in this situation.

From a differential geometry point of view, ω is a 1-form that we use to redefine the parallel transport. In contrast to redefinition of the metric [9,16], it does not modify the orthogonality of the frames.

3.2 Prescribe the Target Field Rotation ω

In this section, we start by reviewing a naive fix: a very local target rotation prescription, and then a global one that gives great quality results.

A Naive Local Fix. The target rotation field ω should promote 1/4 index singularity in places where the smoothest frame field (Eq. (2)) is likely to place an index 1/2 singularity. More precisely, for each boundary vertex v with total angle $\theta_v < \pi/2$, setting its index to 1/4 constrains the sum of field rotation in the 1-ring by Eq. (3): $\sum_{ij \in E(v)} r_{ij} = \theta_v - \pi/2$. We therefore add this constraint to the target rotation, that we write as $d\omega(v) = \theta_v - \pi/2$, where $d\omega(v) = \sum_{ij \in E(v)} \omega_{ij}$ denotes the exterior derivative of ω, extended to the boundary of the surface.

Why is it So Local? If we simply evenly distribute $\theta_v - \pi/2$ on the ω_{ij} of each dual edge $ij \in E(v)$, it indeed moves the singularity away from the boundary, but only as little as possible. The common case of two adjacent boundary triangles i and j (Fig. 8 middle) is very representative of this behavior. As detailed in Fig. 7, imposing $d\omega(v) = \omega_{ji} = \theta_v - \pi/2$ will lead to a matching rotation of $r_{ji} = \theta_v - \pi/2$. As we are looking for the smoothest field, the rotation on neighboring dual edges jk and ki will be $r_{jk} = r_{ki} = \theta_v/2$. By Eq. (3), the index of center vertex is then $-1/4$: the singularity has barely moved away from the boundary.

What happened here is that $d\omega(v)$ is perturbing the energy Eq. (8) needed for choosing the index of v: as observed in [19], it acts as the angle defect. Moreover, if the triangles i, j share the edge v, v', increasing ω_{ij} mechanically increases $d\omega(v)$ and decreases $d\omega(v')$ by the same amount. As a consequence, the sum remains null, i.e. $\sum_v d\omega(v) = 0$. When altering ω only in the 1-ring of v, we are simply moving $d\omega(v)$ to its neighboring vertex... that naturally becomes the new singular vertex.

A Global Solution. Instead of forcing the nearest vertex to become a singularity, it is often better to place it a bit farther (Fig. 8 right). To do so, the

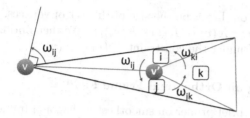

Fig. 7. Local fix of a sharp corner: We set $\omega_{ij} \leftarrow \theta_v - \pi/2$ to force $I(v) = 1/4$. If ω_{jk} and ω_{ki} are null, then $d\omega(v') = \theta_v - \pi/2$. Therefore, the final frame field will have $r_{ij} = \omega_{ij}$, $r_{jk} = r_{ki} = \theta_v/2$, leading to an index $1/4$ at v'.

modification of $d\omega(v)$ that prevents index $1/2$ on sharp corners should not just be transferred to it's nearest neighbor: it would be better to have $d\omega(v) = 0$ for all other vertices. Unfortunately, the constraint $\sum_{ij} d\omega(v) = 0$ makes it impossible, so we instead distribute the constrained $d\omega(v)$ of sharp corner vertices onto all other vertices.

A two step optimization method can be used to determine ω:

- we compute a scalar $K(v)$ per vertex v such that $\sum_v K(v)^2$ is minimal, $K(v) = \pi/2 - \theta_v$ on sharp corners v, and $\sum_v K(v) = 0$. The solution just distributes the sum of the $-K(v)$ of the sharp corners on other vertices. This optimization is done independently for each connected component of the surface (that are likely to be generated when cutting the surface along feature edges).
- we then minimize $\arg\min \sum_{ij} \|\omega_{ij}\|^2$ under the constraint $d\omega(v) = K(v)$. The constraint $\sum_v K(v) = 0$ guarantees the existence of a solution.

| (a) Smoothest field | (b) Constrain only the 1-ring of the sharp corner | (c) Propagate the field curvature |

Fig. 8. On a sharp corner, the smoothest field produces lines of quads that crash in the vertex corner (a). A local fix solves this problem (b), but the propagation of the field curvature is what produces most exploitable lines of quads (c).

This global solution is not always optimal, we don't want the field curvature to spread too far from the sharp corner and produce global distorsions. In practice, we initialize $K(v) \leftarrow \pi/2 - \theta_v$ for sharp corners and $K(v) \leftarrow 0$ for other vertices. Then, for each sharp corner v_s, we compute the set of vertices that can be reached by following less than 5 edges. This tradeoff avoids both local or global high distorsion. Let n be the size of this set of vertices, we update K for all vertices of the set : $K(v) \leftarrow K(v) - K(v_s)/n$. We then optimize omega values $\arg \min \sum_{ij} \|\omega_{ij}\|^2$ under the constraint $d\omega(v) = K(v)$.

3.3   Computing an Orthogonal Frame Field

Let us start with a brief primer on smoothest orthogonal frame field generation (Eq. (2)). The state of the art is to lock boundary frames to have one direction tangent to the boundary, and to minimize the total field rotation. Note that if a triangle has two boundary edges, one can split the triangle in three by adding a vertex at the center to avoid overconstraining the problem .

The smoothest field is the field with minimum rotation r_{ij}. To avoid having to deal with integer variable p_{ij}, a well-known trick is to use a "representation vector" as it is referred to in [18]. The smoothest orthogonal frame field is the one having zero rotation across every dual edge (i.e. $r_{ij} = 0$). Thus in Eq. (1) one can multiply by 4i and take the complex exponential, leading to:

$$e^{4i\alpha_i} = e^{4i\alpha_j} e^{4ic_{ij}} e^{2ip_{ij}\pi}. \tag{6}$$

Since p_{ij} is integer, the last term is equal to one. We can perform a change of variable $z_i = e^{4i\alpha_i}$, representing a frame by a unit complex number per triangle. Then the smoothest frame field is obtained by solving the following optimization problem:

$$\arg \min_{\|z\|=1} \sum_{ij} \|z_i - z_j e^{4ic_{ij}}\|^2 \text{ subject to boundary constraints.} \tag{7}$$

As CAD models have many feature edges that force $\|z_i\| = 1$ on neighboring triangles, a common practice to solve this problem is to use an ordinary least square method and ignore the unit norm constraint. At the end of the process, the variables p_{ij} are set in order to minimize r_{ij} in Eq. (1).

So long for the smoothest frame fields, but recall that we want to compute a frame field whose variation is as close to the prescribed rotation ω as possible. It turns out that this problem can be solved exactly as the smoothest frame field by a simple update of the optimization problem (7):

$$\arg \min_{\|z\|=1} \sum_{ij} \|z_i - z_j e^{4i(c_{ij}-\omega_{ij})}\|^2 \text{ subject to boundary constraints.} \tag{8}$$

As for the variables p_{ij}, they are now set to minimize $r_{ij} - \omega_{ij}$.

4   Relax the Orthogonality

At this point, we generate quad-meshable orthogonal frame fields by minimizing $\sum_{ij}(r_{ij} - \omega_{ij})^2$. The geometry can be further optimized by relaxing the orthogonality constraint. The objective here is to minimize $\sum_{ij} \left(r_{ij}^0\right)^2 + \left(r_{ij}^1\right)^2$ as defined in Eq. (4).

Instead of working with variables ρ_i, α_i, we will optimize the rotation angles to apply to each vector of the frame field: γ_i^0 for even vectors and γ_i^1 for odd vectors. The final frame field will be obtained by updating $\alpha_i \leftarrow \alpha_i + \gamma_i^0$, and setting $\rho_i \leftarrow \gamma_i^1 - \gamma_i^0$.

We can rewrite Eq. (4) for the new variables γ_i^0 and γ_i^1:

$$\begin{cases} r_{ij}^0 = -(\alpha_i + \gamma_i^0) + \alpha_j + \gamma_j^{p_{ij} \bmod 2} + c_{ij} + p_{ij}\frac{\pi}{2} \\ r_{ij}^1 = -(\alpha_i + \gamma_i^1) + \alpha_j + \gamma_j^{(p_{ij}+1) \bmod 2} + c_{ij} + p_{ij}\frac{\pi}{2} \end{cases}$$

The new field is obtained by minimizing:

$$\arg\min \left\{ \sum_{ij} \left[\left(r_{ij}^0\right)^2 + \left(r_{ij}^1\right)^2 \right] + \epsilon \sum_i \left(\gamma_i^0 - \gamma_i^1\right)^2 \right\},$$

where $\epsilon = 10^{-2}$. Note that the term $\sum_i \left(\gamma_i^0 - \gamma_i^1\right)^2$ favors the field to be orthogonal, which is necessary for under-constrained configurations such as ring or torus.

To prevent degenerate frames, once the energy is minimized, we check whether $|\gamma_i^0 - \gamma_i^1| > \alpha$, where $0 < \alpha < \pi/2$ is the maximum deviation from the orthogonality. We use $\alpha = 0.45\pi$ in our experiments. If the condition is not satisfied, we fix the frame locally by applying the smallest possible modification to γ_i^0 and γ_i^1: if $\gamma_i^0 > \gamma_i^1$ then $\gamma_i^0 \leftarrow (\gamma_i^0 + \gamma_i^1 + \alpha)/2$ and $\gamma_i^1 \leftarrow (\gamma_i^0 + \gamma_i^1 - \alpha)/2$, otherwise $\gamma_i^0 \leftarrow (\gamma_i^0 + \gamma_i^1 - \alpha)/2$ and $\gamma_i^1 \leftarrow (\gamma_i^0 + \gamma_i^1 + \alpha)/2$.

5   Results and Applications

The **running time** was not major consideration in this work because, as long as we stick to solving a couple of linear systems, generating the frame field is not the weakest part of the quad meshing process. Our algorithm is 3 to 5 times slower than the fastest way to produce orthogonal frame fields (without taking the representation vector norm into account). The extra time is consumed by computing ω and relaxing the orthogonality. For example, a model of 35K triangles is optimized in 3 s: 0.4 s to compute ω, 0.5 s to optimize the orthogonal field, and 1.3 to relax the orthogonality. As a comparison, computing the global parameterization take 155 s.

5.1   Quad Meshing

A family of quad meshing algorithms takes a frame field as input, computes a global parameterization and extract quads from it. To obtain the presented results, we use quadcover [10]. From a quadcover parameterization, the extracted quad mesh have extraordinary vertices (valence $\neq 4$) only on the singularities of the input frame field.

Previous works like [5,8,17] handled those CAD models cases from traditional orthogonal frame fields, but at the cost of creating more extraordinary vertices in

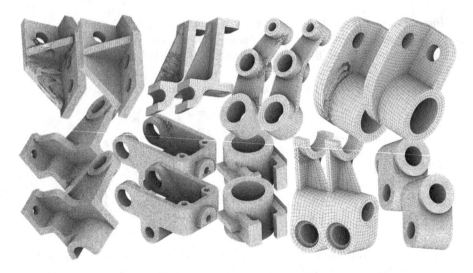

Fig. 9. Each model is remeshed with (foreground) and without (background) fixing sharp corners by our method.

the output quad mesh (see Fig. 10). Instead we handle CAD models with sharp corners, by working on the integrability of the frame field and using simple integration techniques like quadcover [10].

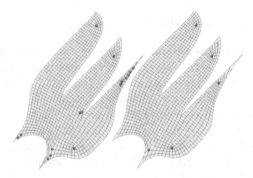

Fig. 10. The quad mesh generated by [5] (left) needs a lot more singularities to deal with feature edges than ours (right).

6   Conclusion

Typical meshing algorithms are not adapted to handle sharp corners configurations that are omnipresent in CAD models. However, previous works show that relaxing the orthogonality constraint on frame fields is sufficient in many cases.

Geometrical approaches for generating non-orthogonal frame field typically rely on solving challenging optimization problems at the cost of high computation time. In comparison, our method only uses linear systems.

Instead of having to optimize non-orthogonal frames, we redefine the parallel transport near every sharp corners to make a classical orthogonal optimization solves non-orthogonal issues. The relaxation of the orthogonality then allows to obtain a geometrically smoothed non-orthogonal frame fields.

The advantages of our approach are that the computation and implementation times are significantly reduced and comparable to classical orthogonal surface frame fields. The resulting fields are guaranteed to be meshable with a small amount of extraordinary vertices on sharp corners.

The drawbacks comes from the fact that it is based on the mesh combinatorix: if the input triangle mesh has inconsistent size, the parameter of the field rotation propagation could be too local or too global. Moreover, if the feature edge detection is of bad quality, the algorithm could try to solve problems that do not exist, and so provide a suboptimal solution.

References

1. Beaufort, P., Lambrechts, J., Henrotte, F., Geuzaine, C., Remacle, J.: Computing two dimensional cross fields - A PDE approach based on the ginzburg-landau theory (2017). CoRR abs/1706.01344, http://arxiv.org/abs/1706.01344
2. Bommes, D., Zimmer, H., Kobbelt, L.: Mixed-integer quadrangulation. ACM Trans. Graph. **28**(3), 77:1–77:10 (2009). https://doi.org/10.1145/1531326.1531383, http://doi.acm.org/10.1145/1531326.1531383
3. Diamanti, O., Vaxman, A., Panozzo, D., Sorkine-Hornung, O.: Designing n-polyvector fields with complex polynomials. Comput. Graph. Forum **33**(5), 1–11 (2014). https://doi.org/10.1111/cgf.12426
4. Diamanti, O., Vaxman, A., Panozzo, D., Sorkine-Hornung, O.: Integrable polyvector fields. ACM Trans. Graph. **34**(4) (2015). https://doi.org/10.1145/2766906
5. Fang, X., Bao, H., Tong, Y., Desbrun, M., Huang, J.: Quadrangulation through morse-parameterization hybridization. ACM Trans. Graph. **37**(4) (2018). https://doi.org/10.1145/3197517.3201354
6. Hertzmann, A., Zorin, D.: Illustrating smooth surfaces. In: PROCEEDINGS OF SIGGRAPH 2000, pp. 517–526 (2000)
7. Iarussi, E., Bommes, D., Bousseau, A.: BendFields: regularized curvature fields from rough concept sketches. ACM Trans. Graph. **34**(3) (2015). https://doi.org/10.1145/2710026, https://hal.inria.fr/hal-01261456
8. Jakob, W., Tarini, M., Panozzo, D., Sorkine-Hornung, O.: Instant field-aligned meshes. ACM Trans. Graph. (Proceedings of SIGGRAPH Asia) **34**(6), 189:1–189:15 (2015). https://doi.org/10.1145/2816795.2818078
9. Jiang, T., Fang, X., Huang, J., Bao, H., Tong, Y., Desbrun, M.: Frame field generation through metric customization. ACM Trans. Graph. **34**(4) (2015). https://doi.org/10.1145/2766927
10. Kaelberer, F., Nieser, M., Polthier, K.: QuadCover - surface parameterization using branched coverings. Comput. Graph. Forum (2007). https://doi.org/10.1111/j.1467-8659.2007.01060.x

11. Knöppel, F., Crane, K., Pinkall, U., Schröder, P.: Globally optimal direction fields. ACM Trans. Graph. **32**(4), 1–10 (2013)
12. Koch, S., et al.: Abc: a big cad model dataset for geometric deep learning. In: The IEEE Conference on Computer Vision and Pattern Recognition (CVPR) (2019)
13. Liu, H., Zhang, P., Chien, E., Solomon, J., Bommes, D.: Singularity-constrained octahedral fields for hexahedral meshing **37**(4) (2018). https://doi.org/10.1145/3197517.3201344
14. Liu, Y., et al.: General planar quadrilateral mesh design using conjugate direction field. ACM Trans. Graph. **30**(6), 1–10 (2011). https://doi.org/10.1145/2070781.2024174
15. Palacios, J., Zhang, E.: Rotational symmetry field design on surfaces. ACM Trans. Graph. **26**(3) (2007). https://doi.org/10.1145/1276377.1276446, http://doi.acm.org/10.1145/1276377.1276446
16. Panozzo, D., Puppo, E., Tarini, M., Sorkine-Hornung, O.: Frame fields: anisotropic and non-orthogonal cross fields. ACM Trans. Graph. **33**(4) (2014). https://doi.org/10.1145/2601097.2601179
17. Ray, N., Li, W.C., Lévy, B., Sheffer, A., Alliez, P.: Periodic global parameterization. ACM Trans. Graph. **25**(4), 1460–1485 (2006)
18. Ray, N., Sokolov, D., Lévy, B.: Practical 3d frame field generation. ACM Trans. Graph. **35**(6) (2016). https://doi.org/10.1145/2980179.2982408
19. Ray, N., Vallet, B., Alonso, L., Levy, B.: Geometry-aware direction field processing. ACM Trans. Graph. **29**(1), 1:1–1:11 (2009). https://doi.org/10.1145/1640443.1640444
20. Ray, N., Vallet, B., Li, W.C., Lévy, B.: N-symmetry direction field design. ACM Trans. Graph. **27**(2), 10:1–10:13 (2008). https://doi.org/10.1145/1356682.1356683
21. Vaxman, A., et al.: Directional field synthesis, design, and processing. In: ACM SIGGRAPH 2017 Courses. SIGGRAPH '17. Association for Computing Machinery, New York (2017). https://doi.org/10.1145/3084873.3084921
22. Zhou, Q., Jacobson, A.: Thingi10k: A dataset of 10,000 3d-printing models (2016). arXiv preprint arXiv:1605.04797

Hierarchical Point Distance Fields

Bastian Krayer[✉][ID] and Stefan Müller

University Koblenz-Landau, Koblenz, Germany
{bastiankrayer,stefanm}@uni-koblenz.de

Abstract. We present an extension to bounding volume hierarchies for fast approximate distance queries on arbitrary objects for which a distance bound is known. Using points on the objects as examples, we compute the relative error of approximating all objects in a node with the node boundary. This scheme can be applied efficiently to the hierarchical structure. We show that both distance queries as well as algorithms relying on those queries are significantly sped up on the CPU and GPU by our algorithm.

Keywords: Distance field · BVH · Implicit representation

1 Introduction

The closest distance to an object provides valuable information in many fields. Collision detection, both of meshes and particles, can rely on distance to check if any intersections have occurred [12,19,20]. Distance fields are related to solvent excluded surfaces in medicine [15] and geometric skeleton extraction [18]. As they are used for surface modeling, especially using constructive solid geometry (CSG), multiple algorithms exist to visualize 3D distance fields with variants of sphere tracing [5,8,17]. Recently, a new method to solve a class of partial differential equations (PDEs) on volumetric domains without meshing was proposed, that requires only distance queries for a random walk through space [16]. For many of these applications, an exact distance field is not necessarily required. In this paper, we present an extension to bounding volume hierarchies (BVH) that allows us to approximate distances up to a specified error while maintaining the important property of being a distance bound for the original objects and significantly speeding up the computation.

2 Related Work

Distance fields can be represented and constructed in various ways. The following is a small overview of some common approaches to these two problems.

© Springer Nature Switzerland AG 2021
G. Bebis et al. (Eds.): ISVC 2021, LNCS 13018, pp. 435–446, 2021.
https://doi.org/10.1007/978-3-030-90436-4_35

Grid-Based Methods. One representation of distance fields is a regular grid-based sampling of the distance values in the object domain. With GPU programming, this is highly beneficial, as these grids can be used as textures with hardware interpolation for fast access. Distance transforms generate such a grid from a binary representation of the input geometry [1,6,13]. Similarly, instead of distances, a cell may store all geometry inside of it to efficiently compute the exact distance for a point, as seen in the complete distance field representation [9]. A fast combined voxelization and distance transform algorithm was introduced in [11], which also propagates the closest cell to optionally compute exact distances for off-grid points with the actual geometry.

Hierarchical Methods. While grid-based methods allow for quick texture-based access, they require a lot of storage for high resolutions, which increases if additional information is stored as well. To alleviate these memory requirements, distance values can be stored in a hierarchical manner, for example as octree-based adaptively sampled distance fields [4,7]. In [10], polynomials are fitted hierarchically to approximate the exact distance up to a specified error.

Hierarchical Object Methods. Another hierarchical approach is to consider a combined distance field made up of multiple distinct objects. The closest distance can then be found with spatial data structures, such as BVHs. In [21], several split heuristics for BVHs are presented to optimize the construction of a tree for distance queries. Our method also works on BVHs. Instead of optimizing the tree, we extend it to allow for approximations with a specified error. The exact distance and closest object can still be efficiently computed in a second step.

3   Data Structure

In this section, we will describe our error metric and how to compute an estimate for it. With that, we define a distance bound for an object that can be applied directly to a BVH.

3.1   Error Bounds

We consider a distance function f for some bounded object $O \subset R^n$.

$$f(\mathbf{x}) = \min_{\mathbf{q} \in O} \|\mathbf{x} - \mathbf{q}\| \tag{1}$$

If needed, we denote the associated object with a superscript, e.g. f^O. Such a distance function is Lipschitz continuous with a Lipschitz constant $L = 1$, which follows immediately from the triangle inequality.

$$|f(\mathbf{x}) - f(\mathbf{y})| \le \|\mathbf{x} - \mathbf{y}\| \tag{2}$$

More generally, Eq. 1 can be replaced by an inequality to define a distance bound, which returns at most the distance to the closest object point.

$$f(\mathbf{x}) \leq \min_{\mathbf{q} \in O} \|\mathbf{x} - \mathbf{q}\| \tag{3}$$

In the following, we will generally use the term distance function for f satisfying either Eq. 1 or inequality 3 to avoid confusion with the bounds of a node. We enclose the object with a bounding object for which a cheap to evaluate distance function b exists. Thus for any point $\mathbf{p}$ outside the bounds we have

$$b(\mathbf{p}) \leq f(\mathbf{p}) \tag{4}$$

We consider the bounding object solid, thus for any point inside, b is equal to 0. For any point outside we use a relative error measure ϵ to compare the actual and the bound distance:

$$\epsilon(\mathbf{p}) = \frac{f(\mathbf{p}) - b(\mathbf{p})}{f(\mathbf{p})}$$
$$= 1 - \frac{b(\mathbf{p})}{f(\mathbf{p})} \tag{5}$$

To estimate ϵ, we take a discrete subset of the bounded object $E = \{\mathbf{q}_i | \mathbf{q}_i \in O, i = 1, \ldots, n\}$. We call the $\mathbf{q}_i$ example points. n is arbitrary. Since $E \subseteq O$, we see from property 3:

$$f(\mathbf{x}) \leq \min_{\mathbf{q} \in O} \|\mathbf{x} - \mathbf{q}\|$$
$$\leq \min_{\mathbf{q}_i} \|\mathbf{x} - \mathbf{q}_i\| \tag{6}$$

Combining this with the relative error 5 we obtain an upper bound u:

$$1 - \frac{b(\mathbf{p})}{f(\mathbf{p})} \leq 1 - \frac{b(\mathbf{p})}{\min_{\mathbf{q}_i} \|\mathbf{p} - \mathbf{q}_i\|} \tag{7}$$
$$= u(\mathbf{p}) \tag{8}$$

From properties 4 and 6 it follows that $\frac{b(\mathbf{p})}{\min_{\mathbf{q}_i} \|\mathbf{p} - \mathbf{q}_i\|}$ will be less than 1, so $u(\mathbf{p}) \geq 0$ for any point strictly outside the volume. Consider the closest point on the bound $\mathbf{p}^c$ for $\mathbf{p}$. Since b is a distance bound, we have $b(\mathbf{p}) \leq \|\mathbf{p} - \mathbf{p}^c\|$ and $\frac{b(\mathbf{p})}{\min_{\mathbf{q}_i} \|\mathbf{p} - \mathbf{q}_i\|} \leq \frac{\|\mathbf{p} - \mathbf{p}^c\|}{\min_{\mathbf{q}_i} \|\mathbf{p} - \mathbf{q}_i\|}$. Letting $\mathbf{p} \to \mathbf{p}^c$, this approaches 0, if none of the example points are $\mathbf{p}^c$ and 1 otherwise. Therefore, $u(\mathbf{p})$ is in $[0, 1]$. A user-defined maximum relative error $\epsilon_{\max}$ in that interval controls the approximation. As the error guarantee holds only outside and to avoid the rare special case of $\frac{0}{0}$ for example points coinciding with the query point itself, we define u to be 1 on the whole bounding object. Computationally it would be more efficient to defer computing the root. The final definition of the upper bound error function then becomes:

$$u(\mathbf{x}) = \begin{cases} 1 - \frac{b(\mathbf{x})}{\sqrt{\min_{\mathbf{q}_i} \|\mathbf{x} - \mathbf{q}_i\|^2}} & \text{if } b(\mathbf{x}) > 0 \\ 1 & \text{else} \end{cases} \tag{9}$$

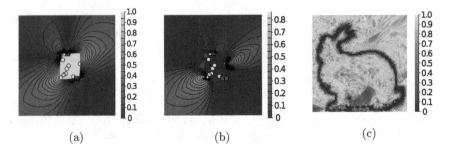

Fig. 1. Figure 1a shows the error estimate for a number of points. Example points are shown as red rectangles. Figure 1b shows the difference between the exact relative error and our estimate. Figure 1c shows the relative errors produced by the final algorithm. Values are divided by $\epsilon_{\max}$ to normalize them between $[0, 1]$. The shell-like structure is due to the hierarchical error estimation. (Color figure online)

Figure 1a shows a visualization of the error estimate u. We see that the error stays very small for points close to the example points, thus even for some points close to the bounds, we do not need to compute the actual distance function f^O of the enclosed object O. Using u we define an approximate distance function $f_{\epsilon_{\max}}$ for the object O as:

$$f_{\epsilon_{\max}}(\mathbf{x}) = \begin{cases} f^O(\mathbf{x}) & \text{if } u(\mathbf{x}) > \epsilon_{\max} \\ b(\mathbf{x}) & \text{else} \end{cases} \tag{10}$$

3.2 Properties

The distance function b is greater than 0 outside of the bounds and thus introduces no additional zeros there. From property 4 it also satisfies inequality 3 for the bounded object. The same is true at any point for f. As $f_{\epsilon_{\max}}$ is a combination of b and f, it is a distance bound for O as well. While the value of $f_{\epsilon_{\max}}$ might differ from the value given by f, it will always be a valid distance bound for the contained object O. This makes it suitable to represent the object itself in any algorithm working on distance bounds, such as Monte Carlo simulations, sphere tracing or CSG operations. Additionally, it allows us to use it in the hierarchical BVH structure. As the object and bounds themselves are finite $\frac{b(\mathbf{x})}{f(\mathbf{x})}$ will tend to 1 as $\mathbf{x}$ moves away from the object. With that $\epsilon(\mathbf{x})$ will tend to 0.

4   Implementation

$f_{\epsilon_{\max}}$ can be used directly in combination with a BVH. A leaf node corresponds to the previous discussion, with the contained objects defining f and the leaf's bounds defining b. An inner node c is the union of all contained objects. These are grouped in the child nodes c_1 and c_2. As stated in Sect. 3.2, $f_{\epsilon_{\max}}$ describes the object contained, so we can use it to compute the union of all contained objects by using the minimum distance of the children's functions.

$$f^c_{\epsilon_{max}}(\mathbf{x}) = \min(f^{c_1}_{\epsilon_{max}}(\mathbf{x}), f^{c_2}_{\epsilon_{max}}(\mathbf{x})) \tag{11}$$

Example points of each sub-object are needed. Using all points of the child nodes would require evaluating a lot of points in the upper hierarchy levels. As we do not require any special properties for the points aside from being part of the objects, any subset of the child nodes is a valid choice for the parent. Section 4.1 will provide one such scheme.

4.1 Choosing Example Points

For our implementation, we chose the common bounding shape of an axis-aligned bounding box (AABB). The closest point from the outside is found by constraining the input point to the minimum and maximum extents. It is then used to compute the distance. From the definition of u, we see that the error will be smaller, the closer the example points are to the closest point on the bound's surface. For the AABB in 3D, we choose six points, the extremal points in each direction. We then order them in pairs of min and max per dimension. In total, this results in $2N$ entries in an N dimensional space. A more sophisticated procedure could take into account the Voronoi regions of the points on the bound's surface. The size of those regions could break up ties between points with similar distance. In our implementation, if multiple points have the same distance, the first point in the list is chosen. Given two sets of ordered points for the child nodes, we compute the parent node's example points by comparing just the corresponding pairs, as seen in Algorithm 1. Algorithm 2 shows the basic construction. Primitives do not need to provide the actual extremal points if that is too difficult to compute. The provided points just need to adhere to the ordering convention. In our implementation, we store all points in one array. Each node then stores six offsets into that array for its example points to reduce the amount of data used.

Since evaluating a node requires only the information of its subtree, updating the example points works similar to other BVH updates. Consider an object stored in a leaf node that is transformed slightly, not requiring a full rebuild of the tree, just propagating the bound changes up to the root node. In the same way, if a change occurs in any node, its example points are recalculated and then propagated upwards.

4.2 Computing the Distance

After gathering the example points for all nodes, distances can be evaluated for arbitrary points. For each node, u computes the upper error bound. To further reduce the number of computations, we use only the points corresponding to the closest sides of the node's AABB. As the example points are ordered, those points can be selected quickly. Algorithm 3 shows this method. If the error bound

---

Algorithm 1: Combine two ordered sets of points. For each dimension, a minimum and maximum point are stored consecutively.

Input: Ordered point sets a and b, dimension dim
Output: Ordered point set that is a combination of the inputs

```
1 Function combine(a, b):
2    if isEmpty(a) then
3        return b
4    result ← copy(a)
5    for i ← 0 to dim − 1 do
6        if b[2i][i] < result[2i][i] then          /* Minimum point */
7            result[2i] ← b[2i]
8        if b[2i +1][i] > result[2i +1][i] then     /* Maximum point */
9            result[2i+1] ← b[2i+1]
10   return result
```

---

is less than the error threshold, the bound distance can safely be returned as a distance. Otherwise, the child nodes have to be traversed. Algorithm 4 shows a basic recursive implementation. Our implementation replaces the recursion with iteration and skips nodes that are further away than the current closest distance. The closest point is found additionally or instead of the distance. When we would return the bound distance, we instead use the closest point on the bound and otherwise compute the closest point of the child nodes or primitives. Figure 1c shows a visualization of the error bounds.

4.3   Multiple Distance Queries

There are two non-exclusive cases that can reuse previous computations to discard nodes that don't have a chance to provide a smaller value than the final result. In the first case, we wish to refine the distance with a smaller maximum error. In the second case, we want to compute the distance at a point in the vicinity. Since $f_{\epsilon_{max}} \leq f$, we can't just use the computed distance to discard anything farther away. We consider a point $\mathbf{y}$ after we processed another point $\mathbf{x}$. We start with the Lipschitz property 2. If $f(\mathbf{y})$ is greater or equal $f(\mathbf{x})$ we have:

$$f(\mathbf{y}) - f(\mathbf{x}) \leq \|\mathbf{x} - \mathbf{y}\|$$
$$f(\mathbf{y}) \leq \|\mathbf{x} - \mathbf{y}\| + f(\mathbf{x}) \tag{12}$$
$$\leq \|\mathbf{x} - \mathbf{y}\| + \min_{\mathbf{q}_i} \|\mathbf{x} - \mathbf{q}_i\|$$

For $f(\mathbf{y})$ less than $f(\mathbf{x})$ we arrive at the same conclusion by adding the non-zero term $\min_{\mathbf{q}_i} \|\mathbf{x} - \mathbf{q}_i\|$. This leads to the upper distance bound function m:

$$m_{\epsilon_{max}}(\mathbf{x}) = \begin{cases} f(\mathbf{x}) & \text{if } u(\mathbf{x}) > \epsilon_{max} \\ \min_{\mathbf{q}_i} \|\mathbf{x} - \mathbf{q}_i\| & \text{else} \end{cases} \tag{13}$$

Algorithm 2: Fill the example point data structure recursively. Leaves are filled immediately from their primitives, while inner nodes first compute their children and then combine the results.

Input: Tree node node, dimension dim
Output: Example points for the node

```
1 Function fill(node):
2 │   pts ← []
3 │   if isLeaf(node) then
4 │   │   forall p in getPrimitives(node) do
5 │   │   └   pts ← combine(pts,getPoints(p), dim)
6 │   else
7 │   └   pts ← combine(fill(left(node)), fill(right(node)))
8 │   setPoints(node, pts)
9 └   return pts
```

Since these values are already computed during evaluation, no additional work is needed. Any node, for which $b(\mathbf{y}) \geq \|\mathbf{x} - \mathbf{y}\| + m_{\epsilon_{max}}(\mathbf{x})$ holds, is skipped immediately. ϵ_{max} here refers to the error threshold chosen for the previous calculation at $\mathbf{x}$, which might be different to the one used in the new query at $\mathbf{y}$.

5   Experimental Results

We implemented the data structure and distance query algorithm on CPU and GPU using C++ and OpenGL. We replaced the recursion in Algorithm 4 with iteration in both cases. The CPU evaluation uses multiple threads and has an alternative version with a priority queue (PQ) instead of the depth-first (DF) traversal. All tests were done in Windows 10 using an Intel i7-6700HQ CPU, 8GB of RAM, and a mobile GeForce GTX 1070 GPU. We tested three different scenarios: A uniform distance field sampling, a Monte Carlo PDE solver, and a sphere tracer.

Uniform Distance Field Sampling. We uniformly sampled a 3D distance field for multiple triangle meshes. These consist of triangles ranging from a few hundred to over 10 million and have different characteristics. Some are compact and densely sampled, others contain large and small triangles and empty spaces. Table 1 shows the used models. For each implementation, we found performance improvements when allowing for errors. The highest rate of increase was found roughly in the range $[0, 0.1]$. Figure 2 shows the measurements of our GPU implementation. On average about $9.5 \cdot 10^6$ queries per second were performed for $\epsilon_{max} = 0$ and $3.5 \cdot 10^7$ for $\epsilon_{max} = 0.1$. To avoid additional branching in a loop, we did not implement the PQ traversal on the GPU. The approximation allows for skipping nodes, even if no other distance is known. That way, branching and loop iterations are avoided. Even with smaller relative errors, speedups between

---

Algorithm 3: The upper error bound function.

Input: Tree node node, dimension dim, query point $\mathbf{x}$

Output: Error bound

1 **Function** u(node, $\mathbf{x}$):
2     $d_{\text{bound}} \leftarrow$ b(node, $\mathbf{x}$)
3   **if** $d_{bound} \leq 0$ **then**
4 | **return** 1
5     $\mathbf{r} \leftarrow \mathbf{x} -$ center(node)
6     $d_{\min}^2 \leftarrow \infty$
7   pts $\leftarrow$ getPoints(node)
8   **for** $i = 0$ **to** dim $- 1$ **do**
9 | off $\leftarrow \mathbf{r}[i] > 0 \,?\, 1 : 0$
10 | $d_{\min}^2 \leftarrow \min(d_{\min}^2, \|\text{pts}[2i + \text{off}] - \mathbf{p}\|^2)$
11   **return** $1 - \frac{d_{bound}}{\sqrt{d_{min}^2}}$

Algorithm 4: Basic algorithm to determine the approximate distance to the object represented by the tree.

Input: Tree node node, dimension dim, query point $\mathbf{x}$, maximum relative error $\epsilon_{\max}$

Output: Approximate distance to the object

1 **Function** dist(node, dim):
2   **if** u(node, dim, $\mathbf{x}$) $< \epsilon_{max}$ **then**
3 | **return** b(node, $\mathbf{x}$)
4     $d_l \leftarrow$ dist(nearChild(node), dim, $\mathbf{x}$, ϵ_{max})
5     $d_r \leftarrow$ dist(farChild(node), dim, $\mathbf{x}$, ϵ_{max})
6   **return** $\min(d_l, d_r)$

---

10 and 100 times can be achieved. Compact models with many triangles, e.g. the dragon and Buddha statue, profit the most. We found the smallest increase for the sphere model. Due to the low triangle count, early discarding might not have much of an impact. Sparser models such as San Miguel and the powerplant perform better in general than dense ones, as the BVH accommodates the free space effectively. Because of this, many far-away nodes are approximated and not traversed any further. The CPU implementations follow a similar pattern, but the overall number of queries per second was less. We sampled the error values at intervals of 0.1 and found the highest speedup of 41.88 (DF) and 6.96 (PQ) for the dragon model with $\epsilon_{\max} = 0.1$. On average about $2 \cdot 10^5$ (DF) and $3.4 \cdot 10^5$ (PQ) queries per second were performed for $\epsilon_{\max} = 0$ and $1.1 \cdot 10^7$ (DF) and $7.9 \cdot 10^5$ (PQ) for $\epsilon_{\max} = 0.1$. We tested a two-step query for the exact distance with property 12. In the first step, an initial distance bound is found with $\epsilon_{\max}$. This is used as a minimum distance for the second step. Our speedup measurements can be seen in Fig. 2b. While not as high as using only

Table 1. Triangle count for the tested models. Aside from the basic sphere, all models are from [14].

Model	San Miguel	Buddha statue	Bunny	Dragon	Powerplant	Sphere
#Triangles	9,980,699	1,087,474	69,664	866,728	12,759,246	960
Image						

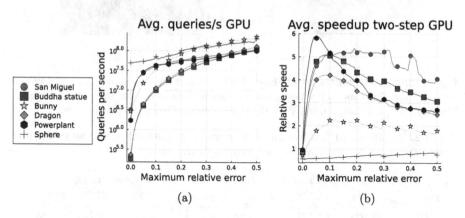

Fig. 2. Figure 2a shows the number of queries per second for different values of ϵ_{max}. Figure 2b shows the speedup of computing the exact distance in a two-step process. The error values were sampled in 0.01 intervals and averaged over 2000 samples each.

an approximate distance, we found it up to six times as fast on the GPU. For two-step queries, the speedup decreases for larger values of ϵ_{max}. These produce larger error bounds, thus counteracting the improved speed of the first step since fewer nodes can be skipped in the second one.

Monte Carlo PDE Solver. A different usage pattern is doing multiple successive queries in close vicinity. We implemented the basic PDE solver described in [16], which performs random walks on the free space spheres given by the distance function until an object point is hit. We chose two Stanford Bunny models with textures representing the boundary conditions. One bunny is smaller and inside of the other one, to provide a more complicated geometric setup with fewer unoccupied regions. Values of the PDE are computed on a 2D plane. Figure 3 shows our setup. Each step in the random walk took into account the previous result with Eq. 12. We used a CPU implementation with errors $0, 0.1, 0.3$. Table 2a shows the results. As the reported distance is generally less than the exact one for larger error values, each walk needs more iterations on average. This is offset by the much faster queries resulting in a significant overall speedup by up to a factor of 31.81.

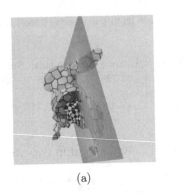

(a)

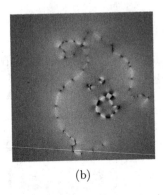

(b)

Fig. 3. Input model for the Monte Carlo PDE solver. Figure 3a shows the input model with the sample plane. The model was cut open to better show the inner geometry. Figure 3b shows a higher quality result of the computation done for the test.

Table 2. Results for PDE solver and sphere tracer. In both cases, we find substantial speed improvements. 100 samples were taken for each entry.

(a) Results of the Monte Carlo PDE solver.				(b) Results of the sphere tracing.			
Type, ϵ_{max}	$\frac{\text{Walks}}{s}$	$\frac{\text{Queries}}{s}$	$\frac{\text{Iterations}}{Walk}$	Type, ϵ_{max}	$\frac{\text{Rays}}{s}$	$\frac{\text{Queries}}{s}$	$\frac{\text{Iterations}}{Ray}$
DF, 0	2,098	60,541	27.86	DF, 0	8,244	59,534	6.22
PQ, 0	2,456	70,873	27.86	PQ, 0	31,819	229,781	6.22
DF, 0.1	49,648	1,571,141	30.64	DF, 0.1	120,132	935,569	6.79
PQ, 0.1	38,006	1,202,615	30.64	PQ, 0.1	107,317	835,766	6.79
DF, 0.3	66,739	2,596,911	37.90	DF, 0.3	212,800	1,967,144	8.24
PQ, 0.3	44,365	1,726,032	37.90	PQ, 0.3	147,502	1,363,519	8.24

Sphere Tracing. Our last test uses a basic sphere tracing algorithm [8] to visualize a triangle mesh of a dragon. In contrast to the Monte Carlo algorithm, where a walk may take various paths through space, a ray in sphere tracing goes in only one direction, each step as big as the distance value at that point. Thus, distances close to the true distance are better, since the ray marcher can take larger steps. The basic setup is the same as with the Monte Carlo example. Table 2b shows the results. Similarly, more steps need to be taken per ray, but each step is less costly, resulting in a maximum speedup of 25.81.

6   Limitations

A limitation of our method is that outside of leaf bounds all distances are unsigned. This can be solved in different ways, though it is dependent on the type of enclosed objects. One way to find a sign is to retrieve the closest object with the two-step method and compute the sign from that. Different methods exist for triangle meshes. If they are closed, the closest triangle with the angle weighted pseudo normal [2] can be used. For more problematic meshes and point clouds, the fast winding numbers algorithm [3] provides a robust and quick sign and can be constructed on the same BVH as our method.

7 Conclusion

In this paper, we presented an extension to BVHs to approximate distances to arbitrary objects defined by distance bounds with a given relative error bound. For that purpose, we chose example points on the objects which act as representatives to guarantee that error bound. Due to the construction, the resulting field is a distance bound, which makes it possible to directly use this data structure for algorithms such as sphere tracing or Monte Carlo PDE computations. Similar to regular BVHs, localized updates to the nodes in the tree require updates to only the nodes on the path to the root node.

References

1. de Assis Zampirolli, F., Filipe, L.: A fast CUDA-based implementation for the euclidean distance transform. In: 2017 International Conference on High Performance Computing & Simulation (HPCS), pp. 815–818. IEEE (2017). https://doi.org/10.1109/HPCS.2017.123, https://ieeexplore.ieee.org/document/8035162/
2. Baerentzen, J., Aanaes, H.: Signed distance computation using the angle weighted pseudonormal. IEEE Trans. Vis. Comput. Graph 11(3), 243–253 (2005). https://doi.org/10.1109/TVCG.2005.49, http://ieeexplore.ieee.org/document/1407857/
3. Barill, G., Dickson, N.G., Schmidt, R., Levin, D.I.W., Jacobson, A.: Fast winding numbers for soups and clouds. ACM Trans. Graph. 37(4), 1–12 (2018). https://doi.org/10.1145/3197517.3201337, http://dl.acm.org/citation.cfm?doid=3197517.3201337
4. Bastos, T., Celes, W.: GPU-accelerated adaptively sampled distance fields. In: 2008 IEEE International Conference on Shape Modeling and Applications, pp. 171–178. IEEE (2008). https://doi.org/10.1109/SMI.2008.4547967, http://ieeexplore.ieee.org/document/4547967/
5. Bálint, C., Valasek, G.: Accelerating Sphere Tracing. In: Diamanti, O., Vaxman, A. (eds.) EG 2018 - Short Papers. The Eurographics Association (2018). https://doi.org/10.2312/egs.20181037
6. Fabbri, R., Costa, L.D.F., Torelli, J.C., Bruno, O.M.: 2d euclidean distance transform algorithms: a comparative survey. ACM Comput. Surv. 40(1) (2008). https://doi.org/10.1145/1322432.1322434
7. Frisken, S.F., Perry, R.N., Rockwood, A.P., Jones, T.R.: Adaptively sampled distance fields: a general representation of shape for computer graphics. In: Proceedings of the 27th Annual Conference on Computer Graphics and Interactive Techniques, SIGGRAPH '00, pp. 249–254. ACM Press/Addison-Wesley Publishing Co., USA (2000). https://doi.org/10.1145/344779.344899
8. Hart, J.C.: Sphere tracing: a geometric method for the antialiased ray tracing of implicit surfaces. Vis. Comput. 12(10), 527–545 (1996). https://doi.org/10.1007/s003710050084, http://link.springer.com/10.1007/s003710050084
9. Huang, J., Li, Y., Crawfis, R., Lu, S.C., Liou, S.Y.: A complete distance field representation. In: Proceedings Visualization, 2001, VIS '01, pp. 247–561. IEEE (2001). https://doi.org/10.1109/VISUAL.2001.964518, http://ieeexplore.ieee.org/document/964518/

10. Koschier, D., Deul, C., Bender, J.: Hierarchical hp-adaptive signed distance fields. In: Proceedings of the ACM SIGGRAPH/Eurographics Symposium on Computer Animation, SCA '16, pp. 189–198. Eurographics Association, Goslar, DEU (2016)

11. Krayer, B., Müller, S.: Generating signed distance fields on the GPU with ray maps. Vis. Comput. **35**(6-8), 961–971 (2019). https://doi.org/10.1007/s00371-019-01683-w, http://link.springer.com/10.1007/s00371-019-01683-w

12. Macklin, M., Müller, M., Chentanez, N., Kim, T.Y.: Unified particle physics for real-time applications. ACM Trans. Graph. **33**(4) (2014). https://doi.org/10.1145/2601097.2601152

13. Manduhu, M., Jones, M.W.: A work efficient parallel algorithm for exact euclidean distance transform. IEEE Trans. Image Process. **28**(11), 5322–5335 (2019). https://doi.org/10.1109/TIP.2019.2916741, https://ieeexplore.ieee.org/document/8718507/

14. McGuire, M.: Computer graphics archive (2017). https://casual-effects.com/data

15. Quan, C., Stamm, B.: Mathematical analysis and calculation of molecular surfaces. J. Comput. Phys. **322**(C), 760–782 (2016). https://doi.org/10.1016/j.jcp.2016.07.007

16. Sawhney, R., Crane, K.: Monte carlo geometry processing: a grid-free approach to pde-based methods on volumetric domains. ACM Trans. Graph. **39**(4) (2020). https://doi.org/10.1145/3386569.3392374

17. Seyb, D., Jacobson, A., Nowrouzezahrai, D., Jarosz, W.: Non-linear sphere tracing for rendering deformed signed distance fields. ACM Trans. Graph. **38**(6), 1–12 (2019). https://doi.org/10.1145/3355089.3356502, https://dl.acm.org/doi/10.1145/3355089.3356502

18. Song, C., Pang, Z., Jing, X., Xiao, C.: Distance field guided l_1 -median skeleton extraction. Vis. Comput. **34**(2), 243–255 (2018). https://doi.org/10.1007/s00371-016-1331-z, http://link.springer.com/10.1007/s00371-016-1331-z

19. Teschner, M.: Collision detection for deformable objects. Comput. Graph. Forum **24**(1), 61–81 (2005). https://doi.org/10.1111/j.1467-8659.2005.00829.x

20. Xu, H., Barbic, J.: 6-DoF haptic rendering using continuous collision detection between points and signed distance fields. IEEE Trans. Haptics **10**(2), 151–161 (2017). https://doi.org/10.1109/TOH.2016.2613872

21. Ytterlid, R., Shellshear, E.: Bvh split strategies for fast distance queries. J. Comput. Graph. Tech. (JCGT) **4**(1), 1–25 (2015). http://jcgt.org/published/0004/01/01/

Parallel Sphere Packing for Arbitrary Domains

Rubén Adrián Cuba Lajo(✉)[ID] and Manuel Eduardo Loaiza Fernández[ID]

Department of Computer Science, Universidad Católica San Pablo, Arequipa, Peru
{ruben.cuba,meloaiza}@ucsp.edu.pe

Abstract. Particle packings are methods used to fill a container with particles. These are used to simulate granular matter, which has various uses. Particle packings seek to be dense, however, particle packings are slow, they don't become completely dense, and most only work in simple containers. Currently, several techniques have been proposed to achieve a dense packing, significantly reducing packing construction time, but little progress has been seen in increasing the density of the packing. Particle packings reach an average maximum density of approximately 70% in rectangular and cylindrical containers, and 60% in arbitrary containers. The density of the packings is also known as compaction or solid fraction. The objective of this work is to make a compact packing that in arbitrary containers reaches between 60% and 70% of compaction. For this, a compact periodic packing of spheres is taken as a basis, which from the use of spheres of the same size achieves the highest compaction, that is, it is the most dense. Searched packing is made following a periodic hexagonal pattern, to this are added three sizes of spheres, which are smaller than the initial size, these spheres go in the empty spaces left by the hexagonal packing. The proposed method, reaches densities in arbitrary containers between 60% and 70% in times less than 5 min using a parallel optimization on GPU resource.

Keywords: Sphere packing · Geometric algorithm · Parallel

1 Introduction

In everyday life it is observed that the products that exists around us usually are mostly granular matter, that is a set of solid particles, for example, sand, seeds, salt, sugar, flour, balls, etc. The behavior of this matter is widely studied in physics, since it can behave as a solid when compacting, as a liquid when flowing, and as a gas when separating. Being widely used it is of utmost importance in the industry [2,7].

Granular matter is made up of a large number of particles, conducting experiments with that number of objects is complex, which is why the discrete element methods (DEM) are used, which are an effective scientific tool to simulate granular matter, DEM's are particle packings with a focus on the simulation of granular matter. In particle packings the granular matter is represented by a

© Springer Nature Switzerland AG 2021
G. Bebis et al. (Eds.): ISVC 2021, LNCS 13018, pp. 447–460, 2021.
https://doi.org/10.1007/978-3-030-90436-4_36

container filled with particles. The container is an arbitrary 3D object, and the particles are 3D objects with known volumes, to facilitate the positioning and calculation of the volume of these.

That is sought in a particle packing is that it be compact, that is, that most of the space occupied by the container is full of particles. The percentage of the container space occupied by particles is called compaction, density or solid fraction. Particle packings vary in the shape of the particle and the shape of containers that can fill. The most used shape is the sphere, due to its simple representation. A compact packing of spheres in cubic containers is one with a compaction greater than 74%, this due to the fact that the maximum density of a packing of spheres of the same size with a periodic distribution reaches a compaction of approximately 74% [5,6], and with an aperiodic distribution, a compaction of approximately 64% is reached [13].

The objective of this article is to present an efficient algorithm that is capable of producing compact packings in arbitrary domains, since, apart from compaction, another limitation of most packings is that they only work with one container. Like any algorithm, the execution time is also taken into account. This algorithm follows a certain size distribution that allows the empty spaces between spheres to be filled efficiently. To fill the empty spaces between the spheres and the container, the spheres that are partially inside the container are reduced or divided into smaller spheres, where some of the new spheres will be found inside the container. The goal is to reach densities between 60% and 70% in arbitrary containers.

This article is organized as follows: Sect. 2 presents the best particle packing methods today along with their limitations. In Sect. 3 the proposed sphere packing method is presented. Section 4 shows the tests performed, as well as their results. Finally, we present the conclusions in Sect. 5.

2 Related Work

The particle packing methods are varied and try to make a compact packing. These can be classified into dynamic and geometric. Dynamic methods use DEMs, which are stable and provide information necessary to perform physical simulations, however, this is time consuming, which restricts the number of particles you can use. Geometric methods do not take much time and provide greater control over the distribution.

2.1 Dynamic Packings

Dynamic methods seek to perform simulations, therefore, they work with different forms of particles, in this way a broader study is covered. In physics, when performing a vibration in a container full of particles, the compaction of the packing increases, based on this it was proposed to use cubes composed of superimposed spheres subjected to mechanical vibration to increase the density of the packing proving to be effective particles for this procedure, it was obtained a maximum density of approximately 70% in a cylindrical container [18]; tetrahedron formed by superimposed spheres subjected to vibration were also used, carrying out a study of the effects of vibration conditions, a maximum density of 74.02% was obtained in a cylindrical container [19].

Another proposed particle model is the cylinder which is also composed of superimposed spheres, for this packing it must be fulfilled that the diameter of the container must be larger than the size of the particle, a variety of filling methods are carried out, when performing the drop filling, it is observed that the density of the packing is sensitive to height, this packing reached a maximum density of approximately 55% [14]. When using ellipsoids as particles, it is observed that using a horizontal orientation, that is, that the elongated part is horizontal, and when increasing the size of the particle increases the density, the maximum density was 70% in a cylindrical container [4].

In particle packings, the size of the particles is usually increased or decreased to increase the density, but modifying the particle is also taken into consideration, as proposed by Zhao et al. [20], which uses shape-shifting ellipsoids to investigate the random packing of monodisperse particles with a wide range of shapes, reaching a maximum density of about 80% in a rectangular container, however, the ellipsoid it achieved this density had a shape similar to a cube, when filling a rectangular container with cubes it can be intuited that it will become compact. Varying the shape of the particles is also used to improve the simulations as is the case of the proposal by Rakotonirina et al. [12], which joins convex particles to build non-convex shapes, collision detection and packing distribution is based on the convex shapes that make up the non-convex shape, getting closer to reality but increasing computational cost.

There are also packings that work in layers with the intention of generating a compact layer and by joining the layers a compact packing is achieved, Campello and Cassares [1] proposed layered packings together with a compaction system using spheres to achieve high-density packings in rectangular containers, these packings reached a maximum compaction of 60%.

The dynamic packings are focused on physical simulations, therefore, they work with one or two domains, which are rectangular and cylindrical, this narrows the focus that is desired in this research.

2.2 Geometric Packings

Geometric methods perform geometric calculations and leave aside simulations, for which reason, it is sought to make a construction with particles that have a simple way to use. Most of the particles are based on the spheres, because this shape only needs the center and the radius to be detected, for this reason there are also particle packings based purely on the use of spheres. Spheres are currently widely used, however most packing uses containers of known shape, be they cylinders or rectangular prisms, therefore, achieving a packing in any container is desirable. A common packing method is the advancing front approach in which an initial set of spheres is generated and a new sphere is inserted with a strategy based on the previously inserted particles.

Lozano et al. [10] proposed an algorithm to fill arbitrary containers derived from a advancing front approach solution in 2D taking it to arbitrary 3D domains using a distance field to achieve that there are contact spheres tangent to the triangles of the container mesh. This method obtains a near constant density of 60% for rectangular containers and 50% for arbitrary containers.

Li and Ji [9] proposed an algorithm based on the advancing front approach to obtain packings in arbitrary containers. It proposes to resize the particles to fit neighboring particles while inserting, based on the trilateration equations. Use a spatial grid to optimize particle detection and speed up their positioning. In a cubic container it reaches a maximum density of 73%.

Weller and Zachmann [17] proposed an algorithm to quickly pack spheres using GPU, successively place spheres as large as possible to fit in the empty spaces. However, it does not show geometric data such as the radii of the spheres or the densities of the packings. Furthermore, due to its behavior, relevant data cannot be entered apart from the container mesh itself.

Geometric containers reach an average density of 60% in rectangular containers and 50% in arbitrary containers, these are based on randomness and work with spheres of various sizes. My goal is to generate compact packings based on Kepler's conjecture that mentions a maximum density of approximately 74% using spheres of the same size in a rectangular container. My packing omits randomness, works with basic geometry, and uses only four sizes of spheres.

3   Packing Generation

Compact packing was made following an orderly distribution. This packing is based on a periodic distribution packing, adding spheres of different sizes, which are coupled to the empty spaces, in order to obtain a better compaction.

To build the sphere packing, first the parameters of this are defined, then a rectangular container that wraps the arbitrary container is filled in layers, finally the spheres that are outside the arbitrary container's mesh are discarded.

3.1   Parameters Definition

In mathematics to work on a dimension it is necessary to review the previous dimension, in this case 2D. The packings of circles were reviewed, which have a very good solution that was demonstrated by L. Fejes Tóth in 1940. This solution is the hexagonal packing, in this packing the centers of the circles are located in a hexagonal grid, and are surrounded for another six circles, this packing has a density of approximately 0.9069 [15]. So in 3D, according to Kepler's conjecture, there are two packing of spheres of equal size that meet the highest density, these are, the face-centered cubic packing and the hexagonal packing where the approximate density is 0.74048 [16]. In Fig. 1a the hexagonal arrangement can be seen, which is the one taken as the basis for the construction of this packing.

The proposed sphere packing works with four radii to reduce the empty spaces left when using a single radius without the radii range being wide. The first radius is max radius (r_{max}), this is the input data and based on this the other three radii are generated $(r_{min}, r_{med}$ and $r_{mid})$. The radii r_{max}, r_{min} and r_{med} are used to fill the enveloping rectangular container, and r_{mid} is used to fill empty spaces of the packing in the container arbitrary.

To calculate the min radius (r_{min}) we will work with the upper right triangle of the hexagon of spheres, using the Eq. 1, where b is the triangle barycenter and c is the center of the central sphere, the insertion of its respective min sphere occurs at the barycenter. The data for r_{min} are shown in Fig. 1b.

$$r_{min} = distance(b, c) - r_{max} \tag{1}$$

Then r_{med} is calculated, for this two points are generated, a point that is given by adding the min radius to the position z of the min sphere $p = (s_{min}.x, s_{min}.y, s_{min}.z + r_{min})$, the other point is obtained by subtracting the max radius of the position z of the max sphere $q = (s_{max}.x, s_{max}.y, s_{max}.z - r_{max})$. The radius r_{med} is equal to half the distance between these points, it is calculated using the Eq. 2. The position of the sphere with radius r_{med} is calculated using the Eq. 3, this is equal to half the distance in z between the min sphere and max sphere. The data for r_{med} and c_{med} are shown in Fig. 1c.

$$r_{med} = \frac{distance(p, q)}{2} \tag{2}$$

$$c_{med} = \left(s_{max}.x, s_{max}.y, \frac{(s_{max}.z - r_{max}) + (s_{min}.z + r_{min})}{2} \right) \tag{3}$$

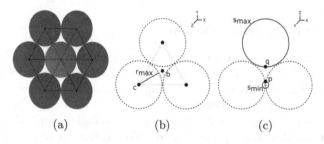

(a)   (b)   (c)

Fig. 1. Data for parameters. (a) Spheres hexagon. (b) Data for r_{min}. (c) Data for r_{med} and c_{med}.

3.2 Layers Generation

In layer generation, a layer is equivalent to a set of max spheres that does not change its position z. Between every three max spheres there are a min sphere and two spheres with radius r_{med} as can be seen in Fig. 2a. The layers begin with the insertion of a max sphere in the minimum point of the enveloping rectangular container and are built based on a structure that was called the hepta-sphere, due to the number of positions seen from above, this can be seen in Fig. 2b.

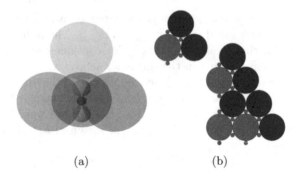

Fig. 2. Data for layers. (a) One min sphere and two med spheres. (b) In the left part, a hepta-sphere and in the right, possible movements to top and right.

The positions of the hepta-sphere are calculated as follows:

$$max_{pos0} = (c.x + 2r_{max}, c.y, c.z)$$

$$max_{pos1} = (c.x + r_{max}, c.y + (2r_{max}sin60°), c.z)$$

$$min_{pos0} = (c.x, c.y + (r_{max} + r_{min}), c.z)$$

$$min_{pos1} = (c.x + r_{max}, c.y + ((r_{max} + r_{min})cos60°), c.z)$$

$$min_{pos2} = (c.x + r_{max}, c.y - ((r_{max} + r_{min})cos60°), c.z)$$

$$min_{pos3} = (c.x, c.y - (r_{max} + r_{min}), c.z)$$

3.3 Spheres in Arbitrary Domain

Once the enveloping rectangular container is filled, the spheres that are not within the mesh of the arbitrary container are discarded. To verify if a sphere belongs to a 3D mesh, raycast is used using the algorithm proposed by Jiménez et al. [8] for the intersection between a segment and a triangle. In the raycast, the intersection of the sphere with the compared triangle is verified, for this it is necessary to find the closest point of a triangle, for this the algorithm proposed by Eberly [3] is used.

If a max sphere intersects a triangle, this sphere is divided into 61 spheres of radius $0.209108658611283u$, the positions and radius of these are recalculated based on a translation of the center of the max sphere and scale of the maximum radius, the resulting radius is the radius r_{mid}. The data for max spheres division are taken from the denser Pfoertner [11] sphere packing. If a sphere with radius r_{med} intersects a triangle, its radius is changed to r_{min}. Once the new spheres with radii r_{mid} and r_{min} have been created, it is verified if they belong to the 3D mesh of the arbitrary container.

3.4 Parallelization

The verification of sphere membership in the container's 3D mesh is the part that is parallelized. Parallelization in both CPU and GPU is done by dividing the number of verified spheres, that is, in parallel the verification of a certain amount of the total spheres is carried out.

As CUDA works with dynamic arrays, the spheres are stored in an array that represents a matrix of size $(n \times 4)$, where n is the number of spheres. As the number of rows will always be 4, the parallelization is worked by dividing the matrix by columns, where each column is a sphere. The implementation of CPU parallelization is in Algorithm 1 and the implementation of GPU parallelization is in Algorithm 2.

In both implementations *valids* are the positions of the spheres inside the arbitrary domain, *spheres* are the spheres generated in the enveloping rectangular container, *triangles* are the triangles of the arbitrary container, $spheres_{size}$ is the number of spheres and $triangles_{size}$ is the number of triangles.

Algorithm 1: Parallel CPU Sphere Inside Mesh

---

1 **Function** ThdSpheresInMesh($valids$, $spheres$, $triangles$, $spheres_{size}$, $triangles_{size}$, s_i, s_f):

2      $sphere[4] \longleftarrow null$;

3   **for** $sphere_{idx} \longleftarrow s_i$ **to** s_f **do**

4          $sphere[0] \longleftarrow spheres[sphere_{idx}]$;

5          $sphere[1] \longleftarrow spheres[spheres_{size} + sphere_{idx}]$;

6          $sphere[2] \longleftarrow spheres[2 * spheres_{size} + sphere_{idx}]$;

7          $sphere[3] \longleftarrow spheres[3 * spheres_{size} + sphere_{idx}]$;

8          $valids[sphr_{idx}] \longleftarrow$ SphereInMesh ($sphere$, $triangles$, $triangles_{size}$);

9 **Function** CPUSpheresInMesh($valids$, $spheres$, $triangles$, $spheres_{size}$, $triangles_{size}$):

10      $csphr \longleftarrow$ number of spheres;

11      $cthd \longleftarrow$ number of threads;

12      $vthd \longleftarrow csphr/cthd$;

13      $lthd \longleftarrow cthd - 1$;

14      $threads[cthd] \longleftarrow null$;

15   **for** $i \longleftarrow 0$ **to** $lthd$ **do**

16          $threads[i]$.Start (ThdSpheresInMesh, $valids$, $spheres$, $triangles$, $i * vthd$, $(i + 1) * vthd$);

17      $threads[lthd]$.Start (ThdSpheresInMesh, $valids$, $spheres$, $triangles$, $lthd * vthd$, $csphr$);

18   **for** $i \longleftarrow 0$ **to** $cthd$ **do**

19          $threads[i]$.Join ();

Algorithm 2: Parallel GPU Sphere Inside Mesh

---

1 **Function** GPUSpheresInMesh($valids$, $spheres$, $triangles$, $spheres_{size}$, $triangles_{size}$):

2      $sphere_{idx} \longleftarrow threadIdx.x + blockIdx.x * blockDim.x$;

3      $sphere[4] \longleftarrow null$;

4   **if** $sphere_{idx} < spheres_{size}$ **then**

5          $sphere[0] \longleftarrow spheres[sphere_{idx}]$;

6          $sphere[1] \longleftarrow spheres[spheres_{size} + sphere_{idx}]$;

7          $sphere[2] \longleftarrow spheres[2 * spheres_{size} + sphere_{idx}]$;

8          $sphere[3] \longleftarrow spheres[3 * spheres_{size} + sphere_{idx}]$;

9          $valids[sphr_{idx}] \longleftarrow$ SphereInMesh ($sphere$, $triangles$, $triangles_{size}$);

---

4 Results

This section presents the tests carried out, as well as the results of the implementation in C++ with OpenGL of the algorithms described that were run on an Intel Core i7-8550U @1.80 GHz with 12 GB of RAM, 8 threads and graphics card NVIDIA GeForce MX130 under Windows 10 64 bits.

First, the tests carried out in a cubic container are presented and then the tests carried out in arbitrary containers are presented to evaluate the density and time of the proposed sequential method. Finally, the results of the proposed parallel method are shown.

4.1 Cubic Container

The methods to be compared are those proposed by Li and Ji [9] and Lozano et al. [10], which are geometric packings for arbitrary domains. All the data of the Li and Ji [9] proposal were taken from the document, since the available algorithm was not obtained and it could not be replicated due to lack of information in the detection of the container, however, it was taken into account due to its high density. The results of these comparisons are shown in Table 1.

Table 1. Comparison in cubic container of $(10u \times 10u \times 10u)$

Algorithm	Machine	Radius	Density	Time
Li and Ji [9]	Intel Core i7, 3.40GHz	$0.5u$	50.30%	–
Lozano et al. [10]	Intel Core i7, 1.80 GHz	$0.5u$	47.12%	16.47 s
Proposed method	Intel Core i7, 1.80 GHz	$0.5u$	58.90%	0.03 s
Li and Ji [9]	Intel Core i7, 3.40 GHz	$0.25u$	59.95%	7.76 s
Lozano et al. [10]	Intel Core i7, 1.80 GHz	$0.25u$	52.38%	56.33 s
Proposed method	Intel Core i7, 1.80 GHz	$0.25u$	60.98%	0.48 s

The results of Table 1 are taking into account a single radius, therefore, in the proposed method, only the spheres with the input radius were counted for the density calculation. These results indicate that the proposed method surpasses the methods of Li and Ji [9] and Lozano et al. [10] both in density and in time for cubic containers. The tests in arbitrary containers are shown below.

4.2   Arbitrary Containers

The method to be compared is the method of Lozano et al. [10] and not that of Li and Ji [9] due to the lack of information on the latter. First, the tests carried out on containers of known volumes are presented, the data for these containers can be found in Table 2. The radii to be used refer to the maximum radius and the minimum radius respectively.

Table 2. Containers with known volumes

Container	Measures (u)	Triangles	Volume (u^3)
Cube	Width (10), height(10), depth(10)	12	1000.00
Cone	Radius (5), height (10)	62	261.80
Cylinder	Radius (5), height (10)	124	785.40
Capsule	Spherical radius (5), cylindrical height (10)	832	245.44
Sphere	Radius (5)	960	523.60
Torus	Max radius (5), min radius (1.25)	1152	154.21

The results of the packing in the previously mentioned containers using as radii $(0.5u, 0.0773503u)$ and $(0.25u, 0.0386751u)$ are shown in Table 3. These results show that the proposed method surpasses the method of Lozano et al. [10] in density and time. The visual results of Table 3 are shown in Fig. 3, where each row from left to right shows the proposed method with radii $(0.5u, 0.0773503u)$, the method of Lozano et al. [10] with radii $(0.5u, 0.0773503u)$, the proposed method with radii $(0.25u, 0.0386751u)$ and the method of Lozano et al. [10] with radii $(0.25u, 0.0386751u)$.

Table 3. Comparison in containers of known volumes

Container	Radii (0.5, 0.0773503)				Radii (0.25, 0.0386751)			
	Lozano et al. [10]		Proposed method		Lozano et al. [10]		Proposed method	
	Density	Time	Density	Time	Density	Time	Density	Time
Cube	53.25%	34.46s	**65.26%**	**0.07 s**	58.40%	208.39 s	**70.63%**	**0.23 s**
Cone	47.87%	21.98 s	**58.49%**	**0.16 s**	55.41%	72.14 s	**67.62%**	**0.74 s**
Cylinder	52.45%	35.50 s	**64.55%**	**0.32 s**	57.81%	172.58 s	**69.57%**	**2.22 s**
Capsule	52.98%	20.71 s	**59.34%**	**1.37 s**	59.47%	67.61 s	**70.67%**	**8.30 s**
Sphere	49.45%	27.16 s	**63.26%**	**3.65 s**	55.36%	125.10 s	**69.42%**	**20.36 s**
Torus	14.71%	20.70 s	**41.58%**	**2.25 s**	49.32%	34.17 s	**57.20%**	**12.60 s**

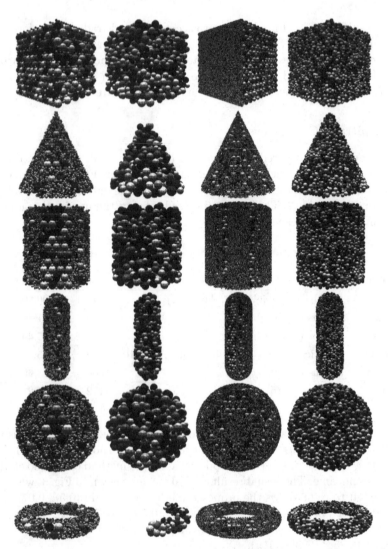

Fig. 3. Containers with known volumes. From top to bottom: Cube, Cone, Cylinder, Capsule, Sphere and Torus. From left to right: Proposed method ($0.5u$, $0.0773503u$), Lozano et al. [10] ($0.5u$, $0.0773503u$), Proposed method ($0.25u$, $0.0386751u$) and Lozano et al. [10] ($0.25u$, $0.0386751u$).

The results of the tests performed on the Stanford Bunny with 7202 triangles, a volume of $109.9030u^3$ and a domain size of $8.07u \times 8.11u \times 6.17u$ are shown in Table 4. The method of Lozano et al. [10] can use as radii ($0.05u$, $0.00773503u$) obtaining a density of 60.37% in a time of 3116.02 s. Smaller radii are not used due to high run time.

Table 4. Comparison in Stanford Bunny

Radii	Lozano et al. [10]		Proposed method	
	Density	Time	Density	Time
0.25u, 0.0386751u	50.69%	**40.64 s**	**62.23%**	76.26 s
0.1u, 0.0154701u	58.08%	**347.45 s**	**70.70%**	969.10 s
0.075u, 0.0116025u	59.37%	**866.34 s**	**72.22%**	2589.61 s

The visual results of the Stanford Bunny with radii (0.25u, 0.00773503u) are found in Fig. 4a and Fig. 4b, in these it can be observed how the method of Lozano et al. [10] does not complete the model correctly, as the ears are missing. In Fig. 4d you can see the Stanford Bunny using the method of Lozano et al. [10] with radii (0.05u, 0.00773503u).

(a)   (b)   (c)   (d)

Fig. 4. Comparison in Stanford Bunny. (a) Proposed method: Radii (0.25u, 0.00773503u), Density (62.23%) and Time (76.26 s). (b) Lozano et al. [10]: Radii (0.25u, 0.00773503u), Density (50.69%) and Time (40.64 s). (c) Proposed method: Radii (0.1u, 0.0154701u), Density (70.70%) and Time (969.10 s). (d) Lozano et al. [10]: Radii (0.05u, 0.00773503u), Density (60.37%) and Time (3116.02 s).

The results of the tests performed on the Stanford Dragon with 21782 triangles, a volume of $6.9508u^3$ and a domain size of $2.24u \times 3.52u \times 5.00u$ are shown in Table 5. The method of Lozano et al. [10] can use as radii (0.025u, 0.00386751u) obtaining a density of 54.21% in a time of 1367.28 s. Smaller radii are not used due to high run time.

Table 5. Comparison in Stanford Dragon

Radii	Lozano et al. [10]		Proposed method	
	Density	Time	Density	Time
0.1u, 0.0154701u	0.00%	**28.53 s**	**53.03%**	384.14 s
0.075u, 0.0116025u	0.00%	**28.72 s**	**58.15%**	825.61 s
0.05u, 0.00773503u	49.21%	**136.85 s**	**64.00%**	2674.20 s

The visual results of the Stanford Dragon are shown in Fig. 5, where you can see the lack of details of the method of Lozano et al. [10] with radii (0.05u, 0.00773503u).

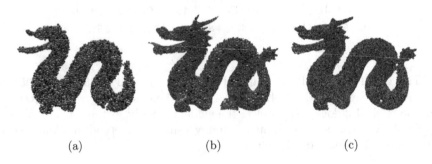

(a)   (b)   (c)

Fig. 5. Comparison in Stanford Dragon. (a) Lozano et al. [10]: Radii (0.05u, 0.00773503u), Density (49.21%) and Time (136.85 s). (b) Proposed method: Radii (0.05u, 0.00773503u), Density (64.00%) and Time (2674.20 s). (c) Lozano et al. [10]: Radii (0.025u, 0.00386751u), Density (54.21%) and Time (1367.28 s).

As can be seen in the results of Tables 4 and 5, the proposed method surpasses the method of Lozano et al. [10] in density, but not in time, therefore, the algorithm was parallelized to reduce the execution time of the packing.

4.3   Parallelization

Two parallelizations were made, the first using CPU threads and the second using GPU threads. The results of these tests are shown in Table 6. In times of parallelization, the parallelization in GPU is greater in some cases, due to the time it takes to pass the data from the CPU to the GPU and viceversa.

Table 6. Parallelization times

Container	Radii	Sequential	CPU Threads	GPU Threads
Cube	0.25u, 0.0386751u	0.23 s	**0.12 s**	0.54 s
Cone	0.25u, 0.0386751u	0.74 s	**0.36 s**	0.79 s
Cylinder	0.25u, 0.0386751u	2.22 s	**0.85 s**	1.25 s
Capsule	0.25u, 0.0386751u	8.30 s	**2.29 s**	2.64 s
Sphere	0.25u, 0.0386751u	20.36 s	6.71 s	**5.73 s**
Torus	0.25u, 0.0386751u	12.60 s	4.24 s	**3.92 s**
Bunny	0.1u, 0.0154701u	969.10 s	292.79 s	**192.27 s**
Dragon	0.05u, 0.00773503u	2674.20 s	**751.14 s**	833.63 s

5   Conclusions

The proposed method works in arbitrary containers, that is, in containers at the request of the user, in this way the flexibility of the method is tested, since it works on any object. The densities are between 60% and 70% in arbitrary containers, surpassing the compared methods in this respect. The times using the sequential method in some cases were high, however, when it works with the parallel method, either in CPU or GPU, these times are considerably reduced, therefore, when reaching densities close to and greater than 60% in shorter times at 5 min in arbitrary containers, the proposed method is considered efficient. As for future work, parallel versions will be reviewed to improve their execution times.

Acknowledgements. M. E. LOAIZA acknowledges the financial support of the CON-CYTEC – BANCO MUNDIAL Project "Mejoramiento y Ampliación de los Servicios del Sistema Nacional de Ciencia Tecnología e Innovación Tecnológica" 8682-PE, through its executing unit PROCIENCIA, within the framework of the call E041-01, Contract No. 038-2018-FONDECYT-BM-IADT-AV.

References

1. Campello, E., Cassares, K.R.: Rapid generation of particle packs at high packing ratios for dem simulations of granular compacts. Lat. Am. J. Solids Struct. **13**(1), 23–50 (2016)
2. Duran, J.: Sands, Powders, and Grains: An Introduction to the Physics of Granular Materials. Springer, New York (2012). https://doi.org/10.1007/978-1-4612-0499-2
3. Eberly, D.: Distance between point and triangle in 3D. Geometric Tools (2020). https://www.geometrictools.com/Documentation/DistancePoint3Triangle3.pdf
4. Gan, J., Yu, A.: Dem study on the packing density and randomness for packing of ellipsoids. Powder Technol. **361**, 424–434 (2020)
5. Hales, T.: Dense Sphere Packings: A Blueprint for Formal Proofs, vol. 400. Cambridge University Press (2012)
6. Hales, T.: Flyspeck. Google Code Archive (2014). https://code.google.com/archive/p/flyspeck/wikis/AnnouncingCompletion.wiki. Accesed 01 Jul 2020
7. Jaeger, H.M., Nagel, S.R., Behringer, R.P.: Granular solids, liquids, and gases. Rev. Mod. Phys. **68**(4), 1259 (1996)
8. Jiménez, J.J., Segura, R.J., Feito, F.R.: A robust segment/triangle intersection algorithm for interference tests. Efficiency study. Comput. Geom. **43**(5), 474–492 (2010)
9. Li, Y., Ji, S.: A geometric algorithm based on the advancing front approach for sequential sphere packing. Granular Matter **20**(4), 1–12 (2018)
10. Lozano, E., Roehl, D., Celes, W., Gattass, M.: An efficient algorithm to generate random sphere packs in arbitrary domains. Comput. Math. Appl. **71**(8), 1586–1601 (2016)
11. Pfoertner, H.: Numerical results for densest packing of n equal spheres in a larger sphere with radius = 1. The Online Encyclopedia of Integer Sequences (2013). http://oeis.org/A084827/a084827.txt. Accessed 02 Aug 2021

12. Rakotonirina, A.D., Delenne, J.Y., Radjai, F., Wachs, A.: Grains3D, a flexible DEM approach for particles of arbitrary convex shape-part iii: extension to non-convex particles modelled as glued convex particles. Comput. Part. Mech. **6**(1), 55–84 (2019)
13. Song, C., Wang, P., Makse, H.A.: A phase diagram for jammed matter. Nature **453**(7195), 629–632 (2008)
14. Tangri, H., Guo, Y., Curtis, J.S.: Packing of cylindrical particles: DEM simulations and experimental measurements. Powder Technol. **317**, 72–82 (2017)
15. Weisstein, E.W.: Circle packing. MathWorld-A Wolfram Web Resource (2020). https://mathworld.wolfram.com/CirclePacking.html. Accessed 01 Jul 2020
16. Weisstein, E.W.: Sphere packing. MathWorld-A Wolfram Web Resource (2020). https://mathworld.wolfram.com/SpherePacking.html. Accessed 01 Jul 2020
17. Weller, R., Zachmann, G.: ProtoSphere: a GPU-assisted prototype guided sphere packing algorithm for arbitrary objects. In: ACM SIGGRAPH ASIA 2010 Sketches, pp. 1–2. Association for Computing Machinery (2010)
18. Wu, Y., An, X., Yu, A.: Dem simulation of cubical particle packing under mechanical vibration. Powder Technol. **314**, 89–101 (2017)
19. Zhao, B., An, X., Wang, Y., Qian, Q., Yang, X., Sun, X.: Dem dynamic simulation of tetrahedral particle packing under 3D mechanical vibration. Powder Technol. **317**, 171–180 (2017)
20. Zhao, S., Zhang, N., Zhou, X., Zhang, L.: Particle shape effects on fabric of granular random packing. Powder Technol. **310**, 175–186 (2017)

Building 3D Virtual Worlds from Monocular Images of Urban Road Traffic Scenes

Ankita Christine Victor and Jaya Sreevalsan-Nair[✉] [iD]

Graphics-Visualization-Computing Lab, International Institute of Information Technology, 26/C, Electronics City, Bangalore 560100, Karnataka, India
jnair@iiitb.ac.in
http://www.iiitb.ac.in/gvcl

Abstract. Three-dimensional (3D) modeling of urban road scenes has warranted well-deserved interest in entertainment, urban planning, and autonomous vehicle simulation. Modeling such realistic scenes is still predominantly a manual process, relying mainly on 3D artists. Cameras mounted on vehicles can now provide images of road scenes, which can be used as references for automating scene layout. Our goal is to use the information from such images from a single camera sensor on a moving vehicle to build an approximate 3D virtual world. We propose a workflow that takes the human out of the loop through the use of deep learning to generate a dense depth map, an inverse projection to correct for perspective distortion in the image, collision detection, and a rendering engine. The engine loads and displays 3D models belonging to a particular type, at accurate relative positions, thus building and rendering a virtual world corresponding to the image. This virtual world can then be edited and animated. Our proposed workflow can potentially speed up the process of modeling virtual environments significantly when integrated with a modeling tool. We have tested the efficacy of our 3D virtual world-building and rendering using user studies with image-to-image similarity and video-to-image correspondences. Even with limited photorealistic rendering, our user study results demonstrate that 3D world-building can be effectively done, with minimal human intervention, using our workflow with monocular images from moving vehicles as inputs.

Keywords: 3D world-building · Modeling · Convolutional neural networks · Deep learning · Depth estimation · Inverse projection · Collision detection · Graphics rendering · Virtual world · Human-in-the-loop

1 Introduction

Building a three-dimensional (3D) world of a scene from a two-dimensional (2D) image is a challenging problem in computer vision. Its technological solutions

© Springer Nature Switzerland AG 2021
G. Bebis et al. (Eds.): ISVC 2021, LNCS 13018, pp. 461–474, 2021.
https://doi.org/10.1007/978-3-030-90436-4_37

have applications in entertainment, digital mapping, urban planning, and training simulations for automated driving systems. Testing of autonomous driving software is critical for validation. It is estimated that autonomous vehicles might have to be tested on up to 17.7 billion kilometers of simulation before one can have valid data on their safety to compare with human drivers [19]. While one could record the footage for this entire (simulated) distance using cameras, it is more advantageous to use virtual worlds that can be modeled from real-world traffic data, edited, and animated to produce a variety of scenarios.

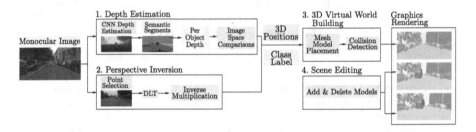

Fig. 1. Overview of our proposed workflow. Given a monocular image, we (1) estimate dense depth using a CNN and obtain per object depth using semantic segments, and (2) correct perspective distortion DLT using selected points. Using the 3D positions and object labels obtained from (1) and (2) for our classes of interest, we (3) place 3D mesh models followed by an AABB collision detection, and lastly, (4) interactively edit the scene. We examine the outcomes of building and editing by rendering the virtual world(s) using a rendering engine, e.g., a basic one using OpenGL, as shown here.

Most methods to automate the process of 3D world-building use data from a combination of sensors and modalities which typically require an elaborate or expensive setup with multiple cameras and sensors. With the onslaught of digital camera devices, the Web has become a source of billions of images and videos of traffic scenes. This image/video data is now used as the starting point for modeling 3D environments, thus eliminating complex data acquisition. In tandem, advances in machine learning and computer vision provide the tools to augment 2D images with 3D information and create new uses for these images.

However, 3D geometric reconstructions from image and sensor data that can directly be used as a high-quality 3D world are still a work in progress. As a result, world-building remains a manual process. Most 3D artists still follow the same workflow that usually starts with gathering inspiration and ideas from the Web, making a simple construction of the scene using basic objects to mock the scene layout. The scene is then lit with the main lights and detailed.

Two important metrics of the modeling process are the extent of visual realism, *i.e.,* how close in appearance an artist can make the virtual environment look when compared to the real world, and performance, *i.e.,* how fast these scenes can be modeled. Sophisticated modeling tools assist in realizing an artist's creative ideas rather than participating in the building process itself. In this regard, a technology that is capable of delivering an animatable, realistic 3D world with minimal human input is an interesting focus of research that we believe has potential for popularizing the usage of 3D worlds. To summarize, there is a demand for production-ready 3D content that resembles real-world scenes and that can be easily edited and animated. We then pose the following research question: Is it possible to design an automated system for world-building from a monocular image captured by a camera in a moving vehicle?

To enable image-to-3D world-building, we propose a workflow that uses a convolutional neural network (CNN) to estimate the depth and computes a matrix to correct the effects of perspective projection using direct linear transform (DLT). Our proposed workflow automates the initial steps of 3D scene modeling up to the stage where the primary objects in the scene have been placed, and the scene is rendered with ambient light. There are four main steps in the workflow, namely, depth estimation, perspective correction, model loading, and interactive editing (Fig. 1). Our workflow exclusively builds 3D virtual worlds of urban road traffic scenes with paved roads, parked or stationary, and moving traffic, people, trees, and buildings. Our novel contributions are in:

- An automated workflow for the building of 3D virtual worlds from monocular images of traffic scenes captured from a moving vehicle, that can be further edited and animated.
- A user study to validate correspondence of the 3D world to its source image.

2   Related Work

We refer to creating an approximate world with the objects of the same type placed, as in the scene, as *3D virtual world-building*. Our approach to image-to-3D world-building is novel. World-building and 3D reconstruction have overlapping solutions as they rely on depth inference and camera approximation. However, the former looks at creating animatable scenes with prefabricated models using relative positions of key objects, and the latter is focused on identifying sizes and types of objects present in the scene. While both can be used in tandem, we focus on the former exclusively here. We discuss literature on both here.

Structure from Motion (SfM). SfM refers to the methods that use observations from two or more viewing directions to derive the position of a point in 3D space by triangulation. Early self-calibrating metric reconstruction systems [2,18] served as some of the first systems on 3D reconstruction from images. Pollefeys *et al.* [20] used monocular video to deliver 3D models as textured meshes. Incremental SfM is a well-accepted strategy for reconstruction from unordered image collections. Unordered photo collections on the Web have been used to generate sparse 3D models [7,23]. As an extension, multibody SfM (MSfM) has been used for the reconstruction of dynamic traffic scenes and vehicle/camera trajectories [3]. The camera in these cases is not necessarily mounted on the moving vehicle. Our workflow uses a monocular image captured by a camera sensor in the moving vehicle, as the input, and gives an approximate 3D world corresponding to the image, unlike the 3D reconstruction of traffic images.

Joint Semantic Segmentation and 3D Reconstruction. Image segmentation and 3D reconstruction can be tightly coupled and jointly implemented, by constraining the solution using priors, thus yielding smoother 3D reconstructions and more precise segmentation. For instance, the surface area has been used as a regularization prior to obtaining the final surface construction indirectly via volumetric optimization [17]. This has been improved by adding class-specific geometric cues guided by image appearances [13]. Joint inference of 3D scene structure and semantic labeling of forward-moving monocular image sequences has been done using class-specific semantic cues and conditional random fields [16]. Geometric cues have been used to simultaneously perform depth estimation from monocular images of traffic scenes and semantic segmentation on a CNN [14].

Generative Adversarial Networks (GANs). GANs have been used as extensions to self-supervised networks for improving depth estimation in monocular images from moving vehicles [12]. Additionally, for image sequences/collections data, GANs are used in image-to-image synthesis tasks and for generating photorealistic images. A noteworthy contribution comes from Isola *et al.* [15] who have proposed a conditional GAN architecture and a corresponding pix2pix software as a general-purpose solution for image-to-image translation. pix2pix has been tested on a variety of tasks and datasets, including the generation of images from semantic labels trained on the Cityscapes dataset [6]. Conditional GANs have been used for video-to-video synthesis [25]. Similar to pix2pix, this method synthesizes images from segmented frames while maintaining temporal coherence. This work has been extended to generate graphics for a driving simulator. One limitation is that the structure of the world is created manually and only the graphics or texture is synthesized. Our work differs in that we infer the scene layout and use off-the-shelf mesh models to create the final scene that can be animated as such. These GAN-based methods predominantly work in cases where the source and destination spaces are of the same dimension, which are not directly applicable for image-to-3D world synthesis.

3D Virtual World-Building. Virtual world rendering from images and LiDAR data has been an active area of research. Modeling of full 3D virtual representations of dynamic events from multiple video streams has been done using a collection of fused visible surface models [21]. There are several methods for the automated extraction of geographic information from LiDAR to support the construction of high-fidelity 3D virtual environment models [1]. Clarke [5] has proposed a pipeline for automated, customized virtual world construction by specifying a set of locations and target style for each location. Our work differs from these in that we consider the construction of approximate environments from a specific data source, namely the monocular images.

Our work is also notably different from the Virtual KITTI dataset generation [4,8]. The Virtual KITTI dataset consists of photo-realistically rendered videos of image sequences from the camera sensor in the moving vehicles, generated using Unity, which enabled manual world-building through crowdsourcing from the activity user community of Unity. Our work builds approximate virtual worlds using a *mostly* human-out-of-the-loop workflow.

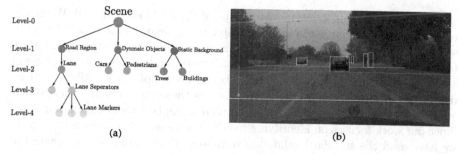

(a)   (b)

Fig. 2. (a) Interpretation of a road scene using a Latent Hierarchical Part-based Model (LHPM) [24] for the choice of objects in the synthesized 3D world. (b) Depth values along the lines $Y = y$ in image space and on the ground plane can be assumed to have the same depth. Each colored line represents a different value, and all points on the line have the same depth. Note that no line is drawn through objects since those pixels do not correspond to ground points. In terms of Y, $a > b > c > d$, whose order reverses in terms of depth.

3 Our Method

3D worlds are traditionally constructed manually by 3D artists who take inspiration from or model parts of the real world. In contrast, we propose a workflow to automatically construct 3D worlds of urban road traffic scenes based on a reference monocular image with minimal user intervention. Our proposed workflow is currently intended for images of urban, outdoor scenes with straight roads, that include objects of interest, namely, people, trees, buildings, and sidewalks. Our work pertains exclusively to straight roads owing to the constraints imposed by our perspective correction methodology. We use the Latent Hierarchical Part-based Models (LHPMs) [24] for the choice of objects in the scene which we include in 3D virtual worlds. All objects in the scene are organized in a hierarchical structure in an LHPM. While we conceptually use the tree data structure given in an LHPM, the indexing of the levels in the tree is different in our workflow to suit our requirements. In our current implementation, we have considered level-1 of road regions (*i.e.,* just the roads without identifying structures at finer levels of granularity, such as lanes, separators, etc.), level-2 of dynamic objects (*i.e.,* pedestrians, cars), and level-2 of static background (*i.e.,* trees, buildings), as shown in Fig. 2(a).

Our workflow has four main steps, as shown in Fig. 1. In step 1, we use the CNN architecture proposed by Godard *et al.* [11] to estimate depth from a monocular image and ground truth semantic segments to compute per-object depth for our classes of interest. In step 2, we approximate the projection matrix of the camera that created the image using DLT and apply an inverse of this to obtain world space coordinates. In step 3, we use the obtained 3D position and the semantic class to load a generic mesh model belonging to that class at the computed location. We additionally run an axis-aligned bounding box (AABB) collision detection to eliminate any mesh intersection in the 3D world-building. In step 4, interactive editing of the world is facilitated. We finally render the synthesized world using a graphics engine or shader-based OpenGL software. The novelty of our workflow is in choosing and integrating appropriate methods for our requirement of image-to-3D world-building. We do not perform a comparison with other methods for subcomponents of our workflow, namely, depth generation or perspective correction, as these methods are already well studied, and equivalent methods can be used to replace them in our workflow. Since our work focuses on identifying relative positions of key objects in a scene, we have used the standard validation technique of user studies to evaluate the closeness of the 3D world from our method to the real world.

Step 1: Depth Estimation. Godard *et al.* [11] have posed depth estimation from a monocular image as an image reconstruction problem instead of a supervised learning problem. Their main idea is that given a set of stereo images captured by a calibrated binocular camera, if a network learns a function that can reconstruct one image of a stereo pair from the other, then the network has learned something about the 3D structure of the input image. If the baseline distance b between the two cameras and the camera focal length f are known then depth, $\hat{d}$ can be trivially recovered from the predicted disparity as, $\hat{d} = \frac{bf}{d}$.

Here, given the novelty of our work in 3D world-building, we choose to use Cityscapes dataset over other similar traffic scene image collection, *e.g.*, KITTI [9], owing to the higher resolution, quality, and variety of the images [11]. The recent GANs that are trained on KITTI and generalized on Cityscapes, provide a marginal improvement in per-pixel accuracy of depth estimation [12]. This is especially because batch normalization that is used for adversarial training does not provide significant improvement for the Cityscapes data [11]. Also, for Cityscapes images to work with the GANs, the images are cropped to resolve the artifacts in the images [12]. Overall, the simpler CNN proposed with lower training time by Godard *et al.* [11] is suitable for our experiments, owing to our requirement of the accuracy of relative depths in pixels for world-building as opposed to the per-pixel accuracy. Since the depth estimation component is decoupled from others in the workflow, a depth estimation model suitable for the input data can be selected and *plugged in.*

We use the model that has been trained for 50 epochs, with a 512 × 256 resolution, a batch size of 8, and a VGG encoder-decoder, using images from both KITTI and Cityscapes datasets [11]. A single input image is run through the depth estimation model to obtain a dense depth map. Using ground truth semantic labels, the average depth of each object of interest is estimated. Depth estimation has been observed to be estimated with higher error especially for occluded objects and objects farther away from the camera [11].

To overcome model limitations and ensure all objects of interest in our work are assigned the right depth value with respect to each other, we propose a post-processing step. Here, we make the assumption that the depth of all points along the same line $Y = y$ in pixel coordinates space and are also on the ground plane in the real world will have the same depth. Y-axis[1] in image space corresponds to

---

[1] We refer to the axes in image space as X-Y, and those in 3D world space as X-Y-Z.

the axis along which height of objects is considered in the world space (+Y-axis). In Fig. 2(b), each colored line represents a different value, and all points on the line (not including the breaks) have the same depth. We compute the bounding box of each segment and consider the Y-coordinate (increases downwards) of the bottom corner to be the point at which the object touches the ground in the image. An object with a higher value of Y must be closer to the camera and have a smaller depth value. We sort the objects in the increasing order of average depth, compare their ground points, and assign depth in the post-processing step, with the following adjustments:

1. If two objects have similar Y values and their average depths differ not less than a certain threshold, δ (we have used $\delta = 1$), then we set the average depth of both to be the average-depth of the closer object.
2. If an object with a higher Y value has greater depth than a closer object, also with a lower Y value, we move the former 'behind' the latter in 3D space, along the +Z-axis from the camera.

Step 2: Perspective Correction. Perspective projection is a non-linear, non-affine transformation in Z-axis as lines that are parallel in the original coordinate space appear to intersect in the transformed coordinate space or the projected image. An accurate synthesis of the corresponding 3D world will require that the image coordinates of each object first be remapped to its original world coordinates using perspective correction.

To localize the objects, we use the Z-coordinate estimated in Step 1 and now approximate the X- and Y-coordinates. Since the scenes here pertain to urban roads, we assume that all objects of interest lie on the ground plane, *i.e.,* $Y = 0$ for these objects in 3D space. We now use inverse projection to estimate X-coordinate. To construct a 3D world out of an image scene, we compute the value of some matrix P using $I_i = PW_i$, where I_i is a set of projected image coordinates, W_i is the corresponding set of world coordinates and P is a projection matrix. Since all objects of interest have been assumed to be on the ground plane, this simplifies to the 2D case of DLT. Given a point i_i in the image space, z_i can be obtained by a lookup from the corresponding depth map, and x_i can be approximated. The approximation is done for a set of 5–6 selected points on the image with reference to the *vanishing point* in the image. Our experiments show that selecting the nearest ground point from the objects of interest in the scene (in 3D world space) provides the best approximation. We compute P by solving a system of equations given by the world space-image space point correspondences with the requirement that $\|P\|^2 = 1$ using the least-squares criterion and its inverse is used. To obtain the position of each object along the X-axis, we multiply the extents of the bounding box around each segment with the inverse matrix obtained and averaged. The center of the object is now *translated* along X by this value, for the placement of the object/instance in the scene.

Step 3: 3D World-Building. We have manually curated a small database of 3D mesh models based on the classes of interest from Cityscapes. These geometric models are triangular meshes of an instance of the expected class and are in the standard OBJ format. We have fixed the orientation of every model in 3D space as well as set the scale of every object with respect to another other by intuitively comparing unit mesh model sizes. The X- and Z-coordinates, and the class label are sent to the rendering engine. The database is looked up using the class label, and a corresponding mesh model is loaded into the scene at the world space coordinates. For example, if an object in the image has been semantically segmented as 'car' the rendering engine loads a generic hatchback or SUV (using a random number generator) to construct the 3D world. A woman in an image is semantically labeled as 'person' and the engine will load a generic model of a male human, Similarly, a generic tree is loaded for 'vegetation' even if the object in the image might be a shrub. This is acceptable in our workflow as we are focused on creating a virtual world, which mimics the scene in the image.

We position the object mesh in the scene using the position coordinates computed in steps 1 and 2, such that the center of the 'base plane' of the mesh (touching the ground) is at the computed position coordinates. We then compute the new centroid of the mesh in the 3D space. We perform a uniform scaling transformation at the centroid, where the scale is computed based on the ratio of the extent of X-coordinates of the road in the image space to that of X-coordinates of the road in the 3D space. This scale value needs to be checked manually and perturbed in some instances to obtain *visually accurate relativeness* of the sizes of the objects in the scene. The automation of the computation of the scale is currently out of the scope of this paper.

Before the final rendering of the scene, we use an AABB collision detector to ensure that no models intersect with each other along the X and Z axes, and accordingly perturb the models. This serves as an additional corrector for predicted depth and horizontal translation. The 3D position coordinates and semantic label of each model in the final scene are written into a text file for future use or loading by a similar, or even advanced, rendering engine.

Step 4: Editing the Virtual World. This 3D scene can be optionally interactively edited to add, delete, or replace mesh models, before or after rendering the scene. In step 4, scene parameters from step 3 can be passed as input to modeling tools and rendering engines, such as Unity or Unreal.

We introduce the notion of "permissible" edits, as the destination mesh model must fit into the space selected for its placement. The fitting of the mesh model is done after it is scaled to a size comparable to the neighborhood of the new position and without distorting its aspect ratio. In the case of replacing a selected mesh model, one can also now place conditions on the semantic class of the object that can replace the object type of the selected model. Thus, the permissible edits also include changing the type of object or position of an existing object.

This editing process in the workflow allows an artist to create a variety of scenes using the same skeleton—a feature that can be particularly useful in autonomous vehicle simulation. Edits can be made to the output of step 3, and the edited scene can be directly fed into external modeling and rendering engines. While we have a rudimentary graphical user interface (GUI) to edit the scene interactively, this can be enhanced in the future scope of work.

Rendering the Virtual World. In the current implementation, we render the 3D virtual world using OpenGL [22] graphics system to visualize and demonstrate it. We render the virtual world without any textures, using a perspective projection in OpenGL, ambient lighting, a Phong shader, and a shadow map. The rendered result in the orientation corresponding to the source monocular image may look slightly different from the source, owing to the known differences between the orientation of the camera sensor in the vehicle and the OpenGL settings, *i.e.*, the camera as well as the perspective projection. In Fig. 3, we observe that the object models have been loaded at approximately correct relative positions, depth, and scale, albeit with minor visually perceptible differences.

4 Experiments, Results and Discussion

We have tested our workflow on images of straight roads from Cityscapes that contain objects of our interest, which are vehicles, trees, sidewalks, people, and buildings. Our current implementation is limited to straight roads without breaks and curves. We have demonstrated our best results of rendering 3D virtual worlds synthesized from four different monocular images using our workflow, namely, S1, S2, S3, and S4 (Fig. 3). These images are also picked for the variety of residential and non-residential areas with straight roads, buildings, trees, vehicles, and sidewalks in the scenes. We have further validated the perceptual similarity of our results of 3D worlds with the corresponding source images. To more comprehensively evaluate the accuracy of our results in terms of inferring the right 3D positions and overall scene layout, we have conducted two user studies. The questionnaire forms for the user studies are available at https://forms.gle/ Zecjbi9UKXTC439Q6 and https://forms.gle/f9LmpzYg3LNjazPu8. We do not use any special methodology to ensure that the samples are representative of all possible traffic scenes. However, given that the results of each study corroborate the accuracy of the generated world we believe it is a useful evaluation.

Fig. 3. 2D input image and corresponding view from the camera of the 3D virtual world, built using our proposed workflow. From top left clockwise: Scene S1, S2, S3, and S4. All four scenes are used for our image-to-image similarity user study; and S2 and S3, for our video-to-image correspondences study.

User Study of Video-to-Image Correspondences (T1). We have generated a video of fly-through of two 3D worlds synthesized using our proposed workflow that starts from the point of capture of the scene and moves forward into the scene before providing an aerial view. Thus, this video has a blend of overhead aerial view and rotation about the Y-axis of the 3D world space for developing the animation using OpenGL rendering. This user study entails viewing the video along with four potential RGB images from which the scene could have been generated, with a task to identify the correct source image.

We have generated a smooth animation of the 3D virtual world, for the best user experience. In the animation, we have additionally included the "source" vehicle where the camera is mounted as an object in the scene, rendered in red. This is to provide the realism and completeness of the virtual world, wherein when the camera is moving outside of the "source" vehicle for the fly-through, the "source" vehicle too is a part of the synthesized virtual world (Fig. 4).

For each question in T1, we include images that are similar to the source image. We identify such images from the image collection using the structural similarity index (SSIM). The three images with ∼0.5 SSIM are selected, and including the source image, we provide four choices for each question (Fig. 4). This is to ensure that the choices available are similar in semantic content, but yet differentiable to perceive the correct image-to-3D world correspondence.

User Study of Image-to-Image Similarity (T2). We have provided the survey respondents with a source RGB image and its corresponding 3D virtual world construction from the view of the camera sensor in the vehicle, rendered using OpenGL. This user study entails assessing the image-to-image similarity on a five-point Likert scale. Having choices 1 and 5 correspond to the worst and best matches, respectively, the Likert scale captures how close the virtual world perceptually matched with the source image, with respect to the presence and relative positions of the objects of interest, *e.g.,* cars, people, sidewalk (Fig. 5).

Outcomes of User Studies. We present our results from a total of 41 survey respondents to both tests. The respondents participated voluntarily in social media groups. In all cases, T1 was administered before T2, in order to provide an appropriate context to the participants. We have used four test monocular images taken from moving vehicles, S1, S2, S3, and S4 (Fig. 3).

For T1, the images chosen for S2 in the question have an SSIM of 0.58, 0.50, and 0.48 with the source image. Similarly, for S3, the selected images have an SSIM of 0.39, 0.43, and 0.39 with the source image. 90.2% of the users correctly identified the source image for S2, and 95.1% of the users correctly identified the source of the second question S3. Participants scored an average of 1.85 points in the study with a standard deviation of 0.48. Out of the 41 participants, 37 respondents got both correct, 2 got one correct, and 2 got both wrong. For the 2 respondents who got one correct answer, they both got the answers correct for S3. The wrong answers for S2 included all the other 3 choices and the wrong answers for S3 included 2 other choices. We observe that the question on S2 was perceptually more difficult than that on S3, which is validated by a relatively

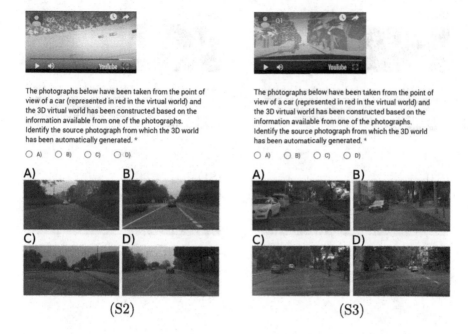

Fig. 4. Questionnaire for the user study of video-to-image correspondences (T1).

higher SSIM index, where the options for S2 are structurally more similar to the source image than that of S3.

For T2, S1, S2, S3, and S4 (Fig. 3) were rated an average of 4.17, 4.24, 4.00, and 3.49 respectively, on the five-point Likert scale. Cronbach's alpha is used for Likert-scale responses to measure latent variables, such as openness and reliability of responses. The alpha value is indicative of whether a designed test accurately measures the variable of interest, which is the perceived similarity between the source image and the synthesized 3D virtual world. We computed a Cronbach's alpha of 0.803 for the responses. By rule of thumb, an alpha of 0.8 is a good goal [10]. We can thus conclude that our survey with ranking questions has been reliable.

Our workflow implementation is a significant improvement over the manually curated scene construction. It takes ~4–7 s to generate the final rendered output for one image. The construction time can be sped up by increased parallelization, particularly during averaging of values within segments. Generation of the depth itself takes to the order of 35 ms for a 512×256 image on a modern GPU [11]. Manual input is required only at the time of perspective inversion where a user selects 5–6 points on the image, and as required, for correcting the relative scales of mesh models of objects of interest. By design, human-in-the-loop is reintroduced in the workflow for editing the scene. We have used untextured models in our user study to focus on relative object placements.

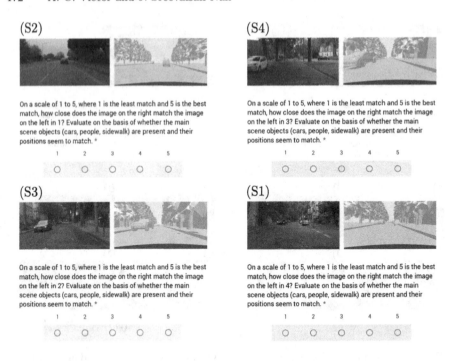

Fig. 5. Questionnaire for the user study of image-to-image similarity (T2).

5   Conclusions

We have proposed a workflow to automatically build 3D virtual worlds based on a reference monocular image with minimal manual intervention to reduce the time and manual effort that goes into scene modeling. The workflow we have proposed can be operated to generate 3D worlds of urban traffic scenes which can be used as simulation environments for autonomous vehicle testing. Given the vast collection of reference images on the Web, our proposed workflow builds approximate 3D virtual worlds from these images efficiently creating a scene that can be detailed and animated. Two key ideas that drive our workflow are the use of deep learning to estimate depth and perspective correction to get real-world positions from an image.

Our proposed workflow can be improved by adding a pose estimation module to automatically detect the orientation of every model and instance-specific labels to load more relevant mesh models. Our prototype implementation works for urban traffic scenes of straight roads, and our results show that our solution presents a useful direction for future research. An important aspect of the rendering of such a world is lighting, which implies determining the lighting parameters from the monocular images is an open problem.

Acknowledgments. The authors are grateful to all members of the Graphics-Visualization-Computing Lab and peers at the IIITB for their support. This work has been financially supported by the Machine Intelligence and Robotics (MINRO) grant by the Government of Karnataka.

References

1. Ahlberg, S., Söderman, U., Elmqvist, M., Persson, A.: On modelling and visualisation of high resolution virtual environments using LIDAR data. In: Proceedings of the 12th International Conference on Geoinformatics, pp. 299–306 (2004)
2. Beardsley, P., Torr, P., Zisserman, A.: 3D model acquisition from extended image sequences. In: Buxton, B., Cipolla, R. (eds.) ECCV 1996. LNCS, vol. 1065, pp. 683–695. Springer, Heidelberg (1996). https://doi.org/10.1007/3-540-61123-1_181
3. Bullinger, S.: Image-based 3D Reconstruction of Dynamic Objects Using Instance-aware Multibody Structure from Motion, vol. 44. KIT Scientific Publishing (2020)
4. Cabon, Y., Murray, N., Humenberger, M.: Virtual KITTI 2. arXiv preprint arXiv:2001.10773 (2020)
5. Clarke, M.P.: Virtual World Construction, US Patent 9,378,296 (28 June 2016)
6. Cordts, M., et al.: The cityscapes dataset for semantic urban scene understanding. In: Proceedings of IEEE Conference on Computer Vision and Pattern Recognition (CVPR), pp. 3213–3223. IEEE (2016)
7. Frahm, J.-M., et al.: Building Rome on a cloudless day. In: Daniilidis, K., Maragos, P., Paragios, N. (eds.) ECCV 2010. LNCS, vol. 6314, pp. 368–381. Springer, Heidelberg (2010). https://doi.org/10.1007/978-3-642-15561-1_27
8. Gaidon, A., Wang, Q., Cabon, Y., Vig, E.: Virtual worlds as proxy for multi-object tracking analysis. In: Proceedings of IEEE Conference on Computer Vision and Pattern Recognition (CVPR), pp. 4340–4349. IEEE (2016)
9. Geiger, A., Lenz, P., Stiller, C., Urtasun, R.: Vision meets robotics: the KITTI dataset. Int. J. Robot. Res. **32**(11), 1231–1237 (2013)
10. Gliem, J.A., Gliem, R.R.: Calculating, interpreting, and reporting Cronbach's alpha reliability coefficient for Likert-type scales. In: Midwest Research-to-Practice Conference in Adult, Continuing, and Community (2003)
11. Godard, C., Mac Aodha, O., Brostow, G.J.: Unsupervised monocular depth estimation with left-right consistency. In: Proceedings of IEEE Conference on Computer Vision and Pattern Recognition (CVPR), pp. 270–279. IEEE (2017)
12. Groenendijk, R., Karaoglu, S., Gevers, T., Mensink, T.: On the benefit of adversarial training for monocular depth estimation. Comput. Vis. Image Underst. **190**, 102848 (2020)
13. Hane, C., Zach, C., Cohen, A., Angst, R., Pollefeys, M.: Joint 3D scene reconstruction and class segmentation. In: Proceedings of IEEE Conference on Computer Vision and Pattern Recognition (CVPR), pp. 97–104. IEEE (2013)
14. He, L., Lu, J., Wang, G., Song, S., Zhou, J.: SOSD-Net: joint semantic object segmentation and depth estimation from monocular images. Neurocomputing **440**, 251–263 (2021)
15. Isola, P., Zhu, J.Y., Zhou, T., Efros, A.A.: Image-to-image translation with conditional adversarial networks. In: Proceedings of IEEE Conference on Computer Vision and Pattern Recognition (CVPR), pp. 1125–1134. IEEE (2017)
16. Kundu, A., Li, Y., Dellaert, F., Li, F., Rehg, J.M.: Joint semantic segmentation and 3D reconstruction from monocular video. In: Fleet, D., Pajdla, T., Schiele, B., Tuytelaars, T. (eds.) ECCV 2014. LNCS, vol. 8694, pp. 703–718. Springer, Cham (2014). https://doi.org/10.1007/978-3-319-10599-4_45

17. Lempitsky, V., Boykov, Y.: Global optimization for shape fitting. In: Proceedings of IEEE Conference on Computer Vision and Pattern Recognition (CVPR), pp. 1–8. IEEE (2007)
18. Mohr, R., Quan, L., Veillon, F.: Relative 3D reconstruction using multiple uncalibrated images. Int. J. Robot. Res. **14**(6), 619–632 (1995)
19. Nidhi, K., Paddock, S.M.: Driving to safety: how many miles of driving would it take to demonstrate autonomous vehicle reliability? Transp. Res. Part A Policy Pract. **94**, 182–193 (2016)
20. Pollefeys, M., et al.: Detailed real-time urban 3D reconstruction from video. Int. J. Comput. Vis. **78**(2–3), 143–167 (2008)
21. Rander, P., Narayanan, P., Kanade, T.: Virtualized reality: constructing time-varying virtual worlds from real world events. In: Proceedings of 8th IEEE Visualization Conference, pp. 277–284. IEEE (1997)
22. Shreiner, D.: OpenGL Reference Manual: The Official Reference Document to OpenGL, version 1.2. Addison-Wesley Longman Publishing Co., Inc. (1999)
23. Snavely, N., Seitz, S.M., Szeliski, R.: Photo tourism: exploring photo collections in 3D. ACM Trans. Graph. (TOG) **25**, 835–846 (2006)
24. Venkateshkumar, S.K., Sridhar, M., Ott, P.: Latent hierarchical part based models for road scene understanding. In: Proceedings of 2015 IEEE International Conference on Computer Vision (ICCV) Workshop, pp. 115–123. IEEE (2015)
25. Wang, T.C., et al.: Video-to-video synthesis. In: Proceedings of the 32nd International Conference on Neural Information Processing Systems (NeurIPS), pp. 1152–1164 (2018). http://dl.acm.org/citation.cfm?id=3326943.3327049

Bodily Expression of Emotions in Animated Agents

Zachary Meyer(✉), Nicoletta Adamo(✉), and Bedrich Benes(✉)

Purdue University, West Lafayette, IN 47906, USA
{meyer204,nadamovi,bbenes}@purdue.edu

Abstract. The goal of this research is to identify key affective body gestures that can clearly convey four emotions, namely happy, content, bored, and frustrated, in animated characters that lack facial features. Two studies were conducted, a first to identify affective body gestures from a series of videos, and a second to validate the gestures as representative of the four emotions. Videos were created using motion capture data of four actors portraying the four targeted emotions and mapping the data to two 3D character models, one male and one female. In the first study the researchers identified body gestures that are commonly produced by individuals when they experience each of the four emotions. In the second study the researchers tested four sets of identified body gestures, one set for each emotion. The animated gestures were mapped to the 3D character models and 91 participants were asked to identify the emotional state conveyed by the characters through the body gestures. The study identified six gestures that were shown to have an acceptable recognition rate of at least 80% for three of the four emotions tested. Contentment was the only emotion which was not conveyed clearly by the identified body gestures. The gender of the character had a significant effect on recognition rates across all emotions.

Keywords: Body language · Emotion expression · Animated

1 Introduction

For several decades, psychologists have studied the emotional displays of people through analysis of facial movements, but research into the ability of the body to convey emotions is relatively scarce. The Facial Action Coding System (FACS) is the primary source of knowledge for facial movements that express emotions in people. The FACS is used by both psychologists and animators as reference for emotions that are conveyed by the face. The body has been mostly ignored in regards to the ability to portray emotion until recently [21].

Creation of coding systems such as the Body Action Coding System (BACS) and Body Action and Posture Coding System (BAP) have aided in the ability to identify expressive actions performed by the human body. This research is in its infancy compared to portrayal of emotion using the face [6, 19]

© Springer Nature Switzerland AG 2021
G. Bebis et al. (Eds.): ISVC 2021, LNCS 13018, pp. 475–487, 2021.
https://doi.org/10.1007/978-3-030-90436-4_38

This paper examines emotion expressive body gestures in animated 3D avatars. We focus on bodily expression of four emotions: happy, content, bored, and frustrated. The goal is to identify a set of affective gestures that animated agents can produce to clearly express the four emotional states.

2   Related Work

Classification of Emotion: The animation of virtual agents has relied heavily on Ekman's classification of emotions. Ekman's theory of universal emotions across cultures was discovered on tests of tribes in New Guinea, resulting in identification of fear, anger, joy, sadness, disgust, and surprise as the basic emotions found in all humans, regardless of culture [10]. The emotional gestures of New Guinean tribes people were recognizable to college students in the United States, validating that American citizens were capable of recognizing distinct emotions in people of other cultures [9]. The emotions identified by Ekman have been the principle focus for animators to showcase emotions in virtual agents, as well as used by researchers in the fields on psychology and anthropology. Other classifications of emotions exist, such as Robert Plutchik's eight basic emotions; fear, anger, joy, sadness, acceptance, disgust, expectation, and surprise [28]. More recent work in the field has concluded that there are only four major emotions; happiness, sadness, fear, and anger. Each of these four is attributed to core effects of either reward, punishment, or stress [15]. There is a continuing trend of researchers unable to agree upon a list of basic emotions that would encompass all humans in previous decades, but more recent work trends towards an agreement of universalities in emotion [11].

The measurement of emotions, independent of the classification system used, has relied on Russell's (2003) model of core affect, in which any particular emotion can be placed along two dimensions–(1) valence–ranging from displeasure to pleasure, and (2) arousal–ranging from activation to deactivation. In particular, the work reported in the paper has focused on affective states based on being exposed to instruction, such as frustration (negative valence, high arousal), happiness (positive valence, high arousal), contentment (positive valence, low arousal) and boredom (negative valence, low arousal).

Emotion Expression: Human emotions are expressed using several modalities: vocal and facial expression, arm and hand gestures, trunk rotation, head rotation, and leg movements. The face is cited as being the most used resource in identification of emotional state [26]. The ability of the face to convey emotional states and the gestures associated with varying emotions have been documented in the Facial Action Coding System (FACS) [12]. The work set forth by the FACS presents ways to express emotion in the face through movements of varying muscles into defined shapes. Facial expression of emotion has been heavily researched, but studies relevant to the body are lesser in comparison to that of facial research. A combination of modalities that include both facial and bodily gestures improves recognition rate of emotion compared to facial gestures alone by 35%. The best rate of recognition uses a combination of both gestures with the inclusion of speech [17]. The hands are an almost equally effective modality of emotion expression as to that of the face. Hands are capable of revealing the emotional state of an individual through gestures alone. The hands themselves can be used for each of the four movement categories previously discussed. The trunk of an individual has the ability to portray a variety of emotions itself. A trunk that is contracted is recognized as sad while anger is a more expanded size and categorized with faster motion [14].

Categorization of emotion expression into databases for research purposes is an emerging trend [21]. Ekman's FACS database is the primary source for facial expression of emotion, and as such, facial expression studies have generally relied on the FACS for verification. Work by psychologists towards a bimodal database of body expression and face expression has been presented to make a readily available collection of affective gestures [16]. The FABO database presented by Gunes and Piccardi is collection of videos that are meant to represent nine different emotional expressions and a neutral expression using a combination of the face and body as stimuli. The FABO database identifies common face and body gestures associated with Ekman's major emotions as well as three other emotions. The emotions identified in the FABO database are uncertainty, anger, surprise, fear, anxiety, happiness, disgust, boredom, and sadness. The Body Action and Posture Coding System (BAP) is a more targeted database that seeks to set forth a collection of identified actions in relation to the modalities that the body is capable producing with the intent of being used in emotion expression research [6]. The BAP database does not identify the emotions that would be associated with movements, but instead identifies the individual motions each modality of the body is capable of producing. The modalities include head orientation, head posture, trunk orientation, trunk posture, whole body posture, arm posture, gaze, head action, trunk action, and arm action. Description are present for each of the behaviors listed. Hand gestures have also been coded into databases, one of which is noteworthy. The Massey Hand Gesture Database is a collection of 2524 images of gestures readily available to the public [1]. The database is comprised of ASL gestures but does not present information pertinent to expression of emotion. Movements of the body can be separated into four categories according to Karg et al. to present information and communicate. The four identified categories are communicative, functional, artistic, and abstract [21]. Each category is used to identify a possible purpose for each of the movements. While communicative can be used to express an emotion of an individual, a functional movement may be as simple as walking to achieve a task. Artistic movements are something you would see at a place such as a ballet performance that have the ability to express an affective state. The final category, abstract, expresses neither emotion nor is used to achieve a task.

Emotion Recognition: Effects of Culture, Gender and Age: Recognition of the emotional state of an individual can be affected by various factors. While Ekman stated that there are basic emotions that people can recognize across cultures, research data show that culture has an effect on recognition of emotion as well as the functional and communicative factors of gestures. Pease and

Pease state that a hand gesture in one culture or country will have a completely different meaning than in other cultures and countries [27]. Researchers such as Archer have identified evidence supporting that while gestures across cultures are interpreted differently, cultures also have a fascination with obscene gestures and that, while the gestures may vary, the purposes behind them remain the same. Cultures will not have the same expressive gestures that convey the same meaning, but cultures will still have a comparable gesture to convey the same meaning [2].

Recent work by psychologists claim that women are better at recognizing gestures and body movements and the emotional state of the individual performing the movements [18, 23]. However, psychologists are not certain if women are more emotionally expressive than men [7]. Researchers found that men use the right hemisphere of the brain for recognition of negative emotions, while women use the left hemisphere of the brain [8]. The researchers noted that the results of the study were noted as not having been replicated at the time of publication. There is also documented difference in how gender affects the perceived valence and arousal levels of emotional gestures. Researchers have found that women are more likely to rate an emotion as a higher valence level than men, but inconclusive about the effect gender has on perceived arousal [4]. Further research into the field of gender and its effect must ultimately continue to have a deeper understanding of the factors that gender attributes to emotional recognition. Age is also another factor that can affect the perceived emotion of an individual. Children who have a higher exposure to older people in their everyday life have a higher rate of recognition of emotion in individuals [29]. The increase of age of an individual lead to the decrease in recognition rate of emotions. Older individuals are significantly less accurate in the recognition of negative emotions such as sadness and anger [24]. The primary modalities tested for emotion recognition in relation to age are the vocal and facial expressions. Younger individuals were more capable of recognition of emotion using vocal modalities as a stimulus, but no significant difference was found across all ages using a facial modality stimulus [20]. The Isaacowitz study also found that individuals were capable of identifying fear, sadness, and a neutral expression, regardless of age group, using vocal stimuli, but the recognition of emotion of anger, disgust, happiness, and surprise were recognized more using facial stimuli. This leads to believe that the modalities present in an individual have varying effects on the recognition of certain emotions. Facial movements and vocal expression are better at expressing different emotions in comparison to one another.

Emotion in Animated Characters: The use of animated characters for studies into recognition and expression of emotion is useful as it allows for a new testing instrument for use in studies as opposed to the use of people. In a study to identify differences between using people as the stimuli or animated characters, work by researchers found that stylized characters are more likely to have the emotion recognized as compared to realistic characters [5]. The study by Cissel also claims that there is little difference between body style of a character being either stylized or realistic. This allows for testing of animated body language using information and databases used in emotion research of realistic bodies. A study conducted by Noel et al. found several important findings related to animated facial expressions. A static or dynamic virtual face is capable of expressing happiness, sadness, and surprise in a recognizable way to a viewer. Disgust was misidentified the most in comparison to the other emotions present in Ekman's classification system [25]. This is supported by findings that disgust is less likely to be identified accurately in an animated character [13]. An animated character is capable of expressing the same emotions that a real person would be capable of presenting to viewers. According to Chaminade, the identification of a motion made by an animated agent is more likely to be seen as biological the less the character is anthropomorphous, and vice versa the more anthropomorphous the character is perceived as being [3]. Usage of virtual characters is then a viable method for emotion recognition and expression research as long as the characters take on the appearance of a person.

3 Methods

Contrary to the early assumption that body movement only indicates emotional intensity, recent studies have shown that body movement and posture also convey emotion-specific information [22]. The goals of this research were to identify and validate body gestures that convey emotion specific information. More specifically, the objectives were to identify and validate four sets of body gestures, each one expressing one of the following four emotional states: happy, content, frustrated and bored. The research comprised of two studies. The objective of the first was to identify those body gestures that are commonly produced when someone is experiencing each of the four individual emotions. The goal of the second study was to validate the emotion-specific information conveyed by the identified sets of body gestures. In the second study, each of the identified 4 sets of gestures were applied to an animated agent and a group of participants were asked to recognize the emotional state of the agent solely from its body gestures.

3.1 Study 1: Affective Body Gestures Identification

Design: The study identified and annotated gestures related to the expression of the four targeted emotions. The researcher reviewed motion capture data of actors to qualitatively determine the emotions specific gestures in the recordings.

Stimuli: The actors were presented with a set of four scenarios; the goal of each scenario was to prompt one of the four emotions. The actors were then asked to express the emotion using body language only, however, they were not given clear instructions on how to perform the body gestures. The performance of each actor was video captured, and motion captured using the Xsens motion capture system and Autodesk Maya. A total of four actors were recruited, two male and two female. Both male actors were students of the Theater program at Purdue University, and one female actor was enrolled in the same program. The second female actor was a dance instructor at Purdue University. The student actors were all in their early twenties, and the fourth actor was middle aged. Each actor was of average height and average build. Each actor portrayed the four emotions being tested three times, resulting in a total of 48 videos and 48 motion captured takes. Motion capture data was extracted from the Xsens system and mapped onto Gabriel Salas' character models David and Dana (Dana & David, 2020). Each character has the facial features obscured by sunglasses and a face mask. Rotation of the sunglasses and face mask were attached to head rotation of the character to maintain head gestures.

Procedure: Recorded motion capture data was analyzed and annotated for each of the 48 videos. Annotations included total time length of gestures, measured using total amount of frames, emotion recognized, forward arm gestures, downward arm gestures, upward arm gestures, outward arm gestures, inward arm gestures, forward body lean, inward body lean, trunk rotation, head rotation, forward head gesture, and inward head gesture. Each gesture, as it is defined for the purpose of this study, is comprised of head, torso and arm movements. For each emotion tested, the gestures that appeared at least three times among the four participants were used in the secondary study. In the absence of repetition of gestures among actors, the researcher selected the two best recognizable gestures for each emotion, utilizing the FABO database as a reference to ensure they are appropriate gestures for testing. The outcome of study 1 was an identified group of body gestures that portray the four selected emotions. The identified gestures included a set of "happy body gestures", e.g. a set of gestures that people are likely to produce when experiencing happiness; a set of "frustrated body gestures", e.g. a set of body gestures that people are likely to produce when experiencing frustration; a set of "bored body gestures", e.g. a set of body gestures that people are likely to produce when experiencing boredom; and a set of "content body gestures", e.g. a set of body gestures that people are likely to produce when experiencing content.

3.2   Study 2: Emotion Recognition

Design: The study used a within-subjects design to examine recognition of emotion through modalities of body gestures in 3D animated characters. The Independent variables were Body Gesture, Participant Gender, Agent Gender; the dependent variable was Emotion Recognition.

Analysis of the data produced by the initial study was used to test the hypotheses listed below. Gesture sets for the study comprised two full-body gestures for each of the four emotions tested. The first gesture was the gesture produced by the majority of the actors. The second gesture was the gesture performed by the majority of actors but appeared less often than the first gesture. Each gesture was validated as representative of that emotion if the emotion recognition rate was 80% or higher.

H1(abcd): Participants are able to accurately recognize affective displays of happiness, frustration, contentment, boredom in an animated agent who is producing the identified (a) "happy body gestures", (b) "frustrated body gestures",

(c) "content body gestures", and (d) "bored body gestures" respectively, and in the absence of facial expressions and speech.

H2(abcd): There are differences in the participants' ability to recognize the emotional state of the agent ((a) happy, (b) frustrated, (c) content, (d) bored) based on participants' gender.

H3(abcd): There are differences in the participants' ability to recognize the emotional state of the agent ((a) happy, (b) frustrated, (c) content, (d) bored) based on the agent's gender.

Participants: 104 participants were recruited using email announcements, through personal connections and through the Prolific participants platform. No screening occurred prior to participation in the study.

Stimuli: The videos presented to participants featured the animated characters performing the identified affective body gestures. Two gestures for each agent gender and for each each of the four emotions resulted in a total of 16 final videos. The faces of the characters were obscured; motion capture data recorded with female actors was applied to the Dana character, and motion capture data recorded with male actors was applied to the David character (Fig. 1).

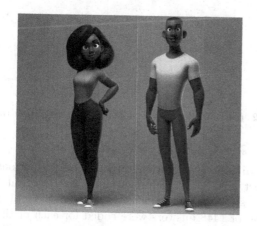

Fig. 1. The character models used in the studies

Procedure: The subjects were sent a link to an online survey which included the stimuli videos and one multiple choice question. The question asked the participant to select the emotion displayed by the animated character from 5 choices, e.g. happy, content, bored, frustrated, and unable to recognize. The presentation order of the videos was randomized and participants could play the videos as many times as needed.

4 Results

Demographics: A total of 104 surveys were collected. 13 surveys were discarded for various reasons such as finishing in under 5 min, or not completing at least one-third of all questions. 91 total surveys were used for the analysis. 50.8% of all respondents had completed high school, with 27.3% having a bachelor's degree. 13% of respondents have acquired a master's degree. Five people indicated they have some high school experience, one had completed trade school, and a further two have a Ph.D. There was almost an even amount of male vs female participants, with 46 females and 44 males. One person identified as non-binary. Out of the 91 participants, 24 indicated that they had some experience with character animation, with the remaining 67 having no experience in animation.

Validity: The data was plotted using a binned residual plot to assess the validity of assumptions, to identify features not captured by the model, and to find problematic data points or clusters. The plot did not reveal any trends in the residual data (Fig. 2).

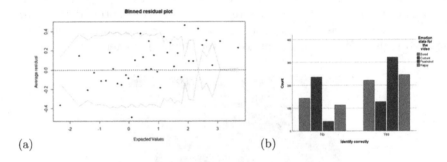

(a)   (b)

Fig. 2. (a) Binned residual plot and (b) recognition rates

Emotion Recognition: Recognition rates of the 4 emotions varied. Participants were correct with their identification if they accurately answered the multiple-choice question, "Cannot identify" answers were placed in the incorrect group. A total of 1448 answers were coded for each of the 16 videos from all 91 participants. For each video, body gestures were identified as being correct representations of the emotions if at least 80% of participants were able to recognize the emotion correctly (see Fig. 2).

Of the four emotions tested, frustrated was the most commonly correctly identified (322 correct responses). Happy followed after with 246 correct responses. Bored was the third most commonly recognized emotion (221 correct responses). Content was the least correctly identified emotion (126 correct responses). The recognition rate for the four emotions were as follows: 60.7% correct recognition rate for bored, 34.6% for content, 88.4% for frustrated, and 67.5% recognition rate for happy. Results support hypothesis H1(b).

Table 1 shows the gestures for each video, with the corresponding emotional state and character gender. Videos identified as having a high recognition rate were videos 5, 6, 9, 10, 11, and 16. Table 2 gives the percentages of correct

Table 1. Video details

Video title	Rand order #	Head action	Trunk action	L-arm action	R-arm action
Female-bored-1	Video 10	Downward head tilt	Forward-backward trunk leaning	Hold	Forward
Female-bored-2	Video 2	Downward head tilt	Trunk action hold	Lateral repetition	Lateral repetition
Female-content-1	Video 15	Upward head tilt	Left-right trunk leaning	Towards the body	Towards the body
Female-content-2	Video 3	Upward head tilt	Left-right trunk leaning	Towards the body	Towards the body
Female-frustrated-1	Video 9	Up-down head shake	Forward trunk lean	Forward	Forward
Female-frustrated-2	Video 5	Up-down head shake	Forward trunk lean	Forward	Hold
Female-happy-1	Video 13	Upward head tilt	Spine straightening	Forward	Forward
Female-happy-2	Video 16	Upward head tilt	Upward/forward chest movement	Upward	Upward
Male-bored-1	Video 1	Downward head tilt	Trunk action hold	Downward	Downward
Male-bored-2	Video 4	Upward head tilt	Trunk action hold	Downward	Downward
Male-content-1	Video 8	Upward head tilt	Trunk action hold	Lateral repetition	Lateral repetition
Male-content-2	Video 12	Upward head tilt	Left-right trunk leaning	Upward	Upward
Male-frustrated-1	Video 11	Head action hold	Forward trunk lean	Frontal repetition	Frontal repetition
Male-frustrated-2	Video 6	Up-down head shake	Forward trunk lean	Frontal repetition	Frontal repetition
Male-happy-1	Video 7	Upward head tilt	Upward/forward chest movement	Upward	Upward
Male-happy-2	Video 14	Upward head tilt	Upward/forward chest movement	Upward	Upward

identification for all 16 videos tested. The videos can be accessed through this link: https://bit.ly/3m9QQCC

All male and female displays of frustrated were identified correctly with a recognition rate of at least 80% for all videos. One video of boredom and one of happiness featuring a female avatar had a similar rate of recognition. Figure 3 shows still frames from videos with 80% or higher recognition rates.

Table 2. Video recognition rates

Video #	Correct identifications	Percentage correct	Emotion state	Avatar gender
1	67/91	73.60%	Bored	Male
2	28/91	30.70%	Bored	Female
3	9/91	9.80%	Content	Female
4	51/91	56.00%	Bored	Male
5	80/91	87.90%	Frustrated	Female
6	80/91	87.90%	Frustrated	Male
7	62/91	68.10%	Happy	Male
8	23/91	25.20%	Content	Male
9	77/91	84.60%	Frustrated	Female
10	75/91	82.40%	Bored	Female
11	85/91	93.40%	Frustrated	Male
12	65/91	71.40%	Content	Male
13	37/91	40.60%	Happy	Female
14	65/91	71.40%	Happy	Male
15	29/91	31.80%	Content	Female
16	82/91	90.10%	Happy	Female

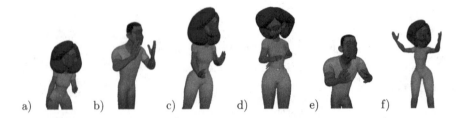

Fig. 3. (a) Video 5-Frustrated gesture with up-down head movement, forward trunk lean, and forward arm actions. (b) Video 6-Frustrated showing up-down head movement, forward trunk lean, and forward arm action with repetition. (c) Video 9-Frustrated showing up-down head movement, forward trunk lean, and forward arm action. (d) Video 10-Bored showing downward head tile, forward-backward trunk leaning, left arm action holding, and a right arm forward action. (e) Video 11-Frustrated showing head action holding, forward trunk lean, and forward arm action with repetition. (f) Video 16-Happy showing upward head tilt, left-right body leaning, and upward arm actions.

An ANOVA test showed that there were significant differences among the recognition rates of the four emotions ata significance level of 0.05 (p-value <.00001). A follow-up post hoc analysis shows the differences to be in frustrated with a P-value of <.00001, content with a P-value of <.00001, and happy with a P-value of 0.048.

Gender of Character. An ANOVA test looking at the recognition rates of emotion based on the gender of the character showed a statistical difference in the ability to recognize emotion (p-value of <.00001). The Male avatar had a considerably higher recognition rate compared to the female avatar across all emotions, hence results support hypotheses H3(abcd).

Participants' Gender, Animation Experience, Education and Age. ANOVA tests showed no significant difference in recognition rate based on participants' gender (p-value = 0.273) across all emotions, hence hypotheses H2 (abcd) were not supported. Further, there was no significant difference based on participants' animation experience (p-value = 0.113), no significant difference based on participants education level (p-value = 0.826), and no significant differences based on participants' age (p-value = 0.168). For each age group, the recognition rates were as follows: 16–25 years old-62%, 26–35 years old- 67%, 36–45 years old- 67%, 46–55 years old-75%, and 56+ years old-88%.

5   Discussion and Conclusion

A key finding of this research is that an animated character can clearly express three of the four targeted emotions (e.g. happy, bored, frustrated) using the body gestures identified by the study. Another finding is that emotions expressed through the identified body gestures have different rates of recognition. The easiest emotion to identify by all participants was frustrated (recognition rate=88.4%). The high recognition rate may be in part due to the fight or flight response of an individual, where a person would benefit from being able to correctly identify hostility towards them. However, additional research would need to be conducted to examine this possibility. Contentment was the only emotion that was misidentified more than it was correctly identified (34.6% recognition rate). This result shows that the identified "content body gestures" are not able to clearly convey the contentment emotion.

The analysis of the videos revealed that an up-down shake of the head with a forward body lean, and a forward movement of the arm either once or in repetition are body movements that convey the frustrated emotional state effectively using an avatar as a means of communication. A bored emotional state can be expressed by downward head movement, with a forward body lean, and the arms having little to no movement at the sides. Avatars that show a happy emotional state may produce upward head movements, with the body moving forward and upward, and the arms having upward actions. Each of these emotional displays were shown to have an emotion recognition rate of at least 80%.

Another important finding is that the avatar gender affects the emotion recognition rate. The emotions displayed by the male avatar were correctly identified 68.8% of the time, while the emotions displayed by the female avatar were correctly identified 57.2% of the time. This finding suggests that male avatars may be better at displaying emotions using body movements than female avatars. However, this might also be due to the male actors who participated in the study being more expressive in their emotional displays than the female actresses, or to the intrinsic design features of the characters.

Although the research yielded important results, it also had several limitations. First, the study used a low number of actors (4) and a relatively small sample size (104 participants). Future studies should include more actors and a larger pool of subjects. Second, the sample did not cover all age ranges (the majority of the participants were young), hence it is not possible to draw meaningful conclusions on the effect of participants' age on emotion recognition. Future studies should use a sample that is more representative of the target population in regard to age.

Third, the characters used for the study were both stylized and their visual style might have influenced the recognition rate. Future studies should include a variety of characters with different visual styles, such as stylized, realistic, iconic. Fourth, several times the avatars had the hands hidden behind another body part due to the motion capture camera placement, which caused an inevitable loss of potential visual stimuli. This could have influenced the ability of the participants to correctly identify the emotion being presented.

The findings from the work reported in the paper have important implications for research and practice. They lay the basis for the development of a coding system of affective body gestures for animated agents. With the growing understanding of the complex interplay between emotions and cognition, there is a need to develop agents that not only provide effective expert guidance/communication, but also believable emotional interactions with the user.

The results of this research can be used to create believable multi modal agents the express emotions effectively through body cues. The findings can also help animation professionals create life-like emotive animated characters for films and games.

References

1. Massey   University   (2012).   https://www.massey.ac.nz/~albarcza/gesture_dataset2012.html
2. Archer, D.: Unspoken diversity: cultural differences in gestures. Qual. Sociol. **20**(1), 79–105 (1997)
3. Chaminade, T., Hodgins, J., Kawato, M.: Anthropomorphism influences perception of computer-animated characters actions. Soc. Cogn. Affect. Neurosci. **2**(3), 206–216 (2007)
4. Cheng, J., Zhou, W., Lei, X., Adamo, N., Benes, B.: The effects of body gestures and gender on viewer's perception of animated pedagogical agent's emotions. In: Kurosu, M. (ed.) HCII 2020. LNCS, vol. 12182, pp. 169–186. Springer, Cham (2020). https://doi.org/10.1007/978-3-030-49062-1_11
5. Cissell, K.: A study of the effects of computer animated character body style on perception of facial expression. Master's thesis, Purdue University, USA (2013)
6. Dael, N., Mortillaro, M., Scherer, K.R.: The body action and posture coding system (BAP). J. Nonverbal Behav. **36**(2), 97–121 (2012)
7. Deng, Y., Chang, L., Yang, M., Huo, M., Zhou, R.: Gender differences in emotional response. PLOS ONE **11**(6), e0158666 (2016)
8. Einstein, G., Downar, J.: Gender/sex differences in emotions. Medicographia **35**(3), 271–280 (2013)
9. Ekman, P.: Universal facial expressions of emotions. Calif. Ment. Health Digest **8**(4), 151–158 (1970). https://www.paulekman.com/wp-content/uploads/2013/07/Universal-Facial-Expressions-of-Emotions1.pdf
10. Ekman, P.: The Face of Man: Expressions of Universal Emotions in a New Guinea Village. Garland STPM Press, University of California (1980)
11. Ekman, P.: What scientists who study emotion agree about. Perspect. Psychol. Sci. **11**(1), 31–34 (2016)
12. Ekman, P., Friesen, E.: Facial Action Coding System: A Technique for the Measurement of Facial Movement. Consulting Psychologists Press, Palo Alto (1978)
13. Fabri, M., Moore, D., Hobbs, D.: Mediating the expression of emotion in educational collaborative virtual environments: an experimental study. Virtual Reality **7**(2), 66–81 (2004)
14. Gross, M.M., Crane, E.A., Fredrickson, B.L.: Effort-Shape and kinematic assessment of bodily expression of emotion during gait. Hum. Mov. Sci. **31**(1), 202–221 (2012)
15. Gu, S., Wang, F., Patel, N.P., Bourgeois, J.A., Huang, J.H.: A model for basic emotions using observations of behavior in Drosophila. Front. Psychol. **10**, 781 (2019)
16. Gunes, H., Piccardi, M.: A bimodal face and body gesture database for automatic analysis of human nonverbal affective behavior. In: 18th International Conference on Pattern Recognition ICPR 2006. vol. 1, pp. 1148–1153 (2006)
17. Gunes, H., Shan, C., Chen, S., Tian, Y.: Bodily expression for automatic affect recognition. In: Emotion Recognition, pp. 343–377. Wiley (2015)

18. Hall, J.A., Matsumoto, D.: Gender differences in judgments of multiple emotions from facial expressions. Emotion 4(2), 201–206 (2004)
19. Huis In't Veld, E.M.J., Van Boxtel, G.J.M., de Gelder, B.: The Body Action Coding System I: muscle activations during the perception and expression of emotion. Soc. Neurosci. 9(3), 249–264 (2014)
20. Isaacowitz, D.M., et al.: Age differences in recognition of emotion in lexical stimuli and facial expressions. Psychol. Aging 22(1), 147–159 (2007)
21. Karg, M., Samadani, A.A., Gorbet, R., Kuhnlenz, K., Hoey, J., Kulic, D.: Body movements for affective expression: a survey of automatic recognition and generation. IEEE Trans. Affect. Comput. 4(4), 341–359 (2013)
22. Lawson, A.P., Mayer, R.E., Adamo-Villani, N., Benes, B., Lei, X., Cheng, J.: Recognizing the emotional state of human and virtual instructors. Comput. Hum. Behav. 114, 106554 (2021)
23. Matsumoto, D., et al.: A new test to measure emotion recognition ability. J. Nonverbal Behav. 24(3), 179–209 (2000)
24. Mill, A., Allik, J., Realo, A., Valk, R.: Age-related differences in emotion recognition ability: a cross-sectional study. Emotion 9(5), 619–630 (2009)
25. Noel, S., Dumoulin, S., Whalen, T., Stewart, J.: Recognizing emotions on static and animated avatar faces. In: 2006 IEEE International Workshop on Haptic Audio Visual Environments and their Applications, HAVE 2006, pp. 99–104 (2006)
26. Noroozi, F., Kaminska, D., Corneanu, C., Sapinski, T., Escalera, S., Anbarjafari, G.: Survey on emotional body gesture recognition. IEEE Trans. Affect. Comput. 12(2), 505–523 (2021)
27. Pease, B., Pease, A.: The Definitive Book of Body Language. Pease International, Australia (2004)
28. Plutchik, R.: A General Psychoevolutionary Theory of Emotion. In: Theories of Emotion, pp. 3–33. Elsevier (1980)
29. Pollux, P.M., Hermens, F., Willmott, A.P.: Age-congruency and contact effects in body expression recognition from point-light displays (PLD). PeerJ. 4, e2796 (2016)

Fast Approximation of Color Morphology

Vivek Sridhar$^{(\boxtimes)}$, Michael Breuss, and Marvin Kahra

Institute for Mathematics, Brandenburg Technical University Cottbus-Senftenberg,
03046 Cottbus, Germany
{sridhviv,breuss,marvin.kahra}@b-tu.de

Abstract. The basic filters in mathematical morphology are dilation and erosion. They are defined by a flat or non-flat structuring element that is usually shifted pixel-wise over an image and a comparison process that takes place within the corresponding mask. The algorithmic complexity of fast algorithms that realise dilation and erosion for color images usually depends on size and shape of the structuring element.

In this paper we propose and investigate an easy and fast way to make use of the fast Fourier transform for an approximate computation of dilation and erosion for color images. Similarly in construction as many other fast algorithms, the method extends a recent scheme proposed for single-channel filtering. It is by design highly flexible, as it can be used with flat and non-flat structuring elements of any size and shape. Moreover, its complexity only depends on the number of pixels in the filtered images. We analyse here some important aspects of the approximation, and we show experimentally that we obtain results of very reasonable quality while the method has very attractive computational properties.

Keywords: Mathematical morphology · Fourier transform · Fast algorithms

1 Introduction

Mathematical morphology is a highly successful field in image processing with abundant applications, see [10,11,13]. An elementary mechanism in morphology is to compare (and order) tonal data within a certain mask sliding over an image. The mask is defined as part of a so-called structuring element (SE), which is fundamental in morphological filtering. The SE is characterised by shape, size and centre location. There are in addition two types of SEs, flat and non-flat [19]. For a given centre pixel a flat SE defines a neighbourhood on which the tonal comparison takes place, whereas a non-flat SE also contains additive offsets in tonal space. The basic operations in morphology are dilation and erosion, where the tonal value at a pixel is set to the maximum and minimum respectively within the SE centred upon it. Many useful morphological processes, like e.g. opening or closing, are formulated by combining dilation and erosion.

Let us briefly review some concepts for color morphology. As mentioned above, a key issue in morphology is to perform a useful comparison of the tonal

© Springer Nature Switzerland AG 2021
G. Bebis et al. (Eds.): ISVC 2021, LNCS 13018, pp. 488–499, 2021.
https://doi.org/10.1007/978-3-030-90436-4_39

values within the SE. In standard grey value morphology this is done relying on the concept of a complete lattice, making use of a total ordering of tonal values [10]. However, the construction of a comparison mechanism is in general a delicate issue when turning to color imagery, since there is no natural total ordering of color values. There are thus basically two approaches to tackle color morphology [5]: *(i)* channel-based, where each channel is individually treated like a grey-value image, and *(ii)* vector-based, where each color is processed as a vector in an underlying color space, see [3,4] for some approaches to construct a vector-based ordering. In this article we will resort to channel-wise filtering as do most fast algorithms.

As indicated, morphological algorithms aiming for computational speed are usually designed methodically for single-channel data, and applied channel-wise for color images. Let us refer to [2] for an example where in addition hardware optimized for channel-wise RGB processing is considered. Most fast (single-channel) methods either aim to reduce the size of a SE or to decompose it, or alternatively they attempt to reduce redundant comparison operations, compare [9]. Most of them refer to specific shape or size of the SE, sometimes also specific hardware like GPUs is addressed, see for instance [15,17,18,20]. There are just a few fast algorithms for non-flat SEs of arbitrary shape and size, even for single-channel data. Let us mention [22] which employs histogram updates during translation of a SE over an image. However, in general the algorithmic complexity of these fast algorithms inherently relies on size and shape of the SE.

Here we will build upon a different approach which eventually leads to a fast method having no limitations with respect to size, shape or flatness of the SE. In [8] it was shown that binary dilation/erosion may be performed employing specific convolutions. By the convolution theorem this enables the possibility of computing binary dilation/erosion using the Fast Fourier Transform (FFT) [12]. In [14] this approach was extended to grey value imagery, by processing each grey value level set as a binary image using the technique from [8], and combining thereafter the results. The proceeding implies that the method is limited to flat SEs. We proposed in [23] an alternative construction that circumvents this limitation by approximating the original convolutions. However, as we observed experimentally in [23], this comes at the expense of a certain shift in grey value data.

Our Contribution. In this paper we extend the method described in [23] to color imagery. The basic construction is extended channel-wise in a straightforward way. We confirm that favourable computational properties are maintained in the color setting. Furthermore, we discuss the occurring tonal shift in detail, as this may be of importance when filtering multiple channels. We derive an estimate for the size of the shift and give experimental evidence that its effect appears to be negligible in practice, since the vast majority of morphological applications naturally relies on combinations of dilation and erosion. In various experiments, we show that our method is extremely fast and yields competitive quality compared to other possible methods for color morphology.

2   Basic Definitions

We start by considering a two dimensional, discrete image domain $\Omega \subset \mathbb{Z}^2$. A single-channel, grey value image can be represented as a function $f : \Omega \to L$, where L is the set of possible grey values. In non-flat morphology, the SE itself can be perceived as a grey value image. A non-flat SE b can thus be defined as a function $b : B \to L$, for B denoting a suitable set centred at the origin. A flat filter is just a special case where $b(x) = 0$ for all $x \in B$.

Dilation, Erosion and its Combinations. The fundamental building blocks of mathematical morphology are dilation and erosion. The *dilation* of an image f by a SE b is given by $f \oplus b : \Omega \to L$, where $(f \oplus b)(x) = \max_{u \in B} \{f(x - u) + b(u)\}$. The *erosion* of an image f by a SE b is given by $f \ominus b : \Omega \to L$ and can be computed by $(f \ominus b)(x) = \min_{u \in B} \{f(x + u) - b(u)\}$.

Many morphological operations of practical interest can be composed by dilation and erosion, cf. [10]. As important examples let us mention here *opening* $f \circ b = (f \ominus b) \oplus b$ and *closing* $f \bullet b = (f \oplus b) \ominus b$. Similarly, composite operation of *white top hat* is defined as $f \boxminus (f \circ b)$, where $(f \boxminus (f \circ b))(x) = f(x) - (f \circ b)(x)$. The *black top hat* is $(f \bullet b) \boxminus f$, and the *Beucher gradient* is $(f \oplus b) \boxminus (f \ominus b)$, *internal gradient* is $f \boxminus (f \ominus b)$ and *external gradient* is $(f \oplus b) \boxminus f$.

Channel-Wise Color Morphology. The most intuitive and simple approach to color morphology we will also follow in this work, is to deal with the image component wise. There are many formats to represent a digital image [6]. We employ here the classic RGB format using three separate channels to store the red, green and blue value for each pixel of an image. On a discrete domain $\Omega \subset \mathbb{Z}^2$, a RGB color image can be thus represented as $f_C : \Omega \to L_C$. Here, $L_C = L_r \times L_g \times L_b$, where L_r, L_g and L_b are the possible values of pixels in red, green and blue channel respectively. For RGB it holds $L_r = L_g = L_b = L$, and L is the set of non-negative integers ≤ 255.

Let us extend the concept of single-channel non-flat SE, to non-flat SE with 3 channels, in a straightforward fashion. A SE is given by the function $b_C : B \to L_C$. Thus an image f_C can be separated into three channels (f_r, f_g, f_b) and each of these channels can be treated like a grey value image. Similarly, a SE b_C can be separated into (b_r, b_g, b_b) and each of the components acts on the corresponding channel of the image. Thus, for instance, we define color dilation of image f_C by SE b_C as $f_C \oplus_C b_C = (f_r \oplus b_r, f_g \oplus b_g, f_b \oplus b_b)$. The definitions of other component-wise color morphological operations follow in accordance.

3   Fast Approximation of Color Morphology

We first recall briefly the basics and implementation of the method from [23]. Observe that by channel-wise extension to color images, we are considering the most general form of color SE with no restriction on its shape or size. After that we investigate an important property of the method, namely the tonal shift arising by approximation in each color channel.

3.1 Fourier-Based Approximative Morphology

We have found in [23] an efficient way to dilate or erode grey scale images by means of Fourier transforms. For this purpose, we approximated the sup contained in the continuous-scale formulation of grey value dilation using

$$\sup(x_1,\ldots,x_k) \doteq \lim_{m\to\infty} \frac{1}{m} \log\left(\sum_{i=1}^{k} e^{mx_i}\right). \tag{1}$$

Thus one may obtain for dilation in an individual channel the representation

$$(f \oplus b)(x) = \lim_{m\to\infty} \frac{1}{m} \log\left(\sum_{y\in E} e^{mf(y)} e^{mb(x-y)}\right)$$

$$= \lim_{m\to\infty} \frac{1}{m} \log \mathcal{F}^{-1}\left[\mathcal{F}\left[e^{mf}\right] \cdot \mathcal{F}\left[e^{mb}\right]\right](x), \tag{2}$$

for which the convolution theorem was applied, and where b was extended to the whole domain by setting $b(x)$ to $-\infty$ outside of the set B. In order to retrieve a flat structuring element, one may set $b(x) = 0$ over B. Let us note, $b(x)$ can be suitable defined to realise any non-flat SE over B.

Following our specifications in [23] for implementation in individual color channels, the method is easily extended to channel-wise processing. In order to consider arbitrary sets B as shapes for the SE, we extend $b(x)$ to the whole image domain by setting $b(x)$ to -256 for implementation. Analogously to [23] let us declare the function Expm$(\cdot)$ as Expm$(f)(x) = e^{(m\cdot f(x))}$. It should be noted that we use functions of the NumPy package [24] to implement all the functions described in this section, unless otherwise mentioned.

To obtain the fast convolution of Expm(f) and Expm(b), we use the FFT as in [23]. To this end we employ the function *scipy.signal.fftconvolve($\cdot$)* from the SciPy package [21]. When using the FFT with large numbers, which may occur during the discrete transformations, it is in principle possible that some overflow errors or errors of the form $0/0$ or ∞/∞ may occur. Though such an error has not occurred during our experiments, one may handle such exceptions in a straightforward manner which can be included in the definition of a function h that yields the discrete convolution of Expm(f) with Expm(b), cf. [23].

Finally, we need the corresponding Fourier-based inverse of Expm$(\cdot)$. For this we define InExpm$(\cdot)$ as InExpm$(h)(x) = \frac{1}{m} \cdot \log(h(x))$. Thus one can completely transfer (1) to the discrete domain in a channel-wise setting.

The fast dilation is therefore given by $f \oplus b \approx$ Inte(h), where Inte$(h)(x) = \lfloor h(x) \rfloor$. So by the well-known complexity of the FFT, the whole process takes place in $O(n \log n)$ if the SE size is smaller than the image under consideration, where n denotes the number of image pixels. This theoretical complexity is confirmed by experiments in Sect. 4.1. The analogous fast erosion technique follows directly from the duality property of erosion and dilation in each channel, as $f \ominus b = 255 - ((255 - f) \oplus \check{b})$, where $\check{b}(-x) = b(x)\ \forall x \in B$.

3.2   Tonal Shift Analysis

We have noted a certain shift of tonal values in our work [23], but not analyzed. In the context of filtering in multiple channels, this shift may represent a major hindrance since shifts of varying magnitude in different channels may potentially spoil results of combinations of dilation and erosion.

By Figs. 1 and 2, one may observe that there is a positive (negative) shift in each channel when the fast approximation method is used for dilation (erosion). By this dilation (erosion) results appear lighter (darker). For this reason, we want to calculate an upper bound for the positive shift with fast dilation in the respective channels. Similar calculation holds for negative shift with fast erosion.

Let A be a finite set of non-negative integers, i.e. $A = \{x_1, x_2, \cdots x_n\}$. Furthermore let the maximum be denoted by $\max A = x_k$ and approximated by $\alpha = \left\lfloor \frac{1}{m_1} \ln \left(\sum_{i=1}^{n} e^{m_1 \cdot x_i} \right) \right\rfloor$, where $m_1 > 0$ is some constant.

Clearly, the difference between the approximation and the actual maximum, $\alpha - x_k$, is non-negative as:

$$x_k = \left\lfloor \frac{1}{m_1} \ln \left(e^{m_1 \cdot x_k} \right) \right\rfloor \leq \left\lfloor \frac{1}{m_1} \ln \left(\sum_{i=1}^{n} e^{m_1 \cdot x_i} \right) \right\rfloor = \alpha. \qquad (3)$$

Thus, we do not observe any negative (positive) shifts during dilation (erosion).

Next, we calculate the *worst-case scenario* for positive shift during dilation, that is, the upper bound of the difference $\alpha - x_k$, as follows:

$$\alpha \leq \left\lfloor \frac{1}{m_1} \ln \left(\sum_{i=1}^{n} e^{m_1 \cdot x_k} \right) \right\rfloor = \left\lfloor \frac{1}{m_1} \ln \left(n \cdot e^{m_1 \cdot x_k} \right) \right\rfloor$$
$$= \left\lfloor \frac{1}{m_1} \ln (n) + \frac{1}{m_1} \ln \left(e^{m_1 \cdot x_k} \right) \right\rfloor = \left\lfloor \frac{1}{m_1} \ln (n) \right\rfloor + x_k. \qquad (4)$$

It follows that $\alpha - x_k \leq \left\lfloor \frac{1}{m_1} \ln (n) \right\rfloor$ and if $m_1 > \ln (n)$ then $\left\lfloor \frac{1}{m_1} \ln (n) \right\rfloor = 0$, i.e. $\alpha = x_k$.

Therefore, in Fig. 1 an upper bound on the positive shift with fast dilation is $\left\lfloor \frac{1}{0.16} \ln (7 \times 7) \right\rfloor = \left\lfloor \frac{1}{0.16} \ln (49) \right\rfloor = 24$. Similarly, the fast erosion in Fig. 1 has a negative shift of magnitude ≤ 24. This estimate is clearly confirmed uniformly over all color channels in the respective histograms, see Fig. 2.

Considering the color histograms, let us comment that a certain smoothing of the color distribution is observed for the fast approximations of dilation and erosion. This is an interesting effect not pointed out in [23]. However, it is clearly observed that major characteristics of the histogram as well as peak magnitudes are largely the same as with the standard channel-wise filtering procedure.

With fast closing as an example for combining dilation and erosion, the tonal shifts are not apparent as they appear uniformly over the color channels. Thus we conjecture that the positive and negative shifts from dilation resp. erosion cancel

Fig. 1. Component-wise morphological operations with flat square 7×7 filter on 512×512 *Pepper* image. **Top row:** Classical method. **Bottom row:** Proposed fast approximations. **From left to right:** Dilation, erosion and closing.

each other out. This is an aspect of high practical relevance, as most applications of morphology rely on suitable combinations of dilation and erosion.

4   Experiments

Let us comment first on the choice of the parameter m. As indicated via formula (1) theory seems to motivate to choose m in accordance to $m \to \infty$. But since we form the maximum over a finite range of discrete values, it is sufficient to choose a finite value of m. Furthermore, the relation (1) is evaluated in the Fourier domain. So in practice, the value of m refers to the implementation of the FFT. Since, we perform the computations using numpy.float datatype, it is observed that the choice of $m = 0.16$ avoids overflow errors and provides reasonable approximations.

For useful comparison we employed a highly efficient channel-wise morphology implementation which we could find openly available, via morphological dilation in the SciPy package [21]. The SciPy routine ndimage.grey_dilation() technically makes use of an efficient implementation of a sliding window technique in the style of [1], to compute channel-wise dilation with arbitrary non-flat SE similarly to the process described in [22]. Note that the worst case complexity of this traditional fast morphological method with non-flat SE, even if optimised in implementation, is theoretically still $O(n_b \times n)$.

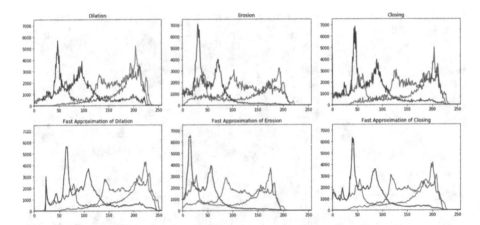

Fig. 2. Histograms of component-wise morphological operations with flat square 7×7 filter on 512×512 *Pepper* image, compare visual results in Fig. 1. **Top row:** Classical method. **Bottom row:** Proposed fast approximations, **From left to right:** Dilation, erosion and closing

4.1   Comparison of Computational Times

Let us briefly recall the asymptotic complexity of our process for approximating component-wise color dilation. We start with the trivial assumption that the size n_b of the filter is $\leq$ size n of the image. For each channel, fast dilation involves a sequence of linear time processes, except for FFT and inverse FFT which are $O(n \log n)$. Erosion, computed using duality, involves two linear time operations preceding and one linear time operation following the dilation. Therefore, fast erosion is also asymptotically $O(n \log n)$. Since most of the other morphological operations are combinations of erosions, dilations and linear in time operations, the fast approximations of combined operations are also performed in $O(n \log n)$.

In the first experiment, Fig. 3 *Left*, we evaluate the time taken by varying size of filter on a fixed size of image. The image used is again *Pepper* of size 512×512. The filter size increases from 1×1 to 43×43. The filters are color filters generated using np.random.randint(), with range of values from 0 to 255. It is clearly visible that the SciPy method behaves linearly with respect to size of filter, taking 0.12 s for filter size 5×5 to around 7.5 s for filter size 43×43. The fast method remains constant with respect to the size of the filter, taking on average about 0.09 s, i.e. 0.03 for each channel.

In the second experiment, Fig. 3 *Right*, we evaluate the time taken for component-wise color dilation by a fixed size of color filter, 51×51, on varying image sizes. The image size increases from 101×101 to 1201×1201. The images and the filters are generated using np.random.randint(), with range of values from 0 to 255. The SciPy method takes 0.08 s for the 101×101 image and increases to about 53 s for the 1201×1201 image. The proposed fast method is efficient overall and the rate of increase in time with respect to the size of the image is very low. It takes 0.02 s for the 101×101 image and 0.48 s for the 1201×1201 image.

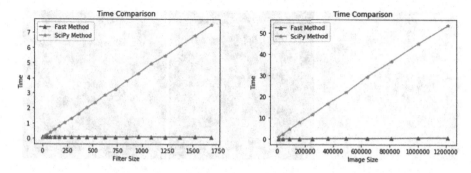

Fig. 3. Time comparison of component-wise color dilation using the proposed fast method versus the dilation function ndimage.grey_dilation() in the SciPy Package. **Left:** Varying SE sizes on an image of size 512×512. **Right:** SE of size 51×51 on varying image sizes.

Let us note that we have not employed GPUs in the above experiments. It is worth pointing out that attempts to use GPUs to compute grey value morphology usually places restrictions of symmetry and/or flatness on the SE, see discussions in [16,20]. However, there are several efficient implementations of FFT and inverse FFT on the GPU, see e.g. [7]. Therefore, our method could be sped up utilising the GPUs, without any restrictions on the SE.

4.2 Visual Quality Comparison

To assess visual quality of filtering, we consider in addition to channel-wise filtering the Loewner ordering method from [25]. For the latter, color images are formulated as fields of symmetric 2×2 matrices and processed by rather complex rules inspired by theoretical physics. We restrict ourselves here to flat SEs and a selection of experiments.

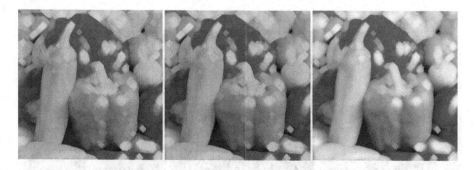

Fig. 4. Dilation of 512×512 *Pepper* image by flat 21×21 diamond shaped SE. **Left:** Loewner. **Centre:** Classic component-wise. **Right:** Proposed fast method

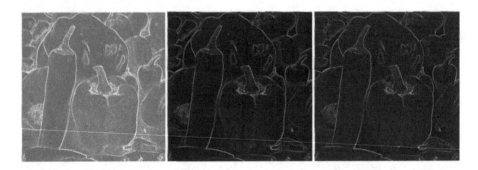

Fig. 5. Beucher Gradient of 512×512 *Pepper* image by flat 3×3 square shaped SE. **Left:** Loewner. **Centre:** Classic component-wise. **Right:** Proposed fast method

Dilation results in Fig. 4 are at first glance qualitatively similar. A careful inspection shows that the Loewner scheme shows few more details than the channel-wise methods, and that the fast approximation result appears as expected a little lighter and smoother.

Let us turn to the Beucher gradient as an example of a morphological process that could be useful (as internal or external gradient) for edge detection or segmentation. Results displayed in Fig. 5 show that the Loewner method gives apparently a different color distribution than the channel-wise methods. Let us note that the Loewner method relies on the underlying structure of a different color space than the RGB-based channel-wise methods. All methods give cleanly the apparent edges of the input image.

Now let us consider another composed filter, the white top hat, see Fig. 6. It is expected that the filtering results highlight points or structures that are lighter than their surrounding (in terms of the individual color channels). This means, it is expected here that results allow to identify shiny highlights as well as the trunks of the two peppers in the foreground of the image. As it can be observed, all the methods give useful results in this respect.

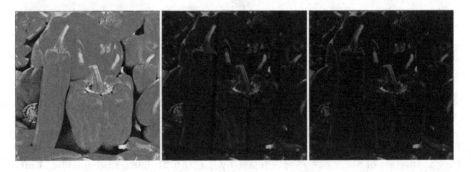

Fig. 6. White top hat of 512×512 *Pepper* image by flat 21×21 diamond shaped SE. **Left:** Loewner. **Centre:** Classic component-wise. **Right:** Proposed fast method

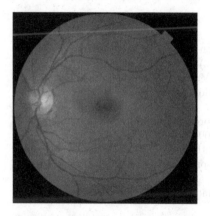 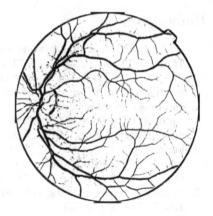

Fig. 7. As an example for potential applications, we take a retinal image of size 1411 × 1411 (source: Wikipedia), set the red channel as 0, and perform a black top hat with the proposed method, using a 25 × 25 flat square S.E. We then do a gamma correction followed by thresholding and an inversion for visualization of the blood vessels. The whole process takes ≤1.6 s, without the use of GPU. **Left:** Retinal test image. **Right:** Inversion after thresholding (≥11) after Gamma Correction with $\gamma = 0.85$.

As a last example for visual quality assessment and at the same time as a proof-of-concept for the usefulness of the developments, we consider to process a retinal image, see Fig. 7. Such images arise in ophthalmic examination, and by advances in medical imaging the image resolution for given tasks of automatic processing is ever-growing. Therefore the need arises for very fast methods for processing such data, compare e.g. [26]. As Fig. 7 shows, our method is capable of useful filtering such images.

5   Conclusion

Our method not only works with complexity $O(n \log n)$ with respect to the size of the image, it is also extremely fast in practice. Let us stress again that it performs overall much faster than standard efficient implementations of morphology as available in SciPy. At the same time it is highly versatile, as there are no restrictions to shape, size or flatness of the SE.

As we have demonstrated, our method may perform very fast with imagery from modern acquisition devices, which may often be of high resolution and in color. By morphological filtering of high resolution images, naturally also the size of useful SEs is at least moderate. We conjecture that a method whose complexity is independent from the SE size parameter may be useful for applications.

Future work may include extension to multi-spectral imagery. In this context it may be important that the method offers high potential to accelerate it even further using GPUs for the incorporated FFT. Furthermore, we aim to study alternative transforms that may reduce the tonal shift visible in pure dilation/erosion filtering.

References

1. Douglas, S.C.: Running max/min calculation using a pruned ordered list. IEEE Trans. Sig. Process. **44**(11), 2872–2877 (1996)
2. Pedrino, E.C., Saito, J.H., Senger, H., Roda, V.O.: Color mathematical morphology in a FPGA. In: Proceedings of the International Conference on Systems, Signals and Image Processing (2010)
3. Aptoula, E., Lefèvre, S.: On lexicographical ordering in multivariate mathematical morphology. Pattern Recogn. Lett. **29**(2), 109–118 (2008)
4. Lezoray, O., Elmoataz, A., Meurie, C.: Mathematical morphology in any color space. In: Proceedings of the International Conference of Image Analysis and Processing - Workshops, pp. 183–187 (2007)
5. Barnett, V.: The ordering of multivariate data. J. Roy. Stat. Soc. Ser. A (Gen.) **139**(3), 318–344 (1976)
6. Sharma, G., Bala, R. (eds.): Digital Color Imaging Handbook. CRC Press (2017)
7. Moreland, K., Angel, E.: The FFT on a GPU. In: Proceedings of the ACM SIG-GRAPH/Eurographics Conference on Graphics Hardware, pp. 112–119 (2003)
8. Tuzikov, A.V., Margolin, G.L., Grenov, A.I.: Convex set symmetry measurement via Minkowski addition. J. Math. Imaging Vis. **7**(1), 53–68 (1997)
9. Van Droogenbroeck, M., Buckley, M.J.: Morphological erosions and openings: fast algorithms based on anchors. J. Math. Imaging Vis. **22**(2), 121–142 (2005)
10. Serra, J., Soille, P. (eds.): Mathematical Morphology and its Applications to Image Processing, vol. 2. Springer, Dordrecht (2012). https://doi.org/10.1007/978-94-011-1040-2
11. Najman, L., Talbot, H. (eds.): Mathematical Morphology: from Theory to Applications. Wiley, Hoboken (2013)
12. Cooley, J.W., Lewis, P.A., Welch, P.D.: Historical notes on the fast Fourier transform. Proc. IEEE **55**(10), 1675–1677 (1967)
13. Roerdink, J.B.: Mathematical morphology in computer graphics, scientific visualization and visual exploration. In: Proceedings of the 10th International Symposium on Mathematical Morphology, pp. 367–380 (2011)
14. Kukal, J., Majerová, D., Procházka, A.: Dilation and erosion of gray images with spherical masks. In: Proceedings of the Annual Conference of Technical Computing (2007)
15. Déforges, O., Normand, N., Babel, M.: Fast recursive grayscale morphology operators: from the algorithm to the pipeline architecture. J. Real-Time Image Proc. **8**(2), 143–152 (2013)
16. Moreaud, M., Itthirad, F.: Fast algorithm for dilation and erosion using arbitrary flat structuring element: improvement of Urbach and Wilkinson's algorithm to GPU computing. In: Proceedings of the International Conference on Multimedia Computing and Systems, pp. 289–294 (2014)
17. Lin, X., Xu, Z.: A fast algorithm for erosion and dilation in mathematical morphology. In: Proceedings of the WRI World Congress on Software Engineering, vol. 2, pp. 185–188 (2009)
18. Van Herk, M.: A fast algorithm for local minimum and maximum filters on rectangular and octagonal kernels. Pattern Recogn. Lett. **13**(7), 517–521 (1992)
19. Haralick, R.M., Sternberg, S.R., Zhuang, X.: Image analysis using mathematical morphology. IEEE Trans. Pattern Anal. Mach. Intell. **9**(4), 532–550 (1987)
20. Thurley, M.J., Danell, V.: Fast morphological image processing open-source extensions for GPU processing with CUDA. IEEE J. Sel. Top. Sig. Process. **6**(7), 849–855 (2012)

21. Virtanen, P., et al.: SciPy 1.0: fundamental algorithms for scientific computing in Python. Nat. Meth. **17**(3), 261–272 (2020)
22. Van Droogenbroeck, M., Talbot, H.: Fast computation of morphological operations with arbitrary structuring elements. Pattern Recogn. Lett. **17**(14), 1451–1460 (1996)
23. Kahra, M., Sridhar, V., Breuß, M.: Fast morphological dilation and erosion for grey scale images using the Fourier transform. In: Proceedings of the 8th International Conference on Scale Space and Variational Methods, pp. 65–77 (2021)
24. Harris, C.R., et al.: Array programming with NumPy. Nature **585**(7825), 357–362 (2020)
25. Burgeth, B., Kleefeld, A.: An approach to color-morphology based on Einstein addition and Loewner order. Pattern Recogn. Lett. **47**, 29–39 (2014)
26. Dachsel, R., Jöster, A., Breuß, M.: Real-time retinal vessel segmentation on high-resolution Fundus images using Laplacian pyramids. In: Proceedings of the 9th Pacific Rim Symposium on Image and Video Technology, pp. 337–350 (2019)

Augmented Reality Gamification of Intra- and Production Logistics

Steffen Moritz[1(✉)], Christoph Schlüter[2], and Benjamin Wagner vom Berg[1]

[1] University of Applied Sciences Bremerhaven, An der Karlstadt 8,
27568 Bremerhaven, Germany
SteffenMoritz@gmx.net

[2] Fraunhofer-Institute for Material Flow and Logistics IML, Joseph-von-Fraunhofer-Straße 2-4,
44227 Dortmund, Germany

Abstract. In intra- and production logistics, monotonous work processes reduce employee motivation and concentration. This leads to errors, decreasing willingness to perform and a decline in productivity. To reduce these deficits, gamification and innovative technologies such as augmented reality (AR) are attracting increasing attention in research and practice.

In the context of this research field, three hypotheses are put forward that assume a positive influence of AR-supported gamification on the work experience, on productivity and on learning speed. To test the hypotheses, the training application TrainAR was gamified to support the learning of a sorting process. The gamification was evaluated by test subjects who conducted three test runs with the gamified application. The test runs each consisted of sorting ten packages for which the trainees achieved scores depending on their performance. Before and after the experiment they answered questionnaires. The results of these experiments supported the hypotheses or provided valuable information towards further research.

Furthermore, a motivating effect of the game elements implemented in TrainAR - rank badges, points, feedback, humanity hero, ranking lists, progress bars, time measurement, achievements and story – were observed among subjects.

Keywords: Gamification · Augmented reality · Logistics

1 Introduction

In intra- and production logistics, operational employees are often confronted with undemanding, monotonous work processes. Repetitive work processes without any significant challenge have a negative impact on concentration during the course of the working day and also on employee motivation. Higher error rates and low motivation are the consequences [1]. However, higher motivation can be assumed to increase employee productivity [2]. Accordingly, an increase in employee motivation is additionally recommendable for companies from an economic point of view. To this day, however, motivational approaches have focused mainly on extrinsic or monetary incentives [3].

© Springer Nature Switzerland AG 2021
G. Bebis et al. (Eds.): ISVC 2021, LNCS 13018, pp. 500–511, 2021.
https://doi.org/10.1007/978-3-030-90436-4_40

An innovative technology that has gained popularity in recent years and can be considered in the context of increasing motivation is augmented reality (AR). Due to the technical progress over the last few years, this technology is increasingly maturing. As a result, interest in logistics practice is growing not only in virtual reality (VR), but also in AR. In the context of intra- and production logistics, AR is mainly implemented using data glasses or head-mounted displays (HMDs) [4].

Another approach to increasing motivation is gamification, which is attracting increasing attention in research and practice [5]. In the future working life, a steadily growing number of people will work who play games every day and have them integrated firmly into their everyday lives. These people learn through games as well as improve their digital skills [6]. Gamification is already being used successfully in many industries, not only to increase employee motivation, and its use has progressed particularly in the healthcare and education sectors [7]. Gamification can be considered as the use of game design elements in a non-game context [8]. Gamification is intended to increase intrinsic motivation in particular, which should achieve the highest possible motivation in conjunction with extrinsic motivators such as monetary compensation.

2 Related Work

The publications by Bräuer and Mazarakis are important pioneering work in the area of AR supported gamification. They conducted a field test within warehouse logistics [9]. In order picking, it was determined that the test subjects described the handling of the AR glasses Microsoft HoloLens as intuitive and satisfactory. Quantitatively, it was also found that the use of a leaderboard led to the subjects working faster. Badges, on the other hand, had no influence on processing speed. In another study, Mazarakis and Bräuer demonstrate a positive impact on motivation using game elements progress indicators, badges and story [11].

Sailer describes the positive influence of game design elements such as "points, badges, leaderboards, team leaderboards, achievement graphs, narratives and avatars" on the fulfillment of basic psychological needs [12]. These needs can be identified as competence, autonomy and social relatedness. Sailer concludes by recommending the consideration of gamification in broader contexts and individual game elements. Bräuer and Mazarakis conclude that there is a need for further research and development regarding the effect of individual game elements, as well as the effect of gamification in combination with AR and logistics [10].

3 Method

3.1 Hypotheses

As this research aims to investigate the impact of gamification on AR supported processes (further referenced to AR supported gamification), the following hypotheses are formulated to support the research goal, which are to be tested during this research.

- H_1: AR-supported gamification leads to a subjectively perceived positive work experience in intra- and production logistics.

- H_2: AR supported gamification leads to a productive work experience in intra- and production logistics.
- H_3: AR assisted gamification has a positive impact on learning speed in intra- and production logistics.

To test these hypotheses, a subject trial with a gamified AR application is conducted. The application TrainAR has been developed by the Fraunhofer Institute for Material Flow and Logistics IML. TrainAR aims to improve the quality of training of workers for a sorting process. This training is then supported by AR and gamification. The goals of TrainAR are to provide more human-centered approach for working conditions in intra- and production logistics and establish a sustainable working environment that appeals to the psychological needs of human workforce.

3.2   Measurements

Two questionnaires were distributed to the participants of the study. The first questionnaire initially collected basic demographic data and the subjects' previous experience and familiarity with AR and HoloLens technologies. In addition, the questionnaire requires input regarding the general well-being of the test subject.

The second questionnaire was handed out after the experimental sessions. Different standardized questionnaires as well as project-specific questions form the second questionnaire that was given out after the experiment sessions. Firstly, it contains questions about the subjects' general well-being and sense of comfort in the context of the simulator sickness questionnaire (SSQ) [13]. The following questions provide an overview of the subjects' intrinsic motivation. For this purpose, the short scale of intrinsic motivation (KIM) based on Wilde et al. is used [14]. This short scale is based on the more comprehensive Intrinsic Motivation Inventory (IMI), validated by McAuley et al. [15]. Brooke's system usability scale (SUS) [16] is a way to assess the usability of a system [17]. To derive a correlation to this, the shorter questionnaire of usability metric for user experience lite (UMUX-Lite) is applied [18]. UMUX-Lite is significantly shorter than SUS with only two items and the Likert scale and is used accordingly to avoid making the overall questionnaire too lengthy. Both SUS and KIM as well as UMUX-Lite are used in this analysis in the version with the Likert scale and five choices. Subsequently, the NASA task load index (NASA-TLX) questionnaire follows, which is a subjective, multidimensional assessment instrument that evaluates perceived workload in order to evaluate the effectiveness of a task or system [19]. Mental, physical and time demands as well as performance, effort and frustration are subjectively assessed. A 20-point scale provides the subjects with precise response options. The corresponding averaging is referred to in the literature as "raw NASA-TLX" [20]. These questions are followed by questions about the subject's immersion and the perceived flow [21]. Following questions regarding the motivational power of the used game elements provide insight. Subsequently questions regarding the impact of TrainAR on the learning experience follow. The subjects' assessments are expressed on a Likert scale. Finally, the question about the subjects' well-being is repeated in order to determine whether there has been a change in the course of the tests. Furthermore, the subjects can list which game elements were particularly memorable and what aspects of the experiment were particularly positive or negative.

3.3 Procedure

After a brief welcome, the subjects were presented with the first questionnaire. As soon as the questionnaire was completed, an explanation of the experimental setup and a briefing on the HoloLens and gesture control was given by the experiment leader. The users then were asked to open the story UI and familiarize themselves with the Christmas-based story that is implemented in the gamified TrainAR application. Thereafter, they were advised to look at the tutorial UI, which displays the classification criteria and can be seen in Fig. 1. The interaction with the TrainAR application in UI contexts is done by the HoloLens interaction gesture (focus point over button and click gesture with thumb and finger). During the training process, the interaction is done by scanning the desired QR-codes as described below.

Fig. 1. TrainAR: tutorial and process sequence

The subjects then started the sorting process. Three test runs were carried out with the training application TrainAR. Within this application the trainees were asked to classify ten different packages into the categories of "transportable" or "not transportable". As a first step, the trainees chose one of the ten packages and scanned the QR-code attached to it. As next step they had to decide wether the package is transportable or not, based on the classification criteria from the tutorial in Fig. 1. To make their choice, the corresponding QR-codes had to be scanned. The choices were indicated by a green QR-code with a check mark (transportable) and a red QR-code with a cross (not transportable). After scanning, subjects received instant feedback on their choice in the form of happy or sad smileys, as displayed in Fig. 1. After ten iterations of picking and classifying packages, the trainees were able to end the current test run by scanning another QR-code. This opened the summary UI as displayed in Fig. 2. The participants obtained a cumulated score they achieved throughout the run and had the option to explore further UI tabs, that include a high score list and an achievement overview. The trainees were asked to report their achieved score, the respective times achieved and the corresponding time bonus points to the experiment leader. After completion of the third test run, the subjects were presented with a second questionnaire. Answering this questionnaire marked the end of the test.

Fig. 2. TrainAR: summary, achievements tabs

3.4 Subjects

The study was conducted with 37 subjects (M: 23, F: 14). Various age groups were represented in the age distribution of the subjects (<25 years: 38%; 25–34: 40%; 35–44: 0%; 45–54: 11%; 55–64: 11%). Furthermore, a wide range of subjects with diverse educational qualifications were included in the study. The largest groups were those with a secondary school diploma (30%), followed by a bachelor's degree (24%) and a general high school diploma (22%). There was also a high variance among the subjects in the occupations they performed.

4   Findings

4.1   Questionnaires

Of the test subjects, only around 8% (3 out of 37) agreed or fully agreed with the statement that they already have manifested prior knowledge with AR. Only around 11% (4 out of 37) of the subjects agreed or fully agreed with the statement that they already have manifested prior knowledge with HoloLens. From this data, an indication can be derived that augmented reality is still far from having arrived in the middle of society.

When asked about the subject's well-being, the average response on a scale from 5 to 100 was significantly more positive after conducting the subject experiment in the second questionnaire (85.81) than at the beginning of the experiment in the first questionnaire (79.32). Male participants gave an average pre-test score of 76.09 which increased in value by 8.55 to 84.64. Female participants gave a higher score early on, but this then only increased from 84.78 to 87.50. The finding from this is that the use of the AR supported gamified application had a positive effect on the mood of the subjects, with the effect on the male participants being greater than on the female participants. This may provide evidence that the design of the application is more appealing to men but may also be due to the argument that men are more quickly attracted to technology or games.

The results of the simplified SSQ showed that ten out of the sixteen symptoms occurred with varying frequency. The most significant symptoms were eye strain (Mean: 0.24; M: 0.14; F: 0.40) and having difficulty in focusing (Mean: 0.16; M: 0.05; F: 0.33), which were mostly described by female test subjects. Rarely emerging symptoms were for example the feeling of being overwhelmed, general discomfort and drowsiness. Severe symptoms rarely occur in AR.

The questions relating to immersion and flow, on a scale of one to five, present a picture of high concentration of all senses (Mean: 3.97; SD: 0.79), partial loss of the sense of time (Mean: 3.73; SD: 0.98) and the absence of irrelevant thoughts or external distractions (Mean: 4.08; SD: 1.00) during the activity.

The evaluation of the UMUX-Lite presents the results on a scale of 5 - 100, where a higher score is a better result. The field tests showed that the capabilities of the system largely meet the requirements of the users (Mean: 75.14; SD: 19.40) and that the system is quite easy to use (Mean: 90.27; SD: 11.03). Interpreting both properties combined results in the total value of the UMUX Lite (Mean: 82,70; SD: 17,50), which can be converted into the SUS value. The achieved mean value is in the percentile range of 80.8−84.0% and corresponds to a percentile range of 90−95 according to the Sauro-Lewis' rating scale [22], which means that TrainAR's usability rating is rated among the top ten percent of all applications.

The twelve items from the short scale of intrinsic motivation can be subsumed under the categories of enjoyment, competence, freedom of choice, and are measured on a scale of one to five. According to the results, enjoyment of the application is perceived as remarkably high (Mean: 4.42; SD: 0.56), and the subjects felt pleasure while using TrainAR. The result of perceived own competence is also in a satisfying range (Mean: 4.11; SD: 0.75). For the perceived freedom of choice (Mean: 3.87; SD: 1.10) and pressure (Mean: 2.29; SD: 1.08) there is a high standard deviation. It should also be noted that the scale is reversed in the case of pressure, and a low value is to be interpreted positively. A gender-specific difference can only be found in the pressure category. On average, female participants had greater concerns about not being able to complete the gamified activity well (M:1.91; F: 3.57) and were more tense during the gamified activity (M: 1.96; F: 3.00). Overall, the gathered data and evaluation on these four pillars of intrinsic motivation hint to an enormously positive effect on the intrinsic motivation generated by TrainAR.

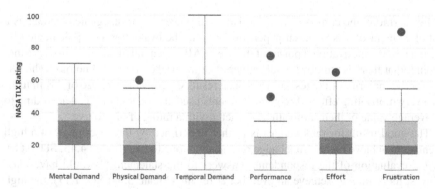

Fig. 3. Raw NASA-TLX results describe a moderate perceived workload.

NASA-TLX is rated on a scale of 5 to 100. A low score represents a minor perceived workload. From the raw NASA-TLX, a moderate stress is obtained (Mean: 27.93; SD: 19.67). This value describes a below-average workload for tasks of this type. The mental workload was found to be higher (Mean: 35.00; SD: 18.42) than the physical workload

(Mean: 22.84; SD: 15.23) by the test subjects. The time pressure was perceived varyingly (Mean: 38.65; SD: 26.90). In the evaluation of the feeling of competence an exception applies since a low value is desirable but corresponds to a high feeling of competence. The feeling of having successfully completed the task was high among the subjects after the experiment (Mean: 20.14; SD: 14.12), although most of the subjects did not feel that they had worked hard for it (Mean: 26.49; SD: 15.20). The measurement of the subjects' sense of frustration was in the lower range (Mean: 24.46; SD: 15.23). These findings are presented in Fig. 3. Overall, a perceived positive influence on learning can be noticed on a scale of one to five. Most of the test subjects stated that they felt supported in learning by the gamified application (Mean: 4.00; SD: 0.66), that it made learning more productive (Mean: 4.38; SD: 0.67) and that the learning success was increased (Mean: 4.14; SD: 0.78). Only one subject responded that the use of the application had a subjectively perceived negative influence on the learning success.

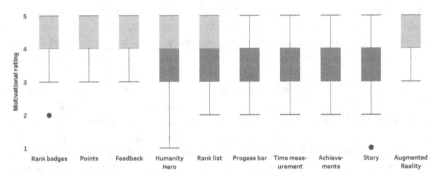

Fig. 4. The subjects describe the motivational power of game elements differently, however on average attest all of them positive impact on motivation.

Furthermore, the comparison of motivational power of various game elements is a central element of this research paper. In addition, the evaluation is supplemented by looking into the motivational power of the use of AR in general, in order to also take into account, that there is a motivational influence of the usage of this technology, which is new for the majority of the test subjects. The result suggests that the use of AR in itself has a very motivating effect. The game elements used are ordered in Fig. 4 according to the average value of their motivating character with a rating of one to five.

The good result for rank badges is further underlined by the description of a high incentive to achieve higher rank badge on a scale of one to five (Mean: 4.43; SD: 0.68). For the evaluation of the respondents' answers to the statement "I would have liked to invest more time to achieve an even better result" (Mean: 3.08; SD: 1.17), the high standard deviation of the answers can be explained by the different achievement of points by the subjects. 22 of the 37 subjects achieved the maximum number of points during the second or third round of the test. Accordingly, the desire to invest more time to perform better is significantly lower (Mean: 2.73; SD: 1.14) than in the group that could not achieve a maximum score (Mean: 3.60; SD: 1.02).

Based on appearance and the way the boxplots are displayed, the result is a grouping as a tier list according to Fig. 5, in which the three leading game elements - rank badges, points and regular feedback - can be described as "S"-tier elements. For each of these game elements more than 75% of the subjects rated them with a score of 4 or higher. Humanity Hero and Rankings form the "A"-tier with 50% ratings of 4 or higher. Finally, the "B"-tier consists of the game elements progress bar, timing, achievements and story. These game elements were given 75% ratings of 4 or lower. This list can serve as a guideline for future (AR) gamification projects.

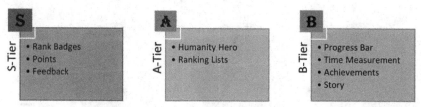

Fig. 5. A Tier list to rank motivational power of investigated game elements in three different tiers.

When asked which of the game elements they remembered most, "smileys" (20 mentions) and "ranking" (16 mentions) were named most often. The frequent mentioning of smileys underlines the importance of feedback, as this is not only perceived as very motivating, but is also particularly memorable. Rankings remain similarly present in the memory of the test subjects but are perceived as less motivating on average.

4.2 Trainees' Performance Results

The evaluation of the achieved scores shows a clear improvement over the course of the three test runs. While the subjects achieved an average of 497.32 points (SD: 54.43) in the first round, this value increased to 544.54 points (SD: 60.92) in the second round. In the third round, the test subjects performed even better and achieved an average of 568.58 out of 600 points (SD: 37.29).

The time bonus points are a crucial factor if a user wants to reach the diamond rank in TrainAR. Diamond represents the highest rank tier in TrainAR followed by gold, silver, bronze and unranked tiers. As the handling of augmented reality and TrainAR in most cases was a new experience for the test subjects, part of the strong increase in the average time bonus points from the first run (Mean: 56.87; SD: 20.25) to the second run (Mean: 81.02; SD: 18.45), Fig. 6, can be assumed to be due to the test subjects' familiarization period. Between the second and third run, the subjects again optimized their speed and improved further (Mean: 92.89; SD: 11.55).

Corresponding to the previously presented results is also the distribution of the achieved ranks. On average, these improved significantly for the test subjects from the first to the third run, as can be seen in Fig. 7. The proportion of subjects who achieved a gold rank or higher grew from 51.35% in the first run to 91.89% in the third run. Every user achieved a gold rank or higher in at least one of the three runs.

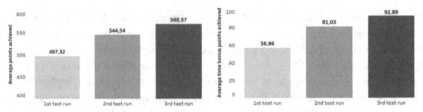

Fig. 6. The change in points and time bonus points during test runs display the improvement of subjects during the experiments.

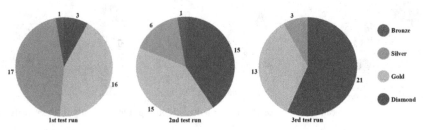

Fig. 7. The rank distribution in three test runs visualizes the steady increasing improvement of subjects.

5   Discussion

5.1   Limitations and Future Research

In this paper, several limitations such as small sample size and the lack of a control group must be considered. On the other hand, it provides valuable findings regarding motivating effects of AR gamification and various specific game elements. It furthermore indicates positive influence of AR Gamification on logistical training.

For future research, dividing a larger group into test and control groups is crucial to determine the effect of gamification. Based on the results of these two groups, the questionnaires and the achieved results of the package classification can be compared to determine which gamification-related differences are measurable.

There are several features to consider for future versions of TrainAR. An additional feature with great improvement potential for the whole application would be a user system for displaying names in the ranking list. This provides the user a stronger feeling of really owning the score he has achieved. The formula for calculating points values the incorrect assignment of a transportable and a non-transportable package equally. Since classifying a non-transportable package as transportable has serious consequences whereas the other way around is only annoying, this should ideally be reflected in TrainAR's scoring system to create awareness among the trainees. In order not to devalue the special feeling of belonging to the elite group, a further balancing of the scores would make sense to increase difficulty to achieve the maximum score. In the test subject trials, 22 out of 37 participants achieved the maximum score. This is not an issue since equal points are not displayed in ranking lists and hence pride in the achievement was high. This can be seen in the answers to the questionnaires.

As Bräuer and Mazarakis also note, AR technology is still new and fascinating for most people, especially when using it for the first time [23]. This may lead to a distortion of the observed positive effects of gamification, especially since the motivating factor of AR was rated very highly by the test subjects. As a result, a longer duration of use or more previous experience with AR is necessary for an experiment. However, even then it is questionable whether an impression of gamification can arise that is detached from the fascination of AR. For this purpose, a study should ideally be conducted with warehouse employees who already work with AR as standard.

The AR gamification of logistical processes is still in its infancy in practice and research in this area is also only progressing slowly. Nevertheless, and especially due to the constantly improving possibilities and opportunities in the technically maturing AR area, it can be assumed that the trend will prevail, and that gamification will be omnipresent in logistics practice in the medium term. For a higher acceptance of AR in logistics practice, it is also important that the wearing comfort of the HMD is improved. An improvement in this area is indispensable to ensure the practical suitability for the desired use in shift operations. Until this point is reached, further research is necessary so that negative effects of AR gamification can be ruled out or reduced to an acceptable level before widespread use.

5.2 Conclusion

H_1 stated that AR supported gamification leads to a subjectively perceived positive work experience in intra- and production logistics. This hypothesis is supported by the significant increase in the subjects' sense of well-being after the experiments. Furthermore, the subjects rate the enjoyment of the application and the perceived, own competence as remarkably high. In the study, the perceived pressure and the feeling of frustration are assessed as low. Based on these results, H_1 can be confirmed.

H_2 claimed that AR supported gamification leads to a productive work experience in intra- and production logistics. This hypothesis is considered from several points of view throughout this paper. On the one hand, motivation correlates with productivity and motivation is increased using various game elements. On the other hand, the improvement in scores over the three runs is a sign of a rapid improvement in productivity. Furthermore, there is evidence of high immersion and a low degree of distraction, which suggests a higher level of concentration on the task.

H_3 refers to the learning speed in intra- and production logistics and can be confirmed if AR gamification has a positive influence on this. Due to the lack of a comparison test group using the non-gamified application, this hypothesis cannot simply be confirmed. However, this hypothesis is supported by the high approval of the test subjects to the questions regarding the learning success. The participants perceived gamification to be supportive and to increase productivity and learning success.

To sum up, this paper contributes to the research regarding AR supported gamification. The results point to significant benefits in motivation and hint towards positive effects in training logistical processes. Additionally, subjects in the experiment rated several game elements and a motivating effect was found in rank badges, points, feedback, humanity hero, ranking lists, progress bars, time measurement, achievements and story.

References

1. Kretschmer, V., Schmidt, M., Schwede, C., Schäfer, S., Müller, G.: Spielerisch zum Trainingserfolg: Evaluationsstudie eines PC-basierten Serious Games für die Verpackungslogistik bei DB Schenker. Logist. J.: Proc. **2018**, 1–8 (2018). ISSN 2192-9084
2. Srivastava, S., Barmola, K.: Role of motivation in higher productivity. Manag. Insight **7**(1) (2011)
3. Günthner, W.A., Mandl, H., Klevers, M.T.M., Sailer, M.: Forschungsbericht GameLog: Gamification in der Intralogistik, Garching (2015). https://www.mw.tum.de/fml/forschung/2015/gamelog-gamification-in-der-intralogistik/
4. Glockner, H., Jannek, K., Mahn, J., Theis, B.: Augmented Reality in Logistics: Changing the way we see logistics - a DHL perspective (2014). https://www.dhl.com/content/dam/downloads/g0/aboutus/logistics_insights/csi_augmented_reality_report_290414.pdf
5. Bozkurt, A., Durak, G.: A systematic review of gamification research. Int. J. Game-Based Learn. **8**(3), 15–33 (2018)
6. Fager, K., Tuomi, P., Multisilta, J.: Gamifying facility service jobs: Using personnel attitudes and perceptions for designing gamification. In: Jonna Koivisto/Juho Hamari (Pub.), GamiFIN Conference 2018: Proceedings of the 2nd International GamiFIN Conference (2018).
7. Chou, Y.-K.: Gamification and behavioral design: a comprehensive list of 90+ gamification cases with ROI stats. https://yukaichou.com/gamification-examples/gamification-stats-figures/. Accessed 4 Apr 2021
8. Deterding, S., Dixon, D., Khaled, R., Nacke, L.: From game design elements to gamefulness. In: Lugmayr, A., Franssila, H., Safran, C., Hammouda, I., (eds.) Proceedings of the 15th International Academic MindTrek Conference Envisioning Future Media Environments, p. S. 9 (2011)
9. Bräuer, P., Mazarakis, A.: AR in order-picking – experimental evidence with Microsoft HoloLens. In: Dachselt, R., Weber, G. (Hrsg.) Mensch und Computer 2018 – Workshopband, 02–05 September 2018, Dresden. Gesellschaft für Informatik e.V. (2018)
10. Bräuer, P., Mazarakis, A.: Gamification und Augmented Reality für Lagerprozesse (2018)
11. Mazarakis, A., Bräuer, P.: Welche gamification motiviert? In: Workshop Gemeinschaften in Neuen Medien (GeNeMe) 2017, pp. 259–268 (2017)
12. Sailer, M.: Die Wirkung von Gamification auf Motivation und Leistung. Springer, Wiesbaden (2016) https://doi.org/10.1007/978-3-658-14309-1
13. Kennedy, R.S., Lane, N.E., Berbaum, K.S., Lilienthal, M.G.: Simulator sickness questionnaire: an enhanced method for quantifying simulator sickness. Int. J. Aviation Psychol. **3**(3), 203–220 (1993). https://doi.org/10.1207/s15327108ijap0303_3
14. Wilde, M., Bätz, K., Kovaleva, A., Urhahne, D.: Überprüfung einer Kurzskala intrinsischer Motivation (KIM). In: Zeitschrift für Didaktik der Naturwissenschaften, pp. 31–45 (2009)
15. McAuley, E., Duncan, T., Tammen, V.V.: Psychometric properties of the Intrinsic Motivation Inventory in a competitive sport setting: a confirmatory factor analysis. Res. Q. Exercise Sport **60**(1), 48–58 (1989)
16. Brooke, J.: SUS - a quick and dirty usability scale. In: Usability Evaluation in Industry. Taylor & Francis, pp. 189–194 (1996)
17. Borsci, S., Federici, S., Lauriola, M.: On the dimensionality of the system usability scale: a test of alternative measurement models. Cogn. Process. **10**(3), 193–197 (2009)
18. Borsci, S., Federici, S., Bacci, S., Gnaldi, M., Bartolucci, F.: Assessing user satisfaction in the era of user experience: comparison of the SUS, UMUX, and UMUX-LITE as a function of product experience. Int. J. Hum.-Comput. Interact. **31**, 484–495 (2015)
19. Hart, S.G., Staveland, L.E.: Development of NASA-TLX (Task Load Index): results of empirical and theoretical research. In: Hancock, P., Meshkati, N. (eds.) Human Mental Workload, pp. 139–183 (1988)

20. Gross, B., Rissler, J.: Beurteilung von Aufgabenlasten von digitalen Informationssystemen auf Flurförderzeugen: Datenbrille (HMD) vs. Monitor (Gundlagenuntersuchung): Deutschen Gesetzliche Unfallversicherung e.V. (DGUV), Berlin (2018)
21. Georgiou, Y., Kyza, E.A.: The development and validation of the ARI questionnaire: an instrument for measuring immersion in location-based augmented reality settings. Int. J. Hum.-Comput. Stud. **98**, 24–37 (2017)
22. Lewis, J.R.: Measuring user experience with 3, 5, 7, or 11 points: does it matter?. Hum. Factors 1–13 (2019)
23. Bräuer, P., Mazarakis, A.: Badges or a leaderboard? How to gamify an augmented reality warehouse setting. In: GamiFIN Conference 2019, Levi, Finland, April 8–10, pp. 229–240 (2019)

Virtual Training System Based on the Physiological Cycle of the Potato INIAP Suprema

Mauricio D. Chiliquinga[1] ⓘ, Edison D. Mañay[1] ⓘ, E. Fabián Rivera[2(✉)] ⓘ, and Marco V. Pilco[2]

[1] Universidad las Fuerzas Armadas ESPE, Sangolquí, Ecuador
{mdchiliquinga,edmanay}@espe.edu.ec
[2] Instituto Superior Tecnológico Universitario Oriente, La Joya de los Sachas EC-220101, Ecuador
{frivera,mpilco}@itsoriente.edu.ec

Abstract. This paper presents the development of a Virtual Reality system oriented to the simulation of the physiological cycle of the INIAP Suprema potato. The developed system allows the user to analyse tuber growth and production under certain conditions such as soil type, seed type and ambient temperature in order to optimize raw material, infrastructure, production time and among other benefits. The conditions set out in the document for virtualization are subject to monitoring and are based on studies previously carried out by agricultural institutions in Ecuador. The immersive system is developed in the graphical environment of Unity 3D using models and scenes that allow the user to visualise the growth simulation, obtain the quantity to be produced, observe the characteristics and physiological conditions of the plant. The results show the efficiency of the system, as the user can combine different conditions for the development of the plant, obtaining a virtual guide to the growth and production of potatoes and can be used as data to obtain quality harvests.

Keywords: Virtual reality · Potato physiological cycle · Immersion systems · Potato production · Agriculture

1 Introduction

The growing technological world is making inroads into the development of industry through the use of technological tools that enable the progress and development of mankind. Through the emergence of Industry 4.0 technologies are implemented to improve industrial processes and increase productivity [1]; e.g.: *a) Internet of Things (IoT)*, based on the collection of data that feeds artificial intelligence algorithms for the benefit of decision making [2]. IoT is used to assess atmospheric conditions and soil variables such as soil condition, composition, temperature and moisture [3]. According to Talavera, IoT applied in agribusiness contributes to creating an informed, connected, developed and adaptive rural community through the use of low-cost devices, IoT is

© Springer Nature Switzerland AG 2021
G. Bebis et al. (Eds.): ISVC 2021, LNCS 13018, pp. 512–521, 2021.
https://doi.org/10.1007/978-3-030-90436-4_41

considered a primary tool for the interaction of people in an agribusiness system [4]. *b) Artificial Intelligence and Vision,* there are studies of existing applications of agricultural robotic systems; where tasks such as sowing, planting, plant treatment, harvesting, yield estimation and phenotyping are analysed [5], therefore, the use of agricultural machines combine computer vision with multitasking processes in order to perform automated tasks such as weeding and irrigation [6]. They also employ Deep Learning algorithms used in image classification tasks and object detection to identify weeds in crops. [7]. *c) Augmented Reality (AR) and Virtual Reality (VR),* considered a growing technology used for training people in various industry sectors. The advantages of employing AR and VR in industry lie in the engagement, speed, preservation of worker integrity, personalisation and cost reduction that immersive digital tools possess [8].

VR applications are growing technologies used to train people in various sectors, including education and agriculture. *i) Education,* through the visualisation of objects designed in 3D, users can interact in previously designed virtual environments; in order to carry out tasks focused on education and training in specific subjects such as training in industrial processes for pumping systems, handling and assembly of machinery, simulation of building construction, among others [9–11]. Additionally, VR provides interactive and safe conditions that enhance teaching and learning processes by engaging students in a motivating environment where there is enjoyment, acquisition and retention of learning [12, 13]. *ii) Agriculture,* immersive technologies applied in agriculture provide an effective way to obtain improvements in precision agriculture education [14], applied not only virtually but using drones for data collection through soil sampling and interactive AR [15]. The use of VR through virtual field demonstrations in applications of tillage, harvesting, field exploration increases the participation of not only students but also farmers in such work [16].

Virtual reality designs focused on agricultural applications allow the design of agricultural environments in order to highlight processes of interest, such as plant growth management through the simulation of an inflatable modular hydroponic greenhouse used by astronauts to emulate the habitat of Mars [17]. In addition to the above, VR simulates models of forest growth development for forest thinning operations [18], allows the evaluation of plant growth impacts [19]; above all, it facilitates the possibility of interacting and experimenting in virtual training environments [18].

For the reasons described above, the present work proposes the development of a virtual system based on the physiological process of the INIAP Suprema potato under different growth conditions such as: soil type, seed type and environmental temperature, in order to emulate and obtain production data of the tuber at the harvest stage through virtual environments. The different growth conditions for the tuber were based on research carried out by competent bodies in Ecuador, such as: Ministerio de Agricultura y Ganadería (MAGAP), Instituto Nacional de Investigaciones Agropecuarias (INIAP).

The paper consists of 6 Sections including the Introduction. Section 2 describes the problem formulation; Sect. 3 presents the structure of the virtual system realised in Unity 3D; while the graphical environment and virtual animation are explained in Sect. 4; Sect. 5 performs the analysis of the experimental results and finally the conclusions are presented in Sect. 6.

2 Problem Formulation

New technological advances evolve over time; even more so in the development of applications that optimise resources such as: training time, training of professionals, budget for the acquisition of high-cost equipment, etc. Immersive technologies allow users to carry out simulations of the real environment while optimising the resources involved; in other words, they are affordable, low-cost systems that enhance technical and technological training processes, including agricultural processes.

On the other hand, farmers, professionals and students argue the importance of improving resources for the benefit of agriculture [14]; as it is the essential livelihood to feed the world, however, the high costs involved in food production, receiving continuous training are not affordable for many farmers; as obtaining a quality product at harvest depends on it.

In order to create a user-friendly tool that contributes to the training and agricultural production processes, we propose the development of a VR system presented to emulate the physiological changes of the potato plant as shown in Fig. 1 and obtain production data at the harvest stage. The interface is designed so that the user can interact and visualise the different physiological cycles of the tuber.

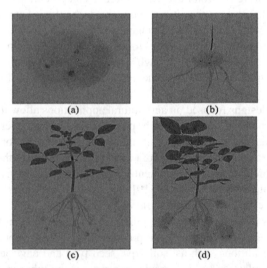

Fig. 1. Stages of potato plant development INIAP Suprema a) Seedling, b) Vegetative growth, c) Beginning of tuber production, d) Tuber grow.

The potential presented in the animation is based on studies carried out in the inter-Andean zones of Ecuador on the production of the INIAP Suprema potato, and has information on factors that involve the development, growth and production of the plant. The growing conditions are determined by: *i) Soil*, three types of soil are considered essential for potato cultivation, such as Andisols and Mollisols, which are found in the Sierra regions and are suitable for potato production [20]. *ii) Seed*, INIAP Suprema distinguishes between three types: certified seed; considered the best in its class as it comes from the genetic mother of the seed [21], selected seed; seed chosen empirically by farmers and degenerated seed; when the seed has already gone through several sowing cycles. *iii) Climate,* environmental temperatures typical of the Andean region, categorised into two groups; normal temperatures ranging from 7 °C to 25 °C and low temperatures below 1.8 °C [22].

3   System Structure

The VR system presented to emulate and obtain production data of potatoes at the harvesting stage; it allows the user to enter the world of agriculture; specifically the INIAP Suprema potato crop in an interactive and easy to manipulate way in order to visualise the morphology of the plant. The application has drop-down menus and easy-to-activate selectors, which are developed using the Unity 3D video game engine, offering resources that integrate the elements of virtual reality and immersion. The block diagram presented in Fig. 2 details the structure of the proposed system; detailing the input and output devices, data simulation, as well as the scripts required for the simulation.

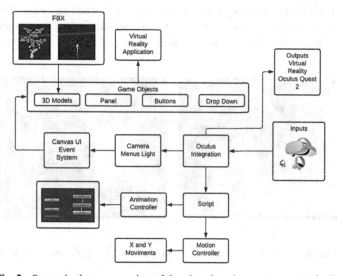

Fig. 2. Stages in the construction of the virtual environment automatically.

The input and output devices (hardware) consist of a virtual reality viewer that allows for a fully immersive interface through the use of the Oculus Quest 2 device with wireless controls that have motion and touch sensors; which operates with the Android-based operating system.

The simulation of the data allows the 3D objects to animate the physiological properties of the plant; virtualising the growth stages through movements and attributes; which have various characteristics depending on the instances that can be modified in the main menu.

The use of scripts allows developing the behaviour of the animations by inputting actions from the real environment, linking the growth conditions of the plant, and additionally linking the 3D models. The scripts allow to control the activation and deactivation functions of the plant animations in order to control the data storage and playback of the 3D objects and to develop the logic of the simulation system within the Unity game engine.

4   Graphic Environment and Virtual Animation

This section details the virtual development of the system, which consists of 2 stages: i) Development of the 3D environment; ii) Animation of the virtual environment.

4.1   3D Environment Development

The 3D objects are designed in Blender, a freely available software, using images of the potato crop with real plants, and then rendering the models to obtain the colours and textures required for the system, as shown in Fig. 3. The developed components are exported in.FBX format and imported into the Unity game engine, where the elements that allow the development of the virtual environment such as scenes, cameras, lights, materials, avatars, scripts and animation control are found.

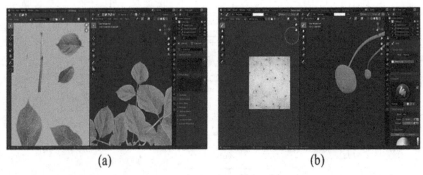

(a)   (b)

Fig. 3. 3D modelling of the INIAP Suprema potato plant: a) Model of leaves and stems, b) Model of the tuber.

Additional 3D elements that are involved in the 3D virtual environment are imported from the Asset Store as the Oculus Integration library and get the necessary resources to develop the environment in Unity. All 3D objects retain the attribute of rigid bodies which have mass and avoid collisions with each other.

4.2   Virtual Environment Interface and Animation

The virtual interface is developed in the Unity 3D video game engine; which works with multiplatform to provide ease of use on other devices, it has an operating system based on Android. Android Software Development Kit and Java Development Kit tools are used to create applications on mobile devices; in this case the virtual reality glasses Oculus Quest 2.

The proposed system has animations that allow the application of technical knowledge focused on the physiological development of potatoes in order to observe their behavior in the face of factors that alter the development of the plant. The con-trol of the animations is done by means of a block based algorithm; which has the inputs controlling the reproduction speed, blocks were assigned with a repetitive loop to visualize the avatar in its beginning stage and also in the end stage so that the user can observe its most relevant characteristics. Additionally, scripts are used in order to have communication between the inputs of the system, such as the control knobs of the vision equipment and the output, the Oculus viewer.

For the interaction of the user with the virtual environment, the fist person controller is used, which applies a capsule and a rigid body in order to imitate the user's movements. To generate the character's movement, the commands attributed to the joystick are used. The transform.translate and transform.rotate are modified simultaneously to assign the movement of the camera to the user. The inputs for the movements are made by inserting the Prefab OVRPlayerController to the scene since the associated script allows to control the movements in first person. To start the animation process of the virtual environment the user can be in any position; sitting or standing.

The training system allows the user to change the behavior of the potato crop by modifying the factors of soil type, seed and weather conditions. The first-person system allows the user to view the interactivity menu, the plant animation, and a summary of the result of the animation. The user has all the attributes of full control to modify any parameter that influences the behavior of the plant.

5   Experimental Results

This section provides evidence of the performance tests performed in the VR environment. The system has alternatives that allow simulating the physiological development of potatoes under different growth conditions, resulting in users (farmers/students) being able to anticipate planting actions and prevent conditions that affect the productive process of the crop. In this way the user manipulates the behavior of a specific plant variety in the face of changes that occur in the stages of its growth; also optimizing the time it takes for a plant to develop, since the simulation has an average travel time of 1 min in which its cycle from seed to production is observed; in comparison with the real cycle of the plant that takes 120 days approximately [7].

The virtual reality application has a main scene as shown in Fig. 4a. in which there are a total of 12 combinations depending on the number of growth factors to control. The scene presents a menu where the user by means of a laser pointer incorporated in the control knob can select the type of soil, type of seed and temperature. With the selected growth parameters, an immersion space where the seed potato is located is created within the system Fig. 4b. The selected characteristics are concatenated and enter the Start section of the animation. By means of Reset the selected data can be deleted and other growth factors can be chosen from the start and the result returned in a drop down with plant information, selected factors and the crop growth animation. By running the VR system you have qualitative results due to the virtualization of the plant and quantitative results regarding the production in a quick and visual way.

(a)   (b)

Fig. 4. Main panel: a) INIAP Suprema potato plant virtual interface and b) Potato plant physiology.

The following section presents the simulations carried out taking into account the factors that are commonly present in the farmers' work as shown in Fig. 5, obtaining the following results. Figure 5a was combined with an Andisol soil type, a certified seed and a temperature of 7 to 25 °C; resulting in the plant foliage presenting large leaves and stems with an approximate production amount of 1.3 kg/plant. Figure 5b was carried out with a Molisol soil type, a certified seed and a temperature of 7 to 25 °C; presenting as a result that the foliage of the plant shows large leaves and stems, its production is 1.1 kg/plant. Figure 5c was combined with an Andisol soil type, a degenerated seed and

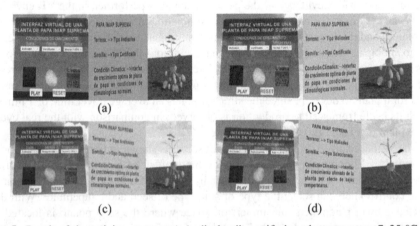

(a)   (b)

(c)   (d)

Fig. 5. Result of the training system: a) Andisol soil, certified seed, temperature 7–25 °C, b) Molisol soil, certified seed, temperature 7–25 °C, c) Andisol soil, degenerated seed, temperature 7–25 °C, d) Molisol soil, selected seed, temperature 1.8 °C.

a temperature of 7 to 25 °C; it presented a potato plant with small leaves and stems and a quantity of less than 1 kg/plant. Figure 5d was carried out by selecting a Molisol soil type, a selected seed and a temperature lower than 1.8 °C resulting in a plant with leaves and stems damaged by low temperatures, additionally the plant presents a dark color, while the amount of production is low.

Finally, a set of 10 questions are asked to determine the usability of the system (SUS); shown in Table 1. The questionnaire applied to the users is weighted from 1 to 5; where 1 is complete disagreement to 5 is complete agreement. The evaluation of the answers is based on subtracting 1 from the result in the case of odd questions; while in the case of even questions the result obtained is subtracted from 5. To obtain the SUS value, the data obtained are added together and multiplied by 2.5 to obtain 100% [11].

Table 1. Questionnaire results.

N°	Questions	Results	Operations
1	Is the information displayed on the screen what is necessary to understand what the site is about?	5	$5 - 1 = 4$
2	Do I understand and comprehend the screen elements presented in the system?	3	$5 - 3 = 2$
3	The application is easy to use?	5	$5 - 1 = 4$
4	Do I need prior knowledge to use the system?	3	$5 - 3 = 2$
5	Does the system provide me with the information I need to learn about the crop?	3	$3 - 1 = 2$
6	Do the icons provide explanatory information?	2	$5 - 2 = 3$
7	Do the interface colours resemble those of the real world?	4	$4 - 1 = 3$
8	How often would you use the application?	3	$5 - 3 = 2$
9	Can anyone use the system?	5	$5 - 1 = 4$
10	The application provides intuitive control of the interface?	2	$5 - 2 = 3$
Total		72,5	

The evaluation of the virtual environment (SUS) obtained a score of 72.5, considered a good system, however, the system needs to implement improvements and data to obtain results similar to the real world and maximise the user experience in immersive environments.

6   Conclusions

The training system allows users to visualize and interact with the physiological behavior of the INIAP Suprema potato plant through a virtual environment. The development of the application has different growth factors, such as soil areas that are fundamental for the development of the plant, depending on the type of seed varies the shape of the tubers, plant height and temperature as a climatological variable incident in the amount of production, since low temperatures affect the natural development of the plant.

The system offers technical knowledge for the development of potato cultivation in users who manipulate and interact with the morphology of the plant. As future work, it is planned to implement in the simulation the affectation of the plant through the application of conventional organic fertilizers and of greater use in the area, additionally to build a sensor network system applied to obtain data in real time and in VR environments in order to obtain data of variables of ambient temperature, soil humidity, relative humidity, UV radiation in order to control production based on timely decision making for the benefit of agriculture.

Acknowledgement. The authors would like to thank the Instituto Superior Universitario Oriente (ITSO) for the research, development and innovation funding provided for this work.

References

1. Garcia, C.A., Naranjo, J.E., Ortiz, A., Garcia, M.V.: An approach of virtual reality environment for technicians training in upstream sector. IFAC-PapersOnLine **52**(9), 285–291 (2019)
2. Saville, R., Hatanaka, K., Wada, M.: ICT application of real-time monitoring and estimation system for set-net fishery. In: OCEANS 2015-MTS/IEEE Washington, pp. 1–5. IEEE (2015)
3. Pang, Z., Chen, Q., Han, W., Zheng, L.: Value-centric design of the internet-of-things solution for food supply chain: value creation, sensor portfolio and information fusion. Inf. Syst. Front. **17**(2), 289–319 (2012). https://doi.org/10.1007/s10796-012-9374-9
4. Talavera, J.M., et al.: Review of IoT applications in agro-industrial and environmental fields. Comput. Electron. Agric. **142**, 283–297 (2017)
5. Oliveira, L.F., Moreira, A.P., Silva, M.F.: Advances in agriculture robotics: a state-of-the-art review and challenges ahead. Robotics **10**(2), 52 (2021)
6. Chang, C.L., Lin, K.M.: Smart agricultural machine with a computer vision-based weeding and variable-rate irrigation scheme. Robotics **7**(3), 38 (2018)
7. Junior, L.C.M., Ulson, J.A.: Weed Detection using Computer Vision and Artificial Inteligence in the Raspberry Pi Plataform as an Edge Device (2021)
8. Naranjo, J.E., Sanchez, D.G., Robalino-Lopez, A., Robalino-Lopez, P., Alarcon-Ortiz, A., Garcia, M.V.: A scoping review on virtual reality-based industrial training. Appl. Sci. **10**(22), 8224 (2020)
9. Quevedo, W., et al.: Virtual reality system for training in automotive mechanics. In: Paolis, L.T.D., Bourdot, P., Mongelli, A. (eds.) Augmented Reality, Virtual Reality, and Computer Graphics, pp. 185–198. Springer International Publishing, Cham (2017). https://doi.org/10.1007/978-3-319-60922-5_14
10. Rivera, E.F., Pilco, M.V., Espinoza, P.S., Morales, E.E., Ortiz, J.S.: training system for hybrid vehicles through augmented reality. In: 2020 15th Iberian Conference on Information Systems and Technologies (CISTI), pp. 1–6. IEEE (2020)
11. Andaluz, V.H., et al.: Multi-user industrial training and education environment. In: Paolis, L.T.D., Bourdot, P. (eds.) Augmented Reality, Virtual Reality, and Computer Graphics: 5th International Conference, AVR 2018, Otranto, Italy, June 24–27, 2018, Proceedings, Part II, pp. 533–546. Springer International Publishing, Cham (2018). https://doi.org/10.1007/978-3-319-95282-6_38
12. Putz, L.M., Hofbauer, F., Treiblmaier, H.: Can gamification help to improve education? findings from a longitudinal study. Comput. Human Behav. **110**, 106392 (2020)

13. Apostolellis, P., Bowman, D.A.: Evaluating the effects of orchestrated, game-based learning in virtual environments for informal education. In: Proceedings of the 11th Conference on Advances in Computer Entertainment Technology, pp. 1–10 (2014)
14. Liu, Y., Rao, G., Chen, J., Hu, H., Ou, Y., Xue, Y.: Teaching reform of precision agriculture technology based on virtual reality. In: 6th Annual International Conference on Social Science and Contemporary Humanity Development (SSCHD 2020), pp. 317–320. Atlantis Press (2021)
15. Huuskonen, J., Oksanen, T.: Soil sampling with drones and augmented reality in precision agriculture. Comput. Electron. Agric. **154**, 25–35 (2018)
16. Hawkins, E.M., Beam, B., Klopfenstein, A.A., Shearer, S.A., Fulton, J.P.: Using virtual reality field demonstrations to increase farmer engagement. In: Precision Agriculture 2021, pp. 85–119. Wageningen Academic Publishers (2021)
17. Bruno, F., Ceriani, A., Zhan, Z., Caruso, G., Del Mastro, A.: Virtual reality to simulate an inflatable modular hydroponics greenhouse on mars. In: International Design Engineering Technical Conferences and Computers and Information in Engineering Conference, vol. 83983, p. V009T09A068. American Society of Mechanical Engineers (2020)
18. Fabrika, M., Valent, P., Scheer, Ľ: Thinning trainer based on forest-growth model, virtual reality and computer-aided virtual environment. Environ. Model. Softw. **100**, 11–23 (2018)
19. Traub, C.: Assessment of the Impacts of Plant Growth on the Air Revitalization System of different sized Space Habitats using the Virtual Habitat (2017)
20. SIGTIERRAS, Sistema Nacional de Información y Gestión de Tierras Rurales e Infraestructura Tecnológica. Memoria explicativa del Mapa de Órdenes de Suelos del Ecuador. Quito, Ecuador (2017)
21. Montesdeoca, F., Andrade, H., Cuesta Subía, H.X., Carrera, E.: Información técnica de la variedad de papa INIAP-Suprema (2000)
22. YARA. Principios agronómicos en el cultivo de la papa (2021). https://www.yara.com.ec/nutricion-vegetal/papa/principios-agronomicos-en-el-cultivo-de-la-papa/

Author Index

Printed in the United States
by Baker & Taylor Publisher Services